REFERENCE GUIDES TO RHETORIC AND COMPOSITION
Series Editors: Charles Bazerman, Mary Jo Reiff, and Anis Bawarshi

REFERENCE GUIDES TO RHETORIC AND COMPOSITION
Series Editors: Charles Bazerman, Mary Jo Reiff, and Anis Bawarshi

The Series provides compact, comprehensive and convenient surveys of what has been learned through research and practice as composition has emerged as an academic discipline over the last half century. Each volume is devoted to a single topic that has been of interest in rhetoric and composition in recent years, to synthesize and make available the sum and parts of what has been learned on that topic. These reference guides are designed to help deepen classroom practice by making available the collective wisdom of the field and will provide the basis for new research. The Series is intended o be of use to teachers at all levels of education, researchers and scholars of writing, graduate students learning about the field, and all, nationally and internationally, who have interest in or responsibility for writing programs and the teaching of writing.

Parlor Press and The WAC Clearinghouse are collaborating so that these books will be widely available through low cost print editions and free electronic distribution. The publishers and the series editors are all teachers and researchers of writing, committed to the principle that knowledge should freely circulate. We see the opportunities that new technologies have for further democratizing knowledge. And we see that to share the power of writing is to share the means for all to articulate their needs, interest, and learning into the great experiment of literacy.

EXISTING BOOKS IN THE SERIES
Invention in Rhetoric and Composition (2004, Lauer)
Reference Guide to Writing across the Curriculum (2005, Bazerman et al.)
Revision: History, Theory, and Practice (2006, Horning and Becker)
Writing Program Administration (2007, McLeod)
Community Literacy and the Rhetoric of Local Publics (2008, Long)
Argument in Composition (2009, Ramage et al.)
Basic Writing (2010, Otte and Mlynarczyk)
Genre: An Introduction to History, Theory, Research, and Pedagogy (2010, Bawarshi and Reiff)
Reconnecting Reading and Writing (2013, Horning and Kraemer)
Style: An Introduction to History, Theory, Research, and Pedagogy (2014, Ray)
Writing Knowledge Transfer: Theory, Research, Pedagogy (2023, Nowacek, Lorimer Leonard, and Rounsaville)

WRITING KNOWLEDGE TRANSFER

Theory, Research, Pedagogy

Rebecca S. Nowacek,
Rebecca Lorimer Leonard, and
Angela Rounsaville

Parlor Press
Anderson, South Carolina
www.parlorpress.com

The WAC Clearinghouse
Fort Collins, Colorado
http://wac.colostate.edu/

Parlor Press LLC, Anderson, South Carolina, USA
The WAC Clearinghouse, Fort Collins, Colorado 80523-1052

© 2024 by Parlor Press and The WAC Clearinghouse
All rights reserved.
Printed in the United States of America

S A N: 2 5 4 - 8 8 7 9

Library of Congress Cataloging-in-Publication Data

1 2 3 4 5

Series logo designed by Karl Stolley. Copyediting by Jared Jameson. This book is printed on acid-free paper.

Parlor Press, LLC is an independent publisher of scholarly and trade titles in print and multimedia formats. This book is available in paperback and eBook formats from Parlor Press on the World Wide Web at https://www.parlorpress.com or through online and brick-and-mortar bookstores. For submission information or to find out about Parlor Press publications, write to Parlor Press, 3015 Brackenberry Drive, Anderson, South Carolina, 29621, or email editor@parlorpress.com.

The WAC Clearinghouse supports teachers of writing across the disciplines. Hosted by Colorado State University, it brings together scholarly journals and book series as well as resources for teachers who use writing in their courses. This book is available in digital formats for free download at wac.colostate.edu

Contents

Series Editors' Preface *xi*
   Anis Bawarshi, Charles Bazerman, and Mary Jo Reiff

Acknowledgments *xiii*

1 Introduction *3*
   Studying Transfer Through a Transdisciplinary
      Lens: Tentative Definitions *7*
   Previewing Transdisciplinary Themes *9*
   Overview of the Book *13*
      Part 1: Outside the Field *13*
      Part 2: Bridges *15*
      Part 3: Inside the Field *16*
      Part 4: Conclusion *19*
   References *19*

2 Cognitive Psychology and Situated Learning: Foundational Research on Transfer of Learning *22*
   Thorndike and the Early History of Transfer *23*
   The Cognitive Revolution *25*
      Concepts and Schemata: Definitions and Methods for Study *25*
      Robust Initial Learning *26*
      An Ability to Move Beyond Surface Details
         to Abstract Schemata *28*
      Hints *28*
      Articulating an Abstract Principle from Comparative Cases *29*
      General Abilities: Heuristics, Mindfulness, and the Value
         of Automatized Cognitive Processes *31*
   Situated Learning Critiques of the Cognitive Approach *35*
      Revised Definitions of Concepts and New Methods for Study *36*

The Role of Hints, Reimagined   38
 Questions of Abstraction, Revisited   39
 Conclusion   42
 References   43

3 Transfer of Training and Knowledge Management: Research from Industrial Psychology, Human Resources, and Management   49

 Transfer of Training: Focusing on Individuals Within a Workplace   50
  Trainee Characteristics   52
  Training Design   59
  Work Environment   65
 Knowledge Management: Focusing on Relationships Among Individuals Within a Workplace   69
  Knowledge Creation   69
  Knowledge Storage   71
  Knowledge Transfer   73
  Knowledge Application   76
 Conclusion   76
 References   78

4 Transfer in Sports, Medical, Aviation, and Military Training   88

 Sports Education   89
  A Paradigm in Sports Education: Teaching Games for Understanding   89
  Tactical Approaches to Transfer in Sports Education: Pedagogical Implications   92
 Simulations in Medical Education, Flight Training, and Military Combat   96
  Medical Education   96
  Fidelity, Situated Learning, and Transfer   96
  Teaching for Transfer in Medical Education   98
  Transfer, Simulations, and Fidelity in Flight Training and Military Combat   100
  Implications for Pedagogy and Methodology from Medical Education, Flight Training, and Military Combat   101
 Conclusion and Avenues for Further Inquiry in Writing Studies   104
 References   106

5 Transfer Implications from Sociocultural and Sociohistorical Literacy Studies   111

 The Impacts of Culture, Power, Ideology, and History in Literacy Transfer   112

Sociocultural Studies of Literacy and New
    Constructs for Transfer   118
  Methodological Implications from Literacy Studies   120
  Pedagogical Implications from Literacy Studies   122
  Conclusion and Avenues for Further Inquiry   124
  References   126

6 Research on Transfer in Studies of Second Language Writing   130
  Influences from Second Language Acquisition   133
    Interference   133
    Cross-Linguistic Influence   134
    Multicompetence   135
  Writing Among Languages   137
    Writing and One-Way Transfer   137
    Writing Across Bi-Directional Transfer   139
    Writing with Holistic Language Repertoires   141
  Instructional and Curricular Design   143
  The Role of Genre   147
  Identity   152
  Paths Forward: Empirically Grounded and
    Theoretically Complex   155
    Implications for Pedagogy and Methodology   157
  References   158

7 Transfer in First-Year Writing   167
  The Role of Local and General Knowledge   168
  The Role of Prior Knowledge   174
    Prior Knowledge, Genre Repertoires, and Transfer   174
    Methods for Prompting and Making Use of Students' Prior
      Writing-Related Knowledge in FYW   177
    Reading, Transfer, and the Role of Prior Knowledge   180
  Transfer and the Role of Dispositions, Attitudes,
    and Emotions in FYW   182
  Transfer, Digital Composing, and Multimodality
    in First-Year Writing   188
  Curricular Recommendations and Innovations for
    Transfer in First-Year Writing   193
  Conclusion   199
  References   200

8 Infrastructure for the Transfer of Writing Knowledge: Writing Across the Curriculum and Writing in the Disciplines   207
  Student Knowledge about Disciplinary Writing Transfer   210
    Single Course Contexts   211

Transfer from General Writing to Disciplinary Courses   *213*
Transfer Across Multiple Courses on Single Campuses   *215*
Transfer in Longitudinal Studies   *217*
Teacher Knowledge about Disciplinary Writing Transfer   *222*
Genre Knowledge in WID/WAC Transfer   *226*
What a Transfer-Based WAC/WID Curriculum
   Is or Should Be   *229*
Infrastructure for the Disciplinary Transfer
   of Writing Knowledge   *234*
References   *236*

9 Writing Centers: An Infrastructural Hub for Transfer   *242*
The Knowledge Tutors Transfer–What Tutors Know   *243*
Transfer in Tutor Education—What Tutors Should Know   *251*
   What: Transfer and Writing Theory as Content   *252*
   How: Activities and Strategies for Tutor Education   *254*
   Why Focus on Transfer in Tutor Education   *258*
A Focus on Student Writers   *260*
Transfer Beyond the Center   *262*
Implications for Pedagogy and Methodology   *264*
References   *266*

10 Writing across Contexts: From School to Work and Beyond   *272*
Theoretical Frameworks for Understanding
   Writing in Workplaces   *273*
Defining the Unit of Analysis for Studying the School-
   to-Work Relationship: Specific Contexts, Specific
   Individuals, and Activity Systems   *277*
   Studying Specific School and Work Contexts   *278*
   Studying Individual Writers Over Time
      and Diverse Contexts   *285*
   Activity Systems in Contact   *289*
Pedagogical Contexts for Examining the School-
   to-Work Transition   *290*
   Professional Writing Courses with a Writing
      About Writing Focus   *291*
   Classroom-Based Interactions with Clients   *292*
   Internships   *298*
   Adult Learning and the "Reverse Commute"   *302*
Conclusion: Implications for Pedagogy and Methodology   *305*
References   *308*

11 Conclusion: Transfer and Transdisciplinarity in Five Themes   *315*

  Individuality   *316*
    Identity   *316*
    Agency   *317*
    Traits, States, and Dispositions   *318*
    Embodied Cognition   *320*
  Intentionality   *321*
    Abstract Schema   *321*
    Metacognition and Self-Monitoring   *323*
    Automaticity   *325*
  Fidelity   *326*
    Situated Learning   *327*
    High and Low Fidelity   *328*
    Scaffolding   *330*
    Modeling   *331*
    Proximity and Perception   *332*
  Directionality   *334*
    Forward: Preparation for Future Learning   *335*
    Forward: Framing   *335*
    Forward: Lateral and Vertical Transfer   *336*
    Backward: Prior Knowledge and Reflection   *337*
    Backward: Negative Transfer and Interference   *339*
    Multidirectional   *340*
  Simultaneity   *341*
    Concurrent Contexts   *341*
    Dynamic Dimensionality   *343*
    Multicompetence   *344*
  Future Frames: Transfer as Orientation   *345*
    Interdependence   *345*
    Ephemerality   *347*
    Orientation   *349*
  References   *350*

Glossary   *363*
  References   *376*

Annotated Bibliography   *382*

Appendix   *403*
  References   *408*

Index   *421*

About the Authors   *437*

Series Editors' Preface

Anis Bawarshi, Charles Bazerman, and Mary Jo Reiff

Rhetoric and Composition scholars have long shared an interest in how the knowledge and writing abilities that students gain in our writing classrooms can transfer to wider university, professional, and public contexts. Over the past two decades, research on "writing knowledge transfer"—on how writing knowledge and abilities learned in one context are repurposed and recontextualized within new writing contexts—has proliferated. A rich body of scholarship has explored the transfer of writing knowledge across multiple contexts: transitions from high school to college composition courses; transitions from first-year writing (FYW) to writing-in-the disciplines (WID) or writing-across-the-curriculum (WAC); and transitions from WAC/WID courses to writing in the workplace and beyond.

While the concept of "learning transfer" has long been a topic of discussion in Education and Educational Psychology, Rhetoric and Composition scholars have looked to the various cognitive, affective, material, linguistic, and social perspectives informing our understanding of writing transfer-ability and the transformation of writing knowledge across situations and contexts. Writing studies scholars, in a series of wide-ranging studies, have explored the relationship between generalizable and local (or situated) writing knowledge; the role of rhetorical awareness, genre knowledge, and metacognition in facilitating transfer; and the influence of dispositional, ecological, material, and affective factors shaping writers' repurposing and reinvention of knowledge in new contexts. Recent transfer scholarship has examined the intersections of various "trans" approaches: knowledge transfer, transmodality, translation, translingualism, with some of the work informed by mobility studies, all of which has added useful layers of complexity to how we understand "trans" as a prefix and as an action.

This reference guide explores the rich body of research conducted on this complex cognitive and social phenomenon, including numerous studies examining the transfer of writing strategies across multiple contexts, such as academic, professional, public, global, and digital contexts. In addition, because research on transfer of learning takes place in a wide range of disciplines, this volume presents an important and much-needed multi-disciplinary overview of transfer scholarship, explaining key issues and concepts in research and theory both within and outside of rhetoric and composition—and exploring intersections with related fields/subfields of education, cognitive psychology, literacy studies, human resources and management, training and professional development, and second-language writing research on transfer. Perhaps of most interest to writing studies scholars and practitioners, the volume includes a comprehensive overview of transfer research within the contexts of FYW, WAC/WID, writing centers, and school-to-work transitions. The authors analyze the methods of current transfer research, synthesize core themes that intersect across transfer scholarship, and suggest areas for future research on writing knowledge transfer. The volume concludes with an inclusive and wide-ranging glossary and annotated bibliography to guide readers in using transfer concepts for research and teaching.

Acknowledgments

The authors wish to thank Parlor Press and editor David Blakesley for his kind handling of the book's timeline and his responsiveness during production. Admiration and gratitude also go to the dedication of Mike Palmquist and the WAC Clearinghouse for their commitment to making our field's scholarship freely available online. Much deep gratitude to series editors Charles Bazerman, Anis Bawarshi, and Mary Jo Reiff for the generosity of their developmental and editorial feedback and their long-term intellectual engagement with this project.

A special thank you to colleague and mentor Elizabeth Wardle, who saw the value of this project from the start and who invited us to present and lead a workshop on Threshold Concepts and Transfer of Knowledge at the Threshold Concepts conference at Miami University of Ohio in 2018. Our conversations there were decidedly formative to the book's shape. We would also like to thank the Brookside Carriage House in Northampton, Massachusetts for serving as homebase during an invigorating writing retreat where we tapped into our collaborative energy and set the final path for our book's completion.

Rebeccca Nowacek would like to thank Anis Bawarshi and Mary Jo Reiff for being early and formative conversational partners about transfer of learning, for suggesting this volume, and for all their critical feedback and encouragement along the way. Thanks also to the many colleagues who've encouraged this project over the years. At Marquette, those colleagues include faculty friends such as Jenn Fishman, Lilly Campbell, Cedric Burrows, and Liz Angeli as well as the fantastic undergraduate writing tutors who offered feedback on chapters in progress, including Margo Higgins, Emily Legan, and Chloe Lipka. A special thanks to librarian extraordinaire, Heather James, whose search-engine wizardry was invaluable and whose friendship is incomparable. Beyond Marquette, those colleagues include Liz Wardle, Mark Hall, Brad Hughes, Julie Christoph, Jessie Moore, the members of Elon's Seminar on Writing Beyond the University (especially 5.5 Scholars), and the members of the Thursday Night Thai Dinner Club. And, of course, she is deeply grateful to Rebecca and Angie for joining this project; together they made the impossible possible and the overwhelming fun.

Rebecca Lorimer Leonard would like to thank her UMass Amherst colleagues and fabulous graduate student research assistants–Lisha Daniels Storey, Jenny Krichevsky, and Stacie Klinowski–for their assistance with library research and copyediting over many years. Thank you to UMass Amherst's Center for Teaching and Learning, Massachusetts Society of Professors, and College of Humanities and Fine Arts for the research funding to support them. She also thanks her sister, Christina Lorimer, for early draft proofreading, and sends deep gratitude to many colleagues-in-conversation–especially Annette Vee, Kate Vieira, and Amy Wan–whose responses like "that sounds like such a contribution" supplied helpful writing energy. Most of all, she thanks Rebecca Nowacek for having the confidence and openness to invite her into this project when she was a graduate student.

Angela Rounsaville would first and foremost like to thank her co-authors, Rebecca and Rebecca, for their professional and personal support and friendship, and for inviting her to join this great team way back in 2016. Immense thanks to friends and colleagues at the University of Central Florida and beyond who helped talk through ideas and stayed excited about this project over the years, especially Dustin Edwards and Mark Hall, who always checked in and gave encouraging words. Thanks also to Corrine Jones, her graduate research assistant at UCF, for Corrine's great help with library research and retrieval and for creating the most useful excel spreadsheet to summarize and organize the (seemingly) countless texts that went into this book's chapters.

We are grateful to our families, as always, for their patient ears and encouraging nods. For Rebecca Lorimer Leonard, a special thank you to the magical Miss Ida and the honorable Mr. Ben; for Angie, loads of love and thanks to her partner and kids, Christian, Tala, and Rizal, and to her parents, Ron and Joan Rounsaville, for always cheering her on; for Rebecca Nowacek, deepest appreciation and boundless love to the whole family—especially Bradley, Zachary, Benjamin, and (most especially) David.

Finally, we all wish to thank each other. Collaborative writing is hard work, but this project was made more rigorous and interesting from our commitments to each other's thinking and writing. The research and writing of this book has been a very long road: babies were born, programs were directed, tenures were awarded, pandemics were endured. We just kept swimming and we still like each other immensely.

Writing Knowledge Transfer

1 Introduction

Writing studies scholars are relatively new to the study of transfer of learning, joining in conversations that date back over a century to the groundbreaking work of psychologist E. L. Thorndike. The current focus on transfer of learning in writing studies is often traced to Smit's (2004) challenge to "construct a writing curriculum so that such instruction in transfer is commonplace, indeed a major feature of the curriculum" (p. 134). In 2007, Beaufort's *College Writing and Beyond* and a trio of articles appearing in *WPA: Writing Program Administration* (Bergmann & Zepernick, 2007; Nelms & Dively, 2007; Wardle, 2007) answered that challenge, making pedagogical suggestions and posing research agendas of their own. Since that time, questions about transfer of learning have taken center stage within the field of writing studies—often, though not always, motivated by an institutional exigence to understand and perhaps defend the value of writing courses, especially first-year writing.

Signs of this interest are visible in multiple ways. Conference sessions devoted to transfer have risen at the Conference on College Composition and Communication as well as the conferences of the International Writing Center Association and the International Writing Across the Curriculum Association; for instance, by our count there were nearly four dozen panels at the 2017 CCCC taking transfer of learning as a central focus. The Elon Seminar on Critical Transitions (2011–2013) facilitated multi-institutional research projects on transfer for more than 40 international participants (with applications from more than 150 scholars); Elon has also launched a second Seminar on Writing Beyond the University: Fostering Writers' Lifelong Learning and Agency (2019–2021). Special issues on transfer of learning have appeared in *Composition Forum* (2012) and *WLN* (formerly known as *Writing Lab Newsletter*) (2018). In 2019, scholars undertaking transfer-related studies were among the recipients of both a CCCC Research Initiative Award (Driscoll, Field-Rothschild, Powell, & Wells) and a CCCC Emergent Researcher Award (Bugdal).

Those seeking to understand how such a "new" area could blossom so quickly might point out that even before transfer of learning was named as a focus in the field, scholars studying writing in the disciplines conducted longitudinal studies of writers, seeking to understand how they repurposed their learning from earlier writing courses when facing subsequent challenges (e.g., Carroll, 2002; Chiseri-Strater, 1991; McCarthy, 1987; Sternglass, 1997). Arguably, the current focus on metacognition and self-monitoring in transfer scholarship has a progenitor in Flower and Hayes's (1981) identification of the monitor as part of their cognitive process theory of writing as well as in Yancey's (1998) work on reflection. Even references to Aristotle's articulation of the *koina topoi*—meant to help rhetors generate arguments in any situation—might be seen as a very early example of how scholars in writing studies[1] have long taken an interest in composition strategies that are transferable across rhetorical contexts. Nevertheless, writing studies scholars seeking to study transfer of learning engage a phenomenon with a long, multidisciplinary history of scholarship—much of which is underrepresented in writing studies. This volume seeks to synthesize and make this wide-ranging scholarship accessible and useful to current and future transfer researchers and teachers in writing studies.

As part of the Reference Guides to Rhetoric and Composition series, the book aims to develop a more capacious understanding of transfer in writing studies, tracing both the distinct ways transfer has been engaged in a wide range of disciplinary fields and drawing connections among similar threads of inquiry. More specifically, we approach transfer research with a transdisciplinary aim. In this volume, we use *transdisciplinary* to mean the result of a systematic reading across disciplinary fields that creates a synthesis of intellectual frameworks that are holistic in their responses to complex problems (Choi & Pak, 2006). Choi and Pak suggest a useful definition: "Transdisciplinarity integrates the natural, social and health sciences in a humanities

---

1. We elect to use the term *writing studies* in an effort to encompass as fully as possible the many dimensions of the field of Rhetoric and Composition.

context, and in so doing transcends each of their traditional boundaries" (p. 359). Such an approach is especially valuable for questions of transfer, as a phenomenon that includes dynamic interplay of task, individual, and context (Wardle, 2007, pp. 66–67) and that matters to any field that seeks to move students from facilitated learning and training to agentive performance and action.

Our transdisciplinary approach is motivated by several goals. First, we aim to point writing studies researchers and teachers toward existing conversations about transfer in other fields. Our reference guide seeks to, in a way, help scholars not reinvent well-tread wheels. As Tardy (2017) aptly puts it, "the use of new terminology for established ideas can ultimately restrict our understanding of an issue by occluding relevant scholarship from view (p. 182; also see MacDonald [2007] and Matsuda [2013]). While Tardy especially wants scholars to avoid creating neologisms for existing terms under long examination, we also find her advice useful for considering how phenomena we name as *transfer* may have been problematized or challenged as such by other fields (see also Wardle [2007] and Nowacek [2011]). We hope to guide scholars to this relevant scholarship, both within writing studies and far afield in disciplines that may not immediately seem relevant to writing, rhetoric, or literacy problems and questions. Thus, our chapters compile and synthesize some of the most salient long-term debates around the term *transfer* that scholars in writing studies could fruitfully cite, challenge, or move forward from.

Second, we take a cue from research we read during the writing of this reference guide (see in particular the chapters on transfer in cognitive and industrial/organizational psychology) and propose that analogical reasoning across disciplines can expand what transfer means in writing studies. Beyond the classical rhetorical roots that will be familiar to many writing studies readers, analogy is taken up across fields to trace how individuals use the concepts and schemata they've developed from previous specific situations to make sense of a new context. Scholars like Nonaka (1991) argue that analogical thinking can help convert tacit knowledge into explicit knowledge "by linking contradictory things and ideas through metaphor" and then "by resolving those contradictions through analogy" (p. 101). Hargadon (1998) argues that analogy serves a linking function in which analogies "highlight non-obvious similarities between two things that appear to be dissimilar" and then prompt an individual facing a new problem to see "non-obvious similarities in other problems he or she has faced in the past" (p. 219). An analogical approach shares a kinship with the transdisciplinary approach we have taken in this Reference Guide. As Choi and Pak (2006) explain, the "ambiguous and incongruous juxtaposition of heterogeneous information elements that are related through the operation of a transdisciplinary interface is likely to stimulate the emergence of new knowledge" (p. 357). The transdisciplinary themes that we present in our conclusion, which emerged as a result of our extensive cross-disciplinary reading, reflect these intellectual processes.

Putting writing studies scholars in the role of the "individual" in the research above, the utility of analogical reasoning about transfer comes into focus: writing studies scholars can convert tacit knowledge about the transfer of writing into explicit knowledge that can be taught, traced, or described; they might link seemingly dissimilar or contradictory transfer phenomena across disciplines for more theoretically grounded conclusions; they could generate new solutions or ideas about the transfer of writing knowledge by analyzing data for non-obvious similarities. As we write in Chapter 4 ("Transfer in Sports, Medical, Aviation, and Military Training"), treating the cross-disciplinary repetition of the term transfer analogically helps writing studies scholars "build out a more holistic and sophisticated theory of transfer to broaden where and how transfer of both writing-related knowledge and writing-related action can matter." By building in analogic thinking about transfer across disciplines, we hope to avoid the missed connections that are common in random database searches for the term. As Hargadon (1998) notes, databases "gather and store information through a process of abstraction and categorization" that sometimes obscure "non-obvious connections between the current problem and past problems" (p. 221). Our aim is to facilitate these connections for readers of this reference guide.

Therefore, our cross-disciplinary presentation of transfer research through individual chapters in this book is motivated by our desire to help scholars link very long and broad transfer conversations, solve transfer problems in their teaching or research that are perhaps stumping them, and support both amplitude (more capacious understandings of writing transfer) and specificity (more detailed and relevant treatments of the term) in research on the transfer of writing knowledge. Optimally, this could lead us all to realize the "untapped potential of a truly transdisciplinary approach" to transfer, fostering the humility to consider what the field may not yet be able to see because of our existing theoretical frames or analytic habits (Tardy, 2017, p. 187).

Studying Transfer Through a Transdisciplinary Lens: Tentative Definitions

Readers have doubtless noticed that in this introduction we have not yet provided a definition of transfer. The transdisciplinary nature of our endeavor leads us to this necessary (if unsatisfying) conclusion: there is no one easy definition, for scholars debate these definitions within and across fields, based on significant differences in their theoretical frameworks and empirical data. Indeed, Baird and Dilger (2018) "inventoried over 20 metaphors for 'adaptive transfer' . . . each with a slightly different understanding of how transfer occurs, is learned, and can be taught" (p. 24). Nevertheless, we can note that any definition of transfer must wrestle with the relationship between transfer of learning and learning itself. A long tradition of scholarship sees these as distinct phenomena. Thorndike and Woodworth (1901), for instance, traced initial learning in one domain and tracked its possible influence on subsequent tasks. Even later cognitive psychologists who rejected the behaviorism of Thorndike's theory of identical elements retained what is often called the two-problem paradigm: tracking the influence of initial learning upon later problem solving. Cognitivist studies of analogical reasoning rely on such a paradigm. The concept of negative transfer—defined as how "prior learning interferes with subsequent learning" (Schunk, 2004, p. 217)—also assumes a distinction between learning and transfer. This distinction is implicit in the entire field of "transfer of training"—whose very name suggests that initial training is a necessary precondition for subsequent transfer.

Other researchers, frequently those adopting a situated learning perspective, are far less likely to distinguish between learning and transfer. It's not uncommon for these scholars to abandon the term transfer (with its resonance of discrete, portable packages of knowledge simply carried over and applied to new contexts) entirely. The language of consequential transitions, generalization, expansive learning, boundary spanning, preparation for future learning, recontextualization, and repurposing are all examples of ways in which scholars reimagine the continuity between earlier and subsequent experiences of learning.

Writing in the wake of situated learning critiques of the earlier learning/transfer distinction, Perkins and Salomon (2012) articulate both the wisdom of the critique and the persistence of the distinction:

> What counts as transfer of learning in contrast with just plain learning? The question arises because all learning involves transfer in some sense. Evidence of learning always entails the learner doing something at least later and under another set of conditions, if not elsewhere, informed by what has been learned; otherwise there would be no basis to claim that learning had occurred. On this reading, transfer has an *inclusive* meaning, always part of learning and a matter of degree—how much later, how far elsewhere, and how different the conditions under which it is displayed. However, transfer as researchers usually use the term takes on a *contrastive* meaning—successful initial learning positively influencing performance on a later occasion and with a different appearance (transfer) versus not influencing (failure to transfer). Yet another case is negative influence, generally called negative transfer. (p. 249)

Ultimately, we have continued to use transfer as the term anchoring this volume, even as it has been both conflated with and distinguished from learning. Although we embrace the critiques of its limitations, we find that—on a very practical level—it remains the term that is threaded through the various disciplinary and methodological approaches synthesized in this volume. Even as we retain the term, we hope through this volume to illuminate its many facets. We treat discrete terms in relation to their disciplinary origins and also place them in conversation with core questions from across writing studies. Through our own analogical reasoning across the literature in this book, we have learned that while binaries may seem initially satisfying—like those referenced in the Perkins and Salomon passage above—transfer processes are never so neat.

For instance, when we place transfer in the stream of a learner's experience over time rather than in discrete moments (i.e., a=initial learning and then b=transfer), we note how transfer opportunities that might be outside the "target context" are occluded from view. When we use the perspective of the learner (e.g., Lobato's 2012 actor-oriented transfer theory) rather than that of the researcher or educator, a priori distinctions between positive and negative transfer are harder to uphold: what did not appear to transfer from a researcher's vantage has perhaps been incorporated by the learner into other practices of invention or resistance.

Thus, throughout this volume we keep the term transfer while also tracing how previous scholars have engaged the phenomenon in ways that hold multiple meanings, even reminding us that not all transfer acts can be captured. As we discuss in our conclusion, such qualities pushed us, in the writing of this book, to especially highlight the interdependent and ephemeral facets that make transfer so tricky to study and teach, but also so interesting. Throughout this writing process, we came to understand that transfer-oriented teaching and research requires not a rigid and uni-positional stance on transfer (one does or does not teach for it) but instead a dialogic and flexible orientation to transfer that includes inevitable relations with other teachers, learners, and writers across multiple transfer contexts.

PREVIEWING TRANSDISCIPLINARY THEMES

Before we turn to a chapter-by-chapter overview of the book, we include below a table of five transdisciplinary themes on writing and transfer that extend across chapters: *individuality* (which raises issues of identity, agency, dispositions, and embodied cognition); *intentionality* (with its focus on abstract schema, metacognition, and automaticity); *fidelity* (in the forms of situated learning, high and low fidelity, scaffolding, modeling, and proximity); *directionality* (including transfer forward, backward, and in both directions); and *simultaneity* (which accounts for concurrent contexts, dynamism, and multicompetence).

These themes emerged during our systematic reading of and conversations about disciplinary scholarship in the multiple fields represented in this volume. The themes echoed across chapters as recurring issues or questions that animate transfer research. Readers will find that although each disciplinary chapter is organized around the history and local debates particular to that field, these five transdisciplinary themes highlight connections across chapters that might otherwise be obscured by terminological and methodological differences. To help readers anticipate these connections, Table 1 offers brief overviews of the transdisciplinary transfer themes and subthemes. The transdisciplinary themes also organize the book's conclusion, offering a framework that demonstrates another layer of scholarly contribution. A more detailed version of Table 1, which includes the chapter locations and representative citations for each theme and subtheme, can be found in Appendix A.

Theme and *Subthemes*	Brief overview
Individuality	
Identity	Transfer of learning cannot be fully understood without considering an individual's full range of linguistic, professional, and personal identifications.
Agency	An emphasis on learner agency focuses on reflection and self-regulated learning, as well as a reconsideration of "failure" and "negative transfer."
Dispositions	Drawing from extensive work in psychology, researchers parse the similarities and differences between traits, states, dispositions, and personality characteristics, all of which play different roles in transfer of learning and exist in dynamic relationship with context.
Embodied Cognition	Theories of embodied cognition, which argue that the body is always active in transfer of learning, play an important role in fields such as medical and aviation education as well as industrial and organizational psychology, and they have become increasingly recognized within writing studies.
Intentionality	
Abstract Schema	Research across fields shows that an abstract schema facilitates transfer, through the use of generalization, hints, and explicit instruction. However, the causal relationship between an abstract schema and transfer of learning is not without some debate.

Metacognition and Self-Monitoring	Studies of metacognition and self-monitoring across fields trace how levels of intentionality affect transfer, focusing on how components of metacognition are related to self-regulation in transfer, including monitoring, regulating, controlling, and evaluating.
Automaticity	Although sometimes dismissed as the cause of low-road negative transfer, automaticity also can be a component of expertise in certain fields; in some knowledge management scholarship, tacit knowledge is crucial for innovation.
Fidelity	
Situated Learning	Situated learning theory, such as communities of practice and legitimate peripheral participation, suggests that fidelity in practice and participation is necessary for learning and for transfer.
High and Low Fidelity	Theories of situated learning generate concern over the similarities or differences among transfer contexts. To name types of likeness among contexts, some fields distinguish high and low fidelity, in which high fidelity indicates a close likeness to the real while low fidelity suggests that the likeness is partial or distant.
Scaffolding	Scaffolding for transfer might involve contriving high-fidelity contexts or moving learners from low to high fidelity contexts; in either case, peers and mentors play an important role.
Modeling	Across a wide range of fields, researchers emphasize the important role that models play for learners constructing abstract schemata that can facilitate transfer of learning across contexts.

Proximity and Perception	Learners' *perceptions* of proximity—closeness or distance of context fidelity—also matter for transfer of learning.
Directionality	
Forward: *Preparation for Future Learning*	Bransford and Schwartz's (1999) notion of *preparation for future learning* explores how to make explicit use of learners' futures to guide them toward successful transfer.
Forward: *Framing*	Drawing on work in linguistics and anthropology, frames are a pedagogical strategy that prime learners for transfer of learning.
Forward: *Lateral and Vertical Transfer*	Lateral transfer links analogous experiences; vertical transfer requires distinguishing simpler and more complex skills and presenting them in a meaningful order over time.
Backward: *Prior Knowledge and Reflection*	Reflection involves looking back to rethink prior knowledge. Writing reflection, in particular, assumes that explicit backward thinking has the potential to reformulate prior experience and make it relevant for supporting the transfer of knowledge.
Backward: *Negative Transfer and Interference*	Negative transfer refers to the ways prior knowledge interferes with learning. Multiple studies (from sociocultural literacy studies and writing studies, and Lobato's [2012] AOT framework), have questioned the ways in which negative transfer privileges the perspective of the researcher.
Multidirectional	Some transfer scholarship indicates both forward *and* backward directionality, including discussions of cross-linguistic influence and writing tutor expertise.
Simultaneity	
Concurrent Contexts	Scholarship suggesting simultaneity in the transfer act, such as Lemke's (2000) heterochrony or Prior and Shipka's (2003) chronotopic lamination, consider how concurrent contexts—situations co-occurring, or happening at the same time—can shape single transfer acts.

Dynamic Dimensionality	This lens attends to the dynamic or multi-dimensional factors that shape a single transfer act, including material factors like noise, psychological factors like bedside manner, physical factors like dexterity or accuracy, and sociocultural factors like educational experiences with writing.
Multicompetence	Multicompetence demonstrates simultaneity in its emphasis on the whole of language relationships rather than the sum of two monolingual parts. The term can reframe the potential of what appear to be language errors, negative transfer, or interference as positive evidence of writers drawing on "existing resources in new combinations," all at once (Hammer et al., 2005, p. 114).

Overview of the Book

Part 1: Outside the Field

The book begins with two chapters that immerse readers in research on transfer of learning in psychology, research with a history that spans 125 years. Tracing the history of behaviorism, the cognitive revolution, and the situated learning critique, the chapter on "Cognitive Psychology and Situated Learning" focuses on issues of concept and schema formation, analogical thinking, attention and cognitive load, and metacognition. After a brief discussion of Thorndike's theory of identical elements, we turn to the laboratory-based research of cognitive psychologists and their focus on mental representations of knowledge. After establishing cognitive psychologists' abiding interest in abstract concepts and analogical thinking and their disappointment in finding relatively few instances of "spontaneous transfer," we identify in their scholarship five conditions that tend to assist people in transferring knowledge. The final condition, a discussion of heuristics and mindfulness, becomes an occasion to critically reassess the role that the work of Perkins and Salomon (1988, 1989) has played in writing studies, by contextualizing their work within ongoing scholarly debates over the nature of attention and cognitive load. We turn then to the situated learning critique of the cognitivist tradition, tracking the ways it changes research methods, terminology, and theories of how individuals build abstract representations. Here we also review work on the value of embodied cognition as a wellspring of transfer.

The second chapter, "Transfer of Training and Knowledge Management: Research from Industrial Psychology, Human Resources, and Management," continues to draw on the long tradition of psychological research—but this time to explore two large areas of scholarly research that are rarely mentioned in writing studies: transfer of training and knowledge management. These terms are rarely if ever used in writing studies—largely, we speculate, because this disciplinary work is grounded in quantitative, survey-based measures; although the situated learning critique has had some influence on the field, industrial/organizational psychology and human resources scholars remain overwhelmingly guided by survey research and statistical analyses to build models of influence. The chapter begins with a focus on "transfer of training," the province of human resources and industrial/organizational psychology scholars seeking to understand whether an organization's investments in employee professional development (or "training") have measurable consequences in the workplace. Although writing studies scholars rarely use the term *transfer of training*, they are in fact increasingly familiar with scholarship central to this field: scholarship focused on dispositions, personality traits, motivation, goal orientations, and more. Human resources scholars identify these as "trainee characteristics." The bulk of the chapter reviews the findings from research on such trainee characteristics, as well as research on the role "training design" and "work environment" might also play in transfer of training. The final pages of the chapter turn from transfer of training to the field of knowledge management; here management scholars focus on how an *organization's* knowledge—one of its greatest assets in the knowledge economy—can be "transferred" from people in one part of the organization to another part and can be used to innovatively meet future challenges (rather than keeping organizations bogged down in their past actions and approaches). Conceiving of transfer as an interpersonal act—taking place between individuals or even groups of individuals, rather than an intrapersonal act, confined within a single individual—these knowledge management scholars significantly challenge the usual assumptions of writing studies scholars.

Part 2: Bridges

Part 2 of the book includes chapters on education, literacy studies, and second language writing that bridge transfer concerns across writing studies and other fields. This section begins with the chapter on transfer in education, which shows how schools mediate transfer from the perspective of sports education, medical education, aviation education, and military education. While this chapter ("Transfer in Sports, Medical, Aviation, and Military Training") draws together four distinct fields, we have placed them all under the capacious heading of education to emphasize the ways that transfer is a core category for learning, research, and scholarship in fields that writing studies may not seek input from, but perhaps should due to their direct investment in undergraduate education. Sports education offers a unique view, mostly unavailable in other fields, of the relationship between mind and body in transfer through its heavy theoretical focus on embodied cognition. Medical education and aviation education likewise complicate transfer through their focus on how to teach for automaticity through simulations. Moving beyond the discursive and deliberative dimensions of transfer, these fields may provide new theoretical and research avenues for the study of writing-related transfer that attune to the embodied and multi-sensory facets of how learners engage past learning to act in new situations.

The next chapter in this section, "Transfer Implications from Sociocultural and Sociohistorical Literacy Studies," addresses how the ideologies of schooling, as embedded in sociocultural and sociohistorical contexts, are a significant but often overlooked set of contextual factors in transfer. In particular, this chapter highlights the range of continuities and discontinuities between learners' community-based repertoires and those expected in mainstream school settings to show that so-called positive and negative transfer are frequently the result of historical power imbalances. Research shows the ways that these imbalances articulate with race and ethnicity, class, language, and geographical location. The value of literacy studies' research on transfer includes theoretical constructs that expand the sociocultural and sociolinguistic dimensions of literacy transfer; theoretical constructs for a range of situated reading and writing contexts; additional methods for exploring the movement of literacy, literacy practices, and literacy learners across situated reading and writing contexts; and pedagogical approaches for facilitating transfer between in- and out-of-school settings.

Our final chapter of Part 2 addresses "Research on Transfer in Studies of Second Language Writing," identifying several themes that commonly motivate or drive research on transfer in the field: (1) students' writing and rhetorical activities, (2) instructional and curricular design, (3) the role of genre, and (4) the impact of identity. The chapter examines how second language writing scholars have traced the movement of writing knowledge among learning contexts and among languages, accounting for how multiple cultural, educational, and linguistic traditions come to bear on the possibility of transfer. Scholars in L2 writing pursue these complexities to understand how language diversity complicates the transfer of writing knowledge and how to best support the linguistically diverse writers who navigate these complexities when they compose. The chapter highlights both what is there in the research—how scholars have navigated the issues—as well as what is implicit—the transfer concerns that appear in L2 writing scholarship whether scholars set out to study them or not. L2 writing transfer research thus suggests not just that language learners make choices among languages when they write, but why they do, how those decisions occur across contexts, and what the consequences of their transfer attempts are for their learning. In the end, the chapter shows that as concepts of language have become more diffuse and research questions have become more precise, several complicating factors remain that researchers of transfer in L2 writing have yet to settle, namely the extent and impact of writers' awareness, intentionality, and agency during the act of transfer.

Part 3: Inside the Field

Part 3 focuses on transfer research inside the field of writing studies. The first chapter in this section, "Transfer in First-Year Writing," traces the ways that scholars have looked at what transfers into and out of first-year writing to offer explicit transdisciplinary connections between FYW and out-of-field scholarship. This chapter reviews literature on (a) the role of prior knowledge; (b) dispositions, attitudes, and emotions in FYW; (c) digital composing and multimodality; and (d) curricular innovations. We attribute the robustness of this line of inquiry to early debates about the efficacy of teaching generalized and local knowledge in FYW and the subsequent theoretical and empirical work on the viability of transfer from FYW. Petraglia (1995), for instance, asked if teaching students generic writing skills could really stand up to the field's growing consensus that writing is situationally, ideologically, and contextually embedded. Smit (2004) later lamented the dearth of communal knowledge about transfer and its role in FYW. As this chapter demonstrates, writing studies has experienced a significant expansion in research and pedagogical knowledge since those early debates and has moved beyond calls to abolish FYW to complex and research-rich responses about what helps or hinders transfer and the role of FYW in that process. As transfer research in FYW is now sufficiently rich though not yet calcified, we suggest it is an ideal time for deliberate transdisciplinary linkage between "core concepts and principles" within and beyond writing studies (Qualley, 2016, p. 69).

The chapter on writing across the curriculum (WAC) and writing in the disciplines (WID) shows how these fields are inescapably shaped by the transfer of writing knowledge. WAC/WID initiatives came into being partly in response to concerns that students did not transfer their writing knowledge beyond first-year writing and thus needed further instruction—whether in general practices of writing to learn (WAC) or disciplinary skills or genres (WID). The chapter reviews scholarship that treats writing as a general learning skill; a socialized disciplinary activity; a process or procedural activity; the activity that compromises the discipline of writing studies itself; or simply as a vessel through which assessment of content occurs. The chapter shows the multi-directionality of transfer, as knowledge moves "up" vertically in a discipline and "out" across courses and extra-curricular writing contexts that students encounter over time, a frame that helps account for the ways that the WAC/WID relationship mirrors what transfer research in other fields argues: that "*general* cognitive skills" exist, but they "function in *contextual* ways" (Perkins & Salomon, 1989, p. 19, emphasis added). The chapter follows this cue by presenting sections organized by WAC/WID researchers' common questions about the transfer of writing knowledge: what students are learning about writing with or through transfer, what instructors are or should be doing to support that transfer, how genre plays a role in that transfer, and which courses or curriculum best support student transfer in and across disciplines or curricular contexts. The chapter shows that WAC and WID approaches to writing education serve as a kind of infrastructure for transfer, creating the architecture that cues students' prior knowledge, scaffolds connections among writing genres, lays down paths for metacognition about writing knowledge, and prompts students to reflect on past, current, and future writing activities across disciplinary contexts, including first-year writing.

The chapter on transfer in writing centers suggests that writing centers are intriguing spaces for attention to transfer because they act as an infrastructural hub of transfer activity. Writing centers' low-stakes atmosphere outside of conventional classrooms, disciplines, and academic hierarchies invites tutors and writers to share and make connections among several forms of writing-related knowledge. For example, writing center tutors transfer knowledge about writing even as they transfer knowledge about tutoring writing; tutors toggle between general writing skills instruction and disciplinary-specific approaches as they work. The chapter reviews the research and thinking that shows this unique potential, with sections organized by common questions and issues in writing center studies: (1) the writing knowledge that tutors transfer, including debates about specialist vs. generalist tutor knowledge; (2) the writing knowledge tutors *should* come to know and transfer through tutor education; (3) studies of writers, themselves, transferring knowledge in writing centers; and (4) the kinds of knowledge, writing and otherwise, tutors and teachers transfer beyond the center into classrooms, workplaces, or community contexts.

The final writing studies chapter has at its heart research on school-to-work transitions. The chapter begins with a review of three theoretical frameworks that dominate scholarship in this area: Lave and Wenger's (1991) concepts of community of practice and legitimate peripheral participation, Miller's (1984) theorization of the rhetorical nature of genres, and Engeström's (2014) model of activity theory. Although we argue that these frameworks are not mutually exclusive and often coexist as complementary frameworks within studies, they also invite very different units of analysis. Thus, we taxonomize in this chapter the copious research analyzing particular school-workplace relationships—but also identify smaller but important traditions of research that follow individuals over much longer periods of time and that focus not on individuals or discrete workplaces but larger activity systems. The bulk of the chapter, though, is devoted to synthesizing empirical research on four pedagogical contexts for facilitating the transition from school to work: writing about writing classrooms, classroom-based interactions with clients, workplace-based internships, and adult learning classrooms where prior work experiences sometimes inform school learning.

Part 4: Conclusion

In the book's final chapter, we synthesize and critically assess the transdisciplinary themes on transfer woven through the previous chapters. Specifically, as we indicated earlier, we identify five concepts as the sites of emerging understandings and intense debates about transfer across fields: *individuality, intentionality, fidelity, directionality,* and *simultaneity*. After synthesizing the scholarship relevant to each of these concepts, we show how a sixth concept—orientation—unites these threads by accounting for the ephemerality and interdependence of transfer concepts. Using a concept of transfer as orientation, we identify several pedagogical implications as well as methods and agendas for future research.

REFERENCES

Aristotle. (2004). *Rhetoric*. (W. R. Roberts, Trans.). Dover Publications.

Baird, N., & Dilger, B. (2018). Dispositions in natural science laboratories: The roles of individuals and contexts in writing transfer. *Across the Disciplines, 15*(4), 21–40. https://wac.colostate.edu/docs/atd/articles/baird-dilger2018.pdf

Beaufort, A. (2007). *College writing and beyond: A new framework for university writing instruction*. Utah State University Press.

Bergmann, L. S., & Zepernick, J. (2007). Disciplinarity and transfer: Students' perceptions of learning to write. *WPA: Writing Program Administration, 31*(1–2), 124–149.

Bransford, J. D., & Schwartz, D. L. (1999). Rethinking transfer: A simple proposal with multiple implications. *Review of Research in Education, 24*(1), 61–100.

Carroll, L. A. (2002). *Rehearsing new roles: How college students develop as writers*. Southern Illinois University Press.

Chiseri-Strater, E. (1991). *Academic literacies: The public and private discourse of university students*. Boynton/Cook Publishing.

Choi, B. C. & Pak A. W. (2006). Multidisciplinarity, interdisciplinarity and transdisciplinarity in health research, services, education and policy: 1. Definitions, objectives, and evidence of effectiveness. *Clinical Investigative Medicine, 29*(6), 351–364.

Engeström, Y. (2014). *Learning by expanding: An activity-theoretical approach to developmental research*. Cambridge University Press.

Flower, L., & Hayes, J. R. (1981). A cognitive process theory of writing. *College Composition and Communication, 32*(4), 365–387.

Hammer, D., Elby, A., Scherr, R. E., & Redish, E. F. (2005). Resources, framing, and transfer. In J. P. Mestre (Ed.), *Transfer of learning from a modern multidisciplinary perspective*, (pp. 89–120). Information Age Publishing.

Hargadon, A. B. (1998). Firms as knowledge brokers: Lessons in pursuing continuous innovation. *California Management Review, 40*(3), 209–227.

Lave, J., & Wenger, E. (1991). *Situated learning: Legitimate peripheral participation*. Cambridge University Press.

Lemke, J. L. (2000). Across the scales of time: Artifacts, activities, and meanings in ecosocial systems. *Mind, Culture, and Activity, 7*(4), 273–290.

Lobato, J. (2012). The actor-oriented transfer perspective and its contributions to educational research and practice. *Educational Psychologist, 47*(3), 232–247.

Matsuda, P. K. (2013). It's the wild west out there: A new linguistic frontier in U.S. college composition. In A. S. Canagarajah (Ed.), *Literacy as translingual practice: Between communities and classrooms* (pp. 128–138). Routledge.

McCarthy, L. P. (1987). A stranger in strange lands: A college student writing across the curriculum. *Research in the Teaching of English, 21*(3), 233–265.

MacDonald, S. P. (2007). The erasure of language. *College Composition and Communication, 58*(4): 585–625.

Miller, C. R. (1984). Genre as social action. *Quarterly Journal of Speech, 70*(2), 151–167.

Nelms, R. G, & Dively, R. L. (2007). Perceived roadblocks to transferring knowledge from first-year composition to writing-intensive major courses: A pilot study. *WPA: Writing Program Administration, 31*(1–2), 214–240.

Nonaka, I. (1991). The knowledge creating company. *Harvard Business Review*, 96-104.

Nowacek, R. S. (2011). *Agents of integration: Understanding transfer as a rhetorical act*. Southern Illinois University Press.

Perkins, D.N., & Salomon, G. (1988). Teaching for transfer. *Educational Leadership, 46*(1), 22–32.

Perkins, D.N., & Salomon, G. (1989). Are cognitive skills context bound? *Educational Researcher, 18*(1), 16–25.

Perkins, D. N., & Salomon, G. (2012). Knowledge to go: A motivational and dispositional view of transfer. *Educational Psychologist, 47*(3), 248–258.

Petraglia, J. (Ed.). (1995). *Reconceiving writing, rethinking writing instruction*. Lawrence Erlbaum.

Prior, P., & Shipka, J. (2003). Chronotopic lamination: Tracing the contours of literate activity. In C. Bazerman & D.R. Russell (Eds.), *Writing selves, writing societies: Research from activity perspectives* (pp. 180–238). The WAC Clearinghouse and Mind, Culture, and Activity.

Qualley, D. (2016). Building a conceptual topography of the transfer terrain. In C. M. Anson and J.L. Moore (Eds.), *Critical transitions: Writing and the question of transfer* (pp. 69–106). The WAC Clearinghouse.

Schunk, D. H. (2004). *Learning theories: An educational perspective* (4th ed.). Pearson.

Smit, D. W. (2004). *The end of composition studies*. Southern Illinois University Press.

Sternglass, M. S. (1997). *Time to know them: A longitudinal study of writing and learning at the college level*. Lawrence Erlbaum.

Tardy, C. M. (2017). Crossing, or creating, divides? A plea for transdisciplinary scholarship. In B. Horner & L. Tetreault (Eds.), *Crossing divides: Exploring translingual writing pedagogies and programs* (pp. 181–189). Utah State University Press.

Thorndike, E. L. & Woodworth, R. S. (1901). The influence of improvement in one mental function upon the efficiency of other functions. (I). *Psychological Review, 8*(3), 247–61.

Wardle, E. (2007). Understanding "transfer" from FYC: Preliminary results of a longitudinal study. *WPA: Writing Program Administration, 31*(1–2), 65–85.

Yancey, K. B. (1998). *Reflection in the writing classroom*. Utah State University Press.

2 Cognitive Psychology and Situated Learning: Foundational Research on Transfer of Learning

This volume begins with a review of the fields of cognitive psychology and situated learning—in part because they offer the earliest instances of empirical research into transfer of learning and more importantly because they establish the foundational arc followed in many other fields from behaviorist assumptions to cognitive investigations to a growing appreciation of the situated nature of learning. We will see the same arc in writing studies and in a number of other areas in the following chapters including industrial and organizational psychology (Chapter 3), and sports, medical, aviation, and military education (Chapter 4). Nonetheless, psychology remains focused primarily on individuals and is dominated by the so-called two-problem paradigm that establishes a baseline of initial learning, then tracks subsequent transfer of that learning to a novel context.

Cognitive studies of transfer are dominated by a few recurring questions.

- What level of abstract understanding best facilitates transfer of learning? How can individuals effectively build such abstract understandings? What is the influence of social and material contexts on those abstractions?
- What types of hints or cues might prompt individuals to recognize similarities between prior learning and new contexts?
- Are there general abilities that will facilitate transfer of learning?

Much of the cognitive research on transfer of learning focuses on analogical reasoning; it was conducted in labs and studies "isomorphic problems"—that is, problems that share a deep underlying structure despite superficial differences. Another tradition of cognitive research into learning—theories of dual processing—doesn't address transfer of learning directly but nevertheless has important implications for understanding how individuals draw on their earlier learning when they approach new contexts. Subsequent research from the situated learning perspective, however, often moved out of the lab, studying, for example, how individuals repurposed their classroom learning of mathematical concepts in homes and in stores.

Although cognitive studies of transfer did not pay much attention to writing, we can see their influence on later writing studies research—for example, in the role attributed to abstraction in high- and low-road transfer and in the imperative for students to develop theories of writing as a means of promoting transfer. Also, the "actor-oriented perspective" (rather than that of teachers and researchers) dominant in writing studies has its origins in cognitive studies. This chapter outlines the history of psychological research on transfer of learning from early behaviorist work by Thorndike, through cognitivist approaches and their situative critiques, to current efforts to synthesize those approaches.

Thorndike and the Early History of Transfer

The first formal empirical study of transfer in the Western tradition is often attributed to Thorndike, who, together with Woodworth, published three studies on how improvement in one "mental function" might influence the "efficiency" of others (Thorndike & Woodworth, 1901a, 1901b, 1901c). These studies interrogated the assumptions of formal discipline theory, which asserted "the mind was a collection of faculties or powers—observation, attention, memory, reasoning, will, and the like—and that any gain in any faculty was a gain for the faculty as a whole" (Thorndike, 1906 / 1916, p. 236). Formal discipline theory regularly invoked metaphors of the mind as a machine (which could be made more efficient) and as a muscle (which could be made stronger). In contrast, Thorndike and Woodworth argued that previous research had established no correlation between relatively distinct skills like spelling and multiplication (1901a, p. 248) and set out to examine participants' ability to transfer between two more closely related skills sets.

Thorndike focused on the similarities between two tasks he believed could facilitate transfer but found that training in one task did not necessarily improve performance in another. One study, for example, found no transfer from the ability to estimate area in rectangles to triangles (Thorndike and Woodworth, 1901a, p. 256). Another study found training in identifying one alphabetic pattern (for example, ER) did not lead to improvement in identifying a different alphabetic pattern (say, AN). However, the study did find improvement in those pairings that had "identical elements" (Thorndike & Woodworth, 1901c, p. 558); for example, if subjects were to first look for instances of ES, participants were subsequently more successful finding ERs or SPs (which share an identical letter) than ANs.

Thorndike later expanded on this theory of identical elements in popular texts that explicitly debunked the tendency to valorize certain subjects of study (like Latin) as a means to general improvement:

> One mental function or activity improves others in so far as and because they are in part identical with it, because it contains elements common to them. Addition improves multiplication because multiplication is largely addition; knowledge of Latin gives increased ability to learn French because many of the facts learned in the one case are needed in the other. (Thorndike, 1906/1916, p. 243)

Put into pedagogical practice, Thorndike's theory of identical elements argued for a series of carefully sequenced tasks meant to establish as much overlap as possible from one context to the next. As the field of psychology developed, however, critics came to condemn Thorndike's theory of identical elements as a hallmark of his behaviorism (e.g., Beach, 1999, p. 105).

An early challenge to the identical elements theory of transfer emerged from Judd's (1908) studies of elementary school boys throwing darts at an underwater target. Because the light refracted under water, the target was not where it appeared to be. Judd explained the principle of refraction to half the participants before they threw the first dart. At first, that explanation made no significant difference in the performance of the two groups. However, when (in a second round of the experiment) the depth of the water changed, the participants armed with a theoretical description of refraction performed considerably better. Judd concluded that it's not identical elements that matter, but rather abstract principles combined with initial learning; Judd's finding began a long tradition of research searching for the optimal sequence of exposure to concrete examples and abstract principles.

Rather than focusing on connections prompted by superficial identical elements, Gestalt theorists understood transfer of learning as the result of an individual's deep understanding. Katona (1940), for instance, compared the "senseless" learning engendered by a "depository of connections" to the "meaningful" learning that results from true understanding of a principle (p. 5-6). Through experiments conducted with card tricks and geometry problems, Katona concluded that meaningful learning occurs when "an integrated knowledge (a whole-principle) [is] acquired and . . . later applied to all tasks involv[ing] the same principle" (p. 127). Werthheimer (1945/1959) similarly argued for the value of whole-quality learning, using the example of children taught to calculate the area of a parallelogram who then struggled to calculate the area of parallelograms with only minute surface-level differences. The problem, he concluded, was that they did not have the kind of "structural understanding" that "plays a decisive role in transfer" (p. 35). This focus on the wholeness of learning was a stark contrast to Thorndike's focus on the match between individual (and often atomized) elements.

The Cognitive Revolution

Thorndike's theory of identical elements held great sway in educational circles during the first half of the twentieth century: it remained "the guiding notion behind a very large number of educational approaches that were especially popular from the period of about 1940 to 1970" (Royer et al., 2005, p. xiii). Not until psychology's so-called cognitive revolution in the 1950s did researchers begin to build significantly different theories of transfer, focusing less on the learning environment and more on individuals' mental representations of that environment.

Concepts and Schemata: Definitions and Methods for Study

The basic unit of analysis in cognitive research is the *concept* (Hammer et al., 2005, p. 95), a mental representation of a category of objects (whether tangible like "dogs" or intangible like "love") that an individual builds or abstracts through exposure to multiple specific examples. Concepts are often understood in relation to each other; these relationships are sometimes called a schema. Concepts and schemata are often referred to as "deep structures"—as opposed to the surface features of various specific situations.

Methodologically, early cognitivist research on transfer frequently focused on analogical reasoning, tracing how individuals use the concepts and schemata they've developed from previous specific situations to make sense of a new situation. Such studies often adopted the two-problem paradigm pioneered by Thorndike, lab studies that tracked whether exposure to task A would have any discernible effect on participants' ability to complete task B. By setting up "isomorphic problems" in which tasks had the same deep structure but significantly different surface features, cognitivist researchers probed participants' ability to recognize the relationships between them. Overwhelmingly, researchers concluded that individuals are unlikely to make spontaneous connections. Reed et al. (1974), for instance, found that despite what seemed to the researchers like obvious parallels between two problems, participants proved unable to solve the second problem any more quickly or accurately than the first and concluded "there was no significant transfer between the two problems" (p. 439). Gick and Holyoak (1980) found that when asked to solve a difficult problem and provided with an analogy, participants noticed and used the analogy to solve the problem only 20% of the time—hardly much better than the 10% of people who came to the solution without any analogy provided.

Despite the persistent difficulties of documenting spontaneous transfer, cognitivist researchers identified at least five conditions that tend to assist people in transferring knowledge: robust initial learning, an ability to move beyond surface details to recognize more abstract concepts and schemata, hints, a process of comparing cases to build an appropriately abstract schema, and general abilities like heuristics and mindfulness.

Robust Initial Learning

One central finding from Gick and Holyoak's (1980, 1983) foundational research on analogical reasoning is that mere exposure to an isomorphic problem does not have the same positive effect as robust learning that results in abstracting the relevant concept. The isomorphic problem at the heart of Gick and Holyoak's research relies on a medical dilemma first posed by Duncker (1945): the radiation required to destroy a tumor must be intense enough to destroy the tumor, but such radiation also destroys healthy tissue it traverses; radiation levels low enough to not harm healthy tissue won't destroy the tumor. How to proceed? The so-called *dispersion solution* sends low-intensity radiation from multiple directions to converge on the tumor. Duncker found that participants rarely generated the dispersion solution spontaneously: of 42 participants, only two generated the dispersion solution—and only with a hint.

To study the conditions under which people could generate a solution to Duncker's radiation problem through analogical reasoning, Gick and Holyoak created an isomorphic problem: a general wants to attack a fortress located at the center of several roads that radiate like spokes from the hub of the fortress; the roads have been mined to explode under the weight of any substantial army. If the general sends too many troops down one road, the mines will detonate; if the general doesn't send enough troops to the fortress, they cannot succeed. The general's solution is to send smaller groups along each road: each group is too small to set off the mines on their road, but collectively they can capture the fortress. Using Duncker's radiation problem and this isomorphic military problem, Gick and Holyoak designed a series of experiments to gauge what kinds of exposure to analogous problems might help participants generate the dispersion solution.

Gick and Holyoak (1983) found that deep learning is necessary for people to draw out the implications of their analogies. In one experiment, before participants were given the radiation problem, they were asked to read and engage with two analogous stories by writing about the similarities between the stories. Researchers then rated the degree to which those descriptions articulated a schema that focused on the convergence of dispersed forces. When subsequently given the medical radiation problem, individuals whose descriptions were rated as good schemata were able to generate the dispersion solution without a hint 91% of the time; those with an intermediate schema could do so only 40% of the time; and those with a poor schema only 30% of the time (pp. 23–24). This finding strongly suggests that robust learning in the form of an emergent abstract schema leads to increased rates of spontaneous transfer. Similarly, Gentner and Gentner (1983) concluded that exposure to an analogy does not have the same effect as robust learning that results in a rich mental representation.

An Ability to Move Beyond Surface Details to Abstract Schemata

Gick and Holyoak's (1980) research also makes clear that surface differences impede transfer. For instance, when they gave participants the story about the general and a second story that had more surface differences despite a deep structural similarity, they found that surface differences impeded (but did not entirely inhibit) analogical reasoning. One means of promoting transfer, then, might be moving beyond, even erasing, surface-level details. This ability to overcome the distractions of surface details is characteristic of expert knowledge. For example, Chi et al. (1981) found that while expert physicists tended to sort physics problems according to deep structural differences (like the laws of physics), novice undergraduate physics students were more likely to focus on surface details (sorting problems according to objects or keywords—like planes or blocks on an incline). One of the characteristics of expertise is the ability to use surface-level features, like springs, to access deep structural knowledge, like the laws of energy.

However, in later research, Gick and Holyoak (1983) identified a tension: although having an abstract schema makes it easier to recognize analogies that might be obscured by surface-level differences, it is also true that particular surface similarities sometimes prompt an individual to make the connection to an abstract schema. (This finding resonates with Nowacek's [2011] claim that genre can be an exigence for transfer and Lindenman's [2015] idea of metagenres, discussed in Chapter 8.) As a result, the "'optimal' level of representation for successful analogical thinking may typically lie at an intermediate level of abstraction" (p. 9).

Hints

Another recurrent finding in the analogical reasoning studies is that people's ability to transfer dramatically increases if they are prompted to use their prior knowledge. Gick and Holyoak's (1980, 1983) research, for instance, is filled with examples of the importance of hints. Throughout their eleven experiments, participants were more likely to achieve the dispersion solution if they were given a hint—that is, if they were told "you may find that the first problem you solved gives you some hints for solving the second problem" (1980, pp. 337–8). This tendency is particularly visible in the fourth experiment of the 1980 study. All participants were asked to memorize three stories—one was the relevant story about the general and two others were distractor stories—and then given the radiation problem to solve; some participants were given the hint that the earlier story might prove helpful; others were not. With the hint, 92% of participants could identify the problem the general faced as useful and generate the dispersion solution—but without the hint, the percentage of participants able to generate the dispersion solution plummeted to 20%. Hints, it appears, can even overcome distractor stories with false analogies. Similarly, Reed et al. (1974) found that most participants given two isomorphic puzzles did not, when left to their own devices, solve the second problem any faster or more accurately than the first, suggesting the lack of any transfer. However, when the second problem "included an additional paragraph that described how the second problem was related to the first" (p. 439), rates of transfer increased dramatically. Together, these studies suggest the power of hints or prompts to facilitate transfer.

Articulating an Abstract Principle from Comparative Cases

In addition to the value of hints, research in the cognitivist tradition argues that prompting participants to draw abstract principles from multiple examples facilitates analogical problem solving/transfer of learning. Although early research (Judd, 1908) argued that participants given a brief explanation of the abstract principle performed better than those without, subsequent research argued that simply providing participants with the abstract principle behind an analogical solution was consistently less effective than requiring participants to compare multiple examples and actively abstract the principle themselves. More specifically, researchers examined multiple factors that might influence the process of abstracting principles, including how many example stories participants were given, whether those stories illustrated the general principle or were "distractor" stories, whether participants were also given an explicit articulation of the abstract principle, and whether the participants were asked to articulate the abstract principle for themselves. Three findings stand out as particularly important for writing studies scholars.

First, providing participants with the abstract principle is not as helpful as providing examples (in the form of stories). Gick and Holyoak (1983) found that participants given only the principle improved their ability to generate the dispersion solution at a lower rate than participants given stories or stories and the principle (66% rather than nearly 80%).

Second, what helps participants most is working with *multiple* examples or stories—especially when participants are asked to abstract a general principle. Gick and Holyoak (1983) found that if participants were given two stories illustrating the dispersion principle from different domains, the frequency of generating the dispersion solution without a hint more than doubled the rates with only one analogy. Furthermore, working to actively compare those examples proves crucial, as illustrated by Gentner and colleagues' research on analogical encoding (the process of not just reading two analogues but actively comparing and connecting them). In a study of business students learning new negotiation strategies, Gentner et al. (2003) found that participants who actively compared cases exemplifying a new principle were more than twice as likely to transfer that principle to a subsequent negotiation than participants asked to describe but never compare sample cases. Gentner's theory of analogical encoding proposes that individuals can inductively build their own schema through comparisons, and that serial exposure to multiple examples is far less effective in facilitating transfer of learning than actively comparing them to build an appropriately abstract schema grounded in specifics.

Third, explicit articulations of the underlying principle provided by the researcher are helpful inasmuch as they ensure that participants' self-generated principles are on the right track. For instance, Gick and Holyoak (1983) evaluated the quality of participants' articulations of their general principle (or "schema"). They concluded that when participants were given an explicit articulation of the general principle in addition to being asked to describe in writing the similarities between the stories, the "addition of the principle had a strong influence on schema quality" (p. 26) as well as eventual transfer. In short, for writing studies scholars interested in helping students "learn how to learn", this finding—that multiple examples combined with an explicit articulation of the principle helped participants increase their rates of transfer—may offer important pedagogical guidance.

General Abilities: Heuristics, Mindfulness, and the Value of Automatized Cognitive Processes

Finally, researchers in the cognitivist tradition asked whether there might be general, portable strategies that can facilitate transfer. After briefly reviewing the idea of general heuristics, we turn to the idea of mindfulness that characterizes Perkins and Salomon's ideas of high-road and low-road transfer. Because Perkins and Salomon receive so much uptake in the field of writing studies, we conclude this section on cognitivist research by contextualizing their work within the cognitivist tradition of "dual processing" research.

One manifestation of the hope for "general skills" that might facilitate transfer was the idea of a general heuristics—or "methods and rules of discovery and invention" (Polya, 1945/1957, p. 112)—for mathematical problem solving. Much like ancient rhetoric's *koina topoi* that serve as a means of invention in any situation whatsoever (Aristotle, 2004, p. 90), Polya's (1945/1957) popular text aimed to articulate a series of questions that could prompt productive mathematical problem solving for any type of problem. The bulk of the book is a dictionary of heuristics—largely consisting of questions (Can you derive the result differently? Do you know a related problem?), prompts (Examine your guess. Look at the unknown.), and significant concepts (corollary, setting up equations). Polya frames this book as a generative catalog of the behaviors of expert mathematical problem solvers, not a narrow prescription. Heuristics like these have had a long shelf life as general strategies that can be used across varied contexts—the ultimate portable, transferrable knowledge.

Polya's work with general heuristics was extended by Schoenfeld in two important ways. First, Schoenfeld (1985) empirically demonstrated the positive effect of Polya's heuristic strategies; students in a classroom focused on five of Polya's heuristics did significantly better on a test designed to probe their problem-solving skills. Second, Schoenfeld worked to help students internalize a series of heuristics *and* learn to choose among them. Working from transcripts of problem-solving sessions, Schoenfeld (1992) argues that experts exhibit extraordinary self-monitoring skills that help them try out and discard a series of possible approaches—and that such self-monitoring strategies can be taught. After taking a course based on his heuristic pedagogy, the number of students who would jump into a solution attempt and pursue it no matter what dropped from 60% to 20%. This self-regulation is another manifestation of a general strategy that might transfer—and facilitate transfer—across problem types. Certainly, writing studies scholars have long been interested in this type of self-monitoring (from Flower and Hayes's [1981] discussion of the monitor onward), and it is increasingly considered in studies of writing transfer (Driscoll & Powell, 2016; Driscoll & Wells, 2012).

While Schoenfeld focused on the portable strategy of self-monitoring, Perkins and Salomon (1988, 1989) focused on mindfulness. Transfer, they note, suffers from a Bo Peep problem: people assume that transfer will automatically follow learning, like sheep trailing after the nursery-rhyme maiden—but such trust is "inordinately optimistic" (1988, p. 23). To explain why transfer does (and does not) take place, they posit two types of transfer: low-road and high-road transfer. Low-road transfer "reflects the automatic triggering of well-practiced routines in circumstances where there is considerable perceptual similarity to the original learning context" (p. 25); for instance, when a person sits down to drive a truck after having only ever driven cars, "the steering wheel begs one to steer it, the windshield invites one to look through it, and so on" (p. 25). High-road transfer "depends on deliberate mindful abstraction of skill or knowledge from one context for application in another" (p. 25) and can be either forward looking or backward reaching.

These are familiar concepts to scholars in writing studies, imported by researchers interested in transfer of writing skills (e.g., Anson, 2016; Beaufort, 2007; Kain & Wardle, 2005; Nelms & Dively, 2007; Nowacek, 2011; Reiff & Bawarshi, 2011; Yancey et al., 2014). What is less well known, though, is how this model of transfer is in quiet conversation with another tradition of cognitivist research, research focused not on the types of analogical problem solving discussed thus far in this chapter, but on attention, memory, and perception. The high-road/low-road model is one among several ways of understanding transfer. On one hand are those scholars who valorize mindfulness and dismiss the more routinized process Perkins and Salomon associated with low-road transfer; on the other are scholars who articulate the value of what they call automaticity in the development of abstract schema and expertise. Salomon explicitly acknowledged the connection of this work to the tradition of attention research by noting that the "construct of mindfulness . . . is based on the distinction between controlled and automatic processes (Schneider & Fisk, 1984; Shiffrin & Schneider, 1977)" (Salomon & Globerson, 1987, p. 625).

To better understand what the work of Perkins and Salomon offers writing studies and what it obscures, it is helpful to also understand theories of dual-processing. Although a wide range of dual-processing theories use different terminologies, they share the idea that every individual possesses "two different modes of processing" characterized by "processes that are unconscious, rapid, automatic, and high capacity, and those that are conscious, slow, and deliberative" (Evans 2008, p. 256). Kahneman (2003, 2011) calls those two processing systems "System 1" and "System 2" and explains that

> The operations of System 1 are typically fast, automatic, effortless, associative, implicit (not available to introspection), and often emotionally charged; they are also governed by habit and are therefore difficult to control or modify. The operations of System 2 are slower, serial, effortful, more likely to be consciously monitored and deliberately controlled; they are also relatively flexible and potentially rule governed. (Kahneman, 2003, p. 698)

Whereas the dual-processing scholarship persistently acknowledges the complementary nature of these two systems, other scholars especially value the flexibility of System 2's effortful, mindful control—suggesting that it is a portable quality or strategy that can facilitate transfer across multiple contexts. (See, for instance, Hatano and Inagaki's [1986] discussion of adaptive expertise.)

Flexibility and control are valorized in Perkins and Salomon's concept of high-road transfer. In an earlier essay, Salomon and Globerson (1987) connected this mindful process with increased levels of abstraction. Referring to research by Gick and Holyoak (1983) on the limited usefulness of providing participants with an already formulated general principle, Salomon and Globerson conclude that it's better for subjects to be "actively engaged themselves in mindfully abstracting the problem's underlying principle. Having an abstraction," they determine, "is not the same as mindfully deriving one" (p. 633). In a similar vein, Salomon (with Perkins) largely dismisses low-road transfer in a subsequent publication, using the stimulus-response language of behaviorism so reviled in cognitivist research.[2]

Other scholars, however, are less dismissive of the value of more automatized processes. Shiffrin and Schneider (1977), for instance, are part of a tradition of inquiry interested in how people manage the cognitive load limitations of short-term memory. Faced with the problem of how individuals divide their attention among multiple sensory inputs, Shiffrin and Schneider distinguished between what they call "automatic detection" and "controlled search."[3] Although controlled processes "may be set up, altered, and applied in novel situations for which automatic sequences have never been learned" (pp. 156–7), the continued advantage of automatic processes is that they are not constrained by the capacity limitations of short-term memory and "their speed and automaticity will usually keep their constituent elements hidden from conscious perception" (p. 160).

The hidden value of automated, even unconscious processes is also at the heart of the work of Kahneman, well known both for the Nobel Prize in Economics he received for his work on decision-making and for his best-selling *Thinking, Fast and Slow* (2011). Kahneman began as a cognitive psychologist "rooted in the psychology of perception" (2011, p. 6) and interested in attention; early in his career (Kahneman, 1973), he argued for a "capacity model" of attention that informed the work of Shiffrin and Schneider and others. In *Thinking, Fast and Slow*, Kahneman calls on that research to defend the importance of System 1 (or "fast") thinking and argue that the routinized automaticity of System 1 is where skilled expertise, built up over long periods of time, resides. Although Kahneman acknowledges that System 1 is also the home of less informed intuitions, he argues this is not a fault of System 1, merely the reality of how Systems 1 and 2 co-exist. Indeed, Kahneman suggests, if blame is to be placed, it should fall at the feet of the mindful abstractions of System 2, which are often too slow to kick in

---

2. "The major difference between the low and the high roads to transfer lies in the processes that yield the transfer: *automatic, stimulus-controlled,* and extensively practiced behaviors or cognitions versus mindful deliberate processes that decontextualize the cognitive elements which are candidates for transfer. The hallmark of the high road is the mindful abstraction it involves." (Salomon & Perkins, 1989, p. 124, emphasis added)

3. Shiffrin and Schneider were by no means the first to offer such a model, as a lengthy section relating their model to previous models (pp. 171–184) indicates. See Evans (2008) for a thorough review of the scholarship.

(2011, pp. 416–7). It is easy to fault System 1 for leading people to intuitive, unconsidered mistakes. After all, Kahneman notes, "When we think of ourselves, we identify with System 2, the conscious, reasoning self that has beliefs, makes choices, and decides what to think about and what to do." But, Kahneman adds, System 1 should not be so easily dismissed: "Although System 2 believes itself to be where the action is, the automatic System 1 is the hero of the book" (2011, p. 21). In short, Kahneman and others in the tradition of research on attention offer an important counterbalance to ways in which the valorization of mindful high-road transfer has often dismissed more automatized low-road transfer. For writing studies scholars, this tradition of cognitivist research may offer a framework for reconsidering both the frequency and the value of unconscious or automatized transfer. (See, for instance, Donahue, 2012; Nowacek et al., 2019; Ringer, 2018).

Situated Learning Critiques of the Cognitive Approach

Although the cognitivist approach to studying transfer has been highly generative, it has not been without criticism. Lave and Wenger's (1991) notions of communities of practice and legitimate peripheral participation have received much attention within writing studies, but it was Lave's (1988) earlier work on mathematics in everyday life that offered a new paradigm in psychological studies of transfer. Critiquing the limitations of cognitivist studies confined to laboratories, Lave established the advantage of "moving into the experienced, lived-in world as the site and source of further investigations of cognitive activity" (p. 44). The Adult Math Project studied how individuals use math in contexts like supermarkets and dieting and concluded that people's mathematical reasoning is profoundly affected by context. As a whole, the Adult Math Project challenged both the theoretical assumptions and methodological approaches of previous scholarship.

Some of these situative critiques are already familiar in writing studies, including Beach's (1995, 1999) idea of "consequential transitions." His study of two generations of shopkeepers studying mathematics in Nepal illustrates the ways in which context matters for cognition. Younger students transitioning from school to work continued to use many written mathematical notations but also added the finger calculation strategies used by experienced shopkeepers. Experienced shopkeepers largely maintained their established finger calculation strategies but added some modified written notations to their practices. In both instances, individuals adapted classroom strategies in ways informed by their identities and contexts (1995). Carraher et al.'s (1985) work is less known in writing studies, but also moved out of the laboratory setting to argue for the importance of context. Researching young people in Brazil who did rapid mental calculations as part of their livelihood on the streets, Carraher and colleagues gave participants mathematical problems in a lab and on the street and found that participants with more context were much more likely to provide the correct answers (36% versus 98%) and used very different problem-solving routines. In subsequent research, Carraher and Schleimann (2002) abandoned the term *transfer* as "misleading" because it "suggests a relatively passive 'carrying over' and deployment of learning from one situation to another," seeking instead a new understanding of transfer as a process of "adjusting and adapting . . . prior knowledge" (p. 19).

Although the situated learning critique dramatically altered transfer research in the field of psychology, we can trace how issues central to the earlier cognitive research evolved in subsequent scholarship. We begin this next section by discussing how the notion of concepts changed and what that means for methods of studying transfer. We then track how situative scholars revisit the importance of two conditions central for transfer of learning in the cognitivist tradition: hints and abstracting general principles.

Revised Definitions of Concepts and New Methods for Study

In light of situated learning critiques, scholars questioned whether the concept was still the most helpful unit of analysis, revising their understanding of what concepts are and where they come from. For instance, Hammer et al. (2005) offer a "resource-based view of learning," arguing that "learning a new idea is not an all-or-nothing acquisition, but involves an activation of existing resources in new combinations" (p. 114). For Hammer and colleagues, concepts are no longer the basic unit of analysis but are "assumed to be built from finer-grained knowledge elements that have become tightly linked" (p. 96).

The situated learning critique brought a significant shift in research methods as well. Bransford and Schwartz (1999), for instance, critiqued previous studies as too focused on direct application to accurately reflect actual processes of learning and argued for a focus on preparation for future learning (discussed within writing studies by Driscoll [2015]). Methodologically, rather than following the usual two-problem paradigm, Schwartz and Martin (2004) developed a "double transfer" study—an approach that not only affirms the value of conceptualizing transfer as preparation for future learning, but also illustrates the need for new methods to investigate those new understandings.

In a similar vein of methodological innovation, Lobato (2003, 2006, 2008, 2012; Lobato & Siebert, 2002) articulates an actor-oriented theory (AOT) that grows out of her desire to extend the theories of Lave (1988) to empirical studies (2003, p. 19). Traditional studies of transfer, Lobato points out, "privilege the perspective of the observer and rely on models of expert performance, accepting as evidence of transfer only specific correspondences defined a priori as being the 'right' mappings" (Lobato, 2006, p. 434). For example, traditional studies might conclude that a student who could state the formula but was unable to accurately calculate slope on the transfer target problem offers no evidence of transfer (Lobato & Siebert, 2002). However, Lobato found that when she stopped looking for the answers she expected based on her own expert knowledge and shifted "to a consideration of the type of conceptions that students could have developed given the instructional treatment," she found considerable evidence of transfer. Her careful analyses revealed how students' incorrect answers were often informed by their efforts to draw on class discussions. Transfer is, in this actor-oriented framework, "in the eye of the beholder" (Lobato, 2008, p. 300). Traditional cognitivist studies aimed to teach participants to think like experts; if participants didn't solve the test problems correctly, researchers saw no transfer and questioned the quality of initial learning, the role of distractor problems in analogical reasoning, and so forth. Lobato changes the paradigm by arguing that even if participants fail to give the expected answer on researchers' tests, that "negative result" does not indicate that there wasn't transfer of learning; it means only that what students learn didn't manifest in the ways researchers expected. Some writing studies scholars may draw connections between this AOT framework and Nowacek's (2011) critique of negative transfer.

The methods of many studies described in the remainder of this chapter follow on this actor-oriented perspective, demonstrating a similar shift in how data are collected and analyzed. Studies take place over weeks or months, rather than during a single visit to a lab; they often rely on interviews and classroom observations; they include discourse analysis to unearth the development of students' understandings over time. The AOT perspective embodied in these studies "emphasizes the interpretive nature of knowing and the transfer of learners' underlying conceptualizations, relinquishes a predetermined standard for judging what counts as transfer and draws upon inductive qualitative methods" (Lobato, 2012, p. 243).

The Role of Hints, Reimagined

The situated learning critique led scholars to reimagine the role of hints by drawing on an idea from linguistics and anthropology: framing. For Hammer and colleagues (2005), frames are "a set of expectations an individual has about the situation in which she finds herself that affect what she notices and how she thinks to act" (p. 98). Similarly, Engle (2006) describes frames as "meta-communicative signals that help establish what the participants are doing together in it, when and where they are doing it, and how each person is participating in it, thus creating a 'frame' in which their activities can be interpreted" (p. 456). Engle tracks how a teacher of fifth-grade students frames their conversations—both in terms of time (reaching forward and back) and in terms of roles (framing them as authors of knowledge)—in ways that later make possible intercontextuality between the initial project and a subsequent project. What Engle calls "expansive framing" has "a family resemblance" to the types of hints described by Gick and Holyoak (1980, 1983), in as much as they "encourag[e] students to orient to what they know as being of continued relevance across times, places, people and topics" (Engle et al., 2011, p. 622).

More recent studies have sought to understand why individuals attend to particular aspects of situations. Lobato et al.'s (2012) study of *noticing* employs striking methodological innovations to learn more about how classroom instruction might influence what seventh graders learning about slope notice. First, in two different classes teaching slope, researchers used three cameras and a four-stage data-coding process to "track what individual students noticed during instruction" (p. 444); then they conducted individual interviews that included prompts to work on transfer tasks. Lobato and colleagues identified different trends in transfer among students in the two classrooms *and* linked those trends as "related conceptually to the divergent centers of focus that emerged across the two classes" (p. 473). What students "noticed mathematically" during the class sessions aligned conceptually with the reasoning they articulated in interviews and influenced (without overdetermining) subsequent transfer. Lobato and colleagues' theory of noticing goes far beyond earlier studies of hints, offering a powerful way to balance the influence of classroom instruction with the idiosyncrasies of individual learning. Pedagogically, framing is a strategy that can be easy to implement; methodologically, Lobato's study of noticing suggests the value of triangulating detailed analysis of classroom discussion with participant interviews and texts to illuminate individual cognition as a profoundly social achievement.

Questions of Abstraction, Revisited

Cognitivist studies of transfer often equated abstract concepts and principles with expertise that allowed participants to look beyond surface details, and much research focused on how participants might build abstract understandings from multiple examples, controlling for as many variables as possible. Did it matter if participants were given a general principle? Did it matter if they were given multiple concrete examples in story form? Did it matter how many? Did it matter if there were distractor stories? Did it matter if participants were coached to abstract principles from the stories? After the situated learning critique, however, researchers increasingly moved outside the laboratory and many began to question the role that material objects and contexts might play in learning and transfer of learning.

Some scholars have argued that abstract examples more effectively facilitate transferable learning than concrete instantiations (Kaminski et al., 2008, 2013). On the other end of the spectrum, scholars of embodied cognition[4] argue that cognition is "deeply dependent upon characteristics of the physical body of an agent, such that the agent's beyond-the-brain body plays a significant causal role, or a physically constitutive role, in that agent's cognitive processing" (Wilson & Foglia, 2017). In many ways, this work resonates with the work of writing studies scholars such as Olinger (2020; Prior & Olinger, 2019) and LeMesurier (2016) and with the discussions of distributed cogni-

---

4. A full review of theories of embodied cognition and their relationship to embedded cognition is beyond the scope of this chapter; see Menary, 2010; Pouw et al., 2014; and Wilson & Foglia, 2017 for three excellent introductions.

tion found in Chapter 3. Nemirovsky (2011), for instance, is interested in the physicality of learning and focuses on *episodic feelings*, that is, "feelings embedded in the specific circumstances of a time/place lived by the participants" (p. 311). He analyzes a moment in which Eleanor (a ten-year-old talking with an interviewer about graphs generated by motion detectors) makes a connection between the two-button motion detector she's currently holding and the one-button version she'd used the previous week. When Eleanor "stretched back her right hand, which [was] precisely the bodily activity that had accompanied her past statement of the one-button rule 'the farther back you hold it the higher it is'" (p. 333), she was prompted to a new understanding of the two-button detector. Nemirovsky argues that "episodic feelings are reexperienced bodily: Often the memory of a past event or situation emerges together with a bodily pose that partially reproduces the one that was adopted during that past event or situation" (p. 314). In this view, transfer of learning is not enabled by abstract principles but cued through concrete instantiations, including material environments and physical poses—a view not unlike Rifenberg's (2014) discussion of "embodied multimodal pedagogies." (See also the discussions of embodied cognition in Chapter 4 and Chapter 11.)

Between those two extremes—between those who insist on the superiority of abstraction and those who focus almost entirely on the value of physical contexts for transfer of learning—are a variety of theories and pedagogical techniques. The pedagogical technique known as concreteness fading (Fyfe et al., 2014) takes students through three stages: enactive (focusing on concrete models and physical experiences), iconic (stripping away details and using graphic symbols to link the concrete experience to the concept), and symbolic (using an abstract model to "highlight relevant structural patterns," p. 12). Goldstone and Son (2005) tested the concreteness fading hypothesis through different sequences of computer simulations. When asked to complete a subsequent transfer task, the students who began with the more concrete simulation demonstrated higher rates of transfer—affirming the concreteness-fading hypothesis that concrete instantiations and abstract learning need not be at odds, particularly if the concrete instantiations appear early in the learning process.

Additional research suggests not only that spatial information in initial learning fosters abstract models that facilitate transfer in subsequent tasks, but also that conscious awareness of the relationship between the concrete instantiation and the more abstract task is not necessary for transfer of learning (Day & Goldstone, 2011, 2012). Day and Goldstone (2011) conducted an experiment in which participants were asked to engage with two computer simulations: a visually based simulation required participants to position a fan to move a ball; a text-based simulation required participants to manage media campaigns that would exert a "force" on population growth. Despite their surface differences, the tasks both used forces (like wind from a fan or ad campaigns) to manipulate an outcome (like ball location or population size). Although moving a ball in one simulation has no obvious correlation to the task of increasing population in the other, individuals from Western societies tend to associate movement to the right with an increase and movement to the left with a decrease. Day and Goldstone therefore hypothesized that "[i]f participants have a natural tendency to translate population increases to rightward movements in space, then a congruent ball training scenario would lead to the development of a spatial model that could be applied to both tasks" (p. 557). This hypothesis was supported by three findings.

- When participants were asked to move the ball to the right in the first simulation, then asked to increase the population in the second, researchers found increased levels of transfer.
- When participants were asked to move the ball to the left (subconsciously perceived as a decrease), the indications of possible transfer disappeared.
- When participants completed the population simulation first, they did not demonstrate the same elevated ability to solve the second task showed by participants who completed the ball task first: because the population task was not "overtly and saliently spatial" in the way the ball simulation was, "no such transfer occurs" (p. 556).

Concrete, spatial instantiations matter—influencing transfer even across very dissimilar contexts.

What proved *not* to matter in Day and Goldstone's study was conscious awareness of the relationship between the concrete instantiation and the more abstract task. In a second version of the experiment, participants were asked several open-ended questions after they finished the experiment in order to determine their level of awareness of any connection between the two simulations. Awareness of the analogous relationship between the simulations was "generally beneficial for performance, [but] was not a necessary condition for transfer" (p. 559). Participants briefly told of the analogous relationship did not demonstrate increased levels of transfer, but participants led through a detailed process of mapping the correspondences between the two simulations demonstrated decreased levels of transfer. Surprised by that finding, Day and Goldstone concluded that perhaps "the intensive focus on explicit correspondences distracts participants from the perceptual and spatial information relevant for the formation of the mental model" (p. 561). The focus in this line of research—on the helpfulness of unconscious knowledge—is reminiscent of perceptual research on the value of automatized, unconscious transfer and of several scholars in writing studies (Donahue, 2012; Nowacek et al., 2019; Ringer, 2018; see also the discussion of automaticity in Chapter 11). In summary, within the ongoing debate over the advantages of abstract versus concrete instantiations, some researchers argue that conscious awareness of connections need not be necessary for—and may even impede—transfer of learning from one context to another.

Conclusion

Our goal in this chapter was to map the vast terrain of research on transfer of learning from the cognitive and situated learning perspectives, highlighting not just the conclusions, but the evolution of theories and methods as well. In the chapters that follow, many of these early studies reappear as touchstones and starting points.

For readers from writing studies, the research synthesized in this chapter suggests at least two lines of methodological innovation. First, the work of Lobato and colleagues underlines the importance of adopting what she calls an actor-oriented perspective. Although it is not unusual to see the actor-oriented perspective cited in writing studies research (e.g., Bromley et al., 2016; DePalma & Ringer, 2011; Driscoll & Wells, 2012; Gorzelsky et al., 2016; Hayes et al., 2016), many studies continue to examine data through the default lens of researcher and instructor expectations rather than centering students' perspectives or highlighting tensions between various participants' perspectives. Lobato's focus on actor perspectives as well as her innovative methods of drawing connections between classroom contexts and individual cognition (Lobato et al., 2012) offer valuable suggestions for future researchers. Second, there is a relatively small but intriguing tradition of research that highlights the important role material contexts may play in the transfer of learning across contexts (e.g., Day & Goldstone, 2011, 2012; Nemirovsky, 2011). These studies suggest the importance of continuing these inquiries within the field of writing studies, following the lead of LeMesurier (2016), Olinger (2020), Rifenburg (2014), and others.

This body of research has important pedagogical implications as well. Instruction—particularly in first-year writing classes—has already been powerfully influenced by arguments that developing conscious vocabulary for (Downs & Wardle, 2007) and even theories of (Yancey et al., 2014) writing might facilitate increased transfer of learning about writing. Such arguments echo Perkins and Salomon's (1988, 1989) ideas of high-road transfer. Studies of analogical encoding (Gentner et al., 2003) and various prompts to abstract principles from provided samples (Gick & Holyoak, 1980, 1983) might suggest to teachers further strategies for helping students to develop abstract schemata that promote transfer. Additionally, work in the dual-processing tradition (Kahneman, 2011; Day & Goldstone, 2011) questions whether such explicitly articulated schemata are always necessary for transfer of learning; such studies might encourage instructors to consider whether carefully scaffolded learning opportunities might still promote transfer of learning even if they stop short of asking students to articulate the schemata explicitly.

References

Anson, C. M. (2016). The Pop Warner chronicles: A case study in contextual adaptation and the transfer of writing ability. *College Composition and Communication, 67*(4), 518–549.

Aristotle. (2004). *Rhetoric*. (W. R. Roberts, Trans.). Dover Publications.

Beach, K. (1995). Activity as a mediator of sociocultural change and individual development: The case of school-work transition in Nepal. *Mind, Culture, and Activity, 2*(4), 285–302.

Beach, K. (1999). Consequential transitions: A sociocultural expedition beyond transfer in education. *Review of Research in Education, 24*(1), 101–139.

Beaufort, A. (2007). *College writing and beyond: A new framework for university writing instruction*. Utah State University.

Bransford, J. D., & Schwartz, D. L. (1999). Rethinking transfer: A simple proposal with multiple implications. *Review of Research in Education, 24*(1), 61–100.

Bromley, P., Northway, K., & Schonberg, E. (2016). Transfer and dispositions in writing centers: A cross-institutional, mixed-methods study. *Across the Disciplines, 13*(1), 1–15.

Carraher, T. N., Carraher, D. W., & Schliemann, A. D. (1985). Mathematics in the streets and in schools. *British Journal of Developmental Psychology, 3*(1), 21–29.

Carraher, D., & Schliemann, A. (2002). The transfer dilemma. *The Journal of the Learning Sciences, 11*(1), 1–24.

Chi, M. T., Feltovich, P. J., & Glaser, R. (1981). Categorization and representation of physics problems by experts and novices. *Cognitive Science, 5*(2), 121–152.

Day, S. B., & Goldstone, R. L. (2011). Analogical transfer from a simulated physical system. *Journal of Experimental Psychology: Learning, Memory, and Cognition, 37*(3), 551–567.

Day, S. B., & Goldstone, R. L. (2012). The import of knowledge export: Connecting findings and theories of transfer of learning. *Educational Psychologist, 47*(3), 153–176.

DePalma, M. J., & Ringer, J. M. (2011). Toward a theory of adaptive transfer: Expanding disciplinary discussions of "transfer" in second-language writing and composition studies. *Journal of Second Language Writing, 20*(2), 134–147.

Donahue, C. (2012). Transfer, portability, generalization: (How) does composition expertise 'carry'? In K. Ritter & P. Matsuda (Eds.), *Exploring Composition Studies: Sites, Issues, and Perspectives* (pp. 145–166). Utah State University Press.

Downs, D., & Wardle, E. (2007). Teaching about writing, righting misconceptions: (Re)envisioning "First-Year Composition" as "Introduction to Writing Studies." *College Composition and Communication, 58*(4), 552–584.

Driscoll, D. L., & Powell, R. (2016). States, traits, and dispositions: The impact of emotion on writing development and writing transfer across college courses and beyond. *Composition Forum, 34.* https://compositionforum.com/issue/34/states-traits.php

Driscoll, D. L., & Wells, J. (2012). Beyond knowledge and skills: Writing transfer and the role of student dispositions. *Composition Forum, 26.* https://compositionforum.com/issue/26/

Driscoll, D. L. (2015). Building connections and transferring knowledge: The benefits of a peer tutoring course beyond the writing center. *Writing Center Journal, 35*(1), 153–181.

Duncker, K. (1945). *On problem-solving.* American Psychological Association.

Engle, R. A. (2006). Framing interactions to foster generative learning: A situative explanation of transfer in a community of learners classroom. *The Journal of the Learning Sciences, 15*(4), 451–498.

Engle, R. A., Nguyen, P. D., & Mendelson, A. (2011). The influence of framing on transfer: Initial evidence from a tutoring experiment. *Instructional Science, 39*(5), 603–628.

Evans, J. S. B. (2008). Dual-processing accounts of reasoning, judgment, and social cognition. *Annual Review of Psychology, 59*, 255–278.

Flower, L., & Hayes, J. R. (1981). A cognitive process theory of writing. *College Composition and Communication, 32*(4), 365–387.

Fyfe, E. R., McNeil, N. M., Son, J. Y., & Goldstone, R. L. (2014). Concreteness fading in mathematics and science instruction: A systematic review. *Educational Psychology Review, 26*(1), 9–25.

Gentner, D., & Gentner, D. R. (1983). Flowing waters or teeming crowds: Mental models of electricity. In D. Gentner & A.L. Stevens (Eds.), *Mental models,* (pp. 99–129). Lawrence Erlbaum Associates.

Gentner, D., Loewenstein, J., & Thompson, L. (2003). Learning and transfer: A general role for analogical encoding. *Journal of Educational Psychology, 95*(2), 393–408.

Gick, M. L., & Holyoak, K. J. (1980). Analogical problem solving. *Cognitive Psychology, 12*(3), 306–355.

Gick, M. L., & Holyoak, K. J. (1983). Schema induction and analogical transfer. *Cognitive Psychology 15*(1), 1–38.

Goldstone, R. L., & Son, J. Y. (2005). The transfer of scientific principles using concrete and idealized simulations. *The Journal of the Learning Sciences, 14*(1), 69–110.

Gorzelsky, G., Driscoll, D. L., Paszek, J., Jones, E., & Hayes, C. (2016). Cultivating constructive metacognition: a new taxonomy for writing studies. In C. M. Anson & J. L. Moore (Eds.), *Critical transitions: Writing and the question of transfer,* (pp. 215–228). WAC Clearinghouse.

Hammer, D., Elby, A., Scherr, R. E., & Redish, E. F. (2005). Resources, framing, and transfer. In J. P. Mestre (Ed.), *Transfer of learning from a modern multidisciplinary perspective,* (pp. 89–120). Information Age Publishing.

Hatano, G., and K. Inagaki. (1986). Two courses of expertise. *Research and Clinical Center for Child Development, 6*, 27–36.

Hayes, H., Ferris, D. R., & Whithaus, C. (2016). Dynamic transfer in first-year writing and "writing in the disciplines" settings. In C. M. Anson & J. L. Moore (Eds.), *Critical transitions: Writing and the question of transfer,* (pp. 181–213). WAC Clearinghouse.

Judd, C. H. (1908). The relation of special training and general intelligence. *Educational Review, 36*, 28–42.

Kahneman, D. (1973). *Attention and effort.* Prentice-Hall.

Kahneman, D. (2003). A perspective on judgment and choice: Mapping bounded rationality. *American Psychologist, 58*(9), 697–720.

Kahneman, D. (2011). *Thinking, fast and slow.* Farrar, Straus and Giroux.

Kain, D., & Wardle, E. (2005). Building context: Using activity theory to teach about genre in multi-major professional communication courses. *Technical Communication Quarterly, 14*(2), 113–139.

Kaminski, J. A., Sloutsky, V. M., & Heckler, A. F. (2008). The advantage of abstract examples in learning math. *Science, 320*(25), 454–455.

Kaminski, J. A., Sloutsky, V. M., & Heckler, A. F. (2013). The cost of concreteness: The effect of nonessential information on analogical transfer. *Journal of Experimental Psychology: Applied, 19*(1), 14–29.

Katona, G. (1940). *Organizing and memorizing: Studies in the psychology of learning and teaching.* Columbia University Press.

Lave, J. (1988). *Cognition in practice: Mind, mathematics and culture in everyday life.* Cambridge University Press.

Lave, J, and E. Wenger. (1991). *Situated learning: Legitimate peripheral participation.* Cambridge University Press.

LeMesurier, J. L. (2016). Mobile bodies: Triggering bodily uptake through movement. *College Composition and Communication, 68*(2), 292–316.

Lindenman, H. (2015) Inventing metagenres: How four college seniors connect writing across domains. *Composition Forum, 31.* http://compositionforum.com/issue/31/inventing-metagenres.php

Lobato, J. (2003). How design experiments can inform a rethinking of transfer and vice versa. *Educational Researcher, 32*(1), 17–20.

Lobato, J. (2006). Alternative perspectives on the transfer of learning: History, issues, and challenges for future research. *Journal of the Learning Sciences, 15*(4), 431–449.

Lobato, J. (2008). When students don't apply the knowledge you think they have, rethink your assumptions about transfer. In M. Carlson & C. Rasmussen (Eds.), *Making the connection: Research and teaching in undergraduate mathematics* (pp. 289–304). Mathematical Association of America.

Lobato, J. (2012). The actor-oriented transfer perspective and its contributions to educational research and practice. *Educational Psychologist, 47*(3), 232–247.

Lobato, J., Rhodehamel, B., & Hohensee, C. (2012). "Noticing" as an alternative transfer of learning process. *Journal of the Learning Sciences, 21*(3), 433–482.

Lobato, J., & Siebert, D. (2002). Quantitative reasoning in a reconceived view of transfer. *The Journal of Mathematical Behavior, 21*(1), 87–116.

Menary, R. (2010). Introduction to the special issue on 4E cognition. *Phenomenology and the Cognitive Sciences, 9*(4), 459–463.

Nelms, G., & Dively, R. L. (2007). Perceived roadblocks to transferring knowledge from first-year composition to writing-intensive major courses: A pilot study. *WPA: Writing Program Administration, 31*(1–2), 214–240.

Nemirovsky, R. (2011). Episodic feelings and transfer of learning. *The Journal of the Learning Sciences, 20*(2), 308–337.

Nowacek, R. S. (2011). *Agents of integration: Understanding transfer as a rhetorical act.* Southern Illinois University Press.

Nowacek, R., Bodee, B., Douglas, J. E., Fitzsimmons, W. V., Hausladen, K. A., Knowles, M., & Nugent, M. (2019). "Transfer talk" in talk about writing in progress: two propositions about transfer of learning. *Composition Forum, 42.* compositionforum.com/issue/42/transfer-talk.php

Olinger, A. R. (2020). Visual embodied actions in interview-based writing research: A methodological argument for video. *Written Communication, 37*(2), 167–207.

Perkins, D. N., & Salomon, G. (1988). Teaching for transfer. *Educational Leadership, 46*(1), 22–32.

Perkins, D.N., & Salomon, G. (1989). Are cognitive skills context bound? *Educational Researcher, 18*(1), 16–25.

Prior, P. A., & Olinger, A. (2019). Academic literacies as laminated assemblage and embodied semiotic becoming. In D. Bloome, L. Castanheira, C. Leung, & J. Rowsell (Eds.), *Retheorizing literacy practices: Complex social and cultural contexts* (pp. 126–139). Routledge.

Polya, G. (1957). *How to solve it: A new aspect of mathematical method* (2nd ed.). Princeton University Press. (Original work published 1945)

Pouw, W. T., Van Gog, T., & Paas, F. (2014). An embedded and embodied cognition review of instructional manipulatives. *Educational Psychology Review, 26*(1), 51–72.

Reed, S. K., Ernst, G. W., & Banerji, R. (1974). The role of analogy in transfer between similar problem states. *Cognitive Psychology, 6*(3), 436–450.

Reiff, M. J., & Bawarshi, A. (2011). Tracing discursive resources: How students use prior genre knowledge to negotiate new writing contexts in first-year composition. *Written Communication, 28*(3), 312–337.

Rifenburg, J. M. (2014). Writing as embodied, college football plays as embodied: Extracurricular multimodal composing. *Composition Forum, 29.* http://compositionforum.com/issue/29/writing-as-embodied.php

Ringer, J. (2018) *Researching transfer: Addressing the challenges of knowing what works.* Conference on College Composition and Communication, 2018, Kansas City.

Royer, J., J. P. Mestre, & R. J. Dufresne. (2005). Framing the transfer problem. In J. Mestre (Ed.), *Transfer of learning from a modern multidisciplinary perspective* (pp. vii–xxvi). Information Age Publishing.

Salomon, G., & Globerson, T. (1987). Skill may not be enough: The role of mindfulness in learning and transfer. *International Journal of Educational Research, 11*(6), 623–637.

Salomon, G., & Perkins, D. N. (1989). Rocky roads to transfer: Rethinking mechanisms of a neglected phenomenon. *Educational Psychologist, 24*(2), 113–142.

Schoenfeld, A. H. (1985). *Mathematical problem solving.* Academic Press.

Schoenfeld, A. H. (1992). Learning to think mathematically: Problem solving, metacognition, and sense making in mathematics. *Handbook of research on mathematics teaching and learning*, 334–370.

Schwartz, D. L., & Martin, T. (2004). Inventing to prepare for future learning: The hidden efficiency of encouraging original student production in statistics instruction. *Cognition and Instruction*, *22*(2), 129–184.

Shiffrin, R. M., & Schneider, W. (1977). Controlled and automatic human information processing: II. Perceptual learning, automatic attending and a general theory. *Psychological Review*, *84*(2), 127–190.

Thorndike, E. L. (1916). *The principles of teaching based on psychology*. AG Seiler. (Original work published 1906)

Thorndike, E. L., & Woodworth, R. S. (1901a). The influence of improvement in one mental function upon the efficiency of other functions. *Psychological Review*, *8*(3), 247–261.

Thorndike, E. L., & Woodworth, R. S. (1901b). The influence of improvement in one mental function upon the efficiency of other functions: II. The estimation of magnitudes. *Psychological Review 8*(4), 384–395.

Thorndike, E. L., & Woodworth, R. S. (1901c). The influence of improvement in one mental function upon the efficiency of other functions: III. Functions involving attention, observation and discrimination. *Psychological Review 8*(6), 553–564.

Wertheimer, M. (1959). *Productive thinking*. Harper. (Original work published 1945)

Wilson, R. A., & Foglia, L. (2017). Embodied cognition. In E. N. Zalta (Ed.), *The Stanford encyclopedia of philosophy* (Spring 2017 Edition). https://plato.stanford.edu/archives/spr2017/entries/embodied-cognition/

Yancey, K., Robertson, L., & Taczak, K. (2014). *Writing across contexts: Transfer, composition, and sites of writing*. Utah State University Press.

3 Transfer of Training and Knowledge Management: Research from Industrial Psychology, Human Resources, and Management

Although writing specialists rarely turn to the fields of human resources and management for research or pedagogical inspiration, scholars in these fields have in fact been researching transfer of learning for several decades as both intra- and inter-personal phenomena. The methods may differ significantly from those valued by writing studies scholars, but the questions asked in human resources and management research are in fact deeply relevant to writing studies. How do the interrelationships of individual characteristics, instructional design, and social context influence transfer of learning? And what obstacles to transfer of learning make it more difficult for individuals or groups to successfully navigate new contexts?

The first portion of this chapter focuses on research conducted on what is known as "transfer of training"—that is, when a company invests in professional development training, do employees actually put those skills and abilities to use? Some writing studies scholars may be vexed by this tradition of research from industrial and organizational (I/O) psychology, because it primarily uses statistical analyses of closed-answer surveys. Nevertheless, we might benefit from understanding several decades of I/O research into dispositions for learning, including self-efficacy. The second portion of the chapter focuses on research from "knowledge management"—that is, the "transfer" of knowledge *among* employees. In writing studies, transfer is nearly always conceptualized as an intra-personal phenomenon, located within a single individual negotiating their own intellectual and social contexts. Interpersonal contexts are generally seen as teaching, not transfer.[5] However, this chapter explores how management scholars conceptualize the interpersonal dimensions of knowledge transfer and might challenge and expand thinking in the field of writing studies.

Together, research from transfer of training and knowledge management might help writing studies scholars better understand the experiences of individual writers, the influence of instructional design, and the possibility of a more collaborative view of transfer.

Transfer of Training: Focusing on Individuals Within a Workplace

Industrial and organizational (I/O) psychologists have taken an interest in the psychology of training since the 1950s. Early transfer-of-training scholarship was informed by a behaviorist framework that advocated techniques such as overlearning and sequencing identical elements (Gagne, 1962; Kraiger, 2003). Mirroring the arc described in Chapter 2, research on transfer of training took a cognitive turn in the late 1980s, to examine how learners are actively involved in their learning. Central to this turn was Bandura's social cognitive theory, which posits that learners operate at the juncture of three mutually influential forces: internal personal factors, behavioral factors, and environmental factors (Bandura, 1986, p. 18). Also central to Bandura's theory is the belief that human beings can learn not only from direct experience but through observation, which helps people abstract "rules for generative and innovative behavior" (Bandura, 1999, p. 25). Consequently, several lines of transfer-of-training scholarship examine the role of models and articulating general principles that can facilitate transfer. (In this, they echo the concerns of many scholars discussed in Chapter 2 as well as writing studies scholars interested in *imitatio* and generalizing principles of writing across contexts.) Social cognitive theory also posits that human beings exercise agency through processes of self-regulation as well as self-efficacy (Bandura, 1986). Writing studies scholars

---

5. For two exceptions, see Nowacek et al. (2019) and Winzenried et al. (2017).

have already begun to consider the role of Bandura's social cognitive theory—especially self-efficacy—in transfer of learning (e.g., Baird & Dilger, 2018; Driscoll & Wells, 2012; Mackiewicz & Thompson, 2013); this chapter argues that I/O scholarship might be more systematically brought to bear on defining dispositions and understanding how they work in models of the transfer-of-training process.

Less familiar to writing studies scholars is Baldwin and Ford's (1988) foundational transfer-of-training model. Baldwin and Ford synthesized existing scholarship into a model that identified three training inputs: trainee characteristics, training design, and work environment. (See figure 1.)

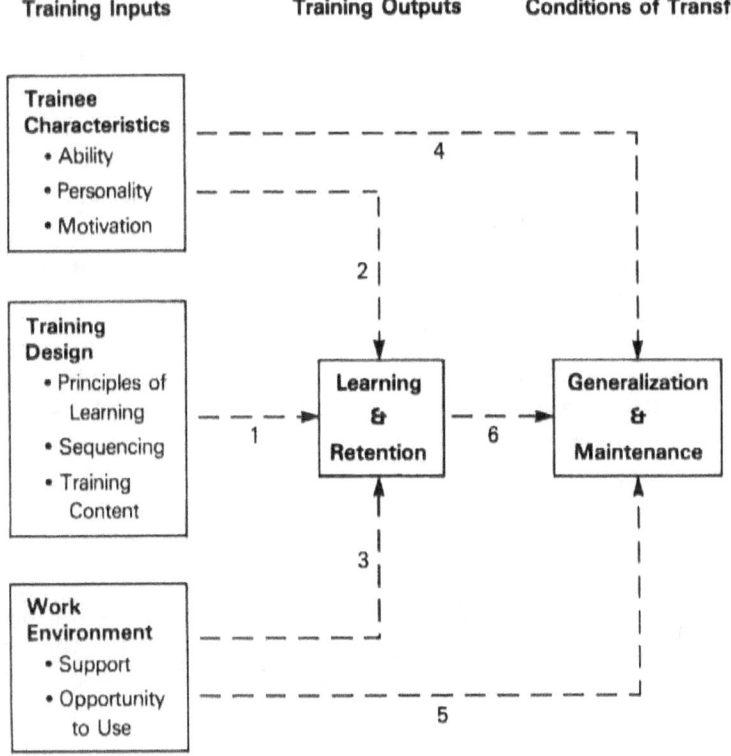

Figure 1: Baldwin and Ford's (1988) model of the transfer process

Writing studies scholars examining this model might note the importance it places on trainee motivation and other characteristics/dispositions, pedagogical considerations such as sequencing, and the distinction between generalization and maintenance. What may be less visible but still ultimately valuable to writing studies scholars is the focus in transfer-of-training scholarship on the importance of environment beyond instructional design and this field's commitment to examining how factors in the three categories of trainees, training design, and environment exist in relation to each other, seeking out correlations and possibly even causal relations.

The remainder of this transfer-of-training section is organized around Baldwin and Ford's three domains: trainee characteristics, training design, and transfer climate. Within the section on trainee characteristics, writing studies scholars will find scholarship that readily speaks to current work on dispositions such as self-efficacy, motivation, and locus of control; they might also be encouraged by the ways in which transfer-of-training scholarship persistently contextualizes these dispositions in relation to each other and to other domains of training design and work environment. Within the section on training design, writing studies scholars may be particularly drawn to discussions of behavioral modeling and error management—traditions of research that speak to writing instructors' long-standing interests in the use of sample texts and the framing of struggle and failure. Within the section on work environment, writing studies scholars may be especially interested in the ways I/O scholars operationalize social context not as a question of genre or discourse communities, but as issues of supervisor support, peer support, and opportunity to perform. Within each domain, we highlight foundational studies and draw out connections of interest for readers in writing studies.

Trainee Characteristics

We begin our review of the transfer-of-training research with the personal characteristics of individual trainees. This first dimension of Baldwin and Ford's influential model overlaps significantly with writing studies scholars' abiding interest in how the qualities of individual students might influence their learning and transfer of learning. For instance, central to the *Framework for Success in Postsecondary Writing* (2011) are eight "habits of mind" that overlap with research into the effects of several personality traits known as the Big Five. Similarly, writing studies scholars may be drawn to I/O scholarship on dispositions such as self-efficacy, motivation, locus of control, and goal orientation; these constructs have been examined at length by I/O scholars and may enrich writing studies scholarship—particularly in terms of how dispositions are defined and identified through diagnostic survey instruments, and how they are understood in relation to one another. Readers from writing studies might also notice that these studies frequently articulate how personality traits and dispositions relate to instructional design and work environments, a move in keeping with Carillo's (2017) call to "go beyond creating curricula and pedagogies that foster the transfer of skills and abilities toward those that also create environments that facilitate the dispositions that are determined to be most germane to transfer" (52).

Big Five Personality Traits. Scholars with an interest in the habits of mind named in the *Framework for Success in Postsecondary Writing* (2011) might consider the longstanding tradition of research into the effects of the Big Five personality traits: openness (a habit explicitly named in *Framework*), as well as conscientiousness, neuroticism, extraversion, and agreeableness. Although research has not established any clear relationships between extraversion or agreeableness and transfer of learning, I/O research does suggest positive relationships with transfer of training for openness, neuroticism, and conscientiousness.

In psychology, openness to experience is defined as "curiosity about one's environment and a willingness to explore new things" as well as a general adaptability to change (Herold et al., 2002, p. 855), which resonates with the *Framework's* definitions of openness and curiosity. Neuroticism is understood as a gauge of emotional stability; low neuroticism is "the absence of feelings of anxiety, insecurity, and nervousness" (p. 856). In their study of the relationship between personality traits and transfer of training for novice pilots, Herold and colleagues tracked participants first in a simulation and then in the actual cockpit. They found that openness to experience combined with emotional stability "accounted for 11.6% of the variance in cockpit performance, even after controlling for . . . the variance explained by previous learning" (p. 864). Furthermore, they found that although emotional stability did not seem to influence performance during the flight simulation, it played a significant role when learners moved to the more anxiety-provoking cockpit. Learners who did well during initial learning and had high emotional stability required 9.4 fewer hours (a reduction of 17%) to obtain their pilot's license (p. 863); however, those with low emotional stability "did only a little better than their colleagues who did poorly in the simulation" (p. 863). Overall, then, low neuroticism (like openness) seems to have a positive relationship with transfer of training.

Conscientiousness reflects "dependability[,] that is, being careful, thorough, responsible, organized, and planful" (Barrick & Mount 1991, p. 4). Some research has questioned the role of conscientiousness in transfer of training. Tziner et al. (2007), for instance, argue that while conscientiousness does have a "direct effect on supervisor evaluation," it has no significant effect on the final training grade (p. 172). This finding raises the question of whether teachers and/or researchers also find their evaluations of students influenced by students' conscientiousness; if so, this may complicate their assessments of students' learning and transfer. On the other hand, conscientiousness may directly impact transfer of training. Herold et al.'s (2002) pilot-training study found that for trainees who struggled during the simulation, high levels of conscientiousness had a positive relationship to performance in the actual cockpit: "conscientiousness acted to compensate for poor earlier performance" (p. 866). In sum, readers extending the implications of this study for writing might consider not only how conscientiousness might influence the evaluations of supervisors, teachers, and researchers, but also how it might influence how the writers themselves experience simulations and internship placements (issues elaborated in Chapters 4 and 10).

Self-Efficacy. Self-efficacy is one of the most commonly studied trainee characteristics in industrial psychology (Judge et al., 2007, p. 107); it has also received considerable uptake in writing studies (Baird & Dilger, 2017, 2018; Bromley et al., 2016; Driscoll & Wells, 2012; Khost, 2017). The I/O tradition of research suggests that writing studies scholars interested in self-efficacy should consider carefully both the nature of the "training" being transferred, as well as the relationship between self-efficacy and motivation.

The construct, first developed by Bandura (1977), indicates an individual's evaluation of their ability to complete a task. The higher the level of self-efficacy, the more strongly that person believes they can accomplish the task at hand. Unlike self-esteem (a more general sense of self [Gist et al., 1991, p. 838]), self-efficacy is tied to the individual's assessment of their ability to complete a *specific* task. Self-efficacy is a self-assessment that often leads people to marshal their resources in strikingly different ways. Indeed, "different people with similar skills or the same person under different circumstances" may perform quite differently, depending on their sense of self-efficacy (Yamkovenko & Holton, 2010, p. 388). Self-efficacy is not a stable trait, but a judgment that can fluctuate over time.

Within the transfer-of-training literature, many studies claim that higher levels of self-efficacy increase transfer of training. Brown's (2005) naturalistic study of government employees cultivating their managerial skills found that "self-efficacy correlated positively with both goal commitment and subsequent performance of the skills learned in training (maintenance)" (p. 382). Velada's (2007) study of Portuguese grocery store employees found a statistically significant, positive relationship between self-efficacy and transfer of training. Gist et al.'s (1989) study of computer self-efficacy established that higher self-efficacy resulted in better subsequent performance, and Gist et al. (1991) affirmed that "initial levels of self-efficacy contributed significantly to skill maintenance as demonstrated by performance 7 weeks following training" (p. 853). Although readers may wonder about the relevance of these studies for writing-related transfer, Blume et al.'s (2010) meta-analysis found that pre-training self-efficacy had a "moderate" relationship with transfer (p. 1090) and that self-efficacy proved more important when the training focused on open rather than closed skills (p. 1093). That self-efficacy has more influence on the transfer of open skills seems to underline the importance of self-efficacy for writing-related transfer. However, there is also some skepticism about the power of self-efficacy: Judge et al.'s (2007) meta-analysis found that "although self-efficacy is moderately correlated with performance, once the individual differences are taken into account, the predictive validity of self-efficacy shrinks dramatically" (pp. 114–5; see also Axtell et al., 1997, and Yamkovenko & Holton, 2010). A more generative line of inquiry has sought to understand self-efficacy as mediating or mediated by various types of motivation (Chiaburu & Marinova, 2005; Chiaburu & Lindsay, 2008; Colquitt et al., 2000; Kirwan & Birchall 2006). Generally, the suggestion seems to be that increasing self-efficacy will increase motivation, which will increase actual transfer of training.

Before we turn to the individual characteristic of motivation, we pause to consider whether it is possible—and whether it is wise—to focus on increasing levels of self-efficacy. Bandura (1977) identified four methods to increase self-efficacy: mastering new skills (individuals feel more confident as they improve their actual skills), vicarious experience (individuals can learn and increase their self-efficacy by watching others, especially peers), verbal persuasion (feedback, especially praise) and management of emotional arousal (staying calm). Driscoll and Powell's (2016) work on the value of faculty facilitating positive emotions in the classroom suggests the value of verbal persuasion; future research might interrogate the other methods as well. The first method—mastering new skills—may be especially important because research suggests that in some cases, high levels of self-efficacy may result in lower levels of motivation; if the self-efficacy was inappropriately high, this may result in poorer performance. Based on analyses of how students studied for a test, Vancouver and Kendall (2006) report that "self-efficacy negatively related to planned and reported study time, as well as performance" (p. 1150). Thus, they conclude that "if external efforts were directed at influencing self-efficacy, independent of learning or skill acquisition, individuals might be misled regarding what they needed to do to adequately prepare or plan" (p. 1151). In sum, efforts to increase self-efficacy can "backfire if care is not taken to align increases in self-efficacy with increases in capacities" (p. 1151)—a finding that instructors considering the role of praise in feedback may find helpful.

Motivation and Perceived Utility. Motivation "refers to the processes that account for an individual's intensity, direction, and persistence of effort toward attaining a goal" (Grossman & Salas, 2011, p. 109). Although the field of writing studies has explored the distinction between intrinsic and extrinsic motivation (e.g., DeCheck, 2012; Robinson, 2009; Sullivan, 2014) that distinction has been less prevalent in industrial/organizational psychology. Instead, I/O researchers distinguish between *motivation to learn* and *motivation to transfer*. Generally, researchers have found that *motivation to learn* has a statistically positive relation to training grades (Blume et al. 2010; Gegenfurtner & Vauras, 2012; Tziner et al., 2007, p. 171). Research exploring the role of choice in motivation to learn concludes that trainees given a choice among training programs had greater motivation to learn—but only if they received the preference they expressed. Trainees ostensibly given a choice but then placed in a training module they did not select "were less motivated and learned less" than those given no choice at all (Baldwin et al., 1991, p. 51). Research suggests that *motivation to transfer* is also a powerful predictor of actual training transfer (Grohmann et al., 2014; Kirwan & Birchall, 2006). Devos et al.'s (2007) study found that motivation to transfer is "the most significant predictor of transfer, and it explained 18.5% of the variance of transfer one to three months after training" (p. 195). Similarly, Axtell et al. (1997) found that motivation to transfer was a "prominent predictor" of individuals' ratings of their training transfer both one month and one year after the training (p. 211).

Certainly, some writing studies scholars have already begun to explore the role of motivation in transfer of learning (see Driscoll, 2011; Driscoll & Wells, 2012). Nevertheless, this review of the research from I/O psychology suggests that writing studies scholarship might helpfully view transfer motivation as a multidimensional characteristic, one that mediates the process of transfer and should be studied over time to fully capture its dynamic nature (Gegenfurtner et al., 2009). It might also suggest the benefit of longitudinal research like Beaufort's (2007) case study of Tim but with a more deliberate focus on dispositions like motivation.

Sometimes also referred to as instrumentality, perceived utility is related to but different from motivation: "an individual's belief that performing a specific behavior will lead to a desired outcome" (Chiaburu & Lindsay, 2008, p. 200). Perceived utility appears to have a positive relationship with transfer of training (Alliger et al., 1997; Velada et al., 2007). More specifically, Chiaburu and Lindsay (2008) found that whereas self-efficacy predicted motivation to learn, instrumentality predicted motivation to transfer—and that instrumentality is "the primary driver" not just of motivation to transfer but also of training transfer (p. 203). Writing instructors often tout the real-world applications of their assignments; writing studies scholars have suggested that increasing the authenticity of assignments in a variety of ways—including a focus on the importance of working with real or imagined clients (see Chapter 10 on simulations and internships) as well as the authenticity of genres assigned in school (Wardle, 2009)—may improve transfer of learning. By focusing on the extent to which a participant's belief that performing a specific behavior may result in a desired outcome, the "perceived utility" construct highlights for writing studies scholars the degree to which participant perceptions matter.

Locus of Control. Locus of control refers to "a stable personality trait that describes the extent to which people attribute the cause or control of events to themselves (internal orientation) or to external environmental factors such as fate or luck (external orientation)" (Kren, 1992,

p. 992). Colquitt et al.'s (2000) meta-analysis found a strong relationship between locus of control and motivation to learn and moderate relationships to declarative knowledge and to transfer; they conclude that "people with an internal locus of control tended to display higher motivation levels" and "people with an external locus of control learned more and had higher transfer levels" (p. 694). Although some writing studies scholars have drawn on the idea of locus of control (Robinson, 2009; see also Baird & Dilger, 2017, on "ownership"), the research from industrial and organizational psychologists suggests that future research might usefully probe the relationships among locus of control, motivation, and transfer of writing-related learning.

Goal Orientation. The trainee characteristic known as goal orientation was first developed and popularized by Dweck's (2008) discussion of mindsets. A goal orientation influences how individuals "construe the situation, interpret events in the situation, and process information about the situation" (Dweck, 1986, p. 1040). Specifically, Dweck and Leggett (1988) identified two goal orientations: learning or mastery oriented and performance oriented. Individuals with mastery goals "are concerned with increasing their competence" while those with performance goals are "concerned with gaining favorable judgments of their competence" (p. 256). Some writing studies scholars have begun to draw directly on Dweck's framework (e.g., Driscoll et al., 2020; Reid, 2017; Sullivan, 2015). Others might be reminded of Wardle's (2012) distinction between problem-exploring and answer-getting dispositions; although their frameworks are not interchangeable, both Dweck and Wardle ask what the genesis and consequences of these goal orientations might be.

I/O scholars have found the performance-goal orientation to be less conducive for both learning and transfer of training. Dweck's early classroom work on goal orientations identified performance goals as "maladaptive" or "helpless" motivational patterns (1986, p. 1040). When researchers gauged how individuals with performance orientations performed on transfer tasks, the results seemed to be mediated by self-efficacy: lower self-efficacy was related to lower transfer performance (Ford et al., 1998) and the higher the self-efficacy the stronger the training program success (Stevens & Gist, 1997). In contrast, many studies have argued for the positive effects of the mastery or learning-goal orientation. Chiaburu and Marinova (2005) argue that a mastery orientation predicts motivation to learn, which in turn predicts skill transfer. Similarly, when Tziner et al. (2007) evaluated outcomes using supervisor feedback, they found a "significant positive effect" of learning goal orientation and performance (p. 172). With these findings in mind, writing researchers might explore the relationship between teacher feedback and student performance goals.

As we conclude this section on the influence of trainee characteristics on transfer of training, we note that the field of writing studies has grown increasingly interested in the role that many of the dispositions reviewed here—self-efficacy, motivation, locus of control, and goal orientation—might play in transfer of learning (e.g., Baird & Dilger, 2017; Driscoll, 2011; Driscoll & Wells, 2012; Wardle, 2012). But the work here also suggests areas for possible research, including the Big Five personality traits and perceived utility. Importantly, the Baldwin and Ford (1988) model of transfer of training—which aims to understand how trainee characteristics interact with training design and with work environment—challenges writing studies scholars to always understand how those individual characteristics exist in a dynamic relationship with social contexts for learning.

Training Design

In addition to the individual characteristics of trainees, a second dimension of transfer of training is training design—that is, how the instruction is organized. Whereas examinations of training design in writing studies tend to qualitatively examine the results of pedagogical interventions like writing about writing (WAW) or teaching for transfer (TFT) on student learning (i.e., Yancey et al., 2014), I/O research generally works to construct quantitative models of the effects of training design. Importantly, these models rarely study training design alone; they are usually multifactor models, including trainee characteristics or the broader work environment. Some principles of training design, such as behavioral modeling and error management, examine the consequences of familiar pedagogical strategies such as building theories of writing and reframing "failure" as an opportunity to learn. Although these theories of training design often focus extensively on conditions for initial learning, scholars in industrial and organizational psychology also draw out implications for subsequent transfer of training; they can thus illuminate for writing studies scholars conditions of initial learning that might facilitate subsequent repurposing of writing-related learning. The remainder of this section on training design will focus on four learning principles with important implications for transfer of training: (1) identical elements, (2) behavioral modeling, (3) error management, and (4) self-management/relapse prevention.

Identical Elements. The theory of identical elements—discussed at some length in Chapter 2—concluded that "one mental function or activity improves others in so far as and because they are in part identical with it" (Thorndike, 1906/1916, p. 243). Unlike learning strategies that focus on helping trainees grasp the principles underlying the transfer task, an identical elements approach led instructors to design assignments to overlap as much as possible from one task and context to the next. In some instances, researchers have focused on fidelity between the training and workplace situations. This can take the form of simulations (Culpin et al., 2014) or even of conducting training in the actual workplace. Saks and Burke-Smalley (2014), for instance, argue that "on-the-job training was the strongest predictor of transfer of training" (p. 112). In other cases, researchers have focused on trainees' *perceptions* of congruity between the training and their workplace—often measured as a question of relevance or validity (Axtell et al., 1997). Taylor et al. (2005) found that "transfer of training . . . was greatest when at least some of the scenarios that trainees practiced were trainee generated" (p. 701) and attributed the value of those trainee-generated scenarios to the likelihood that trainees would generate scenarios with more identical elements (pp. 704–05). Thus, although identical elements are not nearly as popular as Thorndike's work was in the early twentieth century, in these studies of workplace learning, the argument that a close match between the training and target contexts will result in transfer of training persists; as we discuss in subsequent chapters, this belief has persisted in FYW, WAC/WID, and school-to-work pedagogies as well.

Behavioral Modeling. Behavioral modeling (sometimes also called Behavior Modeling Training or BMT) is an instructional approach grounded in Bandura's social learning theory (Baldwin, 1992); as individuals observe others to learn and replicate behaviors, they grapple with multiple processes including attention, retention, motor reproduction, and motivation. To direct attention, encourage retention, and increase motivation, behavioral modeling generally includes five stages: *overviewing* the component parts of the task or skill to be learned, *modeling, practicing, getting feedback,* and *applying* the training in the workplace (Pescuric & Byham, 1996; Taylor et al., 2005, p. 692). The theory of behavioral modeling assumes that with clear instructions, appropriate models, sufficient practice, and useful feedback, trainees will incorporate new information into their long-term memory and on-the-job practice (Taylor et al., 2005).

Several studies that compare behavioral modeling to other instructional methods have found BMT more effective (Burke & Day, 1986; Gist et al., 1989; Meyer and Raich, 1983) and behavioral modeling also seemed to have a particularly positive effect on trainees with low self-efficacy (Gist et al., 1989, p. 890). On the other hand, May and Kahnweiler (2000), who studied behavioral modeling in interpersonal skills training, questioned whether behavioral modeling can effectively prepare trainees to do complex cognitive or interpersonal work that requires adaptation across contexts (see also Tannenbaum & Yukl, 1992, p. 411)—a finding that raises questions about the relevance of BMT for transfer of writing-related learning.

However, a second dimension of behavioral modeling research that may prove more useful to writing studies scholars is the focus on how exactly people learn from observing, analyzing, and manipulating a model. Researchers of behavioral modeling have noted that the process of symbolic coding—in which "individuals organize and reduce the diverse elements of a modeled performance into a pattern of verbal symbols that can be easily stored, retained intact over time, quickly retrieved, and used to guide performance" (Decker, 1980, p. 628)—can be particularly difficult.[6] To help trainees transform their observations of a model into rehearsable and repeatable actions, learning points— that is, "written description of the key behaviors seen performed by the model"—can be helpful (Decker, 1982, p. 324). Written learning points can help trainees grant salience to and focus their attention on certain aspects of the model and nudge the trainee to symbolically encode the model—in ways that perhaps replicate or perhaps revise the written learning points—for themselves (Decker, 1982, p. 324). More specifically, Decker (1980) found that if the trainees generated rule-oriented learning points themselves (rather than receiving pre-existing

---

6. Readers may notice that this description of symbolic coding resonates with discussions of abstract schemata in the "Cognitive Psychology" chapter. Specifically, work in this area of behavioral modeling closely echoes Gentner et al.'s (2003) work on analogical encoding.

rule-oriented learning points or no learning points at all), generalization was statistically more likely to occur (Decker, 1980; findings affirmed by Decker, 1984.) This line of research on how generating such learning points can help individuals transfer their training may resonate with work in writing studies on how generating theories of writing may foster transfer of learning (Yancey et al., 2014).

Finally, writing instructors who use sample essays in their classrooms may learn from the behavioral modeling inquiries into what types of models to provide: solely positive, solely negative, or a mix of both. Early research indicated that a combination of positive and negative models led participants to "scor[e] significantly higher on a behavior generalization measure, taken 4 weeks after training, than did trainees who viewed only positive models" (Baldwin, 1992, p. 151). A subsequent meta-analysis also found that participants using mixed models (rather than only positive models) demonstrated higher levels of transfer of training as measured by job behaviors (Taylor et al., 2005, pp. 700–701).

Error Management. Whereas behavioral modeling sees errors as "needless and time consuming" (Keith & Frese, 2008, p. 60), the error management approach to transfer of training emphasizes the value of errors along the way as a "learning device" (Keith & Frese, 2005, p. 677). Behavioral modeling ensures at least some exposure to positive models to be analyzed and internalized, while error management withholds models and embraces an immediately hands-on, trial-and-error process. These different methods have important implications for the transfer of training. Assuming that novel transfer contexts are themselves "open, disruptive, and ambiguous" (Heimbeck et al., 2003, p. 336), error management training "reduces the distance between the training and transfer environments as it allows and encourages errors to occur in the training process, teaching skills to deal with errors in the training context" (p. 337). Multiple studies have made strong claims for the value of error management (see Keith & Frese's 2008 meta-analysis), and some argue that error management may be specifically well suited to promoting adaptive, not simply analogical, transfer (Keith & Frese, 2005). Given how these claims resonate with the threshold concept that "Failure Can Be An Important Part of Writing Development" (Adler-Kassner & Wardle, 2015) and Robertson et al.'s (2012) discussion of critical incidents, writing studies instructors may be drawn to three specific findings in this approach.

First, encouragement from instructors may help participants maximize the benefits of the error management approach. Heimbeck et al. (2003) compared two types of error management training—one that included "error management *instructions*" highlighting the value of errors with occasional reminders such as "The more errors you make, the more you learn!" and one that did not—with a third "error avoidant" technique that simply provided detailed instructions. Although results for trainees in the plain error management and error avoidant conditions were not significantly different, trainees in the error management *with instructions* condition produced "sizable" positive effects (p. 349); Heimbeck et al. believed this was a result of the instructions keeping trainees focused on the task rather than their own possible anxieties (p. 354), a finding that resonates with Driscoll and Powell's (2016) finding about the importance of instructor support for facilitating positive emotions.

Second, this error management approach may not be equally effective with all learners. Subsequent research highlights the importance of self-regulation techniques for successful error management learning. Specifically, Keith and Frese (2005) found that emotional control (the skill of "keep[ing] performance anxiety and other negative emotional reactions . . . at bay during task engagement" p. 679) and metacognitive activity (which "involves skills of planning and monitoring as well as evaluation of one's progress during task completion" [p. 679]) mediated the effect of the error management training condition. That is, differences in the performance of the two groups "were fully and independently explained by emotion control and metacognitive activity during training" (p. 687). This second finding again resonates with Driscoll and Powell's discussion of the importance of metacognitive monitoring and control.

Finally, for writing studies readers considering the relative merits of behavioral modeling and error management training, one series of studies suggests they are complementary. Studies of how students develop information search skills suggest that for learners starting from scratch, behavioral modeling produces greater self-efficacy and satisfaction, higher quality performance, and involves less wasted effort. But if learners begin with a baseline of preexisting knowledge, enactive exploration approach to error management allows participants to develop more intrinsic motivation, become more efficient, and produce better results (Wood et al., 2000, p. 278). This finding may assist instructors designing courses meant to build on each other over time.

Self-Management and Relapse Prevention. Self-management techniques (also known as behavioral self-management) focus on ways to help individuals use self-regulatory processes such as self-monitoring, judgment, and self-reactive influences to adjust their own actions to achieve intended outcomes. Self-management techniques include multiple stages:

1. identifying and describing a problematic behavior,

2. identifying the circumstances that facilitate the problematic behavior,

3. setting specific goals to overcome the problematic behavior,

4. monitoring progress towards attaining the goal(s), and

5. setting up rewards and punishments to support work towards the goal.

With its focus on problematic behaviors and the situations that trigger them, this self-management approach seems to resonate with writing studies research on negative transfer (e.g., Beaufort, 2007).

Self-management also has a complicated relationship with self-efficacy: some researchers argued that self-management training strengthened self-efficacy (Latham & Frayne, 1989, p. 415), while others found that self-efficacy could have an important moderating effect on self-management interventions (Gist et al., 1991; Stevens & Gist, 1997). Specifically, trainees with low self-efficacy did better maintaining their skills when asked to engage in self-management; they speculate that the self-management program's emphasis on practicing interim behaviors helped those trainees strengthen their skills over time (Gist et al., 1991, p. 857). Trainees with high self-efficacy, however, tended to experience more self-consciousness and reflect on their weaknesses, resulting in "attenuated" (p. 857) performance. Writing studies scholars may reflect on this finding from I/O scholarship as a challenge to further examine how dispositions (like self-efficacy) may have very different consequences in different instructional contexts.

To conclude this section on training design, we observe that writing studies has begun to articulate their own instructional designs meant to promote transfer of learning about writing. Consider, for instance, Downs and Wardle's (2007) WAW approach or Yancey et al.'s (2014) TFT curriculum. Nevertheless, I/O scholarship on training design—especially studies of modeling behaviors and coaching of error—might inspire further pedagogical innovation.

Work Environment

The third training input in Baldwin and Ford's (1988) model is work environment or transfer climate: those "work-environment factors perceived by trainees to encourage or discourage their use of knowledge, skills, and abilities learned in training on the job" (Cromwell & Kolb, 2004, p. 451). In their influential theorization of transfer climate, Rouiller and Goldstein (1993) identified two dimensions of transfer climate: situational cues that might nudge trainees to notice opportunities to use their new training (such as goals, social cues, task cues, and self control) and consequence cues (such as positive feedback, negative feedback, punishment, and no feedback). Importantly, this term focuses on the *perception* (rather than the objective existence) of those conditions. Multiple studies found that organizational transfer climate has a powerful, positive influence on transfer of training (Blume et al., 2010; Colquitt et al., 2000; Prince et al., 2015; Rouiller & Goldstein, 1993; Tracey et al., 1995), and Lim and Johnson (2002) conclude that "ensuring a supportive work climate may be the single most important requirement for the successful transfer of learning" (p. 46).

This focus on how social contexts (including personal relationships) might cue and facilitate transfer of training resonates with work from the situated learning perspective described in Chapter 2 as well as the vast majority of writing studies scholarship influenced by theories of discourse communities, rhetorical genre theory, and activity theory. We anticipate that writing studies readers may be particularly interested in findings on the importance of relationships with peers and supervisors. But how researchers in industrial and organizational psychology go about studying transfer climate differs significantly from work in situative learning and in writing studies—particularly in terms of the effort to develop a closed-question survey instrument (the Learning Transfer System Inventory) to assess the transfer climate of a given workplace. Although such survey-based research methods may be unfamiliar, and perhaps unpersuasive, to some readers from writing studies, there is precedent for large scale, quantitative analyses of transfer of learning within first-year writing classrooms (e.g., Driscoll et al., 2017); this instrument might spark a new line of inquiry within writing studies, particularly studies of workplace writing. In the following pages, we synthesize findings on several factors that might encourage transfer of training (including supervisor support, peer support, and opportunity to use), then turn to describe in more depth the methods and intentions of the Learning Transfer System Inventory.

Supervisor Support. The important role supervisors play has been made clear in studies of writing in the workplace (Chapter 10), but parallels to the writing classroom have yet to be examined. Industrial and organizational psychology finds that supervisor support takes many forms, including feedback, provision of time or resources, sanctions, and assistance setting goals. It is, in essence, "the extent to which supervisors reinforce and support use of learning on the job" (Cromwell & Kolb, 2004, p. 452). Consequently, supervisors (not unlike instructors) can play a "dual role," serving both as gatekeepers and as dispensers of encouragement (Holton et al., 2000, p. 355). Although some studies report no significant relationship between supervisor support and transfer of training (Axtell et al., 1997; Awoniyi et al., 2002; Chiaburu & Marinova, 2005; Devos et al., 2007; Homklin et al., 2014; Velada et al., 2007), multiple empirical studies have found a positive relationship between supervisor support and transfer of training. Supervisor support has been described as being "of crucial importance" (Huczynski & Lewis, 1980, p. 235) and supervisors as "key gatekeepers" (Ford et al., 1992, p. 524). Lim and Johnson (2002) identify supervisor support as a "critical influence" on transfer (p. 46), noting that support can take the form of familiarity with the training, willingness to engage in discussions about how to put the training to use, and offering positive feedback.

Peer Support. The positive effects of peer support—defined as the processes through which "peers produc[e] reinforcement for trainee's use of the learning on the job" (Cromwell & Kolb, 2004, p. 454)— have been consistently documented in the I/O scholarship (Burke & Hutchins 2007, p. 281); such research has obvious parallels to writing studies inquiries into peer talk around writing (Nowacek et al., 2019; Winzenried et al., 2017) in classrooms, writing centers, and beyond. While some I/O research has found peer support exercised less influence on transfer than supervisor support (Huczynski & Lewis, 1980, p. 235), others have found that "peer support and change resistance accounted for significant variance over and above that accounted for by supervisor support and supervisor sanctions" (Bates et al., 2000, p. 32). Both Colquitt et al.'s (2000) meta-analysis and Chiaburu and Marinova's (2005) workplace study found a positive relationship between peer support and motivation to learn, and an even stronger relationship between peer support and transfer of training. Burke and Hutchins' (2007) meta-analysis found that only peer support had a significant relationship with transfer; similarly, Homklin and colleagues' (2014) study found that "only coworker support was significantly positively related to transfer of training" (p. 126) and that co-worker support also served to moderate the relationship between learning and transfer. And although Cromwell and Kolb's (2004) research raised questions about the efficacy of a dispersed "peer network" of other trainees who stayed in touch via a listserv and occasional brown bags, they affirmed that trainees reporting high levels of support from their everyday peers (as well as organization and supervisor support) "also reported applying, to a higher extent, the knowledge and skills learned in the supervisory training program" (p. 463).

Opportunity to Perform. A third element of transfer climate is opportunities to actually use training on the job—opportunities that must be both present and recognized by participants. To the degree that opportunity to perform is seen as part of the environment rather than a quality of the learner, it perhaps resonates with Wardle's (2007) argument that students frequently didn't repurpose knowledge from FYW courses because they didn't feel subsequent courses prompted them to use such knowledge. Opportunity to perform has consistently been theorized as an important contributor to transfer of training (Holton, 1996; Noe, 1986), and much empirical research has demonstrated a positive relationship between opportunities for use and transfer of training (Devos et al., 2007; Gilpin-Jackson & Bushe, 2007; Lim & Johnson, 2002; Rouiller & Goldstein, 1993) and attributed lack of transfer to lack of opportunities to perform (Cromwell & Kolb, 2004). It is generally agreed that supervisors play a crucial role in providing (or not providing) opportunities to perform (Clarke, 2002; Ford et al., 1992); it should also be noted, though, that Ford et al. (1992) found that the importance of supervisor support was somewhat diminished for trainees with higher levels of self-efficacy.

Transfer Climate Instruments and the LTSI. Finally, we conclude this section on work environment by discussing the Learning Transfer System Inventory (LTSI). Holton and colleagues (2000) propose the notion of the transfer *system*, which they define as "all factors in the person, training, and organization that influence transfer of learning to job performance" (p. 335-6)—that is, all three components of Baldwin and Ford's (1988) tripartite model. Holton and colleagues argue that "transfer can only be completely understood and predicted by examining the *entire system* of influences" (p. 336, emphasis added). Noting that "the lack of a well-validated and reasonably comprehensive set of scales to measure factors may be a key barrier to improving organizational transfer systems" (p. 334), Holton and colleagues seek to develop a more consistent means of measuring (and tracking the interactions between) transfer climate, training design, and trainee characteristics.

Towards that goal, Holton and colleagues (Holton & Bates, 1997; Holton et al., 2007; Holton et al., 2000; Holton et al.,1997) have worked to develop the LTSI. They began by drafting a 112-item survey measuring 16 factors from all three components of Baldwin and Ford's (1988) influential transfer of training model, including such constructs as motivation to transfer, peer support, transfer design and opportunity to use, and performance self-efficacy (Holton et al., 2000, p. 340). After piloting the survey, they kept all sixteen factors but reduced the survey to only 68 items (p. 347). Generally, the LTSI has proven consistent across contexts, though some cross-cultural analyses have revealed small but important cultural differences (Bates et al., 2007; Chen et al., 2005; Devos et al., 2007; Khasawneh et al., 2006; Kirwan & Birchall, 2006; Velada et al., 2009; Yamkovenko et al., 2007).

In addition to serving as an instrument to standardize research across studies, Holton and colleagues (2000) concluded that the LTSI might also be used by human resources practitioners (not just researchers) for needs assessments and for program evaluations. Nevertheless, most subsequent studies on the LTSI have focused not on workplace applications, but on the instrument's strengths, limitations (see Tang [1997] and Noe [2000]), and validity. Although many writing studies scholars may find the use of a closed-ended survey questions inappropriate for understanding transfer of learning about writing, the LTSI nevertheless remains one means of examining in a replicable and aggregable way the interrelationships among the characteristics of individual learners, instructional design, and the social context for learning—interrelationships of significant interest for writing studies scholars.

Knowledge Management: Focusing on Relationships Among Individuals Within a Workplace

The interest that management and human resources professionals take in transfer is not limited to transfer of training; there is also a well-established line of inquiry into what is called knowledge management. From a managerial perspective, one of the great challenges of a company's continued success is how it draws on previous experiences when facing new conditions, in ways that learn from but are not constrained by previous failures and successes. This is not unlike the way writing studies scholars frame the problem of learning transfer for writers—but the striking shift here is that knowledge management scholars think of transfer as an inter-personal act, taking place between individuals or even groups of individuals, rather than an intrapersonal act, confined within a single individual. Most knowledge management scholarship has consistently identified four distinct activities that comprise the knowledge management (KM) endeavor: creation of knowledge, storage and retrieval of knowledge, transfer of knowledge, and application of knowledge (Alavi & Leidner, 2001; Nevo & Wand, 2004). In the remainder of this section, we review the scholarship on all four components. Although this knowledge management scholarship, with its focus on the creation and circulation of knowledge among groups within workplaces may seem quite distant from writing studies' usual focus on writing and learning, in fact these studies intersect with several issues of emerging interest within writing studies: tacit vs. explicit articulations of knowledge, material contexts as a prompt for transfer of learning, the relationship between talk and transfer, and how affective, interpersonal relationships may influence transfer of learning.

Knowledge Creation

Some early research into how organizations create knowledge continued to focus on individuals and used constructs developed in cognitive psychology to understand the cognitive activities of individuals (such as interpretive schemes) to understand organizations (Argote et al., 1990; Walsh & Ungson, 1991). Eventually, theories of knowledge creation began to focus on how organizations as a whole work to build collective knowledge based on the knowledge of individual members. Drawing on his study of multiple Japanese firms, Nonaka (1991, 1994) develops a theory of knowledge creation premised on the "knowledge spiral." Invoking Polanyi's observation that "we can know more than we can tell" (qtd. in Nonaka, 1994, p. 16), he defines tacit knowledge as having both cognitive ("schemata, paradigms, beliefs, and viewpoints that provide 'perspectives' that help individuals to perceive and define their world") and technical elements ("concrete know-how, crafts, and skills that apply to specific contexts" (1994, p. 16). Unlike explicit knowledge, which can be articulated and shared, tacit knowledge "has a personal quality, which makes it hard to formalize and communicate. Tacit knowledge is deeply rooted in action, commitment, and involvement in a specific context" (p. 16).

The crux of Nonaka's theory of knowledge creation is that "an organization cannot create knowledge without individuals" (p. 17); organizations amplify knowledge created by individuals, then crystalize that knowledge in the structure and activities of the organization. To do so, they engage in the "spiral of knowledge" (Nonaka, 1991). It can begin with a socialization mode, in which individuals might have tacit knowledge, which they potentially acquired from other people's tacit knowledge. Or it might begin in the combination mode, in which the explicit knowledge of multiple individuals is compiled. Neither of these instances of knowledge creation, Nonaka notes, extend the firm's knowledge base. The interesting and truly "powerful" (1991, p. 99) elements of knowledge creation take place in the two remaining modes. In the articulation mode (called the externalization mode in Nonaka, 1994), individuals make their tacit knowledge explicit for others to understand. In the internalization mode, that explicit knowledge is shared with others in the firm who "begin to internalize it—that is, they use it to broaden, extend, and reframe their own tacit knowledge" (p. 99).

Furthermore, Nonaka argues that metaphors and analogies serve a crucial role in the process of articulation by helping organizations convert tacit into explicit knowledge:

> first, by linking contradictory things and ideas through metaphor; then, by resolving those contradictions through anal-

ogy; and, finally, by crystallizing the created concepts and embodying them in a model, which makes the knowledge available to the rest of the company. (1991, p. 101)

In this way, Nonaka's model not only draws on notions of tacit and explicit knowledge, but also invokes a long tradition of research in cognitive psychology—specifically, research on analogical thinking and dual processing. For writing studies scholars interested in how analogical thinking, the role of tacit knowledge, and the potentially collaborative nature of knowledge creation might influence future inquiries into transfer of learning about writing, Nonaka's theory of knowledge creation merits further consideration.

Knowledge Storage

How organizations store and retrieve knowledge is frequently referred to as organizational memory (OM) or persistence of learning (Argote et al., 1990, p. 141). It is, in essence, "the way organizations store knowledge from the past to support present activities" (Nevo & Wand, 2004, p. 549). Memories can reside in people, but also in procedures and in material artifacts; OM is, therefore, "both an individual- and organizational-level construct" (Walsh & Ungson, 1991, p. 61).

In their foundational discussion of organizational memory, Walsh and Ungson (1991) identify six retention "facilities" (p. 63). *Individuals* can have particular memories of what has transpired within an organization, while *culture* is the organization's shared stories. *Transformations* include things like administrative systems, such as hiring processes and budget allocations; such systems "are the mechanisms for impounding and preserving knowledge" (Jelinek qtd. in Walsh & Ungson, p. 65). Organizational memories are also embedded in *social roles*, as well as in the *ecology* or "actual physical structure" of a workplace. Transformations, social roles, and ecologies work together, as Walsh and Ungson explain, to retain organizational memories. Finally, organizational memories can also be retained outside the organization, in the form of former employees, media coverage, and competitors. Although there is no exact equivalent to the more transitory organizational space of classrooms, these forms of OM resonate with Smart and Brown's (2002) discussion of how "written genres—with their networks of conventionalized texts and discourse practices often . . . functio[n] as vehicles of shared thinking, knowing, and learning . . .

constitut[ing] a significant resource for 'organizational memory,' providing an historical record of work processes, problems/solutions, accomplished knowledge, and decisions" (p. 119).

In framing organizational memory as informed by material contexts and cultural tools, knowledge management scholars intersect with the scholarship on distributed cognition. Like situated cognition, distributed cognition emphasizes the importance of studying individual cognition not in a lab but in its social context (see Chapter 2), but distributed cognition takes a particular interest in how people think in "partnership with others and with the help of culturally provided tools and implements. . . . In other words, it is not just the 'person-solo' who learns, but the 'person-plus'" (Salomon, 1993, p. xiii). The pioneering study in distributed cognition was Hutchins' (1995) account of navigation on a US Navy ship. Taking the entire navigational team as his unit of analysis, Hutchins attends to the layout of the ship, the various tools the team uses (including chronometers, navigation charts, and traditions of celestial observations), and the interactions of the teams. Both tools and teams of individuals working together on a task are sites of distributed cognition; in Hutchins' view, "all divisions of labor, whether the labor is physical or cognitive in nature, require distributed cognition in order to coordinate the activities of the participants" (p. 176). Much of the book is devoted to developing models of the social organization of distributed cognition (p. 262) and understanding the social formation of competence within that organization (p. 279). Through his cognitive ethnography of work aboard a naval ship, Hutchins shows "just how genuinely distributed (between agents) and reshaped (by the use of artifacts, spatial layouts and simple event-response routines) the ship navigation task has become" (Clark, 2017, p. 510). Certainly, the concept of distributed cognition has already had considerable uptake within the field of writing studies—especially but not limited to studies of workplace writing (e.g., Angeli, 2015; Clayson, 2018). But such studies rarely frame distributed cognition as a matter of transfer (see Alexander & William's [2015] conclusion for an exception).

For a deeper dive into how knowledge may be collectively stored by individuals we turn to transactive memory systems. The idea of transactive memory systems (TMS) was originally developed by Wegner to explain the "cognitive interdependence" of individuals in intimate relationships; by studying communications between spouses, Wegner et al. (1985) posited the existence of memories that reside not in a single individual but in the dyad. One of the key features of a TMS is differentiation: both partners in the dyad don't each remember everything. Each remembers some higher-order and some lower-order information, but importantly they both remember the *location* of information—that is, who knows what higher- and lower-order information. That "directory," that knowledge of who knows what, is crucial for the transactive memory system. This transactive memory theory of cognitive interdependence, Wegner (1987) claimed, has important implications not only for understanding intimate relationships, but also for understanding health behaviors (communications between physicians, patients, and family/friends), instructional psychology, and organizational management.

Although TMS has received surprisingly little uptake in cognitive or social psychology studies of memory (Michaelian & Sutton, 2013, p. 7), it has garnered a great deal of attention in management scholarship on how memory functions in work groups and teams. Transactive memory systems are, as Lewis and Herndon (2011) explain, "thought to improve performance in workgroups because they facilitate quick and coordinated access to specialized expertise, ensuring that a greater amount of high-quality and task-relevant knowledge is brought to bear on collective tasks" (p. 1254). This scholarly focus on cognitive interdependence in dyads and groups, while generally focused on organizational performance, has great relevance for understandings of transfer of learning. Studies of transactive memory systems (and theories of distributed cognition more generally) argue that memories are not the province of a single mind locked into an autonomous brain—which opens new possibilities for understanding transfer of learning. TMS research prompts a more collaborative view of how knowledge might be acquired, stored, and repurposed and invites radically new studies of how transfer of learning might unfold in interactions.

Knowledge Transfer

Although early scholarship assumed transfer of knowledge between members of an organization was an automatic and costless process (Szulanski, 2000), later managerial scholarship began to explore the difficulties in knowledge transfer. Szulanski's (2000, 2003) process model identified difficulty, or stickiness, as a "characteristic feature" of transfer (p. 10). Building on four established stages of knowledge transfer—initiation, implementation, ramp-up and integration—Szulanski argued that all four stages "can be difficult in [their] own way" (2000, pp. 12–13) and identified challenges particular to each. Ultimately, Szulanski identified nine causes of stickiness: causal ambiguity, unproven knowledge, source of the information lacks motivation, source lacks credibility, recipient lacks motivation, recipient lacks absorptive capacity, recipient lacks retentive capacity, barren organizational context, and a difficult relationship between source and recipient. He then tested his theoretical framework empirically by surveying employees at eight firms and found that *"Causal Ambiguity* and the lack of recipient's *Absorptive Capacity* appear to be the most important predictors of stickiness" (2000, p. 21). Although scholarship in writing studies has looked at the pedagogical context for transfer of learning, Szulanski's research on phases of transfer and causes of stickiness might invite new types of analysis; for example, interpersonal dimensions such as "source lacks credibility" and "difficult relationship between source and recipient" might encourage researchers to extend Driscoll and Powell's (2016) inquiries into the influence of instructors on writers' emotions and transfer of learning.

In the remainder of this section, we focus on three other trends in scholarship on knowledge transfer. The first has focused on affective dimensions related to some of the challenges Szulanski identified, including the credibility of the source, the motivation of both source and recipient, and the relationship between the two. Lucas (2005), for instance, focuses on how issues of trust and reputation influence transfer of knowledge.

> Knowledge transfer involves asking employees to change the way they do things without any guarantees of success. For employees to adopt new ways of doing things, they must have confidence in the information provided about the new practices. Such confidence . . . is a consequence of the trust employees have in each other, as well as their respective reputations. (p. 88)

Similarly, Haas and Park (2010) and Jarvenpaa and Majchrzak (2008) focus on information withholding in contexts where transfer of knowledge might be possible. For readers outside the field of management, one important take-away from this line of research might be how it draws attention to the role that interpersonal relationships might play in the subsequent transfer of knowledge: to what degree are these same dynamics at play in learning about writing in workplaces—or in classrooms?

Another strand, which takes a particular interest in organizational innovation, has focused on boundaries, boundary objects, and boundary brokers. Carlile (2004), for instance, argues that boundaries sometimes require not just transfer or translation, but transformation of understandings. When such transformations are necessary, Carlile notes the importance of boundary objects. A boundary object—which may be something like a prototype or a process map—"establishes a shared syntax or language for individuals to represent their knowledge . . . . provides a concrete means for individuals to specify and learn about their differences and dependencies across a given boundary, . . . [and] facilitates a process where individuals can jointly transform their knowledge" (2002, pp. 451–2). While boundary objects are not a "magic bullet" (p. 452), they do play an important role in innovation within organizations. (See Chapter 10 for a discussion of how boundary objects may play an important role in transfer of learning within activity systems.)

A third strand of research has focused on knowledge brokering and the "recombinant nature of innovation" (Hargadon, 2002, p. 49). Individuals or organizations who work as knowledge brokers "span multiple markets and technology domains and innovate by brokering knowledge from where it is known to where it is not" (Hargadon, 1998, p. 210), moving established insights or techniques into new contexts. Five key activities allow knowledge brokers to innovate: access, bridging, learning, linking, and implementing. The specific activity of linking in organizations, Hargadon argues, is the same type of analogic thinking studied by cognitive psychologists like Gick and Holyoak (1980, 1983) in individuals. Although Hargadon acknowledges that analogic thinking in organizations requires "intensive interaction between individuals" (p. 220) facilitated by their geographic placement across the country or in the office, his findings largely mirror those from studies of individual cognition. Ultimately, Hargadon is more interested in building a model of knowledge brokering than an understanding of how linking might happen differently for organizations than for individuals.

As we conclude this section, we wish to acknowledge that although the management scholarship brings to writing studies a powerful challenge in its focus on a potentially collaborative dimension of transfer of learning, it also remains mired in some of the earlier problems faced by research in cognitive psychology. For instance, Orlikowski (2002) argues that the field's focus on identifying "best practices" reveals the deeply problematic assumption that "competence [is] something to be 'transferred'" (p. 253). She notes that if practices are understood as "the situated recurrent activities of human agents, they cannot simply be spread around as if they were fixed and static objects" (p. 253). She prefers the term *useful practices* because usefulness is "a necessarily contextual and provisional aspect of situated organizational activity" (p. 253). With this critique, Orlikowski challenges management scholars to move past the two-problem paradigm, beyond the idea that knowledge can be acquired in one context and simply applied in a subsequent context.

Knowledge Application

Knowledge management scholarship tends to assume that "the source of competitive advantage resides in the application of the knowledge rather than in the knowledge itself" (Alavi & Leidner, 2001, p. 122). Explorations of how *exactly* organizational knowledge gets applied, though, seem difficult to tease out from discussions of acquisition, storage, and retrieval. When summarizing existing research on application and implementation, Hargadon (1998) points to Nonaka's work, noting that it provides "a rich description of how the process of implementation turns much of what is tacit about an idea into something explicit that can be shared with the rest of the organization" (Hargadon, 1998, p. 222); however, Nonaka's discussion of tacit-to-explicit knowledge was originally framed as an issue of knowledge *creation*. Perhaps the relative dearth of work in this area reflects a lack of interest from researchers—or perhaps it suggests that "application" is never fully separable from knowledge creation, storage, and transfer.

Conclusion

Our goal in this chapter was to provide readers with an introduction to the various ways in which research in human resources and management is relevant to scholars in writing studies. In terms of research agendas and methods, we identify at least four areas of exploration.

Perhaps most obviously, the I/O tradition of research on trainee characteristics encourages writing studies scholars to grow more precise when studying the role dispositions may play in transfer of learning. Methodologically, I/O scholarship uses survey instruments to identify "high" and "low" presentations of various dispositions, often testing them over time. Although these instruments are not always consistent or validated—a fact that motivates the Learning Transfer System Inventory, which would facilitate replicable and aggregable data over time and various research sites—this tradition of I/O research encourages writing studies scholars to be increasingly precise in their definitions and means of measuring dispositions such as self-efficacy, motivation, and locus of control. Furthermore, although there is a growing discussion of self-regulation as a disposition (Driscoll et al., 2017; Featherstone et al., 2019), future work might helpfully tease out the differences among discussions of self-regulation, self-efficacy (sometimes understood to be a disposition and a part of self-regulation), and self-management (understood in the I/O scholarship to be a matter of training design rather than individual disposition).

Second, although writing studies scholars may not be entirely convinced by the efforts of I/O scholars to use statistical analyses of closed-answer surveys to determine correlations and speculate on causal relationships, writing studies scholars might also be motivated to use different methods to achieve the same goal of better understanding the interrelationships of individual characteristics, instructional design, and social context. Third, work in human resources and management suggests the importance of further exploring the role of affect in transfer of learning—both as a personality trait such as neuroticism and (shifting to the interpersonal perspective of knowledge management research) as a dimension of the relationships between instructors and students, supervisors and employees, or among peers. Finally, knowledge management's view of knowledge transfer as an interpersonal accomplishment suggests the importance of expanding the unit of analysis within writing studies. To some degree, Engeström's (2014) cultural historical activity theory—with its focus on mediational tools and divisions of labor (see more in Chapter 10) has already moved writing studies scholars in this direction. Nevertheless, Hutchins' work on distributed cognition and Wegner and colleagues' work on transactive memory systems suggests that this is a ripe line of inquiry, in workplaces, writing centers (Nowacek et al., 2019), classrooms (Winzenried et al., 2017), and elsewhere.

Many of the obvious links to pedagogy are explored in Chapter 10, which focuses on transitions from writing in school to writing at work. The transfer-of-training inquiries into training design do, however, suggest several additional pedagogical implications for writing instruction. Writing instructors might, for instance, turn to the behavioral modeling research to learn more about how to choose examples and how to scaffold students' interactions with those examples. Writing instructors might also draw on error management research to refine their strategies for responding to drafts. Finally, while research from the transfer of training tradition suggests the important role both peers and supervisors may play in promoting transfer of learning, research from the knowledge management traditions may be especially fertile ground for instructors wishing to consider how the specific issue of trust might influence transfer of learning within and beyond the classroom.

References

Adler-Kassner, L., & Wardle, E. (Eds.). (2015). *Naming what we know: Threshold concepts of writing studies*. Utah State University Press.

Alavi, M., & Leidner, D.E. (2001) Knowledge management and knowledge management systems: Conceptual foundations and research issues. *MIS Quarterly*, *25*(1), 107–136.

Alexander, K. P., Williams, D. M. (2015). DMAC after dark: Toward a theory of distributed invention. *Computers and Composition*, *36*, 32–43.

Alliger, G. M., Tannenbaum, S. I., Bennett Jr, W., Traver, H., & Shotland, A. (1997). A meta-analysis of the relations among training criteria. *Personnel Psychology*, *50*(2), 341–358.

Angeli, E. L. (2015). Three types of memory in emergency medical services communication. *Written Communication*, *32*(1), 3–38.

Argote, L., Beckman, S. L., & Epple, D. (1990). The persistence and transfer of learning in industrial settings. *Management Science*, *36*(2), 140–154.

Awoniyi, E. A., Griego, O. V., & Morgan, G. A. (2002). Person-environment fit and transfer of training. *International Journal of Training & Development*, *6*(1), 25–35.

Axtell, C. M., Maitlis, S., & Yearta, S. K. (1997). Predicting immediate and longer-term transfer of training. *Personnel Review*, *26*(3), 201–213.

Baird, N., & Dilger, B. (2017). How students perceive transitions: Dispositions and transfer in internships. *College Composition and Communication, 68*(4), 684.

Baird, N., & Dilger, B. (2018). Dispositions in natural science laboratories: The roles of individuals and contexts in writing transfer. *Across the Disciplines, 15*(4), 21–40.

Baldwin T.T. (1992). Effects of alternative modeling strategies on outcomes of interpersonal-skills training. *Journal of Applied Psychology, 77,* 147–54.

Baldwin, T. T., & Ford, J. K. (1988). Transfer of training: A review and directions for future research. *Personnel Psychology, 41,* 63–105.

Baldwin, T. T., Magjuka, R. J., & Loher, B. T. (1991). The perils of participation: Effects of choice of training on trainee motivation and learning. *Personnel Psychology, 44*(1), 51–65.

Bandura, A. (1977). Self-efficacy: Toward a unifying theory of behavioral change. *Psychological Review, 84*(2), 191–215.

Bandura, A. (1986). *Social foundations of thought and action: A social cognitive theory.* Prentice-Hall.

Bandura, A. (1999). Social cognitive theory: An agent perspective. *Asian Journal of Social Psychology, 2,* 21–41.

Barrick, M., & Mount, M. (1991). The Big Five personality dimensions and job performance: A meta-analysis. *Personnel Psychology, 44,* 1–26.

Bates, R. A., Holton, E. F. III, Seyler, D. L. and Carvalho, M. A. (2000). The role of interpersonal factors in the application of computer-based training in an industrial setting. *Human Resource Development International, 3*(1), 19–42.

Bates, R., Kauffeld, S., & Holton, E. F. (2007). Examining the factor structure and predictive ability of the German-version of the Learning Transfer Systems Inventory. *Journal of European Industrial Training, 31*(3), 195–211.

Beaufort, A. (2007). *College writing and beyond: A new framework for university writing instruction.* Utah State University Press.

Blume, B. D., Ford, J. K., Baldwin, T. T., & Huang, J. L. (2010). Transfer of training: A meta-analytic review. *Journal of Management, 36*(4), 1065–1105.

Bromley, P., Northway, K., & Schonberg, E. (2016). Transfer and dispositions in writing centers: A cross-institutional, mixed-methods study. *Across the Disciplines, 13*(1), 1–15.

Brown, T.C. (2005). The effectiveness of distal and proximal goals as transfer of training interventions: A field experiment. *Human Resources Development Quarterly, 16*(3), 369–387.

Burke, M. J., & Day, R. R. (1986). A cumulative study of the effectiveness of managerial training. *Journal of Applied Psychology, 71*(2), 232–245.

Burke, L., & Hutchins, H.M. (2007). Training transfer: An integrative literature review. *Human Resource Development Review 6*(3), 263–296.

Carillo, E. (2017). The evolving relationship between composition and cognitive studies: Gaining some historical perspective on our contemporary moment. In P. Portanova, M. J. Rifenburg, & D. Roen (Eds.), *Contemporary perspectives on cognition and writing* (pp. 39–55). The WAC Clearinghouse; University Press of Colorado.

Carlile, P. R. (2002). A pragmatic view of knowledge and boundaries: Boundary objects in new product development. *Organization Science, 13*(4), 442–455.

Carlile, P. R. (2004). Transferring, translating, and transforming: An integrative framework for managing knowledge across boundaries. *Organization Science, 15*(5), 555–568.

Chen, H.C., Holton, E.F. III, & Bates, R. (2005). Development and validation of the Learning Transfer System Inventory in Taiwan. *Human Resource Development Quarterly, 16*(1), 55–84.

Chiaburu, D. S., & Lindsay, D. R. (2008). Can do or will do? The importance of self-efficacy and instrumentality for training transfer. *Human Resource Development International, 11*, 199–206.

Chiaburu, D. S., & Marinova, S. V. (2005). What predicts skill transfer? An exploratory study of goal orientation, training self-efficacy and organizational supports. *International Journal of Training & Development, 9*(2), 110–123

Clark, A. (2017). Embodied, situated, and distributed cognition. *A companion to cognitive science*, 506–517.

Clarke, N. (2002). Job/work environment factors influencing training transfer within a human service agency: Some indicative support for Baldwin and Ford's transfer climate construct. *International Journal of Training & Development, 6*(3), 146–162.

Clayson, A. (2018). Distributed cognition and embodiment in text planning: A situated study of collaborative writing in the workplace. *Written Communication, 35*(2), 155–181.

Colquitt, J. A., LePine, J. A., & Noe, R. A. (2000). Toward an integrative theory of training motivation: A meta-analytic path analysis of 20 years of research. *Journal of Applied Psychology, 85*, 678–707.

Cromwell, S. E., & Kolb, J. A. (2004). An examination of work-environment support factors affecting transfer of supervisory skills training to the workplace. *Human Resource Development Quarterly, 15*, 449–471.

Culpin, V., Eichenberg, T., Hayward, I., & Abraham, P. (2014). Learning, intention to transfer and transfer in executive education. *International Journal of Training and Development, 18*(2), 132–147.

DeCheck, N. (2012). The power of common interest for motivating writers: A case study. *Writing Center Journal, 32*(1), 28–38.

Decker, P. J. (1980) Effects of symbolic coding and rehearsal in behavior-modeling training. *Journal of Applied Psychology, 65*(6), 627–634.

Decker, P.J. (1982). The enhancement of behavior modeling training of supervisory skills by the inclusion of retention processes. *Personnel Psychology, 35*(2), 323–332.

Decker, P.J. (1984). Effects of different symbolic coding stimuli in behavior modeling training. *Personnel Psychology, 37*(4), 711–720.

Devos, C., Dumay, X., Bonami, M., Bates, R., & Holton III, E. (2007). The Learning Transfer System Inventory (LTSI) translated into French: Internal structure and predictive validity. *International Journal of Training & Development, 11*(3), 181–199.

Downs, D., & Wardle, E. (2007). Teaching about writing, righting misconceptions: (Re)envisioning "First-Year Composition" as "Introduction to Writing Studies." *College Composition and Communication, 58*(4), 552–584.

Driscoll, D. L. (2011). Connected, disconnected, or uncertain: Student attitudes about future writing contexts and perceptions of transfer from first year writing to the disciplines. *Across the Disciplines, 8*(2). https://wac.colostate.edu/docs/atd/articles/driscoll2011.pdf

Driscoll, D. L., Gorzelsky, G., Wells, J., Hayes, C., Jones, E., & Salchak, S. (2017). Down the rabbit hole: Challenges and methodological recommendations in researching writing-related student dispositions. *Composition Forum. 35*. https://compositionforum.com/issue/35/rabbit-hole.php

Driscoll, D. L., Leigh, S. R., & Zamin, N. F. (2020). Self-care as professionalization: A case for ethical doctoral education in composition studies. *College Composition and Communication, 71*(3), 453–480.

Driscoll, D. L., & Powell, R. (2016). States, traits, and dispositions: The impact of emotion on writing development and writing transfer across college courses and beyond. *Composition Forum, 34*. https://compositionforum.com/issue/34/states-traits.php

Driscoll, D. L., & Wells, J. (2012). Beyond knowledge and skills: Writing transfer and the role of student dispositions. *Composition Forum, 26*. https://compositionforum.com/issue/26/beyond-knowledge-skills.php

Dweck, C. S. (1986). Motivational processes affecting learning. *American Psychologist, 41*(10), 1040–1048.

Dweck, C. S. (2008). *Mindset: The new psychology of success.* Random House Digital.

Dweck, C. S., & Leggett, E. L. (1988). A social-cognitive approach to motivation and personality. *Psychological Review, 95*(2), 256–273.

Engeström, Y. (2014). *Learning by expanding: An activity-theoretical approach to developmental research.* Cambridge University Press.

Featherstone, J., Barrett, R., & Chandler, M. (2019). The mindful tutor. In K. G. Johnson, & T. Roggenbuck (Eds.), *How we teach writing tutors: A WLN digital edited collection.* https://wlnjournal.org/digitaleditedcollection1/Featherstoneetal.html

Ford, J. K., Quinones, M., Sego, D. & Sorra, J. (1992), Factors affecting the opportunity to perform trained tasks on the job. *Personnel Psychology, 45,* 511–27.

Ford, J. K., Smith, E. M., Weissbein, D. A., Gully, S. M., & Salas, E. (1998). Relationships of goal orientation, metacognitive activity, and practice strategies with learning outcomes and transfer. *Journal of Applied Psychology, 83*(2), 218–233.

Framework for success in postsecondary writing. (2011) Council of Writing Program Administrators, National Council of Teachers of English, and National Writing Project. https://files.eric.ed.gov/fulltext/ED516360.pdf

Gagne, R. M. (1962). Military training and principles of learning. *American Psychologist, 17,* 83–91.

Gegenfurtner, A., Veermans, K., Festner, D., & Gruber, H. (2009). Motivation to transfer training: An integrative literature review. *Human Resource Development Review, 8*(3), 403–423.

Gegenfurtner, A., & Vauras, M. (2012). Age-related differences in the relation between motivation to learn and transfer of training in adult continuing education. *Contemporary Educational Psychology, 37*(1), 33–46.

Gentner, D., Loewenstein, J., & Thompson, L. (2003). Learning and transfer: A general role for analogical encoding. *Journal of Educational Psychology, 95*(2), 393–408.

Gick, M. L., & Holyoak, K. J. (1980). Analogical problem solving. *Cognitive Psychology, 12*(3), 306–355.

Gick, M. L., & Holyoak, K. J. (1983). Schema induction and analogical transfer. *Cognitive Psychology 15*(1), 1–38.

Gilpin-Jackson, Y. & Bushe, G. R. (2007). Leadership development training transfer: A case study of post-training determinants. *Journal of Management Development, 26,* 980–1004.

Gist M.E., Schwoerer C, Rosen B. (1989). Effects of alternative training methods on self-efficacy and performance in computer software training. *Journal of Applied Psychology, 74*(6), 884–891.

Gist, M., Stevens, C. and Bavetta, A. (1991). Effects of self-efficacy and post training interventions of the acquisition and maintenance of complex interpersonal skills. *Personnel Psychology, 44,* 837–861.

Grohmann, A., Beller, J., & Kauffeld, S. (2014). Exploring the critical role of motivation to transfer in the training transfer process. *International Journal of Training & Development, 18*(2), 84–103.

Grossman, R., & Salas, E. (2011). The transfer of training: What really matters. *International Journal of Training & Development, 15*(2), 103–120.

Haas, M. R., & Park, S. (2010). To share or not to share? Professional norms, reference groups, and information withholding among life scientists. *Organization Science, 21*(4), 873–891.

Hargadon, A. B. (1998). Firms as knowledge brokers: Lessons in pursuing continuous innovation. *California Management Review, 40*(3), 209–227.

Hargadon, A. B. (2002). Brokering knowledge: Linking learning and innovation. *Research in Organizational Behavior, 24*, 41–85.

Heimbeck, D., Frese, M., Sonnentag, S. and Keith, N. (2003). Integrating errors into the training process: The function of error management instructions and the role of goal orientation. *Personnel Psychology, 56*, 333–361.

Herold, D. M., Davis, W., Fedor, D. B., & Parsons, C. K. (2002). Dispositional influences on transfer of learning in multistage training programs. *Personnel Psychology, 55*(4), 851–869.

Holton, E.F. (1996). The flawed four-level evaluation model. *Human Resource Development Quarterly, 1*, 5–21.

Holton, I., E., & Bates, R. A. (1997). Toward construct validation of a transfer climate instrument. *Human Resource Development Quarterly, 8*(2), 95–113.

Holton III, E. F., Bates, R. A., Bookter, A. I., & Yamkovenko, V. B. (2007). Convergent and divergent validity of the Learning Transfer System Inventory. *Human Resource Development Quarterly, 18*(3), 385–419.

Holton, I., E., Bates, R. A., & Ruona, W. E. A. (2000). Development of a generalized Learning Transfer System Inventory. *Human Resource Development Quarterly, 11*(4), 333–360.

Holton III, E. F., Bates, R. A., Seyler, D. L., & Carvalho, M. B. (1997). Toward construct validation of a transfer climate instrument. *Human Resource Development Quarterly, 8*(2), 95–113.

Homklin, T., Takahashi, Y., & Techakanont, K. (2014). The influence of social and organizational support on transfer of training: Evidence from Thailand. *International Journal of Training & Development, 18*(2), 116–131.

Huczynski, A. A., & Lewis, J. W. (1980). An empirical study into the learning transfer process in management training. *Journal of Management Studies, 17*(2), 227–240.

Hutchins, E. (1995). *Cognition in the wild*. MIT Press.

Jarvenpaa, S. L., & Majchrzak, A. (2008). Knowledge collaboration among professionals protecting national security: Role of transactive memories in ego-centered knowledge networks. *Organization Science, 19*(2), 260–276.

Judge, T. A., Jackson, C. L., Shaw, J. C., Scott, B. A. & Rich, B. L. (2007). Self-efficacy and work-related performance: The integral role of individual differences. *Journal of Applied Psychology, 92*, 107–127.

Keith, N., & Frese, M. (2005). Self-regulation in error management training: Emotion control and metacognition as mediators of performance effects. *Journal of Applied Psychology, 90*(4), 677–691.

Keith, N. and Frese, M. (2008). Effectiveness of error management training: A meta-analysis. *Journal of Applied Psychology, 93*, 59–69.

Khasawneh, S., Bates, R. A., & Holton, E.F. III. (2006). Construct validation of an Arabic version of the Learning Transfer Systems Inventory for use in Jordan. *International Journal of Training and Development, 10*(3), 180–194.

Khost, P. H. (2017). Researching habits-of-mind self-efficacy in first-year college writers. In P. Portanova, J. M. Rifenburg, & D. Roen (Eds.), *Contemporary Perspectives on Cognition and Writing* (pp. 271–289). WAC Clearinghouse.

Kirwan, C., & Birchall, D. (2006). Transfer of learning from management development programmes: Testing the Holton model. *International Journal of Training & Development, 10*(4), 252–268.

Kraiger, K. (2003). Perspectives on training and development. *Handbook of Psychology*, 171–192.

Kren, L. (1992). The moderating effects of locus of control on performance incentives and participation. *Human Relations, 45*(9), 991–1012.

Latham, G. P., & Frayne, C. A. (1989). Self-management training for increasing job attendance: A follow-up and a replication. *Journal of Applied Psychology, 74*(3), 411–416.

Lewis, K., & Herndon, B. (2011). Transactive memory systems: Current issues and future research directions. *Organization Science, 22*(5), 1254–1265.

Lim, D., & Johnson, S. (2002). Trainee perceptions of factors that influence learning transfer. *International Journal of Training and Development, 6*(1), 36–48.

Lucas, L. M. (2005). The impact of trust and reputation on the transfer of best practices. *Journal of Knowledge Management, 9*, 87–101.

Mackiewicz, J., & Thompson, I. (2013). Motivational scaffolding, politeness, and writing center tutoring. *The Writing Center Journal, 33*(1), 38–73.

May, G. L., & Kahnweiler, W. M. (2000). The effect of a mastery practice design on learning and transfer in behavior modeling training. *Personnel Psychology, 53*(2), 353–373.

Meyer, H. H., & Raich, M. S. (1983). An objective evaluation of a behavior modeling training program. *Personnel Psychology, 36*(4), 755–761.

Michaelian, K., & Sutton, J. (2013). Distributed cognition and memory research: History and current directions. *Review of Philosophy and Psychology, 4*(1), 1–24.

Nevo, D., & Wand, Y. (2005). Organizational memory information systems: A transactive memory approach. *Decision Support Systems, 39*(4), 549–562.

Noe, R. (1986). Trainee's attributes and attitudes: Neglected influences on training effectiveness. *Academy of Management Review, 11*(4), 736–749.

Noe, R. A. (2000). Invited Reaction: Development of a generalized Learning Transfer System Inventory. *Human Resource Development Quarterly, 11*, 361–365.

Nonaka, I. (1991, November–December). The knowledge creating company. *Harvard Business Review*, 96–104.

Nonaka, I. (1994). A dynamic theory of organizational knowledge creation. *Organization Science, 5*(1), 14–37.

Nowacek, R., Douglas, J., Fitzsimmons, W., Hausladen, K., Knowles, M., Bodee, B., & Nugent, M. (2019). "Transfer talk" in talk about writing: How writers engage with prior learning. *Composition Forum, 42*. https://compositionforum.com/issue/42/transfer-talk.php

Orlikowski, W. J. (2002). Knowing in practice: Enacting a collective capability in distributed organizing. *Organization Science, 13*(3), 249–273.

Pescuric, A., & Byham, W. C. (1996). The new look of behavior modeling. *Training & Development, 50*(7), 24–31.

Prince, M., Burns, D., Lu, X., & Winsor, R. (2015). Knowledge and skills transfer between MBA and workplace. *Journal of Workplace Learning, 27*(3), 207–225.

Reid, E. S. (2017). Defining dispositions: Mapping student attitudes and strategies in college composition. In P. Portanova, J. M. Rifenburg, & D. Roen (Eds.), *Contemporary Perspectives on Cognition and Writing* (pp. 291–312). WAC Clearinghouse.

Robertson, L., Taczak, K., & Yancey, K.B. (2012). Notes toward a theory of prior knowledge and its role in college composers' transfer of knowledge and practice. *Composition Forum, 26*. https://compositionforum.com/issue/26/prior-knowledge-transfer.php

Robinson H. M. (2009). Writing center philosophy and the end of basic writing: Motivation at the site of remediation and discovery. *Journal of Basic Writing, 28*(2), 70–92.

Rouiller, J. Z., & Goldstein, I. L. (1993). The relationship between organizational transfer climate and positive transfer of training. *Human Resource Development Quarterly, 4*(4), 377–390.

Saks, A. M., & Burke-Smalley, L. (2014). Is transfer of training related to firm performance? *International Journal of Training & Development, 18*(2), 104–115.

Salomon, G. (1993). Editor's introduction. In G. Salomon (Ed.), *Distributed cognitions: Psychological and educational considerations*, (pp. xi–xxi*).* Cambridge University Press.

Smart, G., & Brown, N. (2002). Learning transfer or transforming learning?: Student interns reinventing expert writing practices in the workplace. *Technostyle, 18*(1), 117–141.

Stevens, C. K., & Gist, M. E. (1997), Effects of self-efficacy and goal-orientation training on interpersonal skill maintenance: what are the mechanisms? *Personnel Psychology*, 50(4), 955–78.

Sullivan, P.A. (2014). *New writing classroom: Listening, motivation, and habits of mind*. Utah State University Press.

Sullivan, P. (2015). "Ideas about human possibilities": Connecticut's PA 12–40 and basic writing in the era of neoliberalism. *Journal of Basic Writing*, 44–80.

Szulanski, G. (2000). The process of knowledge transfer: A diachronic analysis of stickiness. *Organizational Behavior and Human Decision Processes*, 82(1), 9–27.

Szulanski, G. (2003). *Sticky knowledge: Barriers to knowing in the firm*. SAGE Publications Ltd.

Tang, T.L. (1997). Invited reaction: Theory, research, and practice. *Human Resource Development Quarterly*, 8(2), 137–143.

Tannenbaum, S. I., & Yukl, G. (1992). Training and development in work organizations. *Annual Review of Psychology*, 43, 399–441.

Taylor, P. J., Russ-Eft, D. F. and Chan, D. W. L. (2005). A meta-analytic review of behavior modeling training. *Journal of Applied Psychology*, 90, 692–709.

Thorndike, Edward Lee. (1916). *The principles of teaching*. AG Seiler. (Original work published 1906)

Tracey, J. B., Tannenbaum, S. I., & Kavanagh, M. J. (1995). Applying trained skills on the job: The importance of the work environment. *Journal of Applied Psychology*, 80(2), 239–52.

Tziner, A., Fisher, M., Senior, T. & Weisberg, J. (2007). Effects of trainee characteristics on training effectiveness. *International Journal of Selection & Assessment*, 15(2), 167–174.

Vancouver, J. B., & Kendall, L. N. (2006). When self-efficacy negatively relates to motivation and performance in a learning context. *Journal of Applied Psychology*, 91, 1146–53.

Velada, R., Caetano, A., Bates, R., & Holton, E. (2009). Learning transfer—validation of the Learning Transfer System Inventory in Portugal. *Journal of European Industrial Training*, 33(7), 635–656.

Velada, R., Caetano, A., Michel, J. W., Lyons, B. D., & Kavanagh, M. J. (2007). The effects of training design, individual characteristics and work environment on transfer of training. *International Journal of Training & Development*, 11(4), 282–294.

Walsh, J. P., & Ungson, G. R. (1991). Organizational memory. *Academy of Management Review*, 16(1), 57–91.

Wardle, E. (2009). "Mutt genres" and the goal of FYC: Can we help students write the genres of the university? *College Composition and Communication*, 60(4), 765–789.

Wardle, E. (2012). Creative repurposing for expansive learning: Considering 'problem-exploring'and 'answer-getting'dispositions in individuals and fields. In *Composition Forum, 26.* https://compositionforum.com/issue/26/creative-repurposing.php

Wegner, D. M. (1987). Transactive memory: A contemporary analysis of the group mind. In *Theories of group behavior* (pp. 185–208). Springer.

Wegner, D. M., Giuliano, T., & Hertel, P. T. (1985). Cognitive interdependence in close relationships. In W. J. Ickes (Ed.), *Compatible and incompatible relationships* (pp. 253–276). Springer.

Winzenried, M. A. et al. (2017). Co-constructing writing knowledge: Students' collaborative talk across contexts. *Composition Forum, 37.* https://compositionforum.com/issue/37/co-constructing.php

Wood, R., Kakebeeke, B., Debowski, S., & Frese, M. (2000). The impact of enactive exploration on intrinsic motivation, strategy, and performance in electronic search. *Applied Psychology, 49*(2), 263–283.

Yamkovenko, B., & Holton, E. (2010). Toward a theoretical model of dispositional influences on transfer of learning: A test of a structural model. *Human Resource Development Quarterly, 21*(4), 381–410.

Yamkovenko, B.V., Holton, E.F. III, & Bates, R.A. (2007). The Learning Transfer System Inventory (LTSI) in Ukraine: The cross-cultural validation of the instrument. *Journal of European Industrial Training, 31*(5), 377–401.

Yancey, K., Robertson, L., & Taczak, K. (2014). *Writing across contexts: Transfer, composition, and sites of writing.* Utah State University Press.

4 Transfer in Sports, Medical, Aviation, and Military Training

This chapter focuses on the physical performance-oriented fields of sports, medical, aviation, and military education to consider the value in automatic, embodied, and non-verbalized forms of transfer. Fields presented here grapple with questions of embodied and bodily transfer, often in high-stakes professional settings, we believe such a perspective broadens the more conventional approaches to transfer in writing studies that have tended to emphasize transfer's deliberative and discursive features and measures.

We first chronicle how theory and research within sports education accounts for the intersection between bodily performance, in situ and embodied action, and cognition and metacognition. This vein of scholarship has implications for how we in writing studies think about the role of the body and action in writing and helps bridge some theoretical gaps around the teaching of technical skills and situational awareness through its emphasis on embodied cognition. Second, we review transfer research from medicine, aviation, and military training, which likewise emphasizes active, in situ performance and transfer. These fields add the compelling dimension of fidelity through simulation training to conversations about transfer and writing. Such research on the role of real-world fidelity in transfer is especially informative for cases where we seek to connect classroom writing assignments with those found "in the wild." Such work has a strong history and presence in writing studies through focus on internships, service learning, and some professional writing curricula (see Chapter 10 on "Writing across Contexts: From School to Work and Beyond"). Work presented on fidelity in medical, aviation, and military education challenges writing studies to consider broadening types and dimensions of fidelity (e.g., physical, affective, sensory) when building learning environments or simulations that can facilitate transfer. This chapter concludes by offering theoretical and pedagogical constructs from sports, medicine, aviation, and the military and invites readers to consider how embodied cognition, the role of fidelity in planning and teaching for transfer, and approaches to creating simulated environments can all enliven approaches to writing-related transfer.

Sports Education

An important debate for transfer studies in sports education is whether, when, and how to distinguish between teaching isolated technical skills (e.g., dribbling in basketball or a ball toss in tennis) and context-dependent awareness (e.g., decision making within the pass of a live game or the flurry of a throw). Given long-standing discussions within writing studies on transfer of skills versus awareness, this strand of research from sports education is especially resonant. Such debates, which we address in Chapter 6 on "Research on Transfer in Studies of Second Language Writing," Chapter 7 on "Transfer in First-Year Writing," and Chapter 8 on "Infrastructure for the Transfer of Writing Knowledge: Writing Across the Curriculum and Writing in the Disciplines" drove many early conversations about transfer in writing studies. The thrust here was the question of how the teaching of generalized writing skills could transfer into community-specific writing situations while also recognizing literacy as a situated social practice. Sports education research offers insights into this debate for writing studies through its emphasis on how transfer connects bodily performance and embodied action with cognition and metacognition.

A Paradigm in Sports Education: Teaching Games for Understanding

Sports education experienced a significant paradigm shift in the early 1980s related to social constructivist theories of learning and new perspectives on how the body and mind interact with their environment. As a response to long-standing behaviorist approaches in sports education, the new social constructionist focus emphasized situated, contextualized, and participatory learning as critical for transfer of training across games and from practice to performance. Most famously, Bunker and Thorpe (1982) ushered in a changed set of research and pedagogical questions that supplemented the prior dominance of technical and motor skills (connected to behaviorist models) for an additional emphasis on tactical awareness within a whole game context. Questions of transfer moved from a discussion of motor learning in isolation to contextual and active learning through deliberate structuring and scaffolding during game play. Over time, this emphasis on decision-making and tactical awareness in game play has come to drive most questions of transfer theory and pedagogy in sports education. Relevant to writing studies is the question of how to balance skills and tactics when the pedagogical goal is for learners to transfer their knowledge into the messiness and ill-structured nature of real-world activity. The dominant response in sports education has been to design classrooms to teach for tactical awareness primarily, with skill-level instruction embedded within game play. Despite this general level of consensus, we do find variation in how tactical approaches deal with skills. For instance, research asks whether transfer is best achieved when sports-specific skills (e.g., basketball) are taught through those sports alone or whether the teaching of some generalized skills at the level of sports-types (e.g., net games) can transfer across sports. Such multi-variant possibilities in embodied transfer have implications for writing transfer.

In their landmark theoretical article on sports education and transfer research, Bunker and Thorpe (1982) argued that teaching games as "a series of highly structured lessons leaning heavily on the teaching of techniques [specific motor responses]" (p. 5) was too contrived and artificial; those "failed to take into account the contextual nature of games" (p. 5). Light and Fawns (2003) link this shift, in part, to Dewey's (1936/1986) descriptions of "executive intelligence" and "mindful action" (p. 163). Bunker and Thorpe (1982) proposed that players needed learning environments that brought together the individual, the task, and the context for long-term success in game play; they argued that learning within this configuration was more likely to transfer than was mastery over isolated technical skills. Departing from earlier work on motor skills, Bunker and Thorpe (1982) made the radical claim that tactical considerations and tactical awareness, rather than particular skills, should be starting points in games teaching. Bunker and Thorpe (1982) introduced a changed coaching sequence from fronting skills to now fronting game appreciation (i.e., the rules and constraints of the game), tactical awareness, and abstract constructs, which they argued would aid in overall understanding, deeper interest, and motivation to play. This revised sequence didn't reject teaching technical skills altogether; rather, it built up to skills through a focus on *how* games were played. Moreover, their educational model emphasized "sport performance [as] a complex product of cognitive knowledge about the current situation and past events combined with a player's ability to produce the sport skill(s) required" (Thomas et al., 1986, p. 259). From this perspective, types of practice that activate the arena of cognition, decision-making, and tactical awareness within situated activity could prime transfer into a game setting.

This approach—teaching games for understanding (TGfU)—"adopt[s] a more ecological, holistic view of learning" (Light, 2008, p. 22) that foregrounds the body and the body's relationship to cognition and context. Understanding thus arises from the learner's engagement in the world through perception, motor action, and bodily senses" (p. 23). Drawing on work in phenomenology, educational theory, and cognitive science, TGfU is "deeply tied into processes of cognition and the fluid physical context within which they are performed" (Light & Fawns, 2003, p. 164). Thus, teaching for transfer requires activation of embodied cognition. The importance of embodied cognition for transfer has also been developed in the field of cognitive psychology more generally (for more see Chapter 2). In that field, the work of Nemirovsky (2011), for instance, affirms the potential physicality of transfer as an action that resides in the body and can be reignited later under similar contextual and material circumstances.

Broadly, tactical approaches to sports education intertwine body and mind with a focus on situated learning, noting that "inherent [in the] problem of discrete skill practice is that learning is often decontextualized" (Turner & Martinek, 1995, p. 45). Like fields described throughout this book, theories of situated learning inform games teaching and learning, and provide a theoretical connection between "culture, contexts and activities" through its emphasis on communities of practice (Griffin et al., 2005, p. 219). Griffin et al. (2005) argue that "TGfU provides a structure for situated learning to occur within a community of practice, based in the meaningful, purposeful and authentic tasks presented and practiced by students" (p. 219). These theoretical shifts, which bridge embodied and cognitive dimensions of learning with theories of situated learning, are an important base from which tactical approaches address questions of transfer.

Writing studies' long-standing debates over whether and how to teach generalized skills versus situationally and rhetorically specific skills and strategies, especially in first-year writing, may benefit from including theories of embodied cognition into this conversation. Emphasis on holistic learning coupled with decision-making through meta-awareness both supports current sociocultural approaches to teaching writing *and* suggests a need for more attention to the embodied, habituated, and dispositional characteristics of writing and learning to write. In other words, writing skills and strategies are embedded in larger actions, processes, and practices. This work might ask us to consider how disaggregating features of writing from their genres and communities does not necessarily disrupt or support the ways writers have deeply internalized when and how to use certain skills and strategies over others.

Tactical Approaches to Transfer in Sports Education: Pedagogical Implications

Classification Systems and Vertical and Thematic Transfer. Tactical approaches cluster types of individual sports in terms of "fundamental tactical principles [and] structural elements" (Lopez et al., 2009, p. 52). Classification categories include invasion (handball, basketball, netball, soccer, rugby); net/wall (tennis, badminton, table tennis, volleyball, squash); striking/fielding (basketball, softball, cricket, kickball); and target games (golf, croquet, pool, curling, bowling). Scholars and educators focus on theories of transfer that are viable both within and across a given classification: basketball to kickball (within), for instance, or basketball to tennis (across). Oftentimes in sports education, positive transfer, either within or across categories, is linked to physiological similarities between movement patterns across sports (e.g., surfing and skateboarding; tennis and badminton) (Kunzell & Lukas, 2011) in like-to-like bodily movement. As a result of this assumption, it follows that when a player attempts a new game within that category, they would have the requisite prior knowledge (both cognitive and embodied) to draw from because they have practiced at least one sport in each category.

Within this games classification system, transfer can be premised on theories of *vertical transfer* and *thematic transfer*. Vertical transfer suggests that games within each classification system are similar enough in terms of tactics and structure that they can support one another in learning (Holt et al., 2002; Werner & Almond, 1990; Lopez et al., 2009). Vertical transfer requires identifying simple to more complex skills and capacities, then teaching those in a meaningful order. Accordingly, some have suggested that within the games classification system, it's helpful to differentiate between "less tactically complex sport/game categories, such as target games, with subsequent progression to increasing difficulty through net/wall games and fielding/run-scoring games to (finally) invasion games, which are deemed the most complex in tactical terms" (Lopez et al., 2009, p. 52). Relatedly, scholars have also suggested *thematic transfer* in which "transfer occurs from certain mastery to another analogue mastery" (Lopez et al., p. 51). Here, scholars and teachers advocate a "common approach" to a category of games rather than teaching specific games. As Lopez et al. state, "The focus is therefore, [sic] on student learning that which can be deemed [sic] 'common' knowledge, skills and understandings and then transferring their learning to each specialized context" (p. 53).

Mitchell et al. (2013) outline how classifying games according to their tactics—categorizing a tactical over a technical focus—is conducive to carrying knowledge between games. As they describe, for example, "invasion games are tactically similar even though they require completely different skills [and those] similarities enable us to define invasion games as those in which the goal is to invade an opponent's territory. Net and wall games involve propelling an object outward, so an opponent is unable to make a return" and so on (p. 9). The key here is to identify what types of tactics should be taught, how, and in what order within each general category; in other words, a significant part of curriculum development and planning for the transfer of tactical games awareness is identifying constituent parts of a larger tactic and breaking that down in terms of its tactical complexity. Although scaffolding is not a keyword here, researchers and educators do stress that novices cannot jump right into the most highly complex tactical problems. Rather, training should "increase the complexity of each tactical problem as students develop their understanding and skills" of the game (p. 12). In this way, there is a dialogic relationship between increased tactical awareness and an increased understanding of the skills needed for and rules defining each game.

Scholars emphasize social interaction through dialogue and the "action discussion reflective cycle" (Lopez et al., 2009, p. 48) where tactical awareness is raised through dialogue. For instance, interspersing practice with verbalization "integrate[s] the mind expressed in speech and the body expressed in action as an ongoing conversation" (Light, 2008, p. 23). Like authentic writing assessment, sports education embeds assessment in social contexts. Because game play and situational expertise are critical to transfer in sports education, these methods aim to capture authentic action in context and combine all dimensions of play in their assessment: technique and tactics and product and process (Grehaigne et al., 1997, p. 502). For more on sports education assessment, see the Game Performance Assessment Instrument (Oslin et al.,1998) and the Team Sport Assessment Procedure (Grehaigne et al., 1997).

Classification debates resonate with writing studies' conversations on genre and transfer. Specifically, they connect most interestingly with research about meta-genres and genre awareness in first-year writing and writing across the curriculum (see Chapter 6 on "Research on Transfer in Studies of Second Language Writing," Chapter 7 on "Transfer in First-Year Writing," and Chapter 8 on "Infrastructure for the Transfer of Writing Knowledge: Writing Across the Curriculum and Writing in the Disciplines"). Often classification systems cluster sports by bodily movements and game functionality. Writing studies scholars have long debated the teaching of more generalized classifications of genres (like academic writing) versus discipline-specific instantiations of those larger categories (like academic writing as situated within sociology, for example). Russell's (1995) famous lamentation that "there is no autonomous, generalizable skill called ball using or ball handling that can be learned and then applied to all ball games" (p. 57) captures the point of these early debates on writing but takes on a new valence situated next to sports education scholarship. Work within sports education suggests an alternative perspective to teaching general skills within categories, one that could open different research and teaching avenues. Specifically, in drawing from theories of embodied cognition, part of the outcome of putting sports into categories is to prime like-to-like bodily movements. Given the theoretical links between body and mind that are supported through embodied cognition theory, we might extend sport education's approach to work in writing studies by asking about linkages across meta-genres and embodied cognition for thematic transfer. In addition, work on writing transfer and genre uptake might explore the interplay between habituated embodiment as it intersects with habituated cognition for vertical transfer.

Transfer and Declarative and Procedural Knowledge. Transfer of training in sports education also considers how novice and expert learners engage with declarative and procedural knowledge in games-related decision-making processes (Turner & Martinek, 1995, p. 46-47). Because tactical awareness approaches emphasize decision making within context-specific play, encouraging deep and active procedural knowledge is imperative. For instance, relevant studies by McPherson and Thomas (1989) found that while experts were able to connect the network of their declarative knowledge base to make decisions on process and action, novices had too little conceptual foundation to begin the process of decision-making in relation to goals. Because declarative knowledge and procedural knowledge together led to better tactical play, it's important to design a transfer pedagogy that combines them for the interplay of performance and decision-making. Subsequent empirical studies on tactical and decision-making approaches to teaching games have provided positive results for the transfer of procedural knowledge (Holt et al., 2006; Jones & Farrow, 1999; Mitchell & Oslin, 1999). For instance, in their study of net games, Jones and Farrow (1999) monitored how a cohort of eight-year-olds transferred both speed and precision in decision making between volleyball and badminton, reporting strong gains in both areas. Reported results of transfer were significant as participants received explicit instruction in the perceived tactic of interest. While studies have reported good results for the transfer of tactical awareness across games, the most successful results occurred when there was only a slight increase in the level of difference and difficulty (tactical complexity) between games in the same category (Lopez et al., 2009).

Writing studies' conversations on the role of threshold concepts and transfer connect with research on declarative and procedural knowledge in sports education. Threshold concepts research makes a strong case for centering declarative writing-related content knowledge in teaching for transfer. Because threshold concepts provide the conceptual and intellectual grounding for new and deeper learning and more strategic activity, they have potential to undergird and motivate a transfer act (see Chapter 7 on "Transfer in First Year Writing"). Interestingly, and perhaps informed through the conceptual commitment in sports education to embodied cognition, findings emphasize the covalent and synergistic relationship between declarative and procedural knowledge in game play. Perhaps writing studies can think more deeply about a similar relationship and ways to promote pedagogically that symbiosis, such as a focused threshold concept education coupled with process-based instruction with aims toward the transfer of writing-related knowledge.

Simulations in Medical Education, Flight Training, and Military Combat

Medical Education

Within the field of medical education, transfer research has focused heavily on the efficacy of simulations (see Chapter 10 on "Writing across Contexts: From School to Work and Beyond" for more on simulations and professional writing). Medical studies often focus on the role of "fidelity" between simulation and later contexts as well as the types and levels of task complexity—physical and psychological—required for comprehensive knowledge transfer. Like much of the research reviewed from sports education, transfer research within medical education foregrounds issues of situated learning and how changes or differences in contextual variables impact transfer. A key distinction is the role of simulations in medical education, with accompanying questions of whether and how medical simulations help professionals transfer training to real-world contexts and how best to design simulated learning environments. But like sports education, focus on automaticity and embodied cognition often organizes research on simulations, fidelity, and transfer pedagogy. High-stakes work demands that doctors and nurses can not only reason their way to a workplace conclusion but act and react swiftly.

Fidelity, Situated Learning, and Transfer

As we know from work in educational psychology, high-road transfer "depends on deliberate mindful abstraction of skill or knowledge from one context for application in another" (Perkins & Salomon, 1988, p. 25). Importantly, for medical education, so-called high-road transfer must be coupled with low-road transfer for quick thinking and automaticity of action. Simulation in medical training strives to recreate deep characteristics of situated learning and situated cognition for more automatic training in low-road transfer (Teretis et al., 2012, p. 140). Attention to fidelity addresses this transfer goal. Fidelity, that relationship of similarity between the simulated environment and the real-world context, is the core construct for helping students to develop transferable skills, capacities, knowledges, and actions.

Theories of fidelity typically emphasize situated learning and situated cognition (Lave, 1988; Lave & Wenger, 1991) and levels of direct authenticity between a simulated practice and real-world work. Such relationships can be either high (very similar/close likeness) or low (dissimilar/distant/partial). High and low fidelity extends to a context's multi-dimensionality. A nurse or doctor's interaction with a patient includes environment, psychology, and the physical body as well as the use of skills and engagement in actions ranging from motion efficiency, dexterity, economy of movement, quickness, and accuracy to bedside manner, leadership, and communication skills. Concordantly, there are various simulators that are categorized as having low fidelity, high fidelity, engineering (physical) fidelity, psychological (functional) fidelity, and environmental fidelity with the term *fidelity* "used to describe some aspect of the reality of the experience" (Maran & Glavin, 2003, p. 23). Psychological fidelity is also critical and refers to how much the learner perceives the simulation as a real proxy for the target task. Issenberg and Scalese (2008) note that the appropriate "fidelity configuration" (p. 34) is required to maximize transfer.

How fidelity is construed reflects how context and activity are defined and what educators or researchers believe are most applicable to transfer of learning. In some cases, fidelity is constructed through its allegiance to the physicality and functionality of the real-world context. But even within this narrowing, it is still a challenge to name "precisely what aspects of the context should be the focus of attention" (Norman et al., 2012, p. 637). Not only that, but medical professionals are in training for multiple types of care and interaction with patients (e.g., taking blood pressure, discussing health outcomes, performing a range of surgeries). Researchers have identified four connected variables that may aid in transfer between simulations and real-world environments: the amount of initial learning, similarity between learning and performance environments, *perceived* similarity between these environments, and motivation of the learner (Alessi, 1988). These factors all speak to the possibilities and unpredictability of teaching for transfer within medical education. Thus, a guiding question for medical education is this: what kinds of fidelity best support transfer? What kinds of pedagogical approaches best complement the use of simulations in learning? The following section highlights key research findings on the dynamic role of fidelity in learning and transfer of learning.

Teaching for Transfer in Medical Education

In general, research on simulations as proxies for fidelity show the benefit of simulations for transfer (Barsuk et al., 2009[a]; Barsuk et al., 2009[b]; Draycott et al., 2008; McGaghie, 2008; Wayne et al., 2008). There is less consensus on how to structure learning throughout the simulated experience. First, in drawing from research in cognitive science, Teteris and colleagues (2012) suggest that immediate exposure to a comprehensive high-fidelity simulation is too complex and too ambiguous for novice students due to the higher cognitive load of performing all aspects of a complex task. Presenting novice learners with every dimension and real-world complexity may hinder students' ability to progress. Thus, like other fields, an important area of simulation transfer for medical education is how a learner's level of expertise affects their interaction with the simulator and thus the likelihood of transfer to professional, clinical situations. Vygotsky's work on scaffolding and the zone of proximal development informs discussions on how trainees transition from a novice to expert status as "learners are exposed to a series of learning environments of increasing fidelity" (Teteris et al., 2012 p. 141). In fact, "there is evidence . . . that novices may well be better off with simpler models and should gradually move to more complex models as their skills improve, a strategy known as '‘progressive' fidelity" (Norman et al., 2012, p. 644). Learners first work within low-fidelity settings, which decreases the "extraneous and intrinsic cognitive load," in preparation for "when they have mastered this part of the task [and can] progress through increasingly complex environments and tasks until they reach the highest available fidelity" (Teteris et al., 2012 p. 141). A higher cognitive load typically reduces initial learning and, ultimately, transfer—because what has not been learned cannot be transferred. Research draws on cognitive load theory to stress that "many additions to a learning task may detract from learning because of our limited ability to process incoming information" (Norman et al., 2012, p. 644). Research supports starting learners off in low-fidelity situations and moving through fidelity-inspired zones of proximal development (Maran & Glavin, 2003). Thus, a simulated learning environment is effective when parts of a fully realized simulation are broken down into parts or phases and then built back up over time. In this case, discrete simulations are developed through partial exposure to some holistic version of a real-world context.

Research also emphasizes "deliberate practice, reflection and feedback" (Maran & Glavin, 2003, p.22) in conjunction with learning through simulations and apprenticeship models (Porte et al., 2007, p.106). Computer assisted instruction and feedback—through simulations—has gained traction, and research suggests that a combination of expert feedback and computer-assisted technologies are likely the most effective means for learning and transfer (Porte et al., 2007; Xeroulis et al., 2007). As addressed in Xeroulis et al.'s study of computer-based video instruction versus expert feedback in teaching knot-tying and suturing, a combination of computer-assisted learning and expert feedback can be most effective. Despite the usefulness of computer-based simulations in learning, research shows that practitioners still benefit from human feedback throughout the scaffolding process in so-called "performance-related information" because such apprenticeship communication emphasizes the cognitive and social dimensions of the skill being learned (see Chapter 10 on "Writing across Contexts: From School to Work and Beyond" for more on apprenticeship models in writing).

Critically, while feedback appears valuable, "continuous feedback" from either domain may result in "over guidance, leading to learners using concurrent feedback as a crutch [sic], and distraction of attention from the intrinsic feedback naturally present" (Xeroulis et al., 2007, pp. 447–448). Because simulation can "'shape' appropriate technical skill performance" (Xeroulis et al., 2007, p. 448), the same mechanism can be manipulated to monitor and adjust feedback (particularly computer-assisted) through strategies such as "'fading'" which, "initially provide many clues and feedback to trainees at the start of training and slowly fade out as the trainee learns to carry out the task without support" (Xeroulis et al., 2007 p. 448). Aggarwal et al. (2006) provide additional and holistic strategies for teaching with simulations at the level of a comprehensive training curriculum, which they refer to as a scaffolded process of familiarization, training, and assessment. Tellingly, they term the final phase "automation," which "occurs when the learner performs the tasks in a relatively automated fashion with little or no cognitive input" (p. 131). The instructor supports the learner with verbal feedback in all but the final stage.

Transfer, Simulations, and Fidelity in Flight Training and Military Combat

Flight education is an important source field for simulation research. Specifically, studies in aviation further highlight the multiple and interacting dimensions of fidelity. In fact, much of the early medical education research borrowed from flight-training language and theory regarding the roles of physical, psychological, and environmental fidelity for facilitating transfer. But, for flight training, even more focus is placed on transfer at the level of habituated, bodily action and response between simulation and transfer target context. Military training follows a similar focus.

An original theoretical justification for simulations came from Thorndike's (1901) identical elements theory, with special attention to visual and motion cues across the training and the real-world context. Later research pointed to the role of perception in this process, which complicated the use of Thorndike's identical elements to show that "perceptual fidelity is not necessarily induced by exact physical simulation. [Rather,] [i]dentifying ways to induce reality rather than simulating the physics of reality is a scientific challenge to be addressed by all future generations of simulators" (Robinson & Mania, 2007, p. 134).

Attempts to remedy perceptual challenges focus heavily on visual, interactional, and kinesthetic fidelity. As researchers and educators seek more and better ways to create systems and simulations that address the components, they ask, as outlined by Robinson and Mania,

- What makes a simulation feel real to a human observer?
- Can we use what is known about the human visual system and human cognition to help us produce more realistic synthetic images?
- Can our perception of the real world (space and people) around us survive the transition to a graphics environment or to a virtual human?

- How can we use the attributes of the human visual system and human cognition to design computer graphics simulation systems in a way that a sense of "being there" is communicated?
- Are there perceptual commonalities among applications, or are practical applications so independent that we cannot generalize findings from one application to another? (p.124).

The question of perception is further complicated when distinguishing between surface and underlying features of a situation. For instance, some research has found that "the important factor in the transfer of basic flight skills may lie in the transfer of cognitive principles underlying successful task performance rather than transfer of proprioceptive cues from physical identical elements from the device to the aircraft itself" (Koonce & Bramble, 1998, p. 287). Work in military training supports this finding. As Alexander et al. (2005) describe, "surface features of training refer to problem-specific or domain-specific features of training examples. In contrast, deep (structural) features refer to the underlying principles imparted in training" (p. 3). To replicate both surface and deep features, and induce the recognition of those features, but at different times and for different purposes, military training has turned increasingly to virtual games. Through these mechanisms, military education emphasizes scaffolded experiences and levels of fidelity. Alexander et al. note that "[f]idelity is not a simple high/low dichotomy, rather it is multiple compound continua" (p. 6), and that more fidelity does not necessarily mean a better outcome; rather, successful (positive) transfer comes from whether "the level of fidelity captures the critical elements/properties of the skills/tasks you wish to teach, that level of fidelity is sufficient even if it noticeably deviates from the real world" (p. 6).

Implications for Pedagogy and Methodology from Medical Education, Flight Training, and Military Combat

In this section, we have synthesized pedagogical and methodological recommendations as they relate to fidelity and simulations.

- To build scaffolded experiences across simulations, it is important to distinguish between high fidelity and low fidelity. High fidelity means that there is a close likeness to the real while low fidelity means that the likeness is partial or distant. A low-fidelity simulation would have only parts of these types mentioned

above—engineering, environmental, or psychological—while high-fidelity simulations would incorporate all or most for the most realistic version of the real-world experience.
- Distinguishing between types of fidelity allows educators to scaffold a series of increasingly complex simulations over time. While the whole environment, including the learner's interactions with the environment, might be the target context for transfer, breaking context variables down increases the likelihood of on-going learning. The medical literature, for instance, suggests three common types of fidelity to pay attention to: engineering fidelity, environment fidelity, and psychological fidelity. The aviation literature references additional types of fidelity: visual, haptic or kinesthetic, and motion fidelity. While not all these specific context variables are applicable to writing, the broader attention to the full and multiple dimensionalities of context should cue educators to explore elements of context that have been previously neglected.
- To help facilitate transfer, it can be important to begin with a low-fidelity simulation where learners can experience part of the target task, thus reducing both extraneous and intrinsic cognitive load. This is called within the literature "'progressive' fidelity" (Norman et al., 2012, p. 644). When students have mastered a part of the task, they progress through increasingly complex environments and tasks until they reach the highest available fidelity.
- Scaffolded fidelity can be paced over time, with multiple opportunities to practice the new skill, capacity, or action. Reflection and feedback are critical components of this process and include verbal feedback from an expert (Porte et al. 2007) as well as "deliberate practice, reflection and feedback" (Maran & Glavin, 2003, p. 22).
- The place and significance of feedback may shift throughout this process. Aviation training and military combat literature suggests that feedback recedes as students move from low- to high-fidelity simulations given that the goal, in these learning contexts at least, is to train ultimately for automaticity.

Fidelity in and of itself does not create a transfer-rich environment. Rather, fidelity-inspired learning environments require strategy, pedagogy, and monitoring. It is critical to scaffold toward more realistic activities by building up parts of an overall environment carefully, aided by practice, reflection, and feedback. Broadly, these practices also reflect good writing pedagogy. More specifically, writing studies can learn from these fields' attention to the multi-dimensionality of fidelity and the care with which those facets are scaffolded.

Methodologically, two approaches have value for the transfer of writing-related knowledge. These methods include direct observation and the use of haptic sensors. Observation of learner performance is the most common method here, with a researcher watching and taking notes on transfer performance. Such observations are aimed at assessing so-called clinical competence, which aims to not only capture the practitioner's aptitude on the task at hand, but also to generalize to other future tasks. Typically, both inter- and intra-rater reliability are preferred, and video-taped sessions help researchers in this process.

Direct observation of transfer is not nearly as common in writing studies, as a good deal of research relies on either reflective interviews or discursive tracing rather than living accounts of the transfer act. But such a method could fit well with the long history of ethnographic research methods within writing studies. While direct observation cannot capture the meta-cognitive processes of a writer or note a writer's internal dialogue and decision making around when and how to transfer writing-related information, it has the potential to identify extra-discursive features of transfer by focusing on a writer's movements as they relate to the environmental infrastructure. If a researcher is interested in the dynamic between talk, text, and transfer in dyads or groups in action, observation is again a useful tool (see Chapter 9, "Writing Centers: An Infrastructural Hub for Transfer"). The key would be to identify situations in which external transfer data could be gleaned in real time or to theoretically connect (through discourse analysis, for example) talk to transfer. Recent work on "transfer talk" in writing centers illustrates the value of this approach as these researchers sought to use analysis of tutor talk to interrogate "the role of more routine, automated experiences of transfer" (Nowacek et al., 2019.).

Haptic sensors also play a role in how to observe transfer in medical settings. Unlike the direct observation of a participant, these methods have the practitioner interact directly with a technological interface, which is designed to determine the precision and effectiveness of how prior knowledge, especially as expressed through action, transfers to new clinical settings with new patients (Mackel et al., 2007, p. 2133). While haptic methods aren't widely used in writing studies generally, key-stroke logging has made some inroads in process-oriented research (Baaijen et al., 2012) and could be further expanded to include transfer studies like those performed in medical education. Specifically, keystroke-logging can capture "pauses, bursts, and revisions" around text production, with length and duration between activity accounting for some level of comfort, familiarity, or confidence (Baaijen et al., 2012, p. 246). As a more fine-grained and cognitive-theory informed method for transfer research, keystroke-logging between practice and real-world contexts can complement retrospective approaches by providing study of writing-in-action, with fidelity as a guiding principle, to better understand the non-verbalized (the automatic) dimensions of in situ writing across school and workplace contexts. Work in writing studies around emplaced writing processes and the role of space in mobilizing literacy repertoires (Pigg, 2020) or even examining actual medical simulations (Campbell, 2017) may find kinship with the types of haptic methodologies deployed within sports and medical education to expand an understanding of how place, action, writing, and transfer intersect.

Conclusion and Avenues for Further Inquiry in Writing Studies

In this chapter, we brought together transfer studies from the fields of sports education, medical education, and flight and military training. We learn that transfer is both verbalized and not verbalized—it occurs on an embodied and situated level—wherein transfer is defined as including both bodily knowledge as well as conscious and verbalized knowledge. From these perspectives, teaching for transfer requires attention to what is not always articulable and requires linking the automatic with the dialogic and communicative. Given this starting point, the fields in the chapter focus heavily on creating learning environments that deliberately replicate real-world counterparts. This mimicking, described often as establishing fidelity, means fully immersive game play in sports education and the use of simulations in medical, aviation, and military education. Key constructs to pull and apply to writing studies include embodied cognition, fidelity, and simulations. While we have connected these fields' theory and research to writing studies throughout the chapter, we conclude by emphasizing how these constructs open avenues for further inquiry for writing-related transfer. From sports education, writing studies can draw valuable insight into how to think about the scope and approach to transfer. Most critical is the invitation to expand transfer from a cognitive to an embodied and affective practice, which has implications for teaching and research. For scholars and teachers in writing studies, embodied cognition can be linked to work in materiality of technology and its effects on habituated practice (Haas, 2009); textual performance (Arola & Wysocki, 2012; Fishman et al., 2005); the relationship between literacy and rhetorical education and movement (Hawhee, 2005; LeMesurier, 2016); and the intersection between embodied practice, writing process, and material spaces (Campbell, 2017; Pigg, 2020). As emphasized in this section, the body—with its own sense of ritual, memory, and cognition—is always active and present in learning; the insight and challenge, then, is to understand how to develop practices that encourage the integration of body and mind for the purposes of transfer. With a focus on the body and on action, writing studies scholars can build out a more holistic and sophisticated theory of transfer to broaden where and how transfer of both writing-related knowledge and writing-related action can matter. Specifically, sports education can provide additional dimension to the following writing studies transfer-related conversations: (a) the relationship between teaching skills versus teaching rhetorical and contextual awareness, (b) the relationship between teaching specific genres or teaching strategies linked to meta-genres, and (c) understanding how writers' habituated writing and embodied practices and processes impact transfer.

From across medical education, aviation, and military education, we can ask: when could notions of fidelity be applicable to the transfer of writing-related knowledge? As we explore in Chapter 10, writing classrooms often seek to provide realistic real-work, real-world contexts. When starting from the presupposition that writing is an act of situated cognition, which most writing classrooms in the studies we examine later do, fidelity across the procedural and rhetorical dimensions of a writing task becomes imperative. Like a cockpit or a surgery theater, writing contexts are layered with complex material, sensorial, affective, and discursive factors that are likewise realized through human perception. Aviation and medical education suggest that these factors can be parsed in various ways to produce a range of low- to high-fidelity simulations. Drawing from this general insight, writing instructors can be prompted similarly. Specifically, writing studies can make strong use of fidelity and simulations for complex collaborative writing situations. Like physicians, pilots, and team sports players, writers also work in highly charged and urgent situations. For instance, writers are always at work in newsrooms, political and legal spheres, and domains of health and medicine among others. Such situations are not only high stakes and time sensitive, but they also require responsiveness to managers, clients, editors, and other writing colleagues. In *The Rise of Writing*, Brandt (2014) explores such complex and often fraught negotiations that writers have with other writers, with their superiors, and with the public. In a world where everyone writes, it's imperative that educators acknowledge and reckon with the needs of "workaday writers" who "write for pay" (Brandt, 2014, p. 19–20). What types of fidelity do my students need to be introduced to as they increase their facility with engaging in real-world/real-work contexts? How would I break large and complex environment simulations into smaller parts and help students build their competence by moving from low- to high-fidelity over time? Given the ways in which simulations are built to mimic the physical, psychological, and environmental features of the performance context, what characteristics of a writing context map onto such facets? Powerfully, when we combine an interest in fidelity and simulations with embodied cognition, questions of transfer move from a dominantly discursive space to one that includes action, the physical body, and the strong effects of the material environment on transfer. In other words, writing studies scholars can ask: what facets of the writing context and facets of full human experience do I need to interact with to support this transfer act?

References

Aggarwal, R., Grantcharov, T., Moorthy, K., Hance, J., & Darzi, A. (2006). A competency-based virtual reality training curriculum for the acquisition of laparoscopic psychomotor skill. *The American Journal of Surgery*, *191*(1), 128–133.

Alessi, S. M. (1988). Fidelity in the design of instructional simulations. *Journal of Computer-Based Instruction*, *15*(2), 40–47.

Alexander, A. L., Brunyé, T., Sidman, J., & Weil, S. A. (2005). From gaming to training: A review of studies on fidelity, immersion, presence, and buy-in and their effects on transfer in pc-based simulations and games. *DARWARS Training Impact Group, 5,* 1–14.

Arola, K. L., & Wysocki, A. (Eds.). (2012). *Composing media composing embodiment.* University Press of Colorado

Baaijen, V. M., Galbraith, D., & De Glopper, K. (2012). Keystroke analysis: Reflections on procedures and measures. *Written Communication, 29*(3), 246–277.

Barsuk J.H., McGaghie W.C., Cohen E.R., O'Leary K.S., & Wayne D.B. (2009a). Simulation-based mastery learning reduces complications during central venous catheter insertion in a medical intensive care unit. *Critical Care Medicine, 37*(10), 2697–2701

Barsuk J.H., Cohen E.R., Feinglass J., McGaghie W.C., & Wayne D.B. (2009b). Use of simulation-based education to reduce catheter-related bloodstream infections. *Arch Intern Med, 169*(15), 1420–3.

Brandt, D. (2014). *The rise of writing: Redefining mass literacy.* Cambridge University Press.

Bunker, D., & Thorpe, R. (1982). A model for the teaching of games in secondary schools. *Bulletin of Physical Education, 18*(1), 5–8.

Campbell, L. (2017). Simulation genres and student uptake: The patient health record in clinical nursing simulations. *Written Communication, 34*(3), 255–279.

Dewey, J. (1936/1986). How we think: A restatement of the relation of reflective thinking to the educative process. In J. Boydson (Ed.), *John Dewey: The later works, 1925–1953, vol 8* (pp. 105–352). Southern Illinois University Press.

Draycott, T. J., Crofts, J. F., Ash, J. P., Wilson, L. V., Yard, E., Sibanda, T., & Whitelaw, A. (2008). Improving neonatal outcome through practical shoulder dystocia training. *Obstetrics & Gynecology, 112*(1), 14–20.

Fishman, J., Lunsford, A., McGregor, B., & Otuteye, M. (2005). Performing writing, performing literacy. *College Composition and Communication, 57*(2), 224–252.

Grehaigne, J. F., Godbout, P., & Bouthier, D. (1997). Performance assessment in team sports. *Journal of Teaching in Physical Education, 16*(4), 500–516.

Griffin, L. L., Brooker, R., & Patton, K. (2005). Working towards legitimacy: Two decades of teaching games for understanding. *Physical Education and Sport Pedagogy, 10*(3), 213–223.

Haas, C. (2009). *Writing technology: Studies on the materiality of literacy.* New York, NY: Routledge.

Hawhee, D. (2005). *Bodily arts: Rhetoric and athletics in ancient Greece.* University of Texas Press.

Holt, N. L., Strean, W. B., & Bengoechea, E. G. (2002). Expanding the teaching games for understanding. *Journal of Teaching in Physical Education, 21*(2), 162–176.

Holt, J. E., Ward, P., & Wallhead, T. L. (2006). The transfer of learning from play practices to game play in young adult soccer players. *Physical Education & Sport Pedagogy, 11*(2), 101–118.

Issenberg, S. & Scalese, R. (2008) Simulation in health care education. *Perspectives in biology and medicine, 51*(1), 31–46.

Jones, C., & Farrow, D., (1999). The transfer of strategic knowledge: A test of the games classification curriculum model. *Bulletin of Physical Education, 9,* 41–45

Koonce, J. M., & Bramble Jr, W. J. (1998). Personal computer-based flight training devices. *The International Journal of Aviation Psychology, 8*(3), 277–292.

Kunzell, S., & Lukas, S. (2011). Facilitation effects of a preparatory skateboard training on the learning of snowboarding. *Kinesiology, 43*(1), 56–63.

Lave, J. (1988). *Cognition in practice: Mind, mathematics and culture in everyday life.* Cambridge University Press.

Lave, J, and Wegner, E. (1991). *Situated learning: Legitimate peripheral participation.* Cambridge University Press.

LeMesurier, J. L. (2016). Mobile bodies: Triggering bodily uptake through movement. *College Composition and Communication, 68*(2), 292–316.

Light, R. (2008). Complex learning theory—its epistemology and its assumptions about learning: implications for physical education. *Journal of Teaching in Physical Education, 27*(1), 21–37.

Light, R., & Fawns, R. (2003). Knowing the game: Integrating speech and action in games teaching through TGfU. *Quest, 55*(2), 161–176.

López, L. M. G., Jordán, O. R. C., Penney, D., & Chandle, T. (2009). The role of transfer in games teaching: Implications for the development of the sports curriculum. *European Physical Education Review, 15*(1), 47–63.

Mackel, T. R., Rosen, J., & Pugh, C. M. (2007). Markov model assessment of subjects' clinical skill using the E-Pelvis physical simulator. *IEEE Transactions on Biomedical Engineering, 54*(12), 2133–2141.

Maran, N., & Glavin, R. (2003). Low-to high-fidelity simulation–a continuum of medical education? *Medical Education, 37*(s1), 22–28.

McGaghie W.C. (2008). Research opportunities in simulation-based medical education using deliberate practice. *Academic Emergency Medicine, 15*(11), 995–1001.

McPherson, S. L., & Thomas, J. R. (1989). Relation of knowledge and performance in boys' tennis: Age and expertise. *Journal of Experimental Child Psychology, 48*(2), 190–211.

Mitchell, S. A., & Oslin, J. L. (1999). An investigation of tactical transfer in net games. *European Journal of Physical Education, 4*(2), 162–72.

Mitchell, S. A., Oslin, J. L., & Griffin, L. L. (2013). *Teaching sport concepts and skills: A tactical games approach for ages 7 to 18.* Human Kinetics.

Nemirovsky, R. (2011). Episodic feelings and transfer of learning. *The Journal of the Learning Sciences, 20*(2), 308–337.

Norman, G., Dore, K., & Grierson, L. (2012). The minimal relationship between simulation fidelity and transfer of learning. *Medical Education, 46*(7), 636–647.

Nowacek, R., Bodee, B., Douglas, J. E., Fitzsimmons, W. V., Hausladen, K. A., Knowles, M., & Nugent, M. (2019). "Transfer Talk" in talk about writing in progress: two propositions about transfer of learning. *Composition Forum, 42* (Fall). https://compositionforum.com/issue/42/transfer-talk.php

Oslin, J. L., Mitchell, S. A., & Griffin, L. L. (1998). The game performance assessment instrument (GPAI): Development and preliminary validation. *Journal of Teaching in Physical Education, 17*(2), 231–243.

Perkins, D. N, & Salomon, G. (1988). Teaching for transfer. *Educational Leadership, 46*(1), 22–32.

Pigg, S. (2020). *Transient literacies in action: Composing with the mobile surround.* The WAC Clearinghouse and University Press of Colorado.

Porte, M. C., Xeroulis, G., Reznick, R. K., & Dubrowski, A. (2007). Verbal feedback from an expert is more effective than self-accessed feedback about motion efficiency in learning new surgical skills. *The American Journal of Surgery, 193*(1), 105–110.

Robinson, A., & Mania, K. (2007). Technological research challenges of flight simulation and flight instructor assessments of perceived fidelity. *Simulation & Gaming, 38*(1), 112–135.

Russell, D. (1995). Activity theory and its implications for writing instruction. In J. Petraglia (Ed.), *Reconceiving writing, rethinking writing instruction* (pp. 51–78). Lawrence Erlbaum.

Teteris, E., Fraser, K., Wright, B., & McLaughlin, K. (2012). Does training learners on simulators benefit real patients? *Advances in Health Sciences Education, 17*(1), 137–144.

Thomas, J. R., French, K. E., & Humphries, C. A. (1986). Knowledge development and sport skill performance: Directions for motor behavior research. *Journal of Sport Psychology, 8*(4), 259–272.

Thorndike, E. L., & Woodworth, R. S. (1901). The influence of improvement in one mental function upon the efficiency of other functions. (I). *Psychological Review, 8*(3), 247–261.

Turner, A., & Martinek, T. J. (1995). Teaching for understanding: A model for improving decision making during game play. *Quest, 47*(1), 44–63.

Wayne, D.B., Didwania, A., Feinglass, J., Fudala, M. J., Barsuk, J. H., & McGaghie, W. C. (2008). Simulation-based education improves the quality of care during cardiac arrest team responses at an academic teaching hospital: a case-control study. *Chest, 133*(1), 56–61.

Werner, P., & Almond, L. (1990). Models of games education. *Journal of Physical Education, Recreation & Dance, 61*(4), 23–30.

Xeroulis, G. J., Park, J., Moulton, C., Reznick, R. K., LeBlanc, V., & Dubrowski, A. (2007). Teaching suturing and knot-tying skills to medical students: A randomized controlled study comparing computer-based video instruction and (concurrent and summary) expert feedback. *Surgery*, *141*(4), 442–449.

5 Transfer Implications from Sociocultural and Sociohistorical Literacy Studies

Although we have devoted a separate chapter for literacy studies scholarship, we understand work in literacy studies, with its focus on writing instruction, as part of the larger domain of fields dedicated to the study of writing. We believe that readers will benefit from this separation because it provides focus on three critical dimensions of transfer and writing: (a) explicit comparative focus on literacy practices across multiple contexts, especially in and out of school contexts; (b) emphasis on how culture, history, institutions, and personal factors shape literacy and thus heavily impact transfer; and (c) overt commitment to understanding and bettering the lives and literacies of students and communities who have been historically excluded from mainstream school settings.

Importantly, literacy studies emphasize school's role in mediating transfer, but without centering school as a writer's only or primary place of learning. Rather, school is always placed in relation to multiple other domains, all with complex sets of ideological, sociocultural, and historical factors that impact the transfer act, especially for learners whose home and community lives may conflict with the practices and values of mainstream schooling. In focusing on the movement of readers, writers, and literacies across school and non-school domains, we are guided by a question posed by Hull and Schultz (2001): "How can research on literacy and out-of-school learning help us think anew about literacy teaching and learning across a range of contexts, including school?" (p. 575).

Studies of how literacies traverse in and out of school domains elevate the stakes of transfer, with special value for centering diverse and minoritized students in discussions of writing-related transfer. Such a sociocultural orientation challenges notions such as negative and failed transfer. We are invited to construct transfer in conjunction with literacy's varied and multivalent communities and practices to emphasize how transfer is also a generative and deeply cultural process that can build from community practices for school success. While writing studies has done excellent and extensive research on transfer in first-year writing, writing centers, writing across the curriculum, and workplace writing, the field has not pursued transfer as part of an explicit agenda for social and educational justice. Drawing from work in sociocultural literacy studies can change that trajectory and inform an orientation of anti-racist and anti-oppressive approaches to transfer in writing studies.

In what follows, we first synthesize research that illuminates how the cultural, historical, political, and ideological dimensions of literacy shape and motivate the transfer act. Next, we outline a series of methods for capturing literacy practices as they traverse (transfer) across multiple contexts. We then present readers with pedagogical and curricular options for teaching with culture, power, and transfer in mind.

The Impacts of Culture, Power, Ideology, and History in Literacy Transfer

Sociocultural literacies studies have provided groundbreaking examinations of the relationships between in- and out-of-school literacies (Au, 1980; Heath, 1982, 1983; Phillips, 1983; Street, 1993). From these studies, researchers concluded that mainstream schooling and students' home and community literacy practices were often at odds for historically marginalized students. Early studies shifted educational conversations away from assumptions of literacy deficiency in students. Rather, they established that in- and out-of-school literacies are based on differing sets of values, practices, materials, and engagements. This sociocultural viewpoint suggested that (a) when minoritized and working-class students experience disconnection with school, it can often be traced to the institution's lack of support and lack of value for community languages and literacies, and (b) that students' out-of-school repertoires are, in fact, assets to be leveraged by teachers, not deficits to be removed or punished. We can draw two important implications for transfer from these broad findings. First, students are transferring writing-related knowledge across domains that have (at times) radically different practices, uses for, interactions with, attitudes towards, and values for writing and the multiple literacy practices that surround it. Second, literacies associated with mainstream schooling have been historically privileged over community literacies, which sets up a stark divide between students who appear to transfer and those who do not. Without recognizing the sociocultural dimensions of how literacy works in communities and how mainstream schools have promoted a predominantly white and middle-class literacy, transfer studies cannot ask effective questions nor develop useful pedagogical responses to benefit all students.

Cross-cultural studies have shown how literacy practices develop in relation to community needs and through cultural practices and values (Street, 1993). For instance, Heath's (1982) early study of bedtime stories from the communities of Trackton (working-class Black mill community), Roadville (working-class white mill community), and Maintown (middle-class, mainstream, and so-called school-oriented community) was one of the first comparative studies of home and school. Her bedtime story studies, which were also part of her longer, multi-year ethnography of these Carolina Piedmont communities (1983), demonstrated how "each community has rules for socially interacting and sharing knowledge in literacy events" (p. 50). In chronicling those family interactions across Trackton, Roadville, and Maintown, Heath compared children's experiences with school expectations around books, reading, and interpretation. She found that successful transfer of learning was directly linked to when and how children's prior experiences aligned with the school's definitions and practices of literacy; those that were matched (e.g., Maintown children) were welcomed and affirmed. Students whose prior experiences differed from formal environments (Trackton and Roadville, in their own distinct ways) struggled. Heath's work also emphasizes how literacy is part of life. Children do not pull practices on and off like clothing; they are deeply embedded in all ways of interacting and interpreting. In this way, because mainstream schooling in Heath's study developed from white middle-class values and traditions, it was therefore those white, middle-class students who were afforded pathways for home-to-school transfer.

Purcell-Gates (2013) expands studies of in- and out-of-school literacies to include preschool children in migratory farmworker contexts in the US. This study of the literacy practices of children of migrant farmworker communities attending a Head Start Program explores the profound breakdown between community-based knowledge and school programs to expose how racialized and class-based assumptions on the part of school administrators and teachers create barriers to transfer. While camp life was rich with multiple languages and literacies, interviews with Head Start teachers revealed their profound ignorance about camp life and their inability to conceive of literacy development and practice beyond a narrow definition. For instance, the teachers and directors believed that the farm workers did not value reading or writing and that no one at the migrant camps could read or write. These Head Start workers drew from their positions as white, English speaking, and non-mobile (living in one location and in one household) when imagining the lives of these migrant families, who, in this study, spoke mainly Spanish, came mainly and recently from Mexico, and were always relocating from farm to farm and from camp to camp. As Purcell-Gates explains, her case study provides

> a glimpse into how damaging it is to children's future success in mainstream schools if educators fail to understand the fund of knowledge that all children bring from their homes and communities and the ways that early literacy instruction can build on this knowledge to better prepare the children for success. (p. 94)

Migrant farmworkers are integral to the US economy, and yet this Head Start program, a federally based educational program that was designed to teach children of migrant workers, had no resources or culturally specific knowledge for working with these children. This study is a powerful reminder of the sociocultural binds of transfer and how, without careful and deliberate attention to students' funds of knowledge and sociohistorical circumstances, the benefits of transfer may be reserved for those students whose experiences align across contexts. Moreover, it helps emphasize the ways in which schools, as institutions, are ideologically attached to larger political and economic structures that can deny and erase children's and families' literacies.

As these sociocultural studies show, transfer cannot be separated from broader structures and ideologies that shape culture and society. Moreover, the potential to successfully transfer, as was the case in Brandt's (2001) *Literacy in American Lives*, is subject to the economic values attached to the literacies and languages that writers bring to new contexts. For instance, in her study of 80 literacy history interviews of Americans born between the 1890s and 1980s, Brandt shows how changing economic conditions impacted writing development, writings' uses, and the possibilities for transfer when personal knowledge of writing becomes incompatible with changing institutional needs. Transfer, then, should be understood within this process of intertwined trajectories of societies, institutions, and access to power.

Lorimer Leonard's (2018) work on the literacy repertoires of multilingual migrant writers extends our understanding of literacy, value, and transfer to include language more explicitly. She finds that study participants' literacies and languages are intertwined, and together impacted their movement across social domains to produce at different moments fluidity, fixity, and friction, explaining that "fluidity shows writers' values agreeing with others'; fixity shows how values can be mismatched; and friction shows how writers' values simultaneously do and don't correspond to those of others" (p. 124). For transfer studies, the construct of friction is especially helpful, as it adds analysis of "shifting social conditions" and "shifting value" (p. 93) to studies of writing-related transfer.

Of course, such challenges do not negate writers' agency and intention. For instance, Rounsaville (2017), in her lifespan case study of Clara, found that agency and structure interplay in transfer for migrant multilingual writers in complex ways, and that the interplay may shift depending on age, life circumstance, or the writer's development. As Rounsaville reports:

> Findings emphasized the transnational character of how genres-in-use develop dialectically at the nexus of the individual and the social. For Clara, this nexus included legacies of writing from her grandfather and mother, the drive and urgency to make texts produce transnational attachments, as well as more conventionally sanctioned affordances and limitations. This configuration shifted across the lifespan and was influenced by where Clara was positioned on her family's migration trajectory, where she was positioned in life (as a child,

an adolescent, an adult), the contexts she wrote in, and where she was positioned in relation to the accumulating repertoire itself. (p. 334)

Thus, while Clara, a migrant, multilingual writer whose family moved between Argentina, Brazil, and the US, made decisions about when and how to use her genre knowledge, the availability of that knowledge for use was both ideologically and developmentally constrained while at the same time forming through her innovations and life circumstances. Moreover, this study attests to how genre transfer can be formed and circulated in transnational movement, and confirms "that the residue of transnational life persists in, inheres in, and motivates local literacies, even after physical movement across borders has occurred" (p. 337). We might consider transfer as both an active act (i.e., Clara carried and transformed her grandfather's and mother's values about writing into her own writing at school) and as an unpredictably accumulative act (i.e., the more Clara moved her family's relationship with writing into new situations, the more that process became integrated into her everyday).

The story of transfer presented thus far is one of successes, barriers, or mixtures. Literacy practices themselves and the values attributed to them help shape whether transfer will be welcomed or blocked. In other words, the theory of transfer being forwarded implies that if the "sociocultural logic of [literacy] patterns, and the complex relations among them" (Courage, 1993, p. 490), find connection, then out-of-school practices have the chance of finding salience within school activities. It also implies that "how literacy was valued and revalued" (Brandt, 2001, p. 76) will impact whether and how transfer takes place. Of course, if patterns do not relate, if values are hierarchized, then learners are left to manage complex and often contradictory transfer pathways on their own. In writing studies, more work must to done to understand and counter the ways that the transfer act is embedded within and realized through oppressive systems that deny transfer potential for many historically excluded students.

Gonzalez et al. (2006) and Moll and Gonzalez's (2001) valuable work on funds of knowledge—defined as "those historically accumulated and culturally developed bodies of knowledge and skills essential for household or individual functioning and well-being" (Moll & Gonzalez, 2001, p. 160)—bridges the knowledge of language minoritized and working-class students with mainstream, school-based curricula, and literacy tasks. Actively developing relevant curricula based on these rich types of knowing—ranging from knowledge of plant cultivation to masonry to midwifery to biology and chemistry—offers transfer routes not accessible through standardized curricula. Working from funds of knowledge elevates households and the complex networks between households and communities as core sites of culture where literacies are part of the broader sets of experiences that encompass and inform these children's home worlds. Based in a "dynamic, [and] 'processual'" (Moll & Gonzalez, 2001, p. 162) view of culture, funds of knowledge focuses on how young people can be empowered with cultural pathways to bring their practices to school-based tasks. Transfer is bolstered by working with households' knowledge and wisdom.

Multiple studies of the teaching practices stemming from a funds of knowledge paradigm (McCarty et al., 1991; Warren et al., 1994) all attest to positive outcomes. For instance, in their study of a Navajo bilingual program in Rough Rock, Arizona, McCarty et al. (1991) observed how a curricular change that invited Navajo students' language and community-based experiences radically improved student engagement. Counter to long-standing stereotypes about the passive and quiet indigenous student, McCarty and colleagues came to understand how

> Rough Rock's inquiry curriculum taps directly into the socialization experiences and learning predilections Rough Rock children bring to school. This use of children's learning resources, as well as the clear social-cultural relevance of curriculum content, account for the positive responses of Navajo children and their teachers to questioning, inductive/analytical reasoning, and to speaking up in class. (p. 52)

Collaboration, negotiated learning, elevating funds of knowledge, and providing reason and opportunity to use cultural and linguistic resources were all central to students' transfer of out-of-school learning into school contexts. When biliteracy is included in the curriculum, such transfer of funds of knowledge extends further (McCarty et al., 1991, p. 45). McCarty & Watahomigie (2001) suggest strategies for funds of knowledge as a bridge to the classroom, which start with the assumption that bilingualism and multiculturalism are assets (p. 500). For instance, they suggested leveraging the literacy continuum, where native language is valued and activated and "orality and literacy, indigenous and Western narrative forms, are united in ways that allow students to use what they know to develop new language skills and to inquire about the world" (p. 503). Transfer is supported when students' multiple literacies are valued as are the communities, households, and histories they came from (p. 505).

Sociocultural Studies of Literacy and New Constructs for Transfer

In this section, we present sociocultural literacy research that considers transfer as always activated in literacy practice, even when unobserved by a teacher or researcher. Drawing from sociocultural views of teaching and learning (Rogoff, 1990; Wertsch, 1985), Dyson defines transfer from a sociocultural perspective, where "skills and understandings . . . are organized by, and occur in the service of, goal-oriented, socially situated activities" (1999, p. 145). From this base, transfer is an act "interwoven into the background of shared activities within which language itself emerges. . . . If and how learners transfer particular means across activities cannot be separated from the activities themselves and how they are socially framed and arranged" (1999, p. 145-146). Moreover, within this theoretical orientation, literacy events are active events; "they are on-going accomplishments negotiated by children and other participants as they respond to each other" (p. 146). Such redefining provides alternative frameworks for transfer. In this section, we review two constructs with great potential for writing studies: recontextualization (Dyson, 1999) and repurposing (Roozen, 2010).

Dyson (1999) rethinks and redefines transfer: "transfer involves the negotiation between and among teachers and learners, as frames of reference for judging 'relevant' material are themselves differentiated and expanded" (p.142), and challenges the long-held application model of transfer (often linked back to Thorndike). Dyson suggests that educators must radically reimagine the frames of reference that they use to interpret children's actions and to interact with children's intentions and imaginations, with a deliberate turn toward pedagogical "relevance" over "normalcy" (p. 142). In this way, successful transfer is facilitated by an open orientation towards children's diverse worlds. Such a perspective encourages educators to take on the role of negotiator, not arbiter, of meaning-making via children's relevant frames.

This collaborative dimension of literacy learning extends to literacy transfer. Children don't merely bring materials to school settings and place them onto inert activities; rather, they build social worlds (Dyson, 1993, 1997, 2003; Genishi & Dyson, 2009) using materials from across their cultural landscape (Dyson, 2003, p. 25). Dyson's extensive ethnographic work, often with children from poorer African American communities, demonstrates this point through students' creative building from and transformation of popular literacies, characters, and media in ways that deny strict boundaries between home and school. Dyson's research illustrates the fundamentally dialogic and intertextual nature of literacy, which serves as the basis for reimagining transfer as a dynamic act of recontextualization within "collaboratively constructed events" (1999, p. 159) for "a negotiated transformation of *both* school and child worlds" (1999, p. 166). Drawing on such media sources as sports figures and pop culture superheroes, children transformed their out-of-school frames within official school literacy events. What children bring to the classroom, and thus transform through acts of recontextualization, are as diverse as the children themselves. When children's sociocultural worlds are honored ahead of standardized pedagogies, assessments, and assumptions (Genishi & Dyson, 2009), educators ignite transfer potential.

Roozen traces the relationships, patterns, and intertwined trajectories of in- and out-of-school literacy, with particular attention to discipline-specific, university-level writing (Roozen, 2008, 2009, 2010; Roozen & Erickson, 2017). In these fine-grained explorations of how in- and out-of-school practices interact, Roozen prefers the term literate activities, which he defines, drawing from Prior's (1998/2013) work, as activities "not located *in* acts of reading and writing, but *as* cultural forms of life saturated with textuality, that is strongly motivated and mediated by texts" (Prior, 1998/2013, p. 138). When looking across realms of literate activity, Roozen finds that students actively repurpose and interweave activities across personal and academic writing (Roozen, 2009) and public and academic writing (Roozen, 2008, 2010). For transfer studies, this research foregrounds interconnections across private, public, and academic writing. Specifically, Roozen presents the construct of repurposing to emphasize how spheres of writing are not separate; rather, drawing from theories of intertextuality and "nexus of practice," literacy is configured within a "network or matrix of intersecting practices which, although they are never perfectly or inevitably linked into any finalized or finalizable latticework of regular practice, nevertheless form a network or nexus" (Scollon as cited in Roozen, 2009, p. 546). Such a perspective has profound implications for transfer because it assumes that transfer is always happening; transfer is intrinsic to writing and not a separate act. Pedagogically then, the role of the educator is to facilitate students' recognition of the complex and individual ways they pull, reuse, and reshape writing practices from one domain (e.g., diary writing) into another (e.g., school-based essay assignments).

This perspective, also indebted to the earlier work of Prior (1998/2013) and Prior and Shipka (2003), demands that we re-see transfer and repurposing as common. Prior and Shipka's work on chronotopic lamination provides both a theoretical and methodological framework for this vision.

> In this model [of chronotopic lamination] then, a literate act, say reading a newspaper, is both localized in the concrete acts, thoughts, and feelings of the reader(s) and sociohistorically dispersed across a far-flung chronotopic network—including the embodied acts of writing the story, almost certainly spread across multiple chronotopic episodes of individual and collaborative composing; the histories of journalism and the genre of the news story; the actual embodied worlds being represented and their textualized representations; the reader's histories of reading papers and of earlier events relevant to those represented in the story; and so on. (pp. 186–187)

Methodologically, such tracing reveals multi-scalar and multi-temporal interconnections. Moreover, such an account radically widens the realm of prior knowledge and adds layers and networks beyond what is typically considered relevant as sources of transferred knowledge. Recognition of the expanded possibilities for bridging home and school supports a multidimensional, dynamic, and transformative view of transfer.

METHODOLOGICAL IMPLICATIONS FROM LITERACY STUDIES

Literacy studies provides several shared and new methods for studies of writing-related transfer. These methods include ethnographies and multisite ethnographies; meaning-making trajectories and trajectories of practice; and lifespan studies.

Ethnographies of communication and writing and multi-site ethnographies provide an emic view of sociocultural literacy practices from within the logic, historicity, and ideologies of communities and individuals. Methods include interviews, observations, and multiple forms of document collection. Multi-site and comparative studies are especially promising for understanding writing transfer. For instance, in her study on students' in- and out-of-school literacy practices, Schultz (2002) explicitly advocates for the multi-site ethnography to "examine and document the circulation of cultural meanings, objects, and identities across time and space" (p. 363). More recently, transcontextual studies (Kell, 2009) have replaced or supplemented comparative studies. This transition focuses less on the site per se and more on how literacy and writers move among and across contexts. Kell suggested transcontextual analysis could illuminate the ongoing recontextualization of text, practice, and process across contexts. Specifically, Kell (2006) proposed "meaning-making trajectories"—based on earlier discussions of "text trajectories" (Blommaert, 2001; Silverstein & Urban, 1996)—as units of analysis for studying recontextualization. Nordquist (2017) proposed a "multi-sited, mobile ethnography" (p. 47) to not only capture practices that circulate among sites, but also to attune researchers to new developments in in-transit practices (p. 50).

While there are no singular methods attached to studying literacy and transfer across a lifespan (ethnography, interviews, discourse analysis, etc. are all viable), we include this approach to emphasize a benefit from viewing literacy throughout life stages. Bazerman et al. (2018) suggest several research orientations: "look to embodied acts of writing" (p. 8), "look to the medium of written languages" (p. 8), "look to contexts of participation" (p. 9), and "look to the historical and cultural catalysts of writing development" (p. 10). Brandt (2018) more specifically draws from literacy history interviews in combination with the work of Bronfenbrenner (1979, 2005) and others to show what life-course research might reveal about literacy development and transfer. Brandt opts for the construct and theoretical lineage of life-course over lifespan research because "life-course development research focuses on change and aging as continual, multidimensional and mutually influencing processes that are in analyzable relationships to processes and changes in wider environments" (p. 245). Bronfenbrenner's work facilitates this approach and with an added dimension of what Brandt translates as "dispositions for writing development," which "often gather continuity and stability over time; yet they are ever-renewing coproductions of persons and their lifeworlds—constituted out of inner and outer resources, permeable, dynamic, and performative" (p. 262). Brandt references Gonzalez et al.'s (2006) work on funds of knowledge as an example of where researchers might notice developing and changing dispositions. As discussed earlier in this chapter, funds of knowledge treats family as a source of conscious and intuitive knowledge that is shared across and developed through interaction with immediate and extended members. Brandt suggests that we ask how this base grows over time, from what new encounters, and through what age and contextual changes. In fact, she suggests that

> their [Gonzalez, Moll, & Amanti] accounts force an expansion of what is considered transfer in writing, as not merely the ability to carry over writing experiences from one context to another or to translate background knowledge from one task to another but rather a more abstract ability to turn raw experience into 'structuring proclivities' for literacy learning and, indeed, textuality itself. (p. 265)

Pedagogical Implications from Literacy Studies

From research presented in this chapter and beyond, literacy studies scholars have developed promising pedagogical approaches for bridging literacy between home or community and school, thus creating expanded opportunities for transfer. While specific pedagogical recommendations differ, all foreground writer agency and emphasize treating students' out-of-school worlds and repertoires as assets with bridging potential. The goal with each approach is to bring equity to the classroom: equity of opportunity to leverage out-of-school knowledge for in-school learning and equity for transfer potential.

"Cultural modeling" (Lee, 2001; Martínez et al., 2008; Orellana & Reynolds, 2008) encourages deep fidelity between students' cultural funds of knowledge and school-based assignments to activate prior knowledge for tasks such as reading and interpreting literature. For instance, Lee's (2001) work specifically serves African American students by connecting cultural knowledge, such as signify'n and playing the dozens, to African American authors such as Zora Neale Hurston and Toni Morrison who use similar strategies in their writing. As she states, "the idea behind the Cultural Modeling Project is that African American English Vernacular offers a fertile bridge for scaffolding literary response, rather than a deficit to be overcome" (p. 101). The framework "matches" cultural knowledge—rhetorical and linguistic—to school-based readings and assignments to "make public and explicit knowledge of strategies that they routinely use that have been intuitive and implicit" (p. 101). Her work draws from rich scholarship in African American rhetorical and linguistic traditions (Smitherman, 1977) to create what she calls a "mental model" (drawn from Perkins, 1992) link between home and school literacies.

Lee's model has been taken up by other educators in ways that model different cultural and ethnic groups' linguistic and literate funds of knowledge. For instance, Orellana and Reynolds (2008) develop a framework for Latinx immigrants living in the Chicago area to account for the their bilingual immigrant experiences. Thus, in their case, they "focus on the skills that are required as children of Mexican immigrants negotiate across languages and cultures" (p. 50). As Orellana and Reynolds note, while they refer to this as the leveraging of funds of knowledge, other sociocultural literacy research would refer to this as practice for transfer (p. 50). But the goal of such transfer (or leveraging) is neither mere celebration nor direct application of skills. Rather, it's to provide an environment for students to bring their comfort with translation to school contexts. Through cultural modeling, students learn to deliberately engage in the transformation of home and community knowledge when in new contexts; cultural modeling may even "cultivate hybrid abilities that merge different elements from students' repertoires of practice as these elements are displayed across contexts, tasks, and relationships" (p. 50). For such an approach to succeed, there must be empirical work into how students experience their out-of-school communities; these are not instances of guessing at students' prior knowledge.

"Third space" theories of teaching (Gutiérrez, 2008; Gutiérrez et al., 1995) develop pedagogies for an "increasingly complex, transnational, and hybrid world" (Gutiérrez, 2008, p. 148). Within this approach, all social interactions (all classroom dynamics) have the potential to transform from individualistic, sociocultural scripts into distinct ways of knowing that combine multiple dimensions and experiences in third spaces. The formulation is no longer home versus school, but home *and* school as they interact (with an openness from both teacher and student) to generate new linguistic and literacy practices and identities. Third space theory—as with Dyson's notion of transfer as a dynamic act of recontextualization within "collaboratively constructed events" (1999, p. 159) for "a negotiated transformation of *both* school and child worlds" (p. 166)—understands all discursive interaction as fundamentally social, heteroglossic, and intertextual. Likewise, these transformed social spaces—as third spaces—support "expansive learning" (Engeström, 1987), in which the students, teachers, and classroom systems are transformed. Thus, third space approaches (Gutiérrez et al., 1995) foster parity between in- and out-of-school practices and promote new sets of practices and values that benefit all learners. Transfer then, in this method, is the on-going recontextualization of prior knowledge through classroom interaction for the purposes of using out-of-school resources to create a "new sociocultural terrain" that shifts "what counts as knowledge and knowledge representation" (Gutiérrez et al.,1995, p. 445).

In addition to these more comprehensive "named" approaches, many scholars promote a more general approach to bridging that includes honoring and activating students' histories, facilitating metacognitive understandings, and finding transfer routes through low- and high-stakes assignments where students are guided to use and transform their knowledge. Whether a teacher chooses a comprehensively developed pedagogy (e.g., cultural modeling or third space), or whether they work with more general practices for leveraging out-of-school experiences for transfer, they respect the multivariate sociocultural influences that enrich writing.

Conclusion and Avenues for Further Inquiry

There continues to be a need for radical shifts in schools' ideologies, curricula, and valuations of students' funds of knowledge and out-of-school repertoires. This means first viewing students as active, capable, and adept individuals who bring agency and intention to classrooms. Of course, agency is not without its counter—structure—which is a big part of why we need these pedagogies in the first place. As Lorimer Leonard (2018) suggests, "the agency of literate valuation—who is in charge of determining what literacy is worth—is located not in individual migrants or in hegemonic institutions but in the social and economic values held by both" (p. 129). Such a structure-agency relationship has important implications for approaches to the transfer of writing-related knowledge in the classroom. It means that writers can and should reflect on, draw from, and develop metalinguistic and rhetorical awareness. It also means that teachers and administrators have a responsibility to identify structural barriers that deny students their full resources. As writing educators, we can redesign schools, curricula, and classrooms to help students bridge and use rather than leave behind and neglect their vast out-of-school lives, languages, and literacies. Realistically, it also means that agency cannot always overcome structure. Rather, it's a state of on-going negotiation. Transfer, as collectively theorized within literacy studies, can be viewed similarly. Given that, the following theoretical and empirical insights serve as guidelines for how we might research and teach for the transfer of writing-related knowledge between in- and out-of-school contexts. Researchers and educators should consider the following when designing classrooms and curricula for transfer:

- Literacies are dynamic and practice-based in ways that change with factors such as context, purpose, time and place, cultural and linguistic resources and repertoires, and individual and community needs.
- Literacies are socially and historically situated and are impacted by multiple contextual variables that originated from an immediate context to larger shaping forces (e.g., economy, globalization, racialization, language ideologies).
- Literacies index social power relations and those relations are played out (often for the success or detriment of students) in and across in- and out-of-school domains.
- Schools should teach and attend to the linguistic and literate funds of knowledge for all students through some incorporation (broad or narrow) of culturally relevant (Ladson-Billings, 1995) or culturally sustaining pedagogies. (Paris & Alim, 2017)
- Whether it's empirical research into students' households (Gonzalez et al., 2006) or discourse analytic work into students' and their families' brokering practices (Martínez et al., 2008), transfer can be enhanced through a locally developed literacy curriculum.

These suggestions connect to the work we covered in this chapter, which explored how people, practices, and repertoires traverse and are taken up across domains. But it is important to recognize that while this chapter focused primarily on transfer between in- and out-of-school settings, studies have also explored transfer of literacies across generations (Brandt, 2001; Prendergast, 2013; Rounsaville, 2017; Rumsey, 2009; Simon 2017); across religious, bureaucratic, and other non-school institutions (Brandt, 2001; Cushman, 1998; Lorimer Leonard, 2015; Vieira, 2011); through historical and archival studies of transfer and the extracurriculum (Gere, 1994; Peary, 2014); and across genres (Blommaert, 2008; Moss, 1994). These studies, like the ones included in this chapter, provide additional perspectives on how literacy transfer is imbricated in all dimensions of social life. Analysis and inclusion of diverse and multiple social factors in studies of writing-related transfer benefits all students and provides a more realistic view of what helps or hinders transfer.

References

Au, K. H. P. (1980). Participation structures in a reading lesson with Hawaiian children: Analysis of a culturally appropriate instructional event. *Anthropology & Education Quarterly, 11*(2), 91–115.

Bazerman, C., Applebee, A. N., Berninger, V. W., Brandt, D., Graham, S., Jeffery, J. V., & Matsuda, P. K. (2018). *The lifespan development of writing*. National Council of Teachers of English.

Blommaert, J. M. E. (2001). Investigating narrative inequality: African asylum seekers' stories in Belgium. *Discourse and Society, 12*(4), 413–449.

Blommaert, J. (2008). *Grassroots literacy: Writing, identity and voice in Central Africa*. Routledge.

Brandt, D. (2001). *Literacy in American lives*. Cambridge University Press.

Brandt, D. (2018). Writing development and life-course development: The case of working adults. In C. Bazerman, A.N. Applebee, V. W. Berninger, D. Brandt, S. Graham, J. V. Jeffery, & P.K. Matsuda. (Eds.), *The lifespan development of writing* (pp. 244–271). National Council of Teachers of English.

Bronfenbrenner, U. (1979). *The ecology of human development: Experiments by nature and design*. Harvard University Press.

Bronfenbrenner, U. (2005). *Making human beings human: Bioecological perspectives on human development*. Sage.

Courage, R. (1993). The interaction of public and private literacies. *College Composition and Communication, 44*(4), 484–496.

Cushman, E. (1998). *The struggle and the tools: Oral and literate strategies in an inner city community.* SUNY Press.
Dyson, A. H. (1993). *Social worlds of children: Learning to write in an urban primary school.* Teachers College Press.
Dyson, A. H. (1997). *Writing superheroes: Contemporary childhood, popular culture, and classroom literacy.* Teachers College Press.
Dyson, A. H. (1999). Transforming transfer: Unruly children, contrary texts, and the persistence of the pedagogical order. *Review of Research in Education, 24(1),* 141–171.
Dyson, A. H. (2003). *The brothers and sisters learn to write: Popular literacies in childhood and school cultures.* Teachers College Press.
Engeström, Y. (1987). *Learning by expanding: An activity-theoretical approach to developmental research.* Helsinki, Finland: Orienta-Konsultit Oy.
Genishi, C., & Dyson, A. H. (2009). *Children, language, and literacy: Diverse learners in diverse times.* Teachers College Press.
Gere, A. R. (1994). Kitchen tables and rented rooms: The extracurriculum of composition. *College Composition and Communication, 45*(1), 75–92.
Gonzalez, N., Moll, L.C. & Amanti, C. (Eds). (2006). *Funds of knowledge: Theorizing practices in households, communities, and classrooms.* Routledge.
Gutiérrez, K. D. (2008). Developing a sociocritical literacy in the third space. *Reading Research Quarterly, 43*(2), 148–164.
Gutiérrez, K., Rhymes, B., & Larson, J. (1995). Script, counterscript, and underlife in the classroom: James Brown versus Brown v. Board of Education. *Harvard Educational Review, 65*(3), 445–471.
Heath, S. B. (1982). What no bedtime story means: Narrative skills at home and school. *Language in Society, 11*(1), 49–76.
Heath, S. B. (1983). *Ways with words: Language, life and work in communities and classrooms.* Cambridge University Press.
Hull, G., & Schultz, K. (2001). Literacy and learning out of school: A review of theory and research. *Review of Educational Research, 71*(4), 575–611.
Kell, C. (2006). Crossing the margins: Literacy, semiotics, and the recontextualisation of meanings. In K. Pahl & J. Rowsell (Eds.), *Travel notes from the new literacy studies: Instances of practice* (pp. 147–172). Multilingual Matters.
Kell, C. (2009). Literacy practices, text/s and meaning making across time and space. In M. Baynham & M. Prinsloo (Eds.), *The future of literacy studies* (pp. 75–99). Palgrave Macmillan.
Ladson-Billings, G. (1995). Toward a theory of culturally relevant pedagogy. *American Educational Research Journal, 32*(3), 465–491.
Lee, C. D. (2001). Is October Brown Chinese? A cultural modeling activity system for underachieving students. *American Educational Research Journal, 38*(1), 97–141.

Lorimer Leonard, R. (2015). Writing through bureaucracy: Migrant correspondence and managed mobility. *Written Communication*, *32*(1), 87–113.

Lorimer Leonard, R. (2018). *Writing on the move: Migrant women and the value of literacy*. University of Pittsburgh Press.

Martínez R., Orellana, M.F., & Pacheco, M., & Carbone. (2008). Found in translation: Connecting translating experiences to academic writing. *Language Arts*, *85*(6): 421–431.

McCarty, T. L., Wallace, S., Lynch, R. H., & Benally, A. (1991). Classroom inquiry and Navajo learning styles: A call for reassessment. *Anthropology & Education Quarterly*, *22*(1), 42–59.

McCarty, T. L., & Watahomigie, L. J. (2001). Language and literacy in American Indian and Alaskan Native communities. In E. Cushman, E. R. Kintgen, B. M. Kroll, & M. Rose (Eds.), *Literacy: A critical sourcebook* (pp. 488–507). Boston: Bedford/St. Martin.

Moll, L. C, & N. Gonzalez (2001). Lessons from research with language minority children. In E. Cushman, E.R. Kintgen, B.M. Kroll, & M. Rose (Eds.), *Literacy: A critical sourcebook* (pp. 156–171). Boston: Bedford/St. Martin.

Moss, B. (1994). *Literacy across communities*. Hampton Press.

Nordquist, B. (2017). *Literacy and mobility: Complexity, uncertainty, and agency at the nexus of high school and college*. Routledge.

Orellana, M. F., & Reynolds, J. F. (2008). Cultural modeling: Leveraging bilingual skills for school paraphrasing tasks. *Reading Research Quarterly*, *43(1)*, 48–65.

Paris, D., & Alim, H. S. (Eds.). (2017). *Culturally sustaining pedagogies: Teaching and learning for justice in a changing world*. Teachers College Press.

Peary, A. (2014). Walls with a word count: The textrooms of the extracurriculum. *College Composition & Communication*, *66*(1), 43–66.

Perkins, D. N. (1992). *Smart schools: From training memories to educating minds*. The Free Press.

Phillips, S. U. (1983). *The invisible culture: Communication in classroom and community on the Warm Springs Indian Reservation*. Waveland Press.

Prendergast, C. J. (2013). Or you don't: Talents, tendencies, and the pooka of literacy. *Enculturation*, *16*. http://enculturation.net/pooka-of-literacy

Prior, P. (1998/2013). *Writing/disciplinarity: A sociohistoric account of literate activity in the academy*. Lawrence Erlbaum.

Prior, P. A., & Shipka, J. (2003). Chronotopic lamination: Tracing the contours of literate activity. In C. Bazerman, & D. Russell (Eds.), *Writing selves, writing societies: Research from activity perspectives* (pp. 180–238). (Perspectives on Writing). The WAC Clearinghouse and Mind, Culture, and Activity.

Purcell-Gates, V. (2013). Literacy worlds of children of migrant farmworker communities participating in a migrant Head Start Program. *Research in the Teaching of English*, *48*(1): 68–97.

Rogoff, B. (1990). *Apprenticeship in thinking: Cognitive development in social context*. Oxford University Press.
Roozen, K. (2008). Journalism, poetry, stand-up comedy, and academic literacy: Mapping the interplay of curricular and extracurricular literate activities. *Journal of Basic Writing, 27*(1), 5–34.
Roozen, K. (2009). From journals to journalism: Tracing trajectories of literate development. *College Composition and Communication, 60*(3), 541–572.
Roozen, K. (2010). Tracing trajectories of practice: Repurposing in one student's developing disciplinary writing processes. *Written Communication, 27*(3), 318–354.
Roozen, K., & Erickson, J. (2017). *Expanding literate landscapes: Persons, practices, and sociohistoric perspectives of disciplinary development*. Computers and Composition Digital P/Utah State UP.
Rounsaville, A. (2017). Genre repertoires from below: How one writer built and moved a writing life across generations, borders, and communities. *Research in the Teaching of English, 51*(3), 317–340.
Rumsey, S. K. (2009). Heritage literacy: Adoption, adaptation, and alienation of multimodal literacy tools. *College Composition and Communication, 60*(3), 573–586.
Schultz, K. (2002). Looking across space and time: Reconceptualizing literacy learning in and out of school. *Research in the Teaching of English, 36*(3), 356–390.
Simon, K. (2017). Daughters and learning from fathers: Migrant family literacies that mediate borders. *Literacy in Composition Studies, 5*(1), 1–20.
Silverstein, M., & Urban, G. (Eds.). (1996). *Natural histories of discourse*. University of Chicago Press.
Smitherman, G. (1977). *Talkin and testifyin: The language of Black America*. Houghton Mifflin.
Street, B. V. (Ed.). (1993). *Cross-cultural approaches to literacy*. Cambridge University Press.
Vieira, Kate. (2011). Undocumented in a documentary society: Textual borders and transnational religious literacies. *Writing in a Global Context. Spec. Issue of Written Communication, (28)*4, 436–461.
Warren, B., Rosebery, A., & Conant, F. (1994). Discourse and social practice: Learning science in a language minority classroom. In D. Spener (Ed.), *Adult biliteracy in the United States* (pp. 191–210). Center for Applied Linguistics.
Wertsch, J. V. (1985). *Vygotsky and the social formation of mind*. Harvard University Press.

6 Research on Transfer in Studies of Second Language Writing

As an interdisciplinary field that bridges applied linguistics, composition, and TESOL, second language (L2) writing is unique in its study of transfer. In distinction to adjacent fields in linguistics that mainly study speech, L2 writing examines the relationship of writing to L2 learning, often the learning of standard forms of academic English. In many classrooms, monolingual ideology renders communication in English into an unmarked norm. Thus, language—as a kind and a medium of transfer—can become invisible. Studies of transfer in second language research not only serve as a reminder that language is an ever-present element of the transfer act, but also offer ways to re-see different aspects of the transfer of writing knowledge.

In the study of transfer in L2 learning, a focus on writing offers different perspectives than that of speech: writing can be a sloweddown activity and may involve more intentionality than speech; writing by definition produces artifacts to be studied; writing can support learning and the reflection on learning activities often promoted in transfer research; as an expressive form, writing is wound tightly with identity and voice; writing, especially the texts and activities studied in composition and TESOL, is very much caught up in pedagogical, assessment, and institutional mandates and is thus imbued with power and consequence. These unique facets shape a transfer research agenda that at its best seeks an intentional, reflective, and socially situated understanding of how multilingual writers transfer their literate knowledge as they write across assignments, classrooms, disciplines, institutional norms, and countless ways of being an L2 writer.

Therefore, the study of transfer in L2 writing is truly complex: it traces the movement of writing knowledge among learning contexts *and* among languages, even as it considers how multiple cultural, educational, and linguistic traditions come to bear on the possibility of transfer. Scholars in L2 writing pursue these complexities in order to understand how language diversity complicates the transfer of writing knowledge and how to best support the linguistically diverse writers who navigate these complexities when they compose. Researchers and teachers want to know why their multilingual students write the way they do. And writing scholars studying transfer increasingly call for an expanded and nuanced understanding of the role of language(s) in writing transfer (DasBender, 2016; Donahue, 2016; Lorimer Leonard & Nowacek, 2016; McCall, 2016).

The transfer research reviewed below shows that, indeed, the role of language as well as culture has been treated with increasing nuance for the last few decades. Across this chapter's sections, the concepts of "culture" and "language" have, in a way, lost their edges. As variables that may impact writing transfer, they are treated as multiplicities more fluid than bounded, and more ongoing than finite. Nevertheless, many grounding questions in the study of transfer in L2 writing show a tension in how researchers view the role of linguistic or cultural background in writing. Are the differences instructors perceive in their students' rhetorical patterns, stance, word choice, or organizational structure "interference" from writers' other languages or are they simply evidence of second language acquisition in process? Are writers' deviations from standard English mistakes or errors, or are they creative choices of mixing or meshing across their full linguistic repertoires? When writers engage in transfer are they actively "linking" writing knowledge across languages or is their prior knowledge simply "haunting" them (Cozart et al., 2016)? Because responses to these questions may be "both," L2 writing transfer research has set out to understand the dimensions of these choices—not just *that* language learners make choices among languages when they write, but why they do, how those decisions occur across contexts, and what the consequences or outcomes are of their transfer attempts for their learning and academic success. In the end, the chapter shows that as the concept of language has become more diffuse and research questions have become more precise, several complicating factors remain that researchers of transfer in L2 writing have yet to settle, namely the extent and impact of writers' awareness, intentionality, and agency during the act of transfer.

Transfer in L2 writing has been approached through the lenses of several fields, each with different mandates, contexts, goals, and questions. For example, research influenced by TESOL or applied linguistics addresses audiences concerned primarily with language transfer in writing activities, often at the sentence-level, carried out by students who are in the process of acquiring academic English. Transfer research influenced by composition and rhetoric is interested in the practices of multilingual college writers and tends to move beyond the sentence level to consider rhetorical strategies and writing processes. Across these ongoing conversations, some studies follow the skills students transfer among languages, while others examine what teachers should do to facilitate students' transfer among learning contexts. Thus, one could enter L2 writing research from the point of view of units of analysis (type of knowledge transferred; writers' perceptions of transfer), participants studied (student writers; instructors), or curricular or programmatic innovations (genre-based writing instruction; general skills instruction).

But in fact, as James (2008) notes, when it comes to tracing how writing transfer occurs among languages and classroom contexts, "similarity and difference are relative notions" (p. 79). Transfer "tasks that seem different from one angle," he says, "may seem similar from another angle" (p. 79). Because it is a concept that is "highly-situational, context-dependent" and perhaps "unsuited to broader generalizations," research in this area is a challenge to catalogue (DasBender, 2016, p. 277). Is it possible to tease apart the contextual, cultural, linguistic, rhetorical, and educational angles from which to view transfer? The research reviewed below generally does not keep these elements distinct, but instead asks local or language-specific questions while acknowledging that the elements above are inextricably connected. This body of research primarily seeks to understand the activities, perceptions, or conditions that support or inhibit transfer, keeping in mind the unique pressures of cognitive load, cultural multiplicity, and institutional and social stakes that L2 writers also negotiate.

This chapter identifies several themes that organize how scholars in L2 writing have made sense of the phenomenon of transfer: (1) students' writing and rhetorical activities, (2) instructional and curricular design, (3) the role of genre, and (4) the impact of identity. Such an organization highlights both what is there in the research—how scholars have navigated the issues—as well as what is implicit—the transfer concerns that appear in L2 scholarship whether scholars set out to study them or not. These sections are meant to help readers become familiar with the scholarly conversations readers might enter as they ask questions about transfer in their own research and teaching.

INFLUENCES FROM SECOND LANGUAGE ACQUISITION

Within second language writing, research questions, methods, and findings are shaped by epistemological orientations to the languages that writers are transferring from or among: namely whether these languages are separate, connected, or fused systems. These epistemologies have roots in longstanding research on language transfer in the field of second language acquisition (SLA). Although applied linguistics, broadly, is interested in issues of language transfer, SLA's focus on acquisition assumes a transformation of linguistic knowledge, which in turn requires at the least a consideration of the phenomenon of transfer. Studies of language transfer investigate how linguistic knowledge moves from native to target language(s). But within SLA scholarship, the relationships among the elements of language transfer—traditionally a source L1, a language construct, and target languages—are differently conceived along a spectrum of complexity. The brief review of these relationships below shows the range of epistemological patterns from SLA that studies of transfer in L2 writing have followed.

Interference

In early research on language transfer, SLA scholars wanted to understand how language constructs (syntactic, phonetic, morphological, semantic, lexical) from an L1 interfered with the acquisition of an L2. Scholars sought to understand obstacles to the acquisition process, focusing on moments when languages were not successfully acquired and isolating their sources. Research suggested that when learners transferred constructs among languages that were similar (in syntax, morphology, etc.), the transfer, called "positive transfer," was less noticeable; when learners transferred constructs among less similar languages, transfer was visible and was deemed "negative transfer," what might, in writing, appear as an error. Studies largely used contrastive analysis (Lado, 1957) to determine similarities and differences in many pairs of source and target languages. Thus, early transfer was closely associated with language error, wherein evidence of transfer was understood to be interference of the L1 into the target L2 (Gass & Selinker, 1992; Selinker, 1969, 1972; Weinreich, 1953). Negative transfer was considered interference into the process of acquisition, leading to the terms interference and transfer often being used interchangeably. This early orientation to transfer as interference, and interference as error, is remarkably durable throughout studies of language transfer in speech or in writing, remaining in recent studies of transfer in writing. In particular, an understanding of transfer as interference from a source to target language guides L2 writing scholars to look for transfer in writing as text, product, or outcome, rather than in writing as vehicle or phenomenon of transfer in itself.

Cross-Linguistic Influence

More recently, SLA research has sought to understand the influence of similarities or differences between, rather than the interference of, a target language and any other acquired language. As Jarvis (2016) explains, SLA scholars moved from researching transfer as an independent variable to treating transfer as "a dependent variable worthy of investigation in its own right, with its own set of independent variables" (p. 18). Scholars Sharwood-Smith and Kellerman (1986) suggested that the term *cross-linguistic influence* might move the study of language transfer beyond behavioristic and deficit connotations. They describe transfer as "those processes that lead to the incorporation of elements from one language into another" (p. 1), while Odlin (1989) defines transfer as the "influence resulting from similarities and differences between the target language and any other language that has been previously (and perhaps imperfectly) acquired" (p. 27). The word *influence*, it was thought, would stress the interplay among an L1 and L2, or earlier and later acquired languages, as well as the bi- or multi-directional movement of language elements, in that a target language can also influence the source language, which has been called variously the L2 effect, or the reverse or backward transfer of an L2 on an L1 (Cook, 2003; Helfenstein, 2005; Jarvis & Pavlenko, 2008; Pavlenko, 2000; Pavlenko & Jarvis, 2002). According to these scholars and others, cross-linguistic influence is the most widely used term in SLA to describe L1–L2 relationships, although the term *transfer* is sometimes still used interchangeably with it. Research on cross-linguistic influence also has looked at the differing influences—of levels of proficiency, literacy skills, or source language—of an L1 or L2 on the acquisition of an L3, or the other way around, finding bi-directional influences among all three languages, or tracing how third-language acquisition differently reuses language constructs from an L2 or L1 (Alonso Alonso, 2016; Cenoz, 2009; Cenoz & Gorter, 2011; De Angelis, 2007; Jessner et al., 2016; Kobayashi & Rinnert, 2013; Murphy, 2003; Tsang, 2016).

Multicompetence

SLA scholars have pointed to problems in both of these epistemological orientations. Language transfer conceived of as (one-way) interference or as (multi-way) cross-linguistic influence are both "export" models that treat the language learner as a mover of inert language knowledge from one discrete language to another (Larsen-Freeman, 2013; Larsen-Freeman & Cameron, 2008). SLA scholars suggest that this three-point movement—source, language construct, destination—not only concretizes often fluid phenomena but also has several theoretical shortcomings. For example, communication can spring from concurrent or simultaneous use of multiple languages of varying proficiencies. And sometimes languages fade, not because they have been transferred elsewhere but because of time passing or a learner's waning interest. In other words, acts of transfer are more volatile than those depicted as static language constructs moving laterally from one concrete context to another. Therefore, SLA scholars also have proposed theories that can conceptualize language transfer as a fluid and holistic phenomenon.

For example, Cook (1992) proposed the term *multicompetence* to describe language knowledge as a multi-directional system promoting dynamic interrelationships among languages of various proficiencies. Cook (2016) defines multicompetence as "the overall system of a mind or a community that uses more than one language," extending its scope to any other known languages, including interlanguages (p. 2). Influenced by dynamic systems theory and like other theories of bi-, multi-, or translingualism that treat repertoires as holistic systems of interaction (Cenoz & Gorter, 2011; Garcia & Wei, 2014; Grosjean, 1989; Larsen-Freeman, 1997), multicompetence describes a linguistic complex of relationships rather than a sum of two monolingual parts. In terms of transfer, such an approach allows SLA researchers to consider, as Cook (2016) says, the ways that "transfer is not about the acquisition of new knowledge or behavior . . . but about the rejigging of existing knowledge or behavior into new configurations" (p. 33). Contemporary studies of language transfer operating with a multicompetence frame seek to understand interaction of all languages of varying proficiencies in a linguistic repertoire. Such studies redirect "attention to what students do rather than to what they don't do," turning researchers' analysis toward what is happening and why rather than what has gone wrong and why, or reconsidering what is there that might be missed because the transfer act has transformed it (Larsen-Freeman, 2013, p. 108).

Researchers studying transfer in L2 writing are influenced by these epistemological orientations, designing studies to understand how writers transfer activities from one separate language to another, across connected languages that mutually inform each other, or within a holistic language repertoire. As hopefully is clear in the brief review above, these distinctions fall along a spectrum, not into three tidy groups. Importantly, these brief summaries of decades of research are not presented as a progression from the naïve to the accurate. Although chronology plays a role, the order of the orientations above does not imply that the most recent thinking is the only or most frequently used thinking on the myriad issues of language transfer.

The epistemological stances toward second language acquisition described above locate second language writing studies of transfer along a spectrum of epistemologies. On one end, languages are treated as separate, enumerated entities, which guides researchers to look for evidence of transfer of writing skills from a native to a target language. Many of these studies originated in conversations in contrastive rhetoric, laying the groundwork for conceiving of transfer at all in L2 writing (e.g., Connor, 1996; Kang, 2005; Kaplan, 1966, 1967, 1987; Simpson, 2000). These studies primarily understand transfer as the movement of writing or rhetorical knowledge from one language or place to another. On the other end of the spectrum, studies operate under assumptions of multicompetence, leading researchers to look for transfer activities writers enact using their linguistic repertoires. Most studies of transfer in L2 writing exist somewhere in between, or even move from one to the other in the process of a research project.

However, because these epistemological distinctions reveal different compasses with which scholars navigate a study, such a spectrum can show how transfer in L2 writing has been differently conceived.

WRITING AMONG LANGUAGES

L2 writing scholars study the role that writing and rhetorical activities play in the transfer of writing knowledge. The section that follows reviews studies that investigate how L2 writers transfer writing and rhetorical activities—practices or conventions of organization, argument, voice, process, and revision—along the epistemological spectrum sketched above. This section's review proceeds along this epistemological spectrum, from considerations of transfer as one-way L1–L2 movement to examinations of transfer as writing activities springing from a unified, holistic language repertoire.

Writing and One-Way Transfer

Studies of writing knowledge transfer in L2 writing that began in a conversation loosely identified as contrastive rhetoric (Kaplan, 1966) operated on several assumptions: that students from similar language backgrounds are conditioned by cultural conventions that might conflict with English language discourse conventions; that mastery of writing skills on organizational or rhetorical levels can be measured through grammatical proficiency; that L1 language ability affects the quality of content in an L2 or decision-making behaviors in L2 writing; that writing in an L1 is comparable and thus has explanatory power about writing in an L2; that insights about an L1 can be perceived in a standard academic English college essay written by a multilingual writer (Al-Ali, 2006; Berman, 1994; Carson & Kuehn, 1992; Connor, 1996; Cumming, 1989; Gosden, 1998; Johns, 1993; Kang, 2005; Kaplan, 1966, 1967, 1987; Kobayashi & Rinnert, 2008; Kubota, 1998; Mohan & Lo, 1985; Odlin, 1989; Simpson, 2000). In these studies, transfer is conceived of primarily as a linear phenomenon that moves one way, from an L1 to an L2, which is most often English. As Kubota (1998) notes, in looking for the influence of L1 cultural rhetorical patterns on English language writing, contrastive rhetoric assumes that culturally unique rhetorical conventions exist that can be generalized, named, and followed across languages or contexts (p. 69).

For example, Berman's (1994) study of 126 secondary EFL students in Iceland examined how essay organization skills were transferred between Icelandic and English. Grouping three instructional approaches—L1 essay instruction, L2 (English) instruction, no instruction—he looked for differences in pre- and post-intervention organization and grammatical proficiency scores. Berman concluded that students did transfer organization skills from Icelandic to English, showing that the groups with instruction improved regardless of language of instruction. He highlighted that instruction on a particular skill was a more powerful enabler of transfer than was language or grammatical proficiency in that language. While some research continues to position the L1 as a problem to be overcome in pursuit of standard academic English writing, most research pursuing one-way transfer activities adopts a complex understanding of the "dynamic" factors influencing transfer beyond cultural or rhetorical norms (Matsuda, 1997). For example, researchers include considerations of grammatical proficiency (Berman, 1994; Cumming, 1989; Wolfersberger, 2003), educational experiences with writing (Cozart et al., 2016; Kobayashi & Rinnert, 2008; Kubota, 1998; Mohan & Lo, 1985), L1 literacy (Carson & Kuehn, 1992; Mohan & Lo, 1985), and student characteristics, motivations, and intentions (Cozart et al., 2016; Kobayashi & Rinnert, 2008). Even with inclusion of these dynamic factors, by and large these studies proceed from the assumption that writing or rhetorical knowledge is being transferred one-way, among separate language entities.

Writing and rhetorical activities explicitly designed to raise meta-linguistic awareness play an especially important role in high-road, or conscious and effortful, transfer of writing knowledge (DasBender, 2016; Figueredo, 2006; Matsuda, 1997; Negretti & Kuteeva, 2011; Sersen, 2011). For example, Figueredo notes that transfer may be a "conscious, strategic approach" occurring through meta-linguistic abstraction when students relate L1 meta-linguistic skills to ESL spelling skills (p. 893). Sersen claims that helping student writers become "consciously aware" of the "specific aspects" of the L1 that would "appear to affect their English writing products in a direct and negative way" is a kind of meta-linguistic awareness that might mitigate negative transfer (p. 341). Matsuda notes that teaching "ESL students" to write should be considered a method of "raising ESL students' awareness of various factors" involved in writing, including text arrangement and readers' expectations for that arrangement (p. 56). He argues that L2 organization is not always the use of prescribed cultural patterns conditioned from the L1 or imposed by L2 teachers, but is instead a conscious "process of complex decision making" and "understanding of the dynamic nature of the context of writing" (p. 56). DasBender similarly suggests, reporting on two case studies of international multilingual writers in first-year writing courses, that asking students to reflect on the English language experiences in their literacy histories raises a metalinguistic awareness that helps them more intentionally choose writing strategies they had successfully used in past struggles with English-language writing assignments (p. 274). DasBender finds "sufficient evidence" in her results to claim that the "extent of their metacognitive awareness of linguistic and rhetorical differences in writing" plays a "critical role in their development as multilingual writers" (p. 273). To capture the effects of meta-linguistic awareness, such research proceeds from a dynamic understanding of transfer activities, but nevertheless frames awareness as a finished result or outcome of a one-way transfer act.

Writing Across Bi-Directional Transfer

L2 writing research on transfer also studies how writing and rhetorical knowledge moves among connected languages, considering transfer activities that occur "cross-linguistically and bi-directionally" (Gort, 2006, p. 346). For example, Kubota's (1998) study of the negative and positive transfer of rhetorical style between Japanese and English was premised on the possibility of negative transfer or interference from students' L1, Japanese, but its findings moved away from generalizations about Japanese or English and toward the decisions of individual writers. Kubota researched the expository writing of 46 Japanese college students who had studied English for at least eight years in Japan in order to understand how their L1 and L2 interacted in the composing process. Student participants in her study wrote on the same topic in both languages twice, one week apart. She evaluated the location of the main idea and macro-level rhetorical patterns in essays together with survey and interview data. The study's results revealed the nuance of L1 to L2 transfer of writing ability: students who had more experience writing in their L2 produced higher quality essays than students who had more L2 English education. Kubota suggested that this is because English language education focuses on isolated sentence-level concerns, which affected the control over vocabulary and syntax in the L2 essays. Thus, she concluded that students' essay organization that teachers find puzzling may be less a phenomenon of negative L1 transfer and more a factor of little experience with academic L1 writing (p. 88).

Ultimately, Kubota's findings incorporate transfer factors as expansive as those found in Matsuda's (1997) dynamic model of L2 writing, which moves beyond cultural, educational, and linguistic influences to include "variations within his or her native language (i.e., dialect) and culture (i.e., socioeconomic class), his or her knowledge of the subject matter, past interactions with the reader, and the writer's membership to various L1 and L2 discourse communities" (p. 53). Kubota notes, for example, that simply sharing a language background did not lead her research subjects to write in a similar way. Instead, the "students use various organizational patterns" from an L1 with "certain intentions" in their L2 writing (1998, p. 89). The presence and interactivity of these dynamic influences in Matsuda's model and Kubota's conclusions challenge the discrete, one-way, and negative assumptions about how transfer of writing knowledge works among languages.

Building on previous research like Kubota's, Kobayashi and Rinnert (2008) focused on university entrance essay exam instruction to study how writing skills transfer bi-directionally across Japanese and English. They investigated the influence of four types of writing instruction—intensive writing in L1 and L2; intensive writing in only L1; intensive writing in only L2; none in either language—on 28 Japanese students' L1 (Japanese) and L2 (English) exam writing strategies, especially in organizational use of structure and discursive markers. Using textual analysis and post-essay student interviews, Kobayashi and Rinnert concluded that instruction did affect how students approached their exam writing. As students constructed texts in either language, transfer "occurred in both directions," with student interviews showing that students called on both of their languages as sources of knowledge about organization and discursive norms. Thus, Kobayashi & Rinnert (2008) reinforced Berman's (1994) finding that explicit instruction affects the transfer of writing knowledge but extended his findings to show that L1 writing instruction supports writing choices in the L1 and L2, and that instruction that stresses the interaction of an L1 and L2 in writing "led to greater effects" in students' writing than the training that focused on the languages alone or separately (p. 20).

Gort's (2006) research on emergent bilingual first graders in a Two-Way Bilingual Education (TWBE) program's writing workshops details early writers' cross-linguistic transfer that is relevant even for college writers. Gort's intensive data collection and analysis (see p. 333) looked for moments of "positive literacy application" such as strategic lexical codeswitching to connote "unique cultural constructs" (Perez, 2004), or the use of "interliteracy," the application of language-specific elements of literacy among languages (Larsen-Freeman & Long, 1992). Importantly, "when the children began writing in both languages, they employed the majority of their writing-related behaviors and skills cross-linguistically and bi-directionally" (p. 346). Gort claims that these writers developed two written language systems at once by "applying what they knew about writing in one language to the other language" (p. 346). So while transfer of emergent literacy skills was contingent on the stage of biliterate development, the proficiency of interlocutors, and the literacy context, skills transferred when young writers could draw on their "dual language knowledge as they searched for ways to express themselves about things that mattered to them" (p. 341). For Gort, authentic motivation is at the root of the potential of transfer, even for L2 writers early on in their literacy development.

Writing with Holistic Language Repertoires

Another group of L2 scholars studies transfer as a phenomenon among interconnected and mutually informing languages with "soft boundaries" (Manchón & Roca de Larios, 2007). Such research operates from a set of assumptions that are primarily holistic: that transfer processes are general to writing rather than language specific and draw on shared writing knowledge across languages (Cenoz & Gorter, 2011); that the writing knowledge of multilinguals is distinct in its "multicompetence" from that of monolingual writers (Cook, 2003; Kobayashi & Rinnert, 2012); that what appears to be negative transfer or "interference" in writing might be evidence of positive transfer or writers intentionally negotiating meaning (Canagarajah, 2006); that literacy knowledge gained in one language is an asset (rather than an interference) that serves as a foundation and facilitates literacy learning in another (Cummins, 1981, 1991). Taken as a whole, this line of thinking moves beyond monolingualism—languages as singular and separate—to approach the transfer of writing knowledge as a relational phenomenon (Canagarajah, 2011; Ortega & Carson, 2010).

    Researchers who study multilingual writing activities treat transfer as a rhetorical activity that can "co-exist" in multiple languages at once, frustrating the simple tracing of writing knowledge from one language to another (Kobayashi & Rinnert, 2013). For example, Kobayashi and Rinnert's (2013) longitudinal case study examines how one Japanese multilingual writer developed her L1 (Japanese), L2 (English), and L3 (Chinese) writing multicompetence over two and a half years. The researchers analyzed student texts, text-based interviews, and observations to trace "multi-directional interactions" among the student's languages. They concluded that her transfer of writing knowledge was affected by dynamic factors such as proficiency, prior writing knowledge, imagined audience expectations, and perceptions about writing conventions, leading "boundaries [to] become blurred among both the textual and the linguistic features in the three languages" (p. 25). Specifically, Kobayashi and Rinnert found bidirectional lexico-grammatical transfer between the writer's L1 (Japanese) and L3 (Chinese), and the transfer of process-based composing activities from the writer's L2 (English) to her L1. Because the study was designed to capture multiple dimensions of writing development, Kobayashi and Rinnert were able to capture a multi-dimensional understanding of writing transfer as well.

    Studies of codemeshing also draw on holistic notions of language transfer. For example, Canagarajah's (2006) study of a scholar's bilingual academic writing argues that multilingual writers call on rhetorical strategies from multiple languages simultaneously, on purpose. Working against monolingualism, in which successful writing is the error-free performance of writing in a standard, single language, he proposes a negotiation model that recognizes how writers shuttle among their languages to negotiate and achieve social meaning (p. 602). Canagarajah's 2011 study of a student writer interacting with peer and teacher feedback proposed four types of code-meshing strategies in academic writing—recontextualization strategies, voice strategies, interactional strategies, and textualization strategies—that he traced in one student's academic writing. Canagarajah concludes that "what may appear as grammatical deviations or idiomatic novelties are explained as a positive case of transfer from the other languages in one's repertoire rather than a negative case of interference" (p. 402).

Canagarajah's taxonomy of codemeshing strategies is significant for its situating of transfer in the social negotiation among writers rather than in an individual writer's competence. Further, it initiates the agency of negotiation with the student rather than the teacher. In fact, Sánchez-Martín (2016) argues that codemeshing, itself, is evidence of transfer of writing knowledge, as written evidence of students' negotiation of their full repertoire of resources. She follows Rounsaville, Goldberg, and Bawarshi (2008) and Reiff and Bawarshi (2011) to frame codemeshing as a "boundary-crossing" strategy that shows how writers "connect in meaningful ways their prior knowledge (on writing, languages, modalities) to new writing situations" (45). This is because, she says, codemeshing is evidence of multilingual writers explicitly negotiating and then re-adapting their writing knowledge.

Instructional and Curricular Design

In L2 writing, transfer also has been treated as a curricular phenomenon. Many studies in L2 writing examine how students transfer writing strategies and skills from ESL or EAP courses to other college courses, often finding missed transfer opportunities between general and disciplinary courses (Currie, 1993, 1999; Gosden, 1998; James, 2008, 2009, 2010a, 2010b; Johns, 1988, 1993, 1995; Leki, 1995; Leki & Carson, 1994, 1997; Snow, 1993; Snow & Brinton, 1988; Spack, 1988, 1997; Swales, 1984, 1990; Tardy, 2009; Tedick, 1990; Zamel, 1995; Zamel & Spack, 2006). These studies often seek to understand the purpose of an ESL or EAP writing requirement by examining instructional design that supports transfer from one class context to another. Researchers tend to follow two lines of thinking in their conclusions. One suggests that first-year courses should work on general writing skills like revision or voice (e.g., Spack, 1988) while the other promotes conceptual or genre-based activities that might prepare students explicitly for specific disciplinary courses (e.g., Currie, 1993; Johns, 1995).

Several large-scale studies find students experiencing a disconnect between the rhetorical context of their EAP courses and the audience, purpose, and content knowledge of their disciplinary discourse communities (e.g., Hansen, 2000; Tardy, 2009). Spack (1988) anticipates this concern in her review of nascent writing in the disciplines approaches in first-year writing, which she frames in light of what she calls a "problematic trend" in teaching disciplinary preparation in first-year courses. She sets preparation for disciplines in opposition to a humanities focus, saying disciplinary instruction can be overly formulaic and lacking in depth (p. 46). She suggests instead that first-year courses continue to teach general skills like the writing process, writing from sources, and working with data: "general inquiry strategies, rhetorical principles, and tasks that can transfer to other course work" (pp. 40–41). Conducting a longitudinal study to support her initial review, Spack (1997) studied the reading and writing strategies of one ESL student over a three-year period in order to understand how the student's skills learned in the ESL program transferred to her disciplinary courses. Spack analyzed student and instructor interviews, classroom observation, and texts from ten of the student's courses across three disciplines. Spack found that there was no guarantee of application of learned writing knowledge in new situations. She argues that while the student "benefited significantly" from her first-year ESL courses, the general skills strategies learned in those courses—e.g., paraphrasing and quoting—were not taken up when writing about increasingly complex content. In this way, Spack's research added important caveats to her earlier aversion to disciplinary writing: "academic skills are not fixed" and "can be understood only within specific contexts," including the context of first-year writing (p. 50).

Currie (1993) challenges Spack's earlier (1988) work and others who advocate teaching general writing skills by following Swales (1984, 1990) and Johns (1990) to focus on the explicit teaching of disciplinary discursive norms to support transfer. Currie promotes teaching disciplinary "conceptual activities" to support EAP students' disciplinary socialization. In a precursor to Carter's (2007) concept of meta-genres, Currie (1999) describes a sequence of student activities in which students record the disciplinary values they observe and collect by interviewing an instructor: kinds of question-posing, the values around writing and knowledge-making in the discipline, and visual representations of knowledge. In studying students' experiences of these conceptual activities, Currie finds that transfer was more likely when students could build a conscious awareness of disciplinary expectations prior to using them in writing (p. 340). She notes that in terms of transfer, "what might be perceived as writing problems are, in fact, difficulties with the conceptual activities required to write" (pp. 340–341).

Leki (1995), on the other hand, claims that an EAP curriculum shouldn't teach discipline-specific forms but should teach whatever best prepares students to *acquire* discipline-specific forms. Leki and Carson (1994) undertook a large-scale survey of students' perceptions (n=77) at two institutions in order to understand "how well ESL students are able to use what they have learned from our writing classes in their writing tasks across the curriculum" and which elements best transfer to students' disciplines (p. 82). Admitting the limitations of surveys that seek students' perceptions of instruction that is often implicit—simply modeled rather than explicitly taught—their findings remain helpful for understanding students' writing knowledge transfer among curricular contexts. For example, 77% of students felt adequately, well, or very well prepared for disciplinary writing, a perception that their final grades supported. Survey respondents commented that they found instruction in process strategies most helpful (35%) and argument or analytic development least helpful (13%). On the other hand, when asked which writing and language skills students used in later courses, respondents inverted their priorities and listed rhetorical skills first with process skills last, which Leki and Carson interpret as a desire for more language fluency under the time pressure of disciplinary writing.

In a follow-up study, Leki and Carson (1997) examine this seeming inversion by focusing on 27 ESL students, interviewing them at the beginning and end of an academic year. The student interviews reveal the central point that writing classes require more personal writing than writing from source texts. The study found EAP students responding to source texts, but without responsibility for the content, which Leki and Carson argue does not prepare students for disciplinary course's expectations for responding to source content. They suggest an important disconnect regarding transfer: the writing in EAP courses is focused almost entirely on the how—clear writing no matter the accuracy of content—while content courses use writing to demonstrate comprehension of the what—accurate and understood content. Leki and Carson argue that EAP courses must give students practice in learning and grappling with ideas in their writing (pp. 61–62). They conclude that their earlier puzzling inversion—students' perceptions of being prepared more for process than language fluency but using and wanting more of the opposite—is not students' misplaced focus on sentence-level concerns but rather their desire to direct cognitive energy toward the intellectual demands of their disciplines (1994, p. 92).

While Leki and Carson's research sought breadth in students' perceptions, Leki's further qualitative research accomplished depth by focusing on the experiences of five ESL students' "coping strategies" as they move from ESL to courses across the curriculum. In seeking to understand how an EAP curriculum could best prepare students for disciplinary discourses, Leki (1995) identified ten coping strategies reported in interviews by students, some of which focus on interference (relying on past writing experiences) and others that frame students' prior knowledge as useful for transfer: "students came to their studies in the US with a battery of well elaborated strategies for dealing with the work they would face here" (p. 253). Leki notes that these transfer strategies might occur implicitly because participants did not explicitly comment on anything they learned in ESL classes when discussing their writing in disciplinary courses (p. 255). She thus recommends that instructors actively seek out and support students' existing strategies in order to best facilitate their transfer.

Finally, James's extensive research agenda on transfer (2006, 2008, 2009, 2010a, 2010b, 2012) has pursued specificity in understanding curricular articulation. Based on a 2006 study that showed how writing transfer from ESL to other courses was shaped by the subject matter that students wrote about, his 2008 article sought to understand how both subject matter and task similarity/difference influence the transfer of writing skills. Like Leki and Carson's early research, this work focuses on how students' perceptions of task affect transfer between ESL writing courses and "tasks outside the classroom" (p. 76). In other words, James (2008) asked not how subject matter itself affected transfer—how writing about globalization in both an ESL and environmental studies course might affect transfer—but how students' *perceptions* of writing about globalization in both contexts affects transfer. James asked 42 students to complete an out-of-class writing task and subsequent reflective interview, and then analyzed both in terms of transfer. He found (a) that learning transfer did occur between the class writing assignment and out-of-class task, but (b) that transfer was more frequently described and seemingly carried out when students perceived the writing tasks to be of similar difficulty levels (p. 92). Because James found that task difference had less of an impact on transfer than students' understanding of that difference, he concludes that *perception* of writing task difference matters more for transfer than actual difference in the task.

The Role of Genre

Genre as a writing and rhetorical practice of L2 writers is a major line of thinking in scholarship on transfer in L2 writing, (Cheng, 2007; Gentil, 2011; Parks, 2001; Tardy, 2006, 2009) and genre-based writing instruction (GBWI) (Fishman & McCarthy, 2001; Gosden, 1998; Hyon, 2001; Johns, 1988, 1995, 1997, 2011; Johns et al., 2006; Mustafa, 1995; Negretti & Kuteeva, 2011). Findings indicate that genre-based pedagogies can support the transfer of writing knowledge when they explicitly raise students' awareness of textual form and function (Hyland, 2003, 2016). Swales (1984, 1990) laid the groundwork for this line of inquiry by developing text-based genre analysis. Much genre inquiry in L2 writing follows Swales' (1990) understanding that "genre comprises a class of communicative events, the members of which share some set of communicative purposes" (p. 58). Some studies pursue this understanding of genre by tracing the transfer of writing knowledge across genres, or by looking for the replication of genre conventions between an L1 and L2 as evidence of transfer. Other scholars use a Rhetorical Genre Studies (RGS) framework to focus on the transnational and multilingual transfer of writing-related knowledge (Coe, 2002; Coe et al., 2002; Rounsaville, 2014). Scholars investigate genre, and its context-dependent, recurring nature, in order to understand wide-ranging questions about transfer, including about the sociocultural contexts of genre transfer, the institutional conditions that allow the transfer of genre knowledge, or the pedagogies that help L2 writers draw on their prior genre knowledge across multiple languages (Gentil, 2011).

For example, Hyon (2001) conducted interviews with eight L2 writers in a genre-based EAP reading course to understand the effects of this pedagogy. Collecting interviews one year after the course was taken, Hyon traced the extent to which four genres—journalistic news story, feature article, textbook, research article—were useful in students' later course requirements and personal interests. Interviews also asked participants what they remembered about the genre instruction as well as their perceptions of how the genres taught had shaped their reading in English. Hyon noted several lasting features of the pedagogy including a "rhetorical sensitivity" that participants suggested transferred from reading instruction in course genres to their reading in general. Interestingly, even though the course was focused on reading, several participants noted that components of genre instruction, like text organization in research articles, "transferred positively to their academic writing abilities" (p. 431).

Discussions of genre in L2 writing pay special attention to pedagogical concerns. For example, a 2006 commentary section of the *Journal of Second Language Writing* focused on experts' understanding of the state of genre studies (Johns et al., 2006), in which many contributors' "take" on genre in L2 writing was implicitly related to issues of transfer, as in Coe's "culturally typical structure that embodies a socially-appropriate strategy for responding to varied situations" (p. 245). Others explained how explicitly teaching genre in L2 writing courses might support transfer, helping students "anticipate" new rhetorical situations (Reiff, p. 240) or explicitly examine the conventions that shape these situations (Bawarshi, p. 244) in order to lay the groundwork for transfer (Tardy). All contributors admit that teaching with genre or for genre transfer is especially complex in ESL writing, in that L2 writers are grappling with multiple cultural, rhetorical, educational and linguistic perspectives at once (Tardy). These scholars believe that critically engaging L2 students in these complexities may help mitigate the potential for genre analysis to replicate social relations that disadvantage L2 writers (Hyland, p. 241).

Johns (1988, 1995, 1997, 2011) has especially sought to understand how genre-based instruction in ESL writing courses facilitates transfer to content courses. Across her work on genre, she describes how EAP instructors use classroom and "authentic" genres (those that serve clear communicative purposes) to support the transfer of writing knowledge. Challenging a formulaic approach to teaching the writing process, Johns describes a curricular innovation that she calls a "transition package" for students who might benefit from additional English language support in the general education courses (1995). By attaching "adjunct" English language courses, or labs, to general education courses, students benefit from extra time discussing study skills as well as the implicit discourses of their disciplinary content courses. Students are exposed to disciplinary assumptions about speaking, argumentation, and knowledge claims that shape the genres students work with. Ideally, the lab situates students in an "investigative" or "ethnographic" role toward implicit disciplinary genres, which in turn heightens students' awareness of genre conventions and the likelihood of knowledge transfer. To help students avoid replicating only classroom genres, Johns recommends that instructors make clear the "connections and possible transfer of skills among all academic genres" (1995, p. 283). She suggests integrating classroom and authentic genres in portfolio assessment and classroom reflections to allow students to understand differing disciplinary purposes for writing, to be open to styles that depend on situation, and to analyze differing audience expectations in general (p. 289).

Johns (2011) helpfully builds on Hyon's (1996) categories of genre approaches—(1) Systemic Functional Linguistics (SFL) (Halliday, 1978); (2) English for Specific Purposes (ESP) (Swales, 1984); and (3) Rhetorical Genre Studies (Miller, 1984)—to consolidate four main instructional problems or questions that persist in GBWI. Johns first points to the issue of text naming—whether genre means text type and whether naming that type is an effective pedagogy. According to Johns, text naming asks students to identify textual structure, rhetorical mode, and grammatical or lexical elements in order to identify similar structural patterns across their languages or courses. Text naming is an ongoing issue in GBWI because it may support students' memory of text types but lose the social context that give these types meaning. At its best, Johns says, text naming incorporates SFL's link between genre pattern and genre purpose—between structural pattern and the social motive or action that makes the genre meaningful in a specific context (Bawarshi & Reiff, 2010). Johns points to Bhatia's (2002) use of genre in discourse communities and Hyland's (2003) focus on explicit genre instruction as instructional guides to keep text naming linked to specific reading and writing communities.

The second GBWI issue that Johns (2011) says crosses SFL, ESP, and RGS genre theory is genre acquisition vs. genre awareness. Following Macbeth (2009), Johns defines genre acquisition as non-reflective genre learning that may only accomplish low-road transfer; genre awareness then includes explicit instruction in and student reflection on genres' rhetorical purposes and contexts, which can support the high-road transfer that allows for students' genre adaptation in new contexts (Flowerdew, 2011; Hyland, 2011). Johns identifies pedagogy, itself, as the third GBWI issue, pointing to decisions about instructional focus, including the extent to which teachers should teach disciplinary values around genres. Johns suggests that for novice students with lower L2 proficiency, instructors start with pedagogies that focus on text types and then move into the complexity of disciplinary values. Finally, Johns identifies the fourth issue in GBWI as the role of hegemony and ideology around certain genres. Following Luke (1996), Johns highlights the tension around genres that require "assimilation" or "accommodation"—the timed essay, for example—as adhering to the status quo of disciplinary power structures.

Tardy's (2006) review of studies of genre also is relevant to transfer in L2 writing because the gap she locates to justify her review is lack of attention to genre transfer. More specifically, the gap is a lack of studies that follow the same L2 writers across multiple settings to understand their genre learning. She looks across 60 empirical studies that investigate how writers learn genres in order to understand how the movement of genre across domains is relevant to learning. Tardy categorizes her reviewed studies into (1) practice-based settings, how genre-based knowledge is developed without instruction in disciplinary, educational, or workplace practice; and (2) instructional settings, how genre knowledge is built through explicit or implicit classroom instruction. In the category of practice-based contexts, Tardy synthesizes findings that include: drawing on experience and practice in genre learning; oral interactions with peers and experts in building genre knowledge; interacting with text in learning genres; composing strategies; instruction and feedback; transferability and conflict; dimensions of what genre knowledge entails; mentoring; and individuality and identity. In the category of instructional contexts, Tardy synthesizes findings that include: influence of prior experience and exposure on genre learning; textual modeling; explicit instruction; transferability and conflict; and dimensions of genre knowledge. Tardy argues that neither category contains studies that fully explain how learners transfer genre learning to other domains (p. 91), or fully investigate the impact of explicit genre-based teaching approaches like genre analysis or ethnography like those advocated by Johns above (p. 97).

On the topic of transfer, Tardy (2006) finds in her review that both practice-based and instructional studies stress the difficulties of transferring skills among rhetorical situations like workplaces (Smart, 2000) due to differing disciplinary genre expectations. Tardy notes that conflicts among student, peer, and professor expectations seem to impede writing transfer; but conflicts also highlight the pivotal role of students' perceptions of task authenticity in transfer (p. 92). Tardy focuses on Parks' (2001) longitudinal study of francophone nurses in their first year of work at an English-medium hospital as an example of a study that does trace genre learning across practice *and* instruction domains. Because Parks links domains through nursing care plans, a genre explicitly taught in school and then used at work, she is able to trace changes in nurses' use of this genre across domains and over time. Parks finds that discrepancy among school and work genres did not drastically impede nurses' learning. Instead, nurses were able to quickly adapt the genre according to workplace demands and collaboration with colleagues, with the nursing care plans eventually resembling workplace rather than classroom forms. Importantly, Tardy notes that transfer of genre knowledge is not "exclusively an L1 or L2 issue" in that writers and readers struggle to transfer knowledge no matter their language background (p. 95). Studies of genre learning with L1 or L2 writers differ most in their consideration of how factors such as "race, class, and gender, as well as linguistic, ethnic, and cultural background" impact oral interactions and the extent to which access to peer and teacher conversation supports genre learning (pp. 95–96).

Work that takes these factors into account includes Gentil's (2011) literature review that forwards a biliteracy perspective on genre research. Gentil aimed to "untangle" research on genre, writing, and language, using a biliteracy perspective—how bilingualism shapes the cognitive and sociocultural dimensions of reading and writing (Hornberger, 2003)—to examine how L2 writers develop genre expertise across their languages. Such crosslinguistic movement is an issue of transfer for L2 writers: if writers' genre knowledge in one language has a "common underlying proficiency" (Cummins, 2000) with another, "the more it may be acquired in one language and used in another" (p. 7). Gentil's review groups several findings regarding the transfer of genre knowledge: (1) L2 writers are not "conditioned by linguistic codes" but instead have "superior rhetorical savvy" due to their transfer of genre knowledge among codes (p. 17); (2) some discourse communities have preferences for the languages used to accomplish a genre while other communities have the same genre expectations no matter the language; and (3) genre expertise for L2 writers means they can "draw on their whole repertoires of genres and rhetorical strategies across languages strategically" (p. 19). Summarizing these points,

Gentil (2011) concludes that the genre preferences of discourse communities are "not linguistically determined," that is, one language does not condition only certain genre activities (p. 18). Instead, L2 writers develop expertise by transferring genres across (rather than staying within) their languages and recognizing which contexts will validate their genre innovations (p. 10). In the review's pedagogical implications, Gentil concludes that L2 writers can be guided to identify and draw on their crosslinguistic genre knowledge.

Identity

Researchers studying transfer in L2 writing also consider how elements of identity shape the transfer of writing knowledge. Because identity is mutually constitutive with language, writerly identities are bound up in the languages writers are composing among; for many writers labeled L2 or ESL, cultural or sociopolitical aspects of their identities become particularly salient when they enter a writing classroom, sometimes heightening feelings of outsider status or non-native foreignness (Johnstone, 1996; Matsuda, 2015; Norton, 2000). Therefore, transfer in L2 writing is infused with identity concerns (Cozart et al., 2016; Elon statement, 2016). The research reviewed in this section recognizes that L2 writers bring to classrooms lifetimes of experiences with previous English-language instruction and seeks to understand how these experiences complicate or support students' writing transfer.

Because scholarship in L2 writing often seeks better understandings of the cultural and linguistic backgrounds of student writers, such scholarship promotes the validation of these backgrounds to support transfer (Gort, 2006; Jesson et al., 2011; Leki, 1995; Leki & Carson, 1997). For example, in studying the connections between ESL students' extracurricular and classroom writing practices, Leki (1995) argued that research needs "at once closer looks at individual students and broader looks not only at their English classes but at their lives as they negotiate their way through higher education" (p. 236). Such calls to consider student lives aims to recognize writerly identities perhaps not visible through a narrow classroom lens. These scholars also use asset rather than deficit approaches to students' linguistic repertoires, calling for more intentional recognition of multilingual resources to help shape respectful and rigorous curricula (Cozart et al., 2016; Fishman & McCarthy, 2001; Harklau, 1994; Kutz, 2004; Zamel & Spack, 2004, 2006).

For example, Harklau's (1994) ethnography of four high school students transitioning from ESL to mainstream classes found a double bind in these course combinations: While mainstream courses inhibited the extended student and teacher interaction necessary to practice English and socialization skills, well-intentioned ESL courses were stigmatized, perceived by students to be too easy and remedial. The bind resulted in students not fully realizing the linguistic assets they could potentially transfer, while also not further developing their academic English. Harklau recommends integrating the aims of these courses to avoid the marginalization of ESL students. Similarly, Fishman and McCarthy (2001) find that the progress of one ESL student in a writing-intensive philosophy course was shaped by conflicts in the student and professor's interpretations of success in that course. While the professor understood this student's success in terms of written fluency in standard academic English, the student understood her success through multiple lenses including conflicting sociocultural expectations, misunderstandings of assignment genres, and an insultingly easy composition course. Fishman and McCarthy found that the student needed instruction that was respectful, relevant, and collaborative (p. 211).

Other research in L2 writing recommends better recognition of students' linguistic backgrounds to support the transfer of writing knowledge. For example, Leki (1995) identifies cultural multiplicity as a literate "strategy" that L2 student writers already use themselves. She labels the strategy: "taking advantage of first language/culture" (p. 248). Leki noticed this strategy used "in every possible context" by one of the five L2 writers she studied who struggled but who succeeded by calling on "an entire body of knowledge and experience that her classmates and even her professors lacked" (p. 248). In a study of English for Academic Purposes students, Zamel and Spack (2006) argue that an instructor's role in facilitating multilingual students' learning is to invite students to join the classroom conversation by building on their existing linguistic resources (p. 129). Zamel and Spack analyzed collected student surveys, written journals, and interviews to conclude that students "fear that linguistic and cultural difference [masks] their intelligence and knowledge" (p. 129). Zamel and Spack challenge the presumed deficiencies (or interference) caused by L2 writers' languages, concluding that cultural and linguistic repertoires are a source of academic identity and authority in EAP courses. Like Johns (1988), Zamel and Spack suggest that students be taught to view each new classroom through the eyes of ethnographers, looking for the norms and routines of classroom cultures (p. 138).

Studying primary classrooms in New Zealand, Jesson et al. (2011) recommend improving writing instruction for "minoritised cultural groups" by using transfer to make culturally responsive teaching more intentional, to "incorporate the familiar and unlock the unfamiliar" (p. 73). Drawing on Bakhtin (1986) to argue for a focus on intertextuality that includes social and cultural experiences, they suggest incorporating the linguistic resources students bring to school and making clear connections across home and school literacy contexts (p. 66). In their study, an instructional focus on intertextuality supported the transfer of textual knowledge that in turn leveraged students' culture in several ways, allowing students to (1) identify their existing knowledge of textual networks, (2) participate in textual dialogue, (3) create multi-voiced texts with intertextual histories, and (4) borrow techniques and strategies for rhetorical ends (p. 67). Jesson et al. claimed that a linear writing process (brainstorming, writing, revising), a focus on mimicry or emulation (planning, translating, reviewing), or a genre pedagogy that focuses simply on text types can miss prior knowledge that comes from what students actually read (rather than what schools think they should).

Scholars also have sought a more direct relationship between identity and transfer, isolating elements of student identity to investigate their impact on writing transfer. For example, Cozart et al. (2016) reported findings from a multi-institutional project that comprises three separate studies of L2 writing transfer held together by a focus on identities: a study of Danish doctoral students writing in English, a study of American undergraduates writing in Spanish, and a study of Chinese undergraduate students in the US writing in English. Across the three studies, the researchers examine the "possibilities and problems" identity creates in transferring writing knowledge among students' languages (p. 300). For example, in the study of undergraduates writing in Spanish, researchers find that students understand their identities in both languages as a "static" skill but approach writing in their L2 as more physically demanding: "if L1 was driving an automatic car, L2 was driving a stick shift; if L1 was walking, L2 was running" (p. 313). Considering results across the three studies, Cozart et al. find that student writers, both undergraduate and graduate from varying backgrounds, do connect their identities to their writing as an "inextricable link," but they do not perceive of writing in a second language "as an opportunity to experiment with and create new identities" (p. 326). Student writers, researchers say, understand writing in a second language as an act of L1 to L2 translation rather than L1 to L2 meaning making; because their writing identity is more established and malleable in their L1, meaning is made there and then moved over (a translation kind of transfer) to their L2. For the transfer of writing knowledge, this means that fixed or static writerly identities may inhibit the *kinds* of transfer that more recent approaches to writing transfer promote or seek to understand, such as the "remix and repurpose" approach the researchers cite following the Elon Statement on Writing Transfer. Because of this, Cozart et al. suggest writing instructors more purposefully increase students' rhetorical awareness around the phenomenon of language transfer and guide students to approach L2 writing as an opportunity not only to make meaning but also to "expand and enrich one's identity" (p. 327). In other words, writerly identities might be better conceived as a site of meaning-making opportunity, but student writers need to be explicitly taught to recognize and make use of them.

Paths Forward: Empirically Grounded and Theoretically Complex

In the progression of scholarly conversations on transfer in L2 writing, concepts central to this research—language, literacy, expertise, culture, competence—have become increasingly complex even as the research questions asked to attend to them have become quite precise. Studies increasingly aim to examine a small slice of the multilingual writing transfer phenomenon, like student perceptions of one assignment prompt in one kind of disciplinary course. Recent conversations on transfer in L2 writing also bring together increasingly disparate research foci while maintaining the complexity of contemporary scholarly approaches. For example, DePalma and Ringer (2011, 2013, 2014) propose a complex theoretical framework they call adaptive transfer. Aiming to better account for writers' agency in adapting prior writing knowledge to new contexts, DePalma and Ringer propose transfer as a "conscious or intuitive process of applying or reshaping learned writing knowledge in order to help students negotiate new and potentially unfamiliar writing situations" (2011, p. 135). In their formulation, adaptive transfer moves beyond students' application of prior knowledge to the adaptation of writing knowledge in dynamic, idiosyncratic, cross-contextual, rhetorical, multilingual, and transformative ways (2011, p. 141).

In a 2013 response, Grujicic-Alatriste argues that DePalma and Ringer's adaptive transfer is too broad to be useful for workplace or classroom realities. She also lists the model's theoretical components—complexity, sociocultural perspectives, power, Swales' "instantiations"—that she believes are already accounted for in language socialization and genre theory. DePalma and Ringer (2013) respond to Grujicic-Alatriste's critiques that, indeed, theory building was their aim. They acknowledged her concern with adaptive transfer's lack of applicability but resist a "neatly ordered taxonomy" of transfer's dynamic components (p. 465). In their reply and subsequent publications on their theory (2014), DePalma and Ringer stress that writers, including L2 writers, can perform adaptive transfer on a continuum of agency with context transformation on one end and knowledge adaptation on the other (2013, p. 468).

The exchange between DePalma and Ringer and Grujicic-Alatriste displays a common stalemate in scholarly conversation: DePalma and Ringer argue that their framework is meant to be a theoretical push forward, while Grujicic-Alatriste asks important questions about methodology and pedagogy, critiquing the lack of specificity in an overly general model. But such tension between theoretical formulation and demand for utility can lend the energy necessary for empirically grounded and theoretically sophisticated work in transfer research (Lorimer Leonard & Nowacek, 2016). One path forward in L2 writing might focus on how methods unintentionally obscure more complex aspects of L2 writing transfer, such as crosslinguistic writing expertise or recontextualization strategies (Canagarajah, 2011). Sociocultural components that add complexity to L2 writers transfer attempts can also be explored. Much research locates frustrated transfer attempts in the student rather than in the classroom context, student-teacher interaction, linguistic bias, and institutional pressure that L2 writers also negotiate.

Implications for Pedagogy and Methodology

Several pedagogical and methodological suggestions can be distilled from these paths forward for study and teaching in L2 writing transfer. First, researchers and practitioners interested in language issues in the transfer of writing knowledge should consider the influential factor of proficiency, not simply "in terms of how successfully they mimic monolingual native speakers," but as determined by the writers themselves (Cook, 2016). As a field concerned with "the phenomenon of writing in a language that is acquired later in life" (Atkinson et al., 2015, p. 384) and primarily with students "writing in languages they are actively learning" (Matsuda & Hammill, 2014; p. 267), L2 writing continues to suggest that proficiency—a factor of active acquisition in process—is a core analytic component in understanding transfer (Clarke, 1979; Cook, 2003; De Angelis, 2007). Second, the source and target of transferred knowledge should factor into research and pedagogical inquiry around transfer. Investigators should continue to consider how language knowledge is moving—from prior language knowledge to similar more recently acquired knowledge? Among concurrently used languages in different stages of proficiency? Studies should also consider the consequences of that direction: Is that movement creating gain, loss, alteration, insight, systematicity of language knowledge? Rather than thinking of transfer as the linear or lateral portability of fixed knowledge, a focus on language reveals simultaneity, showing that knowledge can move in multiple directions (three, four) at once, revising prior knowledge even as it lays down a path to future knowledge innovations.

Third, considering language in the transfer of writing knowledge can lead educators to reconsider what successful or failed transfer *looks like* in a text and, in turn, who may be concealing or entailing transfer and why. Donahue (2016) reminds readers to consider the role of productive resistance in transfer—that some students may be able to transfer writing knowledge among their languages but may not do so for a range of good reasons. Cook (2016) suggests that transfer acts appearing in text may index not inferior or deficient language users, but instead writers composing from different states or combinations of acquisition. As with all best practices concerning the teaching of writing, in L1 or L2 traditions, practitioners can continue to reflect on empathic inquiries, asking themselves: How can I know about the range of knowledge, including languages, my students are transferring? How does my evaluation account for language acts that may look like error but might also be crosslinguistic influence in process? How might this play a role in culturally responsive or sustaining pedagogies? Finally, rather than thinking of language simply as the transparent medium that communicates transferred knowledge, a focus on language reminds us that language, itself, is additional knowledge that students transfer as they write.

REFERENCES

Al-Ali, M. (2006). Genre-pragmatic strategies in English letter-of-application writing of Jordanian Arabic-English bilinguals. *International Journal of Bilingual Education and Bilingualism*, 9(1), 119–139.

Alonso Alonso, R. (2016). *Crosslinguistic influence in second language acquisition*. Multilingual Matters.

Atkinson, D., Crusan, D., Matsuda, P. K., Ortmeier-Hooper, C., Ruecker, T., Simpson, S., & Tardy, C. (2015). Clarifying the relationship between L2 writing and translingual writing: An open letter to writing studies editors and organization leaders. *College English*, 77(4), 383–386.

Bakhtin, M. M. (1986). The problem of speech genres (V. W. McGee, Trans.). In C. Emerson & M. Holquist (Eds.), *Speech genres and other late essays* (pp. 60–102). University of Texas Press.

Bawarshi, A., & Reiff, M. J. (2010). *Genre: An introduction to history, theory, research, and pedagogy*. Parlor Press.

Bhatia, V. (2002). Applied genre analysis: Analytical advances and pedagogical procedures. In A. M. Johns (Ed.), *Genre in the classroom: Multiple perspectives* (pp. 279–284). Lawrence Erlbaum.

Berman, R. (1994). Learners' transfer of writing skills between languages. *TESL Canada Journal*, 12(1), 29–46.

Canagarajah, A. S. (2006). Toward a writing pedagogy of shuttling between languages: Learning from multilingual writers. *College English*, 68(6), 589–604.

Canagarajah, A. S. (2011). Codemeshing in academic writing: Identifying teachable strategies of translanguaging. *Modern Language Journal*, 95(3), 401–417.

Carson, J., & Kuehn, P. (1992). Evidence of transfer and loss in developing second language writers. *Language Learning*, 42(2), 157–182.

Carter, M. (2007). Ways of knowing, doing, and writing in the disciplines. *College Composition and Communication*, 58(3), 385–418.

Cenoz, J. (2009). *Towards multilingual education*. Multilingual Matters.

Cenoz, J., & Gorter, D. (2011). Focus on multilingualism: A study of trilingual writing. *Modern Language Journal*, 95(3), 356–369.

Cheng, A. (2007). Transferring generic features and recontextualizing genre awareness: Understanding writing performance in the ESP genre-based literacy framework. *English for Specific Purposes, 26*(3), 287–307.

Clarke, M. A. (1979). Reading in Spanish and English: Evidence from adult ESL students. *Language Learning 29*(1), 121–150.

Coe, R. M. (2002). The new rhetoric of genre: Writing political briefs. In A. M. Johns (Ed.), *Genre in the classroom: Multiple perspectives* (pp. 197–210). Lawrence Erlbaum.

Coe, R. M., Lingard, L., & Teslenko, T. (Eds.). (2002*). The rhetoric and ideology of genre: Strategies for stability and change.* Hampton Press.

Connor, U. (1996). *Contrastive rhetoric: Cross-cultural aspects of second-language writing.* Cambridge University Press.

Cook, V. (1992). Evidence for multi-competence. *Language Learning, 42*(4), 557–591.

Cook, V. J. (Ed.). (2003). *Effects of the second language on the first.* Multilingual Matters.

Cook, V. J. (2016) Transfer and the relationship between the languages of multi-competence. In R. Alonso Alonso (Ed.), *Crosslinguistic influence in second language acquisition* (pp. 24–37). Multilingual Matters.

Cozart, S. M., Jensen T. W., Wichmann-Hansen, G., Kupatadze, K, & Chien-Hsiung Chiu, S. (2016). Negotiating multiple identities in second- or foreign-language writing in higher education. In C. M. Anson & J. L. Moore (Eds.), *Critical transitions: Writing and the question of transfer* (pp. 303–334). Perspectives on writing. The WAC Clearinghouse and University Press of Colorado.

Cumming, A. (1989). Writing expertise and second-language proficiency. *Language Learning, 39*(1), 80–135.

Cummins, J. (1981). The role of primary language development in promoting educational success for language minority students. In California State Department of Education (Ed.), *Schooling and language minority students: A theoretical rationale* (pp. 3–49). California State University.

Cummins, J. (1991). Interdependence of first- and second-language proficiency in bilingual children. In E. Bialystok (Ed.), *Language processing in bilingual children* (pp. 70–89). Cambridge University Press.

Cummins, J. (2000). *Language, power and pedagogy: Bilingual children in the crossfire.* Multilingual Matters.

Currie, P. (1993). Entering a disciplinary community: Conceptual activities required to write for one introductory university course. *Journal of Second Language Writing, 2*(2), 101–117.

Currie, P. (1999). Transferable skills: Promoting student research. *English for Specific Purposes, 18*(4), 329–345.

DasBender, G. (2016). Liminal space as a generative site of struggle: Writing transfer and L2 students. In C. M. Anson & J. L. Moore (Eds.), *Critical transitions: Writing and the question of transfer* (pp. 273–298). Perspectives on writing. The WAC Clearinghouse and University Press of Colorado.

De Angelis, G. (2007). *Third or additional language learning*. Clevedon, England: Multilingual Matters.

DePalma, M. J., & Ringer, J. M. (2011). Toward a theory of adaptive transfer: Expanding disciplinary discussions of "transfer" in second-language writing and composition studies. *Journal of Second Language Writing, 20*(2),134–147.

DePalma, M. J., & Ringer, J. M. (2013). Adaptive transfer, genre knowledge, and implications for research and pedagogy: A response. *Journal of Second Language Writing, 22*(4), 465–470.

DePalma, M. J., & Ringer, J. M. (2014). Adaptive transfer, writing across the curriculum, and second language writing: Implications for research and teaching. In M. Cox & T. Zawacki (Eds.), *WAC and second language writers: Research towards linguistically and culturally inclusive programs and practices* (pp. 43–67). The WAC Clearinghouse and Parlor Press.

Donahue, C. (2016). Writing and global transfer narratives: Situating the knowledge transformation conversation. In C. M. Anson & J. L. Moore (Eds.), *Critical transitions: Writing and the question of transfer* (pp. 107–136). Perspectives on writing. The WAC Clearinghouse and University Press of Colorado.

The Elon statement on writing transfer. (2016). Appendix A in C. M. Anson & J. L. Moore (Eds.), *Critical transitions: Writing and the question of transfer* (pp. 107–136). Perspectives on writing. The WAC Clearinghouse and University Press of Colorado.

Figueredo, L. (2006). Using the known to chart the unknown: A review of first-language influence on the development of English-as-a-Second-Language spelling skill. *Reading & Writing, 19*(8), 873–905.

Fishman, S. M., & McCarthy, L. (2001). An ESL writer and her discipline-based professor. *Written Communication, 18*(2), 180–228.

Flowerdew, J. (2011). Reconciling contrasting approaches to genre analysis: The whole can equal more than the sum of the parts. In D. Belcher, A. M. Johns, & B. Paltridge (Eds.), *New directions in English for Specific Purposes research* (pp. 119–144). University of Michigan Press.

Garcia, O. & Wei, L. (2014). *Translanguaging: Language, bilingualism and education*. Palgrave Macmillan.

Gass, S. M., & Selinker, L. (1992). *Language transfer in language learning*. John Benjamins.

Gentil, G. (2011). A biliteracy agenda for genre research. *Journal of Second Language Writing, 20*(1), 6–23.

Gort, M. (2006). Strategic codeswitching, interliteracy, and other phenomena of emergent bilingual writing: Lessons from first grade dual language classrooms. *Journal of Early Childhood Literacy, 6*(3), 323–354.

Gosden, H. (1998). An aspect of holistic modeling in academic writing: Propositional clusters as a heuristic for thematic control. *Journal of Second Language Writing, 7*(1), 19–41.

Grosjean, F. (1989). Neurolinguists, beware! The bilingual is not two monolinguals in one person. *Brain and Language, 36*(1), 3–15.

Grujicic-Alatriste, L. (2013). A response to DePalma and Ringer's article "Toward a theory of adaptive transfer: Expanding disciplinary discussions of transfer in second-language writing and composition studies." *Journal of Second Language Writing, 22*(4) 460–464.

Halliday, M. A. K. (1978). *Language as social semiotic: The social interpretation of language and meaning*. Edward Arnold.

Hansen, J. G. (2000). Interactional conflicts among audience, purpose, and content knowledge in the acquisition of academic literacy in an EAP course. *Written Communication, 17*(1), 27–52.

Harklau, L. (1994). ESL versus mainstream classes: Contrasting L2 learning environments. *TESOL Quarterly, 28*(2), 241–272.

Helfenstein, S. (2005). *Transfer: Review, reconstruction, and resolution.* Unpublished doctoral dissertation, University of Jyväskylä.

Hornberger, N. (Ed.). (2003). *Continua of biliteracy*. Multilingual Matters.

Hyland, K. (2003). *Second language writing*. Cambridge University Press.

Hyland, K. (2011). The presentation of self in scholarly life: Identity and marginalization in academic homepages. *English for Specific Purposes, 30*(4), 286–297.

Hyland, K. (2016). *Teaching and researching writing* (3rd ed.). Routledge.

Hyon, S. (1996). Genre in three traditions: Implications for ESL. *TESOL Quarterly, 30*(4), 693–722.

Hyon, S. (2001). Long-term effects of genre-based instruction: A follow-up study of an EAP reading course. *English for Specific Purposes, 20*(1), 417–438.

James, M. A. (2006). Transfer of learning from a university content-based EAP course. *TESOL Quarterly, 40*(4), 783–806.

James, M. A. (2008). The influence of perceptions of task similarity/difference on learning transfer in second language writing. *Written Communication, 25*(1), 76–103.

James, M. A. (2009). "Far" transfer of learning outcomes from an ESL writing course: Can the gap be bridged? *Journal of Second Language Writing, 18*(2), 69–84.

James, M. A. (2010a). An investigation of learning transfer in English-for-General-Academic-Purposes writing instruction. *Journal of Second Language Writing, 19*(4), 183–206.

James, M. A. (2010b). Transfer climate and EAP education: Students' perceptions of challenges to learning transfer. *English for Specific Purposes, 29*(2), 133–147.

James, M. A. (2012). An investigation of motivation to transfer second language learning. *Modern Language Journal, 96*(1), 51–69.

Jarvis, S. (2016). The scope of transfer research. In L. Yu & T. Odlin (Eds.), *New perspectives on transfer in second language learning* (pp. 17–47). Multilingual Matters.

Jarvis, S., & A. Pavlenko. (2008). *Crosslinguistic influence in language and cognition*. Routledge.

Jessner, U., Megens, M., & Graus, S. (2016). Crosslinguistic influence in third language acquisition. In R. Alonso Alonso (Ed.), *Crosslinguistic influence in second language acquisition* (pp. 193–214). Multilingual Matters.

Jesson, R., McNaughton, S., & Parr, J. M. (2011). Drawing on intertextuality in culturally diverse classrooms: Implications for transfer of literacy knowledge. *English Teaching: Practice & Critique, 10*(2), 65–77.

Johns, A. M. (1988). The discourse communities dilemma: Identifying transferable skills for the academic milieu. *English for Specific Purposes, 7*(1), 55–60.

Johns, A. M. (1990). L1 composition theories: Implications for developing theories of L2 composition. In B. Kroll (Ed.), *Second language writing: Research insights for the classroom* (pp. 24–36). Cambridge University Press.

Johns, A. M. (1993). Reading and writing tasks in English for academic purposes classes: Products, processes, and resources. In J. G. Carson & I. Leki (Eds.), *Reading in the composition classroom* (pp. 274–289). Boston: Heinle and Heinle.

Johns, A. M. (1995). Teaching classroom and authentic genres: Initiating students into academic cultures and discourse. In D. Belcher & G. Braine (Eds.), *Academic writing in a second language: Essays on research and pedagogy* (pp. 277–291). Ablex Publishing Corporation.

Johns, A. M. (1997). *Text, role, and context: Developing academic literacies*. Cambridge University Press.

Johns, A. M. (2011). The future of genre in second language writing: Fundamental, but contested, instructional design. *Journal of Second Language Writing, 20*(1), 56–68.

Johns, A. M., Bawarshi, A., Coe, R. M., Hyland, K., Paltridge, B., Reiff, M. J., & Tardy, C. (2006). Crossing the boundaries of genre studies: Commentaries by experts. *Journal of Second Language Writing, 15*(3), 234–249.

Johnstone, B. (1996). The *linguistic individual: Self-expression in language and linguistics*. Oxford University Press.

Kang, J. Y. (2005). Written narratives as an index of L2 competence in Korean EFL learners. *Journal of Second Language Writing, 14*(4), 259–79.

Kaplan, R. B. (1966). Cultural thought patterns in intercultural education. *Language Learning, 16*(1–2), 1–20.

Kaplan, R. B. (1967). Contrastive rhetoric and the teaching of composition. *TESOL Quarterly, 1*(4), 10–16.

Kaplan, R. B. (1987). Cultural thought patterns revisited. In U. Connor, & R. Kaplan (Eds.), *Writing across languages: Analysis of L2 text* (pp. 9–21). Addison-Wesley.

Kobayashi, H., & Rinnert, C. (2008). Task response and text construction across L1 and L2 writing. *Journal of Second Language Writing, 17*(1), 7–29.

Kobayashi, H., & Rinnert, C. (2012). Understanding L2 writing development from a multicompetence perspective: Dynamic repertoires of knowledge and text construction. In R. M. Manchon (Ed.), *L2 writing development: Multiple perspectives* (pp. 101–134). De Gruyter Mouton.

Kobayashi, H., & Rinnert, C. (2013). L1/L2/L3 writing development: Longitudinal case study of a Japanese multicompetent writer. *Journal of Second Language Writing, 22*(1), 4–33.

Kubota, R. (1998). An investigation of L1–L2 transfer in writing among Japanese university students: Implications for contrastive rhetoric. *Journal of Second Language Writing, 7*(1), 69–100.

Kutz, E. (2004). From outsider to insider: Studying academic discourse communities across the curriculum. In V. Zamel & R. Spack (Eds.), *Crossing the curriculum: Multilingual learners in college classrooms* (pp. 75–93). Lawrence Erlbaum.

Lado, R. (1957). *Linguistics across cultures: Applied linguistics for language teachers*. University of Michigan Press.

Larsen-Freeman, D. (1997). Chaos/complexity science and second language acquisition. *Applied Linguistics, 18*(2), 141–165.

Larsen-Freeman, D. (2013). Transfer of learning transformed. *Language Learning, 63*(1), 107–29.

Larsen-Freeman, D., & Cameron, L. (2008). Research methodology on language development from a complex theory perspective. *Modern Language Journal, 92*(2), 200–213.

Larsen-Freeman, D., & Long, M.H. (1992). *An introduction to second language acquisition research*. Longman.

Leki, I. (1995). Coping strategies of ESL students in writing tasks across the curriculum. *TESOL Quarterly, 29*(2), 235–260.

Leki, I., & Carson, J. G. (1994). Students' perceptions of EAP writing instruction and writing needs across disciplines. *TESOL Quarterly, 28*(1), 81–101.

Leki, I., & Carson, J. G. (1997). "Completely different worlds": EAP and the writing experiences of ESL students in university courses. *TESOL Quarterly, 31*(1), 39–69.

Lorimer Leonard, R., & Nowacek, R. (2016). Transfer and translingualism. *College English, 78*(3), 258–264.

Luke, A. (1996). Genres of power? Literacy education and the production of capital. In R. Hasan & G. Williams (Eds.), *Literacy in society* (pp. 308–338). Longman.

Macbeth, K. P. (2009). Deliberate false provisions: The use and usefulness of models in learning academic writing. *Journal of Second Language Writing*, *19*(1), 33–48.

Manchón, R. M., & Roca de Larios, J. (2007). On the temporal nature of planning in L1 and L2 composing. *Language Learning*, *57*(4), 549–593.

Matsuda, P. K. (1997). Contrastive rhetoric in context: A dynamic model of L2 writing. *Journal of Second Language Writing*, *6*(1), 45–60.

Matsuda, P. K. (2015). Identity in written discourse. *Annual Review of Applied Linguistics*, *35*, 140–159.

Matsuda, P. K., & Hammill, M. J. (2014). Second language writing pedagogy. In G. Tate, A. Rupiper, K. Schick, & H. Brooke Hessler (Eds.), *A guide to composition pedagogies* (2nd ed.). Oxford University Press.

McCall, M. (2016). Bridging the divide: Integrating composition and second language writing approaches to transfer. *Double Helix*, *4*, 1–14.

Miller, C. (1984). Genre as social action. *Quarterly Journal of Speech*, *70*(2), 151–167.

Mohan, B., & Lo, W. (1985). Academic writing and Chinese students: Transfer and developmental factors. *TESOL Quarterly*, *19*(3), 515–534.

Murphy, S. (2003). Second language transfer during third language acquisition. *Studies in Applied Linguistics and TESOL*, *2*(1), 1–21.

Mustafa, Z. (1995). The effect of genre awareness on linguistic transfer. *English for Specific Purposes*, *14*(3), 247–256.

Negretti, R., & Kuteeva, M. (2011). Fostering metacognitive genre awareness in L2 academic reading and writing: A case study of pre-service English teachers. *Journal of Second Language Writing*, *20*(2), 95–110.

Norton, B. (2000). *Identity and language learning: Gender, ethnicity and educational change*. Longman/Pearson Education.

Odlin, T. (1989). *Language transfer*. Cambridge University Press.

Ortega, L., & Carson, J. G. (2010). Multicompetence, social context, and L2 writing research praxis. In T. Silva & P. K. Matsuda (Eds.), *Practicing theory in second language writing* (pp. 48–71). Parlor Press.

Parks, S. (2001). Moving from school to the workplace: Disciplinary innovation, border crossings, and the reshaping of a written genre. *Applied Linguistics*, *22*(4), 405–438.

Pavlenko, A. (2000). L2 influence on L1 in late bilingualism. *Issues in Applied Linguistics*, *11*(2), 175–205.

Pavlenko, A., & Jarvis, S. (2002). Bidirectional transfer. Applied Linguistics, 23(2), 190–214.

Pérez, B. (2004). *Becoming biliterate: A study of two-way bilingual immersion education*. Lawrence Erlbaum.

Reiff, M. J., & Bawarshi, A. (2011). Tracing discursive resources: How students use prior genre knowledge to negotiate new writing contexts in first year composition. *Written Communication*, *28*(3), 312–337.

Rounsaville, A. (2014). Situating transnational genre knowledge: A genre trajectory analysis of one student's personal and private writing. *Written Communication*, *31*(3), 332–364.

Rounsaville, A., Goldberg, R., & Bawarshi, A. (2008). From incomes to outcomes: FYW students' prior genre knowledge, meta-cognition, and the question of transfer. *WPA: Writing Program Administration*, *32*(1), 97–112.

Sánchez-Martín, C. (2016). Proceedings from the II International Colloquium on Languages, Cultures, Identity, in Schools and Society: *A Conceptualization of Transfer for L2 Multilingual Writing from a Translingual Lens: Codemeshing as Evidence of Transfer*. Los Angeles, CA.

Selinker, L. (1969). Language transfer. *General Linguistics*, *9*(2), 67–92.

Selinker, L. (1972). Interlanguage. *IRAL—International Review of Applied Linguistics in Language Teaching*, *10*, 209–231.

Sersen, W. J. (2011). Improving writing skills of Thai EFL students by recognition of and compensation for factors of L1 to L2 negative transfer. *US-China Education Review A*(3), 339–345.

Sharwood-Smith, M., & Kellerman, E. (1986). "Crosslinguistic influence in second language acquisition: An introduction." In M. S. Smith & E. Kellerman (Eds.), *Crosslinguistic influence in second language acquisition* (pp. 1–9). Pergamon.

Simpson, J. M. (2000). Topical structure analysis of academic paragraphs in English and Spanish. *Journal of Second Language Writing*, *9*(3), 239–309.

Smart, G. (2000). Reinventing expertise: Experienced writers in the workplace encounter a new genre. In P. Dias & A. Paré (Eds.), *Transitions: Writing in academic and workplace settings* (pp. 223–252). Hampton.

Snow, M. A. (1993). Discipline-based foreign language teaching: Implications from ESL/EFL. In M. Krueger & F. Ryan (Eds.), *Language and content: Discipline- and content-based approaches to language study* (pp. 37–56). D.C. Heath and Co.

Snow, M. A., & Brinton, D. (1988). The adjunct model of language instruction: An ideal EAP framework. In S. Benesch (Ed.), *Ending remediation: Linking ESL and content in higher education* (pp. 33–52). TESOL.

Spack, R. (1988). Initiating students into the academic discourse community: How far should we go? *TESOL Quarterly*, *22*(1), 29–51.

Spack, R. (1997). The acquisition of academic literacy in a second language: a longitudinal case study. *Written Communication*, *14*(1), 3–62.

Swales, J. M. (1984). Research into the structure of introductions to journal articles and its application to the teaching of academic writing. In R. Williams, J. Swales, & J. Kirkman (Eds.), *Common ground: Shared interests in ESP and communication studies* (pp. 77–86). Pergamon.

Swales, J. M. (1990). *Genre analysis: English in academic and research settings*. Cambridge University Press.

Tardy, C. M. (2006). Researching first and second language genre learning: A comparative review and a look ahead. *Journal of Second Language Writing*, *15*(2), 79–101.

Tardy, C. M. (2009). *Building genre knowledge.* Parlor Press.

Tardy, C. M. (2016). *Beyond convention: Genre innovation in academic writing.* University of Michigan Press.

Tedick, D. J. (1990). ESL writing assessment: Subject-matter knowledge and its impact on performance. *English for Specific Purposes*, *9*(2), 123–143.

Tsang, W. L. (2016). *Crosslinguistic influence in multilinguals: An examination of Chinese English-French speakers.* Multilingual Matters.

Weinreich, U. (1953) *Languages in contact.* The Hague: Mouton.

Wenger (1998). *Communities of practice: Learning, meaning, and identity.* Cambridge University Press.

Wolfersberger, M. (2003). L1 to L2 writing process and strategy transfer: A look at lower proficiency writers. *TESL-EJ, 7*(2). http://www.teslej.org/wordpress/issues/volume7/ej26/ej26a6/

Zamel, V. (1995). Strangers in academia: The experiences of faculty and ESL students across the curriculum. *College Composition and Communication*, *46*(4), 506–521.

Zamel, V., & Spack, R. (Eds). (2004). *Crossing the curriculum: Multilingual learners in college classrooms.* Lawrence Erlbaum.

Zamel, V., & Spack, R. (2006). Teaching multilingual learners across the curriculum: Beyond the ESOL classroom and back again. *Journal of Basic Writing*, *25*(2), 126–152.

7 Transfer in First-Year Writing

This chapter begins our explicit turn to writing studies scholarship on transfer. We start this section of our Reference Guide with first-year writing for two reasons. First, as our readers will recognize, first-year writing is the most visible site for transfer research in writing studies journals, in part due to the long-standing sets of debates around the role of FYW in relation to writing in the university and beyond. And although it's clear that other sites and sub-fields within writing studies have made extensive and important contributions to transfer scholarship, with internal debates of their own, conversations about FYW, and FYW pedagogy, often dominate the field because of the central role that the first-year writing classroom has in the overall disciplinary formation and application of writing studies. Second, because FYW often represents the entry point for students' exposure to teaching for writing-related transfer at the college level, we use this chapter to launch toward our expanded discussions about transfer in writing across the curriculum, transfer in writing centers, and transfer from school to work that follow.

We must acknowledge the number of excellent syntheses on transfer and first-year writing—such as Moore's (2012) "Mapping the Questions: The State of Writing-Related Transfer Research," Moore's (2017) "Five Essential Principles about Writing Transfer," and Qualley's (2016) "Building a Conceptual Topography of the Transfer Terrain"—that have preceded this Reference Guide. This chapter likewise offers a synthesis but focuses almost exclusively on transfer and first-year writing and explores the transdisciplinary possibilities of that focus by referring to findings, insights, and possibilities from out-of-field chapters (1–6). As Moore (2012) has documented in "Mapping the Questions," most transfer scholarship within writing studies centers on seven names: Perkins and Salomon; Beach; Tuomi-Gröhn and Engeström; and Meyer and Land. Yet, as we have documented, transfer research is complex and far-ranging and draws from fields as diverse as human resource management and physical education. Qualley (2016), similarly, and drawing inspiration from Driscoll and Wells' (2012) invitation to "simultaneously focus on multiple theories of transfer," advocates for linkages, connections, and deliberate concept-building both within and beyond writing studies.

In writing this chapter and others throughout this volume, and particularly in synthesizing our conclusion chapter, we found that pursuing such linkages has the potential to not only broaden and enliven our views of transfer but helps stage new transdisciplinary theories altogether. Of happy note are the already existing similarities between research in first-year writing and research on transfer in second language writing; research on transfer in literacy studies; research on transfer in various education-oriented fields (e.g., medicine, sports education); and research in cognitive and organizational psychology. In this chapter, we extend those alignments for the purposes of enhancing transfer research and pedagogy in first-year writing. In what follows, we draw together those connections, illuminate connections as yet unseen, and press for more scholarly and pedagogical exchange between writing studies and this volume's aforementioned fields.

The Role of Local and General Knowledge

The current emphasis on teaching for transfer in the first-year writing classroom stems, in part, from a decades-old debate about the value of first-year writing, and specifically from early critiques of the efficacy of general writing skills instruction (GWSI). In this section, we present earlier debates of the 1980s through the 1990s as they centered around two competing principles: (a) the view that writing was a radically local and situated act that could only be learned through immersion and participation within a discourse community; and (b) the view that there was credence in teaching for generalizable writing skills and that these skills were especially necessary for students at the outset of their college writing trajectory.

As early as 1987, McCarthy's study of Dave, a first-year student who struggled to write across three different and unfamiliar academic writing situations—composition, biology, and poetry—made transfer (or lack of transfer) a central concern for first-year writing. As McCarthy chronicles, Dave struggled to use what he had learned in first-year writing in his other courses; in fact, "in each new class Dave believed that the writing he was doing was totally unlike anything he'd done before" (p. 243) even though the writing tasks had some similarities (e.g., informational assignments written for the instructor as audience). McCarthy's work supports a focus on writing as a social and context-dependent activity and suggests "explicitly training students in [the] assessment process" (p. 262) of contextual and discourse community cues as they construct the rhetorical expectations within each setting.

Dave's experience highlights a core challenge for first-year writing: how can one course address generalized principles of academic writing while also emphasizing the situated and localized conventions and ways of knowing and writing within disciplines? Carter (1990) expounded on this quandary between general and local knowledge—attributing each approach to cognitivist (general) and social (local) theories of writing—and emphasized a pluralistic theory in which general and local knowledge interact in writing development. Building on Carter, Foertsch (1995) also sought to eschew binaries between general (acontextual) and local (context-dependent) writing knowledge for a new basis: a synthesis of social and cognitive theories of writing, memory, and application. In particular, Foertsch called upon cognitive psychology to argue for "a teaching approach that uses higher level abstractions and specific examples *in combination* [for] promoting transfer-of-learning [rather than] either method alone" (p. 364).

Petraglia's (1995) provocative collection, *Reconceiving Writing, Rethinking Writing Instruction*, offered additional perspectives and asked if teaching students generic writing skills in first-year writing made sense if writing is a situated, contextually embedded activity. Contributors questioned how a class based on the autonomous model of literacy (where a universal set of writing skills can be generalized across all contexts) could possibly help students learn to write across contexts. As Russell (1995) famously lamented: "To try to teach students to improve their writing by taking a GWSI course is something like trying to teach people to improve their ping-pong, jacks, volleyball, basketball, hockey, and so on by attending a course in general ball-handling" (p. 58). Interestingly, as we described in our chapter on "Transfer in Sports, Medical, Aviation, and Military Training," these very same debates (literalized in those cases) were also happening in sports education.

These theoretical and pedagogical conundrums evoked discussion about whether FYW had value for transfer and set the tone for the much longer pedagogical debate around the efficacy of teaching general versus local skills and knowledge. They also made clear that transfer must be a key concern for first-year writing. Debates around local and global knowledge remain important for teaching for transfer and are articulated through research on genre pedagogies (Bawarshi, 2003; Bazerman, 1997; Beaufort, 2007, 2012; Clark & Hernandez, 2011; Devitt, 2007; Devitt et al., 2004), writing about writing approaches (Bird et al., 2019; Downs & Wardle, 2007; Wardle, 2009), the teaching for transfer approach (Yancey et al., 2014), and the most recent turn to transfer and threshold concepts (Wardle & Adler-Kassner, 2019). We explore these pedagogical approaches in depth at the end of this chapter.

Ten years after an apex of local and general knowledge debates in the 1990s, Smit (2004) challenged the field directly to engage with questions of transfer by asking: "In what sense can various kinds of knowledge be transferred from one situation to another, or learned in one context and applied to another? (p. 119). This and other questions ushered in a phase of classroom-based research on the paradox of transfer and local/global knowledge. Two prominent studies include Beaufort (2007) and Wardle (2007). Building on the theoretical work of Carter (1990) and Foertsch (1995), Beaufort and Wardle both present the case, derived from qualitative research findings, for a synthesized local-general approach to teaching for transfer in first-year writing through an emphasis on meta-awareness and practices of generalization along with sustained practice in discourse community specific writing.

Beaufort's longitudinal case study of Tim across four years of college and preliminary results from Wardle's longitudinal study that followed seven students from first-year writing to their sophomore year both confirmed that writing within the context of schooling, without the institutional or instructional affordances attuned to prompt the transfer of writing-related knowledge, hindered students' transfer. Beaufort's Tim, for instance, struggled to navigate the changing demands of his courses and instructors, occasionally resulting in "negative transfer" between FYW and subsequent courses. Negative transfer refers here to knowledge inappropriately applied across contexts. For Tim, how the genre conventions of the "essay" were explained in FYW differed from genre expectations in other courses, and yet he brought that knowledge to new courses. Wardle's research participants, while seemingly prepared to transfer writing-related knowledge into their other courses, did not because they "did not *perceive a need* to adopt or adapt most of the writing behaviors they used in FYC for other courses" (2007, p. 76).

Beaufort offers a conceptual model of discourse community knowledge to aid in teaching for transfer that focuses on five knowledge domains: writing process knowledge, subject matter knowledge, rhetorical knowledge, genre knowledge, and discourse community knowledge. Together, these five domains provide writers with the discourse community knowledge needed to meet community-based writing expectations while also serving as a generalized heuristic for writing in new communities. Beaufort suggested designing FYW in ways that both practice discourse community writing and aid students in developing meta-awareness of the shifting types of discourse community expectations they will encounter across school courses and disciplines.

This model aimed to teach general heuristics for writing while also facilitating students' application of those abstractions into localized contexts. Such an approach finds strong resonance with earlier research in both writing studies and psychology on the role of abstract schemata in transfer. For instance, as discussed in Chapter 2, research in the cognitivist tradition argues that prompting participants to draw abstract principles from multiple examples facilitates transfer of learning. That finding pairs closely with Beaufort's suggestion that students work in multiple writing situations and genres to develop an awareness of abstract principles of writing. Moreover, work in both cognitive and industrial/organizational psychology stresses working comparatively with multiple examples. Our upcoming discussion of the role of rhetorical genre awareness and transfer likewise emphasizes this point.

Wardle's findings center on meta-awareness and add an emphasis on institutional affordances in priming for transfer post-FYW. Wardle found that "the only ability that students seemed to consistently generalize from one writing task to another [. . .] was meta-awareness about writing" (p. 76) which was aided by "context-specific supports" such as teacher feedback, peer-to-peer exchange and conversation, and reading or writing in the field of writing studies. These findings led Wardle (2007) to conclude that *"meta-awareness about writing, language, and rhetorical strategies* in FYC may be the most important ability our courses can cultivate" (p. 82). This cultivation depends also on providing a context amenable to transfer—one that treats writing as a situated, sociocultural activity and that takes place within an environment of "context-specific supports." Such findings put strong responsibility on institutions to provide transfer support; without such external facilitation, students may not be able to activate and put into local practice the general writing-related knowledge learned in FYW. Subsequent chapters on transfer in writing centers and writing across the curriculum programs offer precise recommendations for how to scaffold and build such support over time and across learning contexts.

In later work, Wardle draws on genre theory to continue the critique and conversation that writing is highly situated and context-specific at all levels of activity: procedural, rhetorical, cultural, conventional, and in content (Devitt, 2007; Wardle, 2009). For instance, a study by Wardle (2009) on the problem of "mutt genres" in FYW emphasized the challenges of GWSI for providing meaningful writing pedagogy, especially as it related to the question of local and general knowledge in transfer. Wardle, in this second study, bolstered her prior findings and found that when based in "mutt genres," a GWSI course "is not overtly discussing academic genres, is not actively teaching toward them, and is not taking steps to help students achieve useful transfer of genre-related skills. . . . FYC is not, then, achieving its official goal of preparing students to write the genres of the academy" (p. 778). In response, Wardle suggests that the field consider letting go "of the impossible goal of teaching students to write in the academy" (p. 783). Given what we know about the relationship between writing and context as well as the limited time that students participate in FYW, Wardle argues that we teach students *about* writing through focus on meta-awareness, as well as procedural and declarative knowledge about writing as sources of general and local writing-related knowledge. Wardle's suggestion here has subsequently been developed in a recognized FYW approach, writing about writing, with its own theoretical and empirical premises, textbooks, and ongoing lines of inquiry.

While the debate about general and local writing has not been solved, it seems clear that a both/and rather than an either/or formulation is most effective for transfer. It is also apparent that such debates must include context-cues and institutional levers that prompt these cognitive shifts between local and global writing-related knowledge. This final point was first expounded by McCarthy in 1987 and later reaffirmed by Wardle in 2007 and 2009 and highlights how the "the burden for encouraging generalization seems to rest on assignments given in classes beyond FYC" (Wardle, 2007, p. 82). Such a claim requires a stronger relationship between FYW, WAC, WID, and writing centers. Acknowledging the same predicament—the tension between teaching general skills and local genre and discourse community expectations—Fraizer (2010) explores the role that coaching through on-going genre analysis, discourse community analysis, and reflection *beyond* FYW can play in helping students transition from FYW to later situated discourses. Such a suggestion extends Beaufort's work, especially to post-FYW contexts. Facilitating successful transfer of writing-related knowledge is a whole university affair. Models for writing instruction in FYW need to be accompanied by affordances for transfer post-FYW that can prompt perception of task similarity and thus the process of abstraction, localization, and transfer.

Such findings about the complex and intertwined relationship between local and general knowledge and the need for contextual affordances in encouraging transfer strongly echoes the work in sports education and second language writing, in addition to the theories of cognitive psychology previously discussed. Each of these fields has waded through years of similar theoretical debate and related empirical study. For instance, in sports education, the major paradigm shift toward Teaching Games for Understanding was in direct response to debates around teaching technical skills and the teaching of general processes of game play. In that field, the corollary local/general debate turned toward an emphasis on tactical awareness (which echoes much of how meta-awareness is talked about in writing studies) and which dissolved boundaries between cognitive development and physical activity (Light & Fawns, 2003) for a holistic approach to sports education. As we discussed in "Research on Transfer in Studies of Second Language Writing," researchers who've studied these dynamics have reached two conclusions. First, they suggest that first-year courses with emphasis on ESL writing should work on general writing skills like revision or voice (e.g., Spack, 1988); the second promotes conceptual or genre-based activities that might prepare students explicitly for specific disciplinary courses (e.g., Currie, 1993; Johns, 1995). While these findings are starker than those in FYW research, they helpfully demonstrate this ongoing conundrum across multiple fields that focus on student writing development.

The Role of Prior Knowledge

Research into the role of students' prior knowledge and how student writers make use of that prior knowledge plays an important role in this larger puzzle of what helps or hinders transfer into and from FYW. In this section, we first present findings on the role that genres play as students enter new writing situations. Second, we present studies that consider what prompts the transfer of prior writing-related knowledge at all and how methodological shifts in both data collection and analysis can provide new avenues for inquiry into transfer and the role of prior knowledge in FYW.

Prior Knowledge, Genre Repertoires, and Transfer

In the US context, rhetorical genre studies has played a critical role in studies of transfer and first-year writing. From a rhetorical genre theory perspective, genres respond to and provide communicative solutions for specific communities' rhetorical situations. In this way, genres engage and perpetuate historical, cultural, and rhetorical situations through writing (Miller, 1984). Important for questions of transfer, and especially the impact of prior genre knowledge, is how genres tend to fuse the writing situation and the writing artifact in the minds of a writer. Think of it this way: when a student enters a particular school context and is given a writing assignment, they pull and deploy genres from memory that link to the exigence *perceived* in such a context and situation. As Nowacek (2011) has helpfully formulated, genres are an exigence for transfer (p. 30). Perception of situation coupled with practice of antecedent genres play a prominent role in genre transfer. Devitt (2007) theorizes this relationship thusly,

> The writer moving among locations carries along a set of writing experiences, including genres acquired in those various locations. That set of acquired genres, that genre repertoire, serves as a resource for the writer when encountering an unfamiliar genre. Just as writers perceive unique situations as

> somehow similar and so perceive and use the same genre, writers perceive newly encountered situations as sharing some elements with prior situations, and so they use prior genres when writing new ones. It is not the writing skills that are transferring from one situation and genre to another; it is the whole genre. (p. 220)

Because writers interpret new situations from their repertoire of prior genres, it's possible that teaching genres that will repeat or genres that have features that will likely repeat in future genres (like a literature review in academic settings, for instance) will aid in transfer. Devitt (2004) argued that antecedent genres are primers for future genre use and educators have the responsibility to supplement genre repertoires for future writing. For instance, she suggests "if we ask students to write analytic essays in first-year composition, that genre will be available for them to draw on when they need to write a causal analysis in their history class, a report for work, or a letter to the editor" (p. 204–205) because writers draw on genres they know in response to perceived rhetorical exigence.

Devitt's theoretical explanations have been put to empirical research with complex and sometimes uneven results. For instance, Reiff and Bawarshi (2011) and Rounsaville et al. (2008) asked what types of prior genre knowledge student writers bring to college and how students draw on these resources in FYW. Based in surveys and discourse-based interviews, researchers found that students "have a wealth of genre knowledge; They wrote extensively in all three of the domains we supplied—school, work, and outside of school and work—although they wrote most extensively in school and outside of school and work; Their writing did not tend to cross domains, except for a select few genres, most of which represent correspondence-type writing" (Rounsaville et al., 2008, p. 105). Keller's (2013) work on reading echoes these results, as he found that students read richly and robustly across genre, media, platform, and domain *out of school*, and yet students' perceptions of what does and does not count as reading in school limits the transfer of skills, strategies, and broader reading practices. Findings from antecedent genre research also revealed that confidence and self-perception influenced what students would do with their wealth of prior genre knowledge when entering into new situations (Reiff & Bawarshi, 2011). Providing substantive additions to how teachers and researchers should view novice and expert writers, Reiff and Bawarshi (2011) found that boundary crossers (those who were more willing to accept novice status), could disassemble their prior knowledge and pull out what was useful for the present. In this way, boundary crossers "engaged in high-road transfer as they repurposed and reimagined their prior genre knowledge for use in new contexts" (p. 325). Alternatively, students who seemed to pull in old genres whole cloth showed increased confidence (acting more like experts); ironically, for these boundary guarders, their confidence hindered their flexibility when encountering new situations and led to limited high-road transfer. These sets of studies provide a baseline for future studies to consider how the amount and types of prior knowledge work in conjunction with students' changing relationships to and attitudes about writing *in addition to* their growing genre repertoires.

Artemeva and Fox (2010), while not engaged in a study of FYW, have added to this conversation about prior genre knowledge, transfer, and introductory writing courses. Importantly, they find that "students' awareness of genre differences and their ability to identify and report genre features did not enable them to produce a text in the requested genre" (p. 496–497). This has profound implications for popular approaches to genre teaching in FYW that center around genre awareness, which often focuses more on genre analysis and abstraction than on genre production. More specifically, the notion that genre production, the act of repeatedly writing in a genre, is required for students to recall and draw on (transfer) prior knowledge into new situations suggests the need to refine and focus on viable genre repertoires for first-year writers from a curricular perspective. Rather than include all genres encountered, Artemeva and Fox's research suggests that all genres written are what become available for transfer. This substantiates Devitt's (2007) suggestion that instructors and programs carefully consider what genres to require in FYW. Rounsaville's (2012) research on genre transfer and uptake offers additional caveats for delimiting and naming an active genre repertoire through emphasis on how students encounter new writing situations vis-à-vis perceptual valences influenced by history, culture, ideology, language, and other factors shaping background, disposition, and personal perspective. She suggests that it's not only a question of awareness and production, but also an issue of convergence between prior knowledge and present encounters that may determine which genres from a student's repertoire transfer and why.

Methods for Prompting and Making Use of Students' Prior Writing-Related Knowledge in FYW

In addition to research on transfer and antecedent genre knowledge, scholarship also exists around ways transfer is prompted (in the wild) or can be prompted (by teachers or researchers) vis-à-vis prior knowledge. This work is closely supported by scholarship on analogical reasoning within cognitive psychology and situated learning theory, which shows that people's ability to transfer dramatically increased if they were prompted to use their prior knowledge through hints, the explicit use of comparative cases, and framing. In this section, we discuss a similar vein of research that advocates for prompting students' prior knowledge through staging "critical incidents" (Robertson et al., 2012), retrospective interviews, and active questioning and construction of the multivalent factors.

Building on studies of transfer and students' antecedent genre knowledge, Robertson et al. (2012) present constituent elements of what they call a theory of prior knowledge, which rests on the presupposition that "transfer in composition is an 'active, dynamic process." This research was based on interviews conducted and texts collected in a first-year teaching for transfer course. Robertson et al. (2012) are particularly interested in "how students *take up* the new knowledge related to old knowledge," with the caveat that much useful "old knowledge" may be missing from their history. Important to their theory are the following: students often enter into FYW with an absence of prior knowledge, students who do use prior knowledge often fall into one of two typologies of prior knowledge—the assemblage or the remix—and that "critical incidents" can prompt students to "let go of prior knowledge as they rethink what they have learned, revise their model and/or conception of writing, and write anew." (para. 1 in section on "Critical Incidents: Motivating New Conceptions and Practices of Composing"). These findings support a theory of how students "actively make use of prior knowledge and practice" that can be productively put in conversation with research in cognitive psychology on hints, comparative cases, heuristics, and framing.

Hassel and Giordano (2009) provide an important foundation for further research into the range of types of critical incidents that writing students encounter and wrestle with in diverse educational contexts. Their study of students at an open admissions community college provides additional insight into how underprepared writers might encounter "critical incidents," although Hassel and Giordano do not use that construct explicitly. The critical incident covered by Hassel and Giordano includes students transitioning from "developmental and non-degree preparatory courses" (p. 25) to a credit-bearing first-year writing class. Findings here show students struggling with rhetorical adaptability (their term), with some students even reverting to high school writing practices. As Hassel and Giordano note, historically excluded students face challenges beyond the rhetorical nature of writing transfer such as "differing levels of financial, emotional and psychological commitment" (p. 25) needed to successfully move into their college-level coursework. Further research into the range of critical incidents and types of transitions for community college populations is needed.

Drawing from memory studies, Jarratt et al. (2009) forward the construct of "pedagogical memory" as an external and deliberate means to prompt transfer and suggest that researchers interpret interviews about transfer as narrative retellings of prior writing experiences in which "the emotional charge around an event profoundly shapes (or impedes) its reconstruction" (p. 49). As they argued, "remembering is an act of participation, a placing of oneself in a story in a particular way" (p. 49). From this framework, they analyzed and provided implications of retrospective accounts of around one hundred student writers during their final years at university. Perhaps the most intriguing memory group were students who seemed to use the interview itself to make sense of their prior experiences and to "create pedagogical memories linking disparate college writing experiences" (p. 62) in real time. While each grouping provides important insights into how pedagogical memory works, they pull especially from this last group to suggest that "pedagogical memory work" (p. 66)—where students map, translate, and cultivate their own histories and linkages of writing—can bring forgotten memories to the fore. Active and guided remembering becomes a resource for the transfer of prior knowledge. Work by Jarrett et al. resonates strongly with research on framing from situated learning theory (see Chapter 2), defined as "a set of expectations an individual has about the situation in which she finds herself that affect what she notices and how she thinks to act" (Hammer et al., 2005, p. 98). Framing activates sets of resources much like the interviews did for Jarratt et al. Framing can also prompt intercontextual links, which can be primed when two contexts are framed as connected (Engle,

2006). As a valuable force within pedagogical memory work, frames are "meta-communicative signals that help establish what the participants are doing together in it, when and where they are doing it, and how each person is participating in it, thus creating a 'frame' in which their activities can be interpreted" (Engle, 2006 p. 456).

Hannah and Saidy (2014), likewise, provide insight on how prior knowledge and experience may prompt transfer through their innovative study on tracking "shared language development in secondary to postsecondary transitions" (p. 120). Based on a survey of the writing language used by and taught to 112 ninth grade students at a predominantly Hispanic high school, Hannah and Saidy concluded that "the potential boundary posed by language in the transition is not singular. That the boundary has multiple layers and to understand the potential impact of the boundary, it was vital to understand the dimensions of the layers [they] identified: genre, institutional, disciplinary, and personal/familial" (p. 132). This study highlights the complex intertwining of these layers to show the convergence of student's linguistic ecologies and those of the institutions they traverse. Hannah and Saidy's work has strong affinity with research on transfer and second language writing that finds students write among languages, with transfer between languages defined as an interconnected and mutually informing phenomena rather than a process of "interference" (see Chapter 6, "Research on Transfer in Studies of Second Language Writing"). More specifically, Hannah and Saidy make pedagogical recommendations based on students' layered language history. One innovative assignment includes a class corpus of writing vocabulary in which students generate a list of writing-related terms and experiences and define what those mean as a group, with the goal of discourse negotiation.

Studies in this section highlight the range of mediating factors that can prompt transfer at the intersection of a current task and prior knowledge. Like genre knowledge (also a mediating force), critical incidents, transfer-focused interviews, and boundary translation are potential entry points for facilitating transfer and treating students' prior knowledge from an assets-based framework. Students' knowledge is culturally and historically embedded and distributed; the models presented here link transfer to students' sociocultural writing world and prime them for consequential transitions (Beach, 1999). As Beach notes, "transitions are consequential when they are consciously reflected on, often struggled with, and the eventual outcome changes one's sense and social positioning" (p. 114). For instance, as Hannah and Saidy argued, responding to students' language boundaries in ways that support students' transition requires an orientation to students as translators, "as decipherers of language that is teacher-centric" (p. 125). Like Jarratt et al. in their efforts to help students manage their memories in the service of transfer, Hannah and Saidy see a critical role for teachers as helping students develop their boundary translation capacities. In all these prompting methods, boundaries are porous, and transfer is both on-going, active, and agentive. Such transitions are helpfully prompted by deliberate and systematic construction of transfer through methods aimed at drawing out memories, reconfiguring local and general knowledge, and orienting students toward the value of their discursive resources.

Reading, Transfer, and the Role of Prior Knowledge

While less attention has been paid to the transfer of reading-related knowledge, reading transfer does have a role to play in first-year writing as it relates more broadly to a comprehensive literacy education that bundles literacy writing practices. A significant area of reading-related research centers on the role that students' prior knowledge or prior expectations play in how they encounter new and difficult reading assignments in first-year writing courses. A common finding is the need to provide students with culturally and content-familiar readings (Haas & Flower, 1988; Sweeney & McBride, 2015). This seems like a particularly important finding given that many of the teaching for transfer pedagogies suggest writing-related content as course readings (e.g., Downs & Wardle, 2007; Yancey et al., 2014). Thus, an important charge for educators can be to combine writing-related and culturally relevant readings for first-year writers to support prior knowledge in both reading and writing (as these are interlinked practices) by drawing from culturally and linguistically relevant writing studies literature.

While relating course readings to students' prior knowledge, expectations, and values is an effective strategy for transfer, students are also faced with managing today's complex and changing reading practices, which places additional pressure on transfer potential. For instance, Keller (2013) explores how reading practices respond to an age of literacy accumulation—with increasing build-up of literacies past, present, and incoming for students to navigate—coupled with literacy acceleration, how quickly types of accumulations come and go and how many newer literacies "tend toward speed" (p. 7). He argues that questions of transfer are as important for reading as they are for writing and must consider the challenges of genre, media, and domain crossing. Like previous studies on prior writing knowledge, Keller likewise found that his study students have rich and complex reading worlds full of print and digital materials. Prior reading practices span the types of media, genres, and platforms now available in an intermixed digital/non-digital reading world. Yet, students' assumptions about what should be read in school has kept them from bringing their wealth of prior practice into school domains. As he argues, students' perceptions of and narratives about what literacy does, where it belongs, and who values it strongly influence the possibility of transfer.

In response to difficulties that students experience with transferring reading strategies, scholars suggest rhetorical genre awareness for reading (Gogan, 2013). Such reading pedagogies stress meta-awareness and metacognition (see also Carillo, 2015), especially as they relate to how academic values and expectations around reading may be out of step with the realities of the accumulation and speed of reading literacy. Critical reading practices (Keller, 2013) and rhetorical reading strategies can help students both connect to the texts they read as well as identify how and why rhetorical situations and genre expectations differ across classes of texts (Haas & Flower, 1988; Nowacek & James, 2017; Sweeney & McBride, 2015). In fact, many of the suggestions from scholarship on reading transfer align with stated best practices for writing transfer pedagogy. For instance, Sweeney and McBride's finding that students identify a "textual mismatch" (p. 607) between their assigned readings and their compositions (for instance, when a student reads a *New Yorker* essay but is expected to write an analytical argument paper) could be helpfully addressed through Gogan's emphasis on rhetorical genre awareness, which Gogan finds does help students transfer reading skills from FYW into the disciplines. Overall, there is great affinity between how we can teach for the transfer of both reading and writing. As these scholars note, research in both reading transfer on its own and how reading and writing transfer interrelate is a critical next step in transfer studies.

Much of the literature on prior knowledge discussed in this section highlights the complicated alignments and misalignments between students' prior knowledge and activities in first-year writing. Despite the breadth and wealth of research, the role of out-of-school writing and reading, prior knowledge, and transfer is underexplored and can benefit greatly from a transdisciplinary approach. For instance, consideration of prior knowledge is a fundamental part of research on transfer in literacy studies (see Chapter 5), especially as it relates to the role of students' community and cultural knowledge and experience. Pedagogies from literacy studies center on bridging home, community, and school, and thus offer insights on how to build up classroom environments as equity infrastructures to leverage out-of-school and prior knowledge. Literacy studies scholarship could powerfully complement and extend the work presented in this section through its focus on culture, language, and social positioning and the elaboration of what "prior" may mean. For instance, while writing practices may be specific to a context, the ways in which prior knowledge animates practice can include work on students' multi and diverse out-of-school *contexts of activity* and their related ways of being, knowing, and doing, in addition to the text-based focus on types of writing-related knowledge that has been more common in first-year writing research. Readers interested in broadening their approach to prior knowledge in these ways should examine work presented in Chapter 5, "Transfer Implications from Sociocultural and Sociohistorical Literacy Studies."

Transfer and the Role of Dispositions, Attitudes, and Emotions in FYW

Research on the role that individual student and teacher dispositions, attitudes, and emotions have on transfer are a valuable complement to studies on prior knowledge as they deepen our understanding of how students encounter and react to new situations of transfer potential. Such studies reveal how individual students and teachers perceive, manage, and process their navigation of larger educational systems and can help educators extend knowledge on what helps or hinders transfer. In this section, we present studies of two types: first we overview scholarship that considers how attitudes and assumptions influence the possibilities of transfer from the perspective of both teachers and students. Second, we explore the role of disposition and emotions in transfer as "qualities that determine how individuals use and adapt their knowledge" (Driscoll & Wells, 2012, para. 1). Research described in this section has kinship with work on dispositions in industrial and organizational psychology (see Chapter 3) and embodied cognition in situated cognition (see Chapter 2) and sports and medical education (see Chapter 4), all of which can extend writing studies' approaches to dispositions, attitudes, and emotions toward theories and methods as yet unexplored in our field.

Bergmann and Zepernick's (2007) foundational study of the impact of student attitudes and beliefs on transfer from FYW shows the extent to which "individual experience and peer culture" promote "students' conceptions about learning to write" (p. 126). Their study, based on focus group interviews of students who were several years out of their FYW course, treated student interview comments as "representations of students' own perceptions of how and where they learned to write and, most of all, what students believe themselves to be learning" (p. 126). Across four focus groups of 7–10 participants at multiple colleges within a single university, findings highlight how differently students perceived the value and goals of FYW as compared to their discipline-specific courses. Like Driscoll's (2011) study of students' perceptions about FYW's value in relation to later courses in the major, Bergmann and Zepernick found that students placed little value on FYW. Driscoll found that students had uncertain and even declining faith in FYW's potential for transferability. Bergmann and Zepernick (2007) found that students collectively perceived FYW as responsible for "personal and expressive writing" (p. 129) and not something that could be of much use in later classes. The reason for the perceived improbability that FYW could transfer rests in how it was compared to other courses. Discipline specific courses were seen as "part of the socialization into the disciplines" (p. 129), and thus students accepted and expected their rules and conventions to be governed by social and institutional factors.

Findings from these scholars are both troubling and reassuring. They are troubling insofar as they show that students don't see FYW as part of a larger disciplinary universe and thus subordinate that course to others; but findings are reassuring in that students can and do indicate that transfer is possible. Bergmann and Zepernick offer two solutions. First, they suggest instructors help students understand the disciplinarity of FYW—a suggestion echoed elsewhere by Downs and Wardle (2007) in their presentation of a writing about writing first-year writing course. Second, they propose a model to teach students *how to learn to write* (p. 142). Teaching students how to learn to write "would help students learn how to recognize that they are making choices, and how to make those choices consciously, based on knowledge about the discourse community and rhetorical situation in which they are working" (Bergmann and Zepernick, 2007, p. 142). Their suggestion gives a shape to FYW that could hopefully serve as a counterpoint to perceptions about the course that seem to limit its transfer potential. For Driscoll (2011), a possible countervail includes explicit teaching for transfer. Research on prior knowledge and transfer reveals further the ways in which transfer potential is impacted by student attitudes. In their research on transfer and prior genre knowledge, Reiff and Bawarshi (2011) identified boundary crossers (students who were more willing to accept novice status and thus negotiate their prior knowledge more freely), and boundary guarders (students whose confidence hindered their flexibility when encountering new situations and led to stymied and less creative forms of transfer). Clearly, how students approached the course and their relationship to the course content helped determine the course's value and potential as a site of learning and writing across the lifespan.

Teacher and scholar attitudes have also been cited as hindering potential transfer. For instance, Nelms and Dively (2007), in drawing from and comparing and contrasting survey and focus group data of first-year and upper-division writing teachers, found that teachers' assumptions about student motivation and performance (whether founded or not) and their lack of understanding of the total curriculum likely contributed to teachers' own motivation to teach for transfer. With today's increasing numbers of vertical writing curricula across the United States, implications of these findings are especially vital: the "need to concentrate on sharing understandings about writing concepts, skills, and genres as well as course objectives and student attitudes toward writing" (p. 228) cannot be underestimated if we seek for transfer of writing to succeed across the curriculum. Kutney (2008), coming from the position that we ask too much of students, has argued writing studies scholars' assumptions about expertise and first-year writers has created an "unattainable standard for transfer that guarantees the failure of first year composition courses" (p. 223). He asserts that assumptions about writing expertise, most notably that "students possess a meta-awareness of writing that they can use to direct their learning" (p. 223) are too burdensome for practical use. The theoretical premise that scholars and educators expect too much from students, while provocative, has yet to be born out through empirical research. In fact, research such as Yancey et al.'s (2014) study of a teaching for transfer curriculum in first-year courses finds that students do excel in courses that teach for and prompt meta-awareness, transfer, and students' developing their own sophisticated theories of writing.

A promising research strand that asks how perceptions and assumptions affect transfer is disposition research. While the notion of dispositions can be tied back to a number of larger theoretical conversations from sociology, education, and psychology (see a fuller discussion of dispositions in Chapter 3 on "Transfer of Training and Knowledge Management"), two important ways that the construct of dispositions have been taken up in research on FYW comes from Bourdieu's work on disposition and habitus (Wardle, 2012) and Bronfenbrenner and Morris's work on dispositions within the Bioecological Model of Human Development (Driscoll & Wells, 2012). Wardle identifies two qualities that may help or hinder repurposing of writing-related knowledge (a construct she prefers to the term *transfer*): "problem-exploring dispositions," which encourage repurposing, and "answer-getting dispositions," which limit it. Wardle, drawing on Bourdieu, seeks to connect systems with individuals, responding, in part, to Driscoll and Wells' (2012) assertions that attention to "social contexts and curricula" have limited our understanding of individual writers. For Wardle, understanding the ways students' dispositions develop links directly to the social and institutional systems that they have been socialized in and through. Her work points to larger questions about elementary and secondary schooling and how these experiences produce orientations to writing.

Baird and Dilger (2017), who investigated the role of dispositions for writing transfer in internships, determined that "ease and ownership may be two critical dispositions affecting writing transfer" (p. 704). Each disposition is both generative and disruptive and relies on faculty mentoring and curricular infrastructure to aid students in successful transfer. For instance, in their case studies of Mitchell and Ford, both students confidently clung to their writing (ownership), which made it difficult to address complications or misalignments with prior knowledge. Such a disposition made any kind of adaptive or transformational types of transfer more challenging, although the inevitability of such ownership differed for each case study student as Ford yielded to more negotiation between current task and prior knowledge while Mitchell "held onto the approaches to writing he learned in composition as long as possible; then he gave up and tried to give his teachers what they wanted" (704). These findings lend increased credence to Wardle's (2012) argument that US educational systems set students up for unproductive and diminished dispositions for learning and adapting to change and challenges.

Driscoll and Wells (2012), synthesizing studies from two different universities, draw from Bronfenbrenner and Morris to define dispositions as "personal characteristics such as motivation and persistence" that interact with other bio-ecological features of an environment: processes, time, and context (part 1 in section on "Defining Dispositions"). Critically, dispositions refer not to "intellectual traits like knowledge, skills, or aptitude" but rather to how those are practiced (part 2 of section on "Defining Dispositions"). Within this formulation, dispositions are especially salient for transfer study because they "determine students' sensitivity toward and willingness to engage in transfer" (part 3 of section on "Defining Dispositions"). In identifying four dispositions that may impact transfer—how students might value FYW or transfer itself; the extent to which students believe in their own capacities as writers and learners; where and with whom students attribute success or failure; and how disciplined students are in regulating their study and writing habits[7]—Driscoll and Wells further complicate transfer encounters, reminding researchers and teachers that external and internal factors, and their unique combinations, matter for students' ability to transfer. As an interacting factor with dispositions, emotions also play a key role in students' transfer of writing-related knowledge over time (Driscoll & Powell, 2016). Moreover, students' writing is impacted by emotional dispositions, which Driscoll and Powell define as "how emotions are managed across situations," which impacts transfer. Anger, boredom, frustration, or sadness, for example, especially in relation to tough or highly unfamiliar writing situations, are especially inhibitive. In response, these scholars suggest that educators work with students to notice and control their emotional responses in moments of writing frustration to both facili-

---

7. These four dispositions might helpfully be linked to the review of work on motivation and perceived utility, self-efficacy, locus of control, and self-management in Chapter 3 on "Transfer of Training and Knowledge Management."

tate emotion identification and prime them for expecting and cultivating transfer.

Research on dispositions, attitudes, and emotions has made substantial contributions to the field's understanding of transfer and FYW, especially around issues of motivation, persistence, resistance, and problem-solving. Within this growing body of research, transdisciplinary connections with industrial and organizational psychology are especially promising for purposes of refining and broadening the theoretical constructs associated with research on dispositions. In the transfer of training literature, additional areas of research such as general intelligence, the Big Five personality traits, and perceived utility (see Chapter 3) have yet to be pursued and can extend this important research area. For instance, the notion of "perceived utility," which we defined in Chapter 3 as "an individual's belief that performing a specific behavior will lead to a desired outcome" (Chiaburu & Lindsay, 2008, p. 200), is a useful addition to the perception and motivation research on how students view the value and viability of FYW to prepare them for future writing tasks. Using this construct, we can see that Bergmann and Zepernick's (2007) study participants did not perceive the utility (see the value) of their first-year course to help them write in their disciplines. Such findings, when connected to the industrial psychology research on dispositions, provides affirmations to writing studies research and attaches the field's scholarship to longer-standing lines of inquiry associated with dispositions. In the case of perceived utility (or lack of), Chiaburu and Lindsay (2008) found that perceived utility predicted the motivation to transfer. Is this the case for writing students? For instance, Reiff and Bawarshi (2011) suggested that students' self-confidence and assumptions of expertise were responsible for lack of genre transfer. Wardle (2012) has argued that FYW student's prior habitus within US testing regimes limits students' creative repurposing and thus their disposition toward transfer. How would research from industrial and organizational psychology inform these studies? Is perceived utility an additional dimension that we can include in our own analysis? Of course, the value of a construct like perceived utility is just one example of the rich connections between transfer, dispositions, and FYW that could come from such transdisciplinary collaboration. Other examples include further exploration of the multi-dimensionality of types of dispositions already present in FYW literature like self-efficacy, motivation, and locus of control through linkages to long histories of more precise and elaborated definitions as well as extended theoretical connections beyond the more common exposure to Bourdieu and Bronfenbrenner. We encourage readers to return to our synthesis in Chapter 3 to explore further how to grow and complexify their understanding of writing-related dispositions and transfer.

An unusual connection, but one worth pursuing, would be how disposition, attitude, and emotion research in writing studies links to work on embodiment from both sports education and educational psychology. As discussed in our chapter on "Transfer in Sports, Medical, Aviation, and Military Training," Light (2008) argued for an approach to transfer that includes a "holistic view of learning and cognition that extends beyond the mind as a separate entity to include the body and all its senses" (p. 23). Work on embodied cognition within educational psychology argues similarly to the embodied cognition thesis, which states that "Many features of cognition are embodied in that they are deeply dependent upon characteristics of the physical body of an agent, such that the agent's beyond-the-brain body plays a significant causal role, or a physically constitutive role, in that agent's cognitive processing" (Wilson & Foglia, 2017). Disposition and emotion research that foregrounds how histories of practice produce current actions and perceptions could expand those experiential histories to include the habituated development of mind-body-materiality connections in the development and sedimentation of students' dispositions and emotions towards writing. Research on simulations and fidelity, then, might further help writing studies research address ways to either capitalize on or unlearn such connections through its emphasis on the fine-tuned, built environments that interlink cognition, action, and context. Readers interested in broadening their approach to dispositions in these ways should examine work presented in Chapter 4, "Transfer in Sports, Medical, Aviation, and Military Training."

Transfer, Digital Composing, and Multimodality in First-Year Writing

Thus far in this chapter, we have presented work on writing-to-writing transfer: transfer from one mode (alphabetic text) to another similar mode (other genres or occasions of alphabetic text) as well as writing from non-digital to non-digital text and genre. Yet a growing body of research suggests prevalence of transfer from alphabetic text to other modes (non-print based) and vice versa, which opens questions of transfer to include investigation of the "interactions between activity systems, semiotic resources, and media" (DePalma, 2015, p. 617). Semiotic resources are defined here as the available modes (i.e., aural, visual, gestural, linguistic, technological, material, spatial) that writers use to make meaning (DePalma, 2015, p. 637). Transfer and multimodality is an especially vital area because it engages students in their prominent vernacular and extracurricular literacies (which are often multimodal and digital) and attends to the increased presence and near ubiquity of digital composing in school, personal, and professional contexts. Thus, this area of research is critical for supporting students' transfer of prior digital and multimodal composing knowledge into the first-year classroom as well as facilitating students' use of multiple modes in developing writing/composing expertise via transfer across multi-media and literacy domains. In this section, we outline research and pedagogical suggestions that attend to Yancey's 2004 call to (a) "think explicitly about what [students] might "transfer" from one medium to the next: what moves forward, what gets left out, what gets added—and what they have learned about composing in this transfer process [and (b)] consider how to transfer what [students] have learned in one site and how that could or could not transfer to another, be that site on campus or off" (p. 311) through deliberate expansion of writing beyond school walls and beyond traditional texts.

Fine-grained case studies into students' composing practices across modes and literacy domains includes a broad consideration of semiotic resources and is often supported by students' self-sponsored, out-of-school composing practices. Studies include transfer of digital composing between in- and out-of-school domains (Knutson, 2018; Rosinski, 2016), movement across digital and non-digital multimodal genres for writing assignments in school (DePalma & Alexander, 2015; DePalma, 2015; VanKooten, 2020), and impacts of ways of seeing, being, and writing in transfer amongst in- and out-of-school composing contexts (Rifenberg, 2020; Rifenburg & Forester, 2018; Roozen, 2008, 2009, 2010; Roozen & Erickson, 2017; Rounsaville, 2017). Each of these studies reveals the ways in which student writers already participate in acts of transfer in everyday meaning-making, even without explicit instruction. Moreover, due to the fine-grained chronicling of literacy practices through ethnographic methods, they also present opportunities for visualizing the multiple connections and ways of making connections (practices involved in acts of transfer) that writers forge, or are inhibited from forging, across context and modes.

Multimodal, digital transfer is complex and involves the transformation of rhetorical, semiotic, and technological resources. Drawing from classroom data on students' multimodal and digital transfer, De-Palma and Alexander (2015) emphasize the rhetorically, conceptually, compositionally, and technologically messy and changing process of print-to-digital, multimodal transfer. Moreover, they found that the experience of multimodal transfer for students moving from print-based knowledge for digital composing was uneven. As they note, drawing from print-based rhetorical knowledge "worked well for students when they perceived aspects of print-based and multi-modal composing as similar, but it did not work well when they perceived aspects of multimodal tasks as different from their print-based composing experiences" (p. 185). DePalma and Alexander (2015) go on to note that because of some dramatic rhetorical shifts in audience and process between these two modes, "students experienced frustration, anxiety, and feelings of failure" (p. 185). Thus, despite the apparent "naturalness" of such practices, when faced with new forms of multimodal transfer, students may struggle, especially in relation to multimodal audiences, which participants often experienced in direct opposition to academic audiences and as an "ill-defined mass" (p. 186). Students also struggled with the breadth of kinds and types of affordances in multimodal semiotic resources, especially when making complex rhetorical decisions related to audience and purpose. Rosinski (2016) also documents such challenges, especially the rhetorical dimensions of moving between digital, self-sponsored writing and in-school, text-based writing. She finds, through survey data and interviews, that study participants exhibited more rhetorical awareness and sensitivity in their self-sponsored digital composing than in their assigned academic writing, and that this rhetorical knowledge did not appear to transfer between domains. She concludes that the lack of authenticity (in audience and exigence, for example) in in-school settings is partially responsible for the lack of rhetorically oriented transfer. In turn, she offers several suggestions for how teachers can prompt this transfer. Teachers can guide students to "Examine their rhetorical knowledge/strategies in non-academic writing domains; Consider the rhetorical knowledge/strategies they use in their own self-sponsored digital writing; and [r]eflect on these strategies, examine their value and effectiveness, and consider applying them in academic writing" (p. 267).

Importantly, students don't merely transfer digital composing knowledge from discrete text to discrete text. Rather, they often work within digital ecosystems (Davis, 2017), which might include a learning management system (LMS), an online community, or other networked publics that involve substantial digital ecosystems. While all texts are part of an intertextual network (Witte, 1992), the linkages and avenues within digital ecosystems (through hyperlinking, for example) are both immediate and far-reaching, and thus define any starting point in relation to networks of community and expanded audience participation in ways that are not as salient for print texts. Thus, transfer across such "networked communities" presents special challenges for transfer (Davis, 2017). Imagine the rhetorical, semiotic, and technical conundrums experienced within one-to-one digital transfer and then place that within the multitudes of digital ecosystems. Because of the evolving and complexly interlinked nature of such linkages, Davis suggests that students must develop a resilience-type disposition and mindset when writing in digital ecosystems. Universities, too, can play a part in this longer-term instruction by presenting students with a range of digital tools throughout the curriculum (and extended to across the curriculum digital ecosystem) so that students get the consistent, authentic practice they need for acts of transfer within ill-defined online environments.

In addition to research on digital composing as multimodal transfer, scholars document transfer across non-digital multimodal realms. Such work identifies moments of multimodal composition and its related perceptual infrastructure by following writers' practices across a range of literacy domains. For instance, Roozen and Erickson (2017), in their case study of Alexandra, who "acts with tables" across video games, a personal calendar, a variety of tables for making soundtracks and inventing fan novels, and solving puzzles, suggest that these multiple, accumulating, and synergistic practices involve the on-going re-tooling and remediation of inscriptional practices that likewise support her in-school writing development. Rifenburg (2020) has traced the role metacognitive strategies play in helping student athletes connect their athletic experiences with their FYW academic writing. Rounsaville (2017) found, through interview and document analysis, that genre practices and ways of thinking in one student's subculture (his affiliation with maker-culture) constituted a lifeworld experience and provided a discursive and experiential background that yielded taken-for-granted ways of thinking, feeling, and doing in everyday life that supported or hindered transfer between multiple genres in FYW and beyond.

These studies demonstrate how transfer, especially when defined as adaptive, dynamic, transformative, and rhetorical (DePalma & Ringer, 2011), is always integrated into textual, multimodal, and embodied productions. The point, then, is for researchers to observe, document, and name empirically occurring features of such movement and develop pedagogically supportive methods for making transfer more explicit, more conscious, and more purposeful. Students' proclivity toward digital, multimodal, and multiliteracy transfer can be enhanced and supported by dedicated teaching methods to provide some control over these processes. Engaging in self-sponsored multimodal practices does not mean automatic transfer to school writing. Thus, in addition to methods of enhanced reflection on rhetorical processes (Rosinski, 2016), pedagogical suggestions that directly address multimodal-to-print and digital-to-print transfer are needed.

Romanticized notions that students can easily transfer their digital and multimodal composing processes, skills, and strategies should be replaced by systematic teaching practices that can include tracing (DePalma, 2015), semiotic mapping (DePalma & Alexander, 2015), and adaptive remediation (Alexander et al., 2016). These methods add to the growing literature that views transfer as a purposeful, dynamic, and powerful form of agency to transform knowledge across composing contexts and genres in ways that both suit and support writers' goals, identities, sets of knowledge, experiences, and expertise. Tracing (DePalma, 2015), for example, aids students in developing meta-awareness for multimodal transfer through prompting them to inventory their range of semiotic resources as well as trace and name the rhetorical moves of the semiotic resources provided by the texts and compositions they seek to craft. From these activities, "tracing provides a solid basis for decision making and functions as a heuristic for mining rhetorical possibilities" for transfer across media and modes (p. 635). Overall, each of these approaches emphasizes heuristics for adaptation and transformation of rhetorical and semiotic knowledge and also honors students' own self-sponsored literacies in the process.

Curricular Recommendations and Innovations for Transfer in First-Year Writing

Research into transfer and FYW most always has pedagogical implications. While some research yields particular strategies or stand-alone teaching methods, there are several curricular innovations that can be clustered together into more defined "approaches" for FYW. Standalone suggestions that can be incorporated widely include:

- emphasizing increased metacognition and meta-awareness of writing practices, processes, prior experiences, and writing constructs through reflection and portfolios (Keller, 2013; Reiff & Bawarshi, 2011; Rounsaville et al., 2008; Wardle, 2009);
- writing activities and assignments that facilitate students developing abstract schema and generalizations from many local and situated instances of writing (Beaufort, 2007);
- focusing students' attention on the ways that dispositions, attitudes, and emotions toward writing may help or hinder their ability to both draw on prior knowledge and transfer current learning (Baird & Dilger, 2017; Bergmann & Zepernick, 2007; Driscoll, 2011; Driscoll & Wells, 2012; Driscoll & Powell, 2016);
- helping students identify and work with their prior knowledge for the purposes of identifying, applying, and transforming useful skills, strategies, habits of mind, and dispositions that support writing-related transfer (Hannah & Saidy, 2014; Keller, 2013; Reiff & Bawarshi, 2011, Robertson et al., 2012; Rounsaville et. al, 2008).
- attuning students to their range of semiotic resources (aural, visual, gestural, linguistic, technological) developed from self-sponsored composing and community participation and providing opportunities to connect and transform these resources across a range of media, modes, and texts through deliberate practices such as charting, inventorying, coordinating, and literacy linking (Alexander et al., 2016), tracing (DePalma, 2015), and semiotic mapping (DePalma & Alexander, 2015; van Kooten, 2020).

In addition to these recommendations, we have identified four teaching approaches. These include rhetorical genre awareness and genre approaches (Bawarshi, 2003; Bazerman, 1997; Beaufort, 2007, 2012;

Clark & Hernandez, 2011; Devitt, 2007; Devitt et al., 2004; Maimon, 1983); writing about writing (Bird et al., 2019; Downs & Wardle, 2007; Wardle, 2009); threshold concepts (Wardle & Adler-Kassner, 2019); and teaching for transfer (Yancey et al., 2014).

One long-standing approach for teaching towards transfer in FYW is a rhetorical genre and genre awareness approach. Such an approach uses genre analysis and genre production and is supported by theory from educational and cognitive psychology and rhetorical genre studies. This approach centers the interplay of local and general writing knowledge, the development and application of abstract schema through work with genre models and comparative examples, and explicit practice in applying genre heuristics to multiple new writing situations. A goal, as Devitt (2007) suggests, is explicit teaching about genres to facilitate strong genre awareness in first-year writers. The intent is to slow down automatic and unconscious genre transfer, which, like low-road transfer generally, "reflects the automatic triggering of well-practiced routines in circumstances where there is considerable perceptual similarity to the original learning context" (Perkins & Salomon, 1988, p. 25). To wrestle a prior genre from automatic (and perhaps ill-suited) use, Devitt emphasizes the critical role of genre awareness as training in the kind of slowing down and mindful abstraction required for high-road transfer. Thus, genre analysis, and the schemas that students can develop from this rigorous practice, become tools for entering new discourse communities through stages of identifying genres, asking how those genres work in terms of subject matter, rhetorical knowledge, discourse community knowledge, and writing process knowledge (Beaufort, 2007), and then engaging in and producing those genres with the flexibility of localized rhetorical situations in mind.

Beaufort (2007, 2012) has offered several iterations of a genre approach to FYW, with a retrospective culminating in her most refined thinking on the matter. In her 2012 "Retrospective," Beaufort revisits some of her earlier pedagogical recommendations while continuing to emphasize core tenets for teaching for transfer in first-year writing, especially as they relate to genre and transfer. In her earlier work, and in *College Writing and Beyond* (2007) in particular, Beaufort stressed five knowledge domains that students should explore through a carefully scaffolded course sequence. In this review, Beaufort (2012) strengthens and refines her commitment to teaching genre awareness as an integral practice in teaching "learners to frame specific problems and learnings into more abstract principles that can be applied to new situations" (Beaufort, 2007, p. 177). As she notes, "discourse community, genre, and rhetorical situation, [sic] are the kinds of 'abstract principles' that can be taught explicitly and may help writers to frame their knowledge in ways that aid transfer to new writing situations" (p. 178). This approach to transfer is informed by a commitment to (a) teaching abstractions that are applied to multiple writing situations, (b) continued application across multiple situations and contexts, and (c) emphasis on reflection of and awareness about that process.

Beaufort's emphasis on genre is indebted to the work of Bawarshi (2003) and Devitt et al. (2004) who promote sustained and explicit analysis of multiple genres across multiple situations for the express purpose of teaching students how to recognize and respond to recurring rhetorical situations. In the textbook *Scenes of Writing: Strategies for Composing with Genres* (Devitt et al., 2004), for instance, students are guided through a systematic process of collection and analysis that includes collecting multiple genre samples (to show patterns of communication in relation to idiosyncratic features), identifying and describing the genre's context and textual patterns, and analyzing the relationship between the form and function of those patterns. Such an approach merges an intensive study of local writing (through sustained genre analysis) with general schema development (through the abstraction and study of patterns in community genres). As Bawarshi (2003) describes, when genre pedagogy is central in FYW, it becomes a "course in rhetoric, a course that uses genres to teach students how to recognize and navigate discursive and ideological formations. We can do more to help our students write in and beyond the disciplines by teaching them how to position themselves rhetorically within genres so that they can more effectively meet (and potentially change) the desires and practices embedded there" (p. 169). A course based in genre can be a course in writing transfer and transformation. A course in genre is also potentially a course in galvanizing students' vast discursive resources for transfer. As Bazerman (1997) argues, "genre is a tool for getting at the resources that students bring with them, the genres they carry from their educations and their experiences in society, and it is a tool for framing challenges that bring students into new domains that are as yet for them unexplored" (p. 24).

A genre awareness approach is capacious enough to benefit a variety of emphases in transfer pedagogy. For instance, Clark and Hernandez (2011) developed a discipline-oriented genre awareness curriculum to "help students make connections between the type of writing assigned in the Composition course—that is, academic argument—and the writing genres they encounter in other disciplines" (p. 65). Their course adopted many of the suggestions given across transfer-oriented writing pedagogy, but with an explicit target of transfer to other college disciplines. Thus, the central feature of their course was collection, comparison, analysis, and reflection on academic argument in specific disciplines with a focus on identifying how "writer, audience, text, and rhetorical situation interact with one another in constructing a genre" as well as on genre features (p. 69). In studying students' response to this curriculum, they found that genre awareness (not explicit teaching of singular genres) may be an important threshold concept that opens pathways for transfer and is a core characteristic of writers who make significant gains in learning to write in unfamiliar situations.

Bawarshi's admonition that the content of FYW *be writing* is also taken up in Downs and Wardle's (2007) "Teaching about Writing, Righting Misconceptions," which directly addresses the need for a comprehensive pedagogical model that centers transfer. Their approach—more typically called writing about writing—was built from the situated, sociocultural, and activity-based theoretical orientations to writing that Petraglia (1995) and Russell (1995) stressed. This approach teaches writing studies content while also engaging students in discourse community and socially situated writing activity. More specifically, writing about writing foregrounds disciplinary writing and research as a way to (a) provide a context-rich writing environment for students, (b) help students understand that writing is a legitimate object of inquiry and writing studies is a discipline in its own right, and (c) provide writing experts (writing teachers) the real opportunity to serve as teaching and reading experts for their students. As Downs and Wardle (2007) stress, "unlike pedagogies that are so detached from writing studies' specialized knowledge as to deny it, the Intro pedagogy emerges from that knowledge and ethos" (p. 560). Reporting on two instances of this approach's application across two institutions, Downs and Wardle (2007) present positive findings for how this course "teaches potentially transferable conceptions of the activity of writing rather than 'basic' writing skills that are in fact highly specialized and contextualized" (p. 578). These include an increased sense of self-awareness about the activity of writing and students' increased ownership over their first-year experience. Findings also showed students' heightened confidence and ability in reading difficult texts and an increased awareness of the nature of research writing as entering into and contributing to ongoing discipline-specific conversations.

Next Steps: New Directions for/in Writing about Writing (Bird et al., 2019) connects writing about writing with questions of diversity and equity (Grant, 2019; Rudd, 2019; Wilson et al., 2019), a needed and under-researched area. For instance, in their chapter on Latinx writing and writers, Wilson et al., (2019) focus on students at a public Hispanic-serving institution who were introduced to readings from within the field on the language and writing of minoritized writers, and especially minoritized Latinx writers, and then guided to engage with those readings through personal experience. Wilson et al. (2019) found that "WAW allows us to foreground what is generally ignored in our composition handbooks and in our classrooms: the problematic nature of a one-size-fits-all 'standard' of writing and of English" (p. 94). Moreover, the course led to an "increase in the students' self-efficacy" and "their bi- and multiculturalism helped them to understand the readings" (p. 94). Grant (2019), in her study of a writing about writing approach for multilingual students, likewise stresses how her class "help[ed] lift students out of their linguistic dispossession" (p. 84). By connecting students with realistic research about writing and language, such courses counter dangerous literacy myths while also supporting students' potential to transfer their knowledge and confidence elsewhere.

Teaching for transfer (TFT), similarly draws from research and theory in writing studies to center content from the field, with a specific emphasis on reflection, as students build their own theories of writing for future guidance. As Yancey et al. (2014) explain:

> The study of transfer across contexts of writing that we share here is guided by these two questions: what difference does content in composition make in the transfer of writing knowledge and practice? and how can reflection as a systematic activity keyed to transfer support students' continued writing development? (p. 33)

Drawing most strongly from Beaufort's (2007) emphasis on reflecting across courses and situations and her framework for writing expertise, Yancey et al. (2014) developed and implemented their TFT course with the aim of researching its transfer value as compared to two other courses (a themed cultural studies course and an expressivist-centered course) that they study simultaneously. TFT is designed to foreground writing as content and activity, with specific emphasis on "key terms" or "conceptual anchors" (p. 42) that frame students' approaches and reflections. Such anchors guide "specific, reiterative, reflective practice linked to course goals, which themselves take transfer of knowledge and practice as the first priority" (p. 42). Findings from this study are heartening, although more and extended studies are needed. Yancey and colleagues did indeed discover that the students in the TFT course demonstrated increased transfer of writing-related knowledge—in contrast to their study's counterparts. Most revealing is the role that composition content and composition terms (conceptual anchors) played in helping students think about how writing works across contexts. Students' personal theories of writing grew from systematic and persistent reflection across the big picture, as students were cued to think about and imagine applications for other domains of writing in writing-related terms.

A smaller grouping of studies—Johnson & Krase (2012), who studied transfer of argument skills; Jackson (2010), who studied analysis; and Graff (2010), who studied argument development across multiple genres—has looked at the transfer of specific skills from FYW to argue that teaching for transfer is crucial for encouraging it. While not a subset of the teaching for transfer curriculum, these studies do show that when instructors explicitly teach for and talk about developing theories about writing (in addition to teaching the skills themselves), students are inclined to transfer the instructor's chosen focus. Through these cases, we are beginning to understand the importance of writing studies expertise for instructors teaching and designing courses—as writing content, writing practice, and theories of how learning works are likely all necessary for developing a course or curriculum where the explicit goal is to facilitate writing-related transfer.

Conclusion

As we discussed at the beginning of this chapter, the relationship between the possibility of transfer from FYW (or into FYW) had been met early on with skepticism. In *The End of Composition Studies*, Smit (2004) provoked the field when stating: "The question is how to construct a writing curriculum so that such instruction in transfer is commonplace, indeed a major feature of the curriculum" (p. 134). A growing tradition of transfer research in and around FYW is just now beginning to inform such a question; approaches like genre awareness, writing about writing, and teaching for transfer have integrated that research into curricula. These approaches would benefit from further examination, although early findings are positive. One goal now, while also continuing robust research inquiry into prior knowledge, dispositions, and the role of reading, is to push curricular research in a dialogical direction: continuing to move new empirical findings of best practices through pedagogies that are being further refined and sharpened, all the while understanding that a singular pedagogy and a singular writing course is not the panacea.

Beyond continued classroom research of the approaches just outlined, a central goal should be towards a transfer curriculum that centers students' histories, languages, and identities in ways that fully integrate social and linguistic justice in the aims and methods of the course. As extensive research in transfer and L2 writing shows (see Chapter 6, "Research on Transfer and Studies of Second Language Writing"), multilingual and multidialectal students come to writing with holistic and complex language repertoires that are deeply tied to identity and prior experience. A closer and more deliberate connection to L2 transfer research helps center language in the writing classroom and promotes writing studies scholars working from more inclusive research findings. Literacy studies scholarship likewise forwards this goal and, we suggest, should become more integrated into how FYW scholars consider student background, student identities, and students' right to bring their full, complex, and sometimes contradictory selves into acts of transfer (see Chapter 5, "Transfer Implications from Sociocultural and Sociohistorical Literacy Studies).

The foundation for writing transfer in FYW is strong, and while initial turns to transfer may have rested on proving the value of FYW to students and to institutions, it's clear from recent research that the value of teaching for transfer is not simply instrumental and transactional. Of course, it matters that students will be able to use writing-related knowledge gained in FYW in other settings. But as we found in the literature, attention to transfer into and from FYW is also about value to self and community. This latter point is especially prominent in the most recent turns in transfer pedagogy that unite student agency, empowerment, and students' rich discursive resources with writing transfer. As the field broadens to consider *why* transfer matters for first-year writers—to include value to professions and academic settings, value to communities, and value to identities and experiences—we benefit from diversified sets of theory, methods, and rationales for transfer. All of these are enhanced through a transdisciplinary orientation to writing transfer.

References

Alexander, K. P., DePalma, M. J., & Ringer, J. M. (2016). Adaptive remediation and the facilitation of transfer in multiliteracy center contexts. *Computers and Composition, 41,* 32–45.

Artemeva, N., & Fox, J. (2010). Awareness versus production: Probing students' antecedent genre knowledge. *Journal of Business and Technical Communication, 24*(4), 476–515.

Baird, N., & Dilger, B. (2017). How students perceive transitions: Dispositions and transfer in internships. *College Composition and Communication, 68*(4), 684–712.

Bawarshi, A. (2003). *Genre and the invention of the writer: Reconsidering the place of invention in composition.* Utah State University Press.

Bazerman, C. (1997). The life of genre, the life in the classroom. *Genre and writing: Issues, arguments, alternatives,* 19–26.

Beach, K. (1999). Consequential transitions: A sociocultural expedition beyond transfer in education. *Review of Research in Education, 24*(1), 101–139.

Beaufort, A. (2007). *College writing and beyond: A new framework for university writing instruction.* Utah State University Press.

Beaufort, A. (2012, January). College Writing and Beyond: Five years later. *Composition Forum, Vol. 26,* 1–13. https://compositionforum.com/issue/26/college-writing-beyond.php

Bergmann, L. S., & Zepernick, J. (2007). Disciplinarity and transfer: Students' perceptions of learning to write. *WPA: Writing Program Administration, 31*(1–-2), 124–149.

Bird, B., D. Downs, I.M. McCracken, & J. Rieman, eds, (2019). *Next steps: New directions for/in writing about writing.* Utah State University Press.

Carillo, E. C. (2015). *Securing a place for reading in composition: The importance of teaching for transfer.* Utah State University Press.

Carter, M. (1990). The idea of expertise: An exploration of cognitive and social dimensions of writing. *College Composition and Communication, 41*(3), 265–286.

Chiaburu, D. S. & Lindsay, D. R. (2008). Can do or will do? The importance of self-efficacy and instrumentality for training transfer. *Human Resource Development International, 11*(2), 199–206.

Clark, I. L., & Hernandez, A. (2011). Genre awareness, academic argument, and transferability. *The WAC Journal, 22,* 65–78.

Currie, P. (1993). Entering a disciplinary community: Conceptual activities required to write for one introductory university course. *Journal of Second Language Writing, 2*(2), 101–117.

DePalma, M. J. (2015). Tracing transfer across media: Investigating writers' perceptions of cross-contextual and rhetorical reshaping in processes of remediation. *College Composition and Communication, 66*(4), 615–642.

DePalma, M. J., & Alexander, K. P. (2015). A bag full of snakes: Negotiating the challenges of multimodal composition. *Computers and Composition, 37,* 182–200.

DePalma, M. J., & Ringer, J. M. (2011). Toward a theory of adaptive transfer: Expanding disciplinary discussions of "transfer" in second-language writing and composition studies. *Journal of Second Language Writing, 20*(2),134–147.

Davis, R. F. (2017). Pedagogy and learning in a digital ecosystem. *Understanding writing transfer: Implications for transformative student learning in higher education.* Stylus Publishing, LLC, 36.

Devitt, A. J., M. J. Reiff, & A. Bawarshi. (2004). *Scenes of writing: Strategies for composing with genres.* Longman.

Devitt, A. J. (2004). *Writing genres.* SIU Press.

Devitt, A. J. (2007). Transferability and genres. *The locations of composition,* 215–227.

Driscoll, D. L. (2011). Connected, disconnected, or uncertain: Student attitudes about future writing contexts and perceptions of transfer from first year writing to the disciplines. *Across the Disciplines, 8*(2). https://wac.colostate.edu/docs/atd/articles/driscoll2011.pdf

Driscoll, D. L., & Powell, R. (2016). States, traits, and dispositions: The impact of emotion on writing development and writing transfer across college courses and beyond. *Composition Forum, 34*(Summer). https://compositionforum.com/issue/34/states-traits.php

Driscoll, D. L., & Wells, J. (2012). Beyond knowledge and skills: Writing transfer and the role of student dispositions. *Composition Forum, 26*(Fall). http://compositionforum.com/issue/26/beyond-knowledge-skills.php

Downs, D., & Wardle, E. (2007). Teaching about writing, righting misconceptions: (Re)envisioning "First-Year Composition" as "Introduction to Writing Studies." *College Composition and Communication, 58*(4), 552–584.

Engle, R. A. (2006). Framing interactions to foster generative learning: A situative explanation of transfer in a community of learners classroom. *The Journal of the Learning Sciences, 15*(4), 451–498.

Foertsch, J. (1995). Where cognitive psychology applies: How theories about memory and transfer can influence composition pedagogy. *Written Communication, 12(3)*, 360–383.

Fraizer, D. (2010). First steps beyond first year: Coaching transfer after FYC. *WPA: Writing Program Administration, 33*(3), 34–57.

Graff, N. (2010). Teaching rhetorical analysis to promote transfer of learning. *Journal of Adolescent & Adult Literacy, 53*(5), 376–385.

Grant, G. (2019). "I am seen; I am my culture; and I can write": How WAW returns multilingual learners to voice, building self-efficacy, and rhetorical flexibility. In B. Bird, D. Downs, I. M. McCracken, & J. Rieman (Eds). *Next steps: New directions for/in writing about writing* (pp. 75–87). Utah State University Press.

Gogan, B. (2013). Reading at the threshold. *Across the Disciplines, 10*(4). https://wac.colostate.edu/docs/atd/reading/gogan.pdf

Haas, C., & L. Flower. (1988). Rhetorical reading strategies and the construction of meaning. *College Composition and Communication, 39*(2), 167–183.

Hammer, D., Elby, A., Scherr, R. E., & Redish, E. F. (2005). Resources, framing, and transfer. In J. P. Mestre (Ed.), *Transfer of learning from a modern multidisciplinary perspective*, (pp. 89–120). Information Age Publishing.

Hannah, M. A., & Saidy, C. (2014). Locating the terms of engagement: Shared language development in secondary to postsecondary writing transitions. *College Composition and Communication, 66*(1), 120–144.

Hassel, H., & Giordano, J. B. (2009). Transfer institutions, transfer of knowledge: The development of rhetorical adaptability and underprepared writers. *Teaching English in the Two-Year College, 37*(1), 24–40.

Jackson, B. (2010). Teaching the analytical life. *Composition Studies, 38*(2), 9–27.

Jarratt, S. C., Mack, K., Sartor, A., & Watson, S. E. (2009). Pedagogical memory: Writing, mapping, translating. *WPA: Writing Program Administration, 33*(1), 46–73.

Johnson, J. P., & Krase, E. (2012). Articulating claims and presenting evidence: A study of twelve student writers, from first-year composition to writing across the curriculum. *The WAC Journal, 23*, 31–48.

Johns, A. M. (1995). Teaching classroom and authentic genres: Initiating students into academic cultures and discourse. In D. Belcher & G. Braine (Eds.), *Academic writing in a second language: Essays on research and pedagogy* (pp. 277–291). Ablex Publishing Corporation.

Keller, D. (2013). *Chasing literacy: Reading and writing in an age of acceleration*. Utah State University Press.

Knutson, A. (2018). *"It's all part of an education": Case studies of writing knowledge transfer across academic and social media domains among four feminist college students* (Publication No. 11006938). [Doctoral dissertation, The University of Michigan]. ProQuest Dissertations Publishing.

Kutney, J. P. (2008). Guaranteeing the failure of first-year composition: Four assumptions about writing expertise that support an unattainable standard for transfer. *International Journal of Learning, 15*(8), 223–227.

Light, R. (2008). Complex learning theory—its epistemology and its assumptions about learning: implications for physical education. *Journal of Teaching in Physical Education, 27*(1), 21–37.

Light, R., & Fawns, R. (2003). Knowing the game: Integrating speech and action in games teaching through TGfU. *Quest, 55*(2), 161–176.

Maimon, E. P. (1983). Maps and genres: Exploring connections in the arts and sciences. In W.B. Horner (Ed.), *Composition and literature: Bridging the gap* (pp. 110–125). University of Chicago Press.

McCarthy, L. P. (1987). A stranger in strange lands: A college student writing across the curriculum. *Research in the Teaching of English, 21*(3), 233–265.

Miller, C. R. (1984). Genre as social action. *Quarterly Journal of Speech, 70*(2), 151–176.

Moore, J. (2012). Mapping the questions: The state of writing-related transfer research. *Composition Forum, 26.* http://compositionforum.org/issue/26/map-questions-transfer-research.php

Moore, J. (2017). Five essential principles of writing transfer. In J. Moore & R. Bass (Eds.), *Understanding writing transfer: Implications for transformative student learning in higher education,* (pp. 1–12). Stylus.

Nelms, R. G, & Dively, R. L. (2007). Perceived roadblocks to transferring knowledge from first-year composition to writing-intensive major courses: A pilot study. *WPA: Writing Program Administration, 31*(1), 214–240.

Nowacek, R. S. (2011). *Agents of integration: Understanding transfer as a rhetorical act.* Southern Illinois University Press.

Nowacek, R., & James, H. (2017). Building mental maps: Implications from research on reading in the STEM disciplines. In P. Sullivan, H. Tinberg, & S. Blau (Eds.), *Deep reading: Teaching reading in the writing classroom,* (pp. 291–312). NCTE.

Perkins, D. N., & Salomon, G. (1988). Teaching for transfer. *Educational Leadership, 46*(1), 22–32.

Petraglia, J. (Ed.). (1995). *Reconceiving writing, rethinking writing instruction.* Lawrence Erlbaum..

Qualley, D. (2016). Building a conceptual topography of the transfer terrain. In C. M. Anson and J.L. Moore (Eds). *Critical transitions: Writing and the question of transfer* (pp. 69–106). The WAC Clearinghouse.

Reiff, M. J., & Bawarshi, A. (2011). Tracing discursive resources: How students use prior genre knowledge to negotiate new writing contexts in first-year composition. *Written Communication, 28*(3), 312–337.

Rifenburg, J. M. (2020). Student-athletes' metacognitive strategy knowledge. *Composition Forum, 43*(Spring). https://compositionforum.com/issue/43/student-athletes.php

Rifenburg, J. M., & Forester, B. G. (2018). First-year cadets' conceptions of general education writing at a senior military college. *Teaching & Learning Inquiry, 6*(1), 52–66.

Robertson, L., Taczak, K., & Yancey, K. B. (2012). Notes toward a theory of prior knowledge and its role in college composers' transfer of knowledge and practice. *Composition Forum, 26*(Fall). http://compositionforum.com/issue/26/prior-knowledge-transfer.php

Roozen, K. (2008). Journalism, poetry, stand-up comedy, and academic literacy: Mapping the interplay of curricular and extracurricular literate activities. *Journal of Basic Writing,* 5–34.

Roozen, K. (2009). "Fan Fic-ing" English studies: A case study exploring the interplay of vernacular literacies and disciplinary engagement. *Research in the Teaching of English, 44*(2),136–169.

Roozen, K. (2010). Tracing trajectories of practice: Repurposing in one student's developing disciplinary writing processes. *Written Communication, 27*(3), 318–354.

Roozen, K., & Erickson, J. (2017). *Expanding literate landscapes: Persons, practices, and sociohistoric perspectives of disciplinary development.* Computers and Composition Digital Press/Utah State University Press. http://ccdigitalpress.org/expanding/.

Rosinski, P. (2016). Students' perceptions of the transfer of rhetorical knowledge between digital self-sponsored writing and academic writing: The importance of authentic contexts and reflection. In C.M. Anson & J.L. Moore (Eds.), *Critical transitions: Writing and the question of transfer* (pp. 251–276). WAC Clearinghouse.

Rounsaville, A., Goldberg, R., & Bawarshi, A. (2008). From incomes to outcomes: FYW students' prior genre knowledge, meta-cognition, and the question of transfer. *WPA: Writing Program Administration, 32*(1), 97–112.

Rounsaville, A. (2012). Selecting genres for transfer: The role of uptake in students' antecedent genre knowledge. In *Composition Forum, 26*(Fall). compositionforum.com/issue/26/selecting-genres-uptake.php

Rounsaville, A. (2017). Worlding genres through lifeworld analysis: New directions for genre pedagogy and uptake awareness. In *Composition Forum*, *37*(Fall). compositionforum.com/issue/37/worlding.php

Rudd, M. (2019). Why I keep teaching writing about writing in Qatar: Expanding literacies, developing metacognition, and learning for transfer. In Bird, B., D. Downs, I.M. McCracken, & J. Rieman (Eds.), *Next steps: New directions for/in writing about writing* (pp. 101–111). Utah State University Press.

Russell, D. (1995). Activity theory and its implications for writing instruction. In J. Petraglia (Ed.), *Reconceiving writing, rethinking writing instruction* (pp. 51–78). Lawrence Erlbaum.

Spack, R. (1988). Initiating students into the academic discourse community: How far should we go? *TESOL Quarterly, 22*(1), 29–51.

Smit, D. W. (2004). *The end of composition studies*. Southern Illinois University Press.

Sweeney, M. A., & M. McBride. (2015). Difficulty paper (dis)connections: Understanding the threads students weave between their reading and writing. *College Composition and Communication, (66)*4, 591–614.

VanKooten, Crystal. (2020). *Transfer across media: Using digital video in the teaching of writing*. Computers and Composition Digital Press/Utah State University Press. https://ccdigitalpress.org/book/transfer-across-media/index.html

Wardle, E. (2007). Understanding "transfer" from FYC: Preliminary results of a longitudinal study. *WPA: Writing Program Administration, 31*(1–2), 65–85.

Wardle, E. (2009). "Mutt genres" and the goal of FYC: Can we help students write the genres of the university? *College Composition & Communication, 60*(4), 765–789.

Wardle, E. (2012). Creative repurposing for expansive learning: Considering "problem-exploring" and "answer-getting" dispositions in individuals and fields. *Composition Forum, 26*(Fall). http://compositionforum.com/issue/26/creative-repurposing.php

Wardle, E. & Adler-Kassner, L. (2019). Threshold concepts as a foundation for "writing about writing" pedagogies. In B. Bird, D. Downs, I.M. McCracken, & J. Rieman (Eds). *Next steps: New directions for/in writing about writing* (pp. 23–34). Utah State University Press.

Wilson, R. A., & Foglia, L. (2017). Embodied cognition. In E. N. Zalta (Ed.), *Stanford encyclopedia of philosophy* (Spring 2017 Edition). https://plato.stanford.edu/archives/spr2017/entries/embodied-cognition/.

Wilson, N., Jackson, R., & Vera, V. (2019). Vignette: *El ensayo*: Latinxs writing about writing. In B. Bird, D. Downs, I. M. McCracken, & J. Rieman (Eds.), *Next steps: New directions for/in writing about writing* (pp. 88–96). Utah State University Press.

Witte, S. P. (1992). Context, text, intertext: Toward a constructivist semiotic of writing. *Written Communication*, *9*(2), 237–308.

Yancey, K. B. (2004). Made not only in words: Composition in a new key. *College Composition and Communication*, *56*(2), 297–328.

Yancey, K. B., Robertson, L., & Taczak, K. (2014). *Writing across contexts: Transfer, composition, and sites of writing*. Utah State University Press.

8 Infrastructure for the Transfer of Writing Knowledge: Writing Across the Curriculum and Writing in the Disciplines

Writing across the curriculum (WAC) and Writing in the disciplines (WID) approaches to writing education are inescapably shaped by the transfer of writing knowledge. These movements came into being partly in response to concerns that first-year writing courses did not support transfer and continue to exist to support such transfer beyond the first-year writing course—whether through general practices of writing to learn (WAC) or particular practices of writing in discipline-specific genres (WID). Differently put, concerns about the transfer of writing knowledge are central to WAC and WID approaches to writing education. Questions that have motivated the initiation and continued growth of WAC and WID programs—What should first-year writing prepare students for? How do students develop writing knowledge over the course of a college education? How do students learn to write for their disciplines or professions?—are at least in part about transfer, either implicitly or explicitly. In fact, as this chapter will show, much of the research on WAC and WID is premised on the transfer of writing knowledge, which is to say that the transfer—how it does or doesn't happen, across courses, contexts, and curriculum—is a perennial exigency for research on writing education across the curriculum, in the disciplines, and over time.

WAC/WID research that takes up transfer generally follows two main areas of concern: first, that first-year writing as general writing skills instruction (GWSI) is an abstraction with no context or content and cannot offer transferable practices to disciplinary, professional, or extra-curricular contexts (Crowley, 1998; Downs & Wardle, 2007; Petraglia, 1995; Russell, 1995; Wardle, 2009); and second, that college students experience a range of missed connections that inhibits their writing development: among early writing courses and those encountered later in the disciplines,[8] among disciplinary writing courses or genres,[9] among different courses in the same discipline,[10] or among academic, personal, and professional contexts.[11] Scholars who state their exigency for studying transfer in these terms are often responding to pressure from colleagues or stakeholders to justify the existence of writing courses, programs, or the field of writing studies. Because of the ubiquity and assumed expense of such a widely required course as first year writing, writing studies researchers—and the stakeholders they are often gathering data to speak to—often study transfer in WAC and WID programs to better understand what writing skills, practices, or competencies best support later student learning and thus should be taught in a first-year course.

The quiet presence of transfer in much research on student writing development across college curricula indicates that the concept is found in the background rather than the foreground of WAC / WID researchers' purview. Especially in large-scale or longitudinal studies of writing that capture student transfer activity simply by virtue of their scope, transfer appears in study conclusions or implications rather than in design or research questions (Beaufort, 2007; Carroll, 2002; Chiseri-Strater, 1991; Fishman et al., 2005; Herrington & Curtis, 2000; McCarthy, 1987; Soliday, 2011; Sommers & Saltz, 2004; Stern-

---

8. For studies of transfer among early writing courses and those encountered later in the disciplines see Beaufort, 2007; Boone et al., 2012; Carroll, 2002; Herrington & Curtis, 2000; Smit, 2004; Yancey et al., 2014.

9. For studies of transfer among disciplinary writing courses or genres see McCarthy, 1987; Nowacek, 2011; Soliday, 2011; Walvoord & McCarthy, 1990; Zamel & Spack, 2004.

10. For studies of transfer among different courses in the same discipline see Beaufort, 2007; Haas, 1994; Herrington, 1985.

11. For studies of transfer among academic, personal, and professional contexts see Chiseri-Strater, 1991; Collier, 2014; Fishman et al., 2005; Herrington & Curtis, 2000; Reiff & Bawarshi, 2011; Roozen, 2009, 2010; Rounsaville, 2012; Sternglass, 1997.

glass, 1997; Walvoord & McCarthy, 1990). However, to trace writers moving knowledge across or among contexts is to witness transfer, and thus, acknowledging transfer even when it is implicit can give explicit insight into the stops and starts of writing knowledge development and expertise: the complications, disconnects, uneven acquisition, regressions, or unstated connections that students experience as they attempt to transfer their writing knowledge across curricular or disciplinary settings (Boone et al., 2012; Melzer, 2014). Therefore, this chapter, while focusing on WAC/WID research that discusses transfer explicitly, will also include some work that assumes or alludes to transfer implicitly.

The review below includes scholarship that treats writing as a general learning skill (writing as generalizable activities like freewriting, journaling, note-taking, reflecting etc.); a socialized disciplinary activity (largely to do with genres); a process or procedural activity (steps taken through an assignment or in a writer's composition routines); the activity that compromises the discipline of writing studies itself (writing knowledge as a unique research-based domain); or simply as a vessel through which assessment of content occurs. While some of these treatments of writing, which often reveal what researchers think writing is or can do in a college curriculum, are easily separable into more procedural WAC or declarative WID categories, most of them blur these lines between generalizable and situated activities. This is to say that much of the research below weaves in elements of both WAC and WID approaches as scholars pursue questions not about what WAC and WID approaches really are, but about how writing and learning are happening, in varied forms, in their classrooms and programs. This chapter adopts a "synthesis" approach to WAC/WID to highlight WAC/WID relationships in the reviewed work, which in turn shows the multi-directionality of transfer, as knowledge moves "up" vertically in a discipline and "out" across courses and extra-curricular writing contexts that students encounter over time (Bizzell, 1982/2003; Ford, 2004; Teich, 1987). This capacious frame helps account for the ways that the WAC/WID relationship mirrors what transfer research from cognitive psychology shows us: that *general* cognitive skills" exist, but they "function in *contextual* ways" (Perkins & Salomon, 1989, p. 19, emphasis added). This chapter follows that cue by presenting sections organized by researchers' common problems or questions about the transfer of writing knowledge in WAC/WID approaches, which cohere around what students are learning about writing with or through transfer, what instructors are or should be doing to support that transfer, how genre plays a role in that transfer, and the kinds of courses or curricula that best support student transfer and learning in and across disciplines or curricular contexts.

Student Knowledge about Disciplinary Writing Transfer

Much WAC/WID scholarship seeks to understand how students transfer writing knowledge among contexts and over time through their experiences of single courses or programs,[12] across pairs of courses, usually first-year writing and a disciplinary course,[13] or over time on (and off) single campuses.[14] These scholars study students' knowledge of disciplinary writing in order to understand the efficacy of a range of programmatic efforts, including genre instruction, student interpretation of course requirements or sequences, and impact of feedback practices or instructional focus on rhetorical awareness or the writing process. In particular, although these studies offer a range of perspectives into students' disciplinary writing knowledge and the potential for its transfer, the studies largely conclude with a similar take away: that students' transfer of writing knowledge—from general to disciplinary courses, across campus careers, or longitudinally over time—is well supported by intentionally making writing knowledge transparent, explicit, and relevant to students' lives.

---

12. For studies of how students transfer writing knowledge through their experiences of single courses or programs see Bergmann & Zepernick, 2007; Carter et al., 2007; Gilje, 2010; Hilgers et al., 1995; Hilgers et al., 1999; Jarratt et al., 2009.

13. For studies of how students transfer writing knowledge across pairs of courses, usually first-year writing and a disciplinary course, see Adler-Kassner et al., 2012; Ahrenhoerster, 2006; Fallon et al., 2009; Johnson & Krase, 2012; Stretcher et al., 2010.

14. For studies of how students transfer writing knowledge over time on single campuses see Beaufort, 2007; Carroll, 2002; Chiseri-Strater, 1991; Fishman et al., 2005; Herrington & Curtis, 2000; McCarthy, 1987; Nowacek, 2011; Sommers & Saltz, 2004; Spack, 1997; Sternglass, 1997; Walvoord & McCarthy, 1990.

Single Course Contexts

In a study that sought to capture what students come to know in a single course, as shaped through the relationship between disciplinary writing knowledge and more generalized forms of writing to learn activities, Carter et al. (2007) conducted student interviews to understand how writing supports learning in a biology lab. Following a situated approach to cognition and learning (Lave, 1988; Russell, 1995; Russell, 1997), they hypothesized that disciplinary writing, in the sciences in this study, promoted a certain kind of socialization into disciplinary learning. Thus, their study hoped to understand how writing in the disciplines encouraged learning in the disciplines. Interviews with ten students writing lab reports in biology revealed six categories of learning activities, including learning by writing in general, by writing in specific genres (the lab report and "reports for future reference"), by affiliated learning behaviors like reading or searching, and by learning in contrasting contexts or modes. Of these, transfer was most implicated in disciplinary learning enacted through writing reports for future reference and through learning in other contexts. That is, two of their findings show that writing to learn in biology is supported specifically through transfer activities: Students reported using lab reports in future learning situations, transferring the disciplinary writing knowledge to different contexts and continuing to learn from them, sometimes describing an "awareness that the lab reports written for this biology course could be used as a basic reference in more advanced courses in the same or a similar field" (Carter et al., 2007, p. 291). Students also reported that writing biology lab reports "has led or would lead to" their report writing "elsewhere," describing that lab report writing "carried over" to disciplinary writing in other science labs (p. 292). In these ways, students understood the lab report as an activity situating them not only in their immediate lab's community of practice, but also acting as a "vehicle" or a "link" that connected them to a broader scientific community encompassing their other science courses and their future work (p. 297). In essence, the lab report was an "apprenticeship genre" (p. 296) that allowed for students to participate in the biology lab community's ways of knowing, showing that writing is a key form of "legitimate peripheral participation" (Lave & Wenger, 1991) as well as the ways students come to understand disciplines through acts of transfer.

With a similar single-course focus, Gilje (2010) differently complicates writing knowledge by looking at the transfer not of textual or procedural writing knowledge but of "meaning-making" knowledge across modes that include writing. Gilje's study of a filmmaking course in a Danish high school is not concerned with the acquisition of writing or disciplinary knowledge but rather with how students can carry meaning-making practices intentionally across modes and over time, showing "how a specific meaning is transformed and transduced within and across modes" (p. 495). He simply happens to focus on one discipline, which is film. To do this, Gilje collected interactional and textual data around the creation of one film scene in a media education class at an urban secondary school in Oslo. Focusing on students' composing practices across modes, including visual, written, and oral, he traced the "mediated action" occurring during composing—students' negotiations, their deployments of semiotic resources, and their collaboration and distributed agency—while also analyzing the transformation and transduction of meaning across modes (p. 499). Triangulating data sources of recorded observation, student notes, and final films, Gilje traced the trajectory of one particular meaning as it evolved through the composition of one key film scene.

Following a meaning-making trajectory (Kell, 2006) allowed Gilje to see that although students used diverse semiotic resources including synopsis and manuscript writing, storyboard creation, filming, and oral postproduction revision, students were unable to transfer their "particular meaning" across modes and over time because they downplayed the role these resources played in each composing context. For example, the students wrote their film synopsis according to teacher expectations but could not transfer this writing "[tool] for thinking" about plot points when revising the film's eventual narrative. In other words, students' use of semiotic resources, including writing, depended on how intentionally resources were deployed across specific contexts (Gilje, 2010, p. 516). Echoing a common theme across transfer research in and beyond writing studies (see Chapter 2), Gilje's study stresses the level of explicit instruction on transfer that students need to understand how meaning-making carries and shifts across modes, genres, and contexts.

Transfer from General Writing to Disciplinary Courses

Scholars also seek to understand how students transfer writing knowledge from general to disciplinary writing courses, even embedding assumptions about this transferability in "from. . . to" construction in titles (Johnson & Krase, 2012). Such analytic linking occurs in Adler-Kassner et al.'s (2012) examination of the transfer of threshold concepts across linked writing and history general education courses, in which text-based interviews showed that students concurrently enrolled in both courses experienced shifts—from tacit to more consciously discursive—in their rhetorical understanding of audience, purpose, and context. Ahrenhoerster (2006) also used course comparison—first-year writing to communication or history—to study how well first-year writing "proficiencies" (including mastery of punctuation and grammar rules, using diction properly and constructing effective sentences; effective organization; effective argument and idea development; appropriate depth of critical reading and thinking [p. 22]) transferred into subsequent disciplinary essays, finding in analysis of 115 essays and a large-scale student survey that the disciplinary essays were of similar quality to those in the first-year course, with highest proficiency in organization. Because students could have entered the first-year course with these existing proficiencies, Ahrenhoerster's study highlights the correlation of these skills more than a clear transfer of learning from the first-year writing course to a disciplinary course.

In a study that similarly traces transfer from general to disciplinary courses, Fallon et al. (2009) gathered data—students' self-reports of their writing skills and faculty-scored psychology essays—to understand how writing skills transferred from first-year writing to an assignment in a subsequent psychology course. In comparing the survey and scored papers, the researchers found that while students who reported using a drafting process (74%) had higher paper scores, as well as higher final grades in both courses, than those who did not draft, they found it hard to isolate this relationship as evidence of transfer of writing knowledge from English to psychology writing (p. 44). Therefore, in a follow-up intervention, Fallon et al. incorporated elements to support high-road transfer, helping students "bridge" their courses through explicitly modeled drafting in-class and in faculty feedback. The researchers found that this intervention produced a "distinct relationship" between student confidence and performance (p. 47).

Johnson and Krase (2012) similarly designed a study to follow twelve students from first-year writing to a later range of disciplinary writing courses. They collected data from several sources: students' instructor-scored FYW essays, a NSSE questionnaire in which students self-reported their experiences in FYW and WID coursework, three extended qualitative interviews, and portfolios of students' written work. They analyzed this data for the objectives shared by the university's first-year and disciplinary writing courses, finding that ten of the twelve research participants demonstrated "significant progress" toward practicing successful writing, understanding main features of writing, adapting writing to reader expectations, and learning conventions of usage in their fields (p. 7). Researchers attributed this success to a set of motivational characteristics (like willingness to seek out feedback or revise) as well as to appropriate instructional design with clear expectations and guidelines for writing.

Tracing transfer from technical communication to engineering courses, Ford (2004) found evidence of the transfer of rhetorical knowledge—defined as audience awareness, sense of purpose, organization, use of visuals, professional appearance, and style. Analyzing the self-reported conceptual, behavioral, and rhetorical strategies and skills of twelve seniors through group think-aloud protocols, scored student texts, and student and instructor interviews, she found that rhetorical strategies taught in technical communication courses did appear in students' later disciplinary texts, especially in students' process-based and rhetorical approaches to writing like considering audience and purpose. Students reported that they learned these rhetorical strategies in their technical communication courses and did rely on them when completing writing assignments. In particular, they relied on modeled or template-based rhetorical strategies more often than abstract concepts like audience.

Researchers have also enacted this from/to analysis at the graduate level, as in Stretcher et al.'s (2010) research on graduate students' transfer of communication skills from an MBA communication course to a subsequent content-based MBA finance course. Specifically, the researchers followed business communication strategies such as "organizing their ideas, composing coherent messages, and presenting data in a format that is understandable to non-specialists in the finance field" (p. 2). Stretcher et al. were troubled that the MBA students used such communication practices in their jobs but couldn't see the purpose of the communication course in relation to the finance course. Therefore, the group sought to isolate which specific communication strategies students applied to the finance course with the ultimate curricular goal of students building on their communication competencies over time. The authors traced this transfer through several methods: (a) the MBA students' application of the communication course strategies to collaborative assignments in the finance course like written reports, oral presentations, and case studies; (b) a student survey about how they perceived the difficulty of these writing assignments, with an additional survey section for students who had taken the communication course that asked about their recollection of the course and application of its strategies; (c) a group oral presentation of a case study scored by a non-specialist professor; and (d) another student survey about how the communication course prepared them for working in teams. Stretcher et al.'s analysis of this data found that students most frequently mentioned organization and citation strategies from the communication course but found that the course had a minimal impact on students' perceived difficulty of the finance course writing. They did not find significant differences in students' assignment grades whether or not they had taken the communication course.

Transfer Across Multiple Courses on Single Campuses

Several studies also have sought to understand what students come to know across multiple courses in WAC/WID or writing-intensive programs, in effect capturing the culture of writing on their campuses. For example, the extensive writing-intensive course requirements at the University of Hawaii-Manoa led Hilgers et al. (1995) to study their students' experiences of the requirements. Specifically, they looked for evidence that students' writing knowledge was impacted by taking the three or more writing-intensive classes that were required of them. Hilgers and his colleagues interviewed 82 seniors and found through inductive analysis several themes in students' understandings of what they had learned in their writing-intensive courses, including writing-based skills and problem-solving abilities. Their survey data, in which 78% of respondents reported becoming better writers through their writing-intensive curriculum, showed that "the key factor [students] pointed to is not the amount of practice they got or the quantity they wrote; it is the amount of feedback that their course instructors and their peers gave their writing" (p. 79). Compellingly, Hilgers et al. also found that students had typically taken five, rather than the required three, writing-intensive classes, and none complained about the number of these courses required to graduate, showing that students perceived some purpose for so many writing courses, reporting increased confidence as writers and self-efficacy in the learning process.

Hilgers et al.'s (1999) follow-up study, which shared findings from beginning- and end-of-semester interviews with 34 students, aimed to understand first, how the discipline affected students' understanding of writing tasks and second, what students completing the university's five-course writing requirement reported that they know about writing. Their interview data revealed several patterns relevant to students' transfer of disciplinary writing knowledge: (a) students were more invested in writing courses in, rather than outside of, their majors, and that investment extended to writing assignments for which they chose their own topics relevant to their major or future work; (b) students made connections between disciplinary writing and future professional writing, thinking that disciplinary writing tasks predicted their success in similar professional tasks and that they needed to simultaneously write for their teacher and a hypothetical disciplinary audience; and (c) students made connections between disciplinary knowledge and the ways of researching and writing that suited that knowledge, leading them to learn not only about content but about the nature of research, methodology, and questions that matter in their discipline.

In response to their second research question on what students reported they knew about writing in general, the researchers found that students were most of all aware of the writing process, understanding it as "a set of problems to be solved and goals to be reached" (Hilgers et al., 1999, p. 334) although they also were aware of general benefits of writing and believed it promoted learning, thinking (organizing and refining ideas, thinking more deeply), and confidence. From these findings, the researchers conclude that although students seemed much more invested in writing-intensive courses as disciplinary and future preparation rather than as general writing-to-learn practices, the researchers believe students were practicing writing-to-learn across disciplinary contexts without labeling it as such. They suggest more explicit naming of these strategies by instructors would help students make connections, or transfer their writing knowledge, among "apparently disparate" writing and disciplinary contexts that students already do "haphazardly" so that students can write to "solve potentially related sets of epistemological or rhetorical problems" (p. 348).

With findings that highlight instead students' *low* investment in campus writing courses, Bergmann and Zepernick's (2007) study unknowingly captured campus writing perceptions that likely affected transfer. They asked students, in student-led focus groups, how they described their own writing processes, which unexpectedly yielded data about the larger peer culture of writing on their campus. Across six focus groups of seven to ten participants from a variety of departments, the researchers noticed a surprising similarity in student beliefs about writing development that students seemed to be carrying across campus (p. 126). These beliefs, which arose through inductive analysis of focus group transcripts, included: (a) that writing in first-year writing courses (which students conflated with literature courses) is personal and expressive (not academic), and therefore instructor feedback feels subjective and intrusive; (b) this expressive writing is natural, like conversation, and has to do with more personal preference than informed academic judgment; (c) disciplinary writing, on the other hand, has standards, rules, norms, and conventions; and (d) students do transfer writing knowledge about process, audience, and purpose across contexts, but do not locate learning that knowledge in writing courses, first-year or disciplinary, but rather in life and work experience. Bergmann and Zepernick call these beliefs about writing and learning to write an unrecognized element of student peer culture on their campus, concluding that such perceptions may limit students' abilities to recognize the writing knowledge they do learn in first-year writing and transfer it to other writing, particularly disciplinary, contexts. Regarding transfer, they echo findings from psychology regarding students' mindful monitoring of transfer (see Chapter 2), suggesting that the primary obstacle, then, to writing knowledge transfer is "not that students are *unable* to recognize situations outside FYC in which skills can be used, but that students *do not look for* such situations because they believe that skills learned in FYC have no value in any other setting" (p. 139).

Transfer in Longitudinal Studies

Finally, scholars have captured students' transfer of writing knowledge in large-scale, longitudinal studies of writing development that either follow the development of a small number of writers during college or capture the development of a large number of students on a single campus.[15] These large-scale studies all use multiple data sources and methods with a sociocultural theoretical framework, in particular classroom observation, student and teacher interviews, and student text analysis, to understand the writing experiences of one or a handful of college students over time, from a single semester through postgraduate years (Beaufort, 2007; Carroll, 2002; Chiseri-Strater, 1991; Herrington & Curtis, 2000; McCarthy, 1987; Nowacek, 2011; Soliday, 2011; Sternglass, 1997; Walvoord & McCarthy, 1990). Interestingly, as some of the most extensive studies of student writing completed in the US, they are also projects in which the phenomenon of transfer is only implicit. For example, in both McCarthy (1987) and Herrington and Curtis' (2000) reports of their longitudinal research, transfer is somewhat incidental to their research questions—Herrington and Curtis in fact never mention the term explicitly in their book. Instead, Herrington and Curtis present the development of four college writers' identities through extended case studies, showing how academic writing impacts their sense of self during college and beyond. The project's affinities with transfer research appear in the conclusion, when Herrington and Curtis stress that for student writing development to occur, instructors must make explicit the implicit "whys" of academic and disciplinary conventions, not just the "hows" that are more often taught (p. 387). Thus, in addition to an early articulation of the social contours of writing development, Herrington and Curtis argue for what has become one norm of teaching for transfer, that unveiling tacit disciplinary knowledge helps students navigate the "dizzying array" of writing expectations and norms they encounter as they develop their connected personal and academic writing over time (p. 387).

Similarly, McCarthy's (1987) study of one college student, Dave, struggling to apply what he learned in first-year writing to subsequent courses in poetry and cell biology did not set out to understand the transfer of his writing knowledge. In fact, the research article reporting on the study only mentions transfer once, concluding that "skills mastered in one situation, such as the thesis-subpoint organization in Freshman Composition, did not . . . automatically transfer to new contexts with differing problems and language and differing amounts of knowledge that he controlled" (p. 261). Through rigorous analysis

---

15. See Rogers (2010) for a thorough summary of longitudinal studies of writing development.

of Dave's writing behaviors and feedback engagement with his three instructors, including identifying, classifying, and counting his "conscious concerns" as he wrote during a think-aloud protocol, McCarthy concludes that writing success occurs most for students who deduce without being explicitly taught "the content, structure, language, ways of thinking, and types of evidence required in that discipline and by that teacher" (p. 233). That is, she turns to transfer because transfer was *not* occurring for Dave, finding that in each class he encountered, he believed that the disciplinary writing was "totally unlike anything he had ever done before" (p. 234), leading him to write like an academic newcomer or "beginning language user" in each context (p. 261). Like Herrington and Curtis, McCarthy points readers to the "social contexts those classrooms provide for writing," including the social functions writing served there and the social roles available to the student writers when they composed, as one explanation for these missed opportunities for student writing development (p. 261).

With a similar analytic focus on socialization in new writing contexts, the Harvard Study of Undergraduate Writing (Sommers, 2008; Sommers & Saltz, 2004) provides a large-scale institutional example that, due to research design, includes elements of WAC/WID approaches to education in their broad data collection. Although not explicitly invoking transfer, Sommers and Saltz (2004) try to understand why some college students improve and engage with writing over time while others lose interest. The Harvard Study of Undergraduate Writing followed 422 students from the Harvard Class of 2001 through their college careers "to see undergraduate writing through their eyes" (Sommers & Saltz, 2004, p. 126). Researchers randomly sampled 65 of these participants to interview each semester alongside a semester's worth of graded and commented-on writing assignments. In analyzing not just student writing, but also how student language about writing changes over time, Sommers and Saltz isolated two central student perceptions: (a) students who perceive themselves to be novices seem most able to learn new writing skills and (b) students who perceive writing to be a long-term opportunity to "write about something that matters to them" seem most able to remain interested and engaged in their college writing (p. 127). In particular, their analysis shows how engaged first-year novices experience change within themselves as writers rather than in their texts—they adopt an approach of reciprocity, understanding "what they can 'get' and 'give' through writing" (p. 146), which sustains their interest and allows for change over time. Students in the study who were not able to take on a novice role—and were not modeled or granted that role through instructor feedback—and instead relied on already-mastered high school writing methods did not experience change, in themselves or in their texts (p. 140). Sommers and Saltz ultimately conclude that students build on their writing knowledge over time by approaching their first year as novices who are subsequently invited into disciplinary writing and thinking expertise, which helps them move on from their novice position to "question sources, develop ideas, and comfortably offer interpretations" (p. 146).

On the other hand, empirical studies like Beaufort (2007) and Nowacek (2011) do explicitly focus on the transfer of writing knowledge in their research designs and questions. Beaufort's longitudinal case study of Tim, a college student writing in first-year composition, history, and engineering courses, and eventually at work, tracks his struggles transferring writing knowledge across these contexts. The book argues that Tim's struggles are the result of never being explicitly taught the knowledge that supports writing success. Beaufort's contribution is a clear articulation of what that knowledge is, using rich ethnographic detail to concretize the framework of overlapping knowledge domains (previously developed in her ethnography *Writing in the Real World*) she says are necessary for success with writing projects: discourse community knowledge, genre knowledge, rhetorical knowledge, subject matter knowledge, and writing process knowledge. Her conclusion and appendices show how curricula can be designed to explicitly teach writing concepts that live in these domains, aiming to foster a meta-awareness of how they enact those concepts in their writing so they become transferable writing skills in future writing contexts. Like McCarthy (1987) and Herrington and Curtis (2000) above, Beaufort's three principles for facilitating the transfer of writing knowledge anticipated what now are common pedagogical suggestions in transfer research (taken up later in this chapter): (a) generalizing specific writing tasks into abstract writing concepts (e.g. genre) to make instructors' tacit conceptual knowledge explicit to students; (b) providing students opportunities to practice applying those concepts in a variety of writing assignments and situations; and (c) facilitating students' meta-awareness of that practice and potential for application in new writing contexts.

Nowacek's (2011) study of a three-semester interdisciplinary learning community also aims to explicitly study the transfer of writing knowledge but in doing so complicates much of the previous empirical work on transfer. By studying writing in a general education interdisciplinary learning seminar, which linked three courses in history, literature, and religious studies, Nowacek was able to capture both general and discipline-specific writing instruction received and taught by 18 students and three team-teaching instructors in the second semester of the seminar. Building on a theoretical framework informed by rhetorical genre studies, sociocultural approaches to transfer, and activity theory, Nowacek traced how students experienced genres as social and rhetorical resources, but more so as catalysts for making conceptual connections across disciplinary expectations occurring in the same classroom (p. 12). Most centrally, she offers a theory of transfer as dynamic "recontextualization"—not mere application but adaptation and transformation—of writing knowledge, with students as "agents of integration" who enact rhetorical strategies that help them "see" interdisciplinary connections (perceive them) and then "sell" those connections (convey them to others) in their writing, to "justify the value of the connection within the text itself" (p. 53). Nowacek concludes that instructors (and writing center tutors), too, are agents in students' successful transfer of writing knowledge, acting as "handlers" who can cue or fail to cue potential acts of transfer. Expanding on Beaufort's (2007) recommendations regarding meta-awareness, Nowacek reminds readers that transfer is never easily studied or taught: teaching students meta-awareness of their writing knowledge can support but not always guarantee transfer (and sometimes transfer happens without writers' conscious awareness), and even in an intentionally connected interdisciplinary writing community, instructors and students struggle to reconcile contrary or contradictory writing values and conventions.

Interestingly, no matter the design of the studies reviewed above—single course, across general to disciplinary courses, across a single campus, or longitudinally over time—studies about student knowledge of disciplinary writing almost all conclude that explicit instruction of disciplinary writing values, beliefs, genres, expectations, and practices is essential to transfer. For example, studies that trace transfer of writing knowledge from general to disciplinary courses show that students' disciplinary rhetorical knowledge can shift from tacit to more conscious (Adler-Kassner et al., 2012) when that knowledge is made explicit through modeling and clear disciplinary writing expectations (Fallon et al., 2009; Ford, 2004; Johnson & Krase, 2012). Studies of campus writing cultures or programs (Bergmann & Zepernick, 2007; Hilgers et al., 1999) or writers over time (Beaufort, 2007; Herrington & Curtis, 2000; McCarthy, 1987) show that students carry varied implicit writing values and strategies, suggesting that explicitly teaching the "whys" of gained writing knowledge can help students become more aware of writing knowledge, even if that awareness does not guarantee intentionality or transfer success (Nowacek, 2011). While factors such as student dispositions, investment in learning, socialization, and feedback are factors in transfer of writing knowledge, the strong focus across scholarship on explicit instruction is a key takeaway.

Teacher Knowledge about Disciplinary Writing Transfer

A handful of studies show how instructors understand, experience, or support the transfer of their students' writing knowledge (Baird & Dilger, 2017; Carter, 2007; Fraizer, 2010, 2018; Nelms & Dively, 2007; Wolfe et al., 2014). Scholars often focus on teachers or practitioners to understand how to improve faculty or graduate student development, better communicate with faculty colleagues, or simply include another stakeholder perspective on the classroom context. In particular, these studies look for commonalities among disciplinary writing knowledge rather than for differences; they set out to smooth the path for student transfer of writing knowledge rather than point to obstacles that occur after FYW. One way into this comparative work has been to study faculty conversation around disciplinary writing values.

Nelms and Dively's (2007) study seeks instructor perspectives on the transfer of writing knowledge from FYW courses to post-FYW writing contexts. Nelms and Dively surveyed graduate student instructors teaching FYW about the content and skills they teach, and then conducted focus groups with instructors teaching writing-intensive courses in applied sciences about the writing skills they saw in their courses. The TAs reported emphasizing writing process, peer response, the formulation of main ideas, audience analysis, developing ideas, text analysis, argument structure, claim support, organization, source use and citation and most frequently assigning analytic essays, persuasive essays, response journals, and research papers. For their part, the instructors in writing-intensive courses observed that their students did use writing approaches they assumed they learned in FYW—supporting a thesis, text analysis, citation—but also reported that students were unmotivated to write in general. The instructors themselves expressed lacking time to teach writing at all. These findings lead Nelms and Dively to agree with Melzer (2014) and Fraizer (2018) that instructors across programs and departments need a shared vocabulary about writing to dismantle such roadblocks to transfer, suggesting venues like WAC/WID workshops to support increased communication and interdisciplinary exchange around writing concepts, skills, genres, and student attitudes.

Similarly, Wolfe et al.'s (2014) article seeks to move beyond the premise that first-year writing does not promote transfer of writing knowledge to the disciplines. Like Carter (2007) and Thaiss and Zawacki (2006), the authors argue that disciplines similarly value writing knowledge that is argumentative, addresses an insider audience, shows evidence for claims, makes claims about generating new knowledge, and cites existing knowledge. But Wolfe et al. aim to be more specific about these commonalities, using systematic analytic methods to understand the fine-grained expressions of these in disciplinary texts. Using Comparative Genre Analysis (CGA) developed in EAP/ESP, the researchers compared the literary analysis often taught in their local first-year writing courses to conventions found in genres from business, psychology, nursing, biology, engineering, and history textbooks and WID scholarship that describes what practitioners from these disciplines value in student writing, as well as in undergraduate essays from undergraduate journals, conference collections, and instructor websites. Specifically, they used three areas of rhetorical analysis—topoi or lines of argument, macrostructures, and citation conventions—to unearth not only disciplinary writing knowledge but also the values and conventions that index the larger activity systems of which they are a part (p. 45).

Following these three areas, they found several similarities and differences in valued writing knowledge among literary analysis and genres from the disciplines above. They found topoi commonalities like identification and interpretation of a pattern and using a theoretical concept to interpret primary material or analyze phenomena under study. But they observed "dramatic differences" in macrostructures, with thesis-first or thesis-last organizations indexing disciplinary norms for inductive or deductive reasoning, as well as citation differences even among genres within disciplines indexing values around individuality, collaboration, and critique. These nuances lead Wolfe et al. to several pedagogical recommendations to support students' navigation of the transfer of writing knowledge from FYW to these disciplines. They suggest that FYW could do more to support rhetorical similarities such as these even if they are not universal but shared by just a few disciplines, helping students recognize and navigate these similarities and differences, proposing that FYW instructors first develop meta-awareness of differences and commonalities among disciplinary rhetorical knowledge and then pass that meta-awareness on to their students. With suggestions similar to pedagogies like teaching for transfer (Yancey et al., 2014) and genre pedagogies (Bawarshi & Reiff, 2010), they argue that this meta-awareness can be best supported by being explicit about underlying rationale and values rather than arbitrary expectations or random formalities. They suggest activities and assignments that call students' attention to common topoi, macrostructures, and citation norms through analyzing genre features and learning what questions to ask in new rhetorical contexts, always tying these analyses to disciplinary values around writing knowledge.

Carter (2007) describes a project in which departmental faculty worked together to identify their discipline's "ways of doing" that revealed the "ways of knowing and writing" that they valued in turn. Although Carter's ultimate goal is to forward a structure in which "metagenres" and "metadisciplines" help WID professionals guide faculty development in teaching with writing, his description of departmental conversations around writing values reveals implicit assumptions about how writing knowledge accumulates via transfer as students move through a major. In Carter's theory, metadisciplines is a category that emphasizes the procedural knowledge or ways of knowing, doing, and writing, that are common to disciplines. Metagenres are the patterned doing within these, genres of genres or general "ways of doing" that pattern into "similar *kinds* of typified responses to related recurrent situations" (pp. 393). He names four: (a) responses to academic situations that call for problem solving (plans, reports, proposals); (b) responses to academic situations that call for empirical inquiry; (c) responses to academic situations that call for research from sources; and (d) responses to academic situations that call for performance. Importantly, Carter says all of these highlight the relationships among disciplines, thus smoothing the path for transfer to occur. Carter uses his theory essentially to emphasize the intersections and ties both among disciplines and between disciplinary and writing knowledge. He argues that specialized disciplinary knowledge "is not so special" just as generalized writing knowledge "is not so general." Instead, the assumed disjuncture between general writing knowledge and specialized disciplinary knowledge is "porous" and "in flux," with writing located neither fully in nor out of a discipline's more connected boundaries (p. 410).

Fraizer's (2018) study similarly seeks to scaffold faculty professional development around writing. Proposing a model of WAC faculty development which promotes faculty awareness of their students' transfer attempts, Fraizer shows that a "dynamic and contextualized" faculty conversation around writing assignments can help them support both their and their students' transfer of writing knowledge. In designing his study—three stages of student reflections and six faculty members discussion of those reflections—Fraizer sought a strategy to support student transfer as they worked on writing assignments—not after the fact but mid-process. Following Beaufort (2007), Nelms and Dively (2007), and Yancey et al.'s (2014) recommendations to build a shared writing vocabulary to support transfer, Fraizer planned and then studied a dialogic model that promotes faculty awareness of transfer. He (a) designed a student survey based on ongoing faculty conversations about their assignment and larger disciplinary writing goals; (b) administered the survey during class before, during, and after one writing project; (c) synthesized and offered for faculty conversation the "before" and "during" survey results, and then again synthesized and offered the "after" survey results; and (d) met individually with the six faculty participants to reflect on "what was interesting, surprising, or predictable in the data" as well as how their goals were being met and what they might change in the assignment process to better support students' success during the project (para. 13). Studying each of these stages, Fraizer finds that situated and ongoing faculty conversations help them use disciplinary threshold concepts to connect student and disciplinary knowledge. For example, an instructor teaching a healthcare disparities course was able to recognize mid-project that their student needed help building prior knowledge into their literature reviews. Other instructors dispensed with certain aspects of an assignment that weren't working. Ultimately, Fraizer found that his proposed model of faculty development, which required not only awareness of students' needs but the time and space to reflect and then take action on those needs alongside a writing specialist, could more intentionally support their students' transfer of writing knowledge into disciplinary courses.

Genre Knowledge in WAC/WID Transfer

Another cluster of scholarship considers how genre knowledge, in particular, affects writing knowledge transfer across curricula or in disciplines (Bazerman, 2009; Carter et al., 2007; Clark & Hernandez, 2011; Devitt, 2007; Fraizer, 2010; Freedman, 1995; Goldschmidt, 2017; Graff, 2010; Lindenman, 2015; Nowacek, 2011; Reiff & Bawarshi, 2011; Rounsaville, 2014; Rounsaville et al., 2008; Soliday, 2011). Especially for questions about the development of disciplinary writing knowledge, genre is an important unit of analysis (how students carry genre knowledge as they move across their courses, for example) but also one that is especially complex. Devitt (2007) explores what a focus on genre uniquely reveals about the transferability of writing knowledge across disciplines. She presents a central conundrum of transfer and genre: genre must be situated but transfer requires generalization (p. 216). Even though genres are social actions stemming from repetitions, each writing event and situation in which those repetitions occur remains unique. That is to say, because genre emphasizes the situated nature of writing, the notion of genre can frustrate the notion of transfer. Her own response to this puzzle expands a transfer lens—a focus on what is or isn't transferring across contexts—beyond writing skills to the "whole genre," inclusive of writers' perceptions of the similarities of purpose across situations. Devitt explains, "genres capture the ways people categorize those unique writing events as related writing events" (p. 217). So, genres are generalizable to the extent that people perceive similarities and differences in situation and in task. Therefore, because the transferability of genres depends on writers' *perceptions* of generalizability—not just whether a genre is general in fact—studying the transfer of genre can reveal how "writing is at once unique and common, at once situated particularly in a precise writing event and perceived as similar to other writing situations" (219). Devitt uses the complexity built into genre to suggest that writing programs teach critical awareness of the phenomenon of genre for writers' more deliberate and mindful selection among genres in future writing situations.

Devitt's recommendation that courses teach awareness of genre is a common study outcome or recommendation: that instructors should focus on explicitly teaching genre in first-year writing to support writing knowledge transfer to disciplinary courses. For example, Clark and Hernandez (2011) analyzed pre- and post-survey data as well as a final reflective essay from one writing class to understand how explicit teaching of genre theory might help students detect transfer cues (Perkins & Salomon, 1989) in multiple courses. Following Devitt (2004) and Beaufort (2007), they suggest that teaching genre awareness, rather than genre type, might help students develop transferable genre knowledge.

Similarly, Fraizer (2010) designed a study to understand how teaching for transfer strategies like genre and discourse analysis (anticipating Yancey et al., 2014), as well as reflection, support transfer across writing contexts. Specifically, he asked how these writing activities affect transfer when introduced to students not in a FYW course but afterward, and in a smaller group setting. To do this, he followed eight students from a variety of majors during the first semester *after* taking FYW, scheduling group meetings with students to intervene "at opportune developmental moments" (p. 35). These meetings included an orientation to the study, an orientation to the concepts of *reflection* and *genre analysis*, a meeting to discuss these concepts and support each other's ongoing writing from various courses, and a final meeting to reflect on the semester's writing and development. From his conversations with students, as well as a survey of 112 students and six instructors on their perceptions about FYW course content, Fraizer concluded that these strategies can support the transfer of writing knowledge, helping students see "the big picture" of their academic writing (p. 51). But, he argues, such explicit teaching of writing theory might better belong in teaching that occurs after and beyond the first-year writing classroom, with the "richest opportunities for 'bridging' and expanded conceptual thinking" occurring in conversation with other students tackling ongoing writing projects from different writing contexts (p. 52). The need to "reflect across disciplinary boundaries and generalize about what they're learning outside of the activity system of their work in progress" (p. 52) points emphatically to writing center spaces and other informal or extracurricular learning contexts not often captured by transfer research (Grego & Thompson, 2008; Lerner, 2007; Lindenman, 2015; Nowacek, 2011; also see Chapter 9 on writing centers in this volume).

Goldschmidt (2017) also looks to genre to understand cross-disciplinary transfer. Reviewing scholarship that shows students' difficulty transferring genres from first-year writing to disciplinary courses, she asks how programs can best teach for transfer when the differences among humanities- and science-based genres discourage transfer (p. 123). She conducts ten discourse-based interviews with seniors and sophomores at the middle and end of three-course writing-intensive sequences in psychology and computer science, asking them which writing activities they perceived to be the most helpful in negotiating a writing sequence that bridged what she called humanities-based general education writing genres and science-based disciplinary genres. Her thematic analysis of interview transcripts shows that (a) students do not mindfully abstract stylistic and structural norms across first-year writing courses and science writing in their majors; and (b) this difficulty stems in part because they encounter these stylistic and structural differences in new contexts; however, (c) seniors in her study do describe internalizing science-writing norms and repurposing a previously developed sense of authorship for disciplinary contexts once they see themselves "as a member of the new community of practice" (p. 127). Therefore, her findings show that "cross-disciplinary transfer involves a conscious and consequential transformation of participants' identities as contributing members of an academic discourse community" and thus requires students understanding genres not only as situated in a community of practice but also as a type of disciplinary social action (p. 128). To accomplish this understanding, Goldschmidt recommends, like Fraizer (2010) and Carter (2007), teaching metageneric awareness in writing-intensive disciplinary courses and introducing the concept of *genre* as a construct to be observed and analyzed in a variety of contexts.

As a unit of analysis in transfer research, then, genre has been used to reveal the relationships between text and social activity in a disciplinary context, thereby showing the complexity of learning students undertake as they attempt to transfer their writing knowledge within and across courses. Bazerman (2009) helpfully reviews the distinction between genre text types associated with surface-level writing outcomes—that is, list-making associated with increased memory—and genre processes or activities, including task frequency and duration, leading to more complex forms of learning (p. 283). He encourages this latter lens for a more robust understanding of how writing-to-learn skills transfer with students. Lindenman (2015) takes up this approach in her research on genre and transfer. Arguing that writing research often sets up domain categories—home, school, work, etc.—that miss how students forge their own generic connections, her study uses discourse-based interviews to elicit students' understandings of genre relationships, regardless of domain. Lindenman collects data through student surveys (n=319), four focus groups, and ten interviews to understand less how students transfer their writing knowledge across domains (her original research question) and more how students draw on prior knowledge, using intuited relationships among genres, to "figure out" how to compose texts. She finds eight of ten focal participants linking their texts in unconventional ways, creating "metageneric connections" based on texts' purposes, strategies, or rhetorical effect rather than on texts' learning contexts like first-year or disciplinary writing courses (para. 5); students group their texts not by where they take place but by what they do.

Lindenman's findings lead her to suggest that writing instructors support students' creation of their own "organizational schemas" that make connections among writing knowledge. She suggests that instructors could especially draw out what she calls "metageneric reasoning" through activities that ask students to map or cluster their genres, by hand or online, and offer writing opportunities that prompt students to describe their own connections among produced texts. She ultimately agrees with the scholars above that supporting students' development of metageneric reasoning may be a promising avenue to the metacognition researchers say supports transfer.

What a Transfer-Based WAC/WID Curriculum Is or Should Be

Writing studies researchers, teachers, and administrators also have proposed what WAC or WID courses and curricula based in transfer should or could look like (Boone et al., 2012; Downs & Wardle, 2007; Ford, 2012; Hall, 2006; Hayes et al., 2016; Jamieson, 2009; Lettner-Rust et al., 2007; Melzer, 2014; Miles et al., 2008; Smit, 2004; Yancey et al., 2014). Many of these studies and proposals treat transfer as "the very heart of learning—how it occurs and how it is sustained" (Boone et al. 2012, np; also see Smit 2004, p. 119). In designing writing curricula that support student learning across or within disciplines, then, many scholars use transfer as a connective touchstone by which to measure students' development of writing knowledge over time and across curricular contexts.

In something of a manifesto on the state of composition studies in the US, Smit (2004) reviews research on writing and learning to write and concludes that nearly every aspect of writing education in college, from introductory composition courses to graduate education in composition and rhetoric to instructor development, needs to be reimagined to reflect research-based findings on writing education. Following Walvoord and McCarthy (1990), he reiterates conclusions from transfer scholarship that students are more likely to transfer writing knowledge if they can see similarities and differences in the contexts and tasks among which they are writing. To support the "institutionalized instruction" of similarities and differences in "the way writing is done in a variety of contexts" (Smit, 2004, p. 120), Smit says that writing education needs to be better and more intentionally sequenced, exposing students to "an increasing level of domain-specific knowledge" in a hierarchy of thinking and writing skills over time (p. 185). Across these courses, students will come to transfer writing knowledge only if they have constant practice and feedback in a broad range of writing activities and discourse practices. Smit argues that WAC/WID programs are the most effective curricular structure for achieving such learning goals, reminding readers to "spread the responsibility for teaching writing across the curriculum, where it belongs" (p. 213).

Others have implemented similar principles in curricular redesigns that aim to support writing knowledge transfer by redesigning single courses. For example, Ford (2012) aimed to impact a programmatic experience of writing and over a decade redesigned several aspects of a program, including course design, faculty development, student learning outcomes, and faculty joint appointments. She describes a program redesign, shaped by a pluralistic theory of expertise (Carter, 1990) and reflective awareness (Flower, 1989), that evolved over many years from a teaching relationship between technical communication and engineering into an interdisciplinary partnership aiming to support students' writing transfer among multiple instructional contexts. Program stakeholders revised junior and senior design courses in an engineering department by creating connected assignments that "foster building" (assignments that were scaffolded for content and rhetorical knowledge) and a dialogic environment, with a technical writing specialist (Ford) evaluating and responding to assignments alongside instructors who stressed communicative components along the way. Such an instructional partnership aimed to help students become aware of audiences beyond one course, and reinforced consistent feedback on agreed-upon rhetorical strategies. Beyond the author's joint appointment, the program included a technical writing course dedicated to design students, a graduate communication course, and student/faculty designed assignment templates, which served "not only as a style and formatting guide, but as a vehicle for provoking student-faculty conversations regarding communicating their research effectively" because they offered choices in organization, formatting, and style (2012, Faculty and Student Collaboration through Template Creation, para. 4). Ford found that involving students this way, inviting them into the conversation of creating and revising programmatic templates, not only increased student motivation and buy-in, but also helped "cue students' metacognition of higher order rhetorical strategies" that she suggested could ultimately promote high-road transfer (Ford, 2012, para. 4).

Beyond redesigning single courses or lateral writing/discipline partnerships to support transfer, scholars also have reimagined bottom-to-top writing curricula, taking WAC/WID elements into account through integrated "vertical" (Haskell, 2000; Teich, 1987), unified (Hall, 2006), or "connected" (Perkins & Salomon, 2012) curricular approaches to writing education. Vertical curricular models depend on several principles related to transfer: recursion or reiteration of concepts over time and across contexts; experiential learning which affords application of concepts to new or increasingly complex situations; and sequenced learning contexts that increase in complexity (Crowley, 1998; Hall, 2006; Jamieson, 2009; Melzer, 2014; Miles et al., 2008; Smit, 2004). For example, Hall (2006) echoes Carter's (1990) understanding of disciplinary expertise, suggesting that a "unified writing curriculum" supports student learning by increasing rhetorical complexity and disciplinary specificity from first-year writing to major capstone courses. Others provide detailed descriptions and ongoing research of such curricula explicitly based in transfer at such institutions as Dartmouth College (Boone et al., 2012) and UC Davis (Hayes et al., 2016; Melzer, 2014).

Describing the structure of and ongoing research about the Institute for Writing and Rhetoric at Dartmouth, Boone et al. (2012) report on a three-year study that sought to improve course coherence in the first-year writing program by better understanding how students transferred writing knowledge, particularly with the aid of new technologies. The research team structured the study around program and faculty development to center research on knowledge transfer in faculty conversations, creating venues for faculty to experiment with and exchange ideas about research-based approaches to teaching writing. These workshops and conversations aimed to help faculty support their students' transfer of writing knowledge, specifically transfer of rhetorical flexibility (Evolving Directions, para. 5). One innovative aspect of the program and research is use of the program's two-term sequence, which invites first-year writing instructor and first-year seminar instructor pairs to link their courses into a "cohesive learning experience" in the first year, "co-constructing learning environments that may improve students' ability to transfer writing competencies from one course context to the next" (Additional Davis Study Initiatives, para. 2). Because the team's ongoing analysis of first-year students' essays as well as student interviews supports learning research that shows students need writing concepts to be explicitly scaffolded over time, such linked experiences may increase the likelihood that students transfer prior writing knowledge into new contexts.

With an eye to Gagne's (1965) work on vertical curriculum, Melzer (2014) describes a reimagined vertical curriculum at UC Davis based on the transfer of writing knowledge. Melzer explains that a successful form of such a curriculum includes the following components: constant opportunity for student self-reflection and self-monitoring; writing practice over time and embedded in situated, domain-specific contexts; explicit teaching of academic writing threshold concepts like *revision, genre,* and *editing*, introduced and reinforced across contexts and over time; the creation and reinforcement of a shared campus-wide vocabulary about academic writing; and multiple opportunities for peer mentoring. He describes what these principles of a vertical transfer writing curriculum look like at UC Davis, including WAC workshops on supporting student reflection on writing and growth of metacognition; a WAC-focused sophomore composition course that bridges to general education courses and a junior-level WID course that uses forward-reaching transfer strategies; and a shared campus meta-language about writing, reinforced through a university writing rubric, in the student writing handbook, in all course learning outcomes, and tutor-training and outreach workshops in the writing center. (See p. 86 for a comprehensive list.)

In their research on the effect of this curriculum on students' transfer of writing knowledge, Melzer's colleagues found that course learning objectives were being achieved and were aligned with syllabi, assessment portfolios, and model texts found in the course contexts and throughout the program (Hayes et al., 2016). Hayes et al.'s findings were measured through the mechanism of dynamic transfer, what they believe is a theoretical lens that can describe the interaction between inner/cognitive and outer/socially-directed approaches to student learning (Bizzell, 1982/2003, p. 392). To capture moments of dynamic transfer in student learning in their program—acts of coordination between prior knowledge and the creation of new knowledge in new contexts (Martin & Schwartz, 2013)—the researchers looked for dynamic transfer events in data collected from 728 student surveys and 14 text-based student interviews. Tracing dynamic transfer events by isolating student links that influenced the creation of new knowledge or understanding (pp. 197–8), they found that the majority of students described links between their prior writing instruction and their comfort with certain writing skills, contrasting research results like those from Wardle (2009) or Bergmann and Zepernick (2007) in which students report seeing hardly any connections between early writing coursework and later writing. The researchers speculate that these student connections—and the potential subsequent facilitation of transfer—in their study may come from the vertical articulation of the writing program as well as the "programmatic cues" it supplies students: writing assignments that ask students to reflect on prior knowledge but also into future academic careers; explicit connection to writing skill development outside of the writing program; and resources across the university that "highlight the consistent, explicit, and intentional transfer-oriented learning objectives set forth by the multi-year writing requirements" (Hayes, 2016, pp. 208–10).

Infrastructure for the Disciplinary Transfer of Writing Knowledge

This chapter, organized by the common problems or questions that motivate WAC/WID research into the transfer of writing knowledge, has reviewed scholarship about what students do or do not transfer, what instructors are or should be doing to support that transfer, how genre plays a role, and the kinds of courses or curricula that best support student transfer and learning in and across disciplines or curricular contexts. Each section shows the ways that WAC/WID concerns are bound up in the transfer of writing knowledge, with many studies addressing the perennial questions motivating research in writing studies—What should first-year writing prepare students for? How is first-year writing related to students' writing experiences before and after college? How do students develop writing knowledge over the course of a college education and through—even if they raise more questions in the process—their deepening experiences within disciplines?

To support the transfer of writing-to-learn practices that can transform writing knowledge, the reviewed scholarship shares attention to the following instructional foci: modeling and scaffolding writing activities; making writing activities relevant to students' lives including their imagined professional lives; offering frequent but relevantly paced feedback on transfer acts, deep engagement with or intentional learning about writing concepts (Bazerman, 2009; Boscolo & Mason, 2001; Graff, 2010; Wardle, 2007); fostering conversations about writing across disciplinary faculty to develop shared writing vocabulary; and making transparent and explicit (naming and teaching) the writing skills, strategies, values, and meta-cognitive activities that support transfer. Interestingly, many studies note that such metacognition is important (e.g., Ford, 2012; Lindenman, 2015) but others state that it is not essential or required (e.g., Donahue, 2016; Nowacek, 2011) for the transfer of writing knowledge.

Because of its strong affinity to research on disciplinary knowledge, future WAC/WID research focused on transfer could productively continue to call on models from outside of writing studies such as Middendorf and Pace's "Decoding the Disciplines" model (2004) to understand the role that transfer plays as students traverse the "bottlenecks" between expert and novice thinking in a field.[16] Middendorf and Pace's model delineates a "bottleneck approach" that seeks to understand where students experience difficulty in transferring knowledge—moving a concept from one side of a bottleneck to another. In a specific disciplinary context, this looks like faculty in history discussing what counts as teaching and learning in their discipline, using a bottleneck approach to identify where students get stuck in disciplinary learning (Pace, 2011). Such local, disciplinary conversations aim to "decode" unconscious processes into conscious communication about disciplinary knowledge so that concepts can be modeled for students and assessed, in this history case via a written "letter" to a sibling about the course. The model thus assumes that disciplinary learning happens over time and across contexts and thus highlights the role transfer plays in students' acquisition of disciplinary knowledge, including writing knowledge.

One provocative line of thinking for future research is to consider how the transfer of writing knowledge can be differently conceived in a WID context if writing studies is, itself, a discipline. For example, writing about writing approaches to first-year writing are premised on the research-based conclusion that writing learning best occurs in its own disciplinary activity system, and thus first-year writing courses are a kind of WID course that teaches field-specific skills and socialization (Downs & Wardle, 2007; Wardle & Downs, 2013). In other words, what are the implications for the above approaches to transfer if first-year writing is treated as a disciplinary activity system of its own rather than a para-disciplinary course that serves general writing skills or future disciplinary skills? Treated this way, the question of transfer among FYW and disciplinary courses is one of disciplinary rather than general transfer, and future research would need to understand how the disciplinary writing knowledge of writing studies transfers or does not transfer to other disciplinary settings. Perhaps thinking of writing as a discipline itself might help us even better understand the transfer of disciplinary knowledge when it is inclusive of the discipline of writing studies as well.

In fact, this scholarship shows that WAC and WID approaches to writing education can serve as infrastructure for transfer, creating the architecture that cues students' prior knowledge, scaffolds connections

---

16. See http://decodingthedisciplines.org/bibliography/ for a comprehensive list of resources on this model.

among writing genres, lays down paths for metacognition about writing knowledge, and prompts students to reflect on past, current, and future writing activities across disciplinary contexts, including first-year writing. The next chapter demonstrates the pivotal role that writing centers also play in this infrastructure.

References

Adler-Kassner, L., Majewski, J., & Koshnick, D. (2012). The value of troublesome knowledge: Transfer and threshold concepts in writing and history. *Composition Forum, 26*(Fall). http://compositionforum.com/issue/26/

Ahrenhoerster, G. (2006). Will they still respect us in the morning? A study of how students write after they leave the composition classroom. *Teaching English in the Two Year College, 34*(1), 20–31.

Baird, N., & Dilger, B. (2017). How students perceive transitions: Dispositions and transfer in internships. *College Composition and Communication, 68*(4), 684–712.

Bawarshi, A. S., & Reiff, M. J. (2010). *Genre: An introduction to history, theory, research, and pedagogy.* The WAC Clearinghouse and Parlor Press.

Bazerman, C. (2009). Genre and cognitive development: Beyond writing to learn. In C. Bazerman, A. Bonini, & D. Figueiredo (Eds.), *Genre in a changing world*, (pp. 279–294). Perspectives on Writing. The WAC Clearinghouse and Parlor Press.

Beaufort, A. (2007). *College writing and beyond: A new framework for university writing instruction.* Utah State University Press.

Bergmann, L.S., & Zepernick, J. (2007). Disciplinarity and transfer: Students' perceptions of learning to write. *WPA: Writing Program Administration, 31*(1–2), 124–149.

Bizzell, P. (2003). Cognition, convention, and certainty: What we need to know about writing. In V. Villanueva (Ed.), *Cross-Talk in Comp Theory: A reader* (2nd ed., pp. 387–411). National Council of Teachers of English. (Original work published 1982)

Boone, S., Chaney, S. B., Compton, J., Donahue, C., & Gocsik, K. (2012). Imagining a writing and rhetoric program based on principles of knowledge "transfer": Dartmouth's institute for writing and rhetoric. *Composition Forum, 26*(Fall). https://compositionforum.com/issue/26/dartmouth.php

Boscolo, P., & Mason, L. (2001). Writing to learn, writing to transfer. In P. Tynjala, L. Mason, & K. Lonka (Eds.), *Writing as a learning tool: Integrating theory and practice* (pp. 83–104). Dordrecht, The Netherlands: Kluwer Academic.

Carroll, L. A. (2002). *Rehearsing new roles: How college students develop as writers.* Studies in Writing and Rhetoric. Southern Illinois University Press.

Carter, M. (1990). The idea of expertise: an exploration of cognitive and social dimensions of writing. *College Composition and Communication*, *41*(3), 265–286.

Carter, M. (2007). Ways of knowing, doing, and writing in the disciplines. *College Composition and Communication*, *58*(3), 385–418.

Carter, M., Ferzli, M., & Wiebe, E. N. (2007). Writing to learn by learning to write in the disciplines. *Journal of Business and Technical Communication*, *21*(3), 278–302.

Chiseri-Strater, E. (1991). *Academic literacies: The public and private discourse of university students*. Boynton/Cook Publishing.

Clark, I. L., & Hernandez, A. (2011). Genre awareness, academic argument, and transferability. *WAC Journal*, *22*, 65–78.

Collier, L. (2014) Listening to students: New insights on their college-writing expectations. *The Council Chronicle*, *23*(3), 10–12.

Crowley, S. (1998). *Composition in the university: Historical and polemical essays*, University of Pittsburgh Press.

Devitt, A. J. (2004). *Writing genres*. Southern Illinois University Press.

Devitt, A. (2007). Transferability and genres. In C. Keller & C. Weisser (Eds.), *The locations of composition* (pp. 215–227). SUNY Press.

Donahue, C. (2016). Writing and global transfer narratives: Situating the knowledge transformation conversation. In C. M. Anson & J. L. Moore (Eds.), *Critical transitions: Writing and the question of transfer* (pp. 107–136). Perspectives on writing. The WAC Clearinghouse and University Press of Colorado.

Downs, D., & Wardle, E. (2007). Teaching about writing, righting misconceptions: (Re)envisioning "First-Year Composition" as "Introduction to Writing Studies," *College Composition and Communication*, *58*(4), 552–584.

Fallon, D., Lahar, C. J., & Susman, D. (2009). Taking the high road to transfer: Building bridges between English and psychology. *Teaching English in the Two Year College*, *37*(1), 41–55.

Fishman, J., Lunsford, A., McGregor, B., & Otuteye, M. (2005). Performing writing, performing literacy. *College Composition and Communication*, *57*(2), 224–252.

Fishman, J., & Reiff, M. J.. (2015). Taking the high road: Teaching for transfer in an FYC Program"." In M. J. Reiff, A. Bawarshi, M. Ballif, & C. Weisser (Eds.), *Ecologies of writing programs: Program profiles in context* (pp. 69-90). Parlor Press.

Flower, L. (1989). Cognition, context, and theory building. *College Composition and Communication*, *40*(3), 282–311.

Ford, J. D. (2004). Knowledge transfer across disciplines: tracking rhetorical strategies from a technical communication classroom to an engineering classroom. *IEEE Transactions on Professional Communication*, *47*(4), 301–315.

Ford, J. D. (2012). Integrating communication into engineering curricula: An interdisciplinary approach to facilitating transfer at New Mexico Institute of Mining and Technology. *Composition Forum*, *26*(Fall). http://compositionforum.com/issue/26/new-mexico-tech.php

Fraizer, D. (2010). First steps beyond first year: Coaching transfer after FYC. *Writing Program Administration*, *33*(3), 34–57.

Fraizer, D. (2018). Towards a model of building Writing transfer awareness across the curriculum. *Composition Forum*, *38*(Spring). http://compositionforum.com/issue/38/

Freedman, A. (1995). The what, where, when, why, and how of classroom genres. In J. Petraglia (Ed.), *Reconceiving writing, rethinking writing instruction* (pp.121–144). Lawrence Erlbaum.

Gagne, R. M. (1965). *The conditions of learning*. Holt, Rinehart and Winston.

Gilje, Ø. (2010). Multimodal redesign in filmmaking practices: An inquiry of young filmmakers' deployment of semiotic tools in their filmmaking practice. *Written Communication*, *27*(4), 494–522. doi:10.1177/0741088310377874

Goldschmidt, M. (2017). Promoting cross-disciplinary transfer: A case study in genre learning. In R. Bass & J. L. Moore (Eds.), *Understanding writing transfer: Implications for transformative student learning in higher education*, (pp. 122–130). Stylus Publishing.

Graff, N. (2010). Teaching rhetorical analysis to promote transfer of learning. *Journal of Adolescent and Adult Literacy*, *53*(5), 376–385.

Grego, R., & Thompson, N. (2008). *Teaching/writing in thirdspaces: The studio approach*. Southern Illinois University Press.

Haas, C. (1994). Learning to read biology: One student's rhetorical development in college. *Written Communication*, *11*(1), 43–84.

Hall, J. (2006). Toward a unified writing curriculum: Integrating WAC/WID with freshman composition. *The WAC Journal*, *17*, 5–22.

Haskell, R. (2000). *Transfer of learning: Cognition and instruction*. Academic Press.

Hayes, H., Ferris, D. R., & Whithaus, C. (2016). Dynamic transfer in first-year writing and "writing in the disciplines" settings. In C. M. Anson & J. L. Moore (Eds.), *Critical transitions: Writing and the question of transfer*, (pp. 181–213).

Herrington, A. J. (1985). Writing in academic settings: A study of the contexts for writing in two college chemical engineering courses. *Research in the Teaching of English*, *19*(4), 331–361.

Herrington, A. J., & Curtis, M. (2000). *Persons in process: Four stories of writing and personal development in college*. National Council of Teachers of English.

Hilgers, T. L., Bayer, A. S., Stitt-Bergh, M., & Taniguchi, M. (1995). Doing more than "thinning out the herd": How eighty-two college seniors perceived writing-intensive classes. *Research in the Teaching of English, 29*(1), 59–87.

Hilgers, T. L., Hussey, E. L., & Stitt-Bergh, M. (1999). "As you're writing, you have these epiphanies": What college students say about writing and learning in their majors. *Written Communication, 16*(3), 317–353.

Jamieson, S. (2009). The vertical writing curriculum. In J. C. Post & J. A. Inman (Eds.), *Composition(s) in the new liberal arts* (pp. 159–184). Hampton.

Jarratt, S. C., Mack K., Sartor A., & Watson, S. E. (2009). Pedagogical memory: Writing, mapping, translating. *Writing Program Administration, 33*(1–2), 46–73.

Johnson, J. P., & Krase, E. (2012). Coming to learn: From first-year composition to writing in the disciplines. *Across the Disciplines, 9*(2). https://wac.colostate.edu/atd/archives/volume9/

Kell, C. (2006). Crossing the margins: Literacy, semiotics, and the recontextualization of meaning. In K. Pahl & J. Rowsell (Eds.), *Travel notes from the new literacy studies: Instances of practice*, (pp. 147–170). Multilingual Matters.

Lave, J. (1988). *Cognition in practice: Mind, mathematics and culture in everyday life*. Cambridge University Press.

Lave, J., & Wenger, E. (1991). *Situated learning: Legitimate peripheral participation*. Cambridge University Press.

Lerner, N. (2007). Situated learning in the writing center. In W. Macauley & N. Mauriello (Eds.), *Marginal words, marginal work? Tutoring the academy in the work of writing centers* (pp. 53–73). Hampton.

Lettner-Rust, H. G., Tracy, P. J., Booker, S. L., Kocevar-Weidinger, E., & Berges, J. B. (2007). Writing beyond the curriculum: Transition, transfer, and transformation. *Across the Disciplines, 4*. https://wac.colostate.edu/atd/archives/volume4/

Lindenman, H. (2015) Inventing metagenres: How four college seniors connect writing across domains. *Composition Forum, 31*(Spring), http://compositionforum.com/issue/31/inventing-metagenres.php

Martin, L., & Schwartz, D. L. (2013). Conceptual innovation and transfer. In S. Vosniadou (Ed.), *International handbook of research on conceptual change* (2nd ed., pp. 447–465). Routledge.

McCarthy, L. P. (1987). A stranger in strange lands: A college student writing across the curriculum. *Research in the Teaching of English, 21*, 233–265.

Melzer, D. (2014). The connected curriculum: Designing a vertical transfer writing curriculum. *The WAC Journal, 25*, 78–91.

Middendorf, J., & Pace, D. (2004). Decoding the disciplines: A model for helping students learn disciplinary ways of thinking. *New Directions for Teaching and Learning, 2004*(98), 1–12.

Middendorf, J., & Pace, D. (n.d.), Decoding the disciplines: Improving student learning. http://decodingthedisciplines.org/

Miles, L., Pennell, M., Owens, K. H., Dyehouse, J., O'Grady, H., Reynolds, N., Schwegler, R., & Shamoon, L. (2008). Interchanges: Commenting on Douglas Downs and Elizabeth Wardle's "Teaching about writing, righting misconceptions." *College Composition and Communication*, *59*(3), 503–511.

Nelms, G., & Dively, R. L. (2007). Perceived roadblocks to transferring knowledge from first-year composition to writing-intensive major courses: A pilot study. *WPA Writing Program Administration: Journal Of The Council Of Writing Program Administrators*, *31*(1–2), 214–240.

Nowacek, R. S. (2011). *Agents of integration: Understanding transfer as a rhetorical act.* Southern Illinois University Press.

Pace, D. (2011). Assessment in history: The case for decoding the discipline. *Journal of the Scholarship of Teaching and Learning*, *1*(3), 107–119.

Perkins, D. N., & Salomon, G. (1989). Are cognitive skills context-bound? *Educational Researcher*, *18*(1), 16–25.

Perkins, D. N., & Salomon, G. (2012). Knowledge to go: A motivational and dispositional view of transfer. *Educational Psychologist*, *47*(3), 248–258.

Petraglia, J. (1995) *Reconceiving writing, rethinking writing instruction.* Lawrence Erlbaum.

Reiff, M. J., & Bawarshi, A. (2011). Tracing discursive resources: How students use prior genre knowledge to negotiate new writing contexts in first-year composition. *Written Communication*, *28*(3), 312–337.

Rogers, P. (2010). The contributions of North American longitudinal studies of writing in higher education to our understanding and development. In C. Bazerman, R. Krut, K. Lunsford, S. McLeod, S. Null, P.M. Rogers & A. Stansell (Eds.), *Traditions of writing research* (pp. 365–377). Routledge.

Roozen, K. (2009). From journals to journalism: Tracing trajectories of literate development. *College Composition and Communication*, *60*(3), 541–572.

Roozen, K. (2010). Tracing trajectories of practice: Repurposing in one student's developing disciplinary writing processes. *Written Communication*, *27*(3), 318–354.

Rounsaville, A. (2012). Selecting genres for transfer: The role of uptake in students' antecedent genre knowledge. *Composition Forum*, *26*. https://compositionforum.com/issue/26/selecting-genres-uptake.php

Rounsaville, A. (2014). Situating transnational genre knowledge: A genre trajectory analysis of one student's personal and academic writing. *Written Communication*, *31*(3), 332–364.

Rounsaville, A., Goldberg, R., & Bawarshi, A. (2008). From incomes to outcomes: FYW students' prior genre knowledge, meta-cognition, and the question of transfer. *Writing Program Administration*, *32*(1), 97–112.

Russell, D. R. (1995). Activity theory and its implications for writing instruction. In J. Petraglia (Ed.), *Reconceiving writing, rethinking writing instruction* (pp. 51–78). Lawrence Erlbaum.

Russell, D. R. (1997). Rethinking genre in school and society. *Written Communication, 14*(4), 504–554.

Smit, D. W. (2004). *The end of composition studies*. Southern Illinois University Press.

Soliday, M. (2011). *Everyday genres: Writing assignments across the disciplines*. Southern Illinois University Press.

Sommers, N. (2008). "The Call of Research: A Longitudinal View of Writing Development." *College Composition and Communication. 60*(1), 152–164.

Sommers, N., & Saltz, L. (2004) The novice as expert: Writing the freshman year. *College Composition and Communication, 56*(1), 124–149.

Spack, R. (1997). The acquisition of academic literacy in a second language: A longitudinal case study. *Written Communication, 14*(1), 3-62.

Sternglass, M. S. (1997). *Time to know them: A longitudinal study of writing and learning at the college level*. Lawrence Erlbaum.

Stretcher, R., Hynes, G. E., & Maniam, B. (2010). Transfer of learning across courses in an MBA curriculum: A managerial finance case study. *Journal of Instructional Pedagogies, 4*, 1–11.

Teich, N. (1987). Transfer of writing skills: Implications of the theory of lateral and vertical transfer. *Written Communication, 4*(2), 193–208.

Thaiss, C. J., & Zawacki, T. M. (2006). *Engaged writers and dynamic disciplines: Research on the academic writing life*. Boynton/Cook.

Walvoord, B. E., & McCarthy, L. P. (1990). *Thinking and writing in college: A naturalistic study of students in four disciplines*. The WAC Clearinghouse and National Council of Teachers of English.

Wardle, E. (2007). Understanding "transfer" from FYC: Preliminary results of a longitudinal study. *Writing Program Administration, 31*(1–2), 65–85.

Wardle, E. (2009). "Mutt Genres" and the goal of FYC: Can we help students write the genres of the university? *College Composition and Communication, 60*(4), 765–789.

Wardle, E. & Downs, D. (2013). Reflecting back and looking forward: Revisiting teaching about writing, righting misconceptions five years on. *Composition Forum, 27.* https://compositionforum.com/issue/27/reflecting-back.php

Wolfe, J., Olson, B., & Wilder, L. (2014). Knowing what we know about writing in the disciplines: A new approach to teaching for transfer in FYC. *WAC Journal, 25*, 42–77.

Yancey, K. B., Robertson, L., & Taczak, K. (2014). *Writing across contexts: Transfer, composition, and sites of writing*. Utah State University Press.

Zamel, V. & Spack, R. (2004). *Crossing the curriculum: Multilingual learners in college classrooms*. Lawrence Erlbaum.

9 Writing Centers: An Infrastructural Hub for Transfer

The approaches to transfer reviewed across this book's chapters demonstrate the range of intellectual and material infrastructure that supports the transfer of writing knowledge. Writing centers are intriguing spaces for attention to transfer because they act as an infrastructural hub of transfer activity. Writing centers create a space—the tutoring session—where several approaches to writing transfer happen at once. Writing centers encapsulate the complex simultaneity of the transfer of writing knowledge, offering a uniquely "synchronic" window into the transfer phenomenon (Hagemann, 1995, p. 122). For example, writing center tutors transfer knowledge about writing even as they transfer knowledge about tutoring writing; tutors toggle between general writing skills instruction and disciplinary-specific approaches as they work. Working with tutors in sessions, student writers also transfer procedural knowledge about writing and specialized genre knowledge, all the while cultivating dispositions that affect their future writing practices. Stephen North's long-held writing center dictum to support better writers rather than better texts means that writing centers enable one-on-one attention, for both tutor and tutee, to eliciting prior knowledge, facilitating reflection on writing, attending to self-regulation and self-efficacy, and supporting transfer over time, sessions, courses, and texts (Bromley et al., 2016; Busekrus, 2018; Devet, 2015; Driscoll & Devet, 2020; Driscoll & Harcourt, 2012; Hill, 2016; North, 1984).

As Meade (2020) notes, writing centers' origin as a response to the specialization and division that characterizes much of the modern university means that centers are "characterized by [their] inclination to speak back to the features of the university that leave some students behind, keep students from meeting certain expectations, or keep students from reaching their full potential" (para. 9). In other words, writing centers' collaborative and low-stakes atmosphere outside of conventional classrooms, disciplines, and academic hierarchies invites tutors and writers to share and make connections among several forms of writing-related knowledge—discipline-specific writing knowledge, rhetorical knowledge that transcends disciplines, and writing center-informed knowledge about tutoring writing—all at once.

Research on the transfer of writing knowledge in writing centers reveals the vital role centers play not only in the college experience, supporting all students across disciplines over time, but also in lifelong education, as writers (including tutors) continue to transfer writing knowledge learned in writing centers long after graduation (Dinitz & Kiedaisch, 2009; Driscoll, 2015; Hughes et al., 2010; Mattison, 2020; Zimmerelli, 2015). This chapter on transfer in writing centers reviews the research and thinking that shows this unique potential. The majority of transfer-related writing center scholarship is focused on tutors—the writing knowledge they do or should transfer; how they do or do not support tutee transfer—with some research considering the transfer practices of other writers in centers, like student writers and administrative directors. Therefore, the sections below are organized by topics readers are likely to seek out in order to make decisions in their own contexts: (a) the writing knowledge that tutors transfer, including debates about specialist vs. generalist tutor knowledge; (b) the writing knowledge tutors *should* come to know and transfer through tutor education; (c) studies of writers, themselves, transferring knowledge in writing centers; and (d) the kinds of knowledge, writing and otherwise, tutors and teachers transfer beyond the center into classrooms, workplaces, or community contexts. The chapter includes studies that examine transfer both explicitly and implicitly, to best capture the extent of transfer-related thinking in writing center studies.

The Knowledge Tutors Transfer–What Tutors Know

Most writing center transfer research focuses on tutors rather than writers. In a way, this is a natural focus—directors often conduct research to assess the effectiveness of a center and its staff, give guidance to the tutors, and make plans for future tutor hiring and education. For example, Kenzie (2013) conducted a descriptive study of three tutors' use of "transfer talk" (Nowacek, 2011) in 19 sessions, to understand how tutors might use genre pedagogy to support writers' transfer of writing knowledge during sessions. Mackiewicz (2004) conducted a linguistic analysis of four tutoring sessions about engineering writing to understand the impact of disciplinary expertise on the success of a session.

Broadening the scope of what might count as writing knowledge tutors gain and transfer in centers, Bruffee (1978, 2008) describes the personally enriching experience of being a peer writing tutor. Because peer tutoring shows tutors and writers that no one writes alone, that "writing is a form of civil exchange that thoughtful people engage in when they try to live reasonable lives with one another" (2008, p. 8), Bruffee argues that tutoring writing is definitively human, allowing tutors to practice a "helping, care-taking engagement" (2008, p. 6) that tutors take with them to other areas of their life. He names this engagement an "interdependence" (2008, p. 8) that tutors practice, model, hand off to writers, and then carry around to other communicative engagements. Bruffee's essays have shaped how writing center professionals and staff understand the potentials of peer tutoring; it is now assumed that something beyond writing knowledge is being learned in writing centers and carried elsewhere. Bruffee would say that that something is human interdependence, a defining piece of writing center knowledge that shows, if tutors do indeed carry and apply it elsewhere, that transfer might also not be a solitary phenomenon. That is to say, Bruffee's contribution to transfer is the reminder that transfer is deeply social, happening among people rather than solely in the heads of solitary writers.

But perhaps the most prominent presence of transfer in the scholarship on what tutors know is its presence in the debate over tutors' discipline-specific writing knowledge. When writing center directors and researchers discuss whether tutors lead more successful sessions when they have disciplinary knowledge of a tutee's paper—e.g., do they better support a student writing a biology lab report when they are biology majors themselves?—they are also discussing tutors' ability to transfer that disciplinary writing knowledge to the writing center session at hand. Similarly, when writing center professionals promote the merits of generalist tutors, saying that disciplinary specialty is unnecessary or detrimental to the session's success, they assume that tutors are transferring generalized rhetorical knowledge among or outside of disciplinary contexts in that decision. Therefore, tracing transfer's underlying presence in the specialist/generalist tutor debate adds an important dimension to the transfer of writing knowledge in writing center contexts.

The debate generally falls into two categories: (a) essays by writing center directors promoting generalist tutors based on their professional experience (Brooks, 1991; Devet et al., 1995; Healy, 1991; Hubbuch, 1988; Luce, 1986; Pemberton, 1995; Walker, 1998) and (b) empirical research finding that some disciplinary knowledge can support better tutoring (Dinitz & Harrington, 2014; Kiedaisch & Dinitz, 1993; Kohn, 2014; Mackiewicz, 2004; Powers & Nelson, 1995; Shamoon & Burns, 1995; Thonus, 1999; Tinberg & Cupples, 1996). Hubbuch's essay, for example, relies on her decade of direct experience to argue that generalist tutors are better listeners because their job is simply to understand a writer's ideas. She says a tutor who is "ignorant" of subject matter is better able to point to missing information or jumps in logic. Hubbuch worries that there are too many modes for tutors to master even within singular disciplines, "each with an attendant style and rhetorical conventions" (1988, p. 24). She believes specialized disciplinary knowledge also promotes singular understandings of "good" writing (1988, p. 24). Both Hubbuch and others (Brooks, 1991; Kiedaisch & Dinitz, 1993) argue that tutors with disciplinary expertise tend to appropriate a student's text, becoming too invested in its form and substance and act more as an expert evaluator than a "fellow inquirer" (Hubbuch, 1988, p. 24). Thus, Hubbuch concludes that it is more important that tutors develop rhetorical flexibility, recognizing the relationship between discursive conventions and epistemology no matter the discipline, developing an awareness that the "universe of discourse has a varied and diverse terrain," and that they rely on that general rhetorical knowledge for their practices (1988, p. 24).

Seeking to verify and complicate these beliefs, which critics say are based more in lore than research, writing center scholars have sought empirical understandings of how disciplinary knowledge affects the tutoring of writing. Three studies in particular (Dinitz & Harrington, 2014; Kiedaisch & Dinitz, 1993; Mackiewicz, 2004) provide evidence that fluency in the rhetorical norms of a discipline help tutors work more successfully on global (rather than local) issues and give them confidence to gently push a tutee's thinking. While none of these studies evokes transfer explicitly, the studies' data suggest that tutors with disciplinary knowledge are also transferring that knowledge, acting as Nowacek's (2011) "agents of integration" as they tutor.

In the first study, Kiedaisch and Dinitz (1993) recorded twelve tutoring sessions about literature essays, showed them to three English faculty, and gave questionnaires to both the sessions' writers and the faculty who viewed the sessions. While none of the writers saw a connection between the quality of their session and their tutors' disciplinary knowledge, the faculty did, identifying high tutor disciplinary knowledge in sessions they rated excellent and low disciplinary knowledge in weak sessions (p. 64). Based on the faculty's notes and their own analysis, Kiedaisch and Dinitz found that tutors without disciplinary knowledge struggled to move writers beyond summary and struggled to help them find a controlling insight, fully respond to the assignments, move beyond sentence-level concerns, or work on global problems in general. On the other hand, Keidaisch and Dinitz found that tutors with disciplinary knowledge of literature better understood writers' assignments, could lead writers to fully respond to them, and could identify insights that were not supported, especially through close reading. They provide the important caveat, though, that knowledgeable tutors also took more authoritative stances in sessions by being invested in the papers more than other tutors, confirming other writing center professionals' hunches on the matter.

A decade later in 2004, Mackiewicz designed a study focusing on tutor expertise specifically in engineering. She situates her study in Thonus' (1999) and Kiedaisch and Dinitz's (1993) findings that disciplinary knowledge leads to more successful tutoring. However, she looks explicitly for "how the extent of tutors' familiarity with engineering writing influences the extent to which their tutoring is effective" (p. 326). Mackiewicz conducts a linguistic analysis of four tutoring sessions about engineering writing, three with tutors (two undergraduate, one graduate) with no expertise in engineering and one with a graduate tutor with two decades of disciplinary familiarity. Because writing center professionals worry that tutors with expertise tend to be overly directive in their tutoring, she codes for tutoring topics and politeness strategies to gauge tutors' assertions of expertise and control. Mackiewicz found that the tutors with no disciplinary knowledge gave inappropriate advice, which they stated with certainty, while the experienced tutor gave "appropriate and specific" advice that also helped build tutee rapport (p. 316). The non-expert tutors steered sessions toward topics they were familiar with in order to speak with certainty and ended up focusing on surface features in the writing, violating tutoring best practices (p. 320). The expert tutor on the other hand focused on purpose and audience; engaged the tutee's text holistically, including visual components; modulated her suggestions; and built rapport through politeness strategies, praising discipline-appropriate textual strategies like the use of imperative verbs. Importantly, Mackiewicz makes a distinction between tutors' disciplinary rhetorical knowledge and their disciplinary subject matter knowledge, which all the tutors lacked. In other words, Mackiewicz's argument is that it is disciplinary rhetorical knowledge that matters in a session—this is the kind of knowledge the most successful tutor was able to wield.

A decade after Mackiewicz's (2004) study, Dinitz and Harrington (2014) revisited Kiedaisch and Dinitz's (1993) study. Dinitz and Harrington note that tutor "expertise" is used very generally in research, often conflating content knowledge, genre knowledge, and disciplinary knowledge. Like Mackiewicz, they assume that tutor expertise is valuable and thus also seek to understand the *how* of expertise—how it appears in and shapes sessions. Dinitz and Harrington (2014) replicate the methods of Kiedaisch and Dinitz's (1993) study, collecting student papers and session transcripts from seven tutoring sessions (three on political science writing, four on history writing), asking three faculty members from each discipline to view and rate the sessions in terms of the role of disciplinary knowledge and the likelihood of the session resulting in revision. Faculty members made strong connections between "sophisticated" disciplinary knowledge, the quality of a session's agenda, and a session's overall effectiveness (Dinitz & Harrington, 2014, p. 80). These faculty contributions and their own code-based analysis lead Dinitz and Harrington to conclude that disciplinary expertise supports more effective tutoring, "in part because it allows [tutors] to be more directive in ways that enhance collaboration" (p. 74). While tutors lacking disciplinary expertise focused on local issues, moved linearly (rather than recursively) through tutee's texts, and rarely pushed back on tutee thinking, tutors with disciplinary expertise (as evidenced by having taken several courses in the discipline or being majors) were able to accomplish nearly the exact opposite, working at the global level recursively, directing the session agenda, and helping writers draw general rhetorical lessons.

Dinitz and Harrington conclude that contrary to Kiedaisch and Dinitz's 1993 finding (as well as worries from Hubbuch and Brooks), tutor disciplinary knowledge does not always lead to tutors dominating sessions or appropriating tutee texts. Rather, type of directive tutoring matters as much as type of disciplinary expertise. Sophisticated knowledge of writing in a discipline allows tutors to "push back and push forward," being directive by asking writers relevant and complex questions, pushing them to fully respond to an assignment (Dinitz & Harrington, 2014, p. 90). Appropriating tutee texts was an issue of knowledge of disciplinary content, not of disciplinary rhetorical conventions. Kohn (2014) similarly argues for this distinction, citing research from technical communication (i.e., Devitt, 2004; Kain & Wardle, 2005), writing center/science writing collaboration (Hollis, 1991), and transfer studies to claim that rhetorical knowledge, particularly recognition of genres, is the expertise that writing centers can gather in conversation with local disciplinary faculty and that tutors can put into practice.

Walker's (1998) observation that tutors can be simultaneously specialists and generalists foregrounds how the social construction of knowledge helps reframe tutor writing knowledge as adaptable and always in-the-making. She suggests tutors use genre theory, as many practitioners have in genre pedagogies (Bawarshi & Reiff, 2010; Clark, 1999), as an analytic tool to navigate discipline-specific discourse alongside their writers, in a way becoming specialists in that navigation. She recommends genre theory in tutor education as textual analysis, interviewing professors, and using disciplinary models. Anticipating what Nowacek and Hughes (2015) later term the *expert outsider*—tutor generalists who are specialists in the rhetorical functions of writing no matter the discipline—Walker calls for generalists with specialist knowledge in several fields.

Therefore, the tension in specialist/generalist tutor knowledge is less a debate about the efficacy of disciplinary expertise than the evidence of directors' struggle to enact research-based best practices in light of logistical barriers like time, hiring cycles, and professional development budgets. More to the point of this chapter, the conversation mapped above also reveals implicit assumptions about tutors' (and writers') transfer of knowledge. The empirical studies trace enactments of transfer, as tutors and writers engage with papers and with each other by drawing on a wide range of discipline-specific and generalized rhetorical knowledge. The studies seem to show that the interplay of these transfer moves—sifting among specific and general writing knowledge—support the best tutoring: "Disciplinary expertise seemed to permit interplay between general tutoring strategies and disciplinary discourse, leading to more effective sessions" (Dinitz & Harrington, 2014, p. 93). What this implies about transfer is that effective tutors aren't simply transferring disciplinary writing knowledge to sessions depending on the discipline being discussed, but are rather tacking between WID knowledge and WAC knowledge, putting these in conversation for writers to draw both course-specific and generalizable lessons.

Several writing center professionals have acted on the intuition shared by many writing center administrators that working in a writing center impacts the writing knowledge tutors carry elsewhere, especially into their classrooms as teachers (Busekrus, 2018; Moneyhun & Hanlon-Baker, 2012; Shapiro, 2014; Van Dyke, 1997; Weaver, 2018). Scholars wonder how writing knowledge transfers from tutoring to teaching (Shapiro, 2014) or from teaching to tutoring, or even how the teaching of that writing knowledge changes when tutoring begins (Moneyhun & Hanlon-Baker, 2012). For example, Van Dyke (1997) observes that writing center pedagogy is invaluable training for the classroom, arguing that teaching assistants should be exposed to the individualized and formative pedagogical focus of writing centers and be encouraged to transfer these skills to their composition classrooms. In a reflective blog post, Shapiro (2014) agrees, describing a transfer moment—using a tutoring-informed collaborative activity in his own classroom to enliven his students' research process—to show how he transferred into his classroom the kinds of writing-related knowledge tutoring hones: that students can become their own tutors as well as tutors for each other in any given location. As a "teacher in tutor's clothing," Shapiro calls his experiential belief that writing can't really be taught without the focused individualization and flexibility of tutoring as the singular knowledge that he has indeed transferred from tutoring to teaching. Similarly, Busekrus (2018) suggests that teachers can learn feedback-giving strategies—particularly those that promote transfer—from oral feedback that tutors give during writing center sessions. She notes that because tutors are positioned as peer-readers and interlocutors rather than graders and engage directly in students' process of learning, tutor feedback supports intentional goal-setting, increases self-understanding and reflection, and promotes metacognition through a conversational and dialogic dynamic.

Providing empirical backing to the intuitions and reflections above, Weaver (2018) surveyed thirteen graduate tutors who were also teachers; he finds that tutors self-report many benefits of tutoring for teachers, including increased empathy for students and communicative strategies, as well as transfer. He also found that not all participants believed that transfer was conscious or intentional—and concludes by encouraging writing center directors to ask their staff to reflect more regularly on how abilities developed as a tutor might influence classroom teaching. Moneyhun and Hanlon-Baker (2012) examined how five writing teachers' knowledge about giving feedback on writing transferred (which they describe variously through verbs like changed, influenced, translated, and transformed) among teaching and tutoring contexts. The teachers reported transferring the following tutoring-based understandings of writing and learning: assuming less about students' understanding, providing more direct comprehension checks, and writing more explicit assignment prompts. But Moneyhun and Hanlon-Baker found, in analysis of the teachers' interview transcripts and written feedback on texts, that while their tutoring was student-led or student-centered, their teaching for the most part was not. Moneyhun and Hanlon-Baker conclude that while writing-related knowledge can transfer from tutoring to the writing classroom, these moves have to be active and intentional, and likely take time to occur.

Two studies also approach tutors as life-long writers worthy of research attention, examining how writing center work provides a powerful context for a deepening understanding of prior learning about writing. Hall, Romo, and Wardle (2018), for instance, work together to analyze the experience of Mikael (Romo), who was a student in Wardle's advanced writing class, then later became a tutor in the writing center Hall directed. "Mikael's experiences in the center," they report, "deeply impacted his ability to move through the liminal space on some of the most difficult threshold concepts" (para. 17). In particular, they focus on how both the designed curriculum and Mikael's own dispositions and identity influenced his learning over time. Because the writing center "required constant reflection and connection-making" over multiple semesters, it proved a particularly powerful component of learning in his writing studies major (para. 61). Nowacek et al. (2020) similarly conducted research with undergraduate tutors in the writing center, examining how undergraduate tutors who studied threshold concepts of writing may transfer and transform that knowledge over the years they work in a writing center. Their conclusions emphasize how continued engagement with threshold concepts of writing is supported by the activity of tutoring, but how some tutors seem to internalize threshold concepts over time, growing less able to name these. This work thus contributes to showing the variety of ways that writing centers are sites with great potential for the transfer of writing-related knowledge, with tutor education a prime site for discovering this potential.

Transfer in Tutor Education— What Tutors Should Know

As Devet's (2015) primer on transfer for writing center directors states, a more intentional focus on transfer in teaching and research could reveal much about what is accomplished in writing centers. She suggests that deliberately teaching tutors transfer concepts from psychology—near and far, lateral and vertical, conditional and relational, declarative and procedural—and from composition—prior knowledge, dispositions, context, genre—could help tutors become more strategic in their practice, better naming what happened in a session or more thoughtfully anticipating a session to come. Several scholars follow Nowacek's (2011) suggestion that tutors make for especially appropriate "handlers" or "agents of integration" for the transfer of writing knowledge in the writing center (Alexander et al., 2016; Devet, 2015; Kenzie, 2013). By virtue of their location on campus and in conversation with students from across disciplines, tutors become experts not only of tutoring writing but also of generalized writing knowledge, discipline-specific writing knowledge, and sometimes of writing transfer itself.

Many writing center professionals point to tutor education to realize this potential. Primarily, this work is motivated by Bowen and Davis' (2020) important question regarding transfer in writing centers: "How do we best educate tutors to build on and transfer what they know about writing into the tutorial, and to do so in ways that help support transfer for the writers with whom they work?" (para. 37). This section conceives of responses to this question as the what, how, and why of transfer-focused tutor education. That is to say, this section explores (a) *what* might be taught to tutors: transfer- and learning-related concepts such as genre, context, reflection (Bowen & Davis, 2020; Devet, 2015; Hahn & Stahr, 2018; Hill, 2016, 2020; Wells, 2011); (b) *how* or through what pedagogical means that content might be taught (Cardinal, 2018; Clark, 1999; Driscoll, 2015; Driscoll & Harcourt, 2012; Hastings, 2020; Johnson, 2020; Kenzie, 2013; Kohn, 2014; Mackiewicz, 2004); and (c) *why* a focus on transfer in tutor education is appropriate and might matter (Mattison, 2020; Rose & Grauman, 2020; Zimmerelli, 2015). These three conceptions overlap, of course, but this division offers potential inroads for tutor educators to incorporate the transfer-focused approaches to tutor education that are most appropriate to their local constraints and possibilities.

What: Transfer and Writing Theory as Content

Several scholars suggest that tutor education that explicitly uses transfer or writing studies theory as the content of tutor education can support effective tutoring for transfer. Wells (2011) describes a hybrid tutor education and writing studies course she designed to train her tutors in a high school writing center. She taught three units using writing about writing (WAW) content: (a) What is good writing—teaching about writing as dependent on rhetorical situation using rhetorical analysis; (b) WID unit on discourse communities and the future writing expectations in college majors through genre analysis; and (c) creating new knowledge for the field of writing studies through a primary research paper. Her hope was that peer tutoring would support the learning of WAW content, but she also previews how that knowledge transferred both ways, into their tutoring as well. Hahn and Stahr (2018) similarly encourage writing center directors to share concepts related to transfer with tutors in specific and intentional ways. They suggest focusing tutor education to help tutors identify with writers "the rhetorical elements shared by different assignments" (13) and to emphasize how writers' dispositions may influence receptivity to considerations of transfer. They also recommend readings for tutor education (such as Nelms & Dively, 2007, and Wardle, 2007) and advise that tutors prime writers to think and talk about transfer through intake forms that ask writers to articulate connections to previous writing experiences as well as through conversation.

Offering a full description of a tutor education course, Bowen and Davis (2020) argue that a teaching for transfer (TFT) curriculum can be profitably taken up as a frame to support tutors' explicit use of transfer theory for three main reasons: First, they follow Bruffee (1978, 2008) and Ede (1989) in noting that tutoring is highly social in its dependence on collaboration and thus tutors need to develop a social theory of writing to tutor effectively; second, they note that because tutoring requires high-road mindful transfer, tutors' awareness of their own transfer must be raised; and third, they foreground what they call "the dual lens of tutor education . . . an occasion to see, interpret, and act dually, as both students of and tutors of writing" to highlight tutors' "toggling" between tutor and writer subjectivities, an agility helpfully supported with a TFT lens (para. 21). Their chapter thus describes the features of a TFT-focused tutor training course that can support these aspects of tutoring. Following the central tenets of Yancey et al.'s (2014) TFT curriculum, Bowen and Davis say reflection must be central to the course to teach tutors mindfulness and active self-monitoring of how writing transfers across contexts. They also explain that course content must include key terms from writing studies and transfer theory so that tutors engage in evolving conceptual frames of these key terms. They suggest the course culminate in an assignment in which tutors explain not only their theory of writing and their theory of tutoring, but also how these theories work together.

Extending descriptions of tutor courses or workshops, Hill (2016, 2020) studied the effects of such transfer-focused tutor education on the practices of tutors themselves. Building on research findings that claim that transfer needs to be made explicit to be successful, Hill (2016) traces the implicit and explicit uses of transfer talk in tutoring sessions following a one-hour tutor training on transfer theory. Hill's class taught tutors about several techniques that facilitate transfer such as recognizing similarities and differences between learning situations, understanding abstract principles about writing that transcend individual writing situations, and using metacognitive reflection (pp. 79–80). Studying this class, then, Hill used a comparative approach—recording 30 hours of tutoring sessions three months later from those who had attended the workshop vs. those who hadn't—to analyze the viability of this transfer training with Nowacek's (2013) discussion of "transfer talk," which Hill calls "moments when tutors engaged students in talking about their previous knowledge or in talking about how their current learning connected to future tasks" (p. 85). Hill's analysis found that even a one-hour class on transfer theory can support tutors' ability to facilitate transfer for writers: the tutors who had attended explicitly evoked transfer while tutoring far more than tutors who had not attended (2016, p. 88).

While Hill acknowledges that more training than a one-hour class could bring about more explicit transfer talk during tutoring, she suggests in a 2020 follow-up chapter other educational opportunities that might exist. Explaining that her context allows for a one-credit course, rather than the more conventional three-credit model, Hill argues that even courses that mirror a series of workshops could effectively introduce tutors to transfer and genre theory to help them effectively facilitate the transfer of writing-related knowledge for their tutees. She does this not only by assigning scholarly readings on genre, discourse communities, writing across the curriculum, and the rhetorical situation, but also by leading tutors to explicitly apply the readings' concepts to tutoring sessions. For example, she asks tutors to generate questions they might ask tutees about their experience with a particular genre. Along the way, she assigns four short reflection papers to concretize in-class activities and connect readings to their long-term tutoring practices. Hill's (2020) larger point is that even when writing center directors have only small amounts of time for tutor education, a familiarity with transfer, genre, and learning theory can make them better tutors as well as help them become better writers with a more "sophisticated understanding of how writing works" (para. 4).

How: Activities and Strategies for Tutor Education

Other writing center scholars focus more on the active doing of transfer in their tutor education courses and ongoing professional development. In her descriptions and study of transfer-focused tutor education, Driscoll (2015) considered both the content to be taught and activities that help tutors engage with it. For example, Driscoll describes a tutor education course that uses transfer pedagogy to teach writing center and writing studies content (see both Driscoll & Harcourt, 2012 and Driscoll, 2015). Due to the course fulfilling upper-division general education requirements, students enroll not only to prepare for tutoring writing but also to prepare for teaching or writing careers or just for what they perceive as an "easy" gen. ed. credit (Driscoll, 2015, p. 159). Their divergent goals led Driscoll to design a course that focused less on tutor preparation and more on the "knowledge applications" component of the general education requirement, which asked students "to take a course from outside their major and apply that knowledge to their major" (p. 159). To support this knowledge transfer, Driscoll (2015) designed the course around Bransford and Schwartz's (1999) *preparation for future learning*, which emphasizes not specific knowledge or tasks but forward-looking concepts like *adaptability* or *resource use*, and Perkins and Salomon's (2012) *detect-elect-connect model* that relies on three mental bridges: detecting connections between previously learned knowledge/skills/approaches and a new situation, electing to explore that connection, and connecting that knowledge in some way (p. 158; also see this book's chapter "Cognitive Psychology and Situated Learning" for a review of these concepts). Class activities and assignments thus aimed to build connections across prior, current, and future learning contexts with readings about writing and learning research. Frequently assigned reflections brought learning connections to the fore of student thinking.

Driscoll evaluated the course through student writing and retrospective student interviews, one of which is featured in Driscoll and Harcourt (2012). Her thematic analysis showed that the vast majority of her students could build connections among multiple contexts, engage in transfer-focused thinking during the course, and use detect-elect-connect processes after the course (Driscoll, 2015, p. 163). Harcourt, a former student from Driscoll's course, reflects how the course taught her techniques that "became useful as I moved into my student teaching" (Driscoll & Harcourt, 2012, p. 5). As a new first-grade teacher, she transferred what she had learned in the tutor preparation course in new ways, enacting the values of collaboration, reflection, and metacognitive self-monitoring. Therefore, Driscoll deems the transfer-focused pedagogy effective not only for tutoring preparation but for 21st century general education curriculum (Driscoll, 2015, p. 154). She joins Hughes et al. (2010) in arguing that peer tutoring coursework and experiences, taught through transfer-focused pedagogy, can support the "learning of writing, interpersonal, and metacognitive skills that can transfer to broad educational, professional, civic, and personal contexts" (Driscoll, 2015, p. 154).

Writing center scholars also use transfer-related concepts such as genre to structure activities and assignments in their tutor education courses (Clark, 1999; Kenzie, 2013; Kohn, 2014; Hill, 2016). For example, Clark (1999) recommends a focus on genre in tutor training so that genre analysis can become a central component of writing center sessions, claiming that genre knowledge can help students understand writing's social situatedness and "enabling them to understand, deconstruct, and creatively expand upon the requirements of their writing assignments" (1999, p. 13). Clark follows Miller (1984), Devitt (1993; 1997), and Johns (1997) to build a genre pedagogy, in which tutors learn to

- Approach assignments with students in terms of genre, asking about a genre's purpose and features, how its features serve its purpose and whose interests that purpose serves;
- Foster students' awareness of genres in general, making clear their historical and social situatedness, helping students learn to question them and make creative choices;
- Evaluate student texts in terms of function, relating function to a genre's context; and
- Relate genres to discourse communities and the group membership that certain genres enable, turning students' attention to their own discourse communities and familiar genres. (1999, p. 26–27)

Similarly, Kohn (2014) and Mackiewicz (2004), addressing science writing and engineering writing respectively, recommend teaching tutors disciplinary rhetorical norms and genres so that tutors more intentionally transfer that knowledge to their writing center sessions. For example, Mackiewicz recommends introducing tutors to common purposes and conventions of engineering writing like writing intended to inform (instructions and process descriptions) versus writing intended to persuade (recommendation reports); and conventions for numerals, imperative mood, and active voice (p. 327). Kohn recommends not only incorporating rhetorical knowledge like this into tutor education, but folding it into larger writing center functions, like writing across the curriculum conversations with faculty (that would supply the disciplinary knowledge and drive faculty buy-in to the center) and center materials development like handouts that offer tutors disciplinary checklists to review with writers in sessions.

Active-learning and play also have been explored as strategies for teaching tutors about transfer. Cardinal (2018) analyzes the consequences of two transfer-focused tutor education sessions, arguing for the value of active learning about transfer (vs. lecture). She also argues that tutors' self-reports indicate positive changes in both their feelings of preparedness and their willingness to implement those transfer-oriented concepts in their conversations with writers. An extended demonstration of such active learning can be found in Hastings' (2020) description of incorporating play into a tutor education course. Seeking to incorporate conceptions of transfer from learning theory, Hastings describes the domino game "42" that she teaches tutors to help them become more aware of their metacognitive processes while learning something familiar but mostly new. The activity includes a period of time discussing concepts such as novice/expert learning as a group, another period learning and attempting to play the game, and another reflecting backward on the experience and forward to potential tutoring applications. Hastings describes her goals in such active learning (about learning) as supplying to tutors learning-base vocabulary they will hopefully pass on to tutees, engaging in reflection together around a specific learning experience, and modeling for tutors how learning transfer can both succeed and "fail."

Other scholars conceive of tutor education on transfer in theoretical terms, using an adaptive (Alexander et al., 2016) or transformative (Johnson, 2020) lens to organize particular strategies that teach tutors about transfer. Focusing on tutors in multiliteracy centers, Alexander et al. (2016) use one case study to elaborate a theoretical framework for adaptive transfer that provides a set of strategies that could be included in tutor education. Admitting a close alignment with Bolter and Grusin's (1999) remediation, Alexander et al. suggest tutors need knowledge of a particular kind of transfer—adaptive, dynamic reuse of existing knowledge, with adaptive transfer highlighting what knowledge exists or is prior. They offer four concrete approaches to adaptive remediation that tutors could learn and use with writers in sessions: (a) charting, or rhetorical analysis that focuses on what sections of a text are doing or performing; (b) inventorying, or listing of the range of semiotic resources, across modes and media available to them; (c) coordinating, or a rhetorical analysis of the situation around a remediated text (beyond the text itself), inventing additional rhetorical strategies or semiotic resources to be drawn on; and (d) literacy linking, or a consideration of how networks of literacies are connected among domains and could be drawn on for a meaningful integration of multiple literacies.

Using a synthesized theoretical lens of transformation (see her Table 1), Johnson (2020) draws on her practitioner expertise in directing a disciplinary writing center to offer tutoring scenarios in which transfer as transformation occurs. Her scenarios show how tutors discuss genres that are novel to students, leading them to experience "dissonance they must reconcile," which she marks as a kind of transformation (para. 10). She also shows how tutors guide students through adapting concepts or processes from their general knowledge to their immediate projects while also connecting students' subject-based ideas to contexts beyond the course. According to Johnson, these tutor strategies help students transform their knowledge in transfer-supporting ways, blending knowledge across contexts and preparing students to engage their prior knowledge in future situations. Johnson's ultimate point about transfer in tutor education is to demonstrate the small transformations of language and understanding that reveal transfer at work (para. 7). That is, she aims to stress that transfer can be taught through almost incidental opportunities (rather than planned lessons that require longer periods of time) when transfer is recognized more as knowledge transformation than "clear cut moments of knowledge application" (para. 24). In this way, Johnson is in conversation with Alexander et al. (2016) and many transfer scholars who agree that moments of transfer are dynamic and thus need to be taught to tutors as such.

Why Focus on Transfer in Tutor Education

A small set of scholarship on tutor education considers why focusing on transfer in preparing tutors might matter beyond their immediate work in sessions. In a similar manner to Bruffee (1978, 2008), Driscoll (2015), and Hughes et al. (2010), these scholars consider how a focus on transfer-related concepts during tutor education might reverberate beyond writing centers. For example, Rose and Grauman's (2020) study shows that if tutors are explicitly taught to use motivational strategies to support writers' self-efficacy and self-regulation, writers might feel more confident in taking charge of their future writing situations. Rose and Grauman argue that when tutors are equipped to intentionally create an engaging and collaborative tutoring space by using praise, showing empathy, and reinforcing writers' ownership and control, the writers they work with might be more likely to create those spaces for themselves elsewhere. Mattison (2020) similarly argues for making explicit the collaborative and interpersonal skills of tutoring not only to support tutees' and tutors' future endeavors. Noting that professions increasingly value such "soft skills," he suggests that tutor education should intentionally name and foreground the dispositions tutors develop and inevitably transfer to work contexts simply because it makes them more employable.

Claims about the importance of focusing on transfer in tutor education are mainly these: that such a focus can improve tutors' skills, tutees' experiences in and beyond the center, and tutors' future writing lives as well. An interesting demonstration of this last reason is Zimmerelli's (2015) study of her service-learning approach to tutor education, in which she examined a community partnership for its impact on tutors' engagement with social justice. While her course did not focus on transfer, transfer was a theme that arose in her descriptive coding analysis of tutors' final reflective essays. Zimmerelli's coding of tutors' written reflections captured their increased capacity for connection and identification, their recognition of reciprocal and mutual learning, their development of a civic identity, and finally, the prospect of transfer, as tutors described how community tutoring experiences altered their writing center tutoring. Because 83% of tutors' reflection essays displayed features that Zimmerelli said signified transfer—captured in phrases such as "will easily be carried over" or "is applicable to"—she argues that transfer is a central feature in community-engaged tutoring (p. 73). In other words, because tutors articulated how community experiences changed their approaches to tutoring in general, Zimmerelli argues that incorporating more mindfulness about transfer into tutor education, supported by transfer-friendly reflection, might heighten tutors' tendencies to be open and generous, adaptable, empathetic and caring writing collaborators (Bruffee 1978, 2008).

A Focus on Student Writers

Studies that trace student writers' transfer of writing-related knowledge through the lens of the writing center remain spare, although there are several recent indications of a growing research interest in this area (Bromley et al., 2016; Kenzie, 2013; Nowacek et al., 2019;

Rose & Grauman, 2020). For example, Nowacek et al. (2019) examine the "transfer talk" of writers in 30 writing center tutorials. By transfer talk, they mean "the talk through which individuals make visible their prior learning (in this case, about writing) or try to access the prior learning of someone else" (para. 7). Ultimately their article claims that the transfer of learning may be more collaborative and may include more automatized transfer than is generally recognized (para. 2).

Other research focuses on student writers' transfer of learning in more depth. For example, Hagemann's (1995) case study seeks to understand one tutee's transfer of writing knowledge among courses and over time. Arguing that transfer research is too "diachronic," too focused on disconnected singular classrooms, semesters, and courses, Hagemann grounds her transfer study instead in a "synchronic" frame to understand the "synchronous, that is, simultaneous, experiences" of learning to write among multiple academic discourses all at once (p. 122). To accomplish this, Hagemann studies the writing experiences of one undergraduate writer from Taiwan, Lih Mei, who is a fifth-year senior negotiating writing from five courses in three disciplines. Hagemann analyzes tutor records from one fall semester to reconstruct Lih Mei's writing experiences from the point of view of her writing center sessions. Hagemann tracks Lih Mei's courses, assignments, and "writing roles" required in each, reconstructing a timeline of 44 visits and 19–20 assignments.

The tutoring records—notes that tutors write to record what transpired in a session—describe Lih Mei's negotiation of varying expectations for writing in her courses in which writing is assigned to measure content mastery, but also gauge her grasp of disciplinary rhetorical knowledge. The records show Lih Mei negotiating the writing roles of "text processor, decision-maker, debater, counselor and researcher" all in one semester (p. 123). Hagemann also traces which rhetorical strategies Lih Mei could and could not transfer among specific disciplinary genres: Lih Mei easily transferred knowledge of summary writing among summary assignments but struggled with the disciplinary genre of the "tourism plan," which asked for summary writing that Lih Mei did not recognize as such. Similarly, Lih Mei struggled to transfer summary writing knowledge to an assigned reading response, especially struggling to take on the role of conversation contributor. Hagemann finds this bumpy knowledge transfer to be primarily a result of Lih Mei struggling to negotiate too many writing roles simultaneously, suggesting that tutors might best help writers think through types of writing roles or the range of authority being asked of them to support writers' transfer of writing knowledge among tasks and courses.

Rose and Grauman (2020) studied recordings of tutoring sessions to understand how tutors might facilitate transfer-enabling dispositions in writers. Collecting six video-recorded tutoring sessions, they trace when tutors used motivational scaffolding and how those strategies led to writers' self-regulation and self-efficacy. They use Mackiewicz and Thompson's (2018) talk-based motivational scaffolding in tutoring—showing concern, praising, reinforcing student writers' ownership and control, being optimistic or using humor, giving sympathy or empathy—as indications of specific motivational strategies to link to writers' dispositions (p. 58). In the six sessions, they observed tutors using motivational strategies to support transfer-supporting dispositions in several ways. When tutors used praise and empathy, they opened up space for writers to practice self-regulation by choosing what to work on, asking questions, using language that implied confidence, and starting new topic episodes in the session. Tutors who used optimism and humor in developing rapport with writers allowed writers to feel increased comfort in the session and with their text, paving the way for more active involvement in the session that encouraged self-regulation and self-efficacy. And when tutors reinforced writers' ownership and control of their texts and of the session, writers sometimes made different revision decisions than the tutor suggested, which Rose and Grauman claim indicated self-efficacy. About their study, Rose and Grauman conclude that "the most productive moments are conversations where the writers actively engage in collaborative dialogue, demonstrating self-efficacy and self-regulation, rather than letting or expecting tutors to lead" (para. 26). They conclude that incorporating transfer theory into tutor education may heighten the results they witnessed in writers' changed dispositions.

With a slightly different lens, Bromley et al. (2016) examined how student visitors to three centers at different institutions describe the writing knowledge that transferred during and after sessions. The researchers collected students' self-reported perceptions that writing center visits increased their confidence and their meta-awareness through reported acts of writing transfer. Guided by a theoretical framework that incorporated Wardle's (2012) problem-exploring dispositions, Reiff and Bawarshi's (2011) boundary crossers, and Perkins and Salomon's (2012) high-road transfer, they especially focused on writing centers' ability to provide low-stakes contexts to explore and expand problems. Their survey and focus group data from three campuses allowed for a cross-institutional analysis of student transfer, showing most student visitors engaging in transfer, with a "large majority" engaging in far transfer. Their inclusion of focus group quotes shows students' perceptions of how their next steps in an assignment were guided by what they learned in a session as well as of the writing "breakthroughs" they experienced in sessions and continued to call on in later contexts (Bromley et al., 2016, pp. 7–10). Because of the depth and rigorous presentation of the data, their study convincingly shows not only that writing centers do indeed support students' transfer of writing knowledge, but also that writing centers play a central and singular role as a hub of transfer learning and teaching on campus.

Transfer Beyond the Center

The Peer Writing Tutor Alumni Project (PWTARP), conducted by Hughes et al. (2010), takes Bruffee (1987, 2008) seriously by aiming to demonstrate empirically what the impact of tutoring writing looks like on tutors' lives long after graduation. Setting out to understand "what peer tutors take with them" after leaving college, Hughes et al. conducted a large-scale electronic survey of 126 tutor alumni from their three institutions. The survey collects thoughts from alumni who tutored as far back as 1982 (finding former tutors ranging in age from 22 to 77) and thus were able to include a lifespan perspective on the impact of tutoring writing. By relying on the construct "take with them," the survey assumes the presence of knowledge transfer, but moves beyond writing knowledge.

Following Bruffee's notion that tutors practice the kinds of socially-situated communication skills that will serve them in work, family, and civic contexts long after college, the researchers rely on Bruffee (1978) and Cronon's (1998) essay "Only Connect" to structure an analysis of participant reflections that highlighted not only tutors' learned writing knowledge but the kind of learning Cronon characterizes as a liberal education: they "listen and they hear"; "they read and they understand"; "they can talk with anyone"; "they can write clearly and persuasively and movingly"; "they practice humility, tolerance, and self-criticism" and "they nurture and empower the people around them" (pp. 76–78). Like Bruffee, Cronon folds human connectedness into college learning. Hughes et al.'s (2010) findings highlight the presence of these "soft skills," as Mattison (2020) calls them, in tutor alumni, with implications for how tutors transfer intellectual, professional, social, and personal knowledge into other areas of their lives. Specifically, the survey reveals that tutoring writing helped tutors develop intellectual knowledge like deeper revision practices, a willingness to seek out critical conversation around writing, critical reading skills, and a heightened awareness of writing processes in general with a metalanguage to describe them (p. 24–27). But tutoring also led tutors to develop what the researchers call "a listening presence," in which participants describe the active listening and questioning skills they took "with them across the border of graduation and into further studies and into careers, as well as into their family and social lives" (p. 28). Hughes et al. were surprised not that listening was the most frequently reported skill learned but that so many alumni tutors described that listening and writing mattered for them in professions like "sales, social work, acting, management, development work, legal work, and medicine" (p. 32) and in family situations like connecting with their children and in other social relationships. The researchers surmise that this extension of social knowledge stems from tutors' first-hand experience of the impact of collaborative talk. As tutors they have learned "how crucial it is to learning for writers to know that someone cares about, listens to, respects, and empathizes with them" (p. 37).

Hughes et al.'s important research project empirically supports Bruffee's (2008) descriptions of what peer tutoring "can do" for college students, showing not just that tutors develop particular kinds of general and disciplinary-specific writing knowledge, but they develop particular kinds of social knowledge that changes how they move through the world and connect with other humans in it. Similarly, when Dinitz and Kiedaisch (2009) take up PWTARP's framing (available online prior to Hughes et al.'s 2010 publication) to survey 135 tutor alumni on how their tutoring experiences affected their career development in particular, they find that tutor alumni took "interpersonal skills" with them to post-college professional settings (71%). Alumni respondents also report that they carried writing skills such as sophisticated revision practices, awareness of writing and reading habits, and meaningful incorporation of feedback (58%); collaborative and dynamic mentoring and teaching skills (57%); and critical and creative thinking skills (31%). Among their respondents, 73% said tutoring writing in college influenced their choice of profession or graduate work, and when asked to rank "the importance for your occupation of the skills, qualities, or values you developed as a tutor," 90% designated it as "highly important" (p. 4).

Hughes et al. (2010) say that peer tutoring is a "form of liberal education for peer tutors themselves" (p. 14). They mean that tutors aren't just educating others but are experiencing an especially complex and multifaceted form of education themselves. Transfer is an important layer in this tutor-knowledge complex, supporting the connections tutors make among the spaces in which they learn, the disciplines and rhetorical norms they encounter, and the empathetic dispositions that apply elsewhere in life. Hughes et al. say, and other scholars above concur, that all this knowledge, writing and otherwise, "persists" for decades beyond the writing center (p. 38). The persistence or endurance of tutor knowledge is certainly a question of transfer, one that highlights not only the range of knowledge that is gained, or the human-interdependent quality of transfer, but also that tutor knowledge, itself, is particularly durable. Writing center professionals continue to try to understand why this is, and how this knowledge might change or solidify if transfer is explicitly named as one mechanism that supports this knowledge.

Implications for Pedagogy and Methodology

As a distinct infrastructural hub for transfer, writing centers are positioned in the midst of the multidirectional transformation of knowledge (Barron & Grimm, 2002). The scholarship above shows both the complexity and the potential for locating pedagogical and methodological questions about transfer in this spot. Both the instance of the tutoring session, and the ongoing tutor education that envelopes it, together make writing centers a uniquely rich site in which to pursue dynamic, longitudinal, and transdisciplinary treatments of the transfer of writing knowledge.

The scholarship reviewed in this chapter reveals the beginnings of a few patterns of pedagogical insights about transfer from the point of view of the writing center, more as confirmation of existing rather than brand new observations. Most of all, scholars suggest that transfer is already occurring all the time in tutoring, but explicit teaching about transfer can make a difference: teaching tutors about writing studies, learning, and transfer theory as the content of tutor education might shift what tutors become cognizant of and their resulting tutoring practices. From this, writing center directors should not then treat transfer theory as yet another topic to attend to in an already-packed course, but should rather take the cue of many scholars above and refocus a course on a learning concept or two, or reframe the good and important content that likely already exists. For example, if transfer is one theoretical frame for the course, then tutors could analyze the readings in the *St. Martin's Sourcebook for Writing Tutors* for their implications about the transfer of writing knowledge in the tutoring session. Beyond the writing center, expanding the notion of when and where tutoring might occur—peer review, planned or incidental student collaboration—in turn expands the pedagogical potential of teaching for transfer. Teaching student writers to support each other's writing transfer might heighten writers' considerations of themselves as writer-tutors. Such an expansion could move beyond colleges to also consider tutoring interactions in community-based writing centers, professional or job-related writing centers, and more.

When it comes to methodological insights, research on transfer phenomena in writing centers has so far captured isolated pieces of the transfer puzzle. Due to collection methods commonly used—tutor reflections or records, surveys and focus groups, observations and audio/visual recordings of sessions—a single perspective of a collaborative interaction of a session most often is captured. Either a study follows what a tutor transfers, and then usually only one type or strand of knowledge, or what a student transfers, and again usually only their writing knowledge or dispositional performances. Because of the potential of writing centers for revealing the multifaceted nature of transfer, researchers could consider how different methodologies might capture the interaction of multiple study participants, both tutor and tutee, treating both as collaborative writers making knowledge together simultaneously. Research also might center the interaction of strands of knowledge being transferred like tutors' writing and tutoring knowledge. While a focused unit of analysis lends to study clarity, a tight lens on transfer tends to treat the phenomenon somewhat statically. Therefore, future research could profitably ask what data collection methods might best capture the interactivity and synchronicity of transfer that naturally occurs in writing centers? How can studies document both tutors' and tutees' mutually evolving theories of writing based on their transfer of writing knowledge alongside each other? How might study designs account for the other types of knowledge present and potentially being transferred in a writing center space—on the walls, incidentally overheard from other sessions? (See Driscoll & Devet, 2020 for another forward-looking set of questions for a research program on transfer in writing centers.) Here, methods based in complexity, like ethnography, discourse-based interviews, corpus studies, longitudinal studies of writing development, and participatory action research might support study designs that get at the heart of what writing centers can reveal about transfer.

References

Alexander, K. P., DePalma, M., & Ringer, J. M. (2016). Adaptive remediation and the facilitation of transfer in multiliteracy center contexts. *Computers and Composition, 41*, 32–45.

Barron, N., & Grimm, N. (2002). Addressing racial diversity in a writing center: Stories and lessons from two beginners. Writing Center Journal, *22*(2), 55–83.

Bawarshi, A. S., & Reiff, M. J. (2010). *Genre: An introduction to history, theory, research, and pedagogy.* The WAC Clearinghouse and Parlor Press.

Bolter, J. D., & Grusin, R. (1999) *Remediation: Understanding new media.* MIT Press.

Bowen, L.M., & Davis, M. (2020). Teaching for transfer and the design of a writing center education program. In B. Devet, Bonnie & D.L. Driscoll (Eds.), *Transfer of learning in the writing center: A* WLN *digital edited collection.* https://wlnjournal.org/digitaleditedcollection2/.

Bransford, J. D., & Schwartz, D. L. (1999). Rethinking transfer: A simple proposal with multiple implications. *Review of Research in Education, 24*, 61–100.

Brooks, J. (1991). Minimalist tutoring: Making the student do all the work. *The Writing Lab Newsletter, 15*(6), 1–4.

Bromley, P., Northway, K., & Schonberg, E. (2016). Transfer and dispositions in writing centers: A cross-institutional mixed-methods study. *Across the Disciplines, 13*(1), 1–15.

Bruffee, K. A. (1978). The Brooklyn plan: Attaining intellectual growth through peer-group tutoring. *Liberal Education, 64*(4), 447–68.

Bruffee, K. A. (2008). What being a writing peer tutor can do for you. *The Writing Center Journal, 28*(2), 5–10.

Busekrus, E. (2018). A conversational approach: Using writing center pedagogy in commenting for transfer in the classroom. *Journal of Response to Writing*, *4*(1), 100–116.

Cardinal, J. (2018). Transfer two ways: Options and obstacles in staff education for transfer. *Writing Center Journal*, *43*(1–2), 2–9.

Clark, I. L. (1999). Addressing genre in the writing center. *Writing Center Journal*, *20*(1), 7–32.

Cronon, W. (1998). "Only connect...": The goals of liberal education. *American Scholar*, *67*(4), 73–80.

Devet, B. (2015) The writing center and transfer of learning: A primer for directors. *The Writing Center Journal*, *35*(1), 119–151.

Devet, B., Cramer, P., France, A., Mahan, F., Ogawa, M. J., Raabe, T., & Rogers, B. (1995) Writing lab consultants talk about helping students writing across the disciplines. *The Writing lab Newsletter*, *19*(9), 8–10.

Devitt, A. J. (1993). Generalizing about genre: New conceptions of an old concept. *College Composition and Communication*, *44*(4), 573–586.

Devitt, A. J. (1997). Genre as language standard. In W. Bishop & H. Ostrom (Eds.), *Genre and writing: Issues, arguments, alternatives* (pp. 45–55). Boynton.

Devitt, A. J. (2004) *Writing Genres*. Southern Illinois University Press.

Dinitz, S., & Kiedaisch, J. (2009). Tutoring writing as career development. *The Writing Lab Newsletter*, *34*(3), 1–5.

Dinitz, S., & Harrington, S. (2014). The role of disciplinary expertise in shaping writing tutorials. *Writing Center Journal*, *33*(2), 73–98.

Driscoll, D. L. (2015). Building connections and transferring knowledge: The benefits of a peer tutoring course beyond the writing center. *The Writing Center Journal*, *35*(1), 153–181.

Driscoll, D.L., & Devet, B. (2020). Writing centers as a space for transfer: Supporting writing, writers, and contexts. In B. Devet, Bonnie & D.L. Driscoll (Eds.), *Transfer of learning in the writing center: A* WLN *digital edited collection*. https://wlnjournal.org/digitaleditedcollection2/.

Driscoll, D., & Harcourt, S. (2012). Training vs. learning: Transfer of learning in a peer tutoring course and beyond. *The Writing Lab Newsletter*, *36*(7–8), 1–6.

Ede, L. (1989) Writing as a social process: A theoretical foundation for writing centers. *The Writing Center Journal*, *9*(2), 3–15.

Hagemann, J. (1995). Writing centers as sites for writing transfer research. In B. Stay, C. Murphy & E. H. Hobson (Eds.), *Writing center perspectives*. (pp. 120–131). National Writing Center Association.

Hahn, S., & Stahr, M. (2018). Some of these things ARE like the others: Lessons learned from tutor-inspired research about transfer in the writing center. *Writing Center Journal*, *43*(1–2), 10–17.

Hall, R. M., Romo, M., & Wardle, E. (2018). Teaching and learning threshold concepts in a writing major: Liminality, dispositions, and program design. *Composition Forum*, *38*(Spring). https://compositionforum.com/issue/38/threshold.php

Hastings, C. (2020). Playing around: Tutoring for transfer in the writing center. In B. Devet, Bonnie & D.L. Driscoll (Eds.), *Transfer of learning in the writing center: A* WLN *digital edited collection.* https://wlnjournal.org/digitaleditedcollection2/

Healy, D. (1991). Specialists vs. generalists: Managing the writing center-learning center connection. *Writing Lab Newsletter*, *15*: 11–16.

Hill, H. N. (2016). Tutoring for transfer: The benefits of teaching writing center tutors about transfer theory, *The Writing Center Journal*, *35*(3), 77–102.

Hill, H. (2020). Strategies for creating a transfer-focused tutor education program. In B. Devet, Bonnie & D.L. Driscoll (Eds.), *Transfer of learning in the writing center: A* WLN *digital edited collection.* https://wlnjournal.org/digitaleditedcollection2/

Hollis, K. (1991) More science in the writing center: Training tutors to lead group tutorials on biology lab reports. In R. Wallace and J. H. Simpson (Eds.), *The writing center: New directions* (pp. 247–262). Garland Publishing.

Hubbuch, S. M. (1988). A tutor needs to know the subject matter to help a student with a paper: [ ] agree [ ] disagree [ ] not sure. *Writing Center Journal*, *8*(2), 23–30.

Hughes, B., Gillespie, P., & Kail, H. (2010). What they take with them: Findings from the peer writing tutor alumni research project. *Writing Center Journal*, *30*(2), 12–46.

Johns, A. M. (1997). *Text, role, and context: Developing academic literacies.* Cambridge University Press.

Johnson, C. (2020). Transfer(mation) in the writing center: Identifying the transformative moments that foster transfer. In B. Devet, Bonnie & D.L. Driscoll (Eds.), *Transfer of learning in the writing center: A* WLN *digital edited collection.* https://wlnjournal.org/digitaleditedcollection2/.

Kain, D., & Wardle, E. (2005) Building context: Using activity theory to teach about genre in multi-major professional communication courses. *Technical Communication Quarterly*, *14*(2), 113–39.

Kenzie, D. P. (2013, July). *"He just did not listen to me": Authority and resistance in writing tutors' encounters with prior learning.* Presented at the conference of the Council of Writing Program Administrators 2013, Savannah, GA.

Kiedaisch, J., & Dinitz, S. (1993). "Look back and say 'so what'": The limitations of the generalist tutor. *Writing Center Journal*, *14*(1), 63–74.

Kohn, L. L. (2014). Can they tutor science? using faculty input, genre, and WAC-WID to introduce tutors to scientific realities. *Composition Forum*, *29*(Spring). https://compositionforum.com/issue/29/can-they-tutor-science.php

Luce, H. (1986). On selecting peer tutors: Let's hear it for heterogeneity. *Writing Lab Newsletter*, *10*, 3–5.

Mackiewicz, J. (2004). The effects of tutor expertise in engineering writing: A linguistic analysis of writing tutors' comments. *Professional Communication, IEEE Transactions on Professional Communication*, *47*(4), 316–328.

Mackiewicz, J., & Thompson, I. (2018). *Talk about writing: The tutoring strategies of experienced writing center tutors* (2nd ed.). Routledge.

Mattison, M. (2020). Taking the high road to transfer: Soft skills in the writing center. In B. Devet, Bonnie & D.L. Driscoll (Eds.), *Transfer of learning in the writing center: A* WLN *digital edited collection*. https://wlnjournal.org/digitaleditedcollection2/.

Meade, M. (2020). Considering the exigency of transfer and its impact on writing center work. In B. Devet, Bonnie & D.L. Driscoll (Eds.), *Transfer of learning in the writing center: A* WLN *digital edited collection*. https://wlnjournal.org/digitaleditedcollection2/.

Miller, C. (1984). Genre as social action. *Quarterly Journal of Speech*, *70*(2), 151–167.

Moneyhun, C. & Hanlon-Baker, P. (2012). Tutoring teachers. *Writing Lab Newsletter*, *36*(9–10), 1–5.

Nelms, G., & Dively, R. L. (2007). Perceived roadblocks to transferring knowledge from first-year composition to writing-intensive major courses: A pilot study. *WPA Writing Program Administration: Journal of The Council Of Writing Program Administrators*, *31*(1–2), 214–240.

North, S. (1984). The Idea of a Writing Center. *College English*, *46*(5), 433–446.

Nowacek, R. S. (2011) *Agents of integration: Understanding transfer as a rhetorical act*. Southern Illinois University Press.

Nowacek, R. S. (2013). *Transfer as bricolage: Assembling genre knowledge across contexts*. Presented at Conference on College Composition and Communication, Las Vegas, NV.

Nowacek, R. S., Bodee, B., Douglas, J., Fitzsimmons, W., Hausladen, K., Knowles, M., & Nugent, M. (2019). "Transfer talk" in talk about writing in progress: Two propositions about transfer of learning. *Composition Forum 42*. https://compositionforum.com/issue/42/transfer-talk.php

Nowacek, R.S., & Hughes, B.T. (2015). Threshold concepts in writing center work. In L. Adler-Kassner & E. Wardle (Eds.), *Naming what we know* (pp. 171–185). Utah State University Press.

Nowacek, R., Mahmood, A., Stein, K., Yarc, M, Lopez, S., & Thul, M. (2020) Grappling with threshold concepts over time: A perspective from tutor education. In L. Adler-Kassner & E. Wardle (Eds.), *(Re)considering what we know* (pp. 244–260). Utah State University Press.

Pemberton, M. (1995). Writing center ethics: 'The question of expertise'. *Writing Lab Newsletter, 19,* 15–16.

Perkins, D. N., & Salomon, G. (2012). Knowledge to go: A motivational and dispositional view of transfer. *Educational Psychologist, 47*(3), 248–258.

Powers, J., & Nelson, J. (1995). Rethinking writing center conferencing strategies for writers in the disciplines. *Writing Lab Newsletter, 20,* 12–16.

Reiff, M. J., & Bawarshi, A. (2011). Tracing discursive resources: How students use prior genre knowledge to negotiate new writing contexts in first-year composition. *Written Communication, 28*(3), 312–337.

Rose, K. & Grauman, J. (2020). Motivational scaffolding's potential for inviting transfer in writing center collaborations. In B. Devet, Bonnie & D.L. Driscoll (Eds.), *Transfer of learning in the writing center: A* WLN *digital edited collection.* https://wlnjournal.org/digitaleditedcollection2/

Shamoon, L., & Burns, D. (1995). A critique of pure tutoring. *The Writing Center Journal, 15*(2), 134–151.

Shapiro, M. (2014, November). You can take the tutor out of the writing center. . . . *Another Word.* https://writing.wisc.edu/blog/you-can-take-the-tutor-out-of-the-writing-center/.

Thonus, T. (1999). Dominance in academic writing tutorials: Gender language proficiency and the offering of suggestions, *Discourse & Society, 10*(2), 225–248.

Tinberg, H., & Cupples, G. (1996). Knowin' nothin' about history: The challenge of tutoring in a multi-disciplinary writing lab. *Writing Lab Newsletter, 21,* 12–14.

Van Dyke, C. (1997). From tutor to TA: Transferring pedagogy from the writing center to the composition classroom. *The Writing Lab Newsletter, 21*(8), 1–3.

Walker, K. (1998). The debate over generalist and specialist tutors: Genre theory's contribution. *The Writing Center Journal, 18*(2), 27–45.

Wardle, E. (2007). Understanding "transfer" from FYC: Preliminary results of a longitudinal study. *Writing Program Administration, 31*(1–2), 65–85.

Wardle, E. (2012). Creative repurposing for expansive learning: Considering "problem-exploring" and "answer-getting" dispositions in individuals and fields. *Composition Forum, 26*(Fall). http://compositionforum.com/issue/26/creative-repurposing.php

Weaver, B. (2018). Is knowledge repurposed from tutoring to teaching? A qualitative study of transfer from the writing center. *Writing Center Journal, 43*(1–2), 18–24.

Wells, J. (2011). They can get there from here: Teaching for transfer through a "writing about writing" course. *The English Journal, 101*(2), 57–63.

Yancey, K. B., Robertson, L., & Taczak, K. (2014). *Writing across Contexts: Transfer, Composition, and Sites of Writing*. Utah State University Press.

Zimmerelli, L. (2015). A place to begin: Service-learning tutor education and writing center social justice. *The Writing Center Journal*, *35*(1), 57–84.

10 Writing across Contexts: From School to Work and Beyond

In addition to examining transfer of learning in the contexts of first-year writing, writing across the disciplines, and writing centers, writing studies scholars have also focused on transfer of writing-related knowledge from school to workplaces and beyond. Whereas the workplace-based research of industrial and organizational psychologists (described in Chapter 3) was motivated by a financial exigence (do the millions of dollars invested in training influence actual workplace practices?), the research of writing studies scholars tends to be motivated by an institutional exigence: do the classroom experiences of students in FYW and later writing-intensive courses adequately prepare them for the demands of the workplace?

Unlike the work of industrial and organizational psychologists, these studies of workplace writing do not include a shift from behaviorist and then cognitive-inspired studies, adopting instead a focus on social contexts from the start. Specifically, this research on school-to-work transfer of learning about writing has been strongly influenced by three theoretical frameworks: Lave and Wenger's (1991) concepts of community of practice and legitimate peripheral participation, Miller's (1984) theorization of the rhetorical nature of genres, and Engeström's (2014) model of activity theory. Thus, the chapter begins with a brief review of those frameworks.

The remainder of the chapter is organized around methodological and then pedagogical concerns. Methodologically, the research on the transition from school to work can be characterized as focusing on specific contexts (examining particular workplaces or classrooms), specific individuals (often taking a longitudinal view spanning years or even decades), and activity systems (focusing not on the transit of individuals but the interfaces between larger institutional organizations). Much of this research, quite predictably, follows writers into their workplaces, studying how writers learn to understand and succeed with the demands of workplace writing. With some notable exceptions (see the section on *Studying individual writers over time and diverse contexts*), this research tends to focus on new employees and remains focused on the classroom-workplace relationship rather than on self-sponsored or civically engaged writing.

Pedagogically, a large portion of the research (and consequently of this chapter) focuses on instructional choices—perhaps not surprising, given writing studies' scholars abiding interest in the transition from school to work. Specifically, this chapter identifies four pedagogical contexts: writing about writing classrooms, classroom-based interactions with clients, workplace-based internships, and adult learning classrooms where prior work experiences sometimes inform school learning. A recurring concern throughout all four is the question of how authentically the instructional experience can replicate the demands of a workplace. Whereas some approaches seek to maximize verisimilitude (the discussions of simulations here clearly echo the discussion of simulations in Chapter 4 and may even remind some readers of early preoccupations with identical elements in Chapter 2), others question the necessity of verisimilitude as well as the assumption that school will always precede work. Throughout the chapter, the role of personal and professional identities also emerges as central.

Theoretical Frameworks for Understanding Writing in Workplaces

Of the three frameworks that writing studies scholars most often draw on in their studies of the relationship between school and work, the framework most clearly tied to the situative learning perspective articulated in Chapter 2 is Lave and Wenger's (1991) theories of situated learning. Whereas the scholarly tradition synthesized in Chapter 2 turned most often to Lave's work on mathematical reasoning in everyday contexts (Lave, 1988), writing studies scholars seeking to understand how individuals learn to participate in a workplace culture have found Lave's work with Wenger especially generative. Although Lave and Wenger never take up questions of writing or transfer of learning directly, their explorations of apprenticeship and learning in situ have had a profound influence on studies of learning to write in workplaces. More specifically, they began their work with an interest in apprenticeships, studying (sometimes through careful analysis of the previous scholarship of others) how people learn to become midwives, tailors, butchers, and more. Lave and Wenger's analyses suggest that apprentices don't learn through explicit instruction or immediate replication of the practices of an expert; rather they learn from participation in the community of individuals engaged in the activity the apprentice wishes to learn, a group Lave and Wenger term a "community of practice."

> [A]pprentices gradually assemble a general idea of what constitutes the practice of the community. This uneven sketch of the enterprise . . . might include who is involved; what they do; what everyday life is like; how masters talk, walk, work, and generally conduct their lives; how people who are not part of the community of practice interact with it; what other learners are doing; and what learners need to learn to become full practitioners. (p. 95)

The key to successful participation in a community of practice, the "defining characteristic" (p. 29) of situated learning, is legitimate peripheral participation (LPP). LPP refers to "the development of knowledgeably skilled identities in practice" in the context of a community of practice's "characteristic biographies/trajectories, relationships, and practices" (p. 55).

Importantly, these concepts of communities of practice and legitimate peripheral participation are meant to resist the misconception that a community of practice is a static, stable discourse community:

> Given the complex, differentiated nature of communities, it seems important not to reduce the end point of centripetal participation in a community of practice to a uniform or univocal "center" or to a linear notion of skill acquisition. There is no place in a community of practice designated "the periphery" and most emphatically, it has no single core or center. Central participation would imply that there is a center (physical, political, or metaphorical) to a community with respect to an individual's "place" in it. Complete participation would suggest a closed domain of knowledge or collective practice

> for which there might be measurable degrees of acquisition by newcomers. We have chosen to call that to which peripheral participation leads full participation. (Lave & Wenger, pp. 36–7)

Scholars interested in transitions from school to work frequently invoke Lave and Wenger to establish a theoretical framework that privileges a focus on how interactions between newcomers and more established members of a community enable newcomers to make sense of and participate in that community. Through this focus on the learning of apprentices—that is, individuals in transit from earlier communities of practice to a new community of practice—Lave and Wenger's work helps illuminate the complex social dimensions of transfer of learning.

A second theoretical framework proves especially useful for scholars interested in how written documents influence and are influenced by workplace cultures. Such scholars frequently turn to Miller's (1984) work on the rhetorical nature of genres and especially to her definition of genres as "typified rhetorical actions based in recurrent situations" (p. 159). Miller and other rhetorical genre theorists have also elaborated upon the crucial role that "antecedent genres"—those genres already known to an individual—can play in interpreting and generating responses to situations.

Seen as a type of rhetorical action rather than simply a static collection of organizational or stylistic conventions, genres provide a path for understanding and participating in the work of a given community, whether at school (see also Chapter 8 on WAC) or in a workplace. It is not uncommon for researchers examining workplace writing to focus on genre as a site of apprenticeship: like any other apprentice, new employees in an office can learn the values and jargon of a particular workplace by co-authoring or "document cycling"[17] (Paradis et al., 1985) with more senior colleagues. Genres are not straightjackets: individual authors can ignore genred expectations, flouting them to greater or lesser effect. Workplace genres can evolve over time, in response to changing work conditions and the innovations of various individuals. Genres are, nevertheless, stabilized-for-now expectations (Schryer, 1993) that provide an important framework for the learning of new employees. They are also, therefore, a valuable theoretical lens

---

17. An iterative "editorial process by which [managers] helped staff members restructure, focus, and clarify their written work" (p. 285).

for scholars seeking to understand workplace writing and its relationship to school-based writing instruction.

Finally, for scholars seeking to understand the interrelationships between different workplace cultures, or the cultures of school and of work, Engeström's (2014) modeling of activity system theory proves particularly useful. Engeström's framework encourages scholars to understand not only the tensions within an activity system but also, importantly, activity systems in relation to one another. An activity system is diagrammed as a triangle highlighting the relationships between three components: *participants*, working on a particular *object* (towards a particular *motive*), employing specific mediational *tools*. Later (second- and third- generation) representations of activity systems include additional elements such as rules, community, and divisions of labor (See figure 2). Scholars employing an activity theory framework often use this triangular representation to illuminate conflicts within and between systems. For instance, Russell and Yanez (2003) analyze how a single student participates in multiple activity systems—often using what ostensibly seem to be the same mediational tools to achieve very different motives. The motive for writing a book review for a school newspaper, they note, can be very different from the motive for writing a book review for an advanced Irish history course.

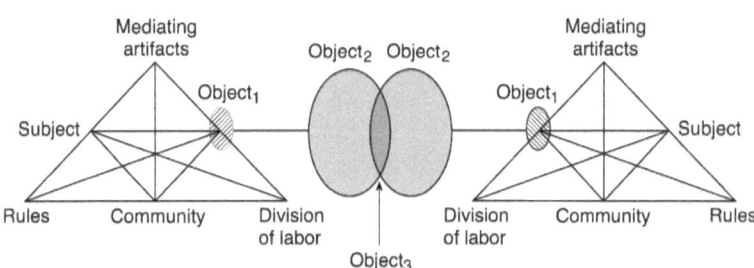

figure 2: Two interacting activity systems as minimal model for the third generation of activity theory, in Y. Engestom (2001) "Expansive Learning at Work"

Individuals participating in multiple activity systems may perceive those conflicts with varying degrees of awareness. In some cases, the conflicts may lead perhaps to a "double-bind," which might lead the individual to shut down from the cognitive dissonance, dismissing the competing expectations as mere idiosyncrasies of individuals. In other cases, the conflict might be transformed into an opportunity for "learning by expanding"—that is, developing a better understanding of how multiple activity systems exist in relation to each other. Thus, while the concepts of *communities of practice, legitimate peripheral participation*, and even *genre* often train their gaze on a single community, cultural historical activity theory prompts scholars to consider the interrelations between multiple communities. By focusing on the potential that participating in multiple activity systems may have (for both doublebinds and learning by expanding), the activity theory framework is particularly useful for illuminating the challenges of moving from school to work when conflicts between those activity systems arise.

Nevertheless, these three frameworks are not mutually exclusive, or even in competition. A significant portion of the scholarship synthesized in the pages that follow invokes two or even all three of these theoretical frameworks. The discussion in the next half of this chapter is organized around the units of analysis adopted in various studies, that is to say, where researchers train their gaze.

Defining the Unit of Analysis for Studying the School-to-Work Relationship: Specific Contexts, Specific Individuals, and Activity Systems

Scholarship on how individuals repurpose what they've learned in school when they enter the workplace can be productively organized around units of analysis—that is, the scope of the data researchers collect. At the risk of oversimplifying, we identify three units of analysis: studies that focus on *specific school and work contexts*, often comparing how writers operate within them; studies that hone in on *particular individuals*, tracking them over long periods of time and across diverse contexts, as they repurpose their knowledge and abilities; and studies that focus not on individual classrooms or workplaces or individuals but on the *interactions between larger activity systems* as a context for transfer of learning.

Studying Specific School and Work Contexts

This category of studies on the transition between school and work envelops so much research that it can be further divided into three subcategories: studies that work to name the particular rhetorical skills necessary for writers transitioning between school and work; studies that use the framework of discourse community to examine the progress of individuals as they work to negotiate the shift from novice to expert in a single workplace; and studies that examine how individuals negotiate the novice-expert transition by focusing on the affordances and constraints of genre.

Rhetorical Skills. Under this heading we group studies that focus on skills or knowledge that individuals might carry from context to context. Ford (2004), for instance, asks "what existing *rhetorical knowledge* do students in engineering classrooms have, and in what ways do students transfer knowledge of these strategies and skills between contexts?" (p. 301, emphasis added); she operationalizes rhetorical knowledge as six textual features highly valued in technical writing courses: "audience awareness, sense of purpose, organization, use of visuals, professional appearance and style" (p. 302). Quick (2012) focuses on *rhetorical adaptability*, a skill that might manifest in the mastery of textual elements or conventions in particular documents—such as mentioning the job for which they are applying in the first paragraph and making more *you* than *I* statements in job application cover letters. The results of these studies that look for the presence of textual conventions in writing consistently disappoint their authors: the students in Quick's study evidence no greater levels of success on a letter writing task; Ford's students dutifully reported that "the writing skills developed in my college English classes helped me during this assignment," but when pressed for details they were unable to identify "higher order rhetorical strategies" (p. 308).

Other studies focus less on evidence of transfer in texts and more on the rhetorical habits of mind students bring to their efforts in the classroom and workplace. Brent (2012), for instance, focuses on *rhetorical judgment*. Following six university students into their co-op semester (an instance of legitimate peripheral participation in the workplace), he finds that although three writers evidenced ability to find and analyze model genres critically, they could not locate a moment in their undergraduate education when they learned to do so: Emma described her knowledge as "a combination of everything I have learned in life" (p. 578) and Christina spoke repeatedly of "common sense," which Brent points out is, in fact, "very sophisticated rhetorical knowledge" (p. 581). Brent's study focuses on the portable rhetorical knowledge that students develop and draw on in their workplaces: "the students seemed to be transferring not so much specific knowledge and skills as a general disposition to make rhetorical judgments" (p. 589).

What these studies share—whether they look for evidence of textual conventions in written documents or evidence of conceptualizations of rhetoric in student interviews—is a focus on the idea of portable rhetorical knowledge which, once acquired, can be put to use across multiple contexts. In this, they echo earlier work in cognitive psychology (Chapter 2) focused on the power of general heuristics, but these findings are somewhat more difficult to reconcile with Perkins and Salomon's (1988) suggestion that high-road transfer involves a mindful abstraction that can be consciously identified and articulated.

Discourse Community. In the tradition of studies that examine school-to-work transitions through the lens of discourse communities, one of the most frequently cited is Anson and Forsberg's (1990) articulation of a developmental schema based on the experiences of six college seniors placed in internships. Students often begin with a sense of *expectation*, entering their internships confident that they will be able to successfully draw on previous writing experiences and strategies. The interns soon enter a stage of *disorientation*, in which they tend to feel isolated and overwhelmed. Ultimately, though, the interns in Anson and Forsberg's study entered into a stage of *transition and resolution*, which allowed them to "finally integrat[e] experience and reflec[t] on the intellectual changes afforded by writing in the new context" (p. 208). Successfully entering and communicating within the discourse community of the workplace, Anson and Forsberg conclude, is about more than simply applying what was learned in school; it involves becoming a student of that particular workplace culture, adapting to the expectations of a particular discourse community.

Winsor (1996) also uses the framework of discourse community to study four engineering students, tracking in more depth and over a longer span of time how new employees navigate the acquisition of writing expertise in a single workplace. After talking with students who were completing an undergraduate degree that included several semesters of co-op placement, Winsor concludes that although all four of her focal students had acquired a richer sense of audience expectations, only one focal student had developed a sense of how workplace documents could create rather than simply document corporate reality. The others persisted in the belief that their jobs were to document data rather than persuade. However, Winsor continued to interview the same four writers—all of whom were offered full-time employment with their co-op companies—at regular intervals over the next several years and found that their sense of the importance of "documentation" increased significantly. Winsor defines documentation as "the representation of past or future action used to build agreement about how that action is to be defined or perceived" (p. 207); documentation, in this view, isn't just paperwork after the fact, but a means for engineers to protect themselves from liability or prompt action from a client or another corporate division. Producing documentation, then, is vital for full-time long-term employees in ways that simply would not register for short-term student workers. In short, Winsor argues that as individuals become increasingly authentic and authorized participants within their discourse community, their writing grows more effective and more richly theorized. Her methodological commitment to tracking writers over many years allows her to illuminate how the understandings of writing that engineers transferred from their classroom studies were, over time, revised.

Beaufort (2007) tracks a similar progress from outsider to insider status by following "Tim" from his first-year writing class, through various history and engineering courses, and eventually into his work as an engineer where he demonstrates rhetorical savvy: "In only two years time and without any formal coaching on his writing by his employer, Tim could articulate many of the social constraints on written texts and the necessary processes and conventions" (p. 140). Beaufort's earlier work (1997, 1999) similarly exemplifies not only the discourse community approach to understanding the school-to-work transition, but also the ways in which researchers often draw on multiple theoretical frameworks. A discourse community, Beaufort explains, is

> a dynamic social entity within which a set of distinctive, yet changeable, writing practices occur in relation to other modes of communication as a result of the community's shared values and goals, the material conditions for text production, and the influence of individual community members' idiosyncratic purposes and skills as writers. (1997, p. 522)

Over multiple publications, Beaufort (1999, 2007) develops a model of writing expertise that identifies discourse community knowledge, genre knowledge, and rhetorical knowledge (as well as subject matter and writing process knowledge) as existing in "symbiotic relation to each other (1999, pp. 63–4); in Beaufort's model, the circle representing discourse community knowledge encompasses the other four overlapping knowledge domains. The primacy of discourse community knowledge over the other domains of knowledge suggests the distinctive quality of studies focused on discourse communities: namely, a focus on how individuals develop increasing expertise in one particular discourse community.

Research indicates that students who have some prior cultural and organizational knowledge may find their way more rapidly into the social complexity of organizations. Artemeva (2005), for instance, argues that novices with enough cultural capital can sometimes follow an alternate path: Sami, a recent engineering graduate whose father and grandfather were both engineers and who possesses a remarkable sense of the kairotic moment available to him in his corporate engineering culture, was able to catapult over several layers of hierarchy to get his implementation plan approved in his first year of employment. Artemeva recounts Sami's savvy use of spoken and written genres (written proposals, oral presentations) and interpersonal connections (he had the support of his manager's supervisor) to critique and alter the expected pathways even as a new employee. From the example of Sami and others, Artemeva (2009) emphasizes the importance of agency (in recognizing kairotic moments in the workplace), "cultural capital, domain content expertise, formal education, private intention, understanding the improvisational qualities of genre, and workplace experiences" (p. 172). Throughout these studies framed by discourse communities is a consistent focus on tracking how individual writers move from novice to expert status, through longer or shorter, bumpier or smoother paths as they transfer knowledge and abilities from the classroom to the workplace.

Genre Knowledge. Taken for granted throughout the studies framed by discourse communities is an interest in the development of individual writers and the existence of a relatively stable disciplinary community, assumptions that are challenged in the studies focused on how the acquisition of professional expertise is mediated through written and spoken genres. Certainly, these are not exclusive categories: many scholars focused on discourse communities also attend to the function of genres in those communities. Nevertheless, what distinguishes these studies is their interest in uncovering how genres function in different contexts (i.e., at school versus in workplaces) to offer affordances and constraints for individuals moving from school to work (and in some cases back again).

In her study of how two employees acclimated to their new positions at the Job Resource Center (JRC), Beaufort (1997) documents how new employees like Ursula and Pam sometimes initially resisted the conventions that reflected community norms, but eventually "demonstrated their understanding of the ways in the which genre . . . needed to reflect the underlying values and standards for accomplishing goals" of JRC (p. 502). Such a finding resonates with the work of Anson and Forsberg and others described in the discourse community section. However, Beaufort also illuminates the exceedingly high stakes of learning not just textual conventions but the community values and identities that constellate around those textual conventions: Beaufort shares how one person was fired because she stayed "in her cubicle and wr[ote] endless internal memos rather than meeting with people face-to-face" (p. 498). Although this employee may have understood the textual conventions of the internal memo, she did not understand how work got done at JRC; in this workplace, the real value of the memo was not in the ideas it put forth, but the consensus that could be built through face-to-face talk *before* the memo codified those conversations. While this particular occurrence may be inflected by the employee's interpersonal skills, Beaufort's larger point ultimately focuses on the work that genres help to accomplish within the workplace. For writing studies scholars interested in transfer of learning, Beaufort's work highlights the ways in which successful transitions from school to work rely not only on knowledge of writing conventions of but the social and rhetorical functions writing plays.

A similar focus on the complex social and personal identity work negotiated through workplace genres emerges from the inquiries conducted by a coalition of Canadian scholars, most prominently gathered in two books: *Transitions* (Dias & Paré, 2000) and *Worlds Apart* (Dias et al., 1999). They examined writing in four professions—public administration, management, architecture, and social work—simultaneously in school and at work. For instance, at the same time they studied how writing was taught and used in a university social work classroom, they also studied how experienced social workers used writing in their daily workplace. From those comparisons, Dias and colleagues conclude that there is "a radical difference" between school and work (1999, p. 199), in terms of goals for the writing (p. 189), processes of scaffolding new colleagues into complex tasks (p. 190), and modes of collaboration and evaluation through document cycling (p. 194, p. 196). School and work are, as the title of the book indicates, worlds apart. This distinction is highlighted in their comparison of distributed cognition in universities and in the workplace of the Bank of Canada: "To put it simply, the . . . Governor of the BOC needs the lowliest analyst's report. The professor, however, does not need any specific student's essay in the same way" (p. 148). Because of these fundamentally different ways of building knowledge, the shift from participation in an academic community to a workplace community is often surprisingly difficult.

Traversing that gap, researchers demonstrate, is a high-stakes project that often relies on the affordances and constraints of genres. Paré (2000), for instance, illuminates the ways in which university students interning as social workers learn, through a process of document cycling with an experienced social work supervisor, genres that "allow students, literally and figuratively, to speak the same language as oldtimers" (p. 149). Parks (2001) tracks the experiences of nurses who were taught one system of writing care plans in school but encounter a very different approach to care plans in the workplace. The changes, including abbreviated diagnoses as well as a shift to medical rather than nursing language, at first appear to simply be shortcuts. Parks demonstrates, however, that for new nurses, the process of adopting these changes is in fact a means of "navigating the boundaries between a school genre and a workplace genre" and consequently a way of "signaling their identities as professionals who were progressively appropriating the culturally accepted ways of doing and seeing" (p. 415). Smart (2000) similarly notes that Bank of Canada employees authoring an article for the *Bank of Canada Review* spoke of "upholding their sense of professionalism in the face of critiques of their texts from more senior reviewers" (p. 243); the processes of collaboration and interaction required to learn workplace genres involve complex negotiations of personal and professional identity.

Like Anson and Forsberg, many of these studies map a trajectory of (un)learning for writers new to workplace writing—but they go even further to illuminate the ways in which genres become a site for the negotiation of identities, especially for new employees working with experienced colleagues. Throughout these studies focused on genre is threaded an interest not simply in the conventions of workplace genres, but how they are necessarily understood in the context of the writer's emerging professional identity. By writing (sometimes alone, sometimes with more experienced colleagues), new employees repurpose their existing genre knowledge in an effort to create for themselves a new identity as a valuable and contributing employee. Although these studies focus primarily on genre, they also suggest that in order to understand the role of genre in transfer we must also closely consider identity.

If genres play such an important role in workplace learning, one logical question is whether genre knowledge might be more effectively developed in university settings through explicit instruction in genre conventions and expectations.[18] In an early article, Freedman (1993) takes up that question directly, drawing on existing research—particularly from Krashen in second language acquisition—to probe two hypotheses. The strong hypothesis proposes that explicit teaching may not be possible and is certainly not helpful; the restricted hypothesis posits that "teaching must always be done either in the context of, or in very close proximity to, authentic tasks involving the relevant discourse" (p. 244). Explicit teaching of genre, Freedman concludes, may be dangerously counterproductive because it can lead writers to overgeneralize and to focus on formal features rather than meaning and function—especially if the instructor is "an outsider" or has an "inaccurate representation of the genre" (p. 245). Freedman et al. (1994) further develop this position in their studies of learning in classroom and workplace contexts. They conclude that simulations unconnected to workplaces can never be more than a fiction disconnected from workplace realities; internships embedded in actual workplaces, however, can provide some powerful opportunities for learning both genres and the workplace values that inform them.

This questioning of the value or necessity of explicit instruction is further developed by Eraut (2004), who studies learning within the

---

18. Some readers may be reminded of Gick and Holyoak's (1980, 1983) work in cognitive psychology on the relative merits of prompting analogical thinking by providing individuals with abstract explanations of principles versus providing them with one or more analogous stories.

workplace, focused both on new hires and midcareer professionals. Combining interviews with workplace observations, Eraut concludes that learning in the workplace is typically informal, invisible, and taken for granted; the resulting knowledge is tacit. There are occasions of non-tacit learning, but they tend to be reactive—"occur[ing] in the middle of the action, when there is little time to think" (p. 250)—rather than deliberate or pre-planned. "Outside formal education and training settings," Eraut concludes, "explicit learning is often unplanned" (p. 250). The suggestion, in Eraut as in Freedman, is that within workplaces explicit instruction in genre is rare and therefore within classrooms can slip into irrelevance. Ultimately, these researchers raise serious questions and express deep skepticism about the ability of schools to prepare writers for work.

Studying Individual Writers Over Time and Diverse Contexts

Under this heading we place studies that focus on an individual moving among many systems, generally over a year or more. On the whole, the studies we collect here tend to resist the novice/expert and insider/outsider dichotomies at the heart of so many other individuals-in-transit studies; they are interested instead in how identities shape and are shaped by writing over time. These studies also resist the casting of school and work as worlds apart; this is the tradition of research most likely to incorporate a focus on self-sponsored writing and other writing activities that aren't clearly academic or for work. To the degree that there is overlap between the school-to-work studies that dominate this chapter and the home-to-school studies discussed at length in Chapter 5 ("Transfer Implications from Sociocultural and Sociohistorical Literacy Studies), that overlap can be seen most clearly in this strand of research.

Lemke's (2000) concept of *heterochrony*, the interlocked nature of various timescales, offers an important reminder of how school and "real" life are always inextricably linked. In Lemke's view, individual students are always in the process of enacting who they are in the world; in any given classroom, students

> are mainly going about the business of learning to be six-year-olds or twelve-year-olds, masculine or feminine, gay or heterosexual, middle-class or working-class, Jewish or Catholic, Irish-American or Jamaican-American, or any of the many

> dozens of stereotypical identities for which there are identity-kits available in a particular community (cf Gee 1992). Whatever we offer in the classroom becomes an opportunity to purpose this longer-term agenda of identity building; our primary affective engagement is with this agenda, with becoming who we want to be, not with learning this or that bit of curriculum, except in so far as it fits our particular agenda or insofar as "being a good student" or "not falling for that bullshit" fits in. (p. 286)

To dichotomize school and work, novices and experts, is to ignore how much overlap people experience in their lives—and how long those overlaps extend. Wertsch's idea of the "spin off" reminds us that the "repurposing of cultural tools across contexts is the rule rather than the exception" (in Roozen, 2010, p. 28). Prior and Shipka (2003) term such overlaps chronotopic laminations—"the simultaneous layering of multiple activity frames and stances . . . which are relatively foregrounded and backgrounded" (p. 187). They provide the example of Melissa Orlie, a professor of political science and women's studies, who had recently published an academic press book wrestling with questions of living ethically and acting politically. Through analysis of interviews, drawings, and the text of Orlie's book, Prior and Shipka illuminate a network of overlapping influences on that book: friends, classmates, and professors from Orlie's undergraduate studies; her "varied moments of writing, reading, walking, and gardening" (p. 201); and the formative experience of living in a not-yet-gentrified neighborhood in Brooklyn. When looked at from this angle, school and work and even home are not worlds apart; they are inseparable. Transfer of learning, from this perspective, is a common, everyday experience.

Roozen's work offers example after example of similarly interconnected reading and writing practices. One student, Kate, finds that her work in her literature and creative writing classes is powerfully influenced by her strong and long-standing identification as a writer of fan fiction and creator of fan art; the interconnections are so strong that they lead Kate to pursue an alternate career path when her fannish commitments are not valued in her creative writing course (Roozen, 2009). Another student, Brian, is an undergraduate math education major who learns about pi and negative infinity in his math class, incorporates those concepts into a recurring comedy sketch performed with his improv group (a poetry slam evaluated with mathematical symbols), and then uses those repurposings as a springboard for instructional work he does as a student teacher in the workplace of his middle-school math classroom. "Brian's use of specialized mathematical discourse," Roozen demonstrates, "is not limited to privileged sites of school and work; rather, it circulates through these extensive nexus of practice that connect the literate activity of his school classes, his sketch comedy, his gaming, his teaching, and perhaps others as well" (2010, p. 48). Charles, a first-year student struggling with speeches in the prerequisite to his Broadcast Journalism major, draws on a complex web of interests and experiences to improve his oral presentation skills: he began reading his high school poetry at the university's African American cultural center's weekly poetry readings, and eventually draws on his journalism experiences as well as the support of friends and his diverse reading interests to develop a standup routine for the university open mic (Roozen, 2008). In this way, Charles improves his speech grade from an F to an A, keeping open a curricular path to the employment in broadcast journalism he desires. The resources Charles, Brian, and Kate draw on as university students stretch back years and connect with a wide range of activities and identities.

In this way, Roozen's research helpfully illuminates how the extra-curriculum might enrich our ideas of transfer—but even within the context of workplace writing, Roozen's research highlights how learning to write as a math teacher, for instance, is not a compartmentalized skill set: it is laminated by all the overlapping engagements of Brian's life. To understand transfer from this research perspective is not about tracking the acquisition of expertise in a single domain but understanding how moments and laminations add up to lives. Consequently, this type of research—focused as it is on how individuals accrue and repurpose knowledge across many different contexts—resonates with other discussions (in psychology [see Chapter 2] and literacy studies [see Chapter 5] and elsewhere) that focus on adaptive expertise and the ability to successfully navigate novel contexts.

Going further, Prior (2018) develops the idea of a "trajectory of semiotic becoming" to challenge the "worlds apart" findings of Dias and colleagues (1999). Tracing the 25-year development of Nora (his daughter) from her kindergarten interests in *Nature* programming on PBS to her field work as a professional biologist in Uganda, he argues that "her emerging patterns of interest, what she chose to read, watch, talk about, and do, what she selectively oriented to in her cultural worlds and what she rejected . . . built her pathways to becoming a biologist." (It may also be that Nora shares cultural capital from her academic family that might bear on the ease of movement in the domains she explored as child and adult, as suggested in Artemeva [2005, 2009].) Based on Nora's example and others in progress, Prior concludes that the "worlds apart" thesis is an "absurd" claim that is "fundamentally wrong"; he argues that transfer of learning is not "a fragile, torturously hard-won achievement" but rather that "continuities of learning across time and setting are a fundamental necessity for any conceivable account of human development." For Prior, these profoundly different views are grounded in different methodological approaches: instead of focusing on discrete discourse communities, he describes his own work as "draw[ing] on sociocultural/CHAT theories that take learning/socialization to be the mediated production and co-genesis of both the person and society across *heterogeneous* times, places, and activities."

Other scholars turning their attention to the development of writing over decades have been guided by other theoretical frameworks, most notably theories of life-course human development. Bazerman and a group of multi-disciplinary colleagues (2018) worked over several years to develop eight principles that might guide future inquiries into writing development across the lifespan. Although their edited collection is filled with essays focusing on different ages and contexts from a range of disciplinary perspectives, of particular interest in this chapter is the work of Brandt who re-analyzed interviews with sixty adult workplace writers in light of life-span development theories. Paying particular attention to workplace roles, historical moments, and dispositions, Brandt (2018) argues that her data—while imperfect—are deeply suggestive and highlight again the co-constructive interactions between personal identifications and writing in the workplace. Not only does Brandt argue that "writing orientations developed through workplace practice [get] incorporated into a person's more general dispositions towards life" (p. 266), she also tracks ways in which early childhood experiences were "creatively transformed into productive orientations to writing" (p. 265). Such findings, she argues, "force an expansion of what is considered transfer in writing" (p. 265). Drawing on the idea of "structuring proclivities"—the idea of prominent lifespan theorist Urie Bronfenbrenner—or dispositions, she calls on future researchers to "expand the search (and what we consider searchable) for the psychological processes that make up life-to-writing transformations, transfers, and amalgamations" (p. 265).

Throughout these studies is an insistence that school and work are not worlds apart, but remain closely tethered and mediated by the dispositions, laminations, and dynamic identities of the writer.

Activity Systems in Contact

In this final category we place studies that are fundamentally interested not in individuals shifting among contexts but in the relationships between those contexts or domains. Whereas Lave and Wenger's idea of communities of practice "emphasizes the practices themselves as a unit of reflection and analysis" (Beach, 1999, p. 114), Engeström and colleagues direct attention to the relationship among various activity systems. In its so-called third generation, activity theory attends not just to activity systems but to their overlaps: "Theories of learning typically speak of the outcomes of learning in terms of knowledge, skills and changed patterns of behavior. In expansive learning, the outcomes are expanded objects and new collective work practices, including practices of thinking and discourse" (p. 339). Tuomi-Gröhn et al. (2003) explain that their unit of analysis for understanding learning becomes "the collective activity system" and that "what is transferred is not packages of knowledge and skills that remain intact; instead the very process of such transfer involves active interpreting, modifying, and reconstructing the skills and knowledge transferred" (p. 4). The focus in such research is no longer individuals shifting among discourse communities or activity systems, but the sustained overlaps between activity systems which are themselves altered by the shuttling of individuals between them.

Particularly useful for this understanding of how activity systems can change one another are the concepts of *boundary zones, boundary encounters,* and *boundary objects.* Boundary objects can be either material or semiotic and are important for transfer because they "have different meaning in different social worlds but their structure is common enough to more than one world to make them recognizable, a means of transition" (Star and Griesemer quoted in Veillard, 2012, p. 257). One use of boundary objects is visible in Ludvigsen et al.'s (2003) study of sales engineers within a Norwegian firm that develops heating and ventilation systems. Sales engineers negotiate with customers, securing business through the writing of bids; such work positions them as boundary spanners within their own firm. The bid is a boundary object that "combines standardization and flexibility" and "creates both common and different meanings depending on the position of the person who 'reads' the bid" (p. 301). Through the genre of the bid, a sales engineer can—indeed must—communicate with their customers as well as their engineering colleagues, negotiating what is possible within the constraints of time and budget.

Another example, taken from Konkola et al.'s (2007) description of an occupational therapy internship, offers an even clearer example of how the various activity systems themselves may be changed by extended contact via boundary objects. In this study, an occupational therapy student interning at a hospital contacted a researcher at a Finnish university to learn more about a relatively untested method: mirror rehabilitation. Working to implement this new rehab technique was the occasion for multiple meetings between the intern, her university professor, and the occupational therapist supervising the intern; together they worked—through their focus on the boundary object of mirror rehabilitation—to develop a practice that changed (in small but discernible ways) both the activity systems of the university and occupational therapy. Such an approach "shifts the emphasis from the individual transfer of knowledge to the collaborative efforts of organizations to create new knowledge and practices" (p. 211) and exemplifies the focus of some researchers on how activity systems themselves can transfer knowledge, practices, and values to one another.

Although this research focus on the interaction between activity systems themselves (rather than on individuals participating in multiple activity systems) is relatively rare, instructors have—as the next section on pedagogical approaches illustrates—sometimes taught students about cultural historical activity theory as a means of helping students understand their own professional, rhetorical situations.

Pedagogical Contexts for Examining the School-to-Work Transition

The first half of this chapter identified three common theoretical frameworks (communities of practice, genre theory, and activity theory) and distinguished three units of analysis for studying transfer of learning from school to work (focus on specific workplaces, focus on specific individuals over time and diverse contexts, and focus on activity systems) that draw on one or more of those frameworks. In the remainder of this chapter, we review the research on transfer of learning in four different pedagogical contexts: writing about writing courses that include observations of workplace writing, classroom-based interactions with clients, workplace-based internships, and adult education.

Professional Writing Courses with a Writing About Writing Focus

We turn first to the professional writing course designed for students from a number of majors. Such courses are a marked contrast to technical writing courses linked to a very particular profession (such as engineering) or subfield (such as industrial engineering). Within multi-major professional writing courses, a focus on the writing about writing (WAW) approach to curriculum design has emerged. More commonly found in first-year writing courses (see Chapter 7), the WAW approach adopts a content focus on research in writing studies as a means of promoting transfer of learning about writing (Downs & Wardle, 2007).

Kain and Wardle (2005), for instance, take up the question of whether "teaching communication in a classroom setting can adequately present (or even represent) the rhetorical and practical realities of complex professional communication situations" (p. 113). Although Wardle's work here with Kain predates her later articulation of WAW with Downs (Downs & Wardle, 2007), this approach does resonate easily with the WAW approach in that the course is grounded in activity theory—not only as the organizing framework, but as content. In their two different courses, Kain and Wardle introduced their students to the principles of activity theory and then asked them to go into workplaces, to observe and interview participants, then to analyze the communicative practices of that workplace. Although documenting instances or patterns of actual transfer is beyond the scope of their study, they find that their students' analyses of workplaces were more complex than those received in previous iterations of the course not informed by activity theory, and they predict that "teaching students to research genre use in complex workplace contexts using activity theory encourages high road transfer" (p. 135).

Several authors aim to complicate and diversify WAW approaches to writing in the workplace: Read and Michaud (2019) inventory ten other instructors already taking a WAW approach in professional writing courses; one commonality that emerges is the emphasis on teaching "students how to do their own research about writing in workplace contexts" (p. 160)—but how they do so varies. Cutrufello (2019) describes a curriculum that privileges reflective writing and cueing of future transfer; its central project is a recommendation report. Research on these WAW approaches to the multi-major professional writing course have not yet systematically documented the consequences of a WAW approach for transfer from the multi-major professional writing course to workplaces; such work is a necessary next step for future research.

Classroom-Based Interactions with Clients

In this group we place pedagogical contexts that promote interactions with clients—either real or imaginary—but remain based within a university classroom. More specifically, we include in this category three distinct types of classroom-based interventions: simulations, client-based projects, and service-learning projects. These pedagogical contexts rely on varying degrees of fidelity to promote transfer of learning from school to work.

Simulations. While simulations may gesture beyond the classroom to fictionalized workplaces, there is no direct contact with actual clients or workplaces. One frequently cited study of the potential for transfer of learning within a simulation-based course offered a scathing critique (Freedman, Adam, & Smart, 1994). Students in this upper-division financial analysis course were asked to take on the role of a management consultant and provide recommendations through written and oral presentations; the textbook that provided the case studies did not prime students to look for applications of any particular theory, potentially allowing a more "naturalistic" context for learning. Furthermore, both the instructor and students went to great lengths to create the fiction of the simulation: designing assignments and providing documents to establish and maintain the fiction of the company, wearing suits to class when making their presentations, and more. Nevertheless, Freedman and colleagues conclude, "the real audience for the students was always the professor—in his role as *professor*" (p. 203), and students "were never deceived about this" (p. 204). The thinness of the fiction was visible both in what appeared in their projects (students elaborated on certain knowledge "to show [they] know the lines of reasoning appropriate for recommending policy within the relevant community" [p. 204]) and in what did not appear in those projects (a student stopped chasing a line of reasoning when he realized "Oh, but that would make it into a marketing case" p. 205). Spinuzzi (1996), drawing on language from Petraglia, terms this persistent challenge facing professional writing instructors psuedotransactionality; pseudotransactional writing "evolve[s] to accomplish the goals of a specific classroom rather than those of the workplace that the classroom supposedly emulates" (p. 302).

Cognizant of the limitations documented by Freedman and colleagues, many scholars still advocate for simulations as a means to promote transfer of learning about writing. Some scholars argue that increasing the verisimilitude of the simulation might increase the possibility of transfer.[19] Paretti (2008), for instance, argues that to succeed, an engineering design course aiming to "engage students in authentic engineering tasks" must have instructors who "interact with students around those assignments in ways that highlight the associated social action—i.e., the purposes documents serve in the design process and in the course" (p. 493). Although Paretti's case study shows that the two teams still experience a disjoint between school and work (echoing conclusions in Freedman and colleagues' research), she proposes that one way to address the gap is to be more mindful of discourse:

> The difference is perhaps shockingly simple—something as slight as replacing "You need to include more detail in your timeline" with "I need to see more detail in the timeline to have a better sense of what you're actually planning to do, what kind of help I can provide, and whether you can realistically meet your deadline." (2008, p. 500)

Whereas Paretti focuses on ways in which the rhetorical context can be made sufficiently realistic, Russell and Fisher (2009) designed a virtual learning environment (VLE) intended to significantly increase the simulation's verisimilitude. They worked to design an online environment that would "afford a much more dynamic circulation of information and a much more complex system of genres than in a traditional VLE" (171). In other words, their fictional company immersed students and instructor not only in roles, but in an emerging "chronotope"—that is "the time-space setting invoked—the landscape

---

19. For more on the possible importance of verisimilitude in simulations hoping to foster transfer of learning, see Chapter 4.

of interactions" (169). The VLE increased verisimilitude by requiring students to complete a series of interlocking assignments that allowed students to experience the genre system of the fictional workplace; it was, Russell and Fisher conclude, "a 'transfer-encouraging' environment" (187).

Campbell (2017) is less focused on verisimilitude than on what (following Crocco) she calls critical simulations; such simulations "produce cognitive dissonance for participants between their assumptions about a specific context and their experience of that context in a simulation" (260). Following a cohort of nursing students through multiple patient-care simulations—simulations in which students know the mechanized patient is voiced by an instructor, in which they both observe and are observed by other students, and after which they will engage in reflective group discussion—Campbell argues that simulations and workplace experiences can be helpfully understood as mutually influential. It's always clear to students that this is a classroom. Indeed, because of financial and technical constraints, the university cannot use the electronic health forms used in hospitals; students instead work in teams to develop their own charting system. Nevertheless,

> the simulation chart draws on students' prior knowledge from their clinical experiences enabling them to repurpose and play with clinical genre knowledge in a context that is focused primarily on learning. . . . [T]he simulation health record is also forward-looking, helping students to better understand how electronic charting will mediate conversations with the patient and other providers in the hospital and consider both the strengths and limitations of the genre. (p. 274)

Students' experiences with simulations may be influenced by their previous workplace experiences as well as prepare students for future workplace experiences.

In sum, throughout the scholarship on simulations runs a disagreement that threads through the workplace scholarship as a whole: are school and work worlds apart, or does communication within school always have a "realness" that can be leveraged to facilitate learning that can successfully transfer?

Client-Based Projects. Whereas simulations rely on a fictionalized client whom the students will never encounter directly, client-based projects serve the needs of an actual client. Acknowledging Freedman and colleagues' critique of simulations, Blakeslee (2001) wonders if client-based assignments "that involve actual workplace projects are different" because they "potentially preserve more of the culture of the workplace while also allowing students to address a variety of audiences" (p. 170). She conducted teacher-research in two of her own professional writing classes, and drawing from interviews and textual analyses, she concludes that although client-based projects don't provide the immersive experience called for by Freedman and colleagues, such courses "still can *expose* students to workplace writing practices, as well as to the activity systems of particular workplaces" (p. 176).

Indeed, although they were extremely critical of the limitations of simulations, Freedman and colleagues were themselves far more optimistic about the promise of client-based projects for facilitating transfer from school to work. Freedman and Adam (2000) describe a systems analysis practicum in which students worked directly with actual clients. In this course, the professor went with the group to their first interview with the client, guiding them when necessary, and spent a lot of time with the students afterwards, reviewing what was learned. Such "authentic" tasks "provided a taste of the complexity of workplace activity" (p. 133)—a difference visible in their comparisons between this client-based project and the business course simulation. For instance, in the simulations class a student discarded a line of reasoning not because it was inappropriate for the problem but because it was not a good fit for the subject matter of the class; the performance of student roles easily trumped the "reality" of the simulation. In the systems analysis practicum, however, when one group discovered that the client's problem could be easily solved by using a piece of existing software, the instructor "simply congratulated the students on their fortuitous find and awarded them the same grade as the other students who ended up putting in countless hours to solve their client's problem" (p. 139). The course emphasis was not on performing certain student roles or obligations; the emphasis was simply on solving the client's problem. Freedman and Adam identify some criteria that helped this client-based curriculum succeed, including an exceptionally skilled instructor who had a small class, considerable autonomy, and connections to a client base.

Research by Dannels makes clear, though, that the mere existence of a client does not automatically eliminate contradictions between the activity systems of school and work. Although the teams of mechanical engineering students Dannels (2003) worked with were in fact designing a project for a real client, they had very little contact with that client; instead they spent their time with the professor, their classmates, and other professors in the engineering department. Whereas the academic context was process oriented and valued displays of knowledge, the engineering context was decidedly product oriented. The conflicts between those two systems became clear when the student engineers prepared and delivered their oral presentations, ostensibly to their clients but delivered in their classroom to their professors and classmates. When confronted by contradictory demands, the importance of identities (a recurring theme in this chapter) once again came to the fore: both faculty and students defaulted to academic identities and values. For instance, faculty evaluated the presentations with a focus on their classroom obligation to make sure students had technical knowledge: after one presentation the faculty responded, "OK, that's good, but talk to me about the real numbers now, not just the ones you prettied up for management" (p. 158).

Sounding much more like Freedman and colleagues' conclusions on simulations, Dannels declares that "School will never be the workplace; it will always be school" (2000, p. 28) and suggests that instructors incorporate more reflection and strengthen ties with the client. Freedman and Adam's research in the systems analysis practicum suggests that this last suggestion—to increase interaction with the client—is important, but that even more than that, client-based projects will only ever begin to bridge the gap between school and work if instructors allow the workplace values (e.g., an emphasis on product, rather than demonstration of process) to govern work in this client-based classroom.

Service Learning. Another significant line of research on the learning—and transfer of learning—that takes place in client-oriented classrooms comes from the field of service learning. Although there is a great deal of scholarship on writing and writing instruction in the context of service learning, much of it is beyond the scope of this chapter. Here we focus on a small subset of articles that explicitly work to understand the transfer of learning between school and service-learning workplaces.

Bacon (1999) frames service-learning placements as an opportunity to disrupt the usual narrative of novice students working to become experts in a single workplace: "In service-learning programs, we create opportunities for students to move back and forth between the campus and the community in the hope that each setting will grant them access to insights that enrich their experience of the other" (p. 55). Framing the study as an inquiry into the "trouble with transfer," Bacon examines the degree to which students' history of academic success might correlate with their work in their service-learning placement. She notes first that "the most proficient academic writers produced the most successful [Community Service Writing] documents," calculating a correlation that was statistically significant and "consistent with the expectation of the faculty participants" (p. 56). But Bacon also argues that her qualitative analyses of reflective essays and interviews suggest that it was not the academic experience of writers that led to successful community writing—but rather qualities like "love for writing, . . . commitment to finding a personal connection with the topic, and . . . willingness to throw [themselves] into the work" (p. 58) that facilitate success in both academic and service-learning workplace contexts. Such findings resonate with research on the role dispositions and identities might play in transfer of learning discussed in the section "Studying Individuals Writers Over Time and Diverse Contexts" in this chapter. (See also Driscoll & Powell, 2016; Driscoll & Wells, 2012; and the discussion of dispositions in Chapter 3.)

In contrast to Bacon's interest in tracking how academic learning might influence writers' abilities to succeed in writing beyond the university, other scholars have focused attention on the degree to which the experience of writing in service-learning placements might influence students' abilities to navigate their academic writing. White (2015), for instance, followed a cohort of eight students from their service-learning oriented first-year writing course into their second semester of college; from these case studies, White argues that service-learning placements can help students develop "transferrable writing knowledge" (p. 26). DePalma (2012) similarly draws on interviews with students from a professional and technical writing course to argue for the existence of "adaptive transfer" while Alexander and Powell (2012) use questionnaires to interrogate what students learned about writing from their service-learning placements.

Service-learning placements, these researchers argue, may be especially powerful sites for two dimensions of learning. First, service learning promotes motivation that in turn facilitates learning about writing. (Readers may be reminded of how the I/O scholarship reviewed in Chapter 3 seeks to understand how training design choices [like service learning] can be correlated with dispositions like motivation.) DePalma quotes students describing how their interpersonal commitments to clients energized them to not give up on difficult projects; Alexander and Powell find that 33% of participants identify "the purpose of [their] service learning project [as] more meaningful than for a traditional assignment" (p. 53). White tracks how students were moved by their projects to negotiate the role of personal experiences and investment in academic writing.

Second, students learned, through their service-learning placements, things about writing that may likely influence their work as writers beyond the placement. DePalma focuses on the ways in which students' understandings of their ethical obligations as communicators were enhanced; Alexander and Powell argue that students identify increased "literacies in teamwork, communication, and project management" (p. 52) that may influence their work in future courses and workplaces. White's research actually follows students longitudinally from one semester to the next, allowing her to identify the ways in which students' learning about writing—including a focus on the need to read broadly in an academic conversation and finding their own investment in a project—was later parlayed into success in other classes. Through her case studies White suggests that the affective dimensions of service-learning placements may influence not simply knowledge acquisition, but a dispositional orientation towards transfer.

Winding through all these pedagogical approaches—service-learning courses, client-based projects, and simulations—is a concern regarding the realness of the work. That concern becomes much less of an issue in internships located within workplaces.

Internships

In this group we place pedagogical approaches that are primarily based not in classrooms but in workplaces through internship or co-op placements. Accounts of internships and co-ops are abundant in the workplace writing scholarship (e.g., Anson & Forsberg, 1990; Bourelle, 2012, 2014; Winsor, 1996). Some of this scholarship focuses on how individual students learn to participate in workplace settings through an internship; other scholarship focuses on the potential of internships to transform not only the individual but also the varied activity systems that come into contact via the internship.

Most commonly, scholars have focused on internships as a site of immersive learning, praising them as opportunities for learning deeply engaged in an authentic community of practice. Freedman and Adam (1996), for instance, compare students in a public administration program with public sector interns, arguing that the different contexts offer very different learning opportunities. In school, they argue, students are offered opportunities for "facilitated performance" that are "oriented entirely toward the learner and to the learner's learning" (pp. 402-3); instructors, for example, lecture to help students learn, not for purposes of their own learning or accomplishing a task beyond instruction. In workplaces, interns and new employees experience attenuated authentic participation in which "no conscious attention is paid to the learner's learning; all attention is directed to the task at hand and its successful completion" (p. 410). Freedman and Adam illustrate this point with the example of a supervisor sitting and writing together with his intern: this collaborative exercise is not undertaken to instruct the intern but rather to compose a document due to a government official within a very short timeframe. What this collaboration offers the intern, though, is an opportunity for the kind of scaffolded learning predicted by Lave and Wenger's model of legitimate peripheral participation.

Other researchers have similarly stressed the importance, for writers transitioning from school to work, of participating in a community of practice. Bremner (2011) tracks the learning curve of an intern placed in a public relations firm, identifying—through analysis of interviews and the intern's reflective journals—a change in her lexicon, a discernible shift from outsider to insider discourse. The two main factors influencing the intern's learning were, Bremner argues, "the opportunity to learn by doing and getting input from her coworkers" (p. 23)—opportunities not easily available in classroom-based projects. Paré and Le Maistre (2006) place a similar importance on apprenticeship in their longitudinal study of social work students moving from their field placement internship into their first full-time jobs. In an effort to determine what accounts for successful transitions, they conclude that "in settings where induction seemed to us most successful . . . newcomers were transformed from students or recent graduates to practitioners through interaction with a number of veteran practitioners" engaged in the central work of the professional community, rather than specially created instructional experiences (p. 364). They conclude that the "movement toward expertise is collaborative" (p. 364) and end with advice for internship students (get actively involved) and instructors (distribute mentorship); Kohn (2015) draws similar lessons for mentoring workplace writing in the context of university-workplace partnerships.

Other scholars suggest that much of an internship's success in fostering transfer may rest not only on the community of practice, but on the role played by the faculty mentor. Teachers, Bourelle (2014) argues, "need to be the bridge between the classroom and the workplace" (p. 172). Rather than being afraid of having too much contact with the students or industrial supervisor ("for fear of stepping on . . . toes" [2012, p. 1185]), instructors should be actively involved in the intern/supervisor connection. More specifically, Bourelle proposes an ambitious two-semester sequence in which students move from a service-learning oriented technical writing course (with a significant client-based project) to an internship focused on similar genres of writing the following semester. Although the increasing levels of fidelity in such a sequence may help "students develop a social consciousness while at the same time learning workplace skills" (Bourelle, 2012, p. 185), designing and sustaining such an integrated course rests on a great deal of organizational work from the instructor who must coordinate the needs and skills of both students and industry partners.

In this way, Bourelle's proposal begins to approximate the integrated vision of internships entailed by the theory of expansive learning developed by Engeström and colleagues (Engeström, 2014; Tuomi-Gröhn & Engeström, 2003). Such an approach focuses on not just individuals but the interfaces between activity systems. For instance, in his study of the advanced education of nurses, Tuomi-Gröhn (2003, 2007) compares different models of internships. The goal of the traditional model is to turn a novice into an expert with the idea that they will be better prepared for the challenges of the workplace. However, some workplaces are "grappling with profound change" and "no one has answers or solutions to the problems encountered" (2003, p. 201); in such cases, the best internships enable "the workplace and the school [to find] a shared object, and a boundary zone activity [is] created . . . which combine[s] two activity systems as collaborative partners" (2007, p. 59). After describing three different nursing internship programs, he concludes that only one meets the criteria of expansive learning. This internship—which resulted in a program implemented in a daycare to better understand the relationship between the development of motor skills and speech—not only influenced the professional growth of the individual intern but also promoted change in the activity systems of both school and work. Such internships appear to be relatively rare (see the earlier explanation of Konkola and colleagues' [2007] research for a second example), but embody a very different, much more integrated, view of the school/workplace relationship navigated by interns.

Several studies have, through their focus on internships, developed analyses that offer critiques of existing theoretical frameworks. For instance, Blythe (2016)—worried that "schools of thought such as activity theory and rhetorical genre theory underestimate the subject, while cognitive theories underestimate context" (p. 65)—works to build a theory of transfer that highlights the subject. Specifically, he supplements Beaufort's (2007) model of writing expertise with a model emphasizing affordances as well as the problem-solving activities of construal, reconciliation, and construction. After using this framework to analyze the experiences of student interns at two American universities, he concludes by highlighting the need for a more "ecological" (p. 65) theory of writing and transfer of learning.

In a similar vein, Baird and Dilger (2017) foreground the importance of dispositions for understanding transfer of learning in writing internships. Building on Beach's (1999/2003) taxonomy of mediational, lateral, collateral, and encompassing transitions, Baird and Dilger offer two case studies that highlight the role played by dispositions related to ease and ownership. Such a framework, they argue, reframes what might otherwise appear as one student's "laziness"; "Under pressure, Mitchell's disposition toward ease cued him to abandon his emerging professional identity and revert to his familiar student identity" (p. 696). A second student, whose "preference for the work side of the work-to-learn experience, intensified by [his] disposition to resist the ease of lateralization and mediation, shaped [his] capstone internship as both collateral and encompassing transitions" (p. 703). Baird and Dilger conclude these case studies of internships with a call for further examinations of the roles of dispositions in transfer.

Finally, Smart and Brown's (2002) study of 24 student interns took a careful, critical view of the role played by the community of practice, leading them to underline its importance but argue that it did not necessarily play out in the ways predicted by Lave and Wenger: namely, the interns in their study "were typically assigned major, rather than ancillary, writing tasks to accomplish, and . . . they were expected to work independently, rather than in an ongoing apprenticing relationship with a mentor" (p. 126). Rather than relying on a close mentor, interns draw on a range of other "cultural artifacts"—such as user manuals, meetings, and software tutorials—to meet expectations. Drawing on their previous learning in the university classroom made it possible for interns to experience "not learning transfer, but rather a transformation of learning that made possible the reinvention of expert practices" (p. 129). Crucial to this transformation of learning was the development of a "knowledgeably skilled identity" (p. 134). In this way, Smart and Brown build on but challenge a prevalent view of internships as an opportunity for extended mentorship, stressing instead the opportunities for distributed cognition embedded in a wide variety of cultural artifacts.

Throughout these studies, though, is a guiding assumption that the authenticity of the workplace helps to facilitate the transfer of learning from school to work and that the development of a professional identity is crucial and may be assisted by learner dispositions.

Adult Learning and the "Reverse Commute"

This final collection of scholarship focuses not on a pedagogy but on a classroom designed for a specific type of student: adult learners. Adult learners are of particular interest for understanding the school/workplace relationship because they disrupt the usual narrative of first-school-then-work. Navarre Cleary (2013) highlights the importance of thoughtfully engaging with the literacy practices adult learners bring to the university classroom: "To ignore how writing in these other contexts influences how students write for school is to unnecessarily impoverish our understanding of our students, their writing development, and the possibilities for transfer" (p. 661). While Prior, Roozen, and others focused on laminations argue that there is never a simple first-work-then-school trajectory, the work of adult learners clearly and frequently brings work and other life experiences back into the classroom. By looking at how work experiences might inform subsequent classroom studies, the research on adult learners both challenges and affirms many of the other findings summarized in this chapter.

One recurring theme in the scholarship on adult learners is the central role of identity—a theme that also appears in other research as the importance of dispositions and emerging professional identities. Navarre Cleary is particularly interested in the understandings of the writing process that adult learners bring to writing classrooms, understandings that she argues are influenced by academic identity, peer cueing, and analogical reasoning. She develops these ideas in her case studies of two returning students: Tiffany (an African American woman without a degree or formal employment beyond her work as a landlord) and Doppel (a White man in his thirties who worked both as a DJ and at an engineering firm creating designs via AutoCAD):

> Both Tiffany and Doppel bring to school the process approaches that they practice outside of school. Tiffany imagines writing as primarily an off-or-on, freeze-or-flow, binary based upon her experience journaling. Doppel employs a collection of analogies for different elements of his process from which he can draw to construct, and when necessary tweak, his writing process. Both are prompted by peers to transfer process knowledge. Tiffany, however, struggles to internalize this input. She sees academic writing as discrete from who she is, what she does, and what she already knows. In contrast, Doppel's sense of himself as an academic writer increases the likelihood that he will look for connections between his prior and new learning. (p. 678)

Metaphors and identities are intertwined in complex ways, but Navarre Cleary finds that a pattern emerges: students with more experience "making things for which others will pay had more ways to think about the various parts of their writing process" (p. 670) and had more success in their academic writing. Prior experiences and antecedent genre knowledge prove crucial for adult learners reentering the academic classroom.

Gillam's (1991) earlier research also suggests the importance of workplace experience for academic success, highlighting the ways in which access to generative antecedent genres and experiences of writing apprehension may be gendered. (This research, published in 1991, assumes a gender binary.) Male returning adult students were more likely to bring into class their work-related writing experience with documents like memos, sales proposals, and personnel evaluations

(40% of men vs. 24% of women); women were more likely to bring experience with personal writing such as letters, diaries, and journals (60% of women vs. 18% of men). As a result, women without work-related writing experience "may treat transactional or persuasive tasks as though they were expressive ones" (p. 8)—posing a significant challenge for their academic success. Gillam further notes that when she administered a writing apprehension test, there were no statistically significant differences between genders in terms of how many writers felt anxious—but there were clear differences in what provoked that anxiety. Female writers were more likely to express anxiety about being evaluated—a consequence, Gillam speculates, of less experience facing evaluation in the workplace. In short, Gillam suggests that workplace experience may offer an academic advantage unequally available to her students based on gender identities; some readers might even see evidence of "negative transfer" grounded in gender identities.

Michaud's (2011) study of what he calls the "reverse commute" also documents the challenges of facing new literacy contexts with old resources, but he frames it not in terms of gendered access, but as an example of Brandt's (2001) account of the challenges of negotiating accumulating literacy practices—a perspective on transfer that (as indicated in Chapter 5, "Transfer Implications from Sociocultural and Sociohistorical Literacy Studies") highlights the economic forces influencing literacy acquisition and repurposing. Like Navarre Cleary, Michaud focuses on the compositional practices of his focal student, Tony, an Emergency Medical Technician whose aspiration to become an EMS educator will require publication in professional EMS journals. Tony's preferred method of composition was assemblage; "right-click-steal" (p. 252) served him well putting together a Competency Manual for work and PowerPoint presentations at school, both cases where he could fill in templates. Michaud finds that Tony struggles, however, with tasks that aren't assemblage—both at work (e.g., documenting problematic workers) and school. Assemblage may be "a difficult habit to break" and "a kind of crutch, allowing students to avoid confronting long-standing difficulties with more extensive forms of writing" (p. 255) or in other cases such a "ubiquitous presence in their professional lives" that the shift is difficult. Nevertheless, if Tony wishes to advance in his career as an EMS educator, Michaud argues, he will need to do less assemblage and more "invention and arrangement of extended original prose" (p. 255). The very same literacy practices that have served Tony well in work and school up until now are the practices that may inhibit his ability to adapt and advance, an indication not of Tony's personal abilities or limitations, but of how Tony's accumulating literacy practices are valued in the larger economic systems in which Tony's school and work participate. Understanding these challenges through the lens of Brandt's argument about accumulating literacy practices highlights the ways in which transfer activities—of knowledge and identities, between work and school—are embedded in larger economic systems.

Conclusion: Implications for Pedagogy and Methodology

This chapter has synthesized findings from researchers adopting a range of complementary theoretical frameworks (communities of practice, rhetorical genre theory, and activity theory) as well as explorations of transfer of learning in four different pedagogical contexts: WAW courses, classroom-based interactions with clients (including simulations, client-based projects, and service learning), internships, and adult learning classrooms. As the second half of this chapter has demonstrated, the pedagogical implications of studying the school-to-work transition have been foregrounded in the research itself. However, as we conclude this chapter, we can identify two crucial pedagogical questions that wind their way through the scholarship.

First, there is an abiding interest in issues of fidelity: with the right rhetorical fictions (in classroom or virtual simulations) or external partnerships (client-based projects or service learning), can a classroom helpfully approximate the experience of workplace writing and facilitate transfer of learning from school to work? Are school and work *necessarily* worlds apart? Or is such a suggestion (in the words of Prior) "absurd" because individuals experience their lives as "laminated" experiences that inform one another? The scholars represented in this chapter have come to no definitive answer on such questions—but these are questions that each instructor will need to consider carefully as they design courses and assignments.

There is far more consensus on a second pedagogical question: what is the role that genres play in transfer of knowledge and abilities from school to work. The answer? They play an enormous—and enormously complex—role. Written genres help get work done in workplaces:

they are sometimes the deliverable and often the tools to produce the deliverable. Working on and talking about writing with more experienced colleagues is a form of legitimate peripheral participation and means of becoming more expert in a workplace. If this is so, instructors might ask themselves a series of questions: what genres might be assigned in the classroom in order to build knowledge and confidence for students moving into subsequent workplaces? And, how might experience with workplace genres inform students' approaches to classroom assignments? In what ways can instructors help students learn to expect that the "same" genre may function in considerably different ways in the context of a classroom and the context of a workplace? And, turning to the issue of identity that recurs throughout this chapter, how do genres work as a site of negotiating identities, especially emergent professional identities?

When we turn to the question of research methods, this body of scholarship raises questions about not only what gets studied but how. To begin with classroom-based research, the existing studies of adult learners have already begun to shift attention from the micro view of workplace writing afforded by most of the research in this chapter, to the macro view offered by Brandt (2014). Writing in workplaces—indeed writing in general—has undergone a profound transformation in the twenty-first century: writing, Brandt argues, has become "a dominant form of labor that is reshaping relationships between writing and reading, and reshaping the character of mass literacy in the process" (p. 18). The labor of writing is valued in complex, even contradictory ways: organizations run on workaday writing, but employee-writers have no legal ownership of or protections for their writing. To be a strong writer can be a means of advancement in a workplace, but often via the process of serving as a ghostwriter for a more powerful, more highly compensated employer. Yet, even as current legal and organizational structures provide no acknowledgement of the influence of writing on the writer herself, Brandt argues that the links between workplace writing and identity formation—what she calls the "residue of writing"—remain. In light of these shifts in the experience of mass literacy, shifts in which "writing seems to be eclipsing reading as the literate experience of consequence" (p. 3), workplace writing—especially studies of workplace writing that look beyond individual experiences to larger social structures, longer sweeps of time, and the role of cultural artifacts—will continue to prove an important site for researchers wishing to understand the transfer and transformation of writing, community membership, and emerging individual identities.

A second line of research, partially grounded in classrooms, might build on the tradition of work-integrated learning (Bleakney, 2019; HEQCO, 2016). Although relatively unfamiliar to researchers in the United States, there is a well-established tradition of work-integrated learning research in Australia, Canada, and elsewhere. Examples of work-integrated learning include internships, co-ops, field experience, and practicum. Although work-integrated learning research has not often focused on writing (see DePalma et al., 2022, for an important exception), its grounding in activity theory and the situated learning perspective suggests that there might be a productive overlap with writing studies concerns and methods.

A third direction for future research might be to deepen explorations that are based in workplaces. To date, writing studies has produced a handful of superb, workplace-based research. Brandt (2014), for instance, interviewed new, mid-, and late-career employees at a wide range of workplaces, and Beaufort (1999, 2007) closely followed several individuals in their workplaces. But relatively few other scholars have offered such systematic studies of post-graduation workplace writing, when participants are no longer participating in internships or coops connected to university studies. The reasons for this gap must surely include the difficulties of access, particularly given the complicated issues of authority and intellectual property that surround much workplace writing; nevertheless, there remains a need for research that centers on post-graduation workplace experiences. Several projects sponsored by Elon University's Research Seminar on Writing Beyond the University, for instance, have begun such work (Bleakney et al., 2022); the Archive of Workplace Writing Experiences may also prove a valuable resource.

A fourth research agenda might take up questions of writing beyond the school/work binary. Anson (2016), for instance, offers an account of his own "frustrated transfer" (p. 532) as he struggles to write summaries of his son's football team's performance for the local paper. Several lines of systematic inquiry have also begun to emerge from Elon University's Research Seminar on Writing Beyond the University and deserve broader uptake. For instance, Yancey et al. (2022) have begun to explore the recursive relationships among spheres that include not only the classroom and workplace but also self-motivated spheres; civic, community, and political spheres; co-curricular spheres; and internship spheres. Diving further into the realm of self-sponsored writing, Reid et al. (2022) have begun to explore the extent to which the functions of self-sponsored writing might be an interplay of the personal, professional, civic, social, and educational. Both projects highlight the degree to which scholars wishing to understand the relationship between school and work have blinkered themselves to the wide range of writing experiences that might be meaningful and influential outside of those two contexts.

Finally, turning to questions of not just what to study but how to study it, writing studies scholars might turn to the knowledge management scholarship described in Chapter 3. The knowledge management perspective frames transfer of learning as an interpersonal phenomenon, one in which colleagues transfer knowledge amongst individuals or even entire workgroups. Although writing studies has focused, *almost* without exception, on transfer as an intrapersonal experience transpiring within a single individual operating within their social contexts, there are indeed exceptions. As discussed earlier in this chapter, work adopting a cultural historical activity theory perspective has already shifted the unit of analysis away from individual learners. By focusing on divisions of labor and the transformation of activity systems, they encourage scholars to examine larger workplace contexts encompassing groups of individuals learning from one another. With its focus on mediational tools and boundary objects, cultural historical activity theory nudges scholars towards considerations of the distributed cognition central to knowledge management. In these ways and others, studies of workplace writing adopting a cultural historical activity theory offer both an argument for and the methods of moving towards a more interpersonal view of transfer.

References

Alexander, K. P., and Powell, B. (2012). Team writing for the community: Literacies developed in a service-learning context. In I. Baca (Ed), *Service learning and writing: Paving the way for literacy(ies) through community engagement* (pp. 47–72). Emerald Group.

Anson, C. M. (2016). The Pop Warner chronicles: A case study in contextual adaptation and the transfer of writing ability. *College Composition and Communication*, 67(4), 518–549.

Anson, C. M., & Forsberg, L. L. (1990). Moving beyond the academic community: Transitional stages in professional writing. *Written Communication, 7,* 200–231.

Archive of Workplace Writing Experiences. www.workplace-writing.org/about/

Artemeva, N. (2005). A time to speak, a time to act: A rhetorical genre analysis of a novice engineer's calculated risk taking. *Journal of Business and Technical Communication, 19*(4), 389–421.

Artemeva, N. (2009). Stories of becoming: A study of novice engineers learning genres of their profession. In C. Bazerman, A. Bonini, & D. Figueiredo (Eds.), *Genre in a changing world* (pp. 158–178). The WAC Clearinghouse and Parlor Press.

Bacon, N. (1999). The trouble with transfer: Lessons from a study of community service writing. *Michigan Journal of Community Service Learning, 6,* 53–62.

Baird, N., & Dilger, B. (2017). How students perceive transitions: Dispositions and transfer in internships. *College Composition and Communication, 68*(4), 684–712.

Bazerman, C., Applebee, A. N., Berninger, V. W., Brandt, D., Graham, S., Jeffery, J. V., Matsuda, P. K., Murphy, S., Rowe, D. W., Schleppegrell, M., & Wilcox, K. C. (2018). *The lifespan of writing development.* NCTE.

Beach, K. (1999). Consequential transitions: A sociocultural expedition beyond transfer in education.

Beaufort, A. (1997). Operationalizing the concepts of the discourse community: A case study of one institutional site of composing. *Research in the Teaching of English, 31*(4), 486–529.

Beaufort, A. (1999). *Writing in the real world: Making the transition from school to work.* Teachers College Press.

Beaufort, A. (2007). *College writing and beyond: A new framework for university writing instruction.* Utah State University Press.

Blakeslee, A. M. (2001). Bridging the workplace and the academy: Teaching professional genres through classroom-workplace collaborations. *Technical Communication Quarterly, 10*(2), 169–192.

Bleakney, J. (2019, September 13.) What is work-integrated learning? [Blog Post]. https://www.centerforengagedlearning.org/what-is-work-integrated-learning/

Bleakney, J., Moore, J. L., & Rosinski, P. (Eds.), 2022. *Writing beyond the university: Preparing lifelong learners for lifewide writing.* Elon, NC: Elon University Center for Engaged Learning.

Blythe, S. (2016). Attending to the subject in writing transfer and adaptation. In C. M. Anson and J. L. Moore (Eds.), *Critical transitions: Writing and the question of transfer* (pp. 49–68).

Bourelle, T. (2012). Bridging the gap between the technical communication classroom and the internship: Teaching social consciousness and real-world writing. *Journal of Technical Writing & Communication*, *42*(2), 183–197.

Bourelle, T. (2014). New perspectives on the technical communication internship: Professionalism in the workplace. *Journal of Technical Writing & Communication*, *44*(2), 171–189.

Brandt, D. (2001). *Literacy in American lives*. Cambridge University Press.

Brandt, D. (2014). *The rise of writing: Redefining mass literacy*. Cambridge University Press.

Brandt, D. (2018). Writing development and life-course development: The case of working adults. In C. Bazerman et al., *The Lifespan Development of Writing* (244–271). NCTE.

Bremner, S. (2011). Socialization and the acquisition of professional discourse: A case study in the PR industry. *Written Communication*, *29*(1), 7–32.

Brent, D. (2012). Crossing boundaries: Co-op students relearning to write. *College Composition & Communication*, *63*(4), 558–592.

Campbell, L. (2017). Simulation genres and student uptake: The patient health record in clinical nursing simulations. *Written Communication*, *34*(3), 255–279.

Cutrufello, G. (2019). Writing about writing pedagogy in a mixed major/nonmajor professional writing course. In B. Bird, D. Downs, I. M. McCracken, & J. Rieman (Eds.), *Next steps: New directions for/in writing about writing* (pp. 155–158). Utah State University Press.

Dannels, D. P. (2000). Learning to be professional: Technical classroom discourse, practice, and professional identity construction. *Journal of Business and Technical Communication*, *14*(1), 5–37.

Dannels, D. P. (2003). Teaching and learning design presentations in engineering contradictions between academic and workplace activity systems. *Journal of Business and Technical Communication*, *17*(2), 139–169.

DePalma, M. (2012). Assessing adaptive transfer in community-based writing. In I. Baca (Ed.), *Service learning and writing: Paving the way for literacy(ies) through community engagement* (pp. 181–203). Emerald Group Publishing Limited.

DePalma, M. J., Mina, L. W., Taczak, K., Eady, M. J., Jaidev, R., & Machura, I. A. (2022). Connecting work-integrated learning and writing transfer: Possibilities and promise for writing studies. *Composition Forum*, 48). http://compositionforum.com/issue/48/work-integrated-learning.php

Dias, P., Freedman, A., Medway, P., & Paré, A. (1999). *Worlds apart: Acting and writing in academic and workplace contexts*. L. Erlbaum Associates.

Dias, P., & Paré, A. (2000). *Transitions: Writing in academic and workplace settings*. Hampton Press.

Downs, D., & Wardle, E. (2007). Teaching about writing, righting misconceptions: (Re) envisioning "First-Year Composition" as "Introduction to Writing Studies." *College Composition and Communication*, *58*(4), 552–584.

Driscoll, D. L., & Powell, R. (2016). States, traits, and dispositions: The impact of emotion on writing development and writing transfer across college courses and beyond. *Composition Forum*, *34*. https://compositionforum.com/issue/34/states-traits.php

Driscoll, D. L., & Wells, J. (2012). Beyond knowledge and skills: Writing transfer and the role of student dispositions. *Composition Forum*, *26*. https://compositionforum.com/issue/26/beyond-knowledge-skills.php

Engeström, Y. (2001). Expansive learning at work: Toward an activity theoretical reconceptualization. *Journal of Education and Work*, *14*(1): 133–156.

Engeström, Y. (2014). *Learning by expanding: An activity-theoretical approach to developmental research*. Cambridge University Press.

Eraut, M. (2004). Informal learning in the workplace. *Studies in Continuing Education*, *26*(2), 247–273.

Ford, J. D. (2004). Knowledge transfer across disciplines: Tracking rhetorical strategies from a technical communication classroom to an engineering classroom. *IEEE Transactions on Professional Communication*, *47*(4), 301–315.

Freedman, A. (1993). Show and tell? The role of explicit teaching in the learning of new genres. *Research in the Teaching of English*, *27*(3), 222–251.

Freedman, A., & Adam, C. (1996). Learning to write professionally "Situated learning" and the transition from university to professional discourse. *Journal of Business and Technical Communication*, *10*(4), 395–427.

Freedman, A., & Adam, C. (2000). Bridging the gap: University based writing that is more than simulation. In P. Dias & A. Paré (Eds.), *Transitions: Writing in academic and workplace settings* (pp. 129–144). Hampton Press.

Freedman, A., Adam, C., & Smart, G. (1994). Wearing suits to class simulating genres and simulations as genre. *Written Communication*, *11*(2), 193–226.

Gick, M. L., & Holyoak, K. J. (1980). Analogical problem solving. *Cognitive Psychology*, *12*(3), 306–355.

Gick, M. L., & Holyoak, K. J. (1983). Schema induction and analogical transfer. *Cognitive Psychology 15*(1), 1–38.

Gillam, A. M. (1991). Returning students' ways of writing: Implications for first-year college composition. *Journal of Teaching Writing*, *10*(1), 1–20.

Higher Education Quality Council of Ontario ("HEQCO"). (2016). *A practical guide for work-integrated learning: Effective practices to enhance the educational quality of structured work experiences offered through colleges and Universities*. Queen's Printer for Ontario.

Kain, D., & Wardle, E. (2005). Building context: Using activity theory to teach about genre in multi-major professional communication courses. *Technical Communication Quarterly, 14*(2), 113–139.

Kohn, L. (2015). How professional writing pedagogy and university–workplace partnerships can shape the mentoring of workplace writing. *Journal of Technical Writing and Communication, 45*(2), 166–188.

Konkola, R., Tuomi-Gröhn, T., Lambert, P., & Ludvigsen, S. (2007). Promoting learning and transfer between school and workplace. *Journal of Education & Work, 20*(3), 211–228.

Lave, J. (1988). *Cognition in practice: Mind, mathematics and culture in everyday life.* Cambridge University Press.

Lave, J., & Wenger, E. (1991). *Situated learning: Legitimate peripheral participation.* Cambridge University Press.

Lemke, J. L. (2000). Across the scales of time: Artifacts, activities, and meanings in ecosocial systems. *Mind, Culture, and Activity, 7*(4), 273–290.

Ludvigsen, S. R., Havnes, A., & Lahn, L. C. (2003). Workplace learning across activity systems: A case study of sales engineers. In T. Tuomi-Gröhn & Y. Engeström (Eds.), *Between school and work: New perspectives on transfer and boundary-crossing* (pp. 292–310). Pergammon.

Michaud, M. J. (2011). The "reverse commute": Adult students and the transition from professional to academic literacy. *Teaching English in the Two-Year College, 38*(3), 244–258.

Miller, C. R. (1984). Genre as social action. *Quarterly Journal of Speech, 70*(2), 151–167.

Navarre Cleary, M. (2013). Flowing and freestyling: Learning from adult students about process knowledge transfer. *College Composition and Communication, 64*(4), 661–687.

Paradis, J., Dobrin, D., & Miller, R. (1985). Writing at Exxon ITD: Notes on the writing environment of an R&D organization. In L. Odell & D. Goswami (Eds.), *Writing in nonacademic settings* (pp. 281–307). Guilford Press.

Paré, A. (2000). Writing as a way into social work: Genre sets, genre systems, and distributed cognition. In P. Dias & A. Paré (Eds.), *Transitions: Writing in academic and workplace settings* (pp. 145–166). Hampton Press.

Paré, A., & Le Maistre, C. (2006). Active learning in the workplace: Transforming individuals and institutions. *Journal of Education and Work, 19*(4), 363–381.

Paretti, M. C. (2008). Teaching communication in capstone design: The role of the instructor in situated learning. *Journal of Engineering Education, 97*(4), 491–503.

Parks, S. (2001). Moving from school to the workplace: Disciplinary innovation, border crossings, and the reshaping of a written genre. *Applied Linguistics, 22*(4), 405–438.

Perkins, D. N., & Salomon, G. (1988). Teaching for transfer. *Educational Leadership, 46*(1), 22–32.

Prior. P. (2018). How do moments add up to lives? Trajectories of semiotic becoming vs. tales of school learning in four modes. In R. Wysocki and M. Sheridan (Eds.), *Making future matters*. Utah State Press/Computers and Composition Digital Press. http://ccdigitalpress.org/book/makingfuturematters/

Prior, P., & Shipka, J. (2003). Chronotopic lamination: Tracing the contours of literate activity. In C. Bazerman & D. R. Russell (Eds.), *Writing selves/writing societies: Research from activity perspectives* (pp. 180–238). The WAC Clearinghouse and Mind, Culture, and Activity.

Quick, C. (2012). From the workplace to academia: Nontraditional students and the relevance of workplace experience in technical writing pedagogy. *Technical Communication Quarterly*, 21, 230–250.

Read, S., & Michaud, M. J. (2019). Negotiating WAW-PW across diverse institutional contexts. In B. Bird, D. Downs, I. M. McCracken, & J. Rieman (Eds.). (2019). *Next steps : New directions for/in writing about writing* (pp. 159-171). Utah State University Press.

Reid, J., Pavesich, M., Efthymiou, A., Lindenman, H., & Driscoll, D. L. (2022). Writing to learn beyond the university: Preparing lifelong learners for lifewide writing. In J. Bleakney, J. L. Moore, & P. Rosinski (Eds.), *Writing beyond the university: Preparing lifelong learners for lifewide writing* (pp. 38-50). Elon University Center for Engaged Learning.

Roozen, K. (2008). Journalism, poetry, stand-up comedy, and academic literacy: Mapping the interplay of curricular and extracurricular literate activities. *Journal of Basic Writing*, 27(1), 5–34.

Roozen, K. (2009). "Fan fic-ing" English studies: A case study exploring the interplay of vernacular literacies and disciplinary engagement. *Research in the Teaching of English*, 44(2), 136–169.

Roozen, K. (2010). The "poetry slam," mathemagicians, and middle school math: Tracing trajectories of actors and artifacts. In P. A. Prior & J. A. Hengst (Eds.), *Exploring semiotic remediation as discourse practice* (pp. 24–51). Palgrave Macmillan.

Russell, D., & Fisher, D. (2009). Online, multimedia case studies for professional education: Revisioning concepts of genre recognition. In D. Stein & J. Giltrow (Eds.), *Genres in the internet: Issues in the theory of genre* (pp. 163–191). John Benjamins Publishing.

Russell, D. & Yanez, A. (2003). "Big picture people rarely become historians": Genre systems and the contradictions of general education. In C. Bazerman & D. R. Russell (Eds.), *Writing selves, writing societies: Research from activity perspectives* (pp. 331–362). The WAC Clearinghouse and Mind, Culture, and Activity.

Schryer, C. F. (1993). Records as genre. *Written Communication*, 10(2), 200–234.

Smart, G. (2000). Reinventing expertise: Experienced writers in the workplace encounter a new genre. In P. Dias & A. Paré (Eds.), *Transitions: Writing in academic and workplace settings* (pp. 223–252). Hampton.

Smart, G., & Brown, N. (2002). Learning transfer or transforming learning? Student interns reinventing expert writing practices in the workplace. *Technostyle, 18*(1), 117–141.

Spinuzzi, C. (1996). Pseudotransactionality, activity theory, and professional writing instruction. *Technical Communication Quarterly, 5*(3), 295–308.

Tuomi-Gröhn, T. (2003). Developmental transfer as a goal in practical nursing. In T. Tuomi-Gröhn & Y. Engeström (Eds.), *Between school and work: New perspectives on transfer and boundary crossing* (pp. 199–232). Pergamon.

Tuomi-Gröhn, T. (2007). Developmental transfer as a goal of collaboration between school and work: A case study in the training of daycare interns. *Actio: An International Journal of Human Activity Theory, 1*, 41–62.

Tuomi-Gröhn, T., & Engeström, Y. (2003). *Between school and work: New perspectives on transfer and boundary-crossing*. Pergamon.

Tuomi-Gröhn, T., Engeström, Y., & Young, M. (2003). From transfer to boundary crossing between school and work as a tool for developing vocational education: An introduction. In T. Tuomi-Gröhn & Y. Engeström (Eds.) *Between school and work: New perspectives on transfer and boundary crossing* (pp. 1–18). Pergamon.

Veillard, L. (2012). Transfer of learning as a specific case of transition between learning contexts in a French work-integrated learning programme. *Vocations and Learning, 5*(3), 251–276.

White, S. (2015). "I stopped writing for myself": Student perspectives on service-learning in composition. Unpublished dissertation, University of Wisconsin Madison.

Winsor, D. A. (2013). *Writing like an engineer: A rhetorical education*. Routledge. (Original work published 1996)

Yancey, K. B., Hart, D. A., Holmes, A. J., Knutson, A. V., O'Sullivan, Í., & Sinha, Y. (2022). "There is a lot of overlap": Tracing writing development across spheres of writing. In J. Bleakney, J.L. Moore, & P. Rosinski (Eds.) *Writing Beyond the University: Preparing Lifelong Learners for Lifewide Writing* (pp. 74-90).

11 Conclusion: Transfer and Transdisciplinarity in Five Themes

Five themes cut across the disciplines reviewed in this volume: individuality, intentionality, fidelity, directionality, and simultaneity. All five are characterized by the situated, sociocultural, and activity-based orientations that studies of writing transfer were originally concerned with. As they emerged for us in the course of writing this volume, these themes provide pathways for writing studies to envision new lines of inquiry, theoretical and methodological paradigms, and teaching commitments through the "untapped potential of a truly transdisciplinary approach" to transfer (Tardy, 2017, p. 187). We hope a transdisciplinary approach to transfer can reposition writing studies at the intersection of multiple transfer research strands rather than (as has typically been the case) in dialogue with limited other fields. As we wrote in our introduction, this volume considers how writing studies' existing theoretical frames or analytic habits can limit the field's understanding of transfer. Our five themes of transdisciplinary transfer research provide readers with entry points into new frames by synthesizing across multiple fields and foregrounding connections to the transfer of writing-related knowledge and activity.

Our five transdisciplinary themes are drawn from the vast landscape of scholarship we discussed in this book's chapters: cognitive psychology and situated learning (65 articles, 14 books); industrial and organizational (I/O) psychology and human resources (128 articles, 10 books); sports, medical, aviation, and military education (44 articles, 6 books); literacy studies (35 articles, 26 books); second language writing (108 articles, 29 books); first-year writing (68 articles, 13 books); writing across the curriculum and in the disciplines (68 articles, 21 books); writing centers (62 articles, 7 books); and school to work (67 articles, 12 books). In this conclusion, we present each of the five themes—individuality, intentionality, fidelity, directionality, and simultaneity—and within each theme, we offer distillations and examples that show how the theme can support agendas for research and teaching in writing studies. We conclude with a look to the future of writing transfer through a framework inspired by our overall synthesis. These future frames—interdependence, ephemerality, and orientation—represent the start of the "untapped potential" for a transdisciplinary approach to transfer for writing studies.

Individuality

Our first transdisciplinary theme, individuality, highlights a common unit of analysis in studies of transfer: the individual. Whether researchers investigate small groups or large cohorts, they almost always look at one individual at a time. Manifestations of individuality have been developed across disciplines and include the uniqueness of identity for transfer of learning, the role of individuals' agency in resistance and failure, the relationships between personal characteristics or dispositions and transfer, and the importance of individuals' bodies and material conditions. Only rarely do researchers turn their attention to dyads, as in transactive memory research (Wegner, 1987; Wegner et al., 1985) or activity systems (Engstrom, 2014; Tuomi-Gröhn & Engeström, 2003). Within writing studies, a focus on collaborative talk has extended the more typical, individual-focused approaches and asked researchers to consider the co-constructed, social, and dialogic nature of students' transfer through interaction (Nowacek et al., 2019, Winzenried et al., 2017). Therefore, as this section chronicles the ways transfer research has consolidated around individuals, it also implies the additional insights that could be gained through pair, group, or community research on transfer.

Identity

The role of identity in transfer recurs throughout this book. For instance, scholars of the school-to-work transition often argue that it is through learning the genres of the workplace that students adopt new identities as professionals in the field. Similarly, second language writing scholars report that for multilingual writers, dimensions of their identities become salient and impact transfer in a writing classroom (Johnstone, 1996; Matsuda, 2015; Norton, 2000).

In some cases, aspects of identities operate as affordances. For instance, across the fields of nursing, social work, or public relations, school-to-work scholars report that an emerging professional identity plays a crucial role in helping students make the transition from writing for school to writing successfully for work (Dias et al., 1999; Dias & Paré, 2000). In other cases, identity aspects operate as constraints. Wardle and Mercer Clement (2016), for example, analyze the ways in which Nicolette elects to "bracke[t] the experiences and values she was exposed to at home" (p. 174) rather than "speaking to her own experiences growing up as a member of 'the masses'" her assignment presumes she will critique (p. 172). Cozart et al. (2016) describe how fixed writerly identities in students' L1 might inhibit meaning-making in transfer, resulting instead in instances of language transfer as surface translation. Drawing from interviews of more than 80 individuals who consider writing a central part of their professional lives, Brandt (2018) proposes a dynamic relationship between identity and transfer of writing-related learning. She reports that the "residues of writing" illustrate a mutually influential relationship between writing and identity: not only do writers' identities potentially influence their writing, but their writing at work potentially influences their emerging identities. Throughout this scholarship, then, is the proposition that transfer of learning cannot be fully understood without considering an individual's full range of linguistic, professional, and personal identifications.

Agency

Scholars in cognitive and socio-cognitive traditions regularly foreground the active cognitive work of individuals who make meaning in social contexts, highlighting the role of agency in transfer of learning. Foundational to Bandura's (1986, 1999) widely influential social cognitive theory is the idea that "human beings have some agency in the ways that they process the information they encounter—and this agency is exercised through processes of self-regulation" (1986, p. 3). Many transfer-oriented writing pedagogies operate from this position through emphasis on reflective writing as a core mechanism for students' transfer (Downs & Wardle, 2007; Yancey et al., 2014). In these approaches, students assume the role of a self-regulated and self-determining learner as they combine writing-related knowledge learned in class with their own experiences with writing to address future writing situations. Implicit in such approaches is the belief that students are agentive in advancing their own writing development.

Our transdisciplinary review of scholarship also suggests that resistance and failure may be important acts of agency. Lobato's (2012) actor-oriented theory (AOT), for instance, asks scholars to look at the ostensible failures of math students from a new perspective. If researchers observe a class session in which students were taught to calculate slope, and then the students later calculate slope incorrectly, that might be seen as a failure to transfer knowledge. But Lobato suggests that if researchers reexamined their data from the perspective of students, students *did* transfer knowledge—just not the knowledge or form researchers expected. Similarly, Nowacek (2011) challenges the common language of "negative transfer," arguing that it unobtrusively validates the instructor's over students' assessment of what counts as transfer. She argues for a conception of student writers as "agents of integration" and proposes a transfer matrix that distinguishes student intention from teacher reception. Donahue (2016) similarly promotes resistance as agency, suggesting that future transfer models need to better understand students' "reuse, adaptation, transformation, and repurposing of knowledge in order to resist educational influences" (p. 113). Importantly, these studies draw on "inductive qualitative methods" to get at the "interpretive nature of knowing" and to "relinquis[h] a predetermined standard for judging what counts as transfer" (Lobato, 2012, p. 243). Empowering student writers' agency in acts of transfer means a shift away from binaries of success or failure. Rather, by centering agency in transfer, we create space for purposeful design of learning, exploration and achievement of intention, and choice-making.

Traits, States, and Dispositions

Writing studies is increasingly attending to the role of an individual's dispositions in transfer of learning. This area is ripe for continued growth and can be enhanced through deeper familiarity with the scholarship in psychology, which could further theoretical precision and extend findings and implications. For instance, psychology researchers have long worked to distinguish traits, which are "behaviors that individuals appear to perform regularly," from states, which are "behaviors that individuals appear to perform as a result of exposure to unusually strong external constraints or the presence of unusual physiological conditions" (Allen & Potkay, 1981, p. 917). While this distinction might be seen as an arbitrary difference between long-term personality traits and moods (Allen & Potkay, 1981; Fridhandler, 1986), the important take-away is that the term disposition has been used—both within writing studies and in other fields—in ways that deserve closer attention.

Psychology researchers often use the term *disposition* in tandem with the word *trait* (e.g., *dispositional traits*)—and indeed dispositions are often meant to describe affective responses that are more predictable than moods over the long term. Allport and Odbert (1936), for instance, argued that traits are "personal dispositions" (p. 13) and their work is often seen as the first step in identifying the Big Five personality traits: openness, conscientiousness, extraversion, agreeableness, and neuroticism. Whether they use the term disposition or not, a range of scholars seem to invoke this type of stable personality trait (e.g., Bacon, 1999; Brent, 2012; White, 2015).

Scholarship on dispositions across disciplines also draws attention to the ways in which dispositions are in a dynamic relationship with context (Bandura, 1977; Bronfenbrenner & Morris, 2006), including in writing studies (Driscoll & Wells, 2012; Driscoll & Powell, 2016; Slomp, 2012; Wardle, 2012). While not using the terminology of dispositions, other writing research emphasizes how personal characteristics might influence a writer's ability to repurpose writing-related knowledge within particular contexts. (See Sommers & Saltz, 2004, on the novice-as-expert paradox; Reiff & Bawarshi, 2011, on how boundary crossers benefit from a certain degree of humility; and Driscoll & Jin, 2018, on the relationship between epistemologies and learning transfer.) Baird and Dilger (2018) argue for a nuanced consideration of dispositions in writing transfer that moves beyond "generative/disruptive binar[ies]" (p. 35) and "represent[s] how dispositions can interact with each other in complex ways" (p. 38). Across all discussions of dispositions, traits, and characteristics, there is a growing recognition that these individual qualities are an important factor in transfer, and that more precise distinctions and applications may yield additional critical insight for writing studies.

Embodied Cognition

One final dimension of individuality in transfer scholarship is a consideration of the role of the individual's body. Despite increased attention to the importance of the material contexts for and the physicality of writing and learning, there is relatively little work in writing studies that integrates theories of embodied cognition into transfer of learning. One exception is LeMesurier's (2016) study of dancers; she argues that "The graffiti artist, or dancer or writer, becomes acclimated to the particular muscle tensions and ways of moving that support the execution of one's repeated tasks. Such bodily acclimations can be used in processes of transfer if there is training in how to recognize and use these movements apart from their original contexts" (p. 312–13). Prior and Olinger (2019) also highlight the role of the body in writing transfer. Drawing on Olinger's analysis of gesture during interviews, they argue that "writers' metaphoric gestures embodied and shaped how they viewed writing styles" (p. 131). Finally, Rifenberg (2014, 2018) offers a detailed study of the transfer of embodied learning in football players, arguing that "student-athletes who thrive with second-nature embodied rhetoric when engaging with multimodality for their sport . . . are often not encouraged to link the body with multimodality for curricular composing" (2014 , para. 3 in section on "Representing the body as a mode of meaning-making in our teaching").

This writing studies research resonates with research in sports education, medical education, and psychology. Sports education draws on theories of embodied cognition where the body is always active and present in learning (see Chapter 4 on "Transfer in Sports, Medical, Aviation, and Military Training"). The teaching games for understanding approach presented in Chapter 4, for instance, rejects the Cartesian split between mind and body and argues that learning games "offers educators a practical means through which they can provide a holistic learning experience. . . centered on the body" (Light & Fawns, 2003, p. 162). Similarly, medical and aviation education have explored the degree to which simulations are able to replicate the physical challenges and stresses of, say, stanching bleeding or landing a plane in turbulence. Within psychology, Day and Goldstone (2011) argue that spatial information—acquired from, for example, tracking balls that move from left to right or from right to left—influences the unconscious perceptual processes at work in transfer of learning. With a case study of a student learning to represent the motion of objects, Nemirovsky (2011) proposes a theory of learning transfer that integrates cognition with "episodic feelings" and bodily context and gestures. Indeed, there is a field of "4E" research—extended, embedded, embodied, and enacted (Menary, 2010)—growing out of work in distributed cognition (Hutchins, 1995) which argues that the body is a crucial element of cognition.

Such transdisciplinary views invite writing studies scholars to continue to expand ideas about how cognition and transfer of learning might be powerfully informed by bodies, other material contexts, and other people. Further areas of connection include more direct engagement with theories of embodied cognition and 4E scholarship, which are a generative avenue for questions of transfer and writing process, transfer and writing technologies, and transfer and writing spaces.

Intentionality

Our second transdisciplinary theme, intentionality, foregrounds two central questions: What is the role of conscious awareness and choice in transfer? What is the role of automaticity and routine in transfer? Such questions have been explored in depth in various subfields of psychology as well as in many fields summarized in this book. Although writing studies scholars have tended to emphasize the importance of conscious intention for repurposing prior learning, research in multiple fields also seeks to understand the role of tacit and automatized knowledge. In this section, we present such discussions and connect them to writing studies through the areas of abstract schema, metacognition and self-monitoring, and automaticity.

Abstract Schema

The claim that a sufficiently abstract schema can promote mindful transfer of learning has a long, vigorous tradition in the field of psychology. In one of the earliest explorations, Judd (1908) suggested that an abstract schema—that is, general principles provided to the participants by the experimenters to help solve their dart-throwing problem—works best when supplemented with concrete experience. Katona (1940) and other Gestalt theorists tended to value an abstract schema even more highly, arguing that specific examples may be clues towards general principles, and those general principles in turn lead to transfer. Much research across fields shows that an abstract schema facilitates transfer, including in sports education (e.g., Bunker & Thorpe's [1982] *Teaching Games for Understanding*), second language acquisition (e.g., Figueredo's [2006] focus on transfer as a "conscious, strategic approach" (p. 893) occurring through meta-linguistic abstraction), and writing studies (e.g., Beaufort, 2007; Van Kooten, 2016). However, the causal relationship between an abstract schema and transfer of learning is not without some debate.

Even without using the language of abstract schema, writing studies has a tradition of teaching for generalizations, especially through emphasis on reflection and theory-building through declarative and procedural knowledge. For instance, Yancey and colleagues have argued that their teaching for transfer curriculum succeeds in promoting writing transfer because transfer requires the ability to contextualize those ideas "in the context of a conceptual framework" (Bransford qtd. in Yancey et al., 2014, p. 137). Their student-developed theory of writing can help students "organiz[e] what they have learned about writing through remixing prior knowledge, new theory, and new practice" in ways that "will support their moving forward to new contexts" (p. 137). Beaufort (2007) similarly argues that "learners need guidance to structure specific problems and learnings into more abstract principles that can be applied to new situations" (p. 151) and that "teaching the practice of mindfulness or meta-cognition" can "increas[e] the chances of transfer of learning" (p. 152). Future writing studies research in this area will especially benefit from engagement with abstract schema research that emphasizes explicit instruction.

Most researchers in cognitive psychology have argued that developing an appropriately abstract schema will help individuals solve novel problems, especially when guided to build and use their schema through explicit instruction like "hints." Hints not only prompt individuals to *use* their existing schemata; they guide individuals in *constructing* their abstract schema. The role of hints in developing an abstract schema has been linked to individuals' capacity to recognize analogies that promote transfer. Working with examples is another mechanism for engaging abstract schema. Experimental designs researched by Schwartz and Martin (2004) established a positive relationship between active engagement with examples and participants' ability to perform well on subsequent tests—a relationship they believe is mediated by the preparation for future learning participants generated by working actively with those examples. Likewise, "noticing" (Lobato et al., 2012) suggests that a teacher's actions can influence student attention in discernible ways that later have consequences for transfer of learning. Development of general heuristics is also connected to transfer through their facilitation of abstract schema.

Explicit instruction fits nicely with current work in writing about writing and teaching for transfer approaches to first-year writing. Both of these pedagogies foreground declarative writing-related knowledge and ask students to use abstractions, such as genre and rhetorical situation, to solve problems across writing situations. Following Engle's notion of expansive framing (2006), for instance, writing instructors can ask students to generate heuristics either from concrete examples or from theoretical premises and dialogue with problems across "times, places, people, and topics" (Engle et al., 2011, p. 622). While this is a common practice in writing-transfer pedagogy, more direct connections with other disciplines not only refines these practices, but also can create alliances across the curriculum. Writing teachers can connect with faculty in education, for example, through a commitment to teaching intentionality via abstract schema and other transfer-related aims and practices. Such a partnership provides productive relationships and common purposes toward a comprehensive project of writing transfer across the university.

Metacognition and Self-Monitoring

Metacognition and self-monitoring are, at their core, about raising levels of intentionality in acts of transfer. Despite metacognition's ubiquity across disciplines, there is "lack of clarity in [its] definition" (Scott & Levy, 2013, pp. 122–1233). Some researchers have identified a range of possible components, including

> *Knowledge* of one's own and others' cognitive processes; *planning* prior to performing a task; *monitoring* one's own thinking, learning and understanding while performing a task; *regulating* one's thinking by making the proper adjustments; *controlling* thinking to optimize performance; and *evaluating* cognitive processes after a solution has been found. (Scott & Levy, 2013, p. 123)

Notably, all these component activities suggest intentional and self-aware decisions about one's own thinking. Of particular relevance to notions of intentionality is research focused on how components of metacognition are related to self-regulation in transfer, including monitoring, regulating, controlling, and evaluating. For I/O psychology scholars interested in transfer of training, the idea of self-regulation has been crucial for training design theories focused on behavioral modeling and error management. Often, self-regulative metacognitive activity is framed as an issue of emotional control (Keith & Freese, 2005). Similarly, theories of transactive memory rely on monitoring which knowledge resides where. In particular, Wegner et al. (1985) describe the emergence of "a personal 'directory' for knowledge held by the dyad" (p. 265); this directory, which must be regularly updated to remain effective, is a mechanism for monitoring who knows what so that shared memories can be accessed when needed.

Writing studies has engaged with metacognition, but with somewhat shifting terminology. Many writing studies scholars use *How People Learn* (Bransford et al., 2000) to treat metacognition as "the ability to monitor one's current level of understanding and decide when it is not adequate" (p. 47). In their analysis of metacognition in writing studies, Gorzelsky et al. (2016) identify planning, monitoring, control, and evaluation as four metacognitive subcomponents that comprise "regulation of cognition" (p. 226). Negretti (2012) finds that writers' "self-regulatory experiences feed back into an increased awareness of conditional and personal strategies" (p. 170). However, Nowacek (2011) describes "faith in unspecified metacognitive abilities [as] tantamount to pointing to a black box in which a general cognitive ability magically operates" (p. 17).

In writing studies, the role of conscious awareness as intentionality has primarily surfaced through uptake of psychologists Perkins and Solomon's articulations of high-road and low-road transfer (Perkins & Salomon, 1988, 1989; see Chapter 2). Although Perkins and Salomon associate the conditions of low-road transfer with a "high level of mastery," by also describing it as a type of "stimulus generalization," they implicitly also associate low-road transfer with the largely discredited theory of behaviorism (1989, p. 22). The work of Kahneman (1973, 2003, 2011), too, has exposed the limitations of what he calls "System 1" thinking: "The operations of System 1 are typically fast, automatic, effortless, associative, implicit (not available to introspection), and often emotionally charged; they are also governed by habit and are therefore difficult to control or modify" (Kahneman 2003, p. 698). However, rather than simply dismissing the automaticity of System 1 operations, he in fact launches a significant defense of System 1, valuing the ways in which System 1's tacit knowledge works in partnership with the explicit knowledge of System 2. So, while deliberate mindful abstraction remains important, the importance and value of the kind of tacit, automatized thinking associated with System 1 also is compelling for future transfer research in writing studies.

Automaticity

Automaticity of transfer would seem the antithesis of the intentional, mindful transfer of learning discussed so far. Indeed, automaticity is the site of considerable tension and even mistrust. Supposed failures in mindful abstraction (an overrun of automatic, low-road, System 1 thinking) result in negative transfer, for instance, which Schunk (2004) defines as when "prior learning interferes with subsequent learning" (p. 217). Beaufort (1999) describes negative transfer as instances in which the "norms of one discourse community were inappropriately transferred to a very different context for writing" (p. 183). Management scholars focused on innovation worry that routines will inhibit innovative responses to new business contexts (Walsh & Ungson, 1991, p. 76).

However, some fields and scholars have also documented significant advantages of automatized learning for transfer of learning. For instance, knowledge management scholars have argued for the crucial role that tacit knowledge plays in innovation, documenting the ways in which tacit knowledge becomes explicit and then—if it is to become a truly sustainable innovation—tacit once again (Nonaka, 1994). In psychology, some scholars have actively praised the importance of deeply internalized, even automatized knowledge. In medical and aviation education, researchers note that automatized learning is desirable; surgeons and pilots make life-or-death decisions so quickly and so often that if they regularly relied on deliberate, mindful, high-road transfer, it would be at their peril.

Writing studies is just beginning to explore the role tacit knowledge and more routine, automatized experiences might play in transfer. Donahue (2012) notes that "although much has been made of . . . meta-awareness as one of the key components of successful transfer, some research is beginning to question its role"; preliminary results from her own study suggest that "mature practices might indeed develop without an accompanying meta-awareness" (p. 155). And although Wardle's claim that "meta-awareness about writing, language, and rhetorical strategies in FYC may be the most important ability our courses can cultivate" (2007, p. 82) is often cited in work spotlighting the value of meta-awareness, she has also noted that her claim was fundamentally about what the FYC course is best suited to do—not a claim that meta-awareness is required for transfer of learning (2018). Schieber (2016) argues that although her two case studies evidenced "excellent use of rhetorical flexibility," that transfer was "unintentiona[l]" and "invisible" not only to the instructor but to the students themselves (p. 480).

Important for future research on writing transfer, then, is balancing an emphasis on mindfulness and automaticity. Metacognition and automaticity, rather than separate faculties at odds with one another, might be reframed as intertwined in lifespan learning. Future research also should examine how so-called failures of transfer (like negative transfer and interference) might be part of a longer and more complex process to capture. Automatic response is not a failure in this view. Rather, it may be, as Kahneman intimated, that automaticity and mindful abstraction in writing rely on one another in long-term writing development. In this way, writing teachers and researchers might gain a more complex vision of writerly intention and agency.

Fidelity

Our third transdisciplinary theme, fidelity, addresses the relational possibilities between learning and performance contexts. Simply put, fidelity is the "likeness" between contexts and the role such similarity plays in transfer. This useful construct comes from studies of transfer and simulations (in medical education, aviation education, military education) where it refers to "the extent to which the appearance and behavior of the simulator/simulation match the appearance and behavior of the simulated system" (Maran & Glavin, 2003, p. 23). While fidelity does imply a match, more often, research is more concerned with the complicated relationships between simulated, classroom practice, and real-world environments, concerns that recall Perkins and Salomon's (1988) pedagogical approaches of "hugging" and "bridging."

Across fields, scholars examine fidelity itself, how to evoke fidelity, and how to help learners enter low-fidelity contexts in order to understand transferable skills, knowledge, and actions. This section sorts fidelity across dimensions: situated learning, high/low fidelity's role in simulations and scaffolding, and context proximity and perception. Each dimension complicates and extends writing studies' questions about how to build connections between learning and performance contexts.

Situated Learning

Situated learning theory, such as Lave (1988) and Lave and Wenger's (1991) work on cognition in practice, communities of practice, and legitimate peripheral participation, suggests that fidelity in practice and participation is necessary for learning and for transfer. For Lave and Wenger, learning happens when newcomers actively engage with a community-defined context. A newcomer must participate with more expert members in order to develop competencies in the group's sociocultural practices. From this perspective, fidelity is critical for learning and includes working with a community expert and receiving on-going feedback on community practices over time. Specifically, the process of legitimate peripheral participation (engaged, social participation) is an example of a high fidelity (high likeness) learning experience. In sports education, situated learning theory has informed questions of what counts as fidelity in training that involves the deep interactions of the body and mind. And medical education builds from situated learning theory to expand its theory of fidelity to questions of how to develop the most effective simulations for learning about medical care.

Writing studies has long debated the utility of general writing skills given overwhelming research on situated learning and situated literacy (Russell, 1995; Petraglia, 1995). A similar debate has animated discussions of transfer in second language writing (Currie, 1993; Spack, 1988). While such debate is not settled, theories of situated learning show that active engagement with communities of practice and their genres provide fidelity of writing contexts through "context-conceptions" rather than "individual" or "task-based" learning models (Wardle, 2007). Teaching for transfer through the lens of situated learning (where writers engage deeply and meaningfully with community practices and members) suggests that fidelity of practice should be complemented by a focus on scaffolding, modeling, awareness, and metacognition to help learners generalize specialized learning to a transferrable outcome.

High and Low Fidelity

Theories of situated learning generate concern over the similarities or differences between types of performance contexts, both classroom and workplace. Thorndike's (1906/1916) early theory of "identical elements" promoted the idea that learners make connections (associations) between tasks or contexts when prompted by identical surface features and that these can work in a complementary way to improve overall performance. As Thorndike argued, "One mental function or activity improves others in so far as and because they are in part identical with it, because it contains elements common to them" (1906/1916, p. 243). Although this work has been subsequently critiqued, identical elements theory provides influential background for work on simulations across education, aviation, military training, and human resources. This tension exemplifies how theories of transfer, moving through cycles of behaviorist, cognitive, and social approaches, retain currency over time when they meet student, practitioner, or trainee needs.

To name types of likeness among identical elements, simulation training has distinguished between high and low fidelity. High fidelity means that there is a close likeness to the real while low fidelity means that the likeness is partial or distant. When comparing contexts, researchers often distinguish between multiple dimensions of high and low fidelity. For example, researchers in military education note that "Fidelity is not a simple high/low dichotomy, rather it is multiple compound continua" (Alexander et al., 2005, p. 6). Dimensions that define high or low fidelity can include "surface features" that are "problem-specific," "domain-specific features of training examples," and "deep (structural) features [that] refer to the underlying principles imparted in training (Alexander et al., 2005, p. 2; see also see Gick & Holyoak, 1987). Importantly, scholars note that more fidelity does not necessarily mean a better transfer outcome. Rather, what matters is how "the level of fidelity captures the critical elements/properties of the skills/tasks you wish to teach;" if it does, then that "level of fidelity is sufficient even if it noticeably deviates from the real world" (Alexander et al., 2005, p. 6).

While other fields may not use the term *fidelity* when studying or creating transfer-friendly contexts for students, scholars and educators have experimented with aspects akin to high and low fidelity in teaching for transfer. For instance, school-to-work studies ask how a classroom's level of authenticity to real work environments can move students from school toward workplace writing, using simulations, client-based projects, service-learning projects, and internships to support transfer of learning. Simulations in these examples differ from simulations in medical, aviation, and military where simulation pedagogy ranges from case studies to highly advanced electronic and digital environments. Rather, simulations in professional and technical writing classrooms provide low fidelity activity through constructed case studies and imagined real-world audiences and exigencies. Such classrooms, while superior to classrooms with no project-oriented assignments (Herrington, 1985), have been criticized as psuedotransactional (Spinuzzi, 1996) spaces where "the real audience for the students was always the professor—in his role as professor" (Freedman et al., 1994, p. 203).

Interestingly, findings from school-to-workplace studies have not found much value for transfer in low fidelity contexts; this contrasts with work in medical education that suggests there are times when high fidelity (high likeness) between the simulated and real-world contexts is too complex for novice students to engage in right away. In fact, Maran and Glavin (2003) have suggested that presenting novice learners with every dimension and real-world complexity may hinder students' ability to progress. But school-to-workplace studies have found more success in higher fidelity contexts such as client-based approaches, in which students work with actual clients in the service of real workplace needs. But even in these higher fidelity situations, scholars have found that any distance or discrepancy between school and workplace activity systems can cause conflict or confusion (Dannels, 2003). Research on internships shows that writers who are more used to being students than workers do not simply apply what they know in the workplace setting; rather, they must move into the culture and activity of the community of practice. For instance, Anson and Forsberg (1990) show that interns need to enter the writing and working culture, participate in its activities over time, and adapt prior knowledge to those new expectations. In this way, fidelity is more than situational likeness; it also accounts for learners' motivations and goals for engagement. Thus, fidelity is a co-constructed phenomenon that includes context, activity, and individual.

Scaffolding

Scaffolding offers one method for moving novices toward more expert status through carefully sequenced activities. While educators can scaffold in multiple ways, this section focuses on how scaffolding for transfer moves learners across low- to high-fidelity contexts. Finding or contriving fidelity-oriented contexts (simulations, client-based approaches, or internships) and determining what they will include is a form of scaffolding for transfer. Two types of fidelity scaffolding rarely taken up in writing studies—progressive fidelity (Norman et al., 2012, p. 644) and concreteness fading (Fyfe et al., 2014)—suggest additional avenues for writing transfer research. In progressive fidelity, developed from research arguing that novices are "better off with simpler models and should gradually move to more complex models as their skills improve" (Norman et al., 2012, p. 644), learners engage in "a series of learning environments of increasing fidelity" (Teteris et al., 2012, p. 141). Scaffolding between low and high-fidelity contexts occurs by building up and out of various context dimensions.

Concreteness fading, on the other hand, employs a combination of concrete and abstract types of scaffolds to transition learners toward transfer potential. Concreteness fading comes from educational psychology research on the value of concrete and abstract learning. Some scholars emphasize that transfer is assisted when concrete examples are not offered (Kaminski et al., 2008, 2013), while others suggest concrete variables—such as the body and bodily action—are required for transfer because they interact with cognition (Nemirovsky, 2011; Pouw et al., 2014). Fyfe et al.'s (2014) work on scaffolding for transfer connects these views through concreteness fading, which moves learners from the concrete to the abstract. Stages include enactive (focusing on concrete models and physical experiences), iconic (stripping away extraneous details and using more formal graphic symbols to link the concrete experience to the conceptual), and symbolic (using an abstract model to "highlight relevant structural patterns" [p. 12]). Fyfe et al.'s findings showed that students who started with concrete simulations/visualizations of activity and ended with more abstract representations of the task had more successful transfer results. Through scaffolding via both concrete and abstract methods, rather than one or the other, transfer was increased.

While scaffolding is commonly used in writing courses to help students transfer their writing-related knowledge, progressive fidelity shows how scaffolding for transfer could impact course sequence design. Concreteness fading also could influence the sequencing and interrelationship of concrete and abstract writing-related knowledge. Engagement with such lesser-known approaches to scaffolding can increase writing studies' theoretical and pedagogical repertoire for building on existing efforts (e.g., writing about writing or teaching for transfer approaches) to empower students' transfer of writing-related knowledge.

An integral element of scaffolding through fidelity is the role of mentors and teachers in these processes. Sports education, for instance, emphasizes the role of teacher dialogue and feedback in the learning process. The teaching games for understanding approach, for instance, stresses the need for coaches and peer guidance in learning, with the ultimate goal of fading the guide's support over time (Lopez et al., 2009). While writing studies has focused less on the role of facilitative learning through scaffolding, recent research suggests that engaging students in "transfer talk" ("the talk through which individuals make visible their prior learning") can be part of a scaffold that primes for transfer (Nowacek et al., 2019, para 7). In writing, which is a complex, ill-structured, and rhetorically variable practice, such dialogic interaction is especially critical in orienting students toward flexible and creative (rather than rigid and application-oriented) acts of writing transfer.

Modeling

Given the importance of context-to-context and task-to-task fidelity in teaching for transfer, modeling (providing examples that model later behavior) also is suggested across fields as an effective transfer tool. For example, psychology research on transfer has long been interested in schemas or concepts: abstract knowledge representations that explain multiple applications of a principle (Hammer et al., 2005, p. 95). Given the importance of schemas for aiding transfer—as they enable a flexible recombination of knowledge for discrete types of local problem-solving—researchers have asked how learners can develop transferable schemas. Gick and Holyoak (1983) found that for learners to articulate a schema, they needed to build an abstract infrastructure from multiple stories and examples. Beyond merely reading examples, learners need to actively compare and draw connections between them (Gentner et al., 2003).

Training design in industrial and organizational (I/O) psychology also relies on behavior modeling that aims to direct attention, encourage retention, and increase motivation. Linked to Bandura's social theory of learning (Baldwin, 1992), behavior modeling involves a trainee overviewing the component parts of the task or skill to be learned, observing models, practicing, getting feedback, and applying the training in the workplace (Pescuric & Byham, 1996; Taylor et al., 2005). Like schema development, behavior-model training seeks generalization from an observation for application in a future context. Additional studies have provided trainees ranges of positive and negative models to learn from, examining the level of generalization achieved.

Implications of modeling for writing transfer are already in play within writing classrooms, writing centers, WAC programs, and first-year writing. For instance, work on "explicit modeling" in WAC/WID contexts highlights the value of students gaining more abstract concepts to guide transfer. Within first-year writing, use of multiple examples (Gick & Holyoak, 1983) and comparing examples (Gentner et al., 2003) are used to help students develop writing-related schemas. In genre approaches to first-year writing, for example, analyzing multiple disciplinary genres for their rhetorical, procedural, formal, structural, and linguistic features provides students with a self-developed schema of that genre in use (Devitt et al., 2004). Other approaches such as teaching for transfer (Yancey et al., 2014) call on schema/theory development as a goal for first-year writing. What becomes clear across fields is just how much teaching writing, even though not always explicitly referenced as such, draws on and works from similar theories of model comparison in efforts to develop abstract theories of writing (schema, concepts, generalizations) to transfer across contexts.

Proximity and Perception

Proximity—closeness or distance in space, time, or association—captures additional aspects of fidelity. Transfer is aided when students perceive the differences and similarities (fidelity) between contexts (Walvoord & McCarthy, 1990) and when they experience "an increasing level of domain-specific knowledge" of thinking and writing skills over time (Smit, 2004, p. 185). Gaps between "expert and novice thinking" (Middendorf & Pace, 2004) are likewise an obstacle to the transfer of writing-related knowledge across the disciplines. The decoding-the-disciplines model sees transfer as intrinsic to disciplinary writing development and seeks to understand where transfer might break down. To break through a "bottleneck" (Middendorf & Pace, 2004), students need help to decode the discipline through explicit faculty intervention like careful sequencing, classroom assignments, and lectures and meta-discussions of discipline-specific writing.

While the above writing studies scholars emphasize the importance of proximity to support the transfer of knowledge, perceptions of that proximity also factor into transfer acts. For example, human resources research on transfer focuses on "work-environment factors perceived by trainees to encourage or discourage their use of knowledge, skills, and abilities learned in training on the job" (Cromwell & Kolb, 2004, p. 451). Such objects of perception can include supervisor support, peer support, and opportunity to perform. Critically, the objective existence of such support is beside the point if trainees do not perceive the support. Just as affordances can be put in place to help writers transfer and expand their writing-related knowledge across the curriculum, human resources scholars suggest that situational and consequential cues can move trainees toward a perception of the fidelity of similar contexts (Rouiller & Goldstein, 1993). Concern with gaps in perception and how to encourage shifts in perception have also been explored in second language writing (James, 2008), first-year writing (Wardle, 2007), and writing across the disciplines (Bergmann & Zepernick, 2007). For instance, Bergmann and Zepernick find a problem of transfer to be "not that students are *unable* to recognize situations outside FYC in which those skills can be used, but that students *do not look for* such situations because they believe that skills learned in FYC have no value in any other setting" (p. 139).

One possible area for further exploration in writing studies is the role of embodied cognition in making transfer possibilities perceptible to writers. Aviation education attempts to remedy perceptual challenges so that trainees are able to experience what would be a perceptual likeness between the simulation and a real flying situation with a focus on visual, interactional, and kinesthetic fidelity. As Robinson and Mania (2007) have opined, "identifying ways to induce reality rather than simulating the physics of reality is a scientific challenge to be addressed by all future generations of simulators" (p. 134). In studies where perception is of core concern for transfer, fidelity between contexts is not made through material likenesses; rather, transfer is prompted by cognitive and embodied recognition in concert with environmental factors.

Directionality

> Transformation, if it is going to happen at all, will happen in multidirectional ways, in no predictable time frame, and often in spaces beyond the institutional gaze. . . . the unpredictability of knowing if or how or where or when these attempts will lead to the kinds of transformations they sought. (Barron & Grimm, 2002, p. 76).

In this quotation, Barron and Grimm are writing about transformation in the writing center, specifically changes in tutors' thinking about racial justice. But the way they tie multidirectionality to transformation sets the stage for our fourth transdisciplinary theme: directionality. Barron and Grimm explain that transformation occurs "in multidirectional ways, in no predictable time frame, and often in spaces" they can't see. They thus place transformation in time and space, stressing the unpredictability of the "where or when" of change. Similarly, the theme of directionality across this book's chapters links time and space to map the movement of transfer. While some transfer concepts explicitly speak of "prior" and "future" times, others are motivated by questions of how knowledge is "moved" or "carried forward" by learners coming from and on their way to future spaces. Thus, our theme of directionality highlights how past contexts—including spatial and embodied elements—influence the learner's present. Like other sections in this conclusion, the theme of directionality challenges one-way application models of transfer in favor of more complex and dynamic ones (Matsuda, 1997), treating writing development as uneven, happening in fits and starts, and transformational when woven through new writing situations (Carroll, 2002).

For example, stressing the directionality of forward and backward reaching transfer highlights how learners seek prior resources for transfer from other times and spaces. Perkins and Salomon (1988) embed forward and backward reaching transfer into the process of high-road transfer, which "depends on deliberate mindful abstraction of skill or knowledge from one context for application in another" (p. 25). In forward reaching transfer, a learner might take from a current situation and abstract requisite skills, strategies, or capacities for future situations. Backward reaching transfer, on the other hand, a learner attempts to link a present task or situation to a memory that might then be pulled forward to help achieve the current task. These contexts and memories are times and places that learners turn to in enacting transfer. Thinking of those turns as directional can help give spatial and embodied dimension to the transfer act. In this section, this potential is categorized in three ways: forward, backward, and multidirectional.

Forward: Preparation for Future Learning

Scholarly conversations across several fields explore how to make explicit use of learners' futures to guide them toward successful transfer. This work pivots around forward-looking terms like "potential," "anticipated," or "imagination." One such conversation is preparation for future learning (PFL) (Bransford & Schwartz, 1999; Schwartz et al., 2005). Bransford and Schwartz argue for helping students learn to be future learners (see Chapter 2). Such research emphasizes that transfer should be treated as forward-looking, leading learners to imagine future times and spaces for knowledge use. Preparation for future learning has been used within writing studies, but only sparingly. Within writing center research, Driscoll (2015) developed and studied a tutor education course that brought together PFL with Perkins and Salomon's (2012) "detect-elect-connect" model. The result was a course that focused on forward-looking concepts like adaptability or resource use while asking students to actively connect learning to new or future contexts. Driscoll and Harcourt (2012) found that such a deliberate, forward-looking approach did activate transfer-like thinking to build connections among multiple contexts.

Forward: Framing

Researchers also have theorized and studied additional types of forward-looking transfer, forwarding concepts like *framing* or *activated resources*. Drawing on the work of Tannen in linguistics and Goffman in anthropology, Hammer et al. (2005) define framing as "a set of expectations an individual has about the situation in which she finds herself that affect what she notices and how she thinks to act" (p. 98). As "meta-communicative signals" (Engle, 2006, p. 456), frames can either keep contexts isolated or help to connect them when cued by intercontextuality (Hammer et al., 2005). To forge connections or build environments that encourage connections, Engle et al. (2011) contrast "expansive" with "bounded" framing to suggest that the former has the potential to activate a constellation of associations to prior knowledge, thus bearing a "family resemblance" to what Gick and Holyoak (1980, 1983) have called hints. In this way, transfer can be prompted when frames connect. Further, while frames are primed for future use, they may remain dormant if they are too bounded. Rather, "encourag[ing] students to orient to what they know as being of continued relevance across times, places, people and topics" (Engle et al., 2011, p. 622) may prompt forward-looking transfer.

Echoing Gick and Holyoak's (1980, 1983) approach to framing connections across resemblances, Lindenman's (2015) work on meta-genres shows how students create connections with genres across domains even when researchers and teachers aren't aware of those connections. In other words, Lindenman shows how student writers generate their own sets of genre family resemblances (meta-genres). Arguing that students more typically work from those affiliations rather than ones imposed through instruction, Lindenman asks writing studies scholars to reconsider the boundaries placed around literacy domains, resonating with Engle's contention that expansive frames are necessary to see and teach for transfer. When educators work within the logic of students' metageneric umbrellas, they follow students' future-looking transfer routes rather than presupposing where and when students will transfer knowledge.

Forward: Lateral and Vertical Transfer

Another set of scholarship that explicitly emphasizes forward-looking transfer is work on lateral and vertical transfer in course and curricular structuring. In writing across the curriculum scholarship, lateral transfer refers to synchronous courses designed to aid transfer of writing-related knowledge by linking analogous writing experiences such as writing classes connected with service-learning experiences (Lettner-Rust et al., 2007). Vertical transfer, on the other hand, addresses student transfer opportunities throughout a curriculum, from first-year writing up to senior year. Vertical models support student writing development through curricular design that explicitly teaches for transfer. Research suggests that students benefit from encountering (a) concepts over time and across contexts; (b) opportunities to apply learned concepts, skills, or strategies to new situations; and (c) sequenced learning contexts that increase in complexity (Crowley, 1998; Hall, 2006; Jamieson, 2009; Melzer, 2014; Miles et al., 2008; Smit, 2004). While researchers advocate for connecting first-year writing to a vertical curriculum, research thus far has not shown students linking the two on their own. This has led to the recommendation for building in "programmatic cues" (Bergmann & Zepernick, 2007; Wardle, 2009) and affordances (Greeno et al., 1993) as catalysts for transfer across the curriculum. Such research suggests that while transfer might happen for students without intervention, educators can encourage students to move their knowledge forward through intentionally designed curricular structures and well-placed transfer affordances.

Sports education also uses a lateral and vertical model, but rather than building connections across courses, scholars are interested in how students build transfer between games. Lateral transfer (Mandler 1954 referenced in Lopez et al., 2009, p. 51) requires a "common approach" to a category of games rather than the teaching of specific games. Theories and studies of "transfer of tactical solutions" have relied on a long-held schema that sorts sports into categories (Thorpe et al., 1984) in terms of "fundamental tactical principles [and] structural elements" (Lopez et al., 2009, p. 52): invasion, net/wall, striking/fielding, and target games (see Chapter 4 in this volume). Here, vertical transfer describes sports similar enough in terms of tactics and structure to be learned sequentially or scaffolded onto one another (Holt et al., 2002; López at al., 2009; Werner & Almond, 1990). In other words, vertical transfer requires identifying simpler to more complex skills and strategies and presenting those in a meaningful order.

Backward: Prior Knowledge and Reflection

In their book *How People Learn: Mind, Brain, Experiences, and School*, Bransford et al. (2000) affirm that "new learning involves transfer based on previous learning" (p. 53). In this way, theories of prior knowledge characterize how writers look back to previous places and times to find a basis for future action. Most prior knowledge scholarship reviewed in this book comes from writing studies, although sports education also relies on the construct of prior knowledge to develop its teaching for vertical or lateral transfer. Writing studies research focusing on the role of prior knowledge confirms that prior writing knowledge shapes the writers' contexts as they encounter new writing tasks. For instance, research has shown that prior writing-related knowledge impacts attitudes toward writing, strategies that writers draw on when encountering new tasks, and the literacy practices that writers associate with a given composing activity or genre. Writers are always making use of prior knowledge, knowingly or not. The use they make impacts writing performances in the present (Jarratt et al., 2009; Nowacek, 2011; Reiff & Bawarshi, 2011; Robertson et al., 2012; Rounsaville et al., 2008).

A set of studies helpful for understanding prior knowledge is found in scholarship on adult learners with lifelong workplace knowledge returning to school (Gillam, 1991; Michaud, 2011; Navarre Cleary, 2013). For example, Michaud's (2011) "reverse commute" study reports on adult learners who bring generationally inflected resources to new writing contexts. Such work-to-school scholarship has close kinship with much literacy research on home-to-school transfer that documents the matches and mismatches between home, school, and work contexts. Literacy studies shows that rather than attribute mismatches to student failure, scholars might look instead to the uneven impact of sociocultural practices and values on students' transfer challenges. Reading even the preceding studies through that lens offers a robust explanation of what is bound up in the prior knowledge that shapes writers' activities in the present.

Reflection involves looking back to rethink prior knowledge. Writing reflection, in particular, assumes that explicit backward thinking has the potential to reformulate prior experience and make it relevant for supporting the transfer of knowledge. Within writing studies, Beaufort (1999, 2007), Downs and Wardle (2007), and Yancey et al. (2014) provide teaching recommendations that take advantage of this deliberate writing move. Beaufort is one of the first writing scholars to connect transfer, mindfulness, and reflection of writing-related knowledge. Based on her case study, Tim, as he moved from first-year writing into his discipline-specific courses, Beaufort (2007) suggests a set of principles for fostering transfer such as principle 3, which suggests "constantly connecting new and already gained knowledge" about writing (p. 182). Beaufort's work serves as a foundation for pedagogies such as writing about writing and teaching for transfer that similarly rely on reflection.

Backward: Negative Transfer and Interference

As a framework for studying and interpreting transfer, negative transfer refers to the ways prior knowledge interferes with or disrupts new learning. While "positive" transfer tends to indicate transfer acts that improve performance—what has been carried forward into the present context supports learning—negative transfer seeks to name a problem. Negative transfer can mean new learning is made worse through such "interference" (Schunk, 2004), with interference being used to indicate syntactic or morphological error as evidence of failed or negative language transfer (Gass & Selinker, 1992; Selinker, 1969, 1972; Weinreich, 1953). The sometimes synonymous use of interference and negative transfer seems to have lasting power as a depiction of transfer in both speech and writing (see Chapter 6 in this volume).

Writing studies scholars also widely engage with notions of negative transfer. Beaufort (2007) shows how case study Tim inappropriately applied genre conventions across contexts as evidence of negative transfer. Nowacek (2011), on the other hand, has questioned the value of negative transfer as a framework and instead warns against the difficulty in determining whether an act is negative or positive transfer, noting that the researchers' answer to that question will depend on their "assessment criteria" (p. 27). When, for example, transfer is only deemed positive if a student accomplishes teacher-defined outcomes, researchers miss other signs of transfer such as emotional moments of "transfer as revelation," as well as how an experience might weave into "the individual student's conception of self and larger trajectory of intellectual and emotional development" (p. 27; see also Lobato, 2012). In fact, scholarship throughout this book shows that the binary of negative and positive transfer is disrupted when learning is studied longitudinally (over time and across contexts) and holistically (involving discursive as well as non-discursive sites of experience).

In a similar vein, sociocultural studies of literacy complicate negative transfer by situating the transfer of writing-related knowledge, and any prior knowledge and writing-related values, within the ideological boundaries between in- and out-of-school literacy. For example, Heath's (1983) ethnography showed that successful transfer of learning was directly linked to when and how children's prior literacy knowledge aligned with the school's definitions and practices of literacy. But using a sociocultural lens for literacy events, Heath did not locate negative transfer within struggling students, but rather in the mainstream school's white, middle-class values. These powerful relations are critical to any discussion of assumed failures of transfer and should inform any robust study of writing transfer.

Multidirectional

While the theme of directionality mostly captures forward- or backward-looking transfer activity, some transfer scholarship reviewed in this book indicates both forward *and* backward directionality. That is, some scholarship considers the two-way movement of transfer acts. For example, cross-linguistic influence (Sharwood-Smith & Kellerman, 1986) suggests that transfer among languages can happen no matter the order of language learned (L1, L2, L3, etc.). In fact, a number of terms in second language acquisition—reverse transfer, backward transfer, the L2 effect—stress how a target language can also influence the source language due to the multi-directional movement of language elements during learning (Cook, 2003; Helfenstein; 2005; Jarvis & Pavlenko, 2008; Pavlenko, 2000; Pavlenko & Jarvis, 2002). In describing "those processes that lead to the incorporation of elements from one language into another," cross-linguistic influence accounts for the unpredictability sometimes absent in uni-directional articulations of language interference or reverse transfer (Sharwood-Smith & Kellerman, 1986, p. 1).

In writing studies, multidirectional movement characterizes Taczak and Robertson's (2016) four-part approach to reflection practices for transfer, including reflecting backward, inward, forward, and outward (p. 46). Dinitz and Harrington's (2014) research on writing center tutors' disciplinary expertise illustrates tutors' ability to guide writers' multidirectional transfer. They found that tutors with disciplinary expertise helped writers generalize rhetorical lessons, facilitating forward *and* backward reaching transfer through a kind of "push back and push forward" tutoring (p. 90).

Most substantially, long-standing research on the transformation of knowledge treats transfer as happening "in multidirectional ways" in that learning cannot be traced along predictable paths or timelines (Barron & Grimm, 2002, p. 76). Much of the research reviewed in this book treats the transfer act as the transformation of knowledge, shaped through "active interpreting, modifying, and reconstructing the skills and knowledge transferred" (Tuomi-Gröhn et al., 2003, p. 4). Transfer as transformation stresses change, unpredictability, multiplicity, reconstruction, and creativity. For example, Nowacek's (2011) principle of reconstruction emphasizes that "both the old and new contexts" for transfer "as well as what is being transferred" all transform during acts of recontextualization (p. 25). DePalma & Ringer's (2011) theory of adaptive transfer rearticulates transfer as transformation, emphasizing the ways that transfer is idiosyncratic, rhetorical, and multilingual (p. 141). In writing center studies, Johnson (2020) emphasizes the seemingly idiosyncratic or incidental transformations of knowledge that reveal transfer at work in the writing center (para 7). She follows Smart and Brown (2002) in defining the "transformation of learning" as "the reinvention of expert practices" (p. 122). She argues that transfer can be taught through incidental opportunities (rather than planned lessons that require longer periods of time) when transfer is recognized to be constant and ongoing knowledge transformation rather than "clear cut moments of knowledge application" (para. 24). From this vantage, transfer must include writers' creative and agentive capacities to negotiate meaning with readers and to shape—transform—knowledge as they learn.

Simultaneity

Our final transdisciplinary theme, simultaneity, characterizes the layered quality of singularity. In terms of transfer this means the single occurrence of multiplicity: multiple contexts, variables, and languages that condition a single transfer act in a particular way. We provide three understandings of simultaneity below, approaching theories of concurrent contexts (multiple contexts shaping a single transfer act), dimensionality (multiple factors shaping a single transfer act), and multicompetence (multiplicity in a single language system) as demonstrations of this holistic understanding of writing transfer.

Concurrent Contexts

Scholars emphasizing simultaneity in the transfer act consider how concurrent contexts—situations co-occurring, existing or happening at the same time—shape single transfer acts. Research that approaches transfer this way highlights the temporal and spatial qualities of transfer—how times and spaces regarded as distinct entities actually bleed into each other, causing writers to be influenced by multiple spaces or times at once. For example, writing center researchers consider concurrent contexts because of the way multiple disciplinary discourses co-occur in a single session. Because tutors and writers bring distinct disciplinary expertise to bear on single writing events (the text or task at hand) the writing center acts as a station through which multiple academic discourses shuttle and stop for collaborative exchange. Tutors are specialists in writing (many having taken full courses in writing center studies prior to tutoring) as well as in a variety of disciplines, and act as "handlers" who guide writing knowledge across these disciplinary backgrounds as well as those of the writers they work with (Nowacek, 2011). Similarly, Alexander et al. (2016) say the multiple literacies that students bring to writing center sessions are inevitably networked, with tutors and writers linking multiple literacies as they collaborate to make meaning in talk and writing. These scholars emphasize that simultaneity helps reframe academic writing knowledge as multiple, adaptable, and emergent (Walker, 1998).

The notion of *networked knowledge*, stemming from multiple contexts but existing in single spaces also resonates with Lemke's (2000) "heterochrony," the interlocked nature of various timescales. Referring to the relationship between school and "real life" contexts, Lemke notes that dichotomizing such spaces, as if students aren't always informed by knowledge from both at the same time, ignores the overlap of these contexts in everyday writing decisions. When writing studies scholars take up heterochronic frames, simultaneity becomes instantiated in theories like chronotopic lamination, Prior and Shipka's (2003) theory which, following Bakhtin's chronotope, foregrounds "the simultaneous layering of multiple activity frames and stances" that inform any single writing moment, all of which together comprise the lifespan development of writing expertise (p. 187). This theoretical stance informs Prior's (2018) rejection of Dias et al.'s (1999) "worlds apart" thesis, saying that any understanding of writers' "becoming" approaches the transfer of writing knowledge not as a tortured reaching-across of distant writing contexts but rather a fact of life. Instead, he treats writing knowledge as sets of already existing "continuities of learning across time and setting" that are a "fundamental necessity for any conceivable account of human development" (in the section on "Worlds Apart vs. Laminated Worlds") and by extension any understanding of the transfer of writing knowledge.

Conclusion

Dynamic Dimensionality

The simultaneous quality of transfer also shapes how scholars in many fields approach the material and sociocultural dimension of transfer. This lens in transfer research attends to the influential factors that shape a single transfer act, variously called dynamism or multi-dimensionality. For example, studies in medical education consider the material factors that influence the ability of medical students to transfer knowledge from simulation to real world healthcare contexts. This aspect of the notion of fidelity (see Chapter 4) attends to a learning context's "multi-dimensionality" when a study considers how a healthcare professional's patient interactions are shaped by environmental factors like noise; psychological factors like bedside manner; and physical factors like motion economy, dexterity, and accuracy. These multiple factors all come to bear on single learning contexts, shaping the fidelity of that context to others and the likelihood of a medical student to transfer skills across them.

In addition to material considerations, research across fields also incorporates the multiple sociocultural dimensions that can shape transfer acts. For example, researchers in second language writing consider multiple dimensions such as grammatical proficiency (Berman, 1994; Cumming, 1989; Wolfersberger, 2003); educational experiences with writing (Cozart et al., 2016; Kobayashi & Rinnert, 2008; Kubota, 1998; Mohan & Lo, 1985); L1 literacy (Carson & Kuehn, 1992; Mohan & Lo, 1985); and student characteristics, motivations, and intentions (Cozart et al., 2016; Kobayashi & Rinnert, 2008). Matsuda's (1997) "dynamic model of L2 writing" expanded the factors that might influence the transfer of writing knowledge among languages, pointing researchers beyond over-determined cultural patterns toward additional factors such as educational background, the shared discourse community of a text's writer and reader, and the genre expectations of that text. Matsuda's model is dynamic in that it centers a written text as an interaction of a writer and reader, who come together to shape the sociocultural conditions for transfer. Other L2 writing research has followed Matsuda's (1997) lead to include "variations within his or her native language (i.e., dialect) and culture (i.e., socioeconomic class), his or her knowledge of the subject matter, past interactions with the reader, and the writer's membership to various L1 and L2 discourse communities" (p. 53).

Other studies of transfer influenced by dynamism include Hayes et al.'s (2016) use of dynamic transfer, which they define as a theoretical lens that can fully account for the interaction of inner/cognitive and outer/social dimensions that shape student learning called for by earlier composition scholars such as Bizzell (1982/2003). Similarly, Martin and Schwartz (2013) frame students' initiation of prior knowledge as dynamic transfer in order to account for the ways learners coordinate prior and new knowledge as they learn in new contexts. In all these studies, researchers use dynamism to incorporate not only multiple factors shaping single transfer contexts, but also to highlight the holistic quality of their interaction. Multiple dimensions do not stay distinct as they shape transfer acts, but instead fuse to create new conditions for transfer that students and writers must navigate anew during each transfer act.

Multicompetence

As is fully defined in the chapter on transfer in second language writing (see Chapter 6), Cook (1992) proposed the term multicompetence to describe language knowledge with more holistic complexity than previous understandings of bilingualism had allowed. He defines multicompetence as "the overall system of a mind or a community that uses more than one language," promoting relationships among languages of various proficiencies including any other known languages and interlanguages (Cook, 2016, p. 24). In other words, multicompetence describes the whole of language relationships rather than the sum of two monolingual parts. In this understanding, a language repertoire is a total linguistic system of interaction rather than a network of isolated individual languages. Therefore, multicompetence demonstrates simultaneity in its fusion of language multiplicity into a single language system. Following this line of thinking, when writers engage in language transfer, they call on multiple languages, of varying proficiencies. This allows researchers to consider the ways that transfer is not an addition of new linguistic knowledge but is instead the "rejigging of existing knowledge or behavior into new configurations," a holistic reimagining of one person's language competence (Cook, 2016, p. 33).

Similarly, second language acquisition scholars who use complexity and dynamism in their theoretical frameworks tend to emphasize fluidity of language transfer. This work argues that lived language transfer is more volatile than one static language construct moving from one concrete context to another (Cenoz & Gorter, 2011; Garcia & Wei, 2014; Grosjean, 1989; Larsen-Freeman, 1997, 2013; Larsen-Freeman & Cameron, 2008). A dynamic understanding of language transfer, with affinities to dynamic and emergent approaches to bilingualism, is resonant with Hammer et al.'s (2005) "resource-based view of learning" in which "learning a new idea is not an all-or-nothing acquisition, but involves an activation of existing resources in new combinations" (p. 114). This view from psychology reframes the potential of what appear to be language errors, negative transfer, or interference as positive evidence of writers drawing on multiple, overlapping language resources all at once (see Chapter 2). With affinities to multi-competence, approaches to multilingualism that emphasize a writer's existing languages resources help scholars consider a linguistic repertoire-in-process, with a writer's language particularities acting as a single kaleidoscope of "new configurations" and "new combinations" through which a writer produces the transfer act.

Future Frames: Transfer as Orientation

We conclude with a final turn of synthesis. This entire reference guide itself is a synthesis of sorts, and in this conclusion, we have suggested five thematic threads that distill commonalities we found uniquely important across the guide's chapters. Now we offer one last step of distillation, suggesting how the shared qualities of these threads might shape future approaches to researching and teaching for transfer.

Interdependence

First, the themes above—individuality, intentionality, fidelity, directionality, and simultaneity—all share an aspect of interdependence that should be accounted for in future studies of transfer and in future transfer pedagogies. Here, interdependence means the inextricable mutuality of aspects of any transfer situation. Aspects like multiple contexts, processes, or dimensions do not just co-occur, but depend on each other to work. The centripetal energy of each element of transfer brings together aspects that seem contradictory: learners transfer knowledge both deliberately and automatically; the transfer of knowledge occurs with both flexibility and control; concepts are best transferred when taught through abstract theories and as concrete skills; transfer skills are transportable but also bound to context. For example, interdependence shapes dual processing theory in psychology, in which every individual uses "two different modes of processing" in order to deal with incoming stimuli: "processes that are unconscious, rapid, automatic, and high capacity, and those that are conscious, slow, and deliberative" (Evans 2008, p. 256). But as transfer research stresses over and over again, across fields, such duality is not contradictory, it is complementary. Elements of transfer that stick together can certainly frustrate the need to isolate factors in an empirical study of transfer. But the point of interdependence is that these elements do not simply sit together in the transfer act; they symbiotically shape what shows up as transferred knowledge during research or teaching. They need each other to make transfer legible.

Therefore, when it comes to researching the transfer of writing knowledge, the interdependent nature of transfer should lead writing studies scholars to consider the ways that transfer might be more interwoven among actors—collaborative, interpersonal, embodied—than writing studies' methods can account for. While long-established approaches—from Giddens' structuration theories to CHAT methodologies—take at their core the co-genesis of both person and society (Prior, 2018), research on the transfer of writing knowledge especially needs to account for the bound nature of individual and social dynamics. One line of research that skillfully models this tension are studies of the body's relation to cognition, which traces learning "beyond the mind as a separate entity to include the body and all its senses" (Light, 2008, p. 23). Such research includes LeMesurier's (2016) studies of embodied rhetorical recognition and response; Nemirovsky's (2011) embodied cognition theories in psychology; or the teaching games for understanding approach in sports education which "links movement in games with the verbalization of understanding through the embodied conversation that takes place between them" (Light & Fawns, 2003, p. 162). While the body and mind are rarely set in opposition to each other in writing transfer research, they are rarely treated as mutually animating elements of the transfer process. Beyond body-mind connections, future research on transfer will need to be able to trace interdependence more capaciously, perhaps by collecting data beyond individual experiences or enactments of transfer, including transfer data that occur in-process (through observation, think-alouds, longitudinal methods) and in groups (through focus groups, teacher research, or online contexts).

Regarding teaching, interdependence might turn practitioners' focus especially toward the collaborative qualities of transfer. Pedagogical approaches across chapters use simulations, awareness of transfer as content, consciousness of transfer acts on the part of students, and reflection that heightens both of these. One can trace how each of these elements have evolved in writing studies, moving from Beaufort's pedagogy (2007) (explicitly teach for transfer) to Yancey et al. (2014)'s teaching for transfer pedagogy (use reflection to do this work) to writing about writing pedagogies (use writing studies research as the content on which to reflect). But future approaches to teaching for transfer need to account especially for the connections among writers in the classroom. That is, beyond the support of individual students reflecting on and transferring writing knowledge, teaching for transfer should be thought of as a distributed pedagogy, in which transfer happens among students as well as the teacher.

This means that writing activities would be designed for groups of students to become aware of and facilitate each other's transfer, or for students to reflect on their instructor's role in their own transfer activities. Nowacek et al. (2019) and Winzenried et al. (2017) have explored the collaborative dimensions of transfer in peer talk, while Driscoll and Jin (2018) have examined the influence of interview conversations on emerging understandings of transfer. Writing assignments could ask students to examine how a past class, as a specific social context, impacts how they transfer writing knowledge to present contexts. Peer review activities could be reflected on as a collaborative transfer event, asking students to address the interpersonal dimensions of peer feedback. Written feedback could be geared to explicitly discuss how student writers and the instructor will *together* transfer learned writing skills to subsequent assignments. The goal would be to acknowledge in each of these activities the ways that teachers and students depend on each other (are interdependent in meaning-making) in the transfer act.

Ephemerality

The second aspect that all five themes above share is a sense of ephemerality in the study and teaching of transfer. Ephemerality is used here to mean that the transfer phenomenon can be fleeting, hard to grasp, and sometimes occurring without the conscious awareness of a researcher or writer (e.g., Day & Goldstone, 2011). When researchers look for transfer, they may see only a part. When instructors aim to teach for transfer, they may support only a piece. Considering ephemerality in transfer research and teaching means giving up some control, acknowledging that in its deeply social nature and close affiliation with learning, transfer can be hard to capture and explain in full. An investigative or pedagogical grasp on the phenomenon might be very brief indeed.

Across this book's chapters, ephemerality often appears in limitations sections of research articles, wherein scholars acknowledge that their study design couldn't quite pin down the phenomenon they were after. In research that stresses individuality, intentionality, and fidelity, findings become nuanced when scholars admit that during transfer individuals are connected to others, in contexts that aim to simulate future realities but never really can. Shades of the ephemeral appear in scholarship like Lobato's (2008) work in psychology, which argues that transfer might occur in a study, but it might not result in the expert behaviors that researchers sought to trace. Lobato suggests that researchers, by choosing a particular learned behavior to trace, may miss the transfer phenomena occurring beyond the researchers' delimited gaze. Similarly, in sports education, Light and Fawns (2003) assert that transfer is both verbalized and not verbalized because it occurs on embodied and situated levels that study subjects might not be able to articulate in words. Think-aloud protocols, interviews, and textual analysis might all miss transfer that exists as bodily, less-conscious, or un-verbalized knowledge. For Keith and Frese (2005) in industrial psychology, "errors" in the transfer behavior they set out to trace do not show a lack of transfer but instead build evidence of a "learning device" (p. 677). They suggest that training programs should "allo[w] and encourage[e] errors to occur" (Heimbeck et al., 2003, p. 337) so that learners develop the skills to work with them in new contexts that are always "open, disruptive, and ambiguous" (p. 336).

In researching the transfer of writing knowledge, such ambiguity means that scholars must reconsider what can be realistically captured by the methods at their disposal. They may need to present analysis and findings with less certainty, being honest about what parts of the transfer of writing were not fully grasped. The role of ephemerality in teaching for transfer might simply be reassuring. Experienced teachers know how much variability and uncertainty is involved in even the grandest of our pedagogical plans.

Orientation

The interdependent and ephemeral qualities of transfer leave researchers and teachers with a bit of a conundrum: it is not necessarily an actionable conclusion that the transfer of writing is too interwoven or fickle to study or teach. We acknowledge that it may not be satisfying to read that pulling out a transfer thread simply unravels transfer's fabric. So, we propose that accounting for orientation in the transfer of writing—on the part of the writer, instructor, and context—might mitigate some of its sticky and slippery qualities.

Brandt (2018) notes that early childhood writing experiences can develop into productive "orientations to writing" (p. 265) that, when combined with later school and workplace practices, eventually become "incorporated into a person's more general dispositions toward life" (p. 266). This forces "an expansion of what is considered transfer in writing," one that sees current orientations to writing through the prism of a lifetime of writing experiences (p. 265). Donahue (2016) defines orientation as "the fundamental cognitive activity" of transfer which is characterized by a "fluidity and anti-determinism" that reminds scholars that "pre-orientation is not pre-direction" (p. 118). In Donahue's terms, orientation unites transfer's cognitive work with the fluidity of social experience: writers accumulate lived knowledge that orients them to the possibilities of writing without determining where, when, or how they will use that knowledge. She explains that because "every learner, every language-user, every writer is pre-oriented by past experiences; every learner can engage in orientation and can recognize his or her orientation" (p. 118). Her repetition of "every" stresses a kind of democratic access to the engaged awareness of being oriented; everyone is both conditioned by past experiences with writing but not limited by them. Following Brandt and Donahue then, orientation places fleeting transfer activity into the durability of transfer occurring across all lives. As Donahue (2016) and others have noted, how something transfers is not the same as what is being transferred—the knowledge itself (the what) is distinct from the nature of its transformation (the how). But orientation unites the what with the how, suggesting that the knowledge that moves affects the shape, direction, or consequences of transfer as it occurs. A transfer act is a realm of possibilities, inclusive of the ways a writer is pulled to apply knowledge, and how they knowingly respond to or resist those tugs.

Orientation provides an architecture for those possibilities, incorporating the interdependent material, sociocultural, and embodied dimensions that condition how writers move their knowledge. Orientation also provides multiple viewpoints into transfer attempts: the teacher's, the writer's, the peer's. Orientation leads us to consider what part of the transfer act we are looking at from which or whose point of view and why. It necessitates including how those views are shaped by the power relations of classed, gendered, racialized positions, leading researchers and teachers to become conscious of their own transfer gaze and aware of which transfer acts they have decided are legible or illegible. Our charge as a field moving forward might be to best determine how to *use* writing to articulate a schema accurate to the experience *of* writing: that interdependence and ephemerality are not qualities that trouble or derail the smooth transfer of writing, but instead are qualities, forged in the activity of lived experience, that remind us what writing always is.

References

Alexander, A. L., Brunyé, T., Sidman, J., & Weil, S. A. (2005). From gaming to training: A review of studies on fidelity, immersion, presence, and buy-in and their effects on transfer in pc-based simulations and games. *DARWARS Training Impact Group*, 5, 1–14.

Alexander, K. P., DePalma, M., & Ringer, J. M. (2016). Adaptive remediation and the facilitation of transfer in multiliteracy center contexts. *Computers and Composition*, 41, 32–45.

Allen, B. P., & Potkay, C. R. (1981). On the arbitrary distinction between states and traits. *Journal of Personality and Social Psychology*, 41(5), 916–928.

Allport, G. W., & Odbert, H. S. (1936). Trait-names: A psycho-lexical study. *Psychological monographs*, 47(1).

Anson, C. M., & Forsberg, L. L. (1990). Moving beyond the academic community: Transitional stages in professional writing. *Written Communication*, 7(2), 200–231.

Bacon, N. (1999). The trouble with transfer: Lessons from a study of community service writing. *Michigan Journal of Community Service Learning*, 6 (1), 53–62.

Baird, N., & Dilger, B. (2018). Dispositions in natural science laboratories: The roles of individuals and contexts in writing transfer. *Across the Dis-*

ciplines, 15(4), 21–41. https://wac.colostate.edu/docs/atd/articles/baird-dilger2018.pdf

Baldwin T. T. (1992). Effects of alternative modeling strategies on outcomes of interpersonal-skills training. *Journal of Applied Psychology, 77,* 147–54

Bandura, A. (1977). Self-efficacy: Toward a unifying theory of behavioral change. *Psychological Review, 84*(2), 191–215.

Bandura, A. (1986). *Social foundations of thought and action: A social cognitive theory*. Prentice-Hall

Bandura, A. (1999). Social cognitive theory: An agent perspective. *Asian Journal of Social Psychology, 2,* 21–41.

Barron, N., & Grimm, N. (2002). Addressing racial diversity in a writing center: Stories and lessons from two beginners. *The Writing Center Journal 22*(2), 55–83.

Beaufort, A. (1999). *Writing in the real world: Making the transition from school to work*. Teachers College Press.

Beaufort, A. (2007). *College writing and beyond: A new framework for university writing instruction*. Utah State University Press.

Bergmann, L. S., & Zepernick, J. (2007). Disciplinarity and transfer: Students' perceptions of learning to write. *WPA: Writing Program Administration, 31*(1–2), 124–149.

Berman, R. (1994). Learners' transfer of writing skills between languages. *TESL Canada Journal, 12*(1), 29–46.

Bizzell, P. (1982 / 2003). Cognition, convention, and certainty: What we need to know about writing. In V. Villanueva (Ed.), *Cross-Talk in comp theory: A reader* (2nd ed., pp. 387–411). National Council of Teachers of English. (Original work published 1982)

Brandt, D. (2018). Writing development and life-course development: The case of working adults. In C. Bazerman et al. (Eds.), *The Lifespan Development of Writing* (pp. 244–271). NCTE.

Bransford, J. D., Brown, A. L., & Cocking, R. R. (2000). *How people learn* (Vol. 11). National academy press.

Bransford, J. D., & Schwartz, D. L. (1999). Rethinking transfer: A simple proposal with multiple implications. *Review of Research in Education, 24*(1), 61–100.

Brent, D. (2012). Crossing boundaries: Co-op students relearning to write. *College Composition & Communication, 63*(4), 558–592.

Bronfenbrenner, U., & Morris, P. A. (2006). The bioecological model of human development. In R. M. Lerner & W. Damon (Eds.). *Handbook of child psychology* (Vol. 1, pp. 793–828). Wiley.

Bunker, D., & Thorpe, R. (1982). A model for the teaching of games in secondary schools. *Bulletin of Physical Education, 18*(1), 5–8.

Carroll, L. A. (2002). *Rehearsing new roles: How college students develop as writers*. Southern Illinois University Press.

Carson, J., & Kuehn, P. (1992). Evidence of transfer and loss in developing second language writers. *Language Learning, 42*(2), 157–182.

Cenoz, J., & Gorter, D. (2011). Focus on multilingualism: A study of trilingual writing. *Modern Language Journal, 95*(3), 356–369.

Cook, V. (1992). Evidence for multicompetence. *Language Learning, 42*(4), 557–591.

Cook, V. J. (Ed.). (2003). *Effects of the second language on the first*. Multilingual Matters.

Cook, V. J. (2016) Transfer and the relationship between the languages of multicompetence. In R.A. Alonso (Ed.), *Crosslinguistic influence in second language acquisition* (pp. 24–37). Multilingual Matters.

Cozart, S. M., Jensen T.W., Wichmann-Hansen, G., Kupatadze, K, & Chien-Hsiung Chiu, S. (2016). Negotiating multiple identities in second- or foreign-language writing in higher education. In C. M. Anson & J. L. Moore (Eds.), *Critical transitions: Writing and the question of transfer* (pp. 303–334). Perspectives on writing. The WAC Clearinghouse and University Press of Colorado.

Cromwell, S. E., & Kolb, J. A. (2004). An examination of work-environment support factors affecting transfer of supervisory skills training to the workplace. *Human Resource Development Quarterly, 15*(4), 449–471.

Crowley, S. (1998). *Composition in the university: Historical and polemical essays*, University of Pittsburgh Press.

Cumming, A. (1989). Writing expertise and second-language proficiency. *Language Learning, 39*(1), 80–135.

Currie, P. (1993). Entering a disciplinary community: Conceptual activities required to write for one introductory university course. *Journal of Second Language Writing, 2*(2), 101–117.

Dannels, D. P. (2003). Teaching and learning design presentations in engineering contradictions between academic and workplace activity systems. *Journal of Business and Technical Communication, 17*(2), 139–169.

Day, S. B., & Goldstone, R. L. (2011). Analogical transfer from a simulated physical system. *Journal of Experimental Psychology: Learning, Memory, and Cognition, 37*(3), 551–567.

DePalma, M. J., & Ringer, J. M. (2011). Toward a theory of adaptive transfer: Expanding disciplinary discussions of "transfer" in second-language writing and composition studies. *Journal of Second Language Writing, 20*(2),134–147.

Devitt, A. J., Reiff, M. J., & Bawarshi, A. S. (2004). *Scenes of writing: Strategies for composing with genres*. Pearson/Longman.

Dias, P., Freedman, A., Medway, P., & Paré, A. (1999). *Worlds apart: Acting and writing in academic and workplace contexts*. L. Erlbaum Associates.

Dias, P., & Paré, A. (2000). *Transitions: Writing in academic and workplace settings*. Hampton Press.

Dinitz, S., & Harrington, S. (2014). The role of disciplinary expertise in shaping writing tutorials. *Writing Center Journal, 33*(2), 73–98.

Donahue, C. (2012). Transfer, portability, generalization: (How) does composition expertise "carry"? In K. Ritter & P. Matsuda (Eds.), *Exploring composition studies: Sites, issues, and perspectives,* (pp. 145–166). Utah State University Press.

Donahue, C. (2016). Writing and global transfer narratives: Situating the knowledge transformation conversation. In C. M. Anson & J. L. Moore (Eds.), *Critical transitions: Writing and the question of transfer* (pp. 107–136). Perspectives on writing. The WAC Clearinghouse and University Press of Colorado.

Downs, D., & Wardle, E. (2007). Teaching about writing, righting misconceptions: (Re)envisioning "First-Year Composition" as "Introduction to Writing Studies." *College Composition and Communication, 58*(4), 552–584.

Driscoll, D. L. (2015). Building connections and transferring knowledge: The benefits of a peer tutoring course beyond the writing center. *The Writing Center Journal, 35*(1), 153–181.

Driscoll, D., & Harcourt, S. (2012). Training vs. learning: Transfer of learning in a peer tutoring course and beyond. *The Writing Lab Newsletter, 36*(7–8), 1–6.

Driscoll, D., & Jin, D. (2018). The box under the bed: How learner epistemologies shape writing transfer. *Across the Disciplines, 15*(4), 1–20. https://wac.colostate.edu/docs/atd/articles/driscoll-jin2018.pdf

Driscoll, D. L., & Powell, R. (2016). States, traits, and dispositions: The impact of emotion on writing development and writing transfer across college courses and beyond. *Composition Forum, 34.* https://compositionforum.com/issue/34/states-traits.php

Driscoll, D. L., & Wells, J. (2012). Beyond knowledge and skills: Writing transfer and the role of student dispositions. *Composition Forum, 26.* http://compositionforum.com/issue/26/beyond-knowledge-skills.php

Engeström, Y. (2014). *Learning by expanding: An activity-theoretical approach to developmental research.* Cambridge University Press.

Engle, R. A. (2006). Framing interactions to foster generative learning: A situative explanation of transfer in a community of learners classroom. *The Journal of the Learning Sciences, 15*(4), 451–498.

Engle, R. A., Nguyen, P. D., & Mendelson, A. (2011). The influence of framing on transfer: Initial evidence from a tutoring experiment. *Instructional Science, 39*(5), 603–628.

Evans, J. S. B. (2008). Dual-processing accounts of reasoning, judgment, and social cognition. *Annual Review of Psychology, 59,* 255–278.

Figueredo, L. (2006). Using the known to chart the unknown: A review of first-language influence on the development of English-As-A-Second-Language spelling skill. *Reading & Writing, 19*(8), 873–905.

Freedman, A., Adam, C., & Smart, G. (1994). Wearing suits to class simulating genres and simulations as genre. *Written Communication, 11*(2), 193–226.

Fridhandler, B. M. (1986). Conceptual note on state, trait, and the state–trait distinction. *Journal of Personality and Social Psychology, 50*(1), 169.

Fyfe, E. R., McNeil, N. M., Son, J. Y., & Goldstone, R. L. (2014). Concreteness fading in mathematics and science instruction: A systematic review. *Educational Psychology Review, 26*(1), 9–25.

Garcia, O. & Wei, L. (2014). *Translanguaging: Language, bilingualism and education.* New Palgrave Macmillan.

Gass, S. M., & Selinker, L. (1992). *Language transfer in language learning.* John Benjamins.

Gentner, D., Loewenstein, J., & Thompson, L. (2003). Learning and transfer: A general role for analogical encoding. *Journal of Educational Psychology, 95*(2), 393–408.

Gick, M. L., & Holyoak, K. J. (1980). Analogical problem solving. *Cognitive Psychology, 12*(3), 306–355.

Gick, M. L., & Holyoak, K. J. (1983). Schema induction and analogical transfer. *Cognitive Psychology 15*(1), 1–38.

Gick, M. L., & Holyoak, K.J. (1987). The cognitive basis of knowledge transfer. In S.M. Cormier & J.D. Hagman (Eds.), *Transfer of learning: Contemporary research and applications*, (pp. 9–46). Academic Press.

Gillam, A. M. (1991). Returning students' ways of writing: Implications for first-year college composition. *Journal of Teaching Writing, 10*(1), 1–20.

Gorzelsky, G., Driscoll, D. L., Paszek, J., Jones, E., & Hayes, C. (2016). Cultivating constructive metacognition: a new taxonomy for writing studies. In C. M. Anson & J. Moore (Eds.),*Critical transitions: Writing and the question of transfer* (pp. 215–246). The WAC Clearinghouse and University Press of Colorado.

Greeno, J. G., Moore, J. L., & Smith, D. R. (1993). Transfer of situated learning. In D.K. Detterman & R.J. Sternberg (Eds.), *Transfer on trial: Intelligence, cognition, and instruction*, (pp. 99–167). Ablex Publishing.

Grosjean, F. (1989). Neurolinguists, beware! The bilingual is not two monolinguals in one person. *Brain and Language, 36*, 3–15.

Hall, J. (2006). Toward a unified writing curriculum: Integrating WAC/WID with freshman composition. *The WAC Journal, 17*, 5–22.

Hammer, D., Elby, A., Scherr, R. E., & Redish, E. F. (2005). Resources, framing, and transfer. In J. P. Mestre (Ed.), *Transfer of learning from a modern multidisciplinary perspective*, (pp. 89–120). Information Age Publishing.

Hayes, H., Ferris, D. R., & Whithaus, C. (2016). Dynamic transfer in first-year writing and "writing in the disciplines" settings. In C. M. Anson & J. L. Moore (Eds.), *Critical transitions: Writing and the question of transfer* (pp. 181–213).

Heath, S. B. (1983). *Ways with words: Language, life and work in communities and classrooms.* Cambridge University Press.

Heimbeck, D., Frese, M., Sonnentag, S., & Keith, N. (2003). Integrating errors into the training process: The function of error management instructions and the role of goal orientation. *Personnel Psychology, 56,* 333–361.

Helfenstein, S. (2005). *Transfer: Review, reconstruction, and resolution.* Unpublished doctoral dissertation, University of Jyväskylä.

Herrington, A. J. (1985). Writing in academic settings: A study of the contexts for writing in two college chemical engineering courses. *Research in the Teaching of English, 19*(4), 331–361.

Holt, N. L., Strean, W. B., & Bengoechea, E. G. (2002). Expanding the teaching games for understanding. *Journal of Teaching in Physical Education, 21*(2), 162–176.

Hutchins, E. (1995). *Cognition in the wild.* MIT Press.

James, M. A. (2008). The influence of perceptions of task similarity/difference on learning transfer in second language writing. *Written Communication, 25*(1), 76–103.

Jamieson, S. (2009). The vertical writing curriculum. In J. C. Post & J. A. Inman (Eds.), *Composition(s) in the new liberal arts* (pp. 159–184). Hampton.

Jarratt, S. C., Mack, K., Sartor, A., & Watson, S. E. (2009). Pedagogical memory: Writing, mapping, translating. *WPA: Writing Program Administration - Journal of the Council of Writing Program Administrators, 33*(1), 46–73.

Jarvis, S., & A. Pavlenko. (2008). *Crosslinguistic influence in language and cognition.* Routledge.

Johnson, C. (2020). Transfer(mation) in the writing center: Identifying the transformative moments that foster transfer. In B. Devet, Bonnie & D.L. Driscoll (Eds.), *Transfer of learning in the writing center: A* WLN *digital edited collection.* https://wlnjournal.org/digitaleditedcollection2/.

Johnstone, B. (1996). The *linguistic individual: Self-expression in language and linguistics.* Oxford University Press.

Judd, C. H. (1908). The relation of special training and general intelligence. *Educational Review, 36,* 28–42.

Kahneman, D. (1973). *Attention and effort.* Prentice-Hall.

Kahneman, D. (2003). A perspective on judgment and choice: mapping bounded rationality. *American Psychologist, 58*(9), 697–720.

Kahneman, D. (2011). *Thinking, fast and slow.* Farrar, Straus and Giroux

Kaminski, J. A., Sloutsky, V. M., & Heckler, A. F. (2008). The advantage of abstract examples in learning math. *Science, 320*(25), 454–455.

Kaminski, J. A., Sloutsky, V. M., & Heckler, A. F. (2013). The cost of concreteness: The effect of nonessential information on analogical transfer. *Journal of Experimental Psychology: Applied, 19*(1), 14–29.

Katona, G. (1940). *Organizing and memorizing: Studies in the psychology of learning and teaching*. Columbia University Press.

Keith, N., & Frese, M. (2005). Self-regulation in error management training: Emotion control and metacognition as mediators of performance effects. *Journal of Applied Psychology, 90*(4), 677–691.

Kobayashi, H., & Rinnert, C. (2008). Task response and text construction across L1 and L2 writing. *Journal of Second Language Writing, 17*(1), 7–29.

Kubota, R. (1998). An investigation of L1-L2 transfer in writing among Japanese university students: Implications for contrastive rhetoric. *Journal of Second Language Writing, 7*(1), 69–100.

Larsen-Freeman, D. (1997). Chaos/complexity science and second language acquisition. *Applied Linguistics, 18*(2), 141–165.

Larsen-Freeman, D. (2013). Transfer of learning transformed. *Language Learning, 63*(1), 107–29.

Larsen-Freeman, D., & Cameron, L. (2008). Research methodology on language development from a complex theory perspective. *Modern Language Journal, 92*(2), 200–213.

Lave, J. (1988). *Cognition in practice: Mind, mathematics and culture in everyday life*. Cambridge University Press.

Lave, J, and E. Wenger. (1991). *Situated learning: Legitimate peripheral participation*. Cambridge University Press.

LeMesurier, J. L. (2016). Mobile bodies: Triggering bodily uptake through movement. *College Composition and Communication, 68*(2), 292–316.

Lemke, J. L. (2000). Across the scales of time: Artifacts, activities, and meanings in ecosocial systems. *Mind, Culture, and Activity, 7*(4), 273–290.

Lettner-Rust, H. G., Tracy, P. J., Booker, S. L., Kocevar-Weidinger, E., & Berges, J. B. (2007). Writing beyond the curriculum: Transition, transfer, and transformation. *Across the Disciplines, 4*. https://wac.colostate.edu/atd/archives/volume4/

Light, R. (2008). Complex learning theory—its epistemology and its assumptions about learning: implications for physical education. *Journal of Teaching in Physical Education, 27*(1), 21–37.

Light, R., & Fawns, R. (2003). Knowing the game: Integrating speech and action in games teaching through TGfU. *Quest, 55*(2), 161–176.

Lindenman, H. (2015). Inventing metagenres: How four college seniors connect writing across domains. *Composition Forum, 31*(Spring). http://compositionforum.com/issue/31/inventing-metagenres.php

Lobato, J. (2008). When students don't apply the knowledge you think they have, rethink your assumptions about transfer. In M. Carlson & C. Rasmussen (Eds.), *Making the connection: Research and teaching in undergraduate mathematics* (pp. 289–304). Mathematical Association of America Washington, DC.

Lobato, J. (2012). The actor-oriented transfer perspective and its contributions to educational research and practice. *Educational Psychologist, 47*(3), 232–247.

Lobato, J., Rhodehamel, B., & Hohensee, C. (2012). "Noticing" as an alternative transfer of learning process. *Journal of the Learning Sciences, 21*(3), 433–482.

López, L. M. G., Jordán, O. R. C., Penney, D., & Chandle, T. (2009). The role of transfer in games teaching: Implications for the development of the sports curriculum. *European Physical Education Review, 15*(1), 47–63.

Maran, N., & Glavin, R. (2003). Low-to high-fidelity simulation–a continuum of medical education? *Medical Education, 37*(s1), 22–28.

Martin, L., & Schwartz, D. L. (2013). Conceptual innovation and transfer. In S. Vosniadou (Ed.), *International handbook of research on conceptual change* (2nd ed., pp. 447–465). Routledge.

Matsuda, P. K. (1997). Contrastive rhetoric in context: A dynamic model of L2 writing. *Journal of Second Language Writing, 6*(1), 45–60.

Matsuda, P. K. (2015). Identity in written discourse. *Annual Review of Applied Linguistics, 35*, 140–159.

Melzer, D. (2014). The connected curriculum: Designing a vertical transfer writing curriculum. *The WAC Journal, 25*, 78–91.

Menary, R. (2010). Introduction to the special issue on 4E cognition. *Phenomenology and the Cognitive Sciences, 9*(4), 459–463.

Michaud, M. J. (2011). The "reverse commute": Adult students and the transition from professional to academic literacy. *Teaching English in the Two-Year College, 38*(3), 244–258.

Middendorf, J. & Pace, D. (2004), Decoding the disciplines: A model for helping students learn disciplinary ways of thinking. *New Directions for Teaching and Learning, 2004*(98), 1–12.

Miles, L., Pennell, M., Owens, K. H., Dyehouse, J., O'Grady, H., Reynolds, N., Schwegler, R., & Shamoon, L. (2008). Commenting on Douglas Downs and Elizabeth Wardle's "Teaching about writing, righting misconceptions". *College Composition and Communication, 59*(3), 503–511.

Mohan, B., & Lo, W. (1985). Academic writing and Chinese students: Transfer and developmental factors. *TESOL Quarterly, 19*(3), 515–534.

Navarre Cleary, M. (2013). Flowing and freestyling: Learning from adult students about process knowledge transfer. *College Composition and Communication, 64*(4), 661–687.

Negretti, R. (2012). Metacognition in student academic writing: A longitudinal study of metacognitive awareness and its relation to task perception, self-regulation, and evaluation of performance. *Written Communication, 29*(2), 142–179.

Nemirovsky, R. (2011). Episodic feelings and transfer of learning. *The Journal of the Learning Sciences, 20*(2), 308–337.

Nonaka, I. (1994). A dynamic theory of organizational knowledge creation. *Organization Science*, 5(1), 14–37.

Norman, G., Dore, K., & Grierson, L. (2012). The minimal relationship between simulation fidelity and transfer of learning. *Medical Education*, 46(7), 636–647.

Norton, B. (2000). *Identity and language learning: Gender, ethnicity and educational change*. Longman/Pearson Education.

Nowacek, R. S. (2011). *Agents of integration: Understanding transfer as a rhetorical act*. Southern Illinois University Press.

Nowacek, R.S., Bodee, B., Douglas, J.E., Fitzsimmons, W, Hausladen, K.A., Knowles, M. & Nugent, M. (2019). "Transfer talk" in talk about writing in progress: Two propositions about transfer of learning. *Composition Forum, 42*. https://compositionforum.com/issue/42/transfer-talk.php

Pavlenko, A. (2000). L2 influence on L1 in late bilingualism. *Issues in Applied Linguistics, 11*(2), 175–205.

Pavlenko, A., & Jarvis, S. (2002). Bidirectional transfer. *Applied Linguistics*, 23(2), 190–214.

Perkins, D.N., & Salomon, G. (1988). Teaching for transfer. *Educational Leadership*, 46(1), 22–32.

Perkins, D. N., & Salomon, G. (1989). Are cognitive skills context bound? *Educational Researcher*, 18(1), 16–25.

Perkins, D. N., & Salomon, G. (2012). Knowledge to go: A motivational and dispositional view of transfer. *Educational Psychologist*, 47(3), 248–258.

Pescuric, A., & Byham, W. C. (1996). The new look of behavior modeling. *Training & Development*, 50(7), 24–31.

Petraglia, J. (Ed.). (1995). *Reconceiving writing, rethinking writing instruction*. Lawrence Erlbaum.

Pouw, W. T., Van Gog, T., & Paas, F. (2014). An embedded and embodied cognition review of instructional manipulatives. *Educational Psychology Review*, 26(1), 51–72.

Prior. P. (2018). How do moments add up to lives? Trajectories of semiotic becoming vs. tales of school learning in four modes. In R. Wysocki and M. Sheridan (Eds.), *Making future matters*. Utah State Press/Computers and Composition Digital Press. http://ccdigitalpress.org/book/makingfuturematters/

Prior, P., & Olinger, A. (2019). Academic literacies as laminated assemblage and embodied semiotic becoming. In Prior P. & Olinger A. R. (Eds.), *Retheorizing literacy practices: Complex social and cultural contexts* (pp. 126–139). Routledge.

Prior, P., & Shipka, J. (2003). Chronotopic lamination: Tracing the contours of literate activity. In C. Bazerman & D. R. Russell (Eds.), *Writing selves, writing societies: Research from activity perspectives* (180–238). The WAC Clearinghouse and Mind, Culture, and Activity.

Reiff, M. J., & Bawarshi, A. (2011). Tracing discursive resources: How students use prior genre knowledge to negotiate new writing contexts in first-year composition. *Written Communication, 28*(3), 312–337.

Rifenburg, J. M. (2014). Writing as embodied, college football plays as embodied: Extracurricular multimodal composing. *Composition Forum, 29.* https://compositionforum.com/issue/29/writing-as-embodied.php

Rifenburg, J. M. (2018). *The embodied playbook: Writing practices of student-athletes*. Utah State University Press.

Robertson, L., Taczak, K., & Yancey, K. B. (2012). Notes toward a theory of prior knowledge and its role in college composers' transfer of knowledge and practice. *Composition Forum, 26.* http://compositionforum.com/issue/26/prior-knowledge-transfer.php

Robinson, A., & Mania, K. (2007). Technological research challenges of flight simulation and flight instructor assessments of perceived fidelity. *Simulation & Gaming, 38*(1), 112–135.

Rouiller, J. Z., & Goldstein, I. L. (1993). The relationship between organizational transfer climate and positive transfer of training. *Human Resource Development Quarterly, 4*(4), 377–390.

Rounsaville, A., Goldberg, R., & Bawarshi, A. (2008). From incomes to outcomes: FYW students' prior genre knowledge, meta-cognition, and the question of transfer. *Writing Program Administration, 32*(1), 97–112.

Russell, D. (1995). Activity theory and its implications for writing instruction. In J. Petraglia (Ed.), *Reconceiving writing, rethinking writing instruction* (pp. 51–78) Lawrence Erlbaum.

Schieber, D. L. (2016). Invisible transfer: An unexpected finding in the pursuit of transfer. *Business and Professional Communication Quarterly, 79*(4), 464–486.

Schunk, D. H. (2004). *Learning theories: An educational perspective* (4th ed.). Pearson.

Schwartz, D. L., Bransford, J. D., & Sears, D. (2005). Efficiency and innovation in transfer. In J.P. Mestre (Ed.), *Transfer of learning from a modern multidisciplinary perspective* (pp. 1–51). Information Age Publishing,

Schwartz, D. L., & Martin, T. (2004). Inventing to prepare for future learning: The hidden efficiency of encouraging original student production in statistics instruction. *Cognition and Instruction, 22*(2), 129–184.

Scott, B. M., & Levy, M. G. (2013). Metacognition: Examining the components of a fuzzy concept. *Educational Research Journal, 2*(2), 120–131.

Selinker, L. (1969). Language transfer. *General Linguistics 9*(2), 67–92.

Selinker, L. (1972). Interlanguage. *IRAL—International Review of Applied Linguistics in Language Teaching 10,* 209–231.

Sharwood, M. S. & E. Kellerman. (1986). "Crosslinguistic influence in second language acquisition: An introduction." In M. S. Smith & E. Kellerman (Eds.), *Crosslinguistic influence in second language acquisition* (pp. 1–9). Pergamon.

Slomp, D. H. (2012). Challenges in assessing the development of writing ability: Theories, constructs and methods. *Assessing Writing, 17*(2), 81–91.

Smart, G. & Brown, N. (2002) Learning transfer or transforming learning?: Student interns reinventing expert writing practices in the workplace. *Technostyle, 18*(1), 117–141.

Smit, D. W. (2004). *The end of composition studies*. Southern Illinois University Press.

Sommers, N. & Saltz, L. (2004) The novice as expert: Writing the freshman year. *College Composition and Communication, 56*(1), 124–149.

Spack, R. (1988). Initiating students into the academic discourse community: How far should we go? *TESOL Quarterly, 22*(1), 29–51.

Spinuzzi, C. (1996). Pseudotransactionality, activity theory, and professional writing instruction. *Technical Communication Quarterly, 5*(3), 295–308.

Taczak, K., & Robertson, L. (2016). Reiterative reflection in the twenty-first-century writing classroom: An integrated approach to teaching for transfer. In K. B. Yancey (Ed.), *A Rhetoric of Reflection* (pp. 42–63). Utah State University Press.

Tardy, C. M. (2017). Crossing, or creating, divides? A plea for transdisciplinary scholarship. In B. Horner & L. Tetreault (Eds.), *Crossing divides: Exploring translingual writing pedagogies and programs*. Utah State University Press.

Taylor, P. J., Russ-Eft, D. F. and Chan, D. W. L. (2005). A meta-analytic review of behavior modeling training. *Journal of Applied Psychology, 90*, 692–709.

Teteris, E., Fraser, K., Wright, B., & McLaughlin, K. (2012). Does training learners on simulators benefit real patients? *Advances in Health Sciences Education, 17*(1), 137–144.

Thorndike, E. L. (1906 / 1916). *The principles of teaching based on psychology*. AG Seiler.

Thorpe, R., Bunker, D., & Almond, L. (1984). A change in focus for the teaching of games. In *Sport pedagogy: Olympic Scientific Congress proceedings* (Vol. 6, pp. 163-169).

Tuomi-Gröhn, T., & Engeström, Y. (2003). *Between school and work: New perspectives on transfer and boundary-crossing*. Pergamon.

Tuomi-Gröhn, T., Engeström, Y., & Young, M. (2003). From transfer to boundary crossing between school and work as a tool for developing vocational education: An introduction. In T. Tuomi-Gröhn & Y. Engeström (Eds.), *Between school and work: New perspectives on transfer and boundary crossing* (pp. 1–18). Pergamon.

VanKooten, C. (2016). Identifying components of meta-awareness about composition: Toward a theory and methodology for writing studies. *Composition Forum* 33. https://compositionforum.com/issue/33/meta-awareness.php

Walker, K. (1998). The debate over generalist and specialist tutors: Genre theory's contribution. *The Writing Center Journal, 18*(2), 27–45.

Walsh, J. P., & Ungson, G. R. (1991). Organizational memory. *Academy of Management Review, 16*(1), 57–91.

Walvoord, B. E., & McCarthy, L. P. (1990). *Thinking and writing in college: A naturalistic study of students in four disciplines*. The WAC Clearinghouse and National Council of Teachers of English.

Wardle, E. (2007). Understanding "transfer" from FYC: Preliminary results of a longitudinal study. *WPA: Writing Program Administration, 31*(1–2), 65–85.

Wardle, E. (2009). "Mutt genres" and the goal of FYC: Can we help students write the genres of the university? *College Composition and Communication, 60*(4), 765–789.

Wardle, E. (2012). Creative repurposing for expansive learning: Considering "problem-exploring" and "answer-getting" dispositions in individuals and fields. *Composition Forum, 26*. http://compositionforum.com/issue/26/creative-repurposing.php

Wardle, E. (2018, March 14-17). *Researching transfer: Addressing the challenges of knowing what works* [paper presentation, respondent]. Conference on College Composition and Communication, Kansas City.

Wardle, E, & Mercer Clement, N. (2016). Double binds and consequential transitions: Considering matters of identity during moments of rhetorical challenge. In C. M. Anson & J. L. Moore (Eds.), *Critical transitions: Writing and the question of transfer* (pp. 161–179). Perspectives on writing. The WAC Clearinghouse and University Press of Colorado.

Wegner, D. M. (1987). Transactive memory: A contemporary analysis of the group mind. In *Theories of group behavior* (pp. 185–208). Springer.

Wegner, D. M., Giuliano, T., & Hertel, P. T. (1985). Cognitive interdependence in close relationships. In Wegner, D. M., Giuliano, T., & Hertel, P. T. (Eds.), *Compatible and incompatible relationships* (pp. 253–276). Springer.

Weinreich, U. (1953) *Languages in contact*. The Hague: Mouton.

Werner, P., & Almond, L. (1990). Models of games education. *Journal of Physical Education, Recreation & Dance, 61*(4), 23–30.

White, S. (2015). "I stopped writing for myself": Student perspectives on service-learning in composition. Unpublished dissertation, University of Wisconsin Madison.

Winzenried, M.A., Campbell, L., Chao, R., & Cardinal, A. (2017). Co-constructing writing knowledge: Students' collaborative talk across contexts. *Composition Forum, 37*, https://compositionforum.com/issue/37/co-constructing.php

Wolfersberger, M. (2003). L1 to L2 writing process and strategy transfer: A look at lower proficiency writers. *TESL-EJ, 7*(2). http://www.tesl ej.org/wordpress/issues/volume7/ej26/ej26a6/

Yancey, K. B., Robertson, L., & Taczak, K. (2014). *Writing across contexts: Transfer, composition, and sites of writing.* Utah State University Press.

Glossary

Activity system. A unit of analysis that includes a subject, an object, and the tools that mediate the subject and object's interaction (Engeström, 1987). Russell (1995) defines an activity system as comprised of goal-directed and historically situated cooperative human interactions. See also *Expansive learning.*

Actor-oriented theory. An alternative to the "traditional transfer paradigm" framework developed by mathematics education researcher Joanne Lobato (Lobato & Siebert, 2002, p. 89). Rather than measuring transfer based solely on what the researcher expects to see, the actor-oriented view of transfer "scrutiniz[es] a given activity for any indication of influence from previous activities" *from the individual actor's perspective.* Nowacek's (2011) critique of negative transfer as affirming the perspective of the teacher rather than considering the experience of the student (and her subsequent articulation of the transfer matrix) makes a similar point.

Analogical reasoning. A mode of thinking and argument that relies on analogies to previous occurrences, in similar or different domains. Within the field of cognitive psychology, Gick and Holyoak (1980, 1983) conducted a series of early and influential experiments on participants' transfer of learning around what is known as the "radiation problem" (with a "dispersion" solution). To a large degree, they focused on participants' ability to recognize isomorphs—that is, similar situations disguised by superficial differences. The ability to reason analogically is often seen as a form of learning transfer.

Automaticity. Automaticity is thinking that is "fast, automatic, effortless, associative, implicit (not available to introspection), and often emotionally charged" as well as "governed by habit and . . . therefore difficult to control or modify" (Kahneman, 2003, p. 698). While automaticity would seem antithetical to the intentional, mindful transfer of learning often promoted in transfer research, some scholars have documented significant advantages of more automatized thinking. For example, Chase and Simon's (1973) perceptual chunking thesis identifies such automatized, unconscious thinking as part of the mental process of expert chess players. In medical and aviation education, researchers note that automatized learning is desirable; surgeons and pilots make life-or-death decisions so quickly and so often that if they regularly relied on deliberate, mindful, high-road transfer, it would be at their peril. Writing studies is just beginning to explore the role that automatized experiences of transfer might play in transfer of writing related knowledge. Donahue (2012) notes that "although much has been made of . . . meta-awareness as one of the key components of successful transfer, some research is beginning to question its role"; preliminary results from her own study suggest that "mature practices might indeed develop without an accompanying meta-awareness" (p. 150).

Boundary crossers and guarders. A distinction articulated by Reiff and Bawarshi (2011) as part of their work studying how first-year university students draw on and potentially repurpose their antecedent genre knowledge when they face novel composition tasks. Informed by Tuomi-Gröhn and Engeström's work on boundary crossing, Reiff and Bawarshi argue that boundary crossers (characterized by a tendency to engage in "not talk," a somewhat lower level of confidence, and a willingness to break down and recombine existing genre knowledge) tend to perform more highly than boundary guarders (characterized by an inappropriately high confidence that their prior composition strategies will be appropriate for new contexts).

Boundary objects. The concept of the boundary object, as developed by Star and Griesemer (1989), gives valuable explanatory power for understanding boundary work practices outside of the application model of metacognition. Specifically, boundary objects re-orient metacognition through its emphasis on how discourses and artifacts (a) have a material, historical, and sociocultural life outside of individual cognition; (b); coordinate specific relationships between people; and thus (c) mediate between disparate social worlds. Star and Griesemer first theorized boundary objects as a way to understand how a group of workers at a natural science museum could collaborate and reach a provisional understanding about ideas and tasks related to running the museum without reaching consensus or straying too far from each person's vision for this communal project. The problem that Star and Griesemer sought to answer was how could actors from a number of distinct and even dissonant social worlds "establish a mutual *modus operandi*" (p. 388). Wardle (2009) suggested that genres could serve as boundary objects, as tools for transfer as writers moved across university-level courses, "actively functioning as bridges to the varied disciplinary genres students will encounter" (p. 783). Boundary objects—and particularly the idea of boundary crossing—are central to the theories of transfer developed by Tuomi-Gröhn, Engeström, and colleagues (Tuomi-Gröhn & Engeström, 2003). The concepts of boundary objects and crossers (Carlile 2002, 2004) and brokering (Hargadon, 1998, 2002; Hargadon & Sutton, 1997) have also received considerable uptake within the field of knowledge management.

Concepts. A construct central to cognitive psychology, a concept is an abstract mental representation that encompasses any number of varied concrete instantiations (Markman & Ross, 2003, p. 593); the concept of a dog, for instance, is built from multiple instances, including experiences with Miniature Schnauzers, Golden Retrievers, and Rotweillers. This notion of a concept as a mental representation of a category of objects (material like *dogs*, or abstract like *love*) abstracted by an individual plays a pivotal role in linguistics and philosophy, as well as psychology (Laurence & Margolis, 1999, p. 3). Concepts are often understood in relation to each other; these relationships are sometimes referred to as schema, or an "organized system of relations" (Gick & Holyoak, 1980, p. 309).

Consequential transitions. A framework developed by Beach (1999) as an alternative to traditional conceptualizations of transfer as the carrying of learning from one context to another; embracing a sociocultural perspective, Beach offers a "reconceptualization of transfer as consequential transition among social activities" (p. 104). He identifies four types of consequential transitions: lateral, collateral, encompassing, and mediational. Indeed, he ultimately rejects the metaphorical entailments of the term *transfer* and instead proposes the term *generalization*, which he defines as "the continuity and transformation of knowledge, skill, and identity across various forms of social organization, involving multiple interrelated processes rather than a single general procedure" (p. 112).

Community of Practice. Developed by Lave and Wenger (1991), the concept of a community of practice emphasizes the ways in which writing (and often genres of writing) emerge from a collective commitment of a group to accomplish a shared goal. Often used in discussions of workplace writing and writing in the disciplines, as well as sports education, to emphasize the situated and dynamic nature of learning.

Declarative and procedural knowledge. Simply put, the what and the how of knowledge: knowing that something is true versus knowing how to do something. Content versus enactment of that content.

Discourse community. A group of people that communicates using shared goals, values, standards, and specialized vocabulary and genres. John Swales (1990) defines discourse communities as a group with an agreed upon set of common goals, mechanisms of communication among members, participatory mechanisms to provide feedback, specialized genres and vocabulary, and a threshold level of expertise for membership participation. James Paul Gee (1999) adds that discourse communities signal membership through saying, doing, being, valuing, and believing in like ways, using combinations of language, actions, interactions, objects, tools, and technologies.

Dispositions. Researchers in psychology and beyond have long worked to distinguish between traits (more long-term qualities) and states (more like moods), but in ways that are not always consistent. Psychology researchers often use the term disposition in tandem with the word *trait* (e.g., dispositional traits)—and indeed dispositions are often meant to describe affective responses that are more predictable over the long term than moods. Driscoll and Wells (2012) explain that dispositions are not intellectual traits, but instead determine how intellectual traits are used. They identify several other key features of dispositions, including that dispositions are dynamic, operate within a larger context, can be generative or disruptive, and can "determine students' sensitivity toward and willingness to engage in transfer" (part 3 of section on "Defining Dispositions").

Distributed cognition. Like work informed by situated cognition, scholarship taking a distributed cognition perspective understands learning to be inseparable from its social context; it takes a particular interest in how individuals use material environments, cultural tools, and even other people to redistribute their cognitive load (Sutton, 2006). One particularly celebrated example is Hutchins' (1995) cognitive ethnography of the collective efforts required to navigate a naval ship. See also embedded cognition; situated learning.

Embodied cognition. A view of cognition in keeping with theories of situated learning and distributed cognition, it is one part of what is sometimes referred to as 4E cognition: embedded, extended, embodied, and enactive cognitions (Menary, 2010). Embedded cognition is often understood as the least radical and most capacious of the four Es; whereas extended cognition extends the boundaries of the mind to include material objects outside the brain, embodied cognition focuses particularly on the role of the physical body in cognition. Theories of embodied cognition play a central role in education that relies on simulations (such as aviation and medical education); they have played an increasing role in writing studies as well (LeMesurier, 2016; Pigg, 2020; Rifenburg 2014, 2018).

Expansive learning. An alternative to the term *transfer of learning*, often preferred by scholars drawing on an activity theory framework. Expansive learning can be understood as the "processes in which an activity system, for example a work organization, resolves its pressing internal contradictions by constructing and implementing a qualitatively new way of functioning for itself" (Engeström,

2007, p. 24); individuals can also go through this process of resolution. Central to the idea of expansive learning is Engeström and colleagues' shift in unit of analysis; whereas the terms *transfer* or even *generalization* of learning (the term often preferred by scholars informed by theories of situated cognition) keep the individual as the unit of analysis, expansive learning focuses on the entire activity system (Tuomi-Gröhn, 2007, p. 201). As Engeström explains, "Theories of learning typically speak of the outcomes of learning in terms of knowledge, skills and changed patterns of behavior. In expansive learning, the outcomes are expanded objects and new collective work practices, including practices of thinking and discourse" (Engeström & Kerosuo, 2007, p. 339).

Fidelity. A term most often associated with transfer and simulations from the fields of aviation and medical education. Fidelity refers to the ways a training or practice context (a lab, a simulation, a classroom) reflects the target context. For many scholars, fidelity is a multi-valent concept that requires educators to name precisely what types of matches they seek between a practice and target context (e.g., motion efficiency, dexterity, economy of movement, quickness, and accuracy).

Generalization. A term sometimes proposed—by varied scholars from varied disciplines—as an alternative to the term *transfer*. It was used as early as Judd (1908) to describe how individuals learned from their experiences. Katona (1940) and other Gestalt theorists also regularly used the term. In the transfer of training scholarship, generalization of learning—which refers to making use of learning in novel contexts (such as the shift from training modules to the workplace)—is distinguished from maintenance of learning over time (Baldwin & Ford, 1988). The term generalization is also favored by scholars taking a situated cognition perspective, including Beach (1999), Carraher and Schliemann (2002), Day and Goldstone (2012), Engle (2006), Lobato (2003), and Wagner (2006). In this tradition, Beach defines generalization as "the continuity and transformation of knowledge, skill, and identity across various forms of social organization, [which] involves multiple interrelated processes rather than a single general procedure" (p. 112).

General writing skills instruction. GWSI refers to writing curricula that attempt to teach universal skills outside of social or rhetorical context. Russell (1995) famously rejected this approach, observing that "To try to teach students to improve their writing by taking a GWSI course is something like trying to teach people to improve their ping-pong, jacks, volleyball, basketball, hockey, and so on by attending a course in general ball-handling" (p. 58). His and others' rejection of general writing skills instruction stems from socially situated theories of writing and learning and has served as a catalyst and conundrum for studies of transfer in both first-year writing and writing across the curriculum/writing in the disciplines.

Genre. See Rhetorical Genre Theory.

Goal orientation. From the research in psychology, a characterization of an individual's approach to learning. Dweck's highly popular *Mindsets* (2008) draws on earlier work (Dweck, 1986; Dweck & Legget, 1988) that distinguishes between mastery orientations and performance orientations. Individuals with mastery goals "are concerned with increasing their competence" while those with performance goals are "concerned with gaining favorable judgments of their competence" (Dweck & Legget, 1988, p. 256). Overwhelmingly the performance-goal orientation has been found to be less conducive for learning and therefore for transfer of training (Fisher & Ford, 1998; Ford et al., 1998; Tziner et al., 2007).

Identical elements. An early theory of transfer articulated by Thorndike (1906/1916, 1913; Thorndike & Woodworth, 1901a, b, c) as a response to earlier formal discipline theories. From this perspective, transfer of learning is made possible not by the strength of a mental muscle (the formal discipline explanation for why studying Latin might improve academic performance in other domains) but by similarities between the two tasks. The more closely related the tasks—the more identical elements they share—the stronger the transfer of learning.

Interference. Early orientations to language transfer in second language acquisition framed evidence of transfer as interference of the L1 into the target L2. This early orientation to transfer as interference, and interference as error, is still frequently used in studies of transfer in writing. See also negative transfer.

Legitimate peripheral participation. A term developed by Lave and Wenger (1991) as a crucial part of their situated learning theory of how individuals become active and knowledgeable members of communities of practice. Lave and Wenger clarify that there is not illegitimate peripheral participation, nor legitimate central participation. Instead, legitimate peripheral participation (LPP) "refers both to the development of knowledgeably skilled identities in practice and to the reproduction and transformation of communities of practice. It concerns the latter insofar as communities of practice consist of and depend on membership, including its characteristic biographies/trajectories, relationships, and practices" (p. 55).

Locus of control. Locus of control refers to "a stable personality trait that describes the extent to which people attribute the cause or control of events to themselves (internal orientation) or to external environmental factors such as fate or luck (external orientation)" (Kren, 1992, p. 992).

Metacognition. A prominent construct in psychological research, which many scholars have noted is defined inconsistently throughout the scholarship. At its core, most researchers acknowledge at least two components: knowledge of cognition and regulation of cognition (Scott & Levy, 2013; Gorzelsky et al., 2016). In his discussion of threshold concepts of writing, Tinberg (2016) defines metacognition as "the ability to perceive the very steps by which success occurs and to articulate the various qualities and components that contribute in significant ways to the production of effective writing" (p. 76); metacognition, he notes, plays an especially important role when writers move into new, unfamiliar contexts.

Metagenres. Carter (2007) defines metagenres as genres of genres or general "ways of doing" that pattern into "similar *kinds* of typified responses to related recurrent situations" (p. 393). He identifies four metagenres: (a) responses to academic situations that call for problem solving (plans, reports, proposals); (b) responses to academic situations that call for empirical inquiry; (c) responses to academic situations that call for research from sources; and (d) responses to academic situations that call for performance. Lindenman (2015) extends the concept to describe the "metageneric connections" that students make for themselves, a type of connection making that may be a promising avenue to the metacognition some researchers say supports transfer.

Motivation. A complex construct defined in the transfer of training scholarship as a trainee characteristic—as opposed to an element of training design or the transfer climate. Developing out of Vroom's (1964) expectancy theory, current theories of motivation generally "refe[r] to the processes that account for an individual's intensity, direction, and persistence of effort toward attaining a goal" (Grossman & Salas, 2011, p. 109). Although researchers often distinguish between motivation to learn and motivation to transfer, they sometimes use the term in broader, less clearly defined ways as well. Scholarship has sought to understand both the causes and the effects of motivation—particularly its effects on transfer of training, which are generally (but not always) seen as positive.

Negative transfer. Negative transfer is considered evidence of interference into the process of language acquisition, what might in writing appear as an error. In psychology, Schunk (2004) defines negative transfer ("prior learning interferes with subsequent learning") in contrast to positive transfer ("when prior learning facilitates subsequent learning") and zero transfer ("one type of learning has no noticeable influence on subsequent learning" [p. 217]). Perkins and Salomon (1989) associate the operations of low-road transfer with negative transfer, noting that "people commonly ignore novelty in a situation, assimilating it into well-rehearsed schemata and mindlessly bringing to bear inappropriate knowledge and skill, yielding negative transfer" (p. 22). Within the field of second language acquisition, when learners transfer constructs among languages that are similar (in syntax, morphology, etc.), the transfer act is called "positive transfer"; when learners transfer constructs among languages that are different, the transfer is deemed more visible and called "negative transfer." L2 researchers often design studies to look for L1 interference or negative transfer that their research might offer pedagogical solutions to. There is a tradition of critiquing the concept of negative transfer, including

Nowacek (2011) in writing studies, Lobato's (2012) actor-oriented theory in mathematical education, and Goldstone and Day's (2012) observation that "All too often, negative transfer is shorthand for 'transfer in a way that conflicts with what the teacher/experimenter intended'" (p. 151).

Organizational memory. A concept central in knowledge management scholarship, it is, in essence, "the way organizations store knowledge from the past to support present activities" (Nevo & Wand, 2004, p. 549). Walsh and Ungson famously identified six repositories of organizational memories, including individuals but also routines, social roles, and the material contexts of work in an organization. In framing organizational memory as informed by material contexts and cultural tools, knowledge management scholars intersect with the scholarship on distributed cognition. See also distributed cognition.

Preparation for future learning. Preparation for future learning (PFL) explores how to make explicit use of learners' futures to guide them toward successful transfer (Bransford & Schwartz, 1999; Schwartz et al., 2005). Informed by situated learning theory, which foregrounds the social and participatory dimensions of learning, PFL approaches emphasize that transfer should be treated as forward-looking, leading learners to imagine future times and spaces for knowledge use. Within writing center research, Driscoll (2015) has developed and studied a tutor education course that brought together PFL with Perkins and Salomon's (2012) "detect-elect-connect" model, resulting in a course that asked students to actively connect learning to new or future contexts and finding that such a deliberate approach did activate transfer-like thinking to build connections among multiple contexts.

Rhetorical genre theory. An approach to genre that focuses on recurrent rhetorical situations—and repeated exigencies in particular—to understand how rhetorical response becomes "stabilized-for-now" (Schryer, 1993, p. 200) as genre. In this formulation, genres facilitate writers in performing socially shared actions made typical across a group based on a "mutual construing of objects, events, interests and purposes" (Miller, 1984, p. 30).

Scaffolding. Scaffolding involves a range of teacher or peer generated building blocks that move a learner through a task, activity, or conceptual problem by building from what a learner knows and forward toward more complex or sophisticated iterations of the task, activity, or conceptual problem. Scaffolding is often connected to Vygotsky's (1978) notion of the zone of proximal development (ZPD), defined as "the distance between the actual developmental level as determined by independent problem solving and the level of potential development as determined through problem solving under adult guidance or collaboration with more capable peers" (p. 86). Scaffolds take many forms, moving from simple to complex, feedback from an instructor, and so on. All aid the learner in moving toward independent action.

Schemata. See Concepts.

Self-efficacy. A concept developed by Bandura (1977) to describe the degree to which an individual believes their efforts will result in accomplishing a desired task. Unlike self-esteem, which is a more generalized and more stable trait, self-efficacy describes an individual's assessment of their capabilities on a particular task and can readily change based on brief interventions. For example, Gist et al. (1989) measured what they called "computer self-efficacy" at the start of a training module, then, after the training module was completed 90 minutes later, measured what they called "software self-efficacy." Many studies claim that higher levels of self-efficacy result in greater transfer of training (e.g., Blume et al., 2010; Brown, 2005; Gist et al., 1989; Gist et al., 1991; Stevens & Gist, 1997; Velada et al., 2007), but some warn that increasing self-efficacy without increasing actual skills can in fact decrease performance (Vancouver & Kendall, 2006). See also dispositions.

Self-regulation. The idea of self-regulation, or self-regulative metacognitive activity, is often framed as an issue of emotional control and has been crucial for industrial and organizational psychology theories focused on behavioral modeling and error management (Keith & Frese, 2005). Similarly, Wegner et al. (1985) describe the emergence of "a personal 'directory' for knowledge held by the dyad" (p. 265), which is a mechanism for monitoring who knows what so shared memories can be accessed when needed. In their analysis of metacognition in writing studies, Gorzelsky et al. (2016) identify planning, monitoring, control, and evaluation as four metacognitive subcomponents that comprise "regulation of cognition" (p. 226). See also dispositions; metacognition.

Simulation. A training strategy used within a variety of educational contexts, simulations attempt to replicate—either through low- or high-tech means—elements of a target performance context. Simulations can be simple (a case study approach) or complex (a virtual world) and work from the concept of context fidelity.

Situated learning. A development of the sociocultural response to the tradition of cognitivist research within psychology (see Beach, 1999; Lave, 1988; Lave and Wenger, 1991), the situated learning perspective turns attention to how cognition unfolds in naturalistic contexts rather than laboratory studies. See also distributed cognition and embodied cognition.

Social cognitive theory. Rejecting both the behaviorist stimulus-response model and a purely cognitive assumption of a self-contained autonomous being, Bandura's (1986, 1999) social cognitive theory posits that learners operate at the juncture of three mutually influential forces: internal personal factors, behavioral factors, and environmental factors that provide affordances or constraints. Also central to Bandura's theory is the belief that human beings can learn not only from direct experience but through observation. Researchers—especially those in psychology—have often turned to this framework to study transfer of learning.

Teaching for transfer. A phrase frequently invoked in transfer of learning scholarship. Within the field of writing studies, it is often associated with a specific curricular approach to first-year writing developed by Yancey et al. (2014) focused on teaching methods, activities, and scaffolded assignments meant to foster transfer of writing knowledge. It is also the title of a frequently cited article by Perkins and Salomon (1988) and an edited collection in psychology (McKeough et al., 1995).

Transactive memory systems. First developed by Wegner (Wegner et al., 1985; Wegner, 1987) as a means of describing "cognitive interdependence" (Wegner et al., 1985, p. 254) between people in an "intimate dyad" (p. 253), the concept was soon expanded to small groups and even larger workplaces (see a listing in Lewis & Herndon, 2011, pp. 1254–1255). Central to the notion of transactive memory is the claim that within a transactive memory system (TMS) the storage of memories is specialized. Not everyone in the system remembers all the information; individuals remember some higher-order and some lower-order information, but they also build "directories" that allow them to know that someone else actually remembers specific lower-order information that can be accessed through interaction. Transactive memory is related to transfer of learning for those who are interested in the more collaborative, interpersonal dimensions of transfer being studied in knowledge management.

Transfer climate. Together with trainee characteristics and training design, transfer climate (sometimes also called work environment) is one of the three major influences on transfer of training studied by researchers in human resources and industrial psychology. The transfer climate is those "work- environment factors perceived by trainees to encourage or discourage their use of knowledge, skills, and abilities learned in training on the job" (Cromwell & Kolb, 2004, p. 451). Importantly, this term focuses not on the objective existence of conditions but the *perception* of those conditions. Although some researchers have conceptualized transfer climate as an aggregate construct (e.g., Tracey & Tews, 2005), most consider it a matter of individual trainee perception (e.g., Cromwell & Kolb, 2004; Holton et al., 1997; Kraiger, 2003).

Transfer of training. A term commonly used by human resources and management scholars to describe the degree to which investments in professional development are put to use in the workplace; training is frequently defined as "a planned learning experience designed to bring about permanent change in an individual's knowledge, attitudes, or skills" (Noe & Schmitt, 1986, p. 497). This field of research draws heavily on work in industrial and organizational psychology. Baldwin and Ford (1988)—in addition to establishing the tripartite taxonomy of features that influence transfer of training including trainee characteristics, training design, and work environment—argue that transfer of training must include both generalization and maintenance: "For transfer to have occurred, learned behavior must be generalized to the job context and maintained over a period of time on the job" (p. 63).

Threshold concepts. Having recently gained traction within writing studies, threshold concepts refer to ways of thinking in a discipline that can fundamentally transform a learner's access to and participation in that discipline's ways of thinking and doing. Described as a "transformed way of understanding, or interpreting, or viewing something without which the learner cannot progress," (Meyer and Land, 2006, p. 3), threshold concepts are transformative, irreversible, integrative, bounded, and troublesome (pp. 7–8). Threshold concepts and transfer are linked through the caveat in the preceding quote that states that "without which the learner cannot progress."

References

Baldwin, T. T., & Ford, J. K. (1988). Transfer of training: A review and directions for future research. *Personnel Psychology, 41*(1), 63–105.

Bandura, A. (1977). Self-efficacy: Toward a unifying theory of behavioral change. *Psychological Review, 84*(2), 191–215.

Bandura, A. (1986). *Social foundations of thought and action: A social cognitive theory.* Prentice-Hall

Bandura, A. (1999). Social cognitive theory: An agent perspective. *Asian Journal of Social Psychology, 2*(1), 21–41.

Beach, K. (1999). Consequential transitions: A sociocultural expedition beyond transfer in education. *Review of Research in Education, 24*(1), 101–139.

Blume, B. D., Ford, J. K., Baldwin, T. T., & Huang, J. L. (2010). Transfer of training: A meta-analytic review. *Journal of Management, 36*(4), 1065–1105.

Bransford, J. D., & Schwartz, D. L. (1999). Rethinking transfer: A simple proposal with multiple implications. *Review of Research in Education, 24*(1), 61–100.

Brown, T.C. (2005). The effectiveness of distal and proximal goals as transfer of training interventions: A field experiment. *Human Resources Development Quarterly, 16*(3), 369–387.

Carlile, P. R. (2002). A pragmatic view of knowledge and boundaries: Boundary objects in new product development. *Organization Science, 13*(4), 442–455.

Carlile, P. R. (2004). Transferring, translating, and transforming: An integrative framework for managing knowledge across boundaries. *Organization Science, 15*(5), 555–568.

Carraher, D., & Schliemann, A. (2002). The transfer dilemma. *The Journal of the Learning Sciences, 11*(1), 1–24.

Carter (2007). Ways of knowing, doing, and writing in the disciplines. *College Composition and Communication, 58*(3), 385–418.

Chase, W. G., & Simon, H. A. (1973). Perception in chess. *Cognitive Psychology, 4*(1), 55–81.

Cromwell, S. E., & Kolb, J. A. (2004). An examination of work-environment support factors affecting transfer of supervisory skills training to the workplace. *Human Resource Development Quarterly, 15*(4), 449–471.

Day, S. B., & Goldstone, R. L. (2012). The import of knowledge export: Connecting findings and theories of transfer of learning. *Educational Psychologist, 47*(3), 153–176.

Donahue, C. (2012). Transfer, portability, generalization: (How) does composition expertise "carry"? In K. Ritter & P. Matsuda (Eds.), Exploring composition studies: Sites, issues, and perspectives, (pp. 145–166). Utah State University Press.

Driscoll, D. L. (2015). Building connections and transferring knowledge: The benefits of a peer tutoring course beyond the writing center. *The Writing Center Journal, 35*(1), 153–181.

Driscoll, D. L., & Wells, J. (2012). Beyond knowledge and skills: Writing transfer and the role of student dispositions. *Composition Forum, 26* (Fall). compositionforum.com/issue/26/beyond-knowledge-skills.php

Dweck, C. S. (2008). *Mindset: The new psychology of success.* Random House Digital.

Dweck, C. S., & Leggett, E. L. (1988). A social-cognitive approach to motivation and personality. *Psychological Review, 95*(2), 256–273.

Engeström, Y. (1987). *Learning by expanding: An activity-theoretical approach to developmental research.* Orienta-Konsultit Oy.

Engeström, Y. (2007). From stabilization knowledge to possibility: Knowledge in organizational learning. *Management learning, 38*(3), 271–275.

Engeström, Y., & Kerosuo, H. (2007). From workplace learning to interorganizational learning and back: The contribution of activity. *Journal of workplace learning, 19*(6), 336–342.

Engle, R. A. (2006). Framing interactions to foster generative learning: A situative explanation of transfer in a community of learners classroom. *The Journal of the Learning Sciences, 15*(4), 451–498.

Fisher, S. L., & Ford, J. K. (1998). Differential effects of learner effort and goal orientation on two learning outcomes. *Personnel Psychology, 51*(2), 397–420.

Ford, J. K., Smith, E. M., Weissbein, D. A., Gully, S. M., & Salas, E. (1998). Relationships of goal orientation, metacognitive activity, and practice strategies with learning outcomes and transfer. *Journal of Applied Psychology, 83*(2), 218–233.

Gee, J. P. (1999). *An introduction to discourse analysis: Theory and method.* Routledge.

Gick, M. L., & Holyoak, K. J. (1980). Analogical problem solving. *Cognitive Psychology, 12*(3), 306–355.

Gick, M. L., & Holyoak, K. J. (1983). Schema induction and analogical transfer. *Cognitive Psychology 15*(1), 1–38.

Gist M. E., Schwoerer, C., & Rosen B. (1989). Effects of alternative training methods on self-efficacy and performance in computer software training. *Journal of Applied Psychology, 74*(6), 884–891.

Gist, M., Stevens, C., & Bavetta, A. (1991). Effects of self-efficacy and post training interventions of the acquisition and maintenance of complex interpersonal skills. *Personnel Psychology, 44*(4), 837–861.

Goldstone, R. L., & Day, S. B. (2012). Introduction to "New conceptualizations of transfer of learning." *Educational Psychologist, 47*(3), 149–152.

Gorzelsky, G., Driscoll, D. L., Paszek, J., Jones, E., & Hayes, C. (2016). Cultivating constructive metacognition: a new taxonomy for writing studies. In C. Anson & J. Moore (Eds.), *Critical transitions: Writing and the question of transfer* (pp. 215–228). The WAC Clearinghouse; University of Press of Colorado.

Grossman, R., & Salas, E. (2011). The transfer of training: What really matters. *International Journal of Training & Development, 15*(2), 103–120.

Hargadon, A. B. (1998). Firms as knowledge brokers: Lessons in pursuing continuous innovation. *California Management Review, 40*(3), 209–227.

Hargadon, A. B. (2002). Brokering knowledge: Linking learning and innovation. *Research in Organizational Behavior, 24*, 41–85.

Hargadon, A., & Sutton, R. I. (1997). Technology brokering and innovation in a product development firm. *Administrative science quarterly, 42*(4), 716–749.

Holton III, E. F., Bates, R. A., Seyler, D. L., & Carvalho, M. B. (1997). Toward construct validation of a transfer climate instrument. *Human Resource Development Quarterly, 8*(2), 95–113.

Hutchins, E. (1995). *Cognition in the wild*. MIT Press.

Judd, C. H. (1908). The relation of special training and general intelligence. *Educational Review, 36*, 28–42.

Kahneman, D. (2003). A perspective on judgment and choice: mapping bounded rationality. *American Psychologist, 58*(9), 697–720.

Katona, G. (1940). *Organizing and memorizing: Studies in the psychology of learning and teaching*. Columbia University Press

Keith, N., & Frese, M. (2005). Self-regulation in error management training: Emotion control and metacognition as mediators of performance effects. *Journal of Applied Psychology, 90*(4), 677–691.

Kraiger, K. (2003). Perspectives on training and development. In W. C. Borman, D. R. Ilgen, & R. J. Klimoski (Eds.), *Handbook of Psychology* (pp. 171–192). John Wiley & Sons.

Kren, L. (1992). The moderating effects of locus of control on performance incentives and participation. *Human Relations, 45*(9), 991–1012.

Laurence, S., & Margolis, E. (1999). Concepts and cognitive science. In E. Margolis & S. Laurence (Eds.), *Concepts: Core readings* (pp. 3–82). MIT Press.

Lave, J. (1988). *Cognition in practice: Mind, mathematics and culture in everyday life.* Cambridge University Press.

Lave, J, and Wenger, E. (1991). *Situated learning: Legitimate peripheral participation.* Cambridge University Press.

LeMesurier, J. L. (2016). Mobile bodies: Triggering bodily uptake through movement. *College Composition and Communication, 68*(2), 292–316.

Lewis, K., & Herndon, B. (2011). Transactive memory systems: Current issues and future research directions. *Organization Science, 22*(5), 1254–1265.

Lindenman, H. (2015) Inventing metagenres: How four college seniors connect writing across domains. *Composition Forum, 31*(Spring). http://compositionforum.com/issue/31/inventing-metagenres.php

Lobato, J. (2003). How design experiments can inform a rethinking of transfer and vice versa. *Educational Researcher, 32*(1), 17–20.

Lobato, J. (2012). The actor-oriented transfer perspective and its contributions to educational research and practice. *Educational Psychologist, 47*(3), 232–247.

Lobato, J., & Siebert, D. (2002). Quantitative reasoning in a reconceived view of transfer. *The Journal of Mathematical Behavior, 21*(1), 87–116.

Markman, A. B., & Ross, B. H. (2003). Category use and category learning. *Psychological Bulletin, 129*(4), 592–613.

McKeough, A., Lupart, J., & Marini, A. (Eds.). (1995). *Teaching for transfer: Fostering generalization in learning.* Lawrence Erlbaum Associates.

Menary, R. (2010). Introduction to the special issue on 4E cognition. *Phenomenology and the Cognitive Sciences, 9*(4), 459–463.

Meyer, J. H. F., & Land, R. (Eds.). (2006). *Overcoming barriers to student understanding: Threshold concepts and troublesome knowledge.* Routledge.

Miller, C. R. (1984). Genre as social action. *Quarterly Journal of Speech, 70*(2), 151–167.

Nevo, D., & Wand, Y. (2005). Organizational memory information systems: a transactive memory approach. *Decision Support Systems, 39*(4), 549–562.

Noe, R. A., & Schmitt, N. (1986). The influence of trainee attitudes on training effectiveness: Test of a model. *Personnel Psychology, 39,* 497–523.

Nowacek, R. S. (2011). *Agents of integration: Understanding transfer as a rhetorical act.* Southern Illinois University Press.

Perkins, D. N., & Salomon, G. (1988). Teaching for transfer. *Educational Leadership, 46*(1), 22–32.

Perkins, D. N., & Salomon, G. (1989). Are cognitive skills context bound? *Educational Researcher, 18*(1), 16–25.

Perkins, D. N., & Salomon, G. (2012). Knowledge to go: A motivational and dispositional view of transfer. *Educational Psychologist*, *47*(3), 248–258.

Pigg, Stacey. (2020). *Transient literacies in action: Composing with the mobile surround*. The WAC Clearinghouse and University Press of Colorado.

Reiff, M. J., & Bawarshi, A. (2011). Tracing discursive resources: How students use prior genre knowledge to negotiate new writing contexts in first-year composition. *Written Communication*, *28*(3), 312–337.

Rifenburg, J. M. (2014). Writing as embodied, college football plays as embodied: Extracurricular multimodal composing. *Composition Forum*, *29*(Spring). compositionforum.com/issue/29/writing-as-embodied.php

Rifenburg, J. M. (2018). *The embodied playbook: Writing practices of student-athletes*. Utah State University Press.

Russell, D. (1995). Activity theory and its implications for writing instruction. In J. Petraglia (Ed.), *Reconceiving writing, rethinking writing instruction* (pp. 51–78) Lawrence Erlbaum.

Schryer, C. F. (1993). Records as genre. *Written Communication*, *10*(2), 200–234.

Schunk, D. H. (2004). *Learning theories an educational perspective* (4th ed.). Pearson.

Schwartz, D. L., Bransford, J. D., & Sears, D. (2005). Efficiency and innovation in transfer. In J.P. Mestre (Ed.), *Transfer of learning from a modern multidisciplinary perspective* (1–51). Information Age Publishing.

Scott, B. M., & Levy, M. G. (2013). Metacognition: Examining the components of a fuzzy concept. *Educational Research Journal*, *2*(2), 120–131.

Star, S. L., & Griesemer, J. R. (1989). Institutional ecology, "translations," and boundary objects: Amateurs and professionals in Berkeley's museum of vertebrate zoology, 1907–1939. *Social studies of science*, *19*(3), 387–420.

Stevens, C. K. & Gist, M. E. (1997), Effects of self-efficacy and goal-orientation training on interpersonal skill maintenance: what are the mechanisms? *Personnel Psychology*, *50*(4), 955–78.

Sutton, J. (2006). Distributed cognition: Domains and dimensions. *Pragmatics & Cognition*, *14*(2),235–247.

Swales, J. M. (1990). *Genre analysis: English in academic and research settings*. Cambridge University Press.

Thorndike, E. L.1916). *The principles of teaching based on psychology*. AG Seiler. (Original work published 1906)

Thorndike, E. L. & Woodworth, R. S. (1901a). The influence of improvement in one mental function upon the efficiency of other functions.(I). *Psychological Review*, *8*(3), 247–261.

Thorndike, E. L. & Woodworth, R. S. (1901b). The influence of improvement in one mental function upon the efficiency of other functions: II. The estimation of magnitudes. *Psychological Review 8*(4), 384–395.

Thorndike, E. L. & Woodworth, R. S. (1901c). The influence of improvement in one mental function upon the efficiency of other functions: III. Functions involving attention, observation and discrimination. *Psychological Review 8*(6), 553–564.

Tinberg, H. (2016) Metacognition is not cognition. In L. Adler-Kassner & E. Wardle (Eds.), *Naming what we know: Threshold concepts of writing studies* (pp. 75–76). Utah State University Press.

Tracey, J. B. & Tews, M. J. (2005). Construct validity of a general training climate scale. *Organizational Research Methods, 8*(4), 353–374.

Tuomi-Gröhn, T. (2007). Developmental transfer as a goal of collaboration between school and work: A case study in the training of daycare interns. *Actio: An International Journal of Human Activity Theory, 1*, 41–62.

Tuomi-Gröhn, T., & Engeström, Y. (2003). Conceptualizing transfer: From standard notions to developmental perspectives. In T. Tuomi-Gröhn & Y. Engeström (Eds.), *Between school and work: New perspectives on transfer and boundary-crossing* (pp. 19–38). Emerald Group.

Tziner, A., Fisher, M., Senior, T. and Weisberg, J. (2007). Effects of trainee characteristics on training effectiveness. *International Journal of Selection & Assessment, 15*(2), 167–174.

Vancouver, J. B. and Kendall, L. N. (2006). When self-efficacy negatively relates to motivation and performance in a learning context. *Journal of Applied Psychology, 91*, 1146–53.

Velada, R., Caetano, A., Michel, J. W., Lyons, B. D., & Kavanagh, M. J. (2007). The effects of training design, individual characteristics and work environment on transfer of training. *International Journal of Training & Development, 11*(4), 282–294.

Vroom, V. H. (1964). *Work and motivation*. Wiley.

Vygotsky, L. S. (1978). *Mind in society: The development of higher psychological processes*. Harvard University Press.

Wagner, J. F. (2006). Transfer in pieces. *Cognition and Instruction, 24*(1), 1–71.

Walsh, J. P., & Ungson, G. R. (1991). Organizational memory. *Academy of Management Review, 16*(1), 57–91.

Wardle, E. (2009). "Mutt genres" and the goal of FYC: Can we help students write the genres of the university? *College Composition and Communication, 60*(4), 765–789.

Wegner, D. M. (1987). Transactive memory: A contemporary analysis of the group mind. In *Theories of group behavior* (pp. 185–208). Springer.

Wegner, D. M., Giuliano, T., & Hertel, P. T. (1985). Cognitive interdependence in close relationships. In *Compatible and incompatible relationships* (pp. 253–276). Springer.

Yancey, K. B., Robertson, L., & Taczak, K. (2014). *Writing across contexts: Transfer, composition, and sites of writing*. Utah State University Press.

Annotated Bibliography

Anson, C. M., & Forsberg, L. L. (1990). Moving beyond the academic community: Transitional stages in professional writing. *Written Communication, 7*(2), 200–231.

Drawing on interviews with six university seniors placed in internships, Anson and Forsberg study the "social and intellectual adaptations" (p. 201) of students moving from school to work by identifying three stages of successful transition into a workplace culture: *expectation* (students entered their internships confident that they would be able to successfully draw on previous writing experiences and strategies), *disorientation* (interns tended to feel isolated and overwhelmed), and *transition and resolution* (interns "finally integrat[ed] experience and reflec[ted] on the intellectual changes afforded by writing in the new context" p. 208).

Anson, C. M., & Moore, J. L. (Eds.). (2016). *Critical transitions: Writing and the question of transfer.* WAC Clearinghouse.

An edited volume representing scholarship produced by participants in Elon University's Seminar on Critical Transitions (2011-2013). See also Moore and Bass's edited collection, *Understanding Writing Transfer: Implications for Transformative Student Learning in Higher Education*, published by Stylus Press (2017). In keeping with the goals of the Elon Seminars, much of the research in both volumes is multi-institutional.

Baldwin, T. T., & Ford, J. K. (1988). Transfer of training: A review and directions for future research. *Personnel Psychology, 41*(1), 63–105.

A seminal literature review that established the taxonomy of trainee characteristics, training design, and work environment that dominated decades of subsequent research for human resources scholars studying transfer of training.

Bandura, A. (1977). Self-efficacy: Toward a unifying theory of behavioral change. *Psychological Review, 84*(2), 191–215.

The article in which Bandura develops the construct of self-efficacy. Helpfully read in tandem with his book, *Social foundations of thought and action* (1986), which develops his social cognitive theory.

Beaufort, A. (2007). *College writing and beyond: A new framework for university writing instruction.* Utah State University Press.

Beaufort's longitudinal case study of Tim, a college student writing in first-year composition, history, and engineering courses, and eventually at work, tracks his struggles transferring writing knowledge across these contexts. The book argues that Tim's struggles are the result of never being explicitly taught the knowledge that supports writing success. Beaufort's contribution is a clear articulation of what that knowledge is: discourse community knowledge, genre knowledge, rhetorical knowledge, subject matter knowledge, and writing process knowledge. This framework of overlapping knowledge domains was previously developed in her ethnography *Writing in the Real World* (1999).

Berman, R. (1994). Learners' transfer of writing skills between languages. *TESL Canada Journal, 12*(1), 29–46.

Berman's study of 126 secondary EFL students in Iceland was one of the first studies in L2 writing to explicitly focus on language transfer by examining how essay organization skills were transferred from English to Icelandic. Grouping three instructional approaches—L1 essay instruction, L2 (English) instruction, no instruction—he looked for difference in pre- and post-intervention organization and grammatical proficiency scores. Berman concluded that students did transfer organization skills between Icelandic and English, showing that the groups with instruction improved regardless of language of instruction, and highlighting that instruction on a particular skill was a more powerful enabler of transfer than was language or grammatical proficiency in that language.

Bromley, P., Northway, K., & Schonberg, E. (2016). Transfer and dispositions in writing centers: A cross-institutional mixed-methods study. *Across the Disciplines, 13*(1), 1–15.

Bromley, Northway, and Schonberg traced the transfer of student writing knowledge by examining how student visitors to three writing centers at different institutions describe the writing knowledge that transferred during and after sessions. The researchers collected students' self-reported perceptions that writing center visits increased their confidence and their meta-awareness through reported acts of writing transfer. Guided by a theoretical framework that incorporated Yancey, Robertson, and Taczak's (2014) connection of Wardle's (2012) problem-exploring dispositions to Reiff and Bawarshi's (2011) boundary crossers and Perkins and Salmon's (2012) high-road transfer, they examined writing centers' ability to provide low-stakes contexts to explore and expand problems. Their survey and focus group data from three campuses allowed for a cross-institutional analysis of student transfer, showing most student visitors engaging in transfer, with a "large majority" engaging in far transfer. Their inclusion of focus group quotes shows students' perceptions of how their next steps in an assignment were guided by what they learned in a session as well as the writing "breakthroughs" they experienced in sessions and continued to call on in later contexts.

Bruffee, K. A. (2008). What being a writing peer tutor can do for you. *Writing Center Journal, 28*(2), 5–10.

Bruffee describes the personally enriching experience of being a peer writing tutor. Because peer tutoring shows tutors and tutees that no one writes alone, that "writing is a form of civil exchange that thoughtful people engage in when they try to live reasonable lives with one another" (p. 8), Bruffee argues that tutoring writing is definitively human, allowing tutors to practice a "helping, care-taking engagement"

(p. 6) that tutors take with them to other areas of their life. He names this engagement an "interdependence" (p. 8) that tutors practice, model, hand off to tutees, and then carry around to other communicative engagements.

Carter, M. (2007). Ways of knowing, doing, and writing in the disciplines. *College Composition and Communication, 58*(3), 385–418.

This essay describes a project in which departmental faculty worked together to identify their disciplines' "ways of doing" that revealed the "ways of knowing and writing" that they valued in turn. Although Carter's ultimate goal is to forward a structure in which "metagenres" and "metadisciplines" help WID professionals guide faculty development in teaching with writing, his description of departmental conversations around writing values reveals implicit assumptions about how writing knowledge accumulates via transfer as students move through a major. Metagenres are the patterned doing within these, genres of genres or general "ways of doing" that pattern into "similar *kinds* of typified responses to related recurrent situations" (p. 393). He names four: (a) responses to academic situations that call for problem solving (plans, reports, proposals); (b) responses to academic situations that call for empirical inquiry; (c) responses to academic situations that call for research from sources; and (d) responses to academic situations that call for performance. Importantly, Carter says all of these highlight the relationships among disciplines, thus smoothing the path for transfer to occur.

Colquitt, J. A., LePine, J. A. and Noe, R. A. (2000). Toward an integrative theory of training motivation: A meta-analytic path analysis of 20 years of research. *Journal of Applied Psychology, 85*(5), 678–707.

A meta-analysis of 106 studies related to training motivation, this article is particularly helpful for the way it works to define and clarify the relationships between motivation, other individual characteristics (such as self-efficacy, locus of control, and anxiety), and transfer.

Courage, R. (1993). The interaction of public and private literacies. *College Composition and Communication*, *44*(4), 484–496.

Courage links out-of-school writing and academic discourse by situating his inquiry within writing studies conversations of the 1980s and 90s that wondered if these two types of literacies could be compatible at all (Bartholomae, 1986; Bizzell, 1982). To address these concerns, Courage (1993) turns to Literacy Studies/New Literacy Studies for how it connects in- and out-of-school writing by evoking the concept of multiple literacies/multiliteracies, which explore how "sociocultural logic of [literacy] patterns, and the complex relations among them" (p. 490) help or hinder home-to-school transfer of writing-related knowledge. In his study of adult-aged college students, Jannette and Ethel, Courage untangles some of the range of how patterned literacy experiences, attitudes towards writing, and senses of identity interact with school and teacher expectations.

DePalma, M. J., & Ringer, J. M. (2011). Toward a theory of adaptive transfer: Expanding disciplinary discussions of "transfer" in second-language writing and composition studies. *Journal of Second Language Writing*, *20*(2), 134–147.

DePalma and Ringer synthesize L2 writers' rhetorical practices, curricular conditions, genre activity, and identity concerns into a complex theoretical framework they call adaptive transfer. DePalma and Ringer aimed to better account for writers' agency in reshaping or reforming of prior writing knowledge as they encounter new contexts, proposing a "conscious or intuitive process of applying or reshaping learned writing knowledge in order to help students negotiate new and potentially unfamiliar writing situations" (p. 135). They relied on studies from writing studies and education, like Matsuda's (1997) dynamic model and Wenger's (1998) concept of brokering, as a theoretical base from which to move beyond transfer as reuse or reinterpretation of static knowledge. In their formulation, adaptive transfer moves beyond students' application of prior knowledge to the adaptation of writing knowledge in dynamic, idiosyncratic, cross-contextual, rhetorical, multilingual, and transformative ways (p. 141).

Detterman, D. K., & Sternberg, R. J. (1993). *Transfer on trial: Intelligence, cognition, and instruction.* Ablex.

In this edited collection, Detterman, Sternberg, and other authors offer a range of critiques of current cognitive approaches to understanding transfer. Detterman's opening chapter takes a cognitive approach, critiquing several landmark studies (including Thorndike, Judd, and Gick and Holyoak) arguing that transfer which must be cued should not be considered transfer. Another chapter by Greeno, Moore, and Smith offers a situated learning critique (and is summarized below).

Devet, B. (2015). The writing center and transfer of learning: A primer for directors. *Writing Center Journal, 35*(1), 119–151.

Devet's primer on transfer for writing center directors states that a more intentional focus on transfer could reveal much about what is accomplished in writing centers. She suggests that deliberately teaching tutors transfer concepts from educational psychology (near and far, lateral and vertical, conditional and relational, declarative and procedural) and from composition (prior knowledge, dispositions, context, genre) could help tutors become more strategic in their practice, better naming what happened in a session or more thoughtfully anticipating a session to come.

Dias, P., Freedman, A., Medway, P., & Paré, A. (1999). *Worlds apart: Acting and writing in academic and workplace contexts.* L. Erlbaum Associates.

A collection of essays generated by four coordinated-yet-distinct research projects undertaken by the authors. They examined writing in four professions—public administration, management, architecture, and social work—simultaneously in school and at work. Through these comparisons, the authors conclude that there is "a radical difference" between school and work (p. 199), that they are, as the title suggests, worlds apart. This collection is heavily influenced by rhetorical genre theory and theories of apprenticeship and distributed cognition.

Dias, P., & Paré, A. (2000). *Transitions: Writing in academic and workplace settings*. Hampton Press.

An edited collection from many of the same researchers involved in *Worlds Apart* (1999). This volume also includes related work by authors similarly informed by rhetorical genre theory and situated learning, focused on engineering (Artemeva), a pharmaceutical company (Ledwell-Brown), and the Bank of Canada (Smart).

Driscoll, D. L. (2015). Building connections and transferring knowledge: The benefits of a peer tutoring course beyond the writing center. *The Writing Center Journal, 35*(1), 153–181.

Driscoll describes a tutor education course that uses transfer pedagogy to teach writing center and writing studies content. Driscoll designed a course that focused on the "knowledge applications" component of a general education requirement, which asked students "to take a course from outside their major and apply that knowledge to their major" (p. 159). To support this knowledge transfer, Driscoll designed the course around Bransford and Schwartz's (1999) preparation for future learning, which emphasizes not specific knowledge or tasks but on forward-looking concepts like adaptability or resource use, and Perkins and Salomon's (2012) "detect-elect-connect" model (p. 158).

Driscoll, D. L., & Wells, J. (2012). Beyond knowledge and skills: Writing transfer and the role of student dispositions. *Composition Forum, 26*(Fall). Retrieved from http://compositionforum.com/issue/26/beyond-knowledge-skills.php

One of the earliest examples in writing studies to highlight the importance of dispositions for transfer of learning. (Wardle, 2016, also does so in the same special issue.) Driscoll and Wells highlight four dispositions discussed at length in the chapter on industrial psychology—value, self-efficacy, attribution, and self-regulation—and illustrate the analytical power of dispositions with examples from their distinct research projects. Driscoll has further developed arguments around dispositions and transfer in Driscoll et al. (2017); Driscoll & Jin (2018); Driscoll and Powell (2016); and Gorzelsky et al. (2016).

Dweck, C. S., & Leggett, E. L. (1988). A social-cognitive approach to motivation and personality. *Psychological review, 95*(2), 256–273.

In this article that predates the best-selling book *Mindsets*, Dweck develops her theory of goal orientation—an individual characteristic which is distinct from the pedagogical intervention of goal setting. She distinguishes between mastery-oriented goals and performance-oriented goals; subsequent research has argued that performance-goal orientation is less conducive for learning and therefore for transfer of training.

Freedman, A., Adam, C., & Smart, G. (1994). Wearing suits to class simulating genres and simulations as genre. *Written Communication, 11*(2), 193–226.

An investigation of an in-class workplace simulation in a financial analysis course. Through analysis of a rich data set (including interviews, texts, classroom observations, and more), the authors conclude that although the instructor and students invest considerable energy in building the fiction of the workplace, students "were never deceived" (p. 204) about the fact that they were doing school for a grade—a reality that influenced both their written and spoken discourse, keeping it at a significant remove from the goals and practices of an actual workplace.

Gick, M. L., & Holyoak, K. J. (1980). Analogical problem solving. *Cognitive Psychology, 12*(3), 306–355.

In a pair of articles—this publication and "Schema induction and analogical transfer" published in the same journal in 1983—Gick and Holyoak share the results of eleven distinct but related examinations of how the problem-solving strategies of individuals might be influenced by their earlier exposure to similar problems—including the oft-cited "radiation problem." An early and widely cited example of the cognitive approach to understanding transfer of learning.

Gist M.E., Schwoerer C, & Rosen, B. (1989). Effects of alternative training methods on self-efficacy and performance in computer software training. *Journal of Applied Psychology, 74*(6), 884–891.

The first in a series of articles Gist published with colleagues (see also Gist et al., 1990; Gist et al., 1991; Stevens & Gist, 1997) that focus on the relationship between self-efficacy and transfer of training as mediated by instructional design differences, such as goal setting and self-management.

Greeno, J. G., Moore, J. L, & Smith, D. R. (1993). Transfer of situated learning. In D.K. Detterman & R.J. Sternberg (Eds.), *Transfer on trial: Intelligence, cognition, and instruction*, (pp. 99–167). Ablex Publishing.

In this chapter, the authors offer a critique of current cognitive approaches to understanding transfer, arguing that cognition is situated and that a robust understanding of transfer must take into account the affordances and constraints offered by the various contexts through which individuals move.

Holton, I. E., Bates, R. A., & Ruona, W. E. A. (2000). Development of a generalized Learning Transfer System Inventory. *Human Resource Development Quarterly, 11*(4), 333–360.

Holton and colleagues explain the development and validation of their Learning Transfer System Inventory (LSTI), a survey instrument of 68 questions meant to help standardize research. More information on its development can be found in Holton et al. (1997); more information on its use in international contexts can be found in Bates et al. (2007), Chen et al. (2005), Devos et al. (2007), Khasawneh et al. (2006), Kirwan & Birchall (2006), Velada et al. (2009), Yamkovenko et al.(2007), and Yamnil (2001).

Hughes, B., Gillespie, P., & Kail, H. (2010). What they take with them: Findings from the Peer Writing Tutor Alumni Research Project. *Writing Center Journal, 30*(2), 12–46.

Setting out to understand "what peer tutors take with them" after leaving college, Hughes et al. describe the Peer Writing Tutor Alumni

Project (PWTARP), for which they conducted a large-scale electronic survey of 126 tutor alumni from their three institutions. The survey collected thoughts from alumni who tutored as far back as 1982, gathering a lifespan perspective on the impact of tutoring writing. By relying on the construct "take with them," the survey assumes the presence of knowledge transfer, but moves beyond writing knowledge. Following Bruffee's (1978) notion that tutors practice the kinds of socially-situated communication skills that will serve them in work, family, and civic contexts long after college as well as constructs from William Cronon's 1998 essay "Only Connect," their analysis of participant reflections highlights not only tutors' learned writing knowledge but the kind of learning Cronon characterizes as a liberal education: they "listen and they hear"; "they read and they understand"; "they can talk with anyone"; "they can write clearly and persuasively and movingly"; "they practice humility, tolerance, and self-criticism"; and "they nurture and empower the people around them" (pp. 76–78). Hughes et al.'s findings show these traits in tutor alumni, with implications for how tutors transfer intellectual, professional, social, and personal knowledge into other areas of their lives.

Hutchins, E. (1995). *Cognition in the wild*. MIT Press.

A "cognitive ethnography" of navigation aboard a US Navy ship, this book is one of the earliest and most often cited analyses of distributed cognition. Hutchins argues that both the navigational tools and the teams of individuals aboard the vessel are sites of distributed cognition. Particularly useful in the field of knowledge management, which focuses on transfer of knowledge among individuals via mediational tools.

James, M. A. (2008). The influence of perceptions of task similarity/difference on learning transfer in second language writing. *Written Communication, 25*(1), 76–103.

Based on findings from his 2006 study that found writing knowledge transfer was partly influenced by the similarity and difference between subject matter that students wrote about in their ESL and other courses, James' article seeks to further understand how both subject matter and task similarity/difference influence the transfer of writing skills. Like Leki and Carson's early research (1994), his research sought to understand how students' perceptions of task similarity affect the transfer of writing knowledge between first-year ESL writing courses and "tasks outside the classroom" (p. 76). Asking 42 students to complete an out-of-class writing task and subsequent reflective interview and scoring both that task and a class writing assignment, James found (a) that learning transfer did occur between the class writing assignment and out-of-class task, but (b) that transfer was more frequently described and seemingly carried out (indicated by higher scores) when students perceived the writing tasks to be of similar difficulty levels (p. 92). Because James found that actual task difference had less of an impact on transfer than students' understanding of that difference, he concludes that perception of writing task difference is more important than actual difference when supporting transfer of writing skills.

Kobayashi, H., & Rinnert, C. (2008). Task response and text construction across L1 and L2 writing. *Journal of Second Language Writing, 17*(1), 7–29.

Kobayashi and Rinnert investigated the transfer of four types of writing instruction—intensive writing in L1 and L2; intensive writing only in L1; intensive writing only in L2; none in either language—on 28 Japanese students' L1 (Japanese) and L2 (English) exam writing strategies, especially in organizational use of structure and discursive markers. The research subjects were novice EFL writers with no prior college L2 writing instruction. Using textual analysis and post-essay student interviews, they conclude that training did affect how students approached their exam writing, but in slightly different ways: L1 essay-level writing practice did transfer to their L2 essays, but L2 (English) writing practice, which focused on the paragraph level, did not transfer back to students' L1 writing (p. 19). In other words, as students constructed texts in either language, transfer "occurred in both directions," with student interviews showing that students called on both of their languages as sources of knowledge about organization and discursive norms. Thus, Kobayashi and Rinnert reinforced Berman's (1994) finding that explicit instruction affects the transfer of writing knowledge but extended his findings to show both that L1 writing instruction supports writing choices in the L1 and L2 and particularly a meta-awareness of making those choices, and that instruction that stresses the interaction of an L1 and L2 in writing "led to greater effects" in students' writing than the training that focused on the languages alone or separately, "perhaps because of the greater confidence it generated for both L1 and L2 writing" (p. 20).

Kubota, R. (1998). An investigation of L1–L2 transfer in writing among Japanese university students: Implications for contrastive rhetoric. *Journal of Second Language Writing, 7*(1), 69–100.

Kubota's 1998 study of the negative and positive transfer of rhetorical style between Japanese and English was premised on the possibility of negative transfer or interference from students' L1, Japanese—but its findings moved away from generalizations about homogeneous languages or cultures and toward the decisions of individual writers. Kubota researched the expository and persuasive writing of 46 Japanese college students who had studied English for at least 8 years in Japan to understand how an L1 and L2 interact in the composing process. Her study's results revealed the nuance of L1 to L2 transfer of writing ability: students who had more experience writing in their L2 produced higher quality essays than students who had more L2 English education. Kubota suggests this is because English language education focuses on isolated sentence-level concerns and translation which affected the control over vocabulary and syntax in the L2 essays. Thus, she concludes that ESL writing organization that teachers and researchers puzzle over may be less a phenomenon of negative L1 transfer and more a factor of little experience with academic L1 writing (p. 88).

Lave, J. (1988). *Cognition in practice: Mind, mathematics and culture in everyday life.* Cambridge University Press.

Lave begins this volume—which predates her subsequent work with Wenger on communities of practice—with a thorough critique of previous cognitive approaches to understanding transfer. Drawing on her work with the Adult Mathematics Project, which followed individuals out of labs and mathematics classrooms and into contexts like grocery stories and weight-loss programs, Lave argues that people's mathematical problem-solving strategies are strongly influenced by context. Through this work, Lave was an early articulator of the theory of situated learning.

Light, R., & Fawns, R. (2003). Knowing the game: Integrating speech and action in games teaching through TGfU. *Quest, 55*(2), 161–176.

Taking up the turn in sports education toward teaching games for understanding, Light and Fawns argue for a more comprehensive theoretical basis that unites teaching for physical skills with cognitive and embodied aspects of learning. As they assert, "we cannot separate the thoughtful activity that has previously been attributed to some inner realm of the mind from the social and material context in which activities or games take place" (p. 172). Moreover, to fully learn the tactical as well as the technical skills of a game, they further challenge the Cartesian split to "argue that the body is not a vessel steered by the mind, but rather that thought expresses itself in and through the body" (p. 173). Ultimately, they challenge the older, behaviorist models for sports education that focused primarily on teaching motor skills to argue that games are a "social-psychological" (p. 174) phenomena.

Lindenman, H. (2015) Inventing metagenres: How four college seniors connect writing across domains. *Composition Forum, 31*(Spring), http://compositionforum.com/issue/31/inventing-metagenres.php

Arguing that writing research often sets up domain categories—home, school, work, etc.—that miss how students forge their own generic connections, Lindenman's study uses discourse-based interviews to elicit students' own understandings of genre relationships, regardless of domain. She collects data through student surveys (n=319), four focus groups, and ten interviews to understand less how students transfer their writing knowledge across domains (her original research question) and more on how students draw on prior knowledge, using intuited relationships among genres, to "figure out" how to compose texts. She finds eight of ten focal participants linking their texts in unconventional ways, creating "metageneric connections" based on texts' purposes, strategies, or rhetorical effect; rather than relying on texts' learning contexts like first-year or disciplinary writing courses, students group their texts not by where they take place but by what they do.

Lobato, J. (2012). The actor-oriented transfer perspective and its contributions to educational research and practice. *Educational Psychologist, 47*(3), 232–247.

One of several articles in which Lobato explains what she has termed an "actor-oriented" perspective on transfer, a theory grounded in her research in mathematics classrooms. Researchers, Lobato notes, often use students' ability to provide a correct solution to a previously encountered mathematical problem to gauge whether transfer has occurred; Lobato argues that if researchers attempt to understand students' thinking as they attempt to solve the problems (e.g., through interviews), there is often evidence of transfer even when the final answers are incorrect.

Maran, N., & Glavin, R. (2003). Low-to high-fidelity simulation–a continuum of medical education? *Medical Education, 37*(s1), 22–28.

Maran and Glavin explain the meaning and value of simulations for medical education and synthesize the more recent uses of simulations in the teaching of medicine. They also emphasize the notion of fidelity in simulation construction and expand the dimensions of fidelity to match the range of context variables and competencies that a medical professional might need. Maran and Glavin concede that assessment in simulator training remains a challenge due to the ultimate unpredictability of working with human patients.

Melzer, D. (2014). The connected curriculum: Designing a vertical transfer writing curriculum. *The WAC Journal, 25*, 78-91.

With an eye to Gagne's (1965) work on vertical curriculum, Melzer describes a reimagined vertical curriculum at UC Davis based in the transfer of writing knowledge. Melzer explains that a successful form of such a curriculum includes the following components: constant opportunity for student self-reflection and self-monitoring; writing practice over time and embedded in situated, domain-specific contexts; explicit teaching of academic writing threshold concepts like revision, genre, editing, introduced and reinforced across contexts and over time; the creation and reinforcement of a shared campus-wide vocabulary about academic writing; and multiple opportunities for peer mentoring. He describes what these principles of a vertical transfer writing curriculum look like at UC Davis, including WAC workshops on supporting student reflection on writing and supporting growth of metacognition; a WAC-focused sophomore composition course that bridges to general education courses and a junior-level WID course that uses forward-reaching transfer strategies; and a shared campus meta-language about writing, reinforced through a university writing rubric, in the student writing handbook, in all course learning outcomes, and tutor training and outreach workshops in the writing center.

Middendorf, J. & Pace, D. (2004), Decoding the disciplines: A model for helping students learn disciplinary ways of thinking. *New Directions for Teaching and Learning, 2004*(98), 1–12.

Middendorf and Pace's "Decoding the Disciplines" model aims to understand how to help students traverse "the gap between expert and novice thinking" in a discipline (http://decodingthedisciplines.org/). In the model, transfer is implicit in disciplinary thinking—those using the model assume that disciplinary learning happens over time and across contexts and thus pursue the role the transfer plays in students' acquisition of disciplinary knowledge. Middendorf and Pace's (1998) model delineates a "bottleneck approach" that seeks to understand where students experience difficulty in transferring knowledge—moving a concept from one side of a bottleneck to another. In a specific disciplinary context, this looks like faculty in history discussing what counts as teaching and learning in their discipline, using a bottleneck approach to identify where students get stuck in disciplinary learning (Pace, 2011). Such local, disciplinary conversations aim to "decode" unconscious processes into conscious communication about disciplinary knowledge so that concepts can be modeled for students and assessed, in this history case via a "letter" to a sibling about the course.

Moll, L.C, & N. Gonzalez (1994). Lessons from research with language minority children. *Journal of Reading Behavior*, 26(4), 439–56.

Moll and Gonzalez helped to develop the notion of funds of knowledge, which includes the historical and cultural experiences, knowledge, and skills that make up home and household life. The concept of funds of knowledge helps educators learn how to bridge the knowledge of language minority and working-class students with mainstream, school-based curricula and literacy tasks. Actively viewing and actively developing relevant curriculum based on the vast, networked, and generationally-rich types of knowing—ranging from knowledge of plant cultivation to masonry to midwifery to biology and chemistry—of language minority and working-class students offers a transfer route that may be inaccessible through standardized schooling. Working from funds of knowledge means elevating households and the complex networks between households in communities as core sites of culture. It also means looking beyond what we would typically view as "literacies" to the broader sets of experiences that encompass and inform these children's home worlds.

Nonaka, I. (1994). A dynamic theory of organizational knowledge creation. *Organization Science*, 5(1), 14–37.

Drawing from experience with Japanese corporations as well as Polanyi's theories of tacit and explicit knowledge, knowledge management scholar Nonaka develops a theory of knowledge creation and innovation. He emphasizes the ways in which, for innovative practices to be adopted by an organization, tacit knowledge must be made explicit, and explicit knowledge must then later be re-internalized.

Norman, G., Dore, K., & Grierson, L. (2012). The minimal relationship between simulation fidelity and transfer of learning. *Medical Education*, 46(7), 636–647.

The goal of this paper was to compare across a range of studies the effectiveness of high and low fidelity simulations in medical education. In their meta-analysis of 24 studies, they found little statistical difference between the effectiveness of high over low fidelity simulations, which challenges the commonly held assumptions that high fidelity would be superior for learning. They posit several theories for their findings, which include: (a) drawing from cognitive load theory, they suggest that too many "additions to the learning task may detract from learning because of our limited ability to process incoming information" (pg. 643); (b) fidelity can be distinguished between engineering fidelity (reflection of the environment) and psychological fidelity (how well the simulator can cue complex mental tasks that allow a learner to recognize the actions required),and to achieve mastery and transfer, a learner needs practice across multiple types of psychological fidelity; and (c) there has been no scaffolding of skills when students are first and only introduced to high fidelity contexts, and as a result, they don't have the hidden skills to perform many of the functions within the simulation system as "training in so-called 'simple' motor skills generally requires considerable practice" (p. 645).

Nowacek, R. S. (2011). *Agents of integration: Understanding transfer as a rhetorical act*. Southern Illinois University Press.

Nowacek's study of a three-semester interdisciplinary learning community also aims to explicitly study the transfer of writing knowledge but in doing so complicates much of the previous empirical work on transfer. By studying writing in a general education interdisciplinary learning seminar, which linked three courses in history, literature, and religious studies, Nowacek was able to capture both general and discipline-specific writing instruction received by 18 students and taught by three team-teaching instructors in the second semester of the seminar. Building on a theoretical framework informed by rhetorical genre studies, sociocultural approaches to transfer, and activity theory, Nowacek traced how students experienced genres as social and rhetorical resources, but more so as catalysts for making conceptual connections across disciplinary expectations occurring in the same classroom (p. 12). Most centrally, she offers a theory of transfer as dynamic "recontextualization"—not mere application but adaptation and transformation—of writing knowledge, with students as "agents of integration" who enact rhetorical strategies that help them "see" interdisciplinary connections (perceive them) and then "sell" those connections (convey them to others) in their writing, to "justify the value of the connection within the text itself" (p. 53).

Petraglia, Joseph. (1995). *Reconceiving writing, rethinking writing instruction*. Lawrence Erlbaum.

This edited collection asked if teaching students generic writing skills in first-year writing could really stand up to the field's growing theoretical and empirical consensus that writing is a situated, contextually embedded activity. Central to this examination is Petraglia and others' challenge to FYW for its lack of rhetorical context within the classroom setting and its lack of any imagined rhetorical context (be they for additional academic or workplace writing) beyond the classroom. In other words, scholars questioned how a class based on the autonomous model of literacy (where writing skills can be generalized across all contexts) could possibly help students learn to write, given that their future writing situations (especially those in workplace and advanced disciplinary settings) could not resemble those in FYW.

Reiff, M. J., & Bawarshi, A. (2011). Tracing discursive resources: How students use prior genre knowledge to negotiate new writing contexts in first-year composition. *Written Communication*, *28*(3), 312–337.

Through a multi-institutional inquiry into students' prior genre knowledge, Reiff and Bawarshi examine how students enrolled in FYW make use of genre knowledge acquired in high school settings. Drawing on analysis of surveys, interviews, and texts collected, Reiff and Bawarshi present a two-part argument. First, they suggest that study students fall into two categories: those who are able to break down prior genres into parts and use those appropriately and those who attempt to import whole genres into new situations. Second, they suggest that these two types of study students are better understood as boundary guarders and boundary crossers. Boundary guarders, who have a difficult time accepting their status as novice writers, may struggle with transfer of prior genre knowledge. Boundary crossers, on the other hand, are more willing to accept their status as novice writers and seem more likely to use elements of prior knowledge in new settings.

Robinson, A., & Mania, K. (2007). Technological research challenges of flight simulation and flight instructor assessments of perceived fidelity. *Simulation & Gaming*, *38*(1), 112–135.

Based in aviation education, Robinson and Mania aim to distinguish between perceptual and technological fidelity and emphasize the role that human perception and judgement has on how a learner interacts with a simulator system. They argue that "perceptual fidelity is not necessarily induced by exact physical simulation" (134), and thus the on-going challenge for creating high fidelity simulators is to understand how to cue learners to experience the simulator as though it were a real task. The challenges here include the multiple types of fidelity required for a flight simulation to be perceived as "real." They suggest differentiating between types of "fidelity metrics" to "ignore certain shortcomings for which the human perceptual system is not sensitive and work on problems that induce high psychophysical sensitivity" (p. 125).

Szulanski, G. (2000). The process of knowledge transfer: A diachronic analysis of stickiness. *Organizational behavior and human decision processes, 82*(1), 9–27.

Working in the field of knowledge management and knowledge transfer, Szulanski draws on his surveys of employees at large corporations to argue that knowledge transfer within an organization is neither automatic or costless. Instead, he identifies a taxonomy of obstacles that result in "stickiness"—that is, knowledge that does not easily transfer from one individual to another.

Tuomi-Gröhn, T., & Engeström, Y. (2003). *Between school and work: New perspectives on transfer and boundary-crossing.* Pergamon, 2003.

An edited collection, informed by Engeström's activity theory model of expansive learning, focused on vocational education and training. In addition to chapters exploring vocational education programs in countries such as Germany, Ireland, Finland, and Norway, the volume is anchored by several theory-building chapters. These include a reprint of King Beach's *RRE* piece on consequential transitions and two early chapters by Tuomi-Gröhn and Engeström arguing for a change in focus from the transfer of knowledge from one context to another to an extended focus on the significant learning that can emerge from the interface between multiple activity systems.

Walsh, J. P., & Ungson, G. R. (1991). Organizational memory. *Academy of Management Review, 16*(1), 57–91.

One of the early taxonomies of organizational memory, this article is frequently cited within the knowledge management scholarship. They define organizational memory as "stored information from an organization's history that can be brought to bear on present decisions" (a view of inter-personal knowledge transfer) and as having identifiable stages of acquisition, retention, and retrieval. Particularly helpful are their six "rentention facilities": individuals, culture, transformations, structures, ecology, and external archives.

Wardle, E. (2009). "Mutt genres" and the goal of FYC: Can we help students write the genres of the university? *College Composition & Communication, 60*(4), 765–789.

In this article, Wardle challenges teachers and scholars to recognize writing assignments in FYW as "mutt genres," defined as "genres that do not respond to rhetorical situations requiring communication in order to accomplish a purpose meaningful to the author" (p. 777). Wardle points to how larger institutional structures of FYW limit teachers' ability to engage students in dynamic and transnational disciplinary genres. She offers several resolutions in response to this paradox. First, teach genres as boundary objects that allow students to connect their writing with that done in other disciplines. Second, teach meta-awareness of genres through genre analysis of university and discipline-specific writing. Here, students "analyze academic genres rather than learn to write academic genres" (p. 783). These suggestions are important features of the writing about writing (WAW) pedagogy introduced here and elsewhere.

Wegner, D. M. (1987). Transactive memory: A contemporary analysis of the group mind. In *Theories of group behavior* (pp. 185–208). Springer.

Here and in an earlier article (Wegner et al., 1985), Wegner sets forth a theory of transactive memory grounded in the experiences of romantic couples who remember more together than they can individually. Rather than each person remembering every experience, they develop "transactive memory systems" that rely on "directories" to help them remember who has remembered what information. Subsequent knowledge management scholars extended this work to small work groups and even larger workplace organizations.

Yancey, K. B., Robertson, L., & Taczak, K. (2014). *Writing across contexts: Transfer, composition, and sites of writing.* Utah State University Press.

This book synthesizes research and theory on transfer in writing studies as well as reports on (and offers suggestions based on) a qualitative study of a teaching for transfer (TFT) course in FYW. Noteworthy features of TFT are "key terms, reflection, and a theory of writing designed as interlocking components aimed at helping students develop a conceptual framework of writing knowledge that would transfer across contexts" (p. 67). According to these authors, the effectiveness of this approach for transfer is heavily influenced by students' prior knowledge and how that knowledge was or was not put to use in new writing situations. Overall, these authors suggest that theoretically informed curricular design can aid in transfer, with the caveat that transfer of writing-related knowledge cannot be guaranteed.

Appendix

Theme	Chapter	Representative Citations
Individuality		
Individuality & *Identity*	Ch 6. Second Language Writing	Cozart et al., 2016; Johnstone, 1996; Matsuda, 2015; Norton, 2000
	Ch 10. From School to Work and Beyond	Brandt, 2018; Dias et al., 1999; Dias & Paré, 2000
Individuality & *Agency*	Ch 2. Cognitive Psychology and Situated Learning	Lobato, 2012
	Ch 3. Transfer of Training and Knowledge Management	Bandura 1986, 1999
	Ch 7. First-Year Writing	Downs & Wardle, 2007; Yancey et al., 2014
	Ch 8. WAC/WID	Donahue, 2016; Nowacek, 2011
Individuality & *Dispositions*	Ch 3. Transfer of Training and Knowledge Management	Bandura, 1977
	Ch 7. First-Year Writing	Driscoll & Powell, 2016; Driscoll & Wells, 2012; Reiff & Bawarshi, 2011; Wardle, 2012
	Ch 8. WAC/WID	Sommers & Saltz, 2004
	Ch 10. From School to Work and Beyond	Bacon, 1991; Baird & Dilger, 2017; Brent, 2012; White, 2015
Individuality & *Embodied Cognition*	Ch 2. Cognitive Psychology and Situated Learning	Day & Goldstone, 2011; LeMesurier, 2016; Menary, 2010; Nemirovsky, 2011; Prior & Olinger, 2019
	Ch 3. Transfer of Training and Knowledge Management	Hutchins, 1995
	Ch 4. Transfer in Education	Light & Fawns, 2003

Theme	Chapter	Representative Citations
Intentionality		
Intentionality & *Abstract Schema*	Ch 2. Cognitive Psychology and Situated Learning	Engle, 2006; Engle et al., 2011; Judd, 1908; Gick & Holyoak, 1980, 1983; Katona, 1940; Lobato et al., 2012; Polya, 1945/1957; Reed et al., 1974; Schwartz & Martin, 2004
	Ch 4. Transfer in Education	Bunker & Thorpe, 1982
	Ch 6. Second Language Writing	DasBender, 2016; Figueredo, 2006; Matsuda, 1997; Negretti & Kuteeva, 2011; Sersen, 2011
	Ch 7. First-Year Writing	Yancey et al., 2014
	Ch 8. WAC/WID	Beaufort, 2007
Intentionality & *Metacognition & self-monitoring*	Ch 2. Cognitive Psychology and Situated Learning	Flower & Hayes, 1981; Kahneman, 1973, 2003, 2011; Perkins & Salomon, 1988, 1989
	Ch 3. Transfer of Training and Knowledge Management	Keith & Freese, 2005; Wegner et al., 1985
	Ch 7. First-Year Writing	Wardle 2007, 2009; Yancey et al., 2014
	Ch 8. WAC/WID	Clark & Hernandez, 2011; Donahue, 2016; Downs & Wardle, 2007; Fishman & Reiff, 2015; Ford, 2012; Fraizer, 2010; Jarratt et al., 2009; Nelms & Dively, 2007; Nowacek, 2011; Rounsaville et al., 2008; Smit, 2004
Intentionality & *Automaticity*	Ch 2. Cognitive Psychology and Situated Learning	Shiffrin & Schneider, 1977
	Ch 3. Transfer of Training and Knowledge Management	Nonaka, 1994; Walsh & Ungson, 1991
	Ch 6. Second Language Writing	Gass & Selinker, 1992; Selinker, 1969, 1972; Weinreich, 1953
	Ch 8. WAC/WID	Donahue, 2016; Nowacek, 2011; Wardle, 2007
	Ch 10. From School to Work and Beyond	Beaufort, 1999

Appendix

Theme	Chapter	Representative Citations
Fidelity		
Fidelity & *Situated Learning*	Ch 2. Cognitive Psychology and Situated Learning	Beach, 1995; Carraher et al., 1985; Lave, 1988; Lave & Wenger, 1991
	Ch 4. Transfer in Education	Griffin et al., 2005; Light & Fawns, 2003
	Ch 6. Second Language Writing	Currie, 1993; Elon Statement on Writing Transfer, 2016; Johns, 1990; Leki, 1995; Leki & Carson, 1994; Spack, 1988; Swales, 1984, 1990
	Ch 7. First-Year Writing	Petraglia, 1995; Russell, 1995; Wardle, 2007, 2009
	Ch 10. From School to Work and Beyond	Tuomi-Gröhn & Engeström, 2003
Fidelity & *High and Low Fidelity*	Ch 2. Cognitive Psychology and Situated Learning	Gick & Holyoak, 1980, 1983; Perkins & Salomon, 1988; Thorndike, 1906/1916
	Ch 3. Transfer of Training and Knowledge Management	Thorndike, 1906/1916
	Ch 4. Transfer in Education	Alexander et al., 2005; Maran & Glavin, 2003
	Ch 8. WAC/WID	Herrington, 1985
	Ch 10. From School to Work and Beyond	Anson & Forsberg, 1990; Dannels, 2003; Freedman et al., 1994; Spinuzzi, 1996
Fidelity & *Scaffolding*	Ch 2. Cognitive Psychology and Situated Learning	Fyfe et al., 2014; Kaminski et al., 2008, 2013; Nemirovsky, 2011; Pouw et al., 2014
	Ch 4. Transfer in Education	Lopez et al., 2009; Norman et al., 2012; Teteris et al., 2012
	Ch 9. Writing Centers	Nowacek et al. 2019

Theme	Chapter	Representative Citations
Fidelity & *Modeling*	Ch 2. Cognitive Psychology and Situated Learning	Gentner et al., 2003; Gick & Holyoak, 1983; Hammer et al., 2005
	Ch 3. Transfer of Training and Knowledge Management	Baldwin, 1992; Decker, 1980; Pescuric & Byham, 1996; Taylor et al., 2005
	Ch 7. First-Year Writing	Devitt et al., 2004; Yancey et al., 2014
Fidelity & *Proximity*	Ch 2. Cognitive Psychology and Situated Learning	Perkins & Saloman, 1988
	Ch 3. Transfer of Training and Knowledge Management	Cromwell & Kolb, 2004; Rouiller & Goldstein, 1993
	Ch 4. Transfer in Education	Robinson & Mania, 2007
	Ch 6. Second Language Writing	James, 2008
	Ch 7. First-Year Writing	Smit 2004; Wardle, 2007
	Ch 8. WAC/WID	Bergmann & Zepernick, 2007; Middendorf & Pace, 2004; Walvoord & McCarthy, 1990
Directionality		
Directionality & *Preparation for Future Learning*	Ch 2. Cognitive Psychology and Situated Learning	Bransford & Schwartz, 1999
	Ch 9. Writing Centers	Driscoll, 2015; Driscoll & Harcourt, 2012; Perkins & Salomon, 2012
Directionality & *Framing*	Ch 2. Cognitive Psychology and Situated Learning	Engle, 2006; Engle et al., 2011; Gick & Holyoak, 1980, 1983; Hammer et al., 2005
	Ch 5. Literacy Studies	Dyson, 1999; Gonzalez et al., 2006
	Ch 8. WAC/WID	Lindenman, 2015

Appendix

Theme	Chapter	Representative Citations
Directionality & *Lateral and Vertical Transfer*	Ch 4. Transfer in Education	Holt et al., 2002; Lopez et al., 2009; Thorpe et al., 1984; Werner & Almond, 1990
	Ch 7. First-Year Writing	Bergmann & Zepernick, 2007; Smit, 2004; Wardle, 2009
	Ch 8. WAC/WID	Crowley, 1998; Ford, 2012; Gagne, 1965; Hall, 2006; Haskell, 2000; Hilgers et al., 1995; Jamieson, 2009; Lettner-Rust et al., 2007; Melzer, 2014; Miles et al., 2008
Directionality & *Transformation of Knowledge*	Ch 2. Cognitive Psychology and Situated Learning	Beach, 1995, 1999
	Ch 5. Literacy Studies	Dyson, 1999
	Ch 6. Second Language Writing	DePalma & Ringer, 2011
	Ch 7. First-Year Writing	Wardle, 2007
	Ch 8. WAC/WID	Nowacek, 2011
	Ch 9. Writing Centers	Johnson, 2020
	Ch 10. From School to Work and Beyond	Smart & Brown, 2002; Tuomi-Gröhn et al., 2003
Directionality & *Prior Knowledge*	Ch 7. First-Year Writing	Robertson et al., 2012; Rounsaville et al., 2008
	Ch 8. WAC/WID	Jarratt et al., 2009; Nowacek, 2011; Reiff & Bawarshi, 2011
	Ch 10. From School to Work and Beyond	Gillam, 1991; Michaud, 2011; Navarre Cleary, 2013
Directionality & *Negative Transfer and Interference*	Ch 2. Cognitive Psychology and Situated Learning	Lobato, 2012
	Ch 5. Literacy Studies	Dyson, 1999; Heath, 1982
	Ch 6. Second Language Writing	Gass & Selinker, 1992; Selinker, 1969, 1972; Weinreich, 1953
	Ch 8. WAC/WID	Beaufort, 2007; Nowacek, 2011
Directionality & *Reflection in Pedagogy*	Ch 7. First-Year Writing	Downs & Wardle, 2007; Yancey et al., 2014
	Ch 8. WAC/WID	Beaufort, 2007
	Ch 10. From School to Work and Beyond	Beaufort, 1999

Theme	Chapter	Representative Citations
Directionality & *Multidirectionality*	Ch 6. Second Language Writing	Cook, 2003; Gort, 2006; Helfenstein, 2005; Jarvis & Pavlenko, 2008; Pavlenko, 2000; Pavlenko & Jarvis, 2002; Sharwood-Smith & Kellerman, 1986
	Ch 9. Writing Centers	Dinitz & Harrington, 2014
Simultaneity		
Simultaneity & *Concurrent Contexts*	Ch 5. Literacy Studies	Prior & Shipka, 2003
	Ch 8. WAC/WID	Nowacek, 2011
	Ch 9. Writing Centers	Alexander et al., 2016; Hagemann, 1995; Walker, 1998
	Ch 10. From School to Work and Beyond	Dias et al., 1999; Lemke, 2000; Prior, 2018
Simultaneity & *Dynamic Dimensionality*	Ch 6. Second Language Writing	Cozart et al., 2016; DePalma & Ringer, 2011; Kobayashi & Rinnert, 2008; Kubota, 1998; Larsen-Freeman & Cameron, 2008; Matsuda, 1997
	Ch 8. WAC/WID	Bizzell 1982/2003; Hayes et al., 2016; Martin & Schwartz, 2013
Simultaneity & *Multicompetence*	Ch 2. Cognitive Psychology and Situated Learning	Hammer et al., 2005
	Ch 6. Second Language Writing	Cook 1992, 2016; Cenoz & Gorter, 2011; Garcia & Wei, 2014; Grosjean, 1989; Larsen-Freeman, 1997, 2013

References

Alexander, A. L., Brunyé, T., Sidman, J., & Weil, S. A. (2005). From gaming to training: A review of studies on fidelity, immersion, presence, and buy-in and their effects on transfer in pc-based simulations and games. *DARWARS Training Impact Group*, 5, 1–14.

Alexander, K. P., DePalma, M., & Ringer, J. M. (2016). Adaptive remediation and the facilitation of transfer in multiliteracy center contexts. *Computers and Composition*, 41, 32–45.

Anson, C. M., & Forsberg, L. L. (1990). Moving beyond the academic community: Transitional stages in professional writing. *Written Communication*, 7(2), 200–231.

Bacon, N. (1999). The trouble with transfer: Lessons from a study of community service writing. *Michigan Journal of Community Service Learning*, 6(1), 53–62.

Baird, N., & Dilger, B. (2017). How students perceive transitions: Dispositions and transfer in internships. *College Composition and Communication*, 68(4), 684.

Baird, N., & Dilger, B. (2018). Dispositions in natural science laboratories: The roles of individuals and contexts in writing transfer. *Across the Disciplines*, 15(4), 21–40. https://wac.colostate.edu/docs/atd/articles/bairddilger2018.pdf

Baldwin T.T. (1992). Effects of alternative modeling strategies on outcomes of interpersonal-skills training. *Journal of Applied Psychology*, 77(2), 147–54

Bandura, A. (1977). Self-efficacy: Toward a unifying theory of behavioral change. *Psychological Review*, 84(2), 191–215.

Bandura, A. (1986). *Social foundations of thought and action: A social cognitive theory*. Prentice-Hall

Bandura, A. (1999). Social cognitive theory: An agent perspective. *Asian Journal of Social Psychology*, 2, 21–41.

Beaufort, A. (1999). *Writing in the real world: Making the transition from school to work*. Teachers College Press.

Beaufort, A. (2007). *College writing and beyond: A new framework for university writing instruction*. Utah State University Press.

Beach, K. (1995). Activity as a mediator of sociocultural change and individual development: The case of school-work transition in Nepal. *Mind, Culture, and Activity*, 2(4), 285–302.

Beach, K. (1999). Consequential transitions: A sociocultural expedition beyond transfer in education. *Review of Research in Education*, 24(1), 101–139.

Bergmann, L. S., & Zepernick, J. (2007). Disciplinarity and transfer: Students' perceptions of learning to write. *WPA: Writing Program Administration*, 31(1-2), 124–149.

Bizzell, P. (2003). Cognition, convention, and certainty: What we need to know about writing. In V. Villanueva (Ed.), *Cross-Talk in comp theory: A reader* (2nd ed., pp. 387–411). National Council of Teachers of English. (Original work published 1982)

Brandt, D. (2018). Writing development and life-course development: The case of working adults. In C. Bazerman et al., *The Lifespan Development of Writing* (244–271). NCTE.

Bransford, J. D., & Schwartz, D. L. (1999). Rethinking transfer: A simple proposal with multiple implications. *Review of Research in Education*, 24(1), 61–100.

Brent, D. (2012). Crossing boundaries: Co-op students relearning to write. *College Composition & Communication, 63*(4), 558–592.

Bunker, D., & Thorpe, R. (1982). A model for the teaching of games in secondary schools. *Bulletin of Physical Education, 18*(1), 5–8.

Carraher, T. N., Carraher, D. W., & Schliemann, A. D. (1985). Mathematics in the streets and in schools. *British Journal of Developmental Psychology, 3*(1), 21–29.

Cenoz, J., & Gorter, D. (2011). Focus on multilingualism: A study of trilingual writing. *Modern Language Journal, 95*(3), 356–369.

Chase, W. G., & Simon, H. A. (1973). Perception in chess. *Cognitive Psychology, 4*(1), 55–81.

Clark, I. L., & Hernandez, A. (2011). Genre awareness, academic argument, and transferability. *WAC Journal, 22*, 65–78.

Cook, V. (1992). Evidence for multi-competence. *Language Learning, 42*(4), 557–591.

Cook, V. J. (Ed.). (2003). *Effects of the second language on the first*. Multilingual Matters.

Cook, V. J. (2016). Transfer and the relationship between the languages of multi-competence. In R. Alonso Alonso (Ed.), *Crosslinguistic influence in second language acquisition* (pp. 24–37). Multilingual Matters.

Cozart, S. M., Jensen, T. W., Wichmann-Hansen, G., Kupatadze, K, & Chien-Hsiung Chiu, S. (2016). Negotiating multiple identities in second- or foreign-language writing in higher education. In C. M. Anson & J. L. Moore (Eds.), *Critical transitions: Writing and the question of transfer* (pp. 303–334). Perspectives on writing. The WAC Clearinghouse and University Press of Colorado.

Cromwell, S. E., & Kolb, J. A. (2004). An examination of work-environment support factors affecting transfer of supervisory skills training to the workplace. *Human Resource Development Quarterly, 15*, 449–471.

Crowley, S. (1998). *Composition in the university: Historical and polemical essays*, University of Pittsburgh Press.

Currie, P. (1993). Entering a disciplinary community: Conceptual activities required to write for one introductory university course. *Journal of Second Language Writing, 2*(2), 101–117.

Dannels, D. P. (2003). Teaching and learning design presentations in engineering contradictions between academic and workplace activity systems. *Journal of Business and Technical Communication, 17*(2), 139–169.

DasBender, G. (2016). Liminal space as a generative site of struggle: Writing transfer and L2 students. In C. M. Anson & J. L. Moore (Eds.), *Critical transitions: Writing and the question of transfer* (pp. 273–298). Perspectives on writing. The WAC Clearinghouse and University Press of Colorado.

Day, S. B., & Goldstone, R. L. (2011). Analogical transfer from a simulated physical system. *Journal of Experimental Psychology: Learning, Memory, and Cognition, 37*(3), 551–567.

Decker, P. J. (1980) Effects of symbolic coding and rehearsal in behavior-modeling training. *Journal of Applied Psychology, 65*(6), 627–634.

DePalma, M. J., & Ringer, J. M. (2011). Toward a theory of adaptive transfer: Expanding disciplinary discussions of "transfer" in second-language writing and composition studies. *Journal of Second Language Writing, 20*(2),134–147.

Devitt, A.J., M. J. Reiff, & A. Bawarshi. (2004). *Scenes of writing: Strategies for composing with genres*. Longman.

Dias, P., Freedman, A., Medway, P., & Paré, A. (1999). *Worlds apart: Acting and writing in academic and workplace contexts*. L. Erlbaum Associates.

Dias, P., & Paré, A. (2000). *Transitions: Writing in academic and workplace settings*. Hampton Press.

Dinitz, S., & Harrington, S. (2014). The role of disciplinary expertise in shaping writing tutorials. *Writing Center Journal, 33*(2), 73–98.

Donahue, C. (2016). Writing and global transfer narratives: Situating the knowledge transformation conversation. In C. M. Anson & J. L. Moore (Eds.), *Critical transitions: Writing and the question of transfer* (pp. 107–136). Perspectives on writing. The WAC Clearinghouse and University Press of Colorado.

Downs, D. & Wardle, E. (2007). Teaching about writing, righting misconceptions: (Re)envisioning "First-Year Composition" as "Introduction to Writing Studies," *College Composition and Communication, 58*(4), 552–584.

Driscoll, D. L. (2015). Building connections and transferring knowledge: The benefits of a peer tutoring course beyond the writing center. *Writing Center Journal, 35*(1), 153–181.

Driscoll, D., & Harcourt, S. (2012). Training vs. learning: Transfer of learning in a peer tutoring course and beyond. *The Writing Lab Newsletter, 36*(7–8), 1–6.

Driscoll, D. L., & Powell, R. (2016). States, traits, and dispositions: The impact of emotion on writing development and writing transfer across college courses and beyond. In *Composition Forum, 34*. https://compositionforum.com/issue/34/states-traits.php

Driscoll, D. L., & Wells, J. (2012). Beyond knowledge and skills: Writing transfer and the role of student dispositions. *Composition Forum, 26*. http://compositionforum.com/issue/26/beyond-knowledge-skills.php

Dyson, A. H. (1999). Transforming transfer: Unruly children, contrary texts, and the persistence of the pedagogical order. *Review of Research in Education, 24(1)*, 141–171.

The Elon statement on writing transfer. (2016). Appendix A in C. M. Anson & J. L. Moore (Eds.), *Critical transitions: Writing and the question of transfer* (pp. 107–136). Perspectives on writing. The WAC Clearinghouse and University Press of Colorado.

Engle, R. A. (2006). Framing interactions to foster generative learning: A situative explanation of transfer in a community of learners classroom. *The Journal of the Learning Sciences, 15*(4), 451–498.

Engle, R. A., Nguyen, P. D., & Mendelson, A. (2011). The influence of framing on transfer: Initial evidence from a tutoring experiment. *Instructional Science, 39*(5), 603–628.

Figueredo, L. (2006). Using the known to chart the unknown: A review of first-language influence on the development of English-as-a-Second-Language spelling skill. *Reading & Writing, 19*(8), 873–905.

Fishman, J. & Reiff, M. J. (2015). Taking the high road: Teaching for transfer in an FYC program. In Reiff M. J., A. Bawarshi, M. Ballif, & C. Weisser (Eds.), *Ecologies of writing programs: Program profiles in context* (pp. 68–90). Parlor Press.

Flower, L., & Hayes, J. R. (1981). A cognitive process theory of writing. *College Composition and Communication, 32*(4), 365–387.

Ford, J. D. (2012). Integrating communication into engineering curricula: An interdisciplinary approach to facilitating transfer at New Mexico Institute of Mining and Technology. *Composition Forum, 26*. http://compositionforum.com/issue/26/new-mexico-tech.php

Fraizer, D. (2010). First steps beyond first year: Coaching transfer after FYC. *Writing Program Administration, 33*(3), 34–57.

Freedman, A., Adam, C., & Smart, G. (1994). Wearing suits to class simulating genres and simulations as genre. *Written Communication, 11*(2), 193–226.

Fyfe, E. R., McNeil, N. M., Son, J. Y., & Goldstone, R. L. (2014). Concreteness fading in mathematics and science instruction: A systematic review. *Educational Psychology Review, 26*(1), 9–25.

Gagne, R. M. (1965). *The conditions of learning.* Holt, Rinehart, and Winston.

Garcia, O., & Wei, L. (2014). *Translanguaging: Language, bilingualism and education.* Palgrave Macmillan.

Gass, S. M., & Selinker, L. (1992). *Language transfer in language learning.* John Benjamins.

Gentner, D., Loewenstein, J., & Thompson, L. (2003). Learning and transfer: A general role for analogical encoding. *Journal of Educational Psychology, 95*(2), 393–408.

Gick, M. L., & Holyoak, K. J. (1980). Analogical problem solving. *Cognitive Psychology, 12*(3), 306–355.

Gick, M. L., & Holyoak, K. J. (1983). Schema induction and analogical transfer. *Cognitive Psychology 15*(1), 1–38.

Gick, M. L., & Holyoak, K.J. (1987). The cognitive basis of knowledge transfer. In S. M. Cormier & J. D. Hagman (Eds.), *Transfer of learning: Contemporary research and applications*, (pp. 9–46). Academic Press.

Gillam, A. M. (1991). Returning students' ways of writing: Implications for first-year college composition. *Journal of Teaching Writing*, *10*(1), 1–20.

Gonzalez, N., Moll, L.C. & Amanti, C. (Eds). (2006). *Funds of knowledge: Theorizing practices in households, communities, and classrooms*. Routledge.

Gort, M. (2006). Strategic codeswitching, interliteracy, and other phenomena of emergent bilingual writing: Lessons from first grade dual language classrooms. *Journal of Early Childhood Literacy*, *6*(3), 323–354.

Griffin, L. L., Brooker, R., & Patton, K. (2005). Working towards legitimacy: Two decades of teaching games for understanding. *Physical Education and Sport Pedagogy*, *10*(3), 213–223.

Grosjean, F. (1989). Neurolinguists, beware! The bilingual is not two monolinguals in one person. *Brain and Language*, *36*, 3–15.

Hagemann, J. (1995). Writing centers as sites for writing transfer research. In B. Stay, C. Murphy, & E. H. Hobson (Eds.), *Writing center perspectives*. National Writing Center Association.

Hall, J. (2006). Toward a unified writing curriculum: Integrating WAC/WID with freshman composition. *The WAC Journal*, *17*, 5–22.

Hammer, D., Elby, A., Scherr, R. E., & Redish, E. F. (2005). Resources, framing, and transfer. In J. P. Mestre (Ed.), *Transfer of learning from a modern multidisciplinary perspective*, (pp. 89–120). Information Age Publishing.

Haskell, R. (2000). *Transfer of learning: Cognition and instruction*. Academic Press.

Hayes, H., Ferris, D. R., & Whithaus, C. (2016). Dynamic transfer in first-year writing and "writing in the disciplines" settings. In C. M. Anson & J. L. Moore (Eds.), *Critical transitions: Writing and the question of transfer* (pp. 181–213). The WAC Clearinghouse/University Press of Colorado.

Heath, S. B. (1982). What no bedtime story means: Narrative skills at home and school. *Language in Society*, *11*(1), 49–76.

Helfenstein, S. (2005). *Transfer: Review, reconstruction, and resolution*. Unpublished doctoral dissertation, University of Jyväskylä.

Herrington, A. J. (1985). Writing in academic settings: A study of the contexts for writing in two college chemical engineering courses. *Research in the Teaching of English*, *19*(4), 331–361.

Hilgers, T. L., Bayer, A. S., Stitt-Bergh, M., & Taniguchi, M. (1995). Doing more than "thinning out the herd": How eighty-two college seniors perceived writing-intensive classes. *Research in the Teaching of English*, *29*(1), 59–87.

Holt, N. L., Strean, W. B., & Bengoechea, E. G. (2002). Expanding the teaching games for understanding. *Journal of Teaching in Physical Education*, *21*(2), 162–176.

Hutchins, E. (1995). *Cognition in the wild*. MIT Press.
James, M. A. (2008). The influence of perceptions of task similarity/difference on learning transfer in second language writing. *Written Communication, 25*(1), 76–103.
Jamieson, S. (2009). The vertical writing curriculum. In J. C. Post & J. A. Inman (Eds.), *Composition(s) in the new liberal arts* (pp. 159–184). Hampton.
Jarratt, S. C., Mack K., Sartor A., & Watson, S. E. (2009). Pedagogical memory: Writing, mapping, translating. *Writing Program Administration, 33*(1–2), 46–73.
Jarvis, S., & A. Pavlenko. (2008). *Crosslinguistic influence in language and cognition*. Routledge.
Johns, A. M. (1990). L1 composition theories: Implications for developing theories of L2 composition. In B. Kroll (Ed.), *Second language writing: Research insights for the classroom* (pp. 24–36). Cambridge University Press.
Johnson, C. (2020). Transfer(mation) in the writing center: Identifying the transformative moments that foster transfer. In B. Devet & D. L. Driscoll (Eds.), *Transfer of learning in the writing center: A* WLN *digital edited collection*. https://wlnjournal.org/digitaleditedcollection2/
Johnstone, B. (1996). The *linguistic individual: Self-expression in language and linguistics*. Oxford University Press.
Judd, C. H. (1908). The relation of special training and general intelligence. *Educational Review, 36*, 28–42.
Kahneman, D. (1973). *Attention and effort*. Prentice-Hall.
Kahneman, D. (2003). A perspective on judgment and choice: mapping bounded rationality. *American Psychologist, 58*(9), 697–720.
Kahneman, D. (2011). *Thinking, fast and slow*. Farrar, Straus and Giroux
Kaminski, J. A., Sloutsky, V. M., & Heckler, A. F. (2008). The advantage of abstract examples in learning math. *Science, 320*(25), 454–455.
Kaminski, J. A., Sloutsky, V. M., & Heckler, A. F. (2013). The cost of concreteness: The effect of nonessential information on analogical transfer. *Journal of Experimental Psychology: Applied, 19*(1), 14–29.
Katona, G. (1940). *Organizing and memorizing: Studies in the psychology of learning and teaching*. Columbia University Press.
Keith, N., & Frese, M. (2005). Self-regulation in error management training: Emotion control and metacognition as mediators of performance effects. *Journal of Applied Psychology, 90*(4), 677–691.
Kobayashi, H., & Rinnert, C. (2008). Task response and text construction across L1 and L2 writing. *Journal of Second Language Writing, 17*(1), 7–29.
Kubota, R. (1998). An investigation of L1-L2 transfer in writing among Japanese university students: Implications for contrastive rhetoric. *Journal of Second Language Writing, 7*(1), 69–100.
Larsen-Freeman, D. (1997). Chaos/complexity science and second language acquisition. *Applied Linguistics, 18*(2), 141–165.

Larsen-Freeman, D. (2013). Transfer of learning transformed. *Language Learning, 63*(1), 107–29.

Larsen-Freeman, D., & Cameron, L. (2008). Research methodology on language development from a complex theory perspective. *Modern Language Journal, 92*(2), 200–213.

Lave, J. (1988). *Cognition in practice: Mind, mathematics and culture in everyday life.* Cambridge University Press.

Lave, J., & Wenger, E. (1991). *Situated learning: Legitimate peripheral participation.* Cambridge University Press.

Leki, I. (1995). Coping strategies of ESL students in writing tasks across the curriculum. *TESOL Quarterly, 29*(2), 235-260.

Leki, I., & Carson, J. G. (1994). Students' perceptions of EAP writing instruction and writing needs across disciplines. *TESOL Quarterly, 28*(1), 81–101.

LeMesurier, J. L. (2016). Mobile bodies: Triggering bodily uptake through movement. *College Composition and Communication, 68*(2), 292–316.

Lemke, J. L. (2000). Across the scales of time: Artifacts, activities, and meanings in ecosocial systems. *Mind, Culture, and Activity, 7*(4), 273–290.

Lettner-Rust, H. G., Tracy, P. J., Booker, S. L., Kocevar-Weidinger, E., & Berges, J. B. (2007). Writing beyond the curriculum: Transition, transfer, and transformation. *Across the Disciplines, 4.* https://wac.colostate.edu/atd/archives/volume4/

Light, R., & Fawns, R. (2003). Knowing the game: Integrating speech and action in games teaching through TGfU. *Quest, 55*(2), 161–176.

Lindenman, H. (2015) Inventing metagenres: How four college seniors connect writing across domains. *Composition Forum, 31(*Spring), http://compositionforum.com/issue/31/inventing-metagenres.php

Lobato, J. (2012). The actor-oriented transfer perspective and its contributions to educational research and practice. *Educational Psychologist, 47*(3), 232–247.

Lobato, J., Rhodehamel, B., & Hohensee, C. (2012). "Noticing" as an alternative transfer of learning process. *Journal of the Learning Sciences, 21*(3), 433–482.

López, L. M. G., Jordán, O. R. C., Penney, D., & Chandle, T. (2009). The role of transfer in games teaching: Implications for the development of the sports curriculum. *European Physical Education Review, 15*(1), 47–63.

Maran, N., & Glavin, R. (2003). Low- to high-fidelity simulation—a continuum of medical education? *Medical Education, 37*(s1), 22–28.

Martin, L., & Schwartz, D. L. (2013). Conceptual innovation and transfer. In S. Vosniadou (Ed.), *International handbook of research on conceptual change.* (2nd ed., pp. 447–465). Routledge.

Matsuda, P. K. (1997). Contrastive rhetoric in context: A dynamic model of L2 writing. *Journal of Second Language Writing, 6*(1), 45–60.

Matsuda, P. K. (2015). Identity in written discourse. *Annual Review of Applied Linguistics, 35*, 140–159.

Melzer, D. (2014). The connected curriculum: Designing a vertical transfer writing curriculum. *The WAC Journal, 25*, 78–91.

Menary, R. (2010). Introduction to the special issue on 4E cognition. *Phenomenology and the Cognitive Sciences, 9*(4), 459–463.

Michaud, M. J. (2011). The "reverse commute": Adult students and the transition from professional to academic literacy. *Teaching English in the Two-Year College, 38*(3), 244–258.

Middendorf, J., & Pace, D. (2004), Decoding the disciplines: A model for helping students learn disciplinary ways of thinking. *New Directions for Teaching and Learning, 2004*(98), 1–12.

Miles, L., Pennell, M., Owens, K. H., Dyehouse, J., O'Grady, H., Reynolds, N., Schweger R. & Shamoon, L. (2008). Commenting on Douglas Downs and Elizabeth Wardle's "Teaching about writing, righting misconceptions." *College Composition and Communication, 59*(3), 503–511.

Navarre Cleary, M. (2013). Flowing and freestyling: Learning from adult students about process knowledge transfer. *College Composition and Communication, 64*(4), 661–687.

Negretti, R., & Kuteeva, M. (2011). Fostering metacognitive genre awareness in L2 academic reading and writing: A case study of pre-service English teachers. *Journal of Second Language Writing, 20*(2), 95–110.

Nelms, R. G, & Dively, R. L. (2007). Perceived roadblocks to transferring knowledge from first-year composition to writing-intensive major courses: A pilot study. *WPA: Writing Program Administration, 31*(1), 214–240.

Nemirovsky, R. (2011). Episodic feelings and transfer of learning. *The Journal of the Learning Sciences, 20*(2), 308–337.

Nonaka, I. (1994). A dynamic theory of organizational knowledge creation. *Organization Science, 5*(1), 14–37.

Norman, G., Dore, K., & Grierson, L. (2012). The minimal relationship between simulation fidelity and transfer of learning. *Medical Education, 46*(7), 636–647.

Norton, B. (2000). *Identity and language learning: Gender, ethnicity and educational change.* Longman/Pearson Education.

Nowacek, R. S. (2011) *Agents of integration: Understanding transfer as a rhetorical act.* Southern Illinois University Press.

Nowacek, R. S., Bodee, B., Douglas, J., Fitzsimmons, W., Hausladen, K., Knowles, M., & Nugent, M. (2019). "Transfer talk" in talk about writing in progress: Two propositions about transfer of learning. *Composition Forum,* 42. https://compositionforum.com/issue/42/transfer-talk.php

Pavlenko, A. (2000). L2 influence on L1 in late bilingualism. *Issues in Applied Linguistics, 11*(2), 175–205.

Pavlenko, A., & Jarvis, S. (2002). Bidirectional transfer. *Applied Linguistics*, 23(2), 190–214.

Perkins, D.N., & Salomon, G. (1988). Teaching for transfer. *Educational Leadership*, 46(1), 22–32.

Perkins, D.N., & Salomon, G. (1989). Are cognitive skills context bound? *Educational Researcher*, 18(1), 16–25.

Perkins, D. N., & Salomon, G. (2012). Knowledge to go: A motivational and dispositional view of transfer. *Educational Psychologist*, 47(3), 248–258.

Pescuric, A., & Byham, W. C. (1996). The new look of behavior modeling. *Training & Development*, 50(7), 24–31.

Petraglia, J. (Ed.). (1995). *Reconceiving writing, rethinking writing instruction*. Lawrence Erlbaum.

Polya, G. (1945 / 1957). *How to solve it: A new aspect of mathematical method* (2nd ed.). Princeton University Press.

Pouw, W. T., Van Gog, T., & Paas, F. (2014). An embedded and embodied cognition review of instructional manipulatives. *Educational Psychology Review*, 26(1), 51–72.

Prior. P. (2018). How do moments add up to lives? Trajectories of semiotic becoming vs. tales of school learning in four modes. In R. Wysocki and M. Sheridan (Eds.), *Making Future Matters*. Utah State Press/Computers and Composition Digital Press. http://ccdigitalpress.org/book/makingfuturematters/

Prior, PA, & Olinger, A.(2019). Academic literacies as laminated assemblage and embodied semiotic becoming. In D. Bloome, L. Castanheira, C. Leung, & J. Rowsell (Eds.), *Retheorizing literacy practices: Complex social and cultural contexts* (pp. 126–139). Routledge.

Prior, P. A., & Shipka, J. (2003). Chronotopic lamination: Tracing the contours of literate activity. In C. Bazerman, & D. Russell (Eds.), *Writing selves, writing societies: Research from activity perspectives* (pp. 180–238). Perspectives on Writing. The WAC Clearinghouse and Mind, Culture, and Activity.

Reed, S. K., Ernst, G. W., & Banerji, R. (1974). The role of analogy in transfer between similar problem states. *Cognitive Psychology*, 6(3), 436–450.

Reiff, M. J., & Bawarshi, A. (2011). Tracing discursive resources: How students use prior genre knowledge to negotiate new writing contexts in first-year composition. *Written Communication*, 28(3), 312–337.

Robertson, L., Taczak, K., & Yancey, K. B. (2012). Notes toward a theory of prior knowledge and its role in college composers' transfer of knowledge and practice. *Composition Forum*, 26. http://compositionforum.com/issue/26/prior-knowledge-transfer.php

Robinson, A., & Mania, K. (2007). Technological research challenges of flight simulation and flight instructor assessments of perceived fidelity. *Simulation & Gaming*, 38(1), 112–135.

Rouiller, J. Z., & Goldstein, I. L. (1993). The relationship between organizational transfer climate and positive transfer of training. *Human Resource Development Quarterly*, *4*(4), 377–390.

Rounsaville, A., Goldberg, R., & Bawarshi, A. (2008). From incomes to outcomes: FYW students' prior genre knowledge, meta-cognition, and the question of transfer. *Writing Program Administration*, *32*(1), 97–112.

Russell, D. (1995). Activity theory and its implications for writing instruction. In J. Petraglia (Ed.), *Reconceiving writing, rethinking writing instruction* (pp. 51–78) Lawrence Erlbaum.

Schwartz, D. L., & Martin, T. (2004). Inventing to prepare for future learning: The hidden efficiency of encouraging original student production in statistics instruction. *Cognition and Instruction*, *22*(2), 129–184.

Selinker, L. (1969). Language transfer. *General Linguistics 9*(2), 67–92.

Selinker, L. (1972). Interlanguage. *IRAL—International Review of Applied Linguistics in Language Teaching*, *10*, 209–231.

Sersen, W. J. (2011). Improving writing skills of Thai EFL students by recognition of and compensation for factors of L1 to L2 negative transfer. *US-China Education Review A*(3), 339–345.

Sharwood-Smith, M., & E. Kellerman. (1986). "Crosslinguistic influence in second language acquisition: An introduction." In M. S. Smith & E. Kellerman (Eds.), *Crosslinguistic influence in second language acquisition* (pp. 1–9). Pergamon.

Shiffrin, R. M., & Schneider, W. (1977). Controlled and automatic human information processing: II. Perceptual learning, automatic attending and a general theory. *Psychological Review*, *84*(2), 127–190.

Smart, G. & Brown, N. (2002). Learning transfer or transforming learning? Student interns reinventing expert writing practices in the workplace. *Technostyle*, *18*(1), 117–141.

Smit, D. W. (2004). *The end of composition studies*. Southern Illinois University Press.

Sommers, N., & Saltz, L. (2004) The novice as expert: Writing the freshman year. *College Composition and Communication*, *56*(1), 124–149.

Spack, R. (1988). Initiating students into the academic discourse community: How far should we go? *TESOL Quarterly*, *22*(1), 29–51.

Spinuzzi, C. (1996). Pseudotransactionality, activity theory, and professional writing instruction. *Technical Communication Quarterly*, *5*(3), 295–308.

Swales, J. M. (1984). Research into the structure of introductions to journal articles and its application to the teaching of academic writing. In R. Williams, J. Swales, & J. Kirkman (Eds.), *Common Ground: Shared Interests in ESP and Communication Studies* (pp. 77–86). Pergamon.

Swales, J. M. (1990). *Genre analysis: English in academic and research settings*. Cambridge University Press.

Thorndike, E. L. (1906 / 1916). *The principles of teaching based on psychology*. AG Seiler.

Thorpe, R., Bunker, D., & Almond, L. (1984). A change in focus for the teaching of games. In *Sport Pedagogy: Olympic Scientific Congress proceedings* (Vol. 6, pp. 163–169).

Tuomi-Gröhn, T., & Engeström, Y. (2003). Conceptualizing transfer: From standard notions to developmental perspectives. In T. Tuomi-Gröhn & Y. Engeström (Eds.), *Between school and work: New perspectives on transfer and boundary-crossing*, (pp. 19–38). Emerald Group.

Tuomi-Gröhn, T., Engeström, Y., & Young, M. (2003). From transfer to boundary crossing between school and work as a tool for developing vocational education: An introduction. In T. Tuomi-Gröhn & Y. Engeström (Eds.), *Between school and work: New perspectives on transfer and boundary crossing* (pp. 1–18). Pergamon.

Walker, K. (1998). The debate over generalist and specialist tutors: Genre theory's contribution. *The Writing Center Journal, 18*(2), 27–45.

Walsh, J. P., & Ungson, G. R. (1991). Organizational memory. *Academy of Management Review, 16*(1), 57–91.

Walvoord, B. E., & McCarthy, L. P. (1990). *Thinking and writing in college: A naturalistic study of students in four disciplines*. The WAC Clearinghouse and National Council of Teachers of English.

Wardle, E. (2009). "Mutt genres" and the goal of FYC: Can we help students write the genres of the university? *College Composition & Communication, 60*(4), 765–789.

Wardle, E. (2012). Creative repurposing for expansive learning: Considering "problem-exploring" and "answer-getting" dispositions in individuals and fields. *Composition Forum, 26*. http://compositionforum.com/issue/26/creative-repurposing.php

Wegner, D. M., Giuliano, T., & Hertel, P. T. (1985). Cognitive interdependence in close relationships. In Wegner, D. M., Giuliano, T., & Hertel, P. T. (Eds.), *Compatible and incompatible relationships* (pp. 253–276). Springer.

Weinreich, U. (1953) *Languages in contact*. The Hague: Mouton.

Werner, P., & Almond, L. (1990). Models of games education. *Journal of Physical Education, Recreation & Dance, 61*(4), 23–30.

White, S. (2015). "I stopped writing for myself": Student perspectives on service-learning in composition. Unpublished dissertation, University of Wisconsin Madison.

Yancey, K. B., Robertson, L., & Taczak, K. (2014). *Writing across contexts: Transfer, composition, and sites of writing*. Utah State University Press.

Index

4E cognition, 46, 357, 367, 379, 422

absorptive capacity, 74
abstract schema, 9–11, 26–28, 30, 32, 43, 61, 171, 193–194, 321–323
abstraction, 6, 23, 28, 32–34, 40, 96, 138, 173, 176, 194–195, 208, 279, 322, 325–326, 334
action discussion reflective cycle, 94
activated resources, 335
actor-oriented theory (AOT), 8, 12, 20, 23, 37–38, 42, 46, 318, 356, 363, 372, 379, 395, 421
Adam, Christine, 292, 295–296, 299, 389
adaptive expertise, 33, 287
adaptive remediation, 192, 257
adaptive transfer, 7, 44, 155–156, 160–161, 201, 257, 297, 310, 341, 352, 386, 417
Adler-Kassner, Linda, 62, 170, 194, 210, 213, 222
adult learning, 19, 273, 291, 305
Adult Math Project, 35
agency, 9–10, 16, 50, 80, 115, 122, 124–125, 128, 132, 143, 155–156, 192, 200, 212, 281, 316, 317–318, 326, 386
Agents of Integration, 221, 246, 251, 318, 398
Ahrenhoerster, Greg, 210, 213
Alexander, Kara Poe, 72, 101, 189–190, 192–193, 251, 257–258, 297–298, 328, 342, 407, 413
alphabetic text, 188–189
amplitude, 6
analogical encoding, 30, 43, 45, 61, 82, 354, 418
analogical encoding (theory of), 30
analogical reasoning, 5–8, 13, 23, 26–28, 37, 71, 177, 284, 303
analogy, 5, 26, 28, 30, 47, 423
Angeli, Elizabeth, xiii, 72
Anson, Chris, 32, 279, 282–283, 298, 307, 329, 382, 405
answer-getting dispositions, 58, 185
antecedent genres, 174–175, 275, 303
apprenticeship, 99, 211, 274–275, 299, 387
Archive of Workplace Writing Experiences, 307, 309
Aristotle, 4
Artemeva, Natasha, 176, 200, 281, 288, 309, 388

assimilation, 150
attention, 13, 23, 32, 34–35, 60, 97, 99, 102,136, 193, 224, 242, 256, 299, 323, 332
audience, 142–143, 149, 161, 169, 190–191, 196, 213–214, 216–217, 222–223, 247, 278, 280, 292, 329
automatic detection, 34
automaticity, 9, 11, 15, 32, 34, 42, 96, 97, 102, 321, 325–326, 364
autonomous model of literacy, 169, 399
aviation education, 10, 15, 22, 88–89, 100, 102, 104–105, 315, 320, 325–326, 328–329, 364, 367–368, 399
awareness, 16, 40–42, 88, 89–93, 95, 105, 132, 138–139, 144, 147, 149, 170–173, 176, 181, 184–185, 192–197, 211, 214, 220–222, 224–228, 230, 245, 253, 256, 261, 263, 276, 278, 321, 324–327, 347, 349, 364, 384, 392, 401

Bacon, Nora, 296, 297, 319, 403
Baird, Neil, 7, 51, 54, 58–59, 185, 193, 222, 301, 319, 403
Bakhtin, Mikhail, 154, 342
Baldwin, Timothy, 51–52, 56, 59, 60, 62, 65, 68, 332, 368, 375, 383, 406
Bandura, Albert, 50–51, 54–55, 60, 79, 317, 319, 332, 351, 373–374, 376, 383, 403, 415
Bank of Canada, 283, 388
Barron, Nancy, 264, 334, 340
Bawarshi, Anis, xiii, 32, 143, 148–149, 170, 175–176, 184, 187, 193, 195–196, 208, 224, 226, 248, 261, 319, 338, 364, 384, 399, 403, 407

Bazerman, Charles, xiii, 121, 170, 193, 195, 226, 228, 234, 288,
Beach, King, 24, 35, 43, 168, 179, 200, 289, 301, 309, 365, 366, 368, 374, 400, 407
Beaufort, Anne, 3,32, 57, 64, 170–171, 173, 193–195, 198, 208, 210, 218, 220, 221–222, 225, 227, 280–281, 282, 301, 307, 322, 325, 338–339, 347, 383, 404, 407,; *College Writing and Beyond*, 3, 194
Behavior Modeling Training (BMT), 60–61
behavioral modeling, 60, 62
behaviorism, 7, 13, 22–24, 34, 50, 89–90, 272, 324, 328, 374, 394
Bergmann, Linda, 3, 183–184, 187, 193, 210, 217, 222, 233, 333, 337,
Berman, Robert, 137–138, 140, 343, 383, 392
Big Five Personality Traits, 53
biliteracy, 117, 129, 151, 160–161
biliterate, 141, 164
Bioecological Model of Human Development, 185
Bird, Barbara: Next Steps; New Directions for/in Writing about Writing, 170, 197
Bizzell, Patricia, 209, 233, 344, 386, 408
Blume, Brian D., 55–56, 65, 373
Boone, Stephanie, 208, 209, 229–230, 232
bottlenecks, 235, 333, 396
boundary: crossers, 176, 184, 261, 319, 364, 384, 399; encounters, 289; guarders, 176, 184, 364, 399; objects, 75, 289–290, 308, 364–365, 380, 401; spanners, 7, 290; zones, 289
Bourelle, Tiffany, 298, 300

Index

Bowen, Lauren Marshall, 251–253
Brandt, Deborah, 106, 115–116, 121–122, 126, 288, 304–307, 317, 349, 403; *Literacy in American Lives*, 115; *The Rise of Writing*, 106
Bransford, John D., 12, 36, 255, 322, 324, 335, 337, 372, 388
Brent, Doug, 278–279, 319, 403
Bromley, Pam, 42, 54, 242, 259, 261–262, 384
Bronfenbrenner, Urie, 121, 185–186, 188, 288, 319
Brown, Travor C., 55, 71, 301–302, 341, 373, 388, 418
Bruffee, Kenneth, 244, 253, 258–259, 262–263, 384, 391
Bunker, David, 90, 322, 404
Burke, Michael J., 60–61, 66, 67, 79
Busekrus, Elizabeth, 242, 249

Campbell, Lillian, xiii, 104–105, 294
campus writing cultures, 222
Canagarajah, Suresh, 141–143, 156
capacity model, 34
Cardinal, Jody, 252, 257
Carillo, Ellen C., 53, 181
Carlile, Paul R., 75, 365
Carolina Piedmont communities, 113
Carraher, Terezinha Nunes, 36, 368, 405
Carroll, Lee Ann, 4, 208, 210, 218, 334
Carson, Joan, 137–138, 142–143, 145–146, 152, 343, 392, 405
Carter, Michael, 144,169–170, 210–211, 222–226, 228, 230–231, 370, 385
categorization, 6
causal ambiguity, 74

charting, 193, 257, 294
CHAT methodologies, 346
Chiaburu, Dan S., 55, 57–58, 66–67, 187
Chiseri-Strater, Elizabeth, 4, 208, 210, 218
Choi, Bernard C. K., 4, 6
chronotope, 293, 342
chronotopic lamination, 12, 20, 120, 128, 286, 313, 342, 358, 423
Clark, Andy, 72, 170, 194, 196, 226–227, 248, 252, 256, 404
classification, 92, 94
client-based projects, 294
cognitive dissonance, 258, 276, 294
cognitive interdependence, 72–73, 374
cognitive load, 13, 34, 98, 102, 132, 367, 397
cognitive psychology, xii, 22, 69, 71, 76, 91, 169, 173, 177, 194, 202, 209, 279, 284, 315, 322, 363, 365
cognitive theories of writing, 169
cognitivist studies, 35, 37
Colquitt, Jason A., 55, 58, 65, 67, 385
Comparative Genre Analysis (CGA), 223
computer-assisted instruction, 99
computer-based simulations, 99
concepts, 5, 13, 16–17, 23, 26, 31, 36, 39, 71, 95, 184, 220, 223, 231– 232, 234, 251–252, 258, 331–332, 336, 345, 365, 376, 387, 396
conceptual anchors, 198
concreteness fading, 40, 330
concurrent contexts, 9, 12, 341–342

Conference on College Composition and Communication (CCCC), 3–4, 47, 269, 361
conscientiousness, 53–54, 319
consequential transitions, 7, 35, 179, 361, 366, 400
context fidelity, 12, 374
contexts of activity, 182
contrastive meaning, 8
controlled search, 34
Cook, Vivian J., 134–136, 141, 157, 340, 344, 408
Cozart, Stacey M., 131, 138, 152, 154–155, 317, 343
critical incidents, 62, 177–179
Cromwell, Susan E., 65–67, 333, 375,
Cronon, William, 262, 263, 391
cross-disciplinary transfer, 228, 238
cross-linguistic influence, 12, 134–135, 340
cultural historical activity theory, 18, 77, 272, 277, 288, 290, 308, 346
cultural modeling, 123–124, 127
Cultural Modeling Project, 123
cultural multiplicity, 132, 153
Currie, Pat, 143–144, 173, 327, 405
Curtis, Marcia, 208, 210, 218–219, 220, 222

dancers, 320
Dannels, Deanna, 295–296, 310
Dartmouth College, 232
DasBender, Gita, 131–132, 138–139, 404
Davis, Matthew, 83, 191, 201, 232, 251–253
Day, Samuel B., 41–43, 61, 320, 348, 368, 372, 403
Decker, Phillip J., 61–62, 406
declarative knowledge, 58, 95, 172

DePalma, Michael-John, 42, 155–156, 189–190, 192–193, 297–298, 307, 341, 386, 407–408, 411,
detect-elect-connect model, 255
Devitt, Amy J., 170, 172, 174–176, 194–195, 226–227, 248, 256, 332, 406; *Scenes of Writing: Strategies for Composing with Genres*, 195
Devos, Christelle, 56, 66–68, 390
dialogue, 94, 103, 154, 261, 315, 323, 331
Dias, Patrick, 282–283, 287317, 342, 387–388, 403, 408
digital ecosystems, 191
digital transfer, 190–191
Dilger, Bradley, 7, 51, 54, 58–59, 185, 193, 222, 301, 319, 403
dimensionality, 97, 103, 187, 341, 343
Dinitz, Sue, 243, 245–249, 263,, 340, 408
direct observation, 103
directionality, 9, 12, 17, 19, 209, 315–316, 334, 340, 345
disciplinary writing, 129, 144–145, 196, 204, 208, 210–211, 213–214, 216–217, 219, 220–223, 225, 226, 229, 235, 240, 244, 249, 258, 270, 394
dispersion solution, 27–30
dispositional traits, 319, 366
dispositions, 14, 16, 49, 51–53, 57, 59, 64, 77, 122, 182–183, 185–188, 193, 199, 222, 242, 250–252, 259, 261, 264, 266,, 288–289, 297–298, 301–303, 316, 318–319, 349,367384, 387–388, 403
distractor problems, 37

distributed cognition, 72–73, 77, 80, 283, 302, 308, 312, 321, 367, 372, 374, 387, 391
Dively, Ronda Leathers, 3, 32, 184, 222–223, 225, 252, 404
document cycling, 275, 283
Donahue, Christiane, 35, 42, 131, 157, 234, 318, 325, 349, 364, 403, 404
double bind, 153
double transfer study, 37
Downs, Douglas, 43, 65, 170, 180, 183, 194, 196, 208, 229, 235, 291, 317, 338, 404, 407
Driscoll, Dana Lynn, 4, 32, 37, 42, 51, 54, 56–59, 63, 65, 74, 77, 168, 182–186, 193, 242–243, 252, 254–255, 258, 297, 319, 335, 347, 367, 372, 388, 403, 406
dual processing theory, 23, 31, 71, 346
Dweck, Carol S., 58, 369, 389
dynamic systems theory, 135
dynamism, 9, 343–344
Dyson, Anne Haas, 118–119, 124, 406, 407

Elon University: Research Seminar, 307; Seminar on Critical Transitions, 3; Statement on Writing Transfer, 155, 407
embodied cognition, 9–10, 14–15, 39, 40, 47, 88–89, 91–92, 94, 96, 104–106, 183, 188, 320–321, 333, 346, 358, 367, 374, 423
emotions, 16, 56, 63, 74, 182–183, 186–188, 193
emulation, 154
Engeström, Yrjö, 18, 77, 124, 168, 272, 276, 289, 300, 316, 363–365, 367–368, 400, 405

engineering, 97, 102, 214, 220, 223, 230–231, 238, 244, 246, 256, 269, 278–281, 290–291, 293, 296, 303, 310–311, 352, 355, 383, 388, 397, 416, 418–419
Engle, Randi, 38, 178–179, 323, 335–336, 368, 404, 406
English as a Foreign Language (EFL) students, 138, 165, 383, 424
English as a Second Language (ESL), 138, 143–146, 148, 152–153, 159–161, 163, 165–166, 173, 391–393, 421
English for Academic Purposes (EAP), 143–148, 154, 161, 163, 165, 223, 421
English for Specific Purposes (ESP), 149, 159, 165, 223, 424
entrance exams, 140
ephemerality, 19, 316, 347–348, 350
episodic feelings, 40, 321
Eraut, Michael, 284–285
Erickson, Joe, 119, 189, 191
error avoidant, 63
error management, 52, 59–60, 62–63, 78, 83–84, 324, 355–356, 373, 378, 420
ethnography, 72, 103, 113, 119–121, 148, 150, 153, 189, 220, 266, 339, 367, 383, 391
executive intelligence, 90
expansive framing, 38, 323
expansive learning, 7, 87, 124, 205, 270, 289, 300–301, 361, 368, 400, 425
expert outsider, 248
explicit instruction, 10, 95, 140, 144, 149–150, 184, 189, 194, 196, 212, 221–222, 227, 232,

265, 274, 284–285, 311, 322, 392, 395
explicit knowledge, 5–6, 70, 71, 76, 123, 325, 397

facilitated performance, 299
fading, 40, 45, 99, 330–331, 354, 418
Fallon, Dianne, 210, 213, 222
Fawns, Rod, 90, 91, 173, 320, 346, 348, 394, 403, 405
fidelity, 9, 11, 19, 60, 88–89, 96–106, 108, 109, 122, 188, 292, 300, 305, 315–316, 326–333, 343, 345, 348, 350, 357–359, 368, 395, 397–400, 413, 421–423
Figueredo, L., 138, 322, 404
first-year composition, 20, 46–47, 175, 202–204, 220, 239–240, 269–270, 359, 380, 383, 399, 422, 423
first-year writing (FYW), 3, 16–18, 43, 45, 60, 65, 67, 92, 94, 139, 143–144, 165, 167–178, 180–187, 193–196, 207, 210, 213–214, 217–218, 222–224, 227–228, 231–236, 238, 240, 272, 280, 291, 297, 323, 332–333, 336–338, 354, 359, 369, 374, 398–399, 403–407
Fisher, David, 293–294, 313
fixity, 115
flight education, 100
Flower, Linda S., 4, 32, 180–181, 230, 404
fluidity, 115, 344, 349
Foertsch, Julie, 169–170
formal discipline theory, 23
Fraizer, Dan, 173, 222–223, 225–228, 404
Framework for Success in Postsecondary Writing (Roen, et al.), 52–53

framing, 20, 38, 39, 45, 52, 72, 177–178, 195, 202, 263, 335–336, 353–354, 372, 418–419
Freedman, Aviva, 226, 284–285, 292–293, 295–296, 299, 329, 387, 389, 405
Frese, Michael, 62–63, 348, 373
friction, 115
funds of knowledge paradigm, 117

Gagné, Robert M., 50, 232, 395, 409
Game Performance Assessment Instrument, 94
game play, 90, 94, 96, 104, 173
general education, 148, 213, 221, 228, 232, 254–255, 313, 388, 396,
general heuristics, 31, 171, 279, 323
general knowledge, 170, 172–173, 180, 258
general principles, 36, 50, 321
generalization, 7, 10, 52, 62, 170, 173, 226, 324, 332, 366, 368, 375, 377
generalized writing knowledge, 225, 251
generalized writing skills instruction (GWSI), 168–169, 172, 208, 369
genre: acquisition, 149; analysis, 147–148, 150, 173, 176, 194–195, 227, 252, 256, 401; awareness, 94, 149, 176, 181, 194, 196, 199, 227; knowledge, 116, 147, 150–152, 171, 174–177, 179, 184, 220, 226–227, 242, 247, 256, 281, 284, 294, 303, 364, 380, 383, ; theory, 149, 156, 172, 227, 248, 254, 290
genre-based writing instruction (GBWI), 132, 147, 149–150
Gentil, Guillaume, 147, 151–152

Index

Gentner, Dedre, 27, 30, 43, 331–332, 406
Gestalt theorists, 25, 321, 368
Gick, Mary L., 26,–28, 30, 33, 38, 43, 75, 284, 328, 331–332, 336, 363, 365, 387, 389, 404, 405, 406
Giddens, Anthony, 346
Gilje, Øystein, 210, 21
Gillam, Alice M., 303–304, 338, 407
Giordano, Joan Baird, 177–178
Gist, Marilyn E., 54–55, 58, 61, 64, 373, 390
Glavin, Ronnie, 97, 99, 102, 326, 329, 395, 405,
globalization, 125, 146
Globerson, Tamar, 33
goal orientation, 14, 52, 58–59, 80, 82–83, 355, 369, 377, 389
Gogan, Brian, 181
Goldschmidt, Mary, 226, 228
Goldstein, Irwin L., 65, 67, 333, 406
Goldstone, Robert L., 40–43, 320, 348, 368, 372, 403
Gonzalez, Norma, 116–117, 122, 125, 396, 406
Gort, Mileidis, 139, 141, 152, 408
Gorzelsky, Gwen, 42, 324, 370, 374, 388
Graff, Nelson, 198, 226, 234
Grauman, Jillian, 252, 258, 260–261
Griffin, Linda L., 91, 405
Grimm, Nancy, 264, 334, 340
Grujicic-Alatriste, Lubie, 156

Haas, Christina, 74, 83, 105, 180–181
habits of mind, 52–53, 193, 278
Hagemann, Julie, 242, 260, 408
Hahn, Scott, 252
Hall, R. Mark, 250, 337

Hammer, David, 13, 25, 36, 38, 178, 331, 335–336, 345, 406, 408
Hanlon-Baker, Patti, 249, 250
Hannah, Mark A., 179–180, 193,
haptic methodologies, 104
haptic sensors, 103
Harcourt, Sarah, 242, 252, 254–255, 335, 406
Hargadon, Andrew B., 5–6, 75–76, 365
Harklau, Linda, 153
Harrington, Susanmarie, 245, 247–249, 340, 408
Harvard Study of Undergraduate Writing, 219
Head Start Program, 114, 128
Heath, Shirley Brice, 112–113, 339, 407
Herrington, Anne J., 208, 218–219, 220, 222, 329, 405
heterochrony, 13, 285, 342
heuristics, 13, 26, 31, 177, 192, 194, 323
high fidelity, 11, 97, 101, 328, 329, 397, 399, 400
Hilgers, Thomas L., 215–216, 222, 407
Hill, Heather N., 242, 252–254, 256
hints, 28–29, 38, 322, 336
Holton, Elwood F., 55, 66–68, 375, 390
Holyoak, Keith J., 26–28, 30, 33, 38, 43, 75, 328, 331–332, 336, 363, 365, 387, 389, 404–406
Homklin, Tassanee, 66–67
How People Learn: Mind, Brain, Experiences, and School (Bransford et al.), 324, 337
Hughes, Bradley, 243, 248, 255, 258, 262–263, 264, 390, 391

human resources, 14, 49, 68–69, 76, 77, 315, 328, 333, 375, 383
Hyland, Ken, 147–149
Hyon, Sunny, 147, 149

identical elements (theory of), 7, 13, 24, 25, 60
identical elements theory, 24–25, 50, 60, 100, 101, 273, 328, 369
imitatio, 50
in- and out-of-school literacy, 112, 114, 119, 121, 339
inclusive meaning, 8
individuality, 9, 19, 150, 224, 315–316, 320, 345, 348
industrial-organizational (I/O) psychology, 5, 14, 49, 50–54, 56–59, 64, 65–66, 77, 171, 298, 315, 324, 332
Institute for Writing and Rhetoric at Dartmouth, 232
institutional affordances, 171
intentionality, 9, 11, 16, 19, 130, 132, 222, 315–316, 321, 323–324, 345, 348
interactional strategies, 142
intercontextuality, 38, 336
Interdependence, 345-347
interference, 13, 131, 134–135, 139, 141–142, 146, 153, 179, 326, 339–340, 345, 369-371, 393
interliteracy, 141
International Writing Across the Curriculum Association (IWAC), 3
International Writing Center Association (IWCA), 3
internships, 19, 57, 79, 88, 185, 236, 273, 279, 284, 291, 298–302, 305, 307, 329–330, 382
interpersonal act, 14
intertextuality, 119, 154
inventorying, 193, 257

isomorphic problem, 23, 26

James, Mark Andrew, 132, 143, 146, 203, 333, 366, 391–392, 406
Jarratt, Susan C., 178, 180, 338, 404, 407
Jarvis, Scott, 134, 340, 408
Jesson, Rebecca, 152, 154
Job Resource Center (JRC), 282
Johns, Ann M., 137, 143–144, 147–150, 154, 158–160, 173, 256, 405
Johnson, Cynthia, 341, 355, 407
Johnson, J. Paul, 198, 210, 213–214, 222
Johnson, Scott D., 65–67
Journal of Second Language Writing, 148
Judd, Charles Hubbard, 24–25, 29, 321, 368, 387, 404
Judge, Timothy A., 54–55

Kahneman, Daniel, 33–35, 43, 324–326, 364, 404; *Thinking, Fast and Slow*, 34
Kain, Donna, 32, 248, 291
Katona, George, 25, 321, 368, 404
Keith, Nina, 62–63, 324, 348, 373, 404
Kell, Cathy, 121, 212
Keller, Daniel, 175, 180–181, 193,
Kellerman, Eric, 134, 340, 408
Kendall, Laura N., 56, 373
Kenzie, Daniel P., 244, 251–252, 256, 259
keystroke-logging, 104
Kiedaisch, Jean, 243, 245–248, 263
knowledge: brokering, 75; creation, 70–71, 76, 397; spiral, 70
knowledge management (KM), 11, 14, 50, 69, 72, 77–78, 308,

Index

325, 365, 372, 375, 391, 397, 400-402
Kobayashi, Hiroe, 135, 137–138, 140–142, 343, 392, 408
Kohn, Liberty L., 245, 248, 252, 256, 300,
koina topoi, 4, 31
Kubota, Ryuko, 137–140, 343, 393, 408

L1 literacy, 133–135, 137–140, 142, 147, 151, 154–155, 157, 317, 340, 343, 371, 383, 392–39
L1–L2 relationships, 135
L2 literacy, 16, 130–134, 136–137, 139–140, 143, 147–148, 150, 152–158, 199, 343, 356–357, 362, 383, 392–39
Land, Ray, 168, 376
language transfer, 132–136, 142, 155, 164, 317, 339, 344–345, 369, 383
lateral transfer, 336–337
Latinx writing, 123, 197
Lave, Jean, 18, 35, 37, 97, 211, 272–275, 289, 299, 302, 327, 366, 370, 374, 393, 405
learning management system (LMS), 191
Learning Transfer System Inventory (LTSI), 65–66, 68, 77, 390
learning, expansive, 276, 289, 300-301, 367-368 ; initial, 7, 8, 22, 25–26, 37, 40, 53, 59, 97–98
Lee, Carol D., 122–123
legitimate peripheral participation (LPP), 11, 18, 35, 211, 272, 274-5, 277–278, 299, 306, 327, 370
Leki, Ilona, 143, 145–146, 152–153, 392, 405
LeMesurier, Jennifer Lin, 39, 43, 105, 320, 346, 367, 403

Lemke, Jay L., 12, 20, 285, 342, 408
Leonard, Rebecca Lorimer, xiv, 115, 124, 126, 131, 156
Lewis, Kyle, 66, 73, 375
life-course development, 121
Light, Richard, 90–91, 94, 173, 188, 320, 346, 348, 394, 403, 405
Lindenman, Heather, 28, 226, 228–229, 234, 336, 371, 394, 406
Lindsay, Douglas R., 55, 57, 187
linear writing process, 154
linguistics, 12, 38, 130, 132–133, 335, 365
literacy linking, 193
literacy studies, 12, 15, 111–112, 122, 125, 168, 182, 287, 315
literate valuation, 124
Lobato, Joanne, 8, 12, 37–39, 42, 318, 323, 339, 348, 363, 368, 372, 395, 403, 404, 407
localization, 173
locus of control, 52, 58–59, 77, 186–187, 370, 385
longitudinal, 4, 57, 142, 144, 151, 170, 208, 217–218, 220, 264, 266, 273, 299, 383
Lopez, Luis, 92–95, 331, 337, 405, 407
low fidelity, 9, 11, 97, 101, 327–328, 329, 397

Mackiewicz, Jo, 51, 244, 245–247, 252, 256, 261
mainstream schools, 113–114
maintenance, 52, 55, 368, 375,
Mania, Katerina, 100, 333, 399, 406
Maran, Nikki, 97, 99, 102, 326, 329, 395, 405
Marinova, Sophia V., 55, 58, 66–67

Martin, Taylor, 37, 322, 344, 404
mastery orientation, 58, 369
Matsuda, Paul Kei, 5, 138, 140, 152, 157, 317, 334, 343, 386, 403, 404, 405,
Mattison, Mike, 243, 252, 259, 263
MBA Program, 85, 214–215,
McBride, Maureen, 180–181
McCarthy, Lucille, 4, 147, 153, 168, 169, 173, 208–210, 218–220, 222, 230, 332, 406
meaning-making trajectories, 121
mediated action, 212
medical education, 15, 96, 98, 100, 104–105, 183, 320, 326–327, 329, 343, 367–368, 395, 397
Melzer, Dan, 209, 223, 229, 231–233, 337, 395, 407
memory, 23, 32, 34, 40, 61, 71–73, 77, 84, 105, 149, 169, 174, 178–179, 228, 316, 324, 335, 372, 374, 375, 381, 401-402
mental model, 42, 123
metagenres, 28, 224, 370, 385, 394,
metaphor, 5, 70
Mexican immigrants, 123
Meyer, Jan, 61, 168, 376,
Michaud, Michael J., 291, 304, 338, 407
Middendorf, Joan, 234–235, 332–333, 396, 406
migrant farmworker communities, 114, 128
military training, 15, 22, 88, 89, 101, 104–105, 315, 326, 328
Miller, Carolyn R., 18, 149, 174, 256, 272, 275, 372
mimicry, 154
mindfulness, 13, 26, 31–32, 90, 253, 259, 322, 326, 338

mindsets, 58
Mitchell, Stephen A., 93, 95, 185, 186, 301
modeling, 9, 52, 59–63, 65, 78, 122–123, 222, 234, 257, 276, 324, 327, 331–332, 373,
Moll, Luis C., 116–117, 122, 396
Moneyhun, Clyde, 249–250
monolingualism, 141–142
Moore, Jessie, 167, 382, 387, 390
Morris, Pamela A., 185–186, 319
motivation, 14, 51, 52, 54–60, 63, 67, 68, 74, 77, 91, 98, 141, 184, 186, 187, 231, 297–298, 332, 371, 385, 389
motor learning, 90
multicompetence, 9, 135, 136, 141–142, 341, 344–345
multidirectional, 264, 334–335, 340
multilingual students, 131, 153, 197
multiliteracy centers, 257
multimodality, 16, 189, 320

National Survey of Student Engagement (NSSE), 214
Navajo students, 117
Navarre Cleary, Michelle, 302–304, 338, 407
negative transfer, 7–13, 15, 37, 64, 133, 138–139, 141, 170, 304, 318, 325–326, 339, 345, 363, 370–371, 372, 393
negotiation, 30, 118, 125, 142–143, 179, 186, 260, 284
Nelms, Ralph Gerald, 3, 32, 184, 222–223, 225, 252, 406
Nemirovsky, Ricardo, 40, 43, 91, 321, 330, 346, 403, 405
networked communities, 191
networked knowledge, 342
neuroticism, 53, 54, 77, 319
New Yorker, The, 181

Nonaka, Ikujiro, 5, 70–71, 76, 325, 397, 404
North, Stephen, 242
noticing, study of, 38–39
novice, 28, 53, 95, 98, 150, 175, 176, 184, 220, 235, 257, 278, 281, 285, 296, 300, 319, 329, 332, 392, 396, 399
Nowacek, Rebecca S., 5, 28, 32, 35, 37, 42, 50, 66, 78, 103, 131, 156, 163, 174, 181, 218, 220–222, 226, 228, 234, 244, 246, 248, 251, 253, 259, 260, 316, 318, 324, 331, 338–339, 341–342, 347, 363, 372, 398, 403-405, 407–408

Odlin, Terence, 134, 137
Olinger, Andrea R., 39, 43, 320, 403
on-the-job training, 60
opportunity to perform, 52, 67, 333
Orellana, Marjorie Faulstich, 122–123
organizational memory (OM), 71
organizational schemas, 229
orientation, 9, 19, 57–58, 112, 118, 134, 180, 200, 227, 298, 316, 349, 369–370, 389

Pace, David, 234-235, 332-333, 396
Pak, Anita W. P., 4, 6
Paré, Anthony, 282, 283, 299, 317, 387–388
peer support, 52, 66–67, 68, 333
Peer Writing Tutor Alumni Project (PWTARP), 262, 390-391
perceived utility, 56-57, 59, 186, 187
perception, 12, 32, 34, 57, 60, 65, 91, 100–101, 105, 132, 142, 145–147, 151, 155, 173-175, 181, 183, 184, 185, 187, 188, 217, 219, 226-227, 261-262, 327, 332-333, 375, 384, 391-392, 399
performance orientation, 58, 369
peripheral participation, see legitimate peripheral participation
Perkins, D. N., 8, 13, 17, 31–34, 43, 96, 123, 168, 194, 209, 227, 231, 255, 261, 279, 324, 326, 334–335, 371, 372, 374, 384, 388, 404, 405, 406
Petraglia, Joseph, 17, 169, 196, 208, 293, 327, 398–399, 405
Pólya, George, 31, 404
positive transfer, 92, 101, 133, 139, 141, 339, 359, 371, 393
Powell, Roger, 4, 32, 56, 63, 74, 186, 193, 297, 319, 388, 403
preparation for future learning (PFL), 7, 12, 37, 255, 322, 335, 372, 388, 406
prior knowledge, 12, 16, 18, 28, 36, 92, 103, 120, 122-124, 131, 143, 146, 154, 156, 157, 174-182, 184-6, 193, 199, 225, 229, 233, 235, 242, 251, 258, 294, 322, 329, 336, 337-339, 344, 386, 387, 394, 399, 402, 407
Prior, Paul A., 12, 39, 119–120, 286–288, 302, 305, 320, 342, 346, 403, 408, 423
problem-exploring dispositions, 58, 185, 261, 384
procedural knowledge, 95-96, 212, 224, 242, 322, 366
progressive fidelity, 98, 102, 330
proximity, 9, 12, 284, 327, 332-333, 406

Qualley, Donna, 17, 167-168

recontextualization, 7, 118, 119, 121, 124, 142, 156, 221, 341, 398

reflection, 4, 10, 12, 99, 102–103, 130, 149, 173, 192–193, 195–198, 227, 232, 242, 250, 252–255, 257, 259, 289, 296, 322, 337-338, 340, 347, 395–396, 307, 402, 407

Reiff, Mary Jo, xiii, 32, 143, 148–149, 175–176, 184, 187, 193, 208, 224, 226, 248, 261, 319, 338, 364, 384, 399, 403, 407

relapse prevention, 60, 64

remix, 155, 177, 322

repurposing, xi, 4, 7, 23, 59, 67, 73, 118, 119-120, 155, 176, 185, 187, 228, 277, 284, 286–287, 294, 304, 318, 319, 321, 364

reverse commute, 302, 304, 338

Reynolds, Jennifer F., 122–123, 240, 357, 422

rhetorical: adaptability, 178, 278; awareness, xi, 125, 155, 190, 210; genre theory, 65, 174, 194, 275, 301, 305, 372, 387, 388; genre awareness, 171, 181, 193; judgment, 278–279; knowledge, 136, 138, 139, 171, 190, 194, 214, 220–221, 224, 231, 243, 245, 247-249, 256, 260, 278–279, 281, 383

rhetorical genre studies (RGS), 147, 149, 174, 194, 221, 398

Rifenburg, J. Michael, 40, 43, 189, 191, 320, 367

Ringer, Jeffrey M., 35, 42, 155–156, 192, 341, 386, 407, 408

Rinnert, Carol, 135, 137–138, 140–142, 343, 392, 408

Robertson, Liane, 62, 177, 193, 338, 340, 384, 402, 407

Robinson, Andrew, 56, 58, 100, 333, 399-400, 406

Roozen, Kevin, 118–120, 189, 191, 208, 286–287, 30

Rose, Kathy, 252, 258, 260–261

Rosinski, Paula, 189, 190, 192

Rounsaville, Angela, xiv, 115, 126, 143, 147, 175, 176, 189, 191, 193, 226, 338, 404, 407, 424

Russell, David, 94, 169, 196, 208, 211, 276, 293–294, 327, 363, 369, 405, 407

Saidy, Christina, 179-180, 193

Salomon, Gavriel, 8, 13, 17, 31–34, 43, 72, 96, 168, 203, 209, 227, 231, 255, 279, 324, 326, 334–335, 371, 372, 374, 388, 404, 405, 406

Saltz, Laura, 208, 210, 219-220, 319, 403

scaffold, 9, 11, 18, 43, 78, 90, 93, 98–103, 123, 172, 194, 225, 231, 232, 234, 235, 261, 283, 299, 327, 330–331, 337, 373, 374, 398, 405

Schneider, Walter, 33–34, 404, 406

Schultz, Katherine, 111, 121

Schwartz, Daniel L., 12, 36–37, 233, 255, 322, 335, 344, 372, 388, 404, 406, 408

second language acquisition (SLA), 131, 133-136, 284, 322, 340, 344, 369, 371

second language writing, 15, 16, 89, 94, 130-158, 160–162, 168, 173, 179, 315, 317, 327, 333, 343, 344, 386, 391, 403, 404, 405, 407, 408, 420

self-efficacy, 49, 50–52, 54–59, 61, 63–64, 67, 68, 77, 186, 187, 197, 216, 242, 258, 261, 373, 383, 385, 388, 390

Index

self-management, 60, 64, 77, 186, 390
self-monitoring, 4, 11, 31-32, 64, 232, 253, 255, 321, 323, 395, 404
self-regulation, 10, 11, 31, 50, 63, 64, 77, 242, 258, 261, 317, 324, 373-374, 388
self-sponsored writing, 189–190, 192–193, 273, 285, 308
semiotic mapping, 192–193
semiotic resources, 189–190, 192, 193, 212, 257
service learning, 88, 259, 292, 296–298, 300, 305, 329, 336
Sharwood-Smith, Mike, 134, 165, 340, 408
Shiffrin, Richard, 33, 34, 404
Shipka, Jody, 12, 120, 286, 342, 408
simulations, 15, 40–42, 53-54, 57, 60, 88-89, 96–102, 104, 10, 188, 273, 284, 292–296, 298, 305,320, 326–330, 333, 343, 347, 367, 368, 374, 389, 395, 397-398, 399-400
simultaneity, 9, 12–13, 19, 157, 242, 315–316, 341–342, 344–345, 408
situated learning, 7–9, 11, 13–14, 22–23, 35–42, 65, 91–92, 96–97, 177–178, 273–274, 307, 315, 327–328, 367, 370, 372, 374, 387, 388, 390, 393, 403-408
Smart, Graham, 71, 150, 283, 292, 301–302, 341, 388, 389, 407
Smit, David W., 3, 17, 170, 199, 208, 229–231, 332, 337, 404, 406, 407
social cognitive theory, 50–51, 317, 374, 383

Sommers, Nancy, 208, 210, 219-220, 319, 403
Spack, Ruth, 143–144, 153–154, 173, 208, 210, 327, 405
Spinuzzi, Clay, 293, 329, 405
spontaneous transfer, 13, 26- 27
sports education, 15, 88, 89-96, 104-105, 168, 170, 173, 188, 320, 322, 327, 331, 337, 346, 348, 366, 394
Sternglass, Marilyn, 4, 208, 210, 218, 241
stickiness, 73–74, 400
Stretcher, Robert, 210, 214–215
structuring proclivities, 122, 288
subject matter knowledge, 140, 171, 194, 220, 245, 247,281, 343, 383
Sullivan, Patrick, 56, 5
supervisor support, 52, 66–67, 77, 78, 333
Swales, John M., 143–144, 147, 149, 156, 366, 45
System 1 & System 2, 33–35, 324-325
Szulanski, Gabriel, 73–74, 400

tacit knowledge, 5–6, 11, 69–71, 76, 213, 218, 220, 221-222, 285, 321, 325, 397
tactical awareness, 90–91, 93–95, 173
Taczak, Kara, 340, 384, 402
Tardy, Christine T., 5, 7, 143, 147–148, 150–151, 315
teaching for transfer (TFT), 59, 170, 177, 180, 185, 194, 197, 224, 253, 322, 323, 331, 332, 338, 347, 374, 402
teaching games for understanding (TGfU), 89-91, 173, 320, 322, 331, 346, 394
technical communication, 214, 230, 248

TESOL (teaching English to speakers of other languages), 130, 132
thematic transfer, 92–93, 95
Thomas, Jerry, 91, 95
Thompson, Isabelle, 51, 261
Thorndike, Edward L., 3, 7, 13, 23–26, 60, 100, 118, 328, 369, 387, 405
Thorpe, Rod, 90, 322, 337, 404, 407
threshold concepts, xiii, 62, 95–96, 170, 194, 196, 213, 225, 232, 250–251, 366, 370, 376, 395
trainee characteristics, 14, 51–59, 68, 77, 371, 375, 383
training design, 14, 51–52, 59-65, 68, 77–78, 298, 324, 332, 371, 375, 383
transactive memory systems (TMS), 72-73, 77, 316, 324, 374-375, 401-402
transdisciplinary, 167-168, 187, 200, 264, 315-316; transdisciplinary approach, 47, 182, 315–316; transdisciplinary connections, 16-17, 187; transdisciplinary themes, 9, 19, 315-350
transfer climate, 52, 65, 67–68, 371, 375
transformation, xi, 71, 75, 119, 123, 124, 133, 156, 185, 190, 192, 195, 212, 221, 228, 258, 264, 289, 302, 306-307, 308, 318, 334, 340–341, 349, 366, 368, 370, 398, 401, 407
transnational, 115-116, 123, 147, 401
Tuomi-Gröhn, Terttu, 168, 289, 300, 316, 340, 364–365, 368, 400, 405, 40
tutoring, 18, 242-266, 340, 342, 384-385, 388, 391

two-problem paradigm, 7, 22, 26, 37, 76
Tziner, Aharon, 54, 56, 59, 369

Ungson, Gerardo Rivera, 70–71, 325, 372, 401, 404

Vancouver, Jeffrey B., 56, 37
Verisimilitude [see also fidelity], 273, 293–294
vertical curriculum, 184, 231-233, 395-396
vertical transfer, 12, 17, 92, 93, 95, 209, 232, 251, 336-337, 387, 395–396, 407
Vygotsky, Lev, 98, 373

Walker, Kristin, 245, 248, 342, 361, 408
Walsh, James P., 70–71, 325, 372, 401, 404
Walvoord, Barbara E., 208–210, 218, 230, 332, 406
Wardle, Elizabeth, xiii, 3, 5, 21, 32, 43, 57–59, 62, 65, 67, 170–173, 180, 183, 185–187, 193–194, 196, 208, 229, 233–235, 248, 250, 252, 261, 291, 317, 319, 326, 327, 333, 337, 338, 365, 384, 388, 401, 403–407
Wegner, Daniel M., 72–73, 77, 316, 324, 373, 374, 401, 404
Wells, Jennifer, 4, 32, 42, 51, 54, 57, 59, 168, 182, 185–186, 193, 252, 297, 319, 367, 388, 403
Wenger, Etienne, 18, 35, 97, 211, 272–275, 289, 299, 302, 327, 366, 370, 374, 386, 393, 405
Wertsch, James, 118, 286
White, Stephanie, 297–298, 319, 403
Wilson, Robert A., 39, 188
Winsor, Dorothy, 279–280, 298

Index

Winzenried, Misty Anne, 50, 66, 78, 316, 347
Woodworth, Robert S., 7, 23, 24, 369
work environment, 14, 51–53, 59, 65-69, 329, 333, 375, 383
workplace writing, 66, 72, 112, 272–308, 329, 366, 399
writing about writing (WAW), 18, 59, 65, 170, 172, 183, 194, 196, 197, 199, 235, 252, 273, 291–292, 305, 323, 331, 338, 347, 401
writing across the curriculum (WAC), xi, xii, 17, 60, 89, 112, 167, 173, 207–210, 215, 219, 223, 225, 226, 229–236, 249, 254, 256, 275, 332, 336, 369, 396, 403-408
Writing Beyond the University (Elon University), 3, 307
writing centers, xii, 18, 66, 78, 103, 112, 167, 172, 173, 221, 227-228, 233, 236, 242–266, 272, 316, 332, 334, 335, 340, 341, 342, 372, 384, 387, 388, 396, 405-408
writing development, 62, 115, 121–122, 142, 169, 174, 191, 197, 208, 217–219, 266, 288, 302, 318, 326, 333, 334–336
writing in the disciplines (WID), xi–xii, 4, 17, 60, 143, 173, 207–211, 214–215, 219, 223–224, 226, 229–231, 232, 233–235, 249, 252, 332, 366, 369, 385, 396, 403-408
writing process knowledge, 171, 194, 220, 281, 383

Yancey, Kathleen Blake, 4, 32, 43, 59, 62, 65, 170, 180, 185, 189, 194, 197–198, 208, 224, 225, 227, 229, 253, 307, 317, 322, 332, 338, 347, 374, 384, 402, 403, 404, 406, 407

Zamel, Vivian, 143, 153–154, 208
Zepernick, Janet, 3, 18-184, 187, 193, 210, 217, 222, 233, 333, 337, 406, 407
Zimmerelli, Lisa, 243, 252, 259

About the Authors

Rebecca Nowacek is a professor of English at Marquette University, where she co-directs the Norman H. Ott Memorial Writing Center. Rebecca's research focuses on writing transfer, writing center studies, and writing across the disciplines. Her publications include *Agents of Integration: Understanding Transfer as a Rhetorical Act* (Southern Illinois University Press, 2011), *Literacy, Economy, and Power* (Southern Illinois University Press, 2013), and *Citizenship Across the Curriculum* (Indiana University Press, 2010). Her work has also appeared in *College Composition and Communication, College English, Research in the Teaching of English*, and the *Journal of General Education*. Rebecca was a Carnegie Scholar with the Carnegie Academy for the Scholarship of Teaching and Learning and a member of Elon University's 2019–2022 Research Seminar on Writing Beyond the University, as well as the 2012 recipient of Marquette University's Robert and Mary Gettel Faculty Award for Teaching Excellence.

Rebecca Lorimer Leonard is Associate Professor of English at the University of Massachusetts Amherst where she teaches undergraduate and graduate courses on language diversity, literacy studies, and research methods. Her current research focuses on the relationship between community-engaged writing and critical language awareness, studies of which have been published in *Community Literacy Journal, College English, Journal of Adolescent & Adult Literacy*, and *Composition Studies*. She also has published on the transfer of writing knowledge (*College Composition and Communication, College English*); language identities and institutional surveys (*Journal of Language, Identity & Education*); and the literate practices of multilingual migrant writers

(*Written Communication, College English, Research in the Teaching of English*). Lorimer Leonard's monograph, *Writing on the Move: Migrant Women and the Value of Literacy,* won the 2019 Outstanding Book Award from the Conference on College Composition and Communication.

Angela Rounsaville is a scholar of transnational literacy, genre studies, and transfer and an associate professor of writing at the University of Central Florida. Her current research focuses on inequities in global knowledge economies and the role of genre in continuing and redressing those imbalances. Her work in this area can be found in journals such as *College English* and *Literacy in Composition Studies.* She has also published on transnational genre knowledge (*Written Communication* and *Research in the Teaching of English*); transfer of writing knowledge (*College Composition and Communication, Composition Forum* and *WPA: Writing Program Administration*); and equity in writing programs (*College English*). Angela served as the University of Central Florida's Director of Composition from 2017 to 2022, and received the 2022–2023 CCCC Writing Program Certificate of Excellence on behalf of UCF's Composition Program and faculty.

www.ingramcontent.com/pod-product-compliance
Lightning Source LLC
Chambersburg PA
CBHW032011300426
44117CB00008B/978